Rural Marketing

THIRD EDITION

Rural Marketing

THIRD EDITION

PRADEEP KASHYAP

Associate Editor—Acquisitions: Varun Goenka
Editor—Production: Vipin Kumar

ISBN 978-93-325-4360-7

First Impression, 2016
Second Impression, 2017
Third Impression, 2018

Published by Pearson India Education Services Pvt. Ltd, CIN: U72200TN2005PTC057128,

Head Office: 15th Floor, Tower-B, World Trade Tower, Plot No. 1, Block-C, Sector 16, Noida 201 301, Uttar Pradesh, India.

Registered Office: 4th floor, Software Block, Elnet Software City, TS -140, Block 2 & 9 Rajiv Gandhi Salai, Taramani, Chennai, Tamil Nadu 600113. Fax: 080-30461003, Phone: 080-30461060, Website in.pearson.com, Email: companysecretary.india@pearson.com

Compositor: D Book Media

Printed in India by Rahul Print O Pack.

ABOUT THE AUTHOR

Pradeep Kashyap, known as the father of rural marketing in India, founded MART in 1993. A transparent, team-based, non-hierarchical, flat organization based on ethical and spiritual principles, MART has emerged as India's leading rural consultancy organization.

He co-created Project Shakti with HUL (erstwhile HLL) to appoint 46,000 poor women from microfinance groups as company dealers. He has pioneered another low-cost, last mile rural distribution model using village volunteers on bicycles for Colgate and Heinz, among others. He has advised many Fortune 500 companies including GE, Intel, John Deere, Shell, Coca-Cola and Pepsi on rural strategy.

He has been Marketing Advisor to the Ministry of Rural Development and has served in the Prime Minister's Office and the Andhra Pradesh Chief Minister's Committee on rural development. He is a World Bank and United Nations consultant. He was Chairman, KVIC National Marketing Committee, and member of the NABARD and SIDBI national advisory committees.

He started Gramshree melas in 1989 for the sale of rural products in urban areas by artisans. Three hundred such melas have been held in 75 cities, benefiting 100,000 producers.

He was the only speaker from India at the Cannes Lions International Festival of Creativity 2008, and among 50 global speakers to address 2,000 participants. The theme of his talk was 'Rural India: The Emerging Market'. He was the keynote speaker at The Third Subsistence Marketplaces Conference, held in 2010 at the University of Illinois, Chicago, where he talked about inclusive marketing. He has given talks at the University of Cambridge and the London Business School.

He is a recipient of the Jamnalal Bajaj Endowment Award 1991 for his outstanding contribution to rural development. His marketing career spans 40 years.

He was the President of Rural Marketing Association of India (2009–14) and was honoured with the Lifetime Achievement Award by the Association. He was also honoured with the Distinguished Alumnus Award 2014 by his alma mater BITS Pilani.

BRIEF CONTENTS

Foreword xix

Preface xxi

Chapter 1 The Call of Rural India 2

Chapter 2 The Rural Marketing Environment 12

Chapter 3 Rural Consumer Behaviour 42

Chapter 4 Rural Marketing Research 64

Chapter 5 Segmenting and Targeting Rural Markets 86

Chapter 6 Product Strategy 108

Chapter 7 Pricing Strategies 132

Chapter 8 Distribution in Rural Markets 152

Chapter 9 Communication Strategies for Rural Markets 196

Chapter 10 Rural Services Marketing 236

Chapter 11 Marketing in Small Towns 270

Chapter 12 Role of Government in Rural India 286

Chapter 13 The Future of Rural Marketing 300

Endnotes 309

Photo Credits 311

Index 313

CONTENTS

Foreword xix

Preface xxi

Chapter 1 The Call of Rural India 2

Defining Rural Markets 4

Rural Myths 5

Rapid Urbanization 5
Rural India is An Agrarian Economy 5

The Rural Marketing Mix: Challenges 6

Affordability 6
Availability 6
Awareness 7
Acceptability 7

The Evolving Rural Consumer 7

Rural India: The Exploding Middle Class 8

RURAL MARKETING SNAPSHOT Changing Rural Settlements 8

RURAL MARKETING MEMO Startling Facts About Rural India 9

Review of Objectives 10
Discussion and Application 11

RURAL MARKETING CASE Rural Markets 11

Chapter 2 The Rural Marketing Environment 12

The Evolution of Rural Marketing 14

Phase I (Prior to the 1960s) 14
Phase II (1960s–1980s) 14
Phase III (1990s–2000) 14
Phase IV (After 2000) 15

The Rural Environment 15

The Demographic Environment 15
The Physical Environment 18
The Social and Cultural Environment 19
The Political Environment 22
The Technological Environment 23

The Rural Economic Environment 24

The Changing Face of Rural Development 25

The Rural Economic Structure 26

The Farm Sector: Agriculture and Allied Activities 27
The Non-farm Sector and Rural Industries 28

CONTENTS

Changing Migration Trends 30
Incomes and Expenditure 30

The Rural Infrastructure 33

RURAL MARKETING SNAPSHOT Rural Infrastructure 34

Road Connectivity 34
Electrification 34

RURAL MARKETING INSIGHT Road Connectivity Bringing Rural Economy on Track in Bihar 35

Rural Housing 35
Telecommunications 35
Drinking Water 36

Rural Employment Generation Programmes: Government Initiatives 36

The Mahatma Gandhi National Rural Employment Guarantee Act (MNREGA) 37
The Swarnjayanti Gram Swarozgar Yojna (SGSY) 37
The Pradhan Mantri Rojgar Yojna 37

Review of Objectives 38

Discussion and Application 39

RURAL MARKETING CASE MNREGA 40

Chapter 3 **Rural Consumer Behaviour 42**

The Consumer Buying Behaviour Model 44

What Influences Consumer Behaviour? 44

Cultural Factors 44
Social Factors 47

RURAL MARKETING MEMO Reference Groups in Rural 48

Personal Factors 49
Psychological Factors 52

The Buyer Decision Process 54

Need Recognition 54
Information Search 54
The Evaluation of Alternatives 55
The Purchase Decision 55
Post-purchase Behaviour 55

RURAL MARKETING SNAPSHOT Key Opinion Leaders 56

The Product Adoption Process 56

RURAL MARKETING INSIGHT Aircel 57

Diffusion of Innovation 57

RURAL MARKETING INSIGHT HPCL Rasoi Ghar 58

CONTENTS

Review of Objectives 59
Discussion and Application 60
RURAL MARKETING CASE HPCL Rasoi Ghar 60
APPENDIX The New SEC System 61

Chapter 4 **Rural Marketing Research 64**

The Rural Marketing Research Process 66

Defining the Objectives 66
Determining the Research Budget 66
Designing the Research 66
Sampling 69
Designing the Research Instrument 73
Organizing the Field and Collecting the Data 74
Collating and Analysing the Data 75
Reporting the Findings 75

Special Tools Used in Rural Marketing Research 76

Participatory Rural Appraisals 76

RURAL MARKETING INSIGHT New Age Innovation in Rural Research 76

Scaling Tools for Rural Quantitative Research 77

Field Procedures and Rural Realities 79

Dos and Don'ts in Rural Marketing Research 79

RURAL MARKETING SNAPSHOT Data Collection in Rural India 80
RURAL MARKETING MEMO Attributes of a Rural Researcher 81

Limitations of Rural Research 81

The Rural Research Business 82

Review of Objectives 83
Discussion and Application 83
RURAL MARKETING CASE Participatory Rural Appraisal 84

Chapter 5 **Segmenting and Targeting Rural Markets 86**

Segmentation 88

Heterogeneity in Rural Markets 88
Pre-requisites for Effective Segmentation 89
Degrees of Segmentation 90
Bases for Segmenting Rural Consumer Markets 91

RURAL MARKETING INSIGHT MART Market Attractiveness Score: Urban and Rural 'Prosperity Plus' Index 99

Targeting 99

Evaluation of Segments 99
Selection of Segments 101

CONTENTS

Coverage of Segments 101
Choosing a Coverage Strategy 103

Positioning 103

Identifying the Positioning Concept 104
Selecting the Positioning Concept 104
Developing the Concept 105
Communicating the Concept 105

Review of Objectives 105

Discussion and Application 106

RURAL MARKETING CASE Bru Instant Coffee Connect 107

Chapter 6 **Product Strategy 108**

The Product Concept and the Classification of Rural Products 110

The Product Concept 110
Rural Product Classification 111

Product Decisions and Strategies 114

Individual Product Decisions 115

RURAL MARKETING SNAPSHOT Product Acceptability 115

Product Line and Mix Decisions 117

RURAL MARKETING INSIGHT Product Designing for Rural Needs—Godrej Chotu Kool 117

Product Lifecycle Strategies 118

Product Branding in Rural Markets 119

Building Brands in Rural Markets 119
Brand Loyalty Versus Brand Stickiness 120
Fake Brands 121

RURAL MARKETING INSIGHT Dealing with Piracy 123

Packaging for Rural Markets 123

Packaging Material 123
Pack Size and Convenience 124

RURAL MARKETING INSIGHT The Sachet Revolution 124

Packaging Aesthetics 125

RURAL MARKETING INSIGHT After-sales Service Initiatives by Companies in Rural Markets 126

Product Warranty and After-sales Service 126

New Product Development in Rural Markets 127

Review of Objectives 128

Discussion and Application 130

CONTENTS

RURAL MARKETING CASE New Product Development: Improved Biomass Stove by Shell Foundation 130

Chapter 7 **Pricing Strategies 132**

Pricing in Rural India 134

RURAL MARKETING INSIGHT Rural Consumers Prefer Value for Money 134

How Do Companies Price? 135
Consumer Psychology and Pricing 135

Setting the Price for Rural Products and Services 136

Internal Factors 136
External Factors 138

Price Setting Strategies 142

Market Entry Strategies 142
Product Mix Pricing Strategies 143
Price Adjustment Strategies 144

RURAL MARKETING MEMO Caution for Marketers Giving Discounts to Rural Consumers 144

RURAL MARKETING SNAPSHOT Rising Consumption of Branded Products 147

Rural-specific Pricing Strategies 147

Review of Objectives 149

Discussion and Application 150

RURAL MARKETING CASE Coca-Cola's Strategy for Rural Markets 150

Chapter 8 **Distribution in Rural Markets 152**

Availability: The Challenge and the Dilemma 154

Distribution Channels 155

The Evolution of Rural Distribution Channels 155
Channel Dynamics 156
Rural Channel Members 156

The Rural Retail Environment 158

Traditional Retail 158

RURAL MARKETING SNAPSHOT The Changing Face of Rural Retail 161

The Emergence of Modern Retail in Rural Areas 163

CONTENTS

Channel Behaviour in Rural Areas 167

Sourcing of Stocks and Purchase Cycles 168
Stocking Behaviour and Seasonality 168
Credit Patterns 169
Transfer of Capital 170
Pricing by Channel 170
Channel Promotion 170
Retailer–Consumer Dynamics 170

Distribution Models in Rural Markets 171

The Distribution Models for FMCGs 171
The Distribution Model for Durables 175

Rural-centric Distribution Models 178

Haats/Shandies 178
Modern Distribution Models 181

RURAL MARKETING INSIGHT Project Shakti 181

Vans 183
The Public Distribution System 184
Cooperative Societies 185
Petrol Pumps and Extension Counters 185
Non-government Organizations 186
Rural Mobile Traders: Last Mile Distribution 186

RURAL MARKETING INSIGHT Gaon Chalo: A Tata Tea Initiative 187

Rural Logistics 188

The Hub and Spoke System 188
Syndicated Distribution 190

RURAL MARKETING INSIGHT Syndicated Distribution for Rural Dominance 190

Review of Objectives 191

Discussion and Application 192

RURAL MARKETING CASE Colgate DISHA: The Evolution of a Sustainable PPP Model in the BoP Market 192

Chapter 9 Communication Strategies for Rural Markets 196

Challenges in Rural Communication 198

Heterogeneity and Spread 198
Low Literacy and Varying Comprehension Abilities 198
Different Media Reach and Habits 198

The Communication Process: An Overview 199

RURAL MARKETING INSIGHT Rural and Urban Responses to Television Advertisements 200

Developing Effective Rural Communication 200

CONTENTS

Identifying and Profiling the Target Audience 200
Determining Communication Objectives 201

RURAL MARKETING INSIGHT Religion: A Key Profiling Factor for Designing Communication 201
Designing the Message 202
Selecting the Communication Channels 207

RURAL MARKETING MEMO Developing an Effective Rural Communication Message 207

Budgeting for Rural Communication 209
Designing the Communication Mix Strategy 209
Measuring the Impact of Communication 211

Creating Advertisements for Rural Audiences 212

RURAL MARKETING INSIGHT Hitting the Bull's Eye 212

Rural Media 213

Conventional Media 213

RURAL MARKETING INSIGHT Increasing Role of DTH in Rural India 214

Rural-centric Non-conventional Media 218

RURAL MARKETING SNAPSHOT Changing Means of Rural Communication 218

RURAL MARKETING INSIGHT Clutter-free Communication at the Mela 221

Sales Promotion and Events and Experiences 224
Sales Promotion 224
Events and Experiences 226

Review of Objectives 229
Discussion and Application 231

RURAL MARKETING CASE Tata Shaktee GC Sheets 231

Chapter 10 Rural Services Marketing 236

Telecommunications in Rural India 238

RURAL MARKETING SNAPSHOT The Telecom Revolution in Rural india 238

Reuters Market Light 241
IFFCO Kisaan Sanchar Limited 241
Nokia Life Tools 242

RURAL MARKETING INSIGHT M-VAS Initiatives in Rural India 242

CONTENTS

Information and Communications Technology (ICT) in Rural Areas 243

- ITC's e-Choupal 243
- Common Service Centres 244
- n-Logue Village Internet Kiosks 245
- Drishtee 246
- The Relevance of ICT Services in Rural India 247

Financial Services in Rural India 248

- Banking Services 248

RURAL MARKETING INSIGHT Cloud Computing for Rural Banking 251

- Microfinance and Credit Services 252
- Insurance 255
- Life Insurance 255

Rural Healthcare Services 257

- An Overview of Rural Healthcare in India 257
- The Challenges in Rural Healthcare 257
- The Healthcare Infrastructure 258
- The Healthcare Market 259
- Government Initiatives in Rural India 259
- Growth Drivers of Rural Healthcare 260

Review of Objectives 265

Discussion and Application 266

RURAL MARKETING CASE Arogya Parivar: A Rural Healthcare Delivery Business Model 267

Chapter 11 Marketing in Small Towns 270

Small Towns: A Definition 272

- The Potential of Small Towns 272

RURAL MARKETING SNAPSHOT The Changing Face of Small-town India 273

Small-town Consumer Behaviour 276

RURAL MARKETING INSIGHT The Dhoni Effect 277

RURAL MARKETING INSIGHT Consumer Behaviour in Small Towns of India 281

The Strategic Importance of Small Towns for Rural Marketers 282

- As Selling and Redistribution Centres 282
- As Servicing Centres 283
- As a Hub for Availing Services 283
- As the Agricultural Linkage 284
- As a Place for Leisure and Entertainment 284

CONTENTS

Review of Objectives 284
Discussion and Application 285

RURAL MARKETING CASE Philips Lighting: Bulb *Ka Badshah* 285

Chapter 12 Role of Government in Rural India 286

Why Is Government's Intervention Important for Rural Development? 288
What is the Government doing? 288

Rural Infrastructure 288

Connecting the Rural 288
Housing in Rural 289
Electrifying the Rural Houses 289
Urbanizing the Rural 290
e-Governance in Rural India 291

Education 291

Health 292

Skill Development 293

Employment 294

National Rural Employment Guarantee Act (NREGA) 294

Financial Inclusion 295

Sanitation 295

Agriculture 296

Conclusion 297

Review of Objectives 298
Discussion and Application 298

RURAL MARKETING CASE Rural Markets 299

Chapter 13 The Future of Rural Marketing 300

The Rural Boom 302

The Way Forward 303

Forward Innovation 303
A New Price–Performance Paradigm 303
Innovative Rural Distribution 303
Inclusive Marketing 304
Dedicated Rural Teams 304

Rural Dividend 304

CONTENTS

RURAL MARKETING MEMO Some Startling Facts 305

New Opportunities 305

Review of Objectives 306

Discussion and Application 306

RURAL MARKETING CASE 3G Video Telephony 306

Endnotes 309

Photo Credits 311

Index 313

FOREWORD

At least 40 per cent of the world's markets are rural markets. They represent more than three billion people whose current consumption is estimated to be at least four trillion dollars per year. Rural markets have been traditionally ignored by most multinationals from advanced countries, as well as by local large-scale manufacturers of packaged branded products, for several reasons.

First, rural markets are still mostly served by unbranded local competitors. These locally entrenched competitors often use non-traditional and unethical tactics to control the market. Also, the fragmented nature of competition as well as the low density of population makes rural markets less attractive to serve.

Second, most consumers still self-produce products and services at home rather than buy them commercially for a variety of historical reasons. For example, rural consumers still make pickles, *papad, chapati*, sweets, snacks, fuel, garments, and most other basic necessities of food, shelter, and clothing. Two exceptions in recent years have been milk (due to the mushrooming of local cooperatives) and mobile telephones (due to the policy-mandated spectrum coverage). It is also true for several livelihood-related products such as tractors and motorcycles.

Finally, a lack of modern infrastructure, including roads, electricity, banks, and media, make accessibility to rural markets very difficult and expensive. In fact, companies that have historically succeeded in rural markets had to organize alternate sales and distribution systems to reach rural consumers. These include Brooke Bond tea, ITC cigarettes, Coca-Cola, as well as government-sector enterprises such as India Post, Life Insurance Corporation of India (LIC) and Indian Railways.

All of this is now changing, and changing rapidly due to several reasons. The first and foremost reason is that rural markets are growing faster than urban markets and with better profitability, as urban markets have become more mature and intensely competitive, especially after the liberalization of the Indian economy. Moreover, if aggregated with cost efficiency, rural markets constitute a very large and untapped market. This has been conclusively proven by Wal-Mart in the USA, which started with small rural towns in America and became the largest retailer, surpassing world-class competitors such as K-Mart and Sears. Rural markets, which used to be neglected by branded manufacturers, are now becoming the core of a company's growth strategy for both multinationals such as Nestlé, Colgate and Unilever, and for Britannia biscuits, Titan watches, Godrej mosquito repellants, and Wipro soaps and lighting products.

The second and equally important factor is the increasing interest of rural consumers in acquiring branded products, especially those that symbolize educated or modern lifestyles. Watches, jeans, cell phones and T-shirts, bottled water, shampoo and toilet soaps, as well as education and healthcare, are part of this list. In other words, rural consumers in India today are less resistant to change. In fact, they seem eager to enter the world of modern consumption, especially those for daily use.

The third factor is the astounding technological advances and affordability of mobile telephony. Mobile phones will have an even greater impact on marketing as they become Internet-enabled. Wireless broadband will increase the reach of the Internet—a very rich medium capable of providing voice and video in addition to data. This is very important, because voice and video transcend literacy. It is also a viral medium, as demonstrated by events in the Middle East. Markets will become increasingly flat, with no level playing advantage for the urban markets. The mobile phone revolution in rural markets is now encouraging investment in other infrastructures, and organizing the otherwise unorganized rural markets all over the world, including in Africa and Latin America.

Finally, as rural markets become more strategic, companies will learn to innovate and experiment with their traditional approaches to the four Ps of marketing: product, price, place, and promotion. This is already happening worldwide. For example, Avon's largest growing market for cosmetics and personal care is Brazil. The company organized an agency-based sales force of a million agents in Brazil alone, who are all self-employed entrepreneurs servicing micro-markets with the help of microfinancing. There are several success stories in India's rural markets as well. Indeed, it is not an exaggeration to assert that companies that succeed in rural markets with non-traditional approaches to products, prices, promotion, distribution, and service will gain a competitive advantage over those who do not, or could not, succeed in rural markets. Reverse innovation from rural markets to urban markets is the key to future growth and profitability.

More than a decade ago, my colleague Rajendra Sisodia and I developed a new customer-centric framework called the 4 As of Marketing.[1] Briefly, the framework suggests that the objective of marketing managers should be to use their marketing and non-marketing resources to improve acceptability, affordability, accessibility, and awareness of their offerings. This framework has been utilized to diagnose more than 500 product failures and successes. This framework is even more relevant in rural markets because of its inherent challenges of reach, awareness, and affordability.

I am very pleased to write this Foreword for three reasons. First, a textbook focused on rural marketing will encourage management institutes to develop separate courses and encourage and prepare students to learn and become passionate about rural marketing in India. Second, there is no other expert better than Pradeep Kashyap as the author of this textbook. Pradeep, over many years, has demonstrated his commitment and dedication to understanding rural marketing, especially through his research and consultancy company, MART. He is one of the very rare individuals who blend theory and practice. Finally, I believe and sincerely hope that this textbook will demonstrate that it is possible to write an Indian book that has the potential to be translated and/or adapted in advanced countries. The reverse innovation in management education is already here!

Jagdish N. Sheth
Charles H. Kellstadt Professor of Marketing
Emory University, USA

[1] Sheth, Jagdish N. and Rajendra S. Sisodia (1999), 'Iridium's 66 Pies in the Sky', *Wall Street Journal*, June.

PREFACE

::: The Rural Marketing Scenario

The first edition of *Rural Marketing* was published in 2005—a time when rural markets were considered a 'black box' as there was very little information or data available, when the rural demand for most categories was just beginning to register high rates of growth. Between then and the second edition in 2011, many companies entered the rural market successfully and a lot of new knowledge was created, which needs to be shared with students and practitioners.

Rural India has undergone a rapid transformation in the last few years. Who would have imagined in 2005 that the rural share of the total market would outstrip the urban share for most categories in a short period of a decade? Or that rural growth would exceed urban growth? Rural India registered a growth of 17 per cent, compared to a modest 12 per cent growth in urban India. Since the introduction of mobile phones in India in the 1990s, it took urban India 10 years to reach a figure of 200 million connections. In contrast, rural India hit 200 million connections in five years, starting in 2005, which was when the first mobile phones were purchased in villages! Today there are 350 million mobile phones in rural India and are growing. As late as 2007–08, Maruti sold less than 20,000 cars in rural India. In 2014–15, it sold 300,000 cars.

The pro-rural government initiatives and schemes, rapid rural infrastructure development, eight good monsoons and a two-fold increase in the minimum support price for food grains have enhanced incomes and fuelled rural growth. Last year alone, the National Rural Employment Guarantee Scheme (NREGA) has put an additional INR 440 billion in the hands of the poor. Rapid electrification has led to enhanced economic activity in rural areas. Seventy-five per cent villages are now connected by high-quality roads, resulting in a spurt in the sale of Hero Honda motorcycles, Maruti cars, Bolero SUVs, and Tata Ace mini goods vehicles. Improved Internet connectivity and the rapid spread of TVs and mobile phones have led to higher awareness levels among rural consumers.

Companies have responded by customizing products for rural consumers—smaller packs, coinage pricing, etc. Some companies such as HUL, ITC, and Tata Tea have innovated new communication and distribution channels.

::: The Theme of the New Edition

The unimaginable transformation of rural India in the last decade prompted me to revise the book, with the view to making it more relevant to today's rural marketing needs and challenges. Unlike the first edition, where the approach was to compare rural markets with urban ones, this edition focusses on capturing the 'changing rural India'. The present edition focuses on the huge opportunity that has already become a reality. The next big growth in demand for the next decade will be mainly from the rural markets. The valuable feedback received from academia and industry has also helped in shaping this edition.

PREFACE

New in this Edition

The present edition, while retaining the key strengths of the previous edition, builds on it by introducing new material relevant for today's readers to enhance and sharpen their learning. The pedagogy of the book has been expanded to make learning easier and interesting.

- Following are the major changes made in this edition of the book.
    - A chapter on 'Role of Government in Rural India' has been added as Chapter 12.
    - The chapter on 'Future of Rural marketing' has now become Chapter 13.
    - New cases and discussion questions have been added to various chapters to bring contemporary knowledge.

Focused **learning objectives** present a convenient overview of the concepts discussed in the chapter.

CHAPTER 1 ::: THE CALL OF RURAL INDIA

one

AFTER READING THIS CHAPTER, YOU WILL BE ABLE TO:

1. Define rural India and rural markets
2. Identify common rural myths
3. Understand the rural marketing mix and the challenges related to it
4. Understand the characteristics of the evolving rural consumer
5. Describe the emerging rural India

Before 2006, Sakamma, a 35-year old lady in a village in Nalgonda district, used to stay in a small house with her husband and three children. Her husband was the sole bread earner for the family of five. His meagre income of INR 10,000 per year was barely sufficient for the family; moreover, the situation worsened due to his alcoholism. With this money, it was a daunting task for Sakamma to meet the needs of her growing children.

When the concept selling meeting of 'Project Shakti' was organized by Hindustan Unilever in the same year in her village, Sakamma was excited, and decided to take up the challenge of becoming a Shakti entrepreneur.

Today, she earns an additional yearly income of INR 10,000 through Shakti. The programme has given her the desired financial independence that has enabled her to plan for the future of her children. 'I want my daughter to become an engineer,' she proudly says.' Sakamma today has independent access to a bank and decides what investments to make. She recently invested in gold jewellery as she has started preparing for her daughter's marriage. Sakamma was recently also chosen to work with the government to help educate the rural population on health issues.

Such initiatives like Project Shakti have not only opened up earning opportunities for rural people like Sakamma, but have also led to rural development in such a way that rural masses are now getting exposed to the right quality products and services, which in turn is adding to their quality of life. Rural markets are no longer a mass of illiterate, poverty-stricken people who are reluctant to change and spend. Instead, they are today becoming the most lucrative markets that every marketer is eyeing.

Project Shakti, HUL's rural initiative, has empowered underprivileged rural women in scores of villages across India by making them financially independent.

Chapter-opening vignettes serve as ice-breakers and narrate the key concepts of the chapter through a powerful story around a consumer, brand or company for a better understanding of the chapter.

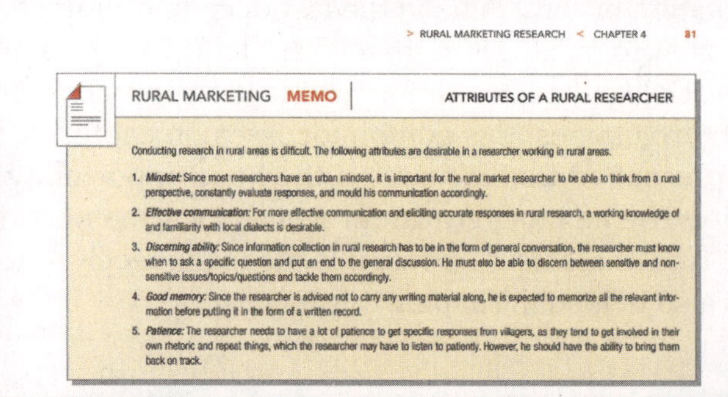

> RURAL MARKETING RESEARCH < CHAPTER 4 81

RURAL MARKETING **MEMO** | ATTRIBUTES OF A RURAL RESEARCHER

Conducting research in rural areas is difficult. The following attributes are desirable in a researcher working in rural areas.

1. ***Mindset:*** Since most researchers have an urban mindset, it is important for the rural market researcher to be able to think from a rural perspective, constantly evaluate responses, and mould his communication accordingly.
2. ***Effective communication:*** For more effective communication and eliciting accurate responses in rural research, a working knowledge of and familiarity with local dialects is desirable.
3. ***Discerning ability:*** Since information collection in rural research has to be in the form of general conversation, the researcher must know when to ask a specific question and put an end to the general discussion. He must also be able to discern between sensitive and non-sensitive issues/topics/questions and tackle them accordingly.
4. ***Good memory:*** Since the researcher is advised not to carry any writing material along, he is expected to memorize all the relevant information before putting it in the form of a written record.
5. ***Patience:*** The researcher needs to have a lot of patience to get specific responses from villagers, as they tend to get involved in their own rhetoric and repeat things, which the researcher may have to listen to patiently. However, he should have the ability to bring them back on track.

Rural Marketing Memo boxes provide practical guidelines and directions in dealing with various decisions at all stages of the rural marketing process.

Rural Marketing Insight boxes bring practical insight through compact rural-centric cases and current research findings, thus supplementing theory and concepts.

Marginalia, or **margin notes**, summarize crucial points and highlight definitions.

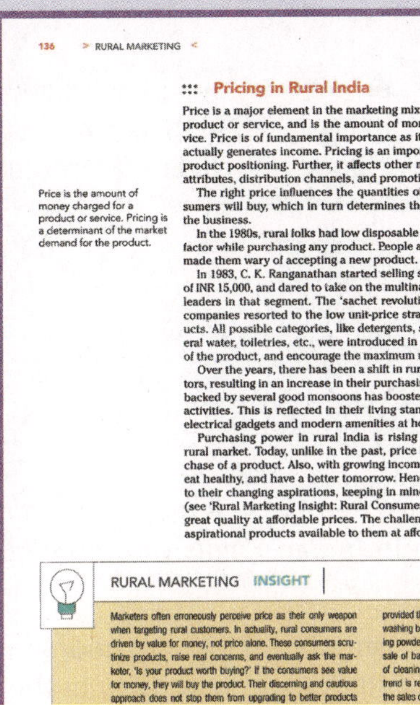

136 > RURAL MARKETING <

Pricing in Rural India

Price is a major element in the marketing mix. It is defined as the exchange value of a product or service, and is the amount of money needed to acquire a product or service. Price is of fundamental importance as it is the only marketing-mix element that actually generates income. Pricing is an important strategic issue since it is related to product positioning. Further, it affects other marketing-mix elements such as product attributes, distribution channels, and promotion strategies.

Price is the amount of money charged for a product or service. Pricing is a determinant of the market demand for the product.

The right price influences the quantities of various products or services that consumers will buy, which in turn determines the total revenues and hence the profit of the business.

In the 1980s, rural folks had low disposable income; hence, affordability was a major factor while purchasing any product. People also had a conservative approach, which made them wary of accepting a new product.

In 1983, C. K. Ranganathan started selling shampoo in a sachet with an investment of INR 15,000, and dared to take on the multinationals HUL and P&G, the unquestioned leaders in that segment. The 'sachet revolution' was a major event of this era. Most companies resorted to the low unit-price strategy, focusing on value-for-money products. All possible categories, like detergents, soaps, toothpaste, sauces, noodles, mineral water, toiletries, etc., were introduced in sachet packaging to ensure affordability of the product, and encourage the maximum number of people to try it.

Over the years, there has been a shift in rural consumers from farm to non-farm sectors, resulting in an increase in their purchasing power. Also, a series of good harvests backed by several good monsoons has boosted rural incomes in agricultural and allied activities. This is reflected in their living standards and possession of assets such as electrical gadgets and modern amenities at home.

Purchasing power in rural India is rising steadily, resulting in the growth of the rural market. Today, unlike in the past, price is not the only consideration in the purchase of a product. Also, with growing incomes, rural consumers aspire to live better, eat healthy, and have a better tomorrow. Hence, marketers have to find a way to cater to their changing aspirations, keeping in mind that rural consumers are value buyers (see 'Rural Marketing Insight: Rural Consumers Prefer Value for Money'). They expect great quality at affordable prices. The challenge for marketers is to make good quality aspirational products available to them at affordable prices.

RURAL MARKETING INSIGHT | RURAL CONSUMERS PREFER VALUE FOR MONEY

Marketers often erroneously perceive price as their only weapon when targeting rural customers. In actuality, rural consumers are driven by value for money, not price alone. These consumers scrutinize products, raise real concerns, and eventually ask the marketer, 'is your product worth buying?' If the consumers see value for money, they will buy the product. Their discerning and cautious approach does not stop them from upgrading to better products delivering higher value for money, as evidenced in the case of dish washing products and mosquito repellents. A few instances where consumers have adopted higher priced products in rural areas to get good value for money are:

1. Dish Washing Products: The shift to bars from local *mitti* cleaners and dish washing powder in rural India clearly indicates that rural consumers are willing to adopt higher priced products, provided that quality is superior. This is despite the fact that dish washing bars are priced at INR 50 per kg as against dish washing powders, which are priced at only INR 19 per kg. Today, the sale of bars is growing at 11 per cent annually, whereas that of cleaning powders is declining steadily (–13 per cent). This trend is reflected in the stocking pattern in rural stores, where the sales of powders is declining.
2. Mosquito Repellents: At 17 per cent, the rural mosquito repellent market is growing much faster than its urban counterpart, which is growing at a mere 8 per cent. Despite the fact that both vapourizers and mats require electricity, we see that the market share of liquid vapourizers is higher, and it continues to grow faster than the other available formats.

Source: FICCI Nielson Report, 2010.

> PRICING STRATEGIES < CHAPTER 7 137

High-value brands too are doing well in rural markets. Rural consumers across income segments are showing a marked propensity towards spending on premium high-quality products backed by strong brand values. For example, rural people have traditionally been '*bidi*' smokers; however, this is slowly changing, and the younger generation is shifting to cigarettes. Rural consumers are upgrading to aspirational products like face wash, deodorants, cream biscuits, and noodles.

How Do Companies Price?

For a company, it is crucial to decide how much to charge for a product. If it charges too much, the product will not sell; if the product is priced very low, the company may not be able to earn a significant revenue, and the product's market value will be diminished.

In rural markets, consumers look at the value for money. So companies have to price their products to meet consumer expectations and generate profits. Nowadays, companies also opt for target pricing in the rural segment. Target pricing involves setting a target price for the product prior to its production. For rural consumers, companies sometimes fix an ideal, affordable price, and then ensure that that price is met. A case in point is the Tata Nano, which holds the distinction of being the cheapest car on Indian roads. It is no secret that the Tatas fixed the price of the car and tweaked features and functionalities to deliver the end product at the pre-determined price point. The

Target pricing is a concept used throughout the product lifecycle, but is primarily used and is most effective at the product development and design stage.

GILLETTE

Gillette[2] commands about 70 per cent of the world's razor and blade sales, but it lags behind rivals in India mainly because rural consumers cannot afford to buy its flagship products. A mere 10 per cent use Gillette blades in India, against about 50 per cent worldwide. To attract and retain more consumers, Gillette has launched a new shaving system—Gillette Guard—comprising a blade and a light plastic handle at INR 15. The replaceable blades cost INR 5. P&G used target costing to develop this product particularly for rural customers. To cut costs, P&G started with a blank piece of paper for the new product, only including features that men in rural India valued and delivered benefits they were willing to pay for. Although most men in the USA and Western Europe prefer a heavy razor handle and lubrication strip, P&G found that men in rural India preferred a safe and affordable shave the most. To meet the key needs of safety and affordability, Gillette Guard was designed. The lighter handle and absence of lubrication strip ensured an efficient manufacturing process and lower product cost to meet the affordability parameter of men in rural India.

Nano uses just one wiper, one side-view mirror, and the seats are not adjustable.

Consumer Psychology and Pricing

A rural marketer should understand consumer psychology before setting the prices of their offerings. They need to keep the following points in mind:

- Rural consumers are very conscious of value for money. They do not always look for cheap products; instead, they want good quality for the money they spend.
- Rural consumers still do not perceive the premium value of brands. They are happy to deal with products, especially consumer durables, which offer basic functions. High-priced products

Gillette Guard was launched to provide high-quality shave at an affordable price and the feel of a premium brand for men in emerging markets.

Rural Marketing Snapshots depict the transition of rural India through powerful visuals.

Caselets highlight best-in-class practices and unique innovative initiatives and solutions that have been adopted by companies successfully.

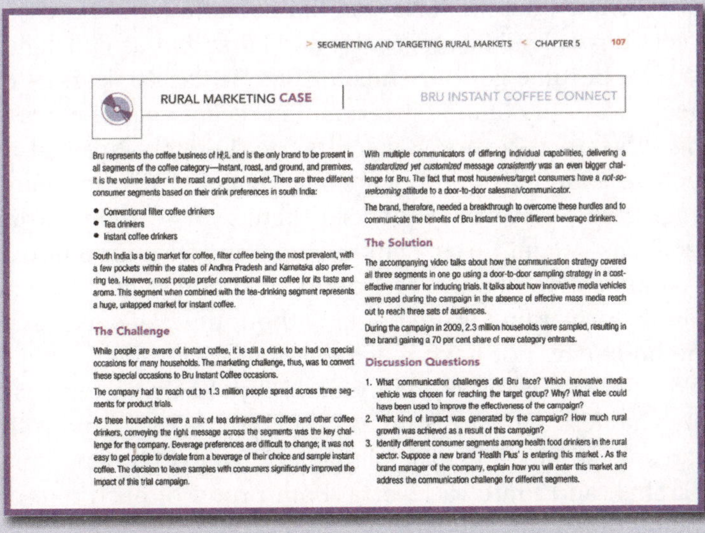

> SEGMENTING AND TARGETING RURAL MARKETS < CHAPTER 5 107

RURAL MARKETING CASE | BRU INSTANT COFFEE CONNECT

Bru represents the coffee business of HUL and is the only brand to be present in all segments of the coffee category—instant, roast, and ground, and premixes. It is the volume leader in the roast and ground market. There are three different consumer segments based on their drink preferences in south India:

- Conventional filter coffee drinkers
- Tea drinkers
- Instant coffee drinkers

South India is a big market for coffee, filter coffee being the most prevalent, with a few pockets within the states of Andhra Pradesh and Karnataka also preferring tea. However, most people prefer conventional filter coffee for its taste and aroma. This segment when combined with the tea-drinking segment represents a huge, untapped market for instant coffee.

The Challenge

While people are aware of instant coffee, it is still a drink to be had on special occasions for many households. The marketing challenge, thus, was to convert these special occasions to Bru Instant Coffee occasions.

The company had to reach out to 1.3 million people spread across three segments for product trials.

As these households were a mix of tea drinkers/filter coffee and other coffee drinkers, conveying the right message across the segments was the key challenge for the company. Beverage preferences are difficult to change; it was not easy to get people to deviate from a beverage of their choice and sample instant coffee. The decision to leave samples with consumers significantly improved the impact of this trial campaign.

With multiple communicators of differing individual capabilities, delivering a *standardized yet customized message consistently* was an even bigger challenge for Bru. The fact that most housewives/target consumers have a *not-so-welcoming* attitude to a door-to-door salesman/communicator.

The brand, therefore, needed a breakthrough to overcome these hurdles and to communicate the benefits of Bru Instant to three different beverage drinkers.

The Solution

The accompanying video talks about how the communication strategy covered all three segments in one go using a door-to-door sampling strategy in a cost-effective manner for inducing trials. It talks about how innovative media vehicles were used during the campaign in the absence of effective mass media reach out to reach three sets of audiences.

During the campaign in 2009, 2.3 million households were sampled, resulting in the brand gaining a 70 per cent share of new category entrants.

Discussion Questions

1. What communication challenges did Bru face? Which innovative media vehicle was chosen for reaching the target group? Why? What else could have been used to improve the effectiveness of the campaign?
2. What kind of impact was generated by the campaign? How much rural growth was achieved as a result of this campaign?
3. Identify different consumer segments among health food drinkers in the rural sector. Suppose a new brand 'Health Plus' is entering this market. As the brand manager of the company, explain how you will enter this market and address the communication challenge for different segments.

Rural Marketing Cases at the end of each chapter helps readers apply their learning from the chapter to real-life situations and problems. The case is divided into two parts: text and video (included in the CD-ROM bundled with the book). Readers are required to read the text and see the video to analyse the case and answer the discussion questions.

::: The Teaching and Learning Package

The second edition of *Rural Marketing* includes a teaching and learning package.

For Instructors

PowerPoint lecture slides, for use by instructors, provide an overview of key chapter concepts and examples, and include additional notes to help instructors explain various rural marketing concepts. This is designed to deliver classroom sessions in an interesting and engaging manner.

::: A Note on the Language and Terms Used in the Book

I have used the ISO 4217 code for the Indian currency—INR—instead of Rs throughout the book.

The terms million and billion have been used to represent large numbers, and the use of lakh and crore, although common in Indian English have been avoided.

In the interest of gender equality, I have avoided using terms like he and she when the pronoun is indefinite. Instead I have used they, their, and them in the singular sense.

::: Acknowledgements

I am grateful to Jagdish N. Sheth, a world-renowned authority on marketing, for agreeing to write the Foreword. It is brilliant and reflects a deep understanding of rural markets. He is a true master and a great source of inspiration for all of us.

I am indebted to Bhalender Singh Nayyar, IIM Calcutta (1971 batch), for guiding the book project through all its stages. He and I first met as colleagues at MICO-Bosch in 1976 and became good friends for life. He has 40 years of rich marketing experience in a variety of industries, and in recent years he has been teaching marketing subjects at several B-schools. He therefore brought a wonderful blend of practical experience and academic rigour to the assignment. Pankaj Mishra, Partner, MART deserves a special thanks for leading a young team of MART professionals—Rajni Teriar, Pankita Uppal and Deepika Sharma, and Pratigya Kwatra—who contributed the first drafts of chapters and case studies, and mined data and information for the book. Without the painstaking coordination of Pankaj, the book may not have reached completion. The young team—supported by Nikhil Sharma, Satya Mohanty, and Divya Kashyap, who wrote the first drafts of some chapters and case studies—worked tirelessly and with total commitment and responsibility. My special thank is due to Pradeep Kumar, Poulomy Roy, Dharmik Shah and Pratigya Kwatra. I am proud of each one of them and amazed at their enthusiasm and energy.

I am grateful to my publisher Pearson, particularly Varun Goenka, Associate Acquisition Editor and Vipin Kumar, Production Editor, for their help and support throughout the writing of this book. Both the editors were very patient and respectful in their dealings. I want to thank them for their input and enthusiasm.

I offer this book to the very source of knowledge from where I have drawn my inspiration.

Pradeep Kashyap

AFTER READING THIS CHAPTER, YOU WILL BE ABLE TO:

1. Define rural India and rural markets
2. Identify common rural myths
3. Understand the rural marketing mix and the challenges related to it
4. Understand the characteristics of the evolving rural consumer
5. Describe the emerging rural India

CHAPTER 1 ::: THE CALL OF RURAL INDIA

one

Before 2006, Sakamma, a 35-year old lady in a village in Nalgonda district, used to stay in a small house with her husband and three children. Her husband was the sole bread earner for the family of five. His meagre income of INR 10,000 per year was barely sufficient for the family; moreover, the situation worsened due to his alcoholism. With this money, it was a daunting task for Sakamma to meet the needs of her growing children.

When the concept selling meeting of 'Project Shakti' was organized by Hindustan Unilever in the same year in her village, Sakamma was excited, and decided to take up the challenge of becoming a Shakti entrepreneur.

Today, she earns an additional yearly income of INR 10,000 through Shakti. The programme has given her the desired financial independence that has enabled her to plan for the future of her children. 'I want my daughter to become an engineer,' she proudly says.[1] Sakamma today has independent access to a bank and decides what investments to make. She recently invested in gold jewellery as she has started preparing for her daughter's marriage. Sakamma was recently also chosen to work with the government to help educate the rural population on health issues.

Such initiatives like Project Shakti have not only opened up earning opportunities for rural people like Sakamma, but have also led to rural development in such a way that rural masses are now getting exposed to the right quality products and services, which in turn is adding to their quality of life. Rural markets are no longer a mass of illiterate, poverty-stricken people who are reluctant to change and spend. Instead, they are today becoming the most lucrative markets that every marketer is eyeing.

Project Shakti, HUL's rural initiative, has empowered underprivileged rural women in scores of villages across India by making them financially independent.

A habitation with a population density of less than 400 per sq. km, where at least 75 per cent of the male working population is engaged in agriculture and where there exists no municipality or board, is defined as a rural habitation.

Defining Rural Markets

The Census of India (2001) defines any habitation with a population density of less than 400 per sq. km, where at least 75 per cent of the male working population is engaged in agriculture and where there exists no municipality or board, as a rural habitation. Thus, the rural population consists of 800 million inhabitants, accounting for 70 per cent of India's population. Depending on their requirements, different organizations ascribe different meanings to the term *rural*. LG Electronics, for instance, defines any population centre other than the seven metros as semi-urban or rural. This definition is in stark contrast to that of the Census. It is important for a marketer to look beyond these definitions at the underlying limitations of each. Table 1.1 captures important definitions and limitations that marketers should be familiar with.

While defining a market as *rural*, the following facts and figures should be considered:

- As per the 2011 Census, India has more than 20,000 villages whose population ranges from 5,000–10,000. So any population cut-off criteria should definitely include these villages as rural areas. The majority of rural institutions, agricultural markets and rural banks are located in larger villages and towns, which have a population of up to 10,000. As the population crosses this figure, characteristics

| TABLE **1.1** |
Definitions of Rural

Organization	Definition of Rural	Limitations
Census	*Village:* Basic unit for rural areas is the revenue village, which might comprise several hamlets demarcated by physical boundaries. *Town:* Towns are actually urban areas that satisfy the following criteria: • Minimum population ≥ 5,000 • Population density ≥ 400/ sq. km • 75% of the male population engaged in non-agricultural activities	The term 'rural' is not defined. It does not specify the population strata. It does not rule out 5,000+ population villages.
IRDA	Similar to the Census definition *Village:* Basic unit for rural areas is the revenue village, which might comprise several hamlets demarcated by physical boundaries. *Town:* Towns are urban places that satisfy the following criteria: • Minimum population ≥ 5,000 • Population density ≥ 400/ sq. km • 25% rather than 75% of the male population engaged in non-agricultural activities	Widening of definition has allowed a larger market to be considered for rural products.
RBI	*Rural:* All locations with a population up to 10,000 will be considered rural, irrespective of whether village or town. *Semi-urban:* All locations with a population between 10,000 and 100,000 will be considered semi-urban, irrespective of whether village or town.	Village and town characteristics are not defined: • Towns with less than 10,000 population are defined as rural. • Villages with more than 10,000 population are defined as semi-urban.
Planning Commission	Towns with population up to 15,000 are considered rural.	Town characteristics are not defined.
Sahara	Locations with shops/commercial establishments up to 10,000 population size are treated as rural.	No town or village characteristics defined.
LG Electronics	All population centres other than the 7 metros are considered rural or semi-urban.	Population criteria is not considered.

such as occupation, consumption and buying behaviour show a marked change, indicative of the transition from a rural to an urban/semi-urban set-up.

- Many villages, although now notified as towns due to their economic growth over the last three or four decades, continue to retain their rural character.
- Leaving aside Hindustan Unilever and ITC, most companies in the FMCG sector define a rural set-up as any place with a population of up to 20,000. Similarly, durables and agri-input companies set this limit at 50,000.

Rural Myths

Although there has been a great deal of interest in rural markets over the past few years, a few big myths remain regarding the size and potential of rural markets.

Rapid Urbanization

It is widely believed that the pace of migration from rural to urban centres is very rapid, which of course means that rural India is shrinking at a very rapid pace. If this were to continue, rural India would eventually become insignificant in size, and perhaps not worth the effort of entering.

The truth is somewhat different. Up until 1980, there was indeed rapid urbanization. However, since that time, there has been a massive slowdown. In fact, in 2010 the UN population database revealed that the urban population had only a slight increase (0.75 times) over the rate of increase of the rural population, suggesting that migration levels were very low (see Fig. 1.1).

The trend also suggests that in the near future, there may even be reverse migration, which ties in with recent field observations. As earning possibilities increase in rural areas, as has happened through the National Rural Employment Guarantee Scheme (NREGS) in the last few years, there is less incentive to leave for urban markets in search of work, or, if migration does occur, it is only for a short period of time spanning agricultural lean months.

Predictions (United Nations' population database 2010) suggest that while the urban population will continue to grow, the share of rural will come down only marginally till the year 2020, and nearly two-thirds of the country's population will continue to live in villages. So, it would be better for marketers to enter the arena sooner rather than later.

Rural India is An Agrarian Economy

Traditionally, rural India was an agrarian economy. However, this is no longer true. Already the non-farm sector accounts for higher incomes in rural India than the farm sector. This is only expected to increase further (see Fig. 1.2). The increased earning opportunities in rural India have decreased the dependence of agriculture on the vagaries of a good monsoon, suggesting that rural markets will be more

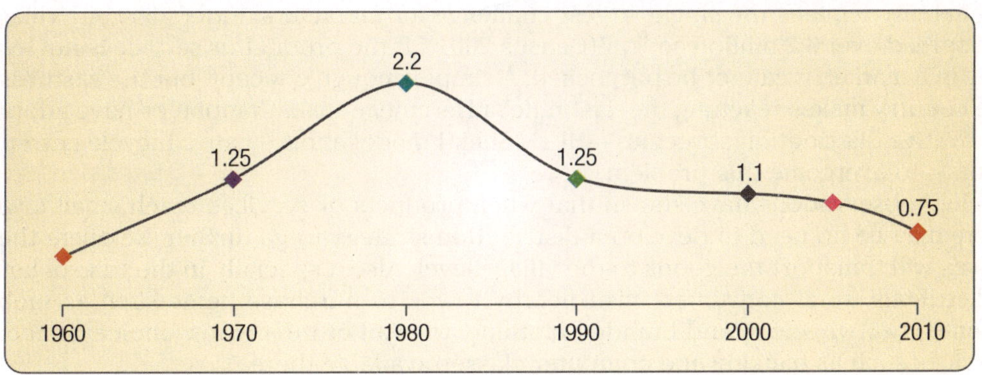

| FIG. 1.1 |
The Pace of Urbanization in India
Source: United Nations' population database.

| FIG. 1.2 |
Growing Non-farm Income

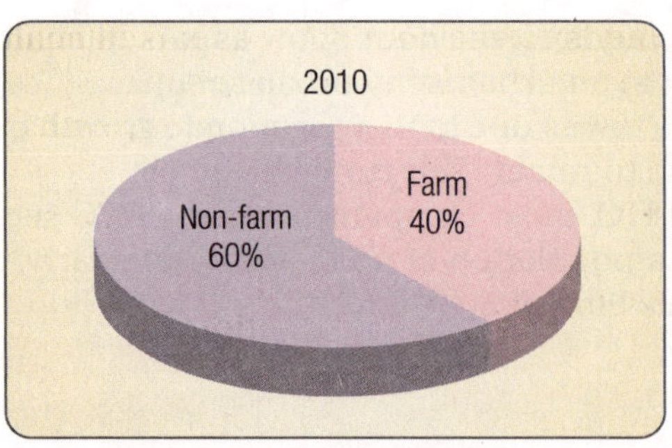

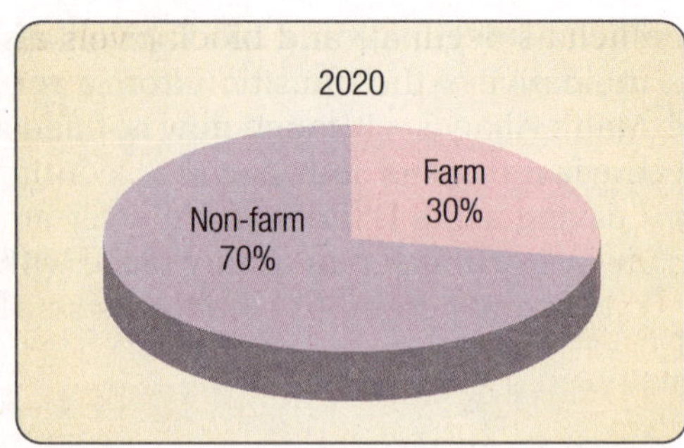

resilient to fluctuations in rainfall.

Field observations have indicated that multiple sources of income for a household are increasingly becoming the norm, with only one family member involved in agriculture as owner or daily wage labourer, while other earning members in the family run a small business or shop or work as salaried employees. Apart from increasing the household income, this has the added benefit of buffering the household from risks occurred in farming, and providing a more constant stream of income to the household rather than only at harvest times.

::: The Rural Marketing Mix: Challenges

The 4 Ps of marketing—price, product, place, and promotion—have been the standard by which every marketing strategy has been developed in the past. This approach was designed for urban markets, but the distinctiveness of rural consumers means that something different was required.

The 4 As of rural marketing are affordability, availability, awareness, and acceptability.

The 4 As of marketing—affordability, availability, awareness, and acceptability—have evolved as a more customer-oriented solution to designing an appropriate marketing strategy for rural markets.

Affordability

It is a fact that per capita rural incomes are still only half of urban incomes, and all products and services designed for rural markets must keep affordability in mind. However, it is important to realize that creating an affordable product or service is not the same as creating a low-cost–low-quality version of an urban product or service. It is vital to design a product or service that caters to the needs of the rural consumers in their unique environment and provides value as perceived by them. Rural consumers are driven by the value proposition, and not just by cost. Affordability here simply means that it should be within their purchasing capacity.

Thus, branded personal care items have been successful in rural areas through 'sachet packaging' by increasing affordability. Companies like Max Vijay now offer life insurance through 'sachet purchasing', small frequent payments made to local retailers.

Availability

Availability remains the single largest challenge for marketers. India's 640,867 villages are spread over 3.2 million sq. km (Census 2001). If the product or service is not available in a market, it cannot be purchased. A simple enough concept, but the vastness of the country makes reaching the 'last mile' a Herculean task. Companies have adopted innovative distribution strategies—HUL's Shakti model and Colgate's bicycle entrepreneurs—to overcome this problem.

Field observations have shown that when products or services reach small towns, there may be no need to develop a distribution strategy to go further. Retailers themselves will transport the goods to the village level. Also, especially in the case of larger ticket items, rural consumers visit nearby towns to purchase items such as mobile phones, two wheelers, and branded clothing, to avail of the greater choice or access services such as banking and computer classes available there.

Thus, the question is, which small towns to target? The paucity of secondary data available at the village and block levels also adds to the confusion, as it is difficult to determine where distribution efforts would reveal a viable market. A 'Small Town Index' to rate the attractiveness of one location versus another would be an invaluable tool in determining where to make the product or service available.

Awarenes

Low levels of literacy remain a stumbling block for any communications message for rural consumers. However, literacy rates are rising, indicating that comprehension levels will rise, too. Access to mass media, especially television, is very high in rural India, with half of all television sets being sold in rural India. This means that rural consumers are exposed to the same advertising designed for urban markets, increasing the demand for typically urban products and services such as fairness creams, etc. However, alternative rural means of communication such as wall paintings, vans, road shows, and *nautankis* in the local language also play an important role in creating interest amongst rural consumers.

Acceptability

A rural marketer should design his products keeping in mind the rural environment and needs, so that his products become acceptable and affordable to the target audience.

Acceptability of a product or service vis-à-vis rural consumers is critical. As mentioned earlier, a product or service developed and designed for urban consumers may not necessarily be successful in rural markets. The rural environment must be borne in mind, in terms of their living conditions and how they would perceive and use the product or service. A productive asset, one that adds to earnings rather than a mere consumption product, would have greater acceptability in a typical rural household. Products that show greater versatility and adaptability to rural conditions have an advantage over others. For example, Chinese models of mobile phones have been an instant hit in rural markets without any advertising or promotion as they are low cost, durable, easy to use, have a built-in torch, and loudspeakers for playing music. So the mobile phone transforms into a personal portable entertainment system operable in 'no electricity' conditions.

Once a product or service fulfils rural concerns on all aspects of the marketing mix, it becomes suitable for rural markets. However, the size of the target rural consumer segment and the cost implications need to be considered to determine if this has the potential to become a successful product or service for the company.

The Evolving Rural Consumer

The rural consumer is becoming more literate and value driven. The greatest change is taking place amongst the rural youth, who are rapidly getting exposed to urban products and services.

The rural consumer is evolving from the poverty-stricken, illiterate stereotype, with a fear of change and a reluctance to spend. Today's rural consumer is value driven. A product is worth purchasing if it enhances his life in a meaningful way. Either it should add to his earning capability (like mobile phones), or it should enhance his status (like readymade clothing). Literacy is rising, and exposure to the same commercials as urban consumers has created a demand for typically urban products and services. Villagers are willing to adopt new products or services if they can clearly see the benefits that accrue. Better road infrastructure has led to increased mobility, with people travelling more often and further afield in search of entertainment in the form of cinema, and not just for visiting family or pilgrimages.

The change has been greatest amongst the rural youth. They are the most educated and most savvy of all rural consumers, emulating their urban cousins and demanding the same high quality in the products and services they require. They are the key drivers for expenditure on mobile phones, two wheelers, computers, personal care items, and education in rural areas, leading to an improved quality of life.

In some households, it is the young children who are the only educated members of the family. In this capacity, they play a large role in decision-making for a variety of products and services, including food and personal care. For example, rural children's 'pester power' has become a driver for the purchase of Horlicks, a health drink, in many households, although mothers are the decision-makers for this product category in urban areas. Children are also the educators of their mothers where health and sanitation messages are concerned, influencing behavioural changes affecting the whole household.

Cultural and social norms are slowly changing, with nuclear families creating new roles for women. Traditionally, males were the decision-makers for all household purchases, but now women do participate in decision-making for the items they use, such as cooking utensils, food items, and soaps, as a result of greater exposure. There are seven million self-help groups (SHGs) in India, which means approximately 70 million SHG members. This averages out to one SHG member in every two rural households. The overwhelming majority of these SHG members are women, many of whom travel to nearby towns for federation meetings as a result of their membership, and in the process gain exposure to advertising and the products available. The 50 per cent reservation for women in the Panchayati Raj has also played a similar role for the participants. This greater level of exposure influences purchase behaviour for the complete household, and creates a willingness to try out new products, services, and brands. Some corporations have already identified this sizeable new target consumer and are designing appropriate communication to create awareness for their brands.

Companies should focus on creating awareness and excitement for their brands amongst the women, youth, and children, rather than focusing on the older generations which remain more resistant to change, if they are to thrive in rural markets. See 'Rural Marketing Snapshot: Changing Rural Settlements' to understand how rapidly rural India is progressing.

Rural India: The Exploding Middle Class

The sleeping giant has woken up, and rural India has finally emerged as a market worth chasing in its own right. 'Rural Marketing Memo: Startling Facts About Rural India' captures some interesting and relatively unknown facts about rural India. For years, its sheer size had captivated the imagination of marketers, but a population of 800 million, consisting of approximately 164 million households, had yet to prove that it had the spending power to emerge as a vital force to compete with urban markets in the eyes of marketers. Rural India has, as a result, been isolated from its urban counterpart, as a

RURAL MARKETING **SNAPSHOT** | CHANGING RURAL SETTLEMENTS

A *kuccha* dwelling

A permanent house

Rural India has come a long way from the *kuccha*, mud houses of the past. Today 62 per cent of rural houses are *pucca*. The dramatic change in trend in the type of house is indicative of the changing lifestyle, and increasing consumerism and asset possession. This large base of pucca-house dwellers presents a huge opportunity to rural marketers.

RURAL MARKETING **MEMO** | STARTLING FACTS ABOUT RURAL INDIA

- 377 million rural mobile users, more than the total number of subscribers in Brazil
- 27 million mobile internet users in Dec 2013
- Of the 22 million DTH subscribers, 60 per cent reside in rural areas and small towns
- 96 million Kisan Credit Cards issued, which exceeds the total number of (credit + debit) cards in urban areas
- Rural India is growing faster than urban India. Durables (25 per cent vs 10 per cent urban growth in 2009); FMCGs (18 per cent vs 12 per cent urban growth in 2009)
- 11 per cent car sales coming from rural areas and small towns
- There are 42,000 rural supermarkets (*haats*) in India, which exceed the total number of retail chain stores in the United States (35,000).

wide range of products and services were considered by marketers to be beyond their purchasing capacity. Today, this has changed. Now rural India has emerged as one of the largest markets to be tapped on the global scale.

The present income pyramid is predicted to change its shape to a diamond as the proportion of the poor earning less than USD 1 per day drastically shrinks over the next decade to almost half.

The rural market is now an acknowledged viable market that has captured the attention of marketers. It already accounts for 56 per cent of India's total income, 64 per cent of expenditure and 33 per cent of savings. Infrastructure is also developing fast, leading to better connectivity by road (67 per cent villages are connected by all-weather roads), by phone (30 per cent tele-density in rural areas), and access to mass media through television. Increased electrification of households (60 per cent) has opened up the rural markets for durables. All of these factors have increased purchasing power and the demand for and access to new goods and brands, as seen over the past decade (2001–2010).

The future of the rural market looks even brighter. Future predictions of income are very positive, suggesting that the present income pyramid will actually change shape to a diamond as the proportion of the poor earning less than USD 1 per day drastically shrinks over the next decade to almost half (see Fig. 1.3). The majority of the rural population will be earning between USD 1 to 5 per day, and the proportion with incomes of over USD 5 per day will increase three-fold. Rural India is fast moving from poverty to prosperity.

The rural population earning more than USD 5 per day per capita on top of the income pyramid holds great promise for marketers. Although it translates into a monthly household income of USD 750 or INR 33,750, it is more than earners with similar

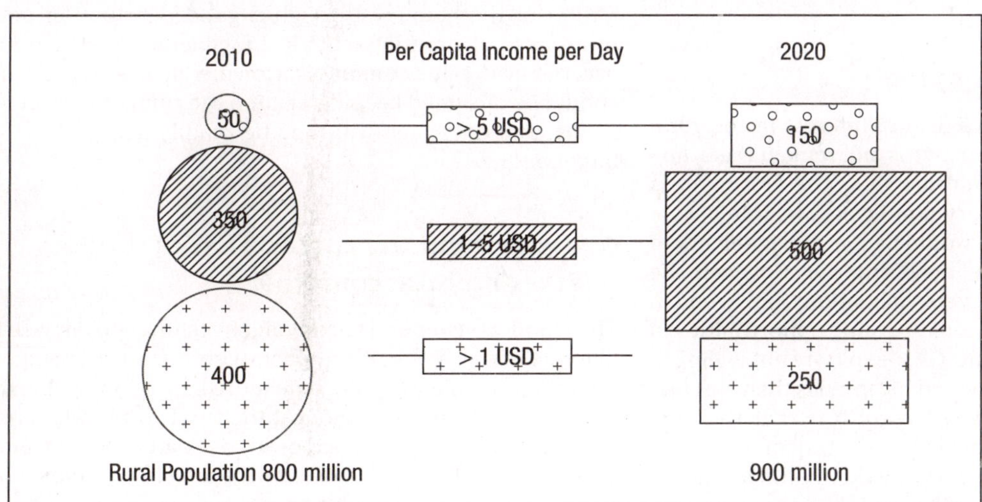

| FIG. **1.3** |
Changing Rural Income Pyramid

incomes in urban areas, as the cost of living in rural areas is far less. In rural areas, almost all own their homes, so there is no rent to be paid. Some food may be grown, saving on household expenditure. Primary healthcare and education are subsidized or even free. As a result, the level of disposable income could be significant for a marketer.

Other growth factors have also contributed. Eight good monsoons and a two-fold increase in the support price of food grains in the last decade have contributed to improving agriculture prosperity as well as to a INR 720 billion loan waiver, which benefited 40 to 45 million farmers. Higher literacy levels, increased mobility, rising aspirations, and a greater linkage between urban and rural India have increased demand, and will continue to do so. An increasing labour force participation in non-farm activities has led to more income earning opportunities, and this trend is likely to continue to grow.

Government focus on poverty alleviation and the rural population has led to significant spending on initiatives. The Rural Employ ment Guarantee Scheme was launched in 2006 to ensure 100 days of employment at a rate of INR 100 per day. The scheme has boosted Base of Pyramid (BoP) incomes and created 1.34 billion man days of work for 38 million people in the year 2013–14.

Over the next decade, it is expected that rural infrastructure will improve drastically with approximately 100 per cent road connectivity, electrified households, literacy, television households, 80 per cent *pucca* households, and 50 per cent mobile penetration. An integration of rural and small town India with urban India is expected, as well as a 100 per cent increase in agricultural productivity, where India will emerge as the food basket of the world. A major shift to cash crops will increase incomes from agriculture. Of course, these predictions will not be fulfilled if there is a change in government to one with less focus on development, or if there is a monsoon failure upsetting the upward growth trend. But, if all goes well, India will emerge as the fifth largest consumer economy of the world by 2020.

REVIEW OF OBJECTIVES

1. Define rural India and rural markets

The Census of India defines rural as any habitation with a population density of less than 400 per sq. km, where at least 75 per cent of the male working population is engaged in agriculture and where there exists no municipality or board. Thus, the rural population today consists of 800 million inhabitants accounting for 70 per cent of India's population. Instead of following the census definition, many organizations and companies define rural markets as per their own marketing requirements.

2. Identify common rural myths

Although there has been a great deal of interest in the rural over the past few years, a few big myths still remain regarding the size and potential of the rural markets. The first myth is that the rural is shrinking at a very rapid pace and if this were to continue, eventually the rural would become insignificant in size and perhaps not worth the effort of entering. However, the truth is that there is a trend of reverse migration from urban to rural and with the increase in income-earning opportunities in rural through programmes like NREGA, people are not willing to move to urban areas now. The second big myth is that the rural is an agrarian economy. However, the truth is that the non-farm sector already accounts for 60 per cent income in rural India, and this is expected to increase further in the future.

3. Understand the rural marketing mix and the challenges related to it

The 4 As of Rural Marketing—affordability, availability, awareness, and acceptability—have evolved as a more customer-oriented solution to designing an appropriate marketing strategy for rural markets. Affordability means that products and services designed for rural markets should be affordable and within their purchasing capacity. They should be easily available and should reach the rural masses even in the interiors of the country through a good distribution network. Awareness of products should be generated using rural-centric, below-the-line communication media. Lastly, the products should be designed keeping in mind the rural environment and needs, and only then will they be readily acceptable to their target audience.

4. Understand the characteristics of the evolving rural consumer

The rural consumer is evolving from the poverty-stricken, illiterate stereotypes of the past, with a fear of change and a reluctance to spend, to become more literate and value driven. The change is greatest amongst the rural youth, who are more educated and are getting exposed to urban products and services. Also, cultural and social norms are slowly changing, with nuclear families creating new roles for women. Therefore, rural marketers should focus on creating awareness and excitement for their brands amongst women, youth and children, rather than focusing on the older generations who remain more resistant to change.

5. Describe the emerging rural India

The rural market is now an acknowledged viable market capturing the attention of marketers. It accounts for 56 per cent of India's total income, 64 per cent of expenditure, and 33 per cent of savings. Fast developments in infrastructure, household electrification, rapid growth in tele-density, and media penetration is leading to the opening up of rural markets at a fast pace. Increased purchasing power and demand for and access to new goods and brands have been observed over the past decade. The future of the rural markets is even brighter, with predictions of the present income pyramid changing to a diamond as the proportion of the poor earning less than USD 1 per day drastically shrinks over the next decade to almost half. Over the next decade, it is also expected that rural infrastructure will improve drastically, along with literacy, mobile and television penetration, and more income to agriculture from cash crops. If all goes well, India will emerge as the fifth largest consumer economy of the world by 2020.

DISCUSSION AND APPLICATION

Discussion of Concepts

1. How do you define rural? Describe how rural has been defined by different organizations.
2. Explain with facts and figures the various myths about rural markets.
3. What are the 4 As of rural marketing? Explain.
4. 'Future lies in rural markets'. Discuss with illustrations.
5. How do the governments in different parts of the world define 'rural'? What differences do you see when you compare rural India to those of other countries?
6. What would be the implications of the 'Changing Rural Income Pyramid' on marketers?

Application of Concepts

1. Which of the 4 As is most difficult to address and replicate in a competitive scenario in rural areas? Explore and discuss with practical examples.
2. Enlist some of the major investments made by corporates in rural India in the past few years. Develop a business case around these investments.

RURAL MARKETING **CASE** | RURAL MARKETS

In India, 70 per cent of the Indian population—800 million-living in approximately 600,000 villages is considered rural. Rural people mostly live in inherited houses which is not the case with their urban counterparts. Rural India lacks basic infrastructure such as electricity and roads. The rural population continues to be largely illiterate with low exposure to products and services.

However, rural India is gaining importance as it accounts for 56 per cent of the total income and 64 per cent of total spending in India. Today, more than 50 per cent of FMCG and durables, 100 per cent of agricultural inputs and 40 per cent of two-wheeler sales come from rural markets.

The accompanying video talks about unity in diversity present in the country in terms of religions, ethnic groups, languages and dialects. At the same time, it talks about the huge potential vested in the rural as a result of which marketers are going rural.

Discussion Questions

1. Despite the diverse heterogeneous nature of rural markets, why are marketers focusing on rural markets?
2. How should marketers tackle the huge diversity seen in rural markets?
3. What steps should a company take to tap the huge potential in rural markets? Discuss this with regard to the 4 Ps of marketing.

AFTER READING THIS CHAPTER, YOU WILL BE ABLE TO:

1. Describe the evolution of rural marketing
2. Track the rural marketing environment in terms of demographic, physical, social, cultural, political, and technological aspects
3. Understand the rural economic environment, the changing rural economic structure, and income spending pattern
4. Understand rural infrastructure, government support, and its relevance to marketing
5. Describe the initiatives in the rural employment generation programme

CHAPTER 2 ::: THE RURAL MARKETING ENVIRONMENT

two

Puttanna, aged 40, lives in Harnahalli village, located 25 km from the Shimoga district centre in Karnataka. Earlier he used to grow groundnuts and vegetables on his small farm (less than one acre) and sell the produce in a mandi to commission agents at very low prices. The low income from his farm forced Puttanna to look for other sources of income. He noticed that the existing transport link between his village and the district centre was insufficient. Due to the increase in economic activity within the village, more people were travelling to Shimoga on a regular basis. Puttanna decided to start a taxi service to improve the connectivity of the village with the district centre, for which he had to sell his farm. Since the proceeds from the land sale were not enough to buy a taxi, he took a loan from an MFI with the help of his wife, who was a member of a self-help group.

The business plan worked, and he is now generating a revenue of INR 1,500 per day. After accounting for diesel, taxi maintenance, and the salary of the driver, he earns INR 400 in a day. He has also opened a grocery shop to supplement his income, which helps him to pay the EMI regularly. The increased, regular income has significantly improved the lives of Puttanna and his family. He now sends his children to a better school.

A number of Puttannas in different parts of rural India are shifting from the farm to the non-farm sector in search of higher incomes and better lives.

The new-generation rural chief wage earner is modern in thought and entrepreneurial in spirit. They believe in leading a simple life and working as smart businessmen.

::: The Evolution of Rural Marketing

The rural environment in India is undergoing a massive change. There has been a significant growth in purchasing power, change in lifestyle, increase in brand consciousness, change in consumption patterns, improvement in infrastructural facilities, and spread of the communication network. These changes have resulted in shifting the marketing battlefields from cities to villages. 'Go Rural' seems to be the latest slogan. The rural market has grown in the following phases from a dark economy to a vibrant economy.

Phase I (Prior to the 1960s)

Prior to the 1960s, the term *rural marketing* referred to the marketing of rural products in rural and urban areas, and agricultural inputs in rural markets. It was considered synonymous with agricultural marketing.

Agricultural produce such as food grains and industrial inputs like cotton, oilseeds, and sugarcane were the primary products marketed during this period. The rural economy was in a primitive stage, with traditional farming methods being used in agriculture. There was limited scope for agricultural marketing. The marketing of earthen and metallic utensils, agricultural tools (ploughs, bamboo baskets, etc.), ropes and wooden products (bullock carts, window and door frames) by skilled workers in rural areas (blacksmiths, carpenters, potters) was not given much importance. This was a totally unorganized market.

Phase II (1960s–1980s)

The Green Revolution changed the face of rural India, ushering in scientific farming practices. Better irrigation facilities, use of fertilizers, pesticides, and high-yield variety seeds, coupled with the application of implements like tractors, power tillers, harvesters, pump sets, and sprinklers resulted in an exponential growth in agricultural production, changing the very content of rural markets.

The White Revolution was initiated by the government with the aim of achieving self-sufficiency in the area of milk production. The cornerstone of the government dairy development policy was producing milk in rural areas through producer cooperatives and moving processed milk to urban demand centres. The formation of producers' cooperatives has played a significant role in institutionalizing milk production and processing.

A new area—marketing of agricultural inputs—emerged. This period saw the emergence of companies such as Mahindra & Mahindra, Escorts, Eicher, Shriram Fertilisers (now DCM Shriram Consolidated Ltd), and Indian Farmers Fertiliser Cooperative Limited (IFFCO).

During this period, marketing of rural products received considerable attention through agencies like the KVIC (Khadi and Village Industries Commission), *bunkar* (weaver) societies, and handicrafts emporia. The promotion of village industries, supported by the government through exhibitions and 'Gram Shree Melas' and 'Shilp Melas', resulted in the inflow of products like handicrafts, handloom textiles, leather products, etc., into urban markets on a large scale.

It was in this phase that a few FMCG companies began establishing a distribution network in the rural segment. In 1970, Nirma became the first company to initiate and produce products for rural consumers. There was also a limited exposure of home appliance companies like Usha, Philips, and Murphy.

Phase III (1990s–2000)

During the first two phases, the marketing of consumables & durables to rural markets was not considered seriously. The prime reasons for this were:

- The growth of urban markets during this period kept marketers busy.
- The potential of rural markets was not visible. The existing rural markets for these

products were not sizeable enough to attract the attention of urban marketers.

- Rural markets were not very accessible. The poor infrastructure of widely scattered villages made them unreachable and expensive in terms of logistics.

Consequently, rural markets were conveniently ignored, as they were seen as extensions of the urban markets.

However, from the 1990s, India's industrial sector gained in strength and maturity. A new service sector emerged, signifying the transition of an agricultural society into an industrial one. Meanwhile, the increased Plan outlay of central and state governments for rural development and for strengthening local governance accelarated socio-economic progress. In addition, economic reforms further accelerated the process by introducing competition into the markets. All these factors resulted in the growth of rural markets for household consumables and durables.

In this phase, most companies (both Indian and multinational) began realizing the enormous potential of rural markets, brought about by a saturation in urban markets.

Rural marketing began assuming importance in Phase III and came to the centre-stage in Phase IV with the government's pro-rural initiatives, and the arrival of global and Indian corporations with customized offerings for rural markets.

Phase IV (After 2000)

After the proven success of marketing models like Project Shakti and e-Choupal, rural marketing has become an agenda for most global and Indian corporations. Rural marketing has taken the centre-stage, as companies that had been serving the urban markets for long have now begun planning to enter the rural market.

Several fast moving consumer goods (FMCG) companies such as Hindustan Unilever, Godrej Consumer Products, Dabur, Marico, and ITC have planned for increased visibility, and have also hired people in rural areas and small towns to establish local connections. Durables companies like LG and Samsung have employed a rural thrust. Automobile companies like Maruti, Hero Honda, and Bajaj are planning a major initiative in rural India by launching more models in the affordable price range. Other companies like GE, Intel, Honeywell, Shell Foundation, Microsoft, and HPCL are planning to come out with new products for rural areas, using low-cost technologies. Reliance has entered the rural market with mobile connections. Private insurance companies are also interested in the market.

The government is taking serious steps to develop the rural market. Government initiatives like farm loan waivers, and employment and rural infrastructure development programmes received a major thrust after 2000. These initiatives attempt to bridge the gap between the rich and the poor.

There is a huge rural market waiting to be served, ready to splurge, and wanting to explore new products and services. The market size of rural India is expected to increase from USD 0.5 trillion to USD 1 trillion by 2020 (MART Knowledge Centre).

::: The Rural Environment

The rural environment comprises demographic, physical, economic, social, cultural, political, and technological aspects of rural markets.

Rural Demography: Understanding the population size, age groups, gender dynamics, family structure, education level, occupation, landholdings pattern, and income structure of rural masses.

The Demographic Environment

In this section, we will discuss the rural population in terms of its size, age, gender, education, occupation, landholdings, and incomes.

- ***Growth in the rural population.*** The rural population has grown by over 200 million over the last two decades (see Table 2.1). The proportion of rural households continues to be 70 per cent, and is expected to stabilize in the event that the rural thrust continues.
- ***Change in the rural family structure.*** Traditionally, households in rural India were joint families. But with the rise in population, the resulting pressure on land, and

| TABLE **2.1** |
The Rural Population in India

Parameter	1991	2001	2011	2015	2021
Total population (in million)	848	1029	1210	1254	1423
Rural population (in million)	629	742	833	866	935
Rural proportion to total population (per cent)	74	72	69	6	66
Male (in million)	NA	381	427	445	479
Female (in million)	NA	360	405	4	456
Number of rural households (in million)	112	138	168	NA	205
Family size (number)	5.55	5.36	4.85	NA	4.4

Source: Census 1991, 2001, and Population Projections for India 2001–26

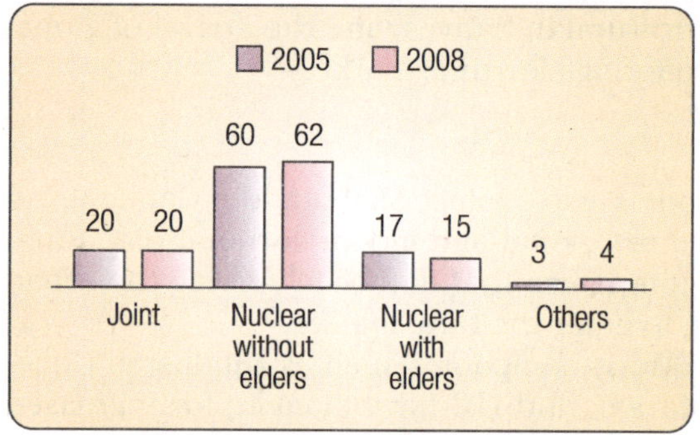

| FIG. **2.1** |
A Break-up of the Type of Households in India
Others include siblings living together, etc.
Source: Indian Readership Survey

several other socio-economic factors (education, separate sources of income, migration, etc.), joint families are now breaking apart. Families are now gradually moving towards the nuclear model in rural areas (see Fig. 2.1). A new concept, that of 'individualized joint families', is emerging, in which families stay in the same house, but have separate kitchens in order to avoid conflicts, pursue individualized choices, and nurture their children better. With the increase in 'individualized joint' and nuclear families, the range and number of branded products entering the family is likely to increase.

- ***Age.*** Thirty-five per cent of the rural population is in the consuming age group of 15–34 yrs (see Table 2.2). This is expected to grow further in the coming years.
- ***Education.*** Twenty-one per cent of the rural population is SSC/HSC and higher pass out (see Fig. 2.2). The literacy rate has gone up from 53 per cent in 2000 to 65 per cent in 2011 (see Table 2.3). The literacy rate is higher in the southern region of the country as compared to the north.
- ***Occupation.*** Agriculture was the principal occupation in rural India. It is now being replaced by non-traditional occupations, including shop/trade, skilled work, and salaried jobs. Rising literacy levels, improved and upgraded skill sets, and new technology have encouraged rural people to take up new occupations. As can be seen from Table 2.4, an increasing number of people have given up farming (decline from 63 to 50 per cent during 2000–2010) on account of land fragmentation, declining profitability in the farm sector, and increasing nuclearization

| TABLE **2.2** |
Distribution of Rural Population by Age Groups

Age Groups (in years)	1991 (in per cent)	2001 (in per cent)	2008 (in per cent)	2011 (in per cent)
0–4	13	11	10	9
5–14	26	26	24	22
15–19	9	10	11	10
20–34	23	23	24	25
35–54	19	20	20	22
55+	10	10	12	12

Source: Census 1991, 2001, and DLHFS 2007–08 (Ministry of Health and Family Welfare)

of families. India is no longer an agrarian economy. There is an increasing incidence of supplementary occupation—an occupation pursued either in addition to the primary occupation, or on a seasonal basis to augment income. As per an Edelweiss-MART survey (2010), 30 per cent of rural households have a supplementary occupation. Out of these, 56 per cent stated self-employment in agriculture as their supplementary occupation.

- ***Landownership.*** Land in rural India is more than a basic input for agriculture; it is also a symbol of security, power, prestige, and social standing. A strong attachment to land, which arises from the fact that land is scarce whereas people are not, has direct economic consequences. As can be seen from Table 2.5, although the total land area has remained nearly constant between 2000–01 and 2010–11, the number of landholdings has increased for smaller landholdings. This highlights the land fragmentation and the increasingly uneconomic nature of agriculture. Landownership in India is extremely fragmented—

	2005	2011
Illiterate	42	35
Up to 9th	43	44
SSC/HSC	12	16
Under-graduate	1	2
Graduate and above	2	3

| FIG. **2.2** |
The Level of Education in Rural India
Source: IRS

Quality education for children is assuming high priority in rural areas, leading to an impressive rise in literacy levels and better informed new-generation customers.

| TABLE **2.3** |
Literacy among Individuals of Age 12 years and Above

Year	Literacy (in per cent)
2000	53
2005	58
2010	63
2011	65

Source: IRS

| TABLE **2.4** |
Occupation Break-up in Rural Areas

Occupation	2000 (in per cent)	2010 (in per cent)
Self-employment in agriculture	36	38
Agricultural labourers	27	12
Non-agricultural labourers	9	31
Self-employment in non-agriculture	14	11
Others	14	8

Source: NSSO 2000– 01 (56th round). Salaried and Edelweiss-MART Survey wage earners are included in others.

| TABLE 2.5 |
The Landholding Pattern in Rural India

Size Category	No. of Landholdings in Millions (per cent)			Area in Million Hectares (per cent)		
	*2000-01**	*2005-06**	*2010-11*	*2000-01**	*2005-06**	*2010-11*
Marginal (Below 1 ha)	75.4 (62.9)	83.7 (64.8)	92.8 (67.1)	29.8 (18.7)	32 (20.2)	35.9 (22.5)
Small (1–4 ha)	36.7 (30.6)	38.1 (29.5)	38.7 (28)	70.3 (44.1)	71 (44.8)	72.9 (45.7)
Medium (5–10 ha)	6.6 (5.5)	6.4 (4.9)	5.9 (4.2)	38.2 (24)	36.6 (23.1)	33.8 (21.2)
Large (10ha & Above)	1.2 (1)	1.1 (0.8)	1 (0.7)	21.1 (13.2)	18.7 (11.8)	16.9 (10.6)
Total	119.9 (100)	129.2 (100)	138.3 (100)	159.4 (100)	158.3 (100)	159.6 (100)

Source: Ninth Agriculture Census 2010–11 * Excluding Jharkhand

small and marginal farmers, who constitute 95 per cent of the population, control only 68 per cent of the land. The average landholding size in India is just 1.2 hectares.

- ***Income.*** Rural income constitutes around 56 per cent share of the total incomes in India. The per capita income for rural India has increased from INR 4,860 in 1994–95 to INR 11,227 in 2004-05. In 2010, the per capita income was estimated at INR 15,173 (Edelweiss MART Survey, 2010). The urban–rural disparity ratio has declined from 2.41 in 1995 to 1.96 in 2005, narrowing down the income gap. According to the McKinsey Report, the middle class and above (seekers, strivers, and global) will grow six-fold from 32 million in 2005 to 208 million in 2025. Income growth per HH is expected to accelerate from the current 2.8 per cent to 3.6 per cent by 2025 (see Fig. 2.3).

The Physical Environment

The physical environment in rural areas comprises settlement size and rural housing structures.

SETTLEMENTS (SCATTERED AND CLUSTERED) Villages comprise homestead land (*abadi*) and cultivated land. The settlement pattern of households is either in a cluster or in individualized landholdings, or a combination of both. Farmers normally live in an abadi. In a village, it is quite common to find houses ordered according to kinship, caste, or religious groups. Sometimes entire villages are classified on the basis of dominant caste groups, or some other predominant characteristic.

Physical environment in rural areas entails the study of the settlement patterns of households and types of dwellings. Table 2.6 provides rich insights to a marketer:

- Villages with a population of less than 500 generally do not have any shop, but the number of such villages has decreased by 4 per cent over the last 10 years. Twenty-two thousand villages in the 'less than 500 population' category have upgraded to the 500+ population category.

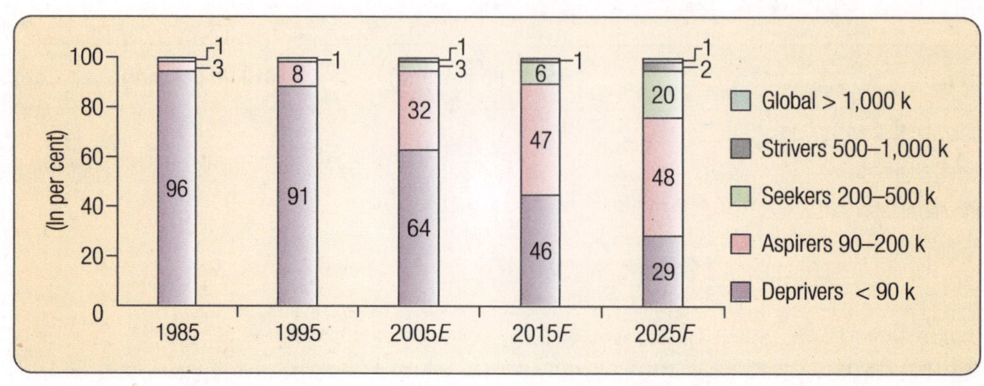

| FIG. 2.3 |
Share of Rural Population by Income Class
Source: This was originally published in the report *The Bird of Gold: The Rise of India's Consumer Market* prepared by the McKinsey Global Institute. Copyright© 2007 McKinsey & Company. All rights reserved. Reprinted with permission.

| TABLE **2.6** |
Spread of Villages in Rural India

Population Size	Villages in Size Group (1991)		Villages in Size Group (2001)		Villages in Size Group (2001)	
	Number	***Per cent***	***Number***	***Per cent***	***Number***	***Per cent***
Less than 200	103,952	17.9	92,541	15.6	82,151	13.74
201–500	141,143	24.3	127,054	21.4	114,732	19.19
501–1,000	144,998	25.0	144,817	24.4	141,800	23.72
1,001–2,000	114,395	19.7	129,662	21.9	139,164	23.28
2,001–5,000	62,915	10.8	80,313	13.5	96,428	16.13
5,000 +	13,376	2.3	18,758	3.2	23,333	3.90
Total no. of inhabited villages	580,779	100.0	593,154	100.0	597,608	100
Total no. of villages (includes uninhabited villages)	**634,321**	-	**638,588**	-	**640,867**	-

Source: Census of India 1991, 2001, 2011

- Villages in the 2,000+ population strata are the most prosperous. The number of such villages is increasing very rapidly. Over the last 10 years, almost 21,000 villages have been upgraded to the 2,000+ population category. These villages have around 16 shops.
- As per the 2011 Census, the 20 per cent villages in the 2,000+ population category account for 50 per cent of the rural population and 60 per cent of rural wealth. A marketer going rural should target this category first.

THE RURAL HOUSING PATTERN The types of houses in rural areas are very strong indicators of economic growth. Over the last 20 years, the trend in house type has changed dramatically, from less permanent, semi-pucca or *kuccha*, to more permanent pucca types.

A majority of low-income groups live in kuccha houses. However, as incomes increase, the number of kuccha houses comes down; low-income groups gradually move towards semi-kuccha houses and then finally, pucca houses. Today, 63 per cent of rural houses are pucca as depicted in Fig. 2.4. Statistics indicate that the owners of such houses possess sufficient disposable income.

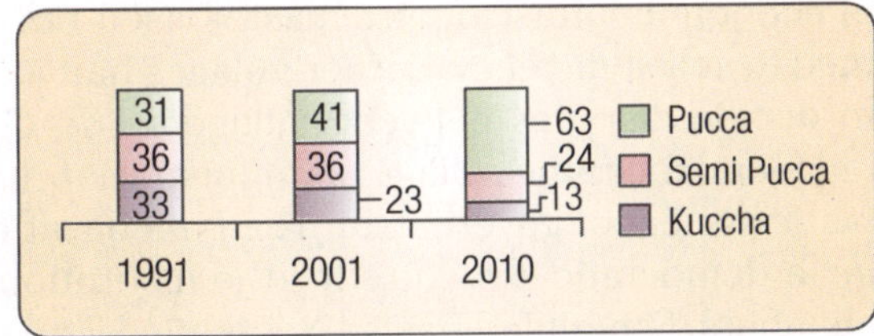

| FIG. **2.4** |
The Housing Pattern in Rural Areas
Source: Census of India and Indian Readership Survey.

The Social and Cultural Environment

SOCIO-CULTURAL REGIONS Society and polity across the country vary between regions and sub-regions, as well as between different religious, caste, and linguistic groups. Although there are no strict boundaries for identifying cultural differentials, common socio-cultural behaviour has been mapped as distinct socio-cultural regions (SCRs).

A socio-cultural region (SCR) is a group of districts clubbed together, based on linguistic homogeneity combined with geographical contiguity, financial, economic and administrative homogeneity, and regionalization of culture and lifestyle.

India has been primarily divided into 56 SCRs. However, some larger SCRs were later divided into two regions to ensure that each SCR used for town\village selection is not too large, and that no SCR is spread across two states. This resulted in a total of 90 distinct regions. The National Readership Survey uses these 90 regions as the stratum for media survey across the country.

A socio-cultural region (SCR) is a group of districts clubbed together, based on linguistic homogeneity combined with geographical contiguity, financial, economic and administrative homogeneity, and regionalization of culture and lifestyle, which is unique to them and differentiates them from other districts and caste and class considerations.

Rural settlements are mostly semi-pucca and pucca dwellings, clustered around castes and kinship.

While the urban environment across SCRs reflects degrees of homogeneity, the rural environment is distinctly different, as reflected in Table 2.7. Marketers use SCRs as a yardstick for market segmentation and targeting. We discuss this in detail in Chapter 5. Within each SCR, there is a spectrum of rural and urban communities on the continuum of socio-economic variables.

THE VILLAGE COMMUNITY Historically, villages have in many ways been self-sufficient and autonomous. While agricultural surplus contributed to the sustenance of economic infrastructure, caste-based occupations and trades collectively contributed to self-sufficiency. Earlier villages had a council of elders (panchayat), which used to decide disputes between villagers and discuss matters of common interest. Post independence, the village administration has undergone changes under the democratic system of governance. The panchayat members are now elected, thereby ensuring a democratic structure for the institution. There is reservation for disadvantaged members, Scheduled Castes/Scheduled Tribes, and women. All villagers above the age of 18 are eligible to vote.

Gram panchayats today have a statutory base with a range of regulatory and developmental functions, as declared in the Constitution of India. They are part of the state administration in a three-tier Panchayati Raj structure: district, block, and village level.

Earlier, because of their experience and maturity, the elderly were considered more capable of advising and leading the village. Now, the role of the educated, informed youth, and knowledgeable persons (headmaster, teachers, retired military personnel, etc.) has increased within the community, as well as within the family. They play an important role in popularizing a brand.

Gender bias is declining, and hence, the female child's education is also being given equal importance. The status of women in villages is changing. Today, women in rural areas are not only taking care of household work, but are also contributing to the family income and ensuring the well-being of the family. Their role in decision-making has also increased.

| TABLE **2.7** |
Urban and Rural Differentiators

Urban India	Rural India
Size and Characteristics	
• City has a large population size growing at a fast growth rate due to migration from rural areas for education and employment. The population density is high. • Towns are smaller urban units.	• Village is a human settlement with a small administrative unit comprising a few hundred households. • Migration from village to city/town is for better education and employment.
Settlement Pattern	
• The city settlement is compact, though spread over a larger area. • Land use is for residential, commercial, industrial, roads and streets, institutional and community facilities. • Structure of houses is permanent and mostly more than one storey. • Housing on rental is highly prevalent. • Clustering pattern in cities is more on the basis of class. In the initial phases of urbanization of a human settlement, neighbourhoods and streets indicated some caste/sub-caste and extended family influences. • Primary resource base is production and distribution of industrial goods and services.	• Village has land for human settlement and for cultivation. • The settlements are predominantly clustered, but in some areas households settle on respective cultivable landholdings. • Houses earlier were largely semi-pucca or kachha, but now there are more pucca houses. • They are owner occupied. • Houses in villages are clustered according to kinship, caste, or religious groups. Some villages are locally referred to as '*thakur gaon*' or '*harijan basti*', depending on the numerically major caste residing in the village. • Land is the primary resource for livelihoods. Others are water bodies, forests, and mountains. Cows, buffaloes, and poultry are kept for household needs like milk, eggs, and meat.
Occupation	
• Occupation is diverse, ranging from professionals, skilled, semi-skilled, to unskilled workers. • Specialization is achieved through higher education, training, and skill development.	• Predominant occupation was agriculture, but now people are shifting to non-traditional occupations like shop/trade, skilled work, salaried job. • Skill upgradation is gradually improving with exposure to new technology.
Realms of Activities	
• Interaction and mobility is spread over a large geographical, social, and economic area. • Relationship is more complex with differentiation in personal and professional life. • There is an erosion of the role of custom, tradition, and religion. Formal mechanisms of social control are needed in the absence of community influence. • Women have a freedom of choice vis-à-vis activity and interest.	• Restricted to smaller geographical, social and economic area. • Individuals are recognized by family, caste, and village. Individual behaviour is governed by custom, tradition and religion. • Conformance and compliance to mechanisms of social control is through family, kinship, and community. • Women have limited freedom of choice of activity or interest.

THE CASTE SYSTEM Indian society had a definite scheme of social gradation, with the Brahmins at the head of the hierarchy, followed by Kshatriyas (warriors) and Vaishyas (business class and traders), and then the Shudras (involved in low-skilled and odd jobs) at the bottom. Individual castes themselves are further divided into sub-castes, each claiming social supremacy over the other. Claims of social supremacy were usually exploitative, and accompanied the humiliation of social groups lower in the hierarchy, whose basic human rights were denied.

The Shudras suffer from social and economic disadvantages, and are even treated as untouchables. Access to certain public places like temples, parts of the village, and even drinking water from wells used by upper castes are denied to them. Settlements of the lower castes are located mostly on the outskirts of the village.

Post independence, the development process in the social, economic, and political arenas have initiated changes in the traditional systems; however, caste hegemony continues to affect rural polity. The abolition of zamindari and other legislation related to land and labour have brought about changes to empower the deprived.

However, over the last few years the influence of the caste system appears to be reducing. Now we can see mixed hamlets, with Brahmins and Kshatriyas living at the same place in villages. Untouchability is also phasing out, except in a few states like Rajasthan, where it is highly prevalent.

As the impact of the caste system has diluted, it is no longer of much importance from a marketer's point of view.

The Political Environment

The political environment in rural areas focuses on understanding the Panchayati Raj System and its functioning, as it plays a critical role in many spheres of rural consumers' lives.

Historically, the panchayat and the village pradhan/sarpanch had represented rural India. Dominated largely by the upper castes, they lorded over the political scene until the panchayats became part of the administrative machinery of the Government of India. Under the Panchayati Raj system, all government departments (education, health, agriculture, rural development, social justice, livelihoods) form an integrated approach for the development of rural areas.

PANCHAYATI RAJ INSTITUTIONS The salient features of Panchayati Raj under the 73rd Amendment are:

- To provide a three-tier system of Panchayati Raj for all states with a population of over two million.
- To hold panchayat elections regularly every five years.
- To provide reservation of seats for Scheduled Castes, Scheduled Tribes, and women (not less than 33 per cent).
- To appoint a State Finance Commission to make recommendations with regard to the financial powers of panchayats.
- To constitute a District Planning Committee to prepare draft development plans for the district.
- According to the Constitution, panchayats shall be given powers and authority to function as institutions of self-government.
- Preparation of a plan for economic development and social justice.
- Implementation of schemes for economic development and social justice in relation to the 29 subjects given in the Eleventh Schedule of the Constitution.
- To levy, collect, and appropriate taxes, duties, tolls, and fees.

Gram Sabha A general assembly of villagers called the Gram Sabha has to be organized, involving people's participation and necessarily including the rural poor, women and marginalized communities in decisions on matters affecting their lives. The active functioning of the Gram Sabha will ensure participatory democracy with transparency, accountability, and achievement.

The Gram Sabha should meet at least once in each quarter, preferably on Republic Day, Labour Day, Independence Day, and Gandhi Jayanti. Role of the Gram Sabha:

- Decides the developmental work to be undertaken by panchayats, based on a needs assessment.
- Suggests remedial measures for economy and efficiency in the functioning of the panchayats.
- Questions and scrutinizes the decisions of panchayats in its meetings.
- Discusses the annual financial statement of gram panchayats.

The structure of the panchayat ensures the participation of villagers in electing their representatives to the panchayat as well as in its functioning, thereby making them politically aware and active.

| TABLE **2.8** |
Rapid Growth of Farm Mechanization

	1994	2002	2006
Total cropped area (million hectares)	187	190.5	190.3
Tractors (thousands)	1540	2450	2749
Threshers (thousands)	1351	1551	1614
Harvesters (thousands)	407	422	427

Source: Agricultural Machinery Sector in India, FICCI Report

Villages with a population of 5,000 or a cluster of smaller villages with a cumulative population of 5,000 form a panchayat. Villages are segmented to form wards, from where ward members are elected to the panchayat. The ward members select their leader, who becomes the sarpanch. The sarpanch represents the village at the *tehsil/ taluka*/block level.

The Technological Environment

The changes in the rural technological environment were triggered by rapid mechanization in farming after the Green Revolution (see Table 2.8), and the information and communication technology revolution in the last decade.

Technological environment catalyses the adoption of new technology, like farm mechanization and ICT, leading to the transformation of rural consumers with increased consumption of new products and services.

RAPID MECHANIZATION There has been a sustained increase in the adoption of mechanization to ensure greater returns on investment (RoI) and sustainability of agriculture. Mechanization, primarily driven by the increased use of tractors, is replacing manual and animal labour.

As a consequence of the mechanization of agriculture, the share of animal power has declined from 16 to 7 per cent, and the share of tractor power has increased from 30 to 46 per cent between 1990–91 and 1995–96, as depicted in Fig. 2.5. India is the second largest manufacturer of tractors in the world, with annual sales of 342,000 tractors (2009–10). There are 16.7 tractors per 1,000 hectares at present.

All these factors have resulted in better productivity in agriculture.

| FIG. **2.5** |
Increasing Mechanization: Source of Power

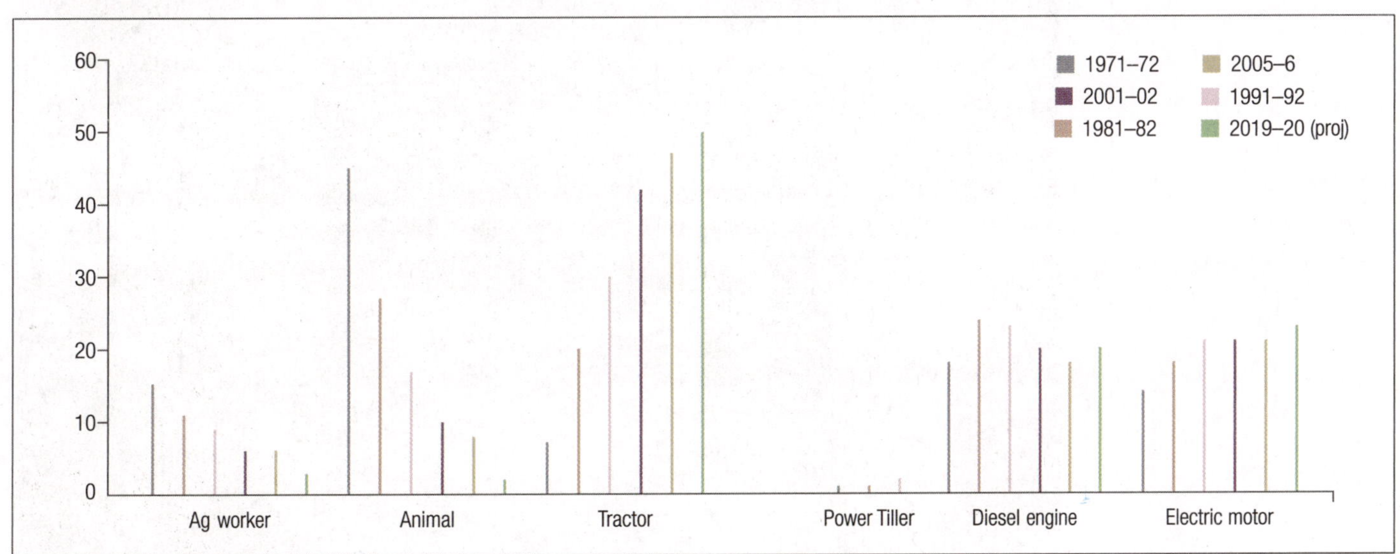

THE INFORMATION AND COMMUNICATION TECHNOLOGY REVOLUTION

Information and communication technology is making inroads into, and changing the face of, rural India.

The evolution of the computer, Internet, and mobile phones has had a tremendous impact on the lives of rural people. It is connecting farmers to food retailers, enabling them to sell the produce at high farm gate prices without delay. They receive market information at the touch of the button.

Before ITC introduced e-Choupal, farmers were restricted to selling their produce to middlemen in the local mandi at low prices. Today they have formed a community of e-farmers who have access to the daily prices of a variety of crops, wider markets, weather forecasts, the latest farming techniques, crop insurance, etc. This is transforming the Indian farmer into a progressive, knowledge-seeking netizen.

The e-Choupal project is currently benefiting four million farmers in 40,000 villages through 6,500 e-choupals. This initiative is discussed in Chapter 10 in greater detail.

Today's rural children and youth will grow up in an environment where they have 'information access' to education opportunities, exam results, career counselling, job opportunities, government schemes and services, health and legal advice, worldwide news and information, land records, mandi prices, weather forecasts, bank loans, and livelihood options.

::: The Rural Economic Environment

The rural economy has changed from a slow-growth, subsistence agriculture economy to a fast-growth economy. Economic liberalization and government-led infrastructure development have opened up the rural economy. Better access to goods, markets, and funds has kickstarted the more resilient non-farm sector. This, combined with better farm earnings due to a sharp minimum support price (MSP) increase for crops and crop diversification, has led to more money for rural pockets, which transformed the rural economy into a vibrant and growing economy with rapidly rising incomes. This has brought India's cities much closer to their hinterlands, more than people might imagine.

Information and communication technology is revolutionizing rural India by enhancing the skills of rural youth through vocational training.

Parameter	Contribution of Rural India (in per cent)
Total population	70
Total income	56
Total expenditure	64
Total savings	33

| TABLE 2.9 | The Contribution of the Rural Economy

Today, the rural economy is undergoing a favourable transformation in terms of rising and stabilizing rural income, fuelling consumption growth at faster pace than in urban areas. The importance of the rural economy can be gauged from the fact that nearly 70 per cent of India's population, 56 per cent of its income, 64 per cent of its expenditure, and 33 per cent of its savings come from rural India, as evident from Table 2.9.

MSP stands for minimum support price, announced by the government for major agri commodities every year, at which procurement of produce takes place. It is perceived as a guaranteed price by farmers.

The resilience of the rural economy during the recent economic recession suggests that rural India will be a significant contributor to this rapid rate of growth. In recent times, the Central government has made substantial progress in creating rural infrastructure in accordance with the commitment to faster social-sector development, in order to remove disparities under the Eleventh Five-Year Plan and numerous other initiatives. In addition, the private sector has played a significant role in providing greater access to information via telecommunications.

In the following section, we will discuss the changing face of rural development, changes in the rural economic structure, the phenomenon of migration, and the impact of these changes on rural income and the consumption pattern.

The Changing Face of Rural Development

Nominal rural GDP has increased to over 12 per cent p.a. in the last few years, the highest for any three-year period in several decades.

Over the past two decades, the rural economy in India has graduated from being a 'barter economy' to a cash-rich economy. In the recent global meltdown, the rural economy acted as the saviour for the Indian economy, and helped India to stamp its mark on the global economy.

Due to a host of favourable cyclical factors, growth in nominal rural GDP has increased to over 19 per cent p.a. in the last few years, the highest for the last three decades, even higher than urban, as depicted in Fig. 2.6. (In the figure, the per capita consumption has been used as a proxy for nominal rural per capita GDP since the split of rural–urban GDP is unavailable.) This is forcing corporate India to focus its strategies on rural India, in part also to beat the slowdown in urban India. While cyclical factors could turn adverse, the political environment is extremely favourable for pro-rural policies. Rural India has moved to the core of both the government's policies and corporate India's strategies.

Rapid increase in rural literacy levels, improvement in health indicators, increase in per capita expenditure, improvement in housing, decline in poverty levels, and increase in life expectancy are factors that have resulted in the improvement of human development indicators in rural India.

Persons living below the poverty line have declined both in terms of percentage (27 per cent to 22 per cent) and absolute number (193 mn to 170 mn) between 1999–20 and 2004–05.

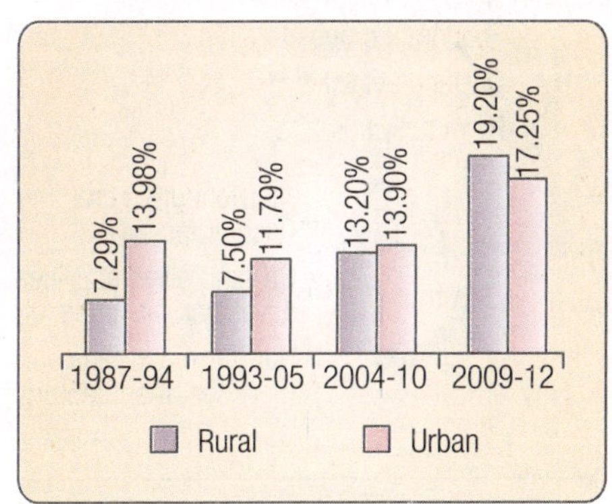

| FIG. 2.6 | Percentage increase in monthly per capita expenditure
Source: Masters of Rural Markets: Profitably Selling to India's Rural Consumers, Accenture Report 2013

THE DEVELOPMENT EXERCISE: THE FIVE-YEAR PLANS To improve the quality of life

| TABLE 2.10 |
Sectoral Allocations During Five-year Plans (billion, INR)

Heads of Development	8th Plan	9th Plan	10th Plan	11th Plan	12th Plan
	(1992–97)	(1997–02)	(2002–07)	(2007–12)	(2012–2017)
Agriculture	225	372	589	1216	3632
Rural development	344	890	1219	1903	4574

Source: Planning Commission, 2010

| TABLE 2.11 |
Percentage Share of Different Sectors in GDP (at 1993–94 prices)

Year	Primary (Agri and Allied)	Secondary (Manufacturing)	Tertiary (Services)	Total
1990–91	32.0	24.3	43.7	100.0
2001–02	23.9	26.6	49.5	100.0
2009–10*	15.7	28.1	57.2	100.0
2013–14	14.0	26.1	59.9	100.0

Source: Planning Commission, 2013

in rural areas, allocations for rural development and agriculture have been increased substantially over consecutive Five-Year Plans. The increase in budget allocation has been multi-fold, both for agriculture and rural development sectors between the Eighth and Eleventh Plans, as shown in Table 2.10.

The rural economy has undergone a structural shift, from predominantly farm-based to a mix of farm, off-farm, and services economy, a change that is reflected in the decreasing contribution of the primary sector, whose GDP share halved in the last two decades as demonstrated in Table 2.11. On the other hand, the GDP share of the services sector increased (it employs 34 per cent of the workforce) during the same period.

While the direct contribution of agriculture is limited and declining, its influence on the overall economic growth has been immense. Most non-farm activities are dependent on agricultural income.

THE TRANSITION OF THE RURAL ECONOMY The transition of the rural economy has occurred at three levels (see Fig. 2.7).

The transition at all three levels were linked to the high opportunity for value addition, resulting in high rural incomes. The farm sector now contributes only 40 per cent of the rural income, whereas the non-farm sector contributes 60 per cent of the total rural income. This transition has important positive implications for employment and productivity, both within the farm and non-farm sectors, which have grown substantially.

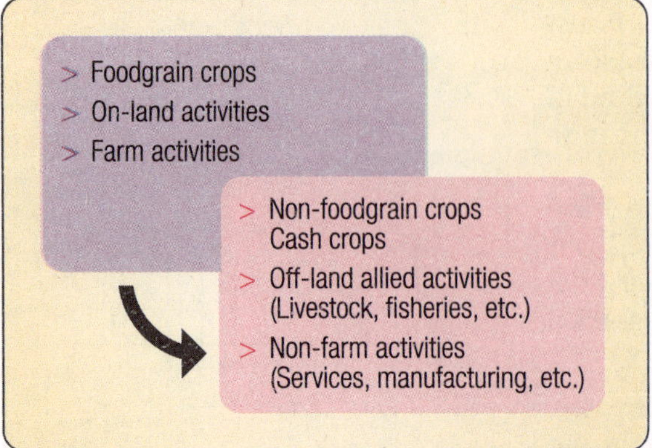

| FIG. 2.7 |
The Transition of the Rural Economy

The Rural Economic Structure

Farm and non-farm are two basic constituents of the rural economy, as shown in Fig. 2.8. We will discuss the changing trends in the agriculture economy and non-farm economy in this section.

The Farm Sector: Agriculture and Allied Activities

Indian agriculture has graduated rapidly from a food grain-scarce economy to a food grain-surplus economy. Today, India is the largest producer of coconuts, mangoes, bananas, milk and dairy products, cashew nuts, pulses, ginger, turmeric, and black pepper. It is also the second largest producer of rice, wheat, sugar, cotton, fruits, and vegetables.

There has been a significant shift from staples to more lucrative cash crops in recent years. Since 1990–91, due to the new economic policies, the area under food grains and coarse grains have declined by 2 and 18 per cent, respectively, while the area under non-food cash crops such as cotton and sugarcane have increased by 25 and 10 per cent, respectively.

This shift has partly been a result of lower minimum support prices (MSPs) in the past, which has resulted in a lower production of staples. In order to stop this trend, the government recently provided a large increase in the value of MSPs, which has had a significant impact on farm incomes.

The MSP has doubled in the last decade. A closer look at Fig. 2.9 reveals that in the last three years, farmers have witnessed an increase in MSP at the rate of 10 per cent per annum, resulting in increased farm incomes. The increase in MSPs has meant that the majority of farmers have realized greater incomes from their crops, and more money is being injected into the rural economy.

India's agriculture and allied sector grew by 3.8 per cent in the first six months of 2010–11, as against 1 per cent in the previous year because of a better Kharif crop

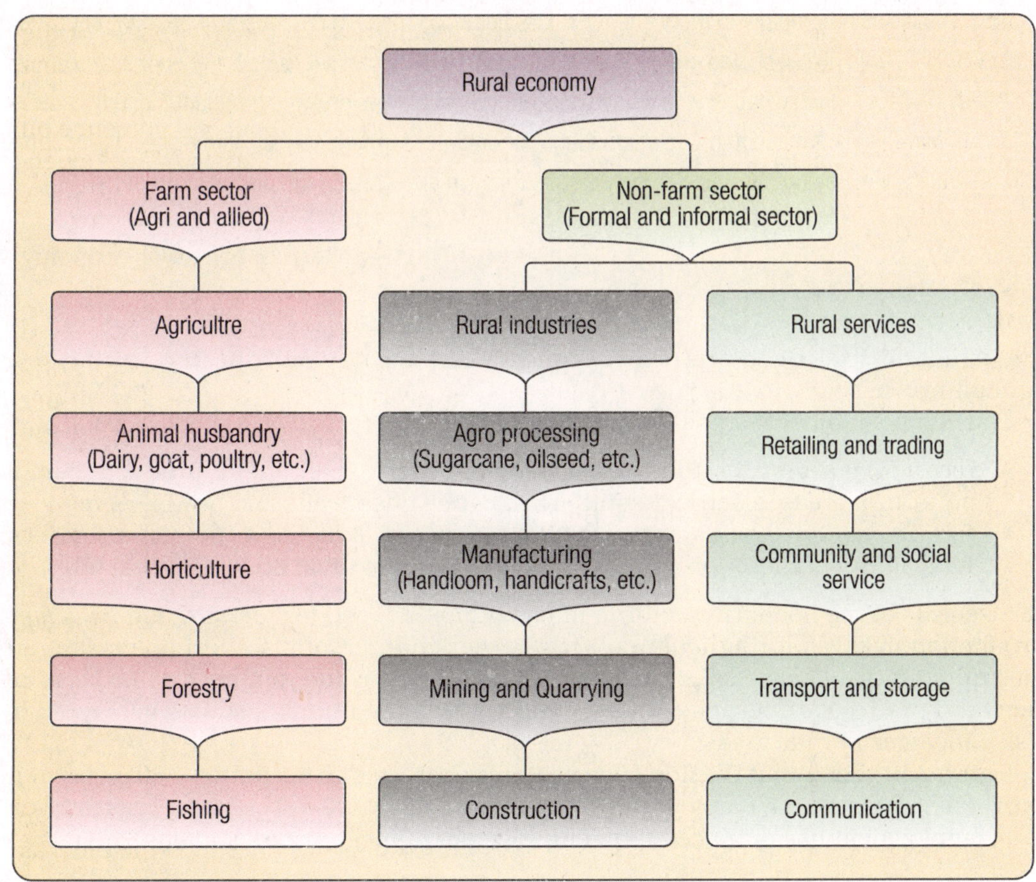

| FIG. **2.8** |
The Rural Economic Structure
Source: MART Knowledge Centre

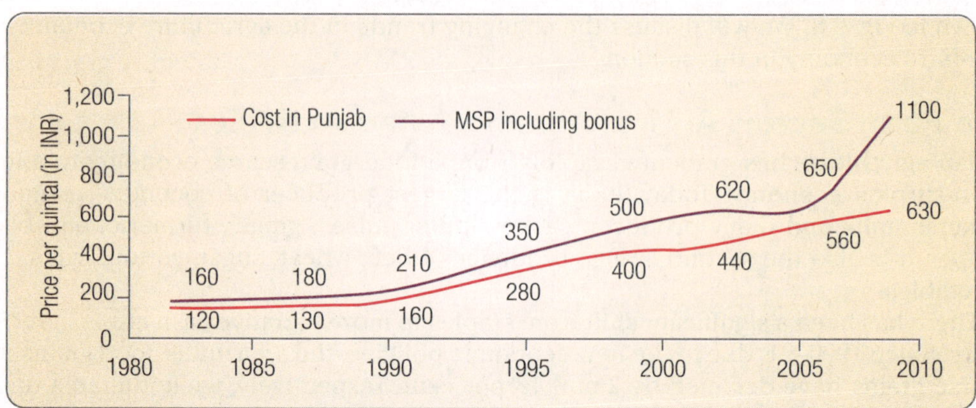

| FIG. **2.9** |
Changes in Minimum Support Price from 1980 to 2010
Source: Credit-Suisse

output. According to Annual Report 2009--10 of the Ministry of Agriculture, production of food grains during 2009–10 is estimated at 216.8 million tonnes (MT).

The agri–allied sector has also grown significantly, particularly dairy, poultry, fish and meat products. India has become the largest milk producer in the world. India is also the second largest producer of inland fish and the sixth largest in the overall production of fish in the world.

CONTRACT FARMING

Narayanappa Maranna lives in Mallenamadagu village, about 155 km away from Bangalore. He owns five acres of land on which he cultivated groundnut, paddy and ragi. Few years ago his friends told him about a new way of farming that yielded higher prices, returns and margins. He then signed a deal with The Global Green Company to grow gherkins. This company ranks third globally in gherkin production. In very little time he raised two crops on an acre of land that he had set aside for gherkins, and earned three times more than what he would have pocketed when he was growing groundnut, paddy and ragi. Today Maranna is a mascot in Mallenamadagu for contract farming. Higher earning has transformed his family's life. Seeing his success, his neighbours have also gone in for contract farming.

The Non-farm Sector and Rural Industries

The non-farm sector comprises all secondary and tertiary activities not included in agriculture.

The composition of the non–farm sector includes:

- ***Secondary sector.*** cotton textiles, wood, pottery, food, metal products, handicrafts; new areas: electrical equipment, paper, chemicals, and power looms
- ***Tertiary sector.*** trade, transport, food business, education, personal services; the majority of these jobs are informal (60 per cent of all non-farm rural jobs)

The genesis of the non-farm sector in India was in the need for forward and backward production linkages for agricultural activity. Agricultural inputs and implements are part of backward linkages. Forward linkages arise either due to a need to process agricultural produce, or because of the need for non-agricultural products generated by rising incomes in rural areas.

Figure 2.10 shows that the non-farm sector is estimated to account for 60 per cent of the rural GDP, whereas it employs only 27 per cent of the rural workforce at present. Non-farm employment has outpaced farm employment in recent years and has grown over

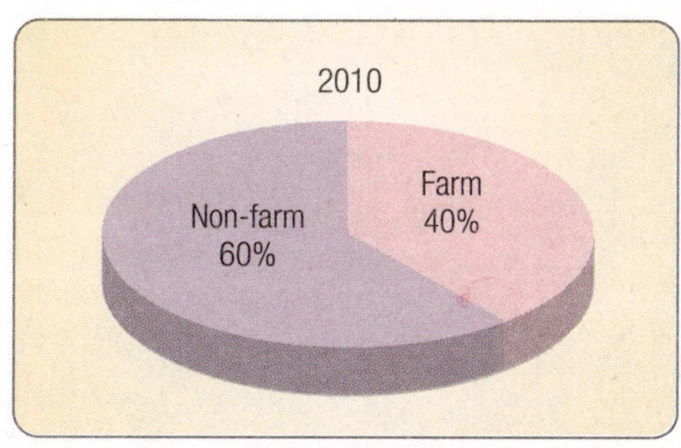

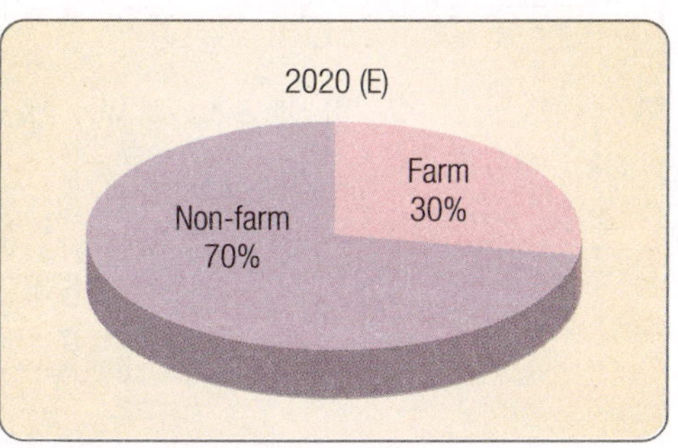

| FIG. **2.10** |
Change in Income Trend from Farm to Non-farm
Source: MART Knowledge Centre

5 per cent between 2000–05, whereas agriculture labour growth was less than 1 per cent in the same period (Planning Commission).

Further, there are multiple sources of income in a typical household, some from agriculture and others from non-farm sources. Typically, at least one person from farming households is employed in the non-farm sector, bringing in a regular income which allows for more planned expenditure. Thus, there is less dependence on erratic agriculture and seasonal incomes.

As a result of the economic transformation, the rural non-farm sector is estimated to contribute 70 per cent of the rural income by 2020. Higher wages and more employment opportunities in the non-farm sector are likely to drive this growth in the next decade.

Households moving out of the farm sector are finding opportunities largely in non-farm areas, as it ensures reliability and regularity of incomes higher than farm incomes. Also, government programmes focused on rural areas, like Bharat Nirman (Rural Infrastructure development) and MGNREGA (Livelihood security), are creating huge opportunities in non-farm employment.

RURAL ENTERPRISES According to the 2014 Economic Census Report, out of a total of 58 million enterprises in the country, 35 million (60 per cent) are located in the rural area (see Table 2.12). In the non-farm establishment, retail trade (39 per cent) was the dominant activity, followed by manufacturing (26 per cent) and community, and social and personal services (8 per cent), as shown in Fig. 2.11.

The number of workers has increased by 35 million between 1990–2014, largely in services like trading, social services, and transport, which have emerged as rapidly growing sectors.

In the face of an ever-expanding population, the limited availability of cultivable land, a shrinking labour pool, and the declining absorptive capacities of the farm sector, it is certain that the non-farm sector will continue to be the driving force for improving income and employment opportunities in rural India.

Rural enterprises are defined as agricultural and non-agricultural establishments engaged in the production and/or distribution of goods and/or services for commercial purposes.

| TABLE **2.12** |
The Status of Rural Enterprises in India

Rural Enterprises in India	1990	1998	2005	2014
Agricultural Enterprises (million)	2.08	3.18	5.71	-
Non-agricultural Enterprises (million)	12.28	14.01	19.83	-
Total Rural Enterprises (million)	14.36	17.19	25.54	35.02
Total Number of Workers Employed (million)	32.17	38.13	52.07	66.29
Growth of Workers (%)	2.88	2.15	4.55	31.59

Source: Economic Census, 2005, Provisional Results of 6th Economic Census, 2014

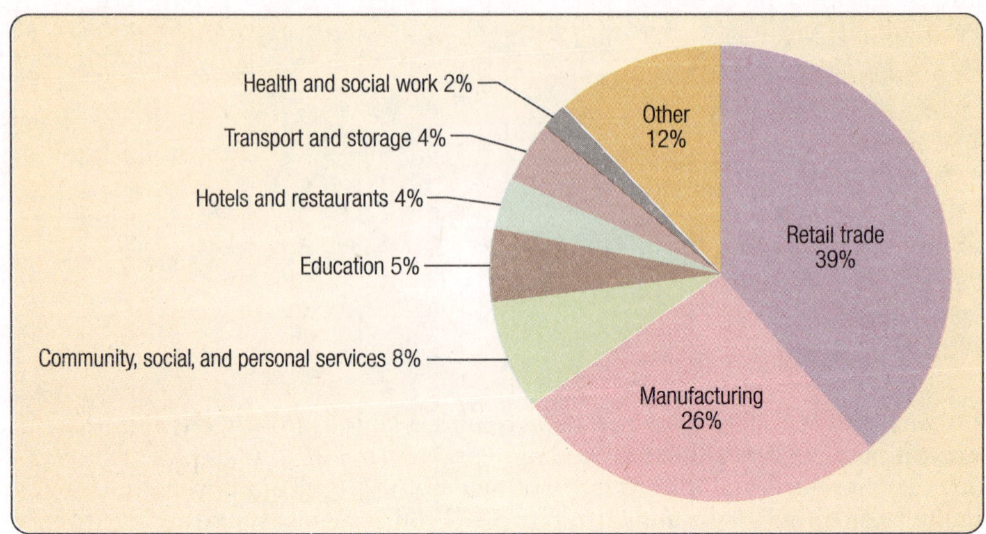

| FIG. **2.11** |
Non-agricultural Establishments in Rural India
Source: Economic Census, 2005.

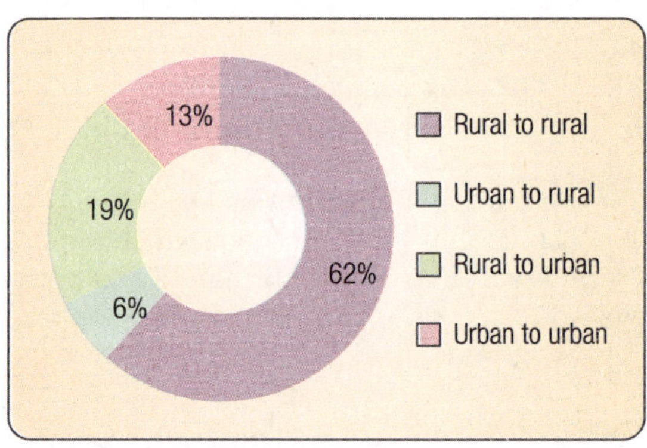

| FIG. **2.12** |
Migration Pattern
Source: Based on 'Migration in India, 2007–08,' NSSO.

Changing Migration Trends

Migration from rural areas has a positive effect on rural incomes, as the purpose of migration is to generally explore better employment opportunities for remitting money back home. Nearly 57 per cent of households in rural areas have migrated to urban areas, the majority for employment-related reasons, in 2007–08, according to the National Sample Survey report (64th round). The migration rate (proportion of migrants in the population) in rural areas stands at 26 per cent.

As seen in Fig. 2.12, a greater portion of migrant workers go to other rural areas (62 per cent) in search of jobs or better jobs, followed by migration from rural to urban centres (19 per cent). This implies that opportunities in some villages were more favourable than in others. This difference in the ability of a village to attract migrant workers depends on better working opportunities and a better investment climate, which in turn depends on a host of factors like infrastructure, electricity supply, support of the common people, etc.

On an average, a migrant from rural areas residing abroad remitted about INR 52,000 during the year, whereas those residing within India remitted INR 21,000.

It is interesting to note that as many as 24 per cent male migrants in rural areas have reported returning to their home land in 2007–08 with the improvement in rural employment opportunities.

Incomes and Expenditure

Changes in the rural economic environment discussed above have led to a healthy increase of 50 per cent in rural incomes in the last five years (see Fig. 2.13). Spending has also gone up by 33 per cent during the same period as consumption increased in rural areas. While rural incomes have grown at 8 per cent CAGR in line with GDP growth, consumption growth has lagged at 5 per cent CAGR (Rural India: Transcending Boundaries, Edelweiss–MART Survey 2010).

Table 2.13 explains that among occupation groups, non-farm households are reporting higher incomes led by the salaried and self-employed; however, maximum income growth is experienced by labourers (includes both farm and non-farm), whose income

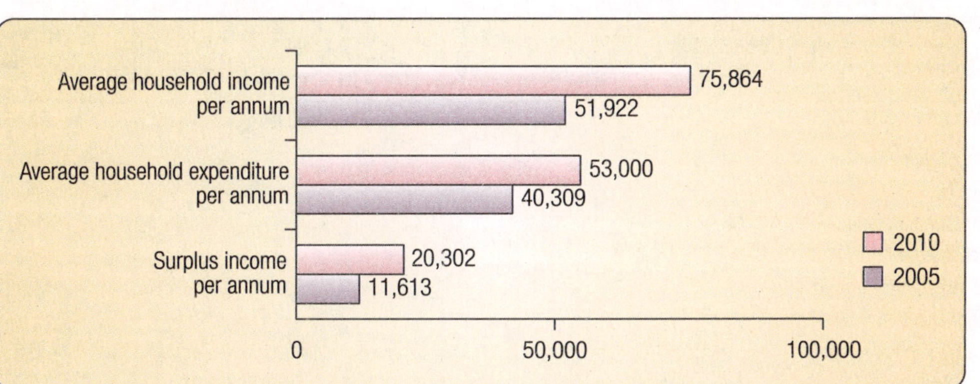

| FIG. **2.13** |
The Rural Income–Expenditure Profile (in INR)
Source: Max–NCAER and Edelweiss–MART Survey.

doubled in the last five years largely due to increased days of employment and better wages.

It is important to note that regular salaried/wage earner-headed households contribute twice to rural income as compared to labourer-headed households who contribute on half of the total income in proportion to their population, as evident from Fig. 2.14. This leads to more buying power among non-farm households (salaried and self-employed).

INCOME DISPARITY Table 2.14 reveals a huge income disparity in rural areas as the top quintile's household income is seven times that of the bottom quintile. Also, 14 per cent belonging to the top quintile have the highest (40 per cent) contribution to the total rural income, whereas the contribution is least (8 per cent) for one-fourth households in the bottom quintile. The top two quintiles (Q4 and Q5), which translates to 217 million rural consumers, contribute more than 60 per cent of the rural income.

Fifty per cent growth in rural income at eight per cent CAGR in line with GDP growth is testimony to the strength of rural buying power.

RURAL SPENDING According to the Edelweiss–MART survey, at an annual household consumption expenditure level of INR 53,000, the rural consumption market was

| TABLE **2.13** |
Changes in Rural Income by Occupation Groups

OCCUPATION	Average Annual Household Income—2005 (INR)	Average Annual Household Income—2010 (INR)
Self-employment in agriculture	55,880	73,574
Labour	30,480	68,885
Regular salary/wages	96,520	1,44,220
Self-employment in non-agriculture	66,040	63,796
Average HH Income	**51,922**	**75,864**

Source: Max-NCAER survey, 2004-05, & Edelweiss-MART Survey 2010

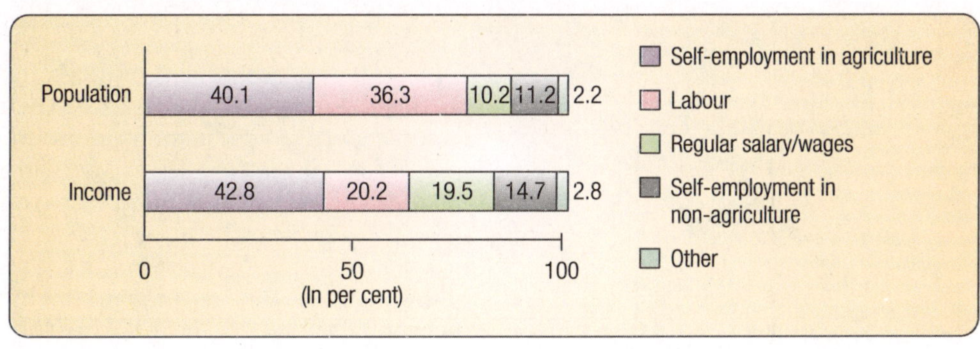

| FIG. **2.14** |
Distribution of Household and Incomes by Major Source of Household Income
Source: Max–NCAER Survey, 2005.

| TABLE 2.14 |
Distribution of Rural Population and Income by Income Quintiles

	Q1 (Bottom) (0–20%)	Q2 (21%–40%)	Q3 (21%–40%)	Q4 (21%–40%)	Q5 (Top) (21%–40%)	Total
Population (in million)	187	170.7	157.1	116.8	100.3	731.9
Population share (in per cent)	25.5	23.3	21.5	16.0	13.7	100
Household income (INR per annum)	18,967	29.212	40,841	64,200	138,427	51,922
Income share (in per cent)	8.4	12.8	17.4	20.6	40.7	100.0
Large (10 hectares and above)	2 (1)	1.4 (1.2)	1.2 (1)	29 (17)	24.2 (14.8)	21.1 (13.2)
Total	106 (100)	115.6 (100)	120.1 (100)	166 (100)	163.4 (100)	159.9 (100)

Source: NSHIE 2004–05 data: NCAER–CMCR Analysis

estimated at USD 190 billion in 2010, which is greater than the GDP of Singapore and Hungary.

The share of the rural wallet displays a dramatic shift in consumption from food to non-food items over the last decade. Fig. 2.15 reveals that there has been a substantial decrease in the proportion of spending on food and beverages—from 58 per cent to 42 per cent—with the increasing incomes of rural households resulting in a movement away from basic consumption needs. The lost share of food has shifted in favour of the travel and transport, education and recreation categories.

The recent improvements in rural road infrastructure triggered the ownership of personal transport and leisure travel (pilgrimage), which has led to a more than threefold increase in spending on travel and transportation.

The share for education has doubled, with an increased spending on higher education for children taking place with the improvement in higher educational facilities.

It is interesting to observe that the sharpest growth among all categories was witnessed in recreation, which multiplied seven-fold in the last decade. This growth is attributed to the disproportionately high expenditure on ceremonies like weddings, in which high-end durables like motorcycles, televisions, refrigerators, and washing machines are purchased as dowry gifts. In addition, the rapid explosion of DTH/cable connections (14 million rural connections out of the 20 million total DTH connections) has also contributed to this growth, as these categories were non-existent earlier.

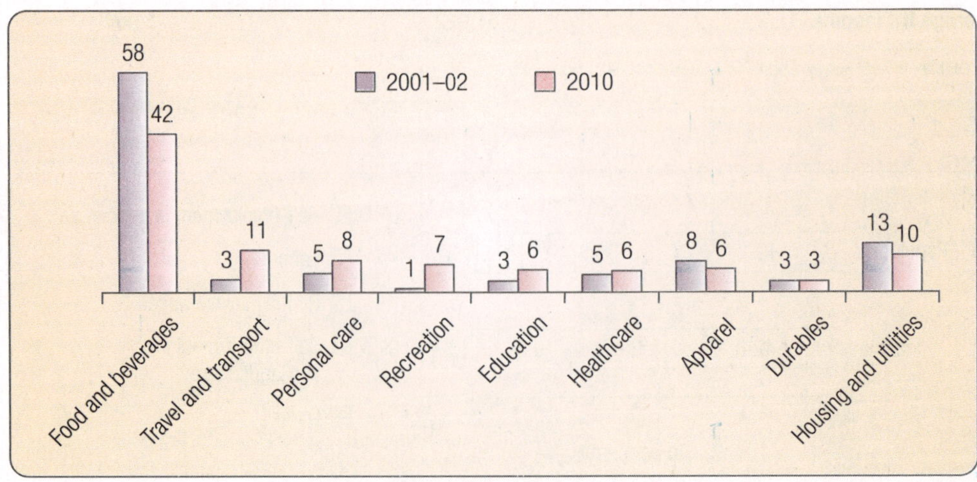

| FIG. 2.15 |
The Changing Wallet Share in Rural India
Source: NSSO and Edelweiss–MART Survey.

Also, a healthy growth is noticed in the personal care category, with consumers shifting from unbranded to branded products or to new products like shampoo, toothpaste, hair oil, and talcum powder. Rising aspirations, which unleashed a latent demand for these products, were instrumental in the mushrooming of provision stores, cosmetics shops, and beauty parlours in the rural marketplace over the last decade.

It is important to note that the durables category has not shown any growth in wallet share, although asset ownership has grown during this period. One important reason for this trend is the entry of household durables in many rural households as dowry gift in weddings, for which these households had not spent any money. At the same time, a continuous decline in durables prices has also made such goods more affordable, resulting in the ownership of more assets with the same proportion of spending.

Rising and reliable income streams, coupled with an aspiration to lead an urban lifestyle, will get the expenditure growth rate to pick up momentum, transforming rural India into one big and growing consumption market. According to Edelweiss' estimates, the rural consumption market will triple by 2020 to USD 600 billion.

::: The Rural Infrastructure

This section focuses on the infrastructural facilities available in rural India, and their relevance for marketing. The poor state of rural infrastructure in terms of poor road connectivity, inadequate power supply, poor market infrastructure, lack of quality drinking water, and poor access to sanitation facilities has often discouraged corporations to venture into rural markets. However, pro-rural long-term policies and programmes (for example, Bharat Nirman, MGNREGA, NRHM) in the last five years have brought with them the promise of sustainable infrastructural and social development of rural India, bringing rural markets back to the centre-stage of the corporate world.

In the following section, we will discuss the major infrastructural developments in rural India, in terms of road connectivity, house construction, electrification, telecommunication, and other initiatives. See 'Rural Marketing Snapshot: Rural Infrastructure' to see and understand the changes that the rural environment has undergone.

In 2005, the introduction of the flagship programme **Bharat Nirman**, which focused on an all-round infrastructure development, has brought about a remarkable transformation in the rural landscape. The programme aims at building infrastructure and basic amenities in rural areas to reduce the gap between rural and urban areas. It covers rural housing, irrigation potential, drinking water, rural roads, electrification, and rural telephony (see Table 2.15).

| TABLE **2.15** |
Areas of Development Under Bharat Nirman

Component	Target
Irrigation	To create 10 million hectares of additional irrigational potential
Roads	To provide all-weather connectivity to all habitation with over a 1,000 population (500 for hilly areas)
Electricity	To provide electricity to 125,000 villages (23 million) households
Housing	To construct six million houses
Drinking water	To provide drinking water to 55,067 uncovered habitations by 2009. All habitation with failed sources and water quality problems will be addressed
Telephone connectivity	To connect all habitations

Source: www.bharatnirman.gov.in

RURAL MARKETING **SNAPSHOT** | RURAL INFRASTRUCTURE

Kuccha road leading to a village

Pucca, metalled roads have improved connectivity

Improved road connectivity is transforming rural areas. Better connectivity means more income-generating opportunities within and outside villages. It also means higher market accessibility for organizations, which means they can take their products and services to rural markets.

Road Connectivity

Roads are the backbones of rural market development, paving the way for all support infrastructure like electricity, water, telecommunication, transportation, health, and education facilities to reach remote villages, leading to a transformation of the rural economy. 'Rural Marketing Insight: Road Connectivity Bringing Rural Economy on Track In Bihar' elucidates how improved road connectivity has benefitted rural India.

Road connectivity is a useful indicator of the 'inclusionary' aspect of the development process, and perhaps the reach of the market as well. It is particularly relevant in the Indian context, where over 70 per cent of the population continues to live in rural areas, and only about 67 per cent of the villages are connected by roads at present (World Bank Report). The tiniest villages with populations of less than 500 are yet to be connected by roads.

Rural roads account for more than 61 per cent of the total road length in India (the second largest road network in the world, with 3.3 million km road length). Rural roads have witnessed the highest growth as road length has more than doubled in the last two decades with long-term government initiatives like PMGSY, discussed below.

The **Pradhan Mantri Gram Sadak Yojna (PMGSY)** was launched in December 2000. The programme aims to provide connectivity to about 180,000 habitations through the construction of about 372,000 km of roads, and upgrade about 370,000 km of the existing core rural network to provide full farm-to-market connectivity. A total of 3,99,979.14 km road length has been completed and 97,838 habitations have been provided all weather roads upto March 2014. The PMGSY aims to provide all-weather connectivity to all habitations with a population of 500 by 2015.

Electrification

The quality of power supply has remained poor in villages as power outages and erratic supply are common.

There has been considerable improvement in the pace of electricity coverage at the household level in recent years. The proportion of rural households with access to electricity increased from 48 per cent in 1998–99 to 60 per cent in 2008 (IRS, 2010).

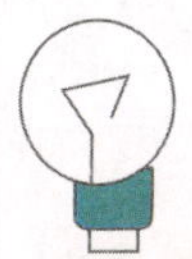

RURAL MARKETING INSIGHT | ROAD CONNECTIVITY BRINGING RURAL ECONOMY ON TRACK IN BIHAR

Some of the quickest consequences of new roads and bridges have been better connectivity to markets, and to service providers such as schools and hospitals. With connectivity, economic activity in villages has changed, tending towards growth in high-value agriculture, traditional services, and even manufacturing.

Better roads have opened new markets for perishable goods. Sudha Dairy, the state's leading dairy firm, has been able to go national, spreading to 10 cities outside Bihar in the past 18 months. Having spurred a White Revolution in Bihar, the dairy sold 30,000 litre of milk in Delhi and Kolkata within a month.

Due to better roads, Sudha now collects 1.2 million litre of milk from the remotest of villages, in contrast to 400,000 litre before the infrastructure was improved. Now, Sudha is even planning to reach flood-prone districts in the state and as far as Kathmandu (the capital of Nepal).

Experts also predict that improved roads will boost the food processing industry. A 10-year vision document identifies 100 villages to be developed as rural agribusiness centres, bearing an investment potential of around INR 15 billion in the food processing sector alone. At the primary school in Mobarakpur Sahajpura in Nawada, enrolment has risen from 160 children to 195 in the six months since the road outside the school was laid.

Created in April 2005 by merging all ongoing electrification schemes, the **Rajiv Gandhi Grameen Vidyutikaran Yojna** aims to electrify all villages and habitations, providing access to electricity to all rural households and providing electricity connections to Below Poverty Line (BPL) families free of charge, and reliable power by the end of the Eleventh Plan. More than 1 lakh villages have been electrified and more than 200 lakh free electricity connections have been released under RGGVY by September 2014.

Rural Housing

Housing constitutes a very basic requirement for the rural populace. The 2001 Census places the rural housing shortage figure in India at 14.8 million. The Bharat Nirman Programme has recognized and accorded due priority to the needy to end the problem of homelessness.

Under the **Indira Awas Yojna**, 7.2 million houses have been constructed between 2005–06 and 2008–09 against the 6 million envisaged. The Centre has allocated over INR 17,000 crore to be used for construction of nearly 25 lakh houses under IAY in 2014–15.

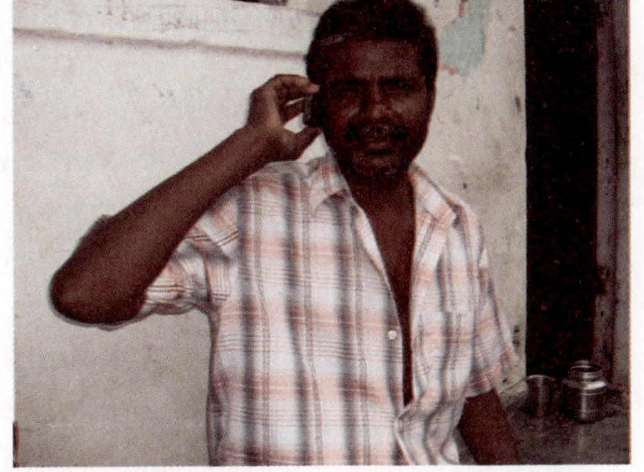

Rural telephony has been transformed by the entry of mobile phones.

Telecommunications

Rural telephony has seen a dramatic transformation with the opening of the telecom sector, which has witnessed a 44-fold growth in teledensity in the last twelve years (see Table 2.16). The 383 million rural users number more than the total subscribers in Brazil.

| TABLE **2.16** |
Rural Teledensity Growth

Parameter	2002	2008	Dec 2009	June 2010	Dec 2013	June 2014
Rural teledensity	1.2	9.5	21.2	26.4	42.7	44.5
Rural subscriber base (in millions)	-	62	175	219	365.8	383

Source: TRAI Report, 2015

Today, India is the fastest growing telecommunication industry in the world with more than 943 million subscribers. Between 2006 and 2014, rural India outpaced urban India in mobile growth as the rural subscription base grew several times as against the urban growth. According to National Telecom Policy 2012, the government aims to increase rural teledensity from the current level to 70 by the year 2017 and 100 by the year 2020.

Drinking Water

Rural India may lack infrastructure for power, telecommunications, and other basic services, but almost all (95 per cent) villages have access to drinking water. However, the challenge lies in providing safe drinking water to all villages and ensuring the maintenance of water sources.

To address this challenge, the Rajiv Gandhi National Drinking Water Mission (RGNDWM) under Bharat Nirman adopted an integrated approach, so that conservation and augmentation of water sources is interrelated with rural water supply schemes to provide a sustainable supply of safe drinking water to the rural population. The Mission seeks to provide a supply of 40 litre of safe drinking water per capita per day to rural households.

::: Rural Employment Generation Programmes: Government Initiatives

The pro-rural focus of the government has led to the implementation of mega employment generation programmes. The important ones among these are listed below. Several poverty alleviation and employment generation programmes are being implemented by the government.

MNREGA

A couple belonging to Tonk district near Jaipur in Rajasthan have been working in construction sites away from their village. The husband works as a mason and the wife as a helper. Due to gender discrimination, the wife earned very little in comparison to the husband. As the work is seasonal, the whole family migrates to a nearby semi-urban area to work, and once it is completed after a few months, they return to their village. With their low income, they were just about able to sustain the basic needs of the family. Some time ago they came to know about the MNREGA scheme, which was offering employment opportunities in their own village. The wife approached the officials and was enrolled in construction work. The husband continued working in nearby semi-urban areas, as only one person in the family can avail of the scheme. Now the wife earns much more than she was earlier as the MNREGA does not discriminate between men and women. The family stays in the village throughout the year and only the husband travels whenever he finds work outside. The children are now going to the village school. Earlier they could not go to school as they had no permanent set-up. The MNREGA is a breakthrough innovation in a government scheme. It is a law under which an intended beneficiary can sue the government if they do not receive their entitlement. The scheme is designed to be inherently customizable, wherein the beneficiaries can decide new ways to use the wages provided under the scheme. The scheme has provided employment to 50 million households. It has taken up nearly 4.3 million work projects, of which 1.8 million have been completed. The scheme's budget has risen to INR 410 billion in 2010.

The Mahatma Gandhi National Rural Employment Guarantee Act (MNREGA)

Launched in February 2006, the MNREGA is the flagship livelihood programme operational throughout the country (619 districts) at present. The Act provides 100 days of guaranteed wage employment in a financial year to every rural household. The objective is to guarantee a minimum income for economically weak rural households. The major achievement of the programmes are:

- Wage rate has risen to INR 177/day in 2014–15 from INR 69/day in 2006–07.
- The average wage earned per beneficiary has risen from INR 65 per person day in 2006 to INR 124 by 2013.
- During 2013–14, 38 million households have been provided for employment and 1.34 billion person days created under the scheme.
- Seventy-four per cent of the fund spent under the programme was in the form of wages to labourer, providing cash benefits to the rural poor.
- Spending on MNREGA has declined over the period of 2012–14 to INR 330 billion from INR 400 billion in the previous years.

The Swarnjayanti Gram Swarozgar Yojna (SGSY)

Launched in April 1999 as a self-employment programme for the rural poor, the scheme was restructured as National Rural Livelihood Mission (NRLM) in 2010 has been renamed as '**Aajeevika**' in 2014. Partly aided by the World Bank, the programme aims at creating effective institutional platforms for the rural poor to help them to increase their household income. The programme targets to bring at least one member of each rural BPL household, preferably a woman member, under the SHG net.

The Pradhan Mantri Rojgar Yojna

The Prime Minister's Rojgar Yojna (PMRY) for providing self-employment to educated, unemployed youth from economically weaker sections has been in operation since

MNREGA guarantees hundred days of employment in a year to rural people.

October 1993. The scheme aims to assist the eligible youth to set up self-employment ventures in the industry, service and business sectors, and intends to cover urban and rural areas.

REVIEW OF OBJECTIVES

1. Describe the evolution of rural marketing

The evolution of rural marketing has been described in four different phases. Before the 1960s, rural marketing was considered synonymous with agricultural marketing. The period between the 1960s and 1980s saw the Green Revolution, which changed the face of rural India with its scientific farming practices and marketing of agricultural inputs. After the 1990s, the industrial sector gained in strength and maturity. There was a demand for consumables and durables. People then realized the enormity of the rural market.

After 2000, several FMCG, durables, automobile, telecom, insurance, and service-sector companies adopted a rural thrust. They are now coming up with products/services using low-cost technology.

Currently, the rural market is undergoing a massive change. There is a huge opportunity waiting to be tapped. Government initiatives are also supporting rural market development. The future looks bright for rural India.

2. Track the rural marketing environment in terms of demographic, physical, social, cultural, political, and technological aspects

Demographics in rural areas have shown an overall increase in population by over 200 million in the last two decades. The joint family is being phased out and the number of individualized joint and nuclear families is increasing. The literacy rate is rising, which is having an overall impact on the socio-economic status of the people. Agriculture, once the primary occupation, is being replaced by non-traditional occupations like shop/trade, skilled work, salaried jobs, etc. The type and size of rural settlement and clusters, that is, villages comprise the physical environment. The housing pattern is changing from kuccha to semi-pucca and pucca.

The social and cultural environment plays a significant role in determining the behaviour of marketers. A new market segmentation of Indian households has been carried out on the basis of socio-cultural regions (SCR), where the country has been divided into 90 SCRs based on certain common parameters.

The political environment consists of laws or groups who influence marketing actions. The Panchayat and Gram Sabha form part of the political arena in rural areas.

Technology is making inroads into and changing the face of rural India. Exposure to technology is revolutionizing the market. First came the Green Revolution, which resulted in the modernization and mechanization of the farm sector, followed by the White Revolution, which increased the production of milk in the country, making it the second largest producer. Non-Government Organizations (NGOs) assisted in technology reaching the grassroots level. The evolution of the computer, Internet and mobile phones has had a tremendous impact in the lives of rural people. The concept of e-Choupal is transforming the Indian farmer into a progressive, knowledge-seeking netizen.

3. Understand the rural economic environment, the changing rural economic structure, and income spending pattern

The rural economy has undergone a transformation from a slow-growth, subsistence agrarian economy to a vibrant non-farm economy in the last six decades. Today, rural India accounts for 70 per cent of India's population, 56 per cent of the national income, 64 per cent of the total expenditure, and 33 per cent of the total savings. The traditional vision of rural economies as purely agricultural is clearly obsolete. The share of agriculture has declined to 15.7 per cent, and almost half the workforce has moved out of agriculture. This has led to a diversification of the rural economy and a growth of the non-farm sector in rural areas. The non-farm sector, which today accounts for 60 per cent of the rural GDP, has outpaced farm employment, and is likely to account for 70 per cent of the rural GDP by 2020.

Eight good monsoons, a two-fold increase in MSP in the last decade, diversification to non-cash crops, and rapid growth in farm mechanization has led to moderate growth in the agricultural sector. The sector is estimated to achieve an average growth of 4 per cent per annum during the Eleventh Plan period.

On the other hand, rural enterprise (especially non-farm) has doubled to 25 million between 1990–2005, absorbing an additional 20 million workforce largely in services like trading and transport. The rise of the non-farm sector is helping to reduce over-dependence on the farm sector (which has led to disguised unemployment over the years in the farm sector), and is also helping to improve the reliability and seasonality of rural incomes.

With 50 per cent growth in rural incomes and 38 per cent growth in expenditure, the rural consumption market is expected to triple to USD 600 billion by 2020. The share of wallet has been rapidly shifting from food to non-food items over the last decade, primarily in favour of education, travel, recreation, and personal care. With rising aspirations towards an urban lifestyle, rural India's consumption story is likely to be characterized by the rise of discretionary spending in rural households.

4. Understand rural infrastructure, government support, and its relevance for marketing

The government's thrust towards improving the poor state of rural infrastructure in recent years through the ambitious 'Bharat Nirman' programme, which has led to an impressive growth in telecommunication, rural connectivity, pucca houses, and electrified households, has compelled the corporate sector to take another look at the changing face of rural markets. The fast improving rural landscape is creating an enabling environment for the corporate sector, promising future growth.

At present, rural India has achieved universal telephone connectivity with a 219 million subscriber base, over 95 per cent electrified villages and 60 per cent electrified households, 60 per cent road connectivity, and almost universal availability of potable drinking water. These infrastructural improvements, coupled with improving social indicators, like health and education through NRHM and SSA, are rewriting the rural India growth story, showcasing the promise of future growth.

The delivery of promises on infrastructure growth on most fronts indicate that rural India will achieve its target of 40 per cent teledensity by 2014, road connectivity up to 500 population habitations by 2015, universal electrification by 2012, 12 million additional houses by 2012 to end homelessness, and universal access to safe drinking water by the end of 2011.

This means that rural India will become as lucrative as urban India in the next five years, not only in terms of purchasing power, but also in physical and social infrastructure development.

5. Describe the initiatives in the rural employment generation programme

The pro-rural government employment programme spearheaded by MNREGA has become the largest employment programme in the world, with an annual spending capacity of INR 400 billion, providing livelihood opportunities to more than 45 million economically weak rural households every year at present. The programme has provided large-scale employment to unskilled workers in their vicinity, increasing their incomes by 30 per cent in the last two years, and depositing the money directly to the beneficiaries' bank accounts. Thus, the programme is creating buying power among the rural poor, who are becoming the new breed of BOP consumers and are joining the mainstream consumption market.

::: DISCUSSION AND APPLICATION

Discussion of Concepts

1. What have been the developments in the marketing environment in rural areas in the last five years?
2. How should marketers respond to the changes taking place in the environment?
3. What have the changes in the rural economic structure been in the last decade? What are their implications for marketers?
4. What were the three major changes in rural infrastructure in recent years? What opportunities will they provide to rural markets, and how?
5. Explore how the telecommunications industry made inroads into rural markets in the last decade while other sectors like durables have been struggling since a long time. What are the key lessons learned?
6. Which is the most remarkable government initiative in rural India? Why? How will it supplement the marketing efforts of corporate India?
7. Discuss the impact of the economic slowdown on rural India. 'Rural India has not been impacted by the economic slowdown'. State a reason in support of and against this argument.

Application of Concepts

1. The economic environment is fast changing in rural India. How will these changes affect consumption patterns among customers?
2. A durables company wants to sell its products in rural markets. Which critical factors in the socio-economic environment should it examine to design its market entry strategy?
3. What is the significance of SCRs in the rural context? Develop a communication plan for a FMCG company for the state of Bihar based on SCRs.
4. What will happen to the rural growth agenda if the government withdraws or scales down its rural spending on flagship programmes like MNREGA and Bharat Nirman? How will rural growth be sustained? How will the corporate sector respond to this change?

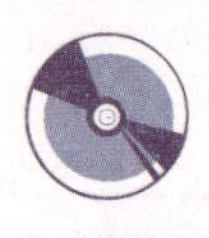

RURAL MARKETING CASE | MNREGA

The Mahatma Gandhi National Rural Employment Guarantee Act (MNREGA) guarantees one hundred days of employment in every financial year to adult members of any rural household willing to do public work-related unskilled manual work at the statutory minimum wage. This act was introduced to improve the purchasing power of rural people, primarily through providing semi- or unskilled work to rural people, whether or not they are below the poverty line.

The accompanying video shows how MNREGA is transforming the lives of the unskilled rural workforce by providing large-scale employment opportunities in and around their villages, and increasing their income by 30 per cent in the last two years. This flagship programme is creating buying power among the BoP consumers – the new entrants in the mainstream consumption market.

Discussion Questions

1. What are the key success factors of MNREGA? How is MNREGA different from other income-generation programmes and initiatives of the past?
2. If the MNREGA programme is discontinued in a couple of years, what will happen to the growth story of rural India? Describe the scenario with appropriate reasons.

AFTER READING THIS CHAPTER, YOU WILL BE ABLE TO:

1. Describe the customer buying behaviour model in rural India in terms of cultural, social, personal, and psychological factors
2. List and define the major types of buying decision behaviour and the stages in the buyer decision process
3. Describe the adoption and diffusion process for new products

CHAPTER 3 ::: RURAL CONSUMER BEHAVIOUR

three

Ramkishan—a farmer from Bulandshahr, Uttar Pradesh—had to replace one of the tyres of his five-year-old tractor. He consulted the progressive farmers in his village to get an idea of the latest brands that offered the best value for money. Armed with this information, he visited the closest town to evaluate the available options. He asked questions, checked prices, and went back to discuss these with the others in the village.

Having satisfied himself that all possible pros and cons had been identified, he proceeded to actually purchase the tyre. He managed adequate cash and, accompanied by his brother and two friends, set out early in the morning to the nearby town market. He went from shop to shop checking the brands and prices. He scrutinized the tyres to ensure that they were free of any manufacturing defects. Although the dealers did not proffer any assurances, the discreet 'OK' sticker convinced him that the product had been put through a quality check by the manufacturer. Finally, he was convinced of it being flawless.

He tried his utmost to drive a hard bargain with the aim of securing the best possible price for what he considered the best brand. The entire process was time-consuming, but Ramkishan was happy with his purchase, secure in the knowledge that he had taken a sensible decision.

The purchase of high-involvement products such as tractor tyres is a long, well-researched, and discussed process in rural India.

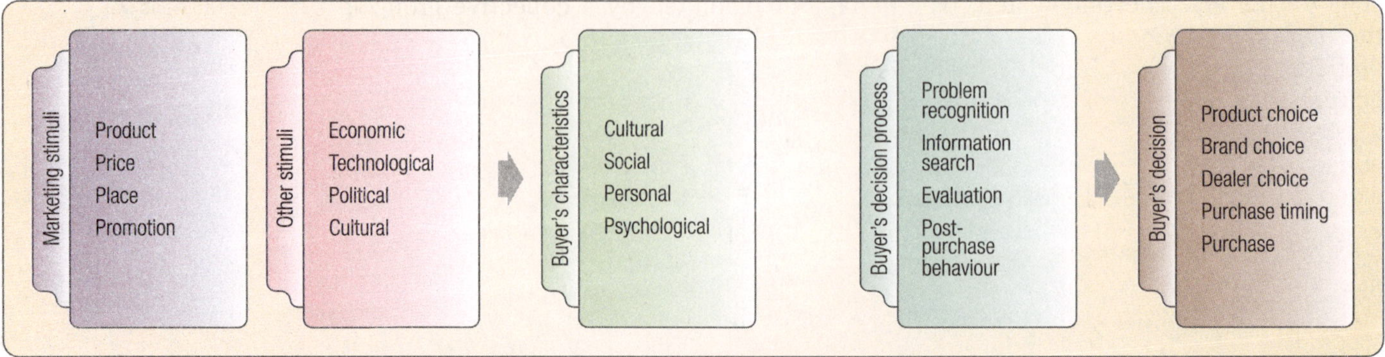

| FIG. **3.1** |
The Consumer Buying Behaviour Model

::: The Consumer Buying Behaviour Model

It is relatively easy to measure what rural consumers buy, where they buy from, and how much they buy. Understanding why they buy is the most difficult in rural India. This has to be the focal point of any marketer's efforts. Marketers have to study the consumer response to marketing stimuli regularly, and look into the 'buyers' black box' to adapt their marketing strategies to elicit the required response.

The starting point for understanding consumer behaviour is the basic model applicable to consumers universally, as given in Fig. 3.1. Although this model explains consumer behaviour in rural India, which is far from being a homogenous mass on account of factors such as caste, culture, and social groups, it is difficult to categorize behavioural patterns of rural consumers into the universally defined modules. Rural India has its own customs, traditions, and beliefs, which impact the decision-making process. It is only in the last two decades, due to investments in transportation, telecommunication, and media, that this impact has been acutely felt. Marketers also have to understand the changes in opinion leaders in rural India.

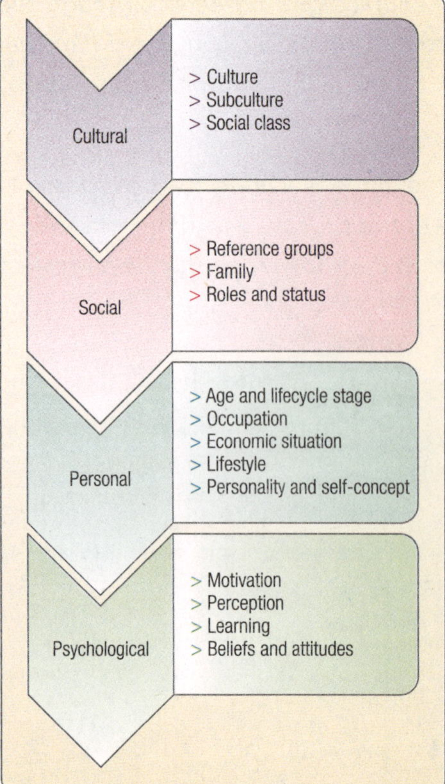

| FIG. **3.2** |
Factors Influencing Consumer Behaviour

::: What Influences Consumer Behaviour?

Consumer behaviour, particularly in rural India, is influenced by a whole gamut of factors stemming from the heterogeneous nature of rural set-ups (see Fig. 3.2). These factors can be classified as cultural, social, personal, and psychological. We examine each of these here.

Cultural Factors

Cultural factors can be further divided into three subclasses—culture, subculture, and social class.

CULTURE Culture is the most fundamental determinant of a person's behaviour in rural India. As a child grows up in the rural environment, he acquires a set of values, perceptions, preferences, and behaviours through the family and other key institutions involved at each stage of his life. The time-tested, true behaviour exhibited by a collective group is therefore determined by culture. However, the degree of impact that culture will have on behaviour will depend on the insularity of a culture, or its intermingling with other cultures, the influence of subcultures, and the evolution of a hybrid culture.

Marketers have to spot ongoing cultural shifts in rural India. The shift towards basic education and the breakdown of the joint family system in rural India have to be recognized in terms of communication, distribution, and other factors.

India's culture is still preserved in rural life. Advancement of technology, western influence, and globalization have not affected rural people significantly.

Social Customs Customs are socially accepted norms that have been in practice over a long period of time. Rural India, being largely isolated from new practices and customs, tends to follow age-old, traditional customs. Urban marketers are not always able to identify with these customs, and may find it difficult to understand the need to continue with these customs.

For example, in many parts of India, touching another person's body with one's feet, even accidentally, is considered taboo. The person seeks to apologize by placing his hand on his head. This is done because of the belief that there is God in all of us; however, most people do it as a ritual. This custom is practised by some in urban India, too, but it is gradually fading away. Many young people find it awkward to follow this social custom, fearing that others may look upon it as curious and old-fashioned. Others simply discard it because their 'set' doesn't do it.

Traditions Traditions are long-standing beliefs that are accepted as true in nature, and often practised in a ritualistic manner without knowing their origins, or questioning the need to do so. However, traditions do influence the way humans behave, and could therefore lead to the acceptance or rejection of behaviour (and, therefore, the product associated with it). People in rural India are definitely staunch believers in tradition, and therefore do not view its violation with any degree of positive association.

For example, in India, a guest is considered the equivalent of God. So welcoming a guest is no less than an event. The guest is given a very warm, traditional welcome in which he/she is garlanded and given a welcome drink. Then a *tikka* (vermillion) is applied on the forehead and a small '*aarti*' performed. The Indian phrase for this is '*Atithi Devo Bhava*'. This phrase is also used in a campaign launched by the Tourism Ministry of India to highlight the rich culture of India.

SUBCULTURE Subcultures are groups of people within a culture who have shared value systems based on common life experiences and situations.

Caste Caste plays a key role in the behaviour of the community. In rural India, upper and lower caste differences still continue, and are considered an important facet

Hariyali Kisaan Bazaar had to discontinue the practice of offering water to potential customers.

of everyday life. The difference is also evident in the dwellings of the different castes in rural India. The upper-caste houses will be located on one side of the village, whereas the houses of the lower castes will be on the other. For instance, there would be a *harijan basti* or a *dom para*. There will be a clear demarcation between the two areas, including that of natural resources such as drinking water and grazing lands for cattle.

SOCIAL CLASS Social classes are defined on the basis of occupation and education in the urban sector. In rural India, it is difficult to do so due to the multiple and changing occupations related to opportunities in different seasons. This creates difficulties in estimating their annual income with accuracy and consistency. Also, the fact that they do not file income tax returns complicates the problem. For example, in many parts of Mayurbhanj, Orissa, during particular times of the year farmers (especially those of tribal origin) take off from the fields to earn an additional income picking 'sal' leaves from the forest to make leaf plates, or to make ropes from 'bobai' grass. A similar phenomenon is found in Athamalik, Orissa, where agricultural daily wage earners are lured into picking uncut gem stones for a part of the year by traders from Haryana.

Socio-economic Classification Socio-economic classification (SEC) is the most widely preferred and accepted consumer classification in India. Based on the education of the chief wage earner and the type of house he stays in, the SECs—created in the early 1980s by MRSI (Market Research Society of India)—in rural India have been divided on a scale of R1 to R4. R1 and R2,[1] which constitute 19 per cent of the rural population, form the major consuming class, while R3 and R4, the remaining 81 per cent form the relatively poor class.

In urban areas, it is occupation and education that form the basis for defining social classes (SEC A, B, C, etc). Income and occupation variables are not used in rural classification, as they are not well-defined and distinctive among rural people.

The SEC grid (shown in Fig. 3.3) is easy to read as all the chief wage earners who are college-educated and living in a pucca house are classified under SEC R1. Figure 3.4 shows the SEC break-up in rural India. Purchase behaviour across various SEC classes is often different. SEC R1 generally makes bulk purchases from nearby town markets as they look for more variety and better quality products. SEC R2 and R3 prefer to purchase from weekly haats, which offer opportunities to bargain. Marketers can use the SEC classification to:

- target the right segments for a product category, especially while launching the product;
- conduct market research activities with the most appropriate respondent segment for a given product category; and
- design different marketing strategies for different consumer segments.

| FIG. **3.3** |
SEC Grid in Rural
Source: Market Research Society of India. Reproduced with permission.

Education	Type of house		
	Pucca	Semi-pucca	Kuchha
Illiterate	R4A	R4A	R4B
Below SSC	R3A	R3B	R4A
SSC/HSC	R2	R3A	R3B
Some college not graduate	R1	R2	R3B
Graduate/PG (General)	R1	R2	R3A
Graduate/PG (Professional)	R1	R2	R3A

As rural India is graduating towards building pucca dwellings, the relevance of socio-economic classification based on type of house is reducing. This segmentation approach is currently being relooked into. The Media Research Users Council (MRUC) has come up with a new SEC system applicable to both rural and urban markets to address the limitations of the current system. See 'Appendix: The New SEC System' for more details.

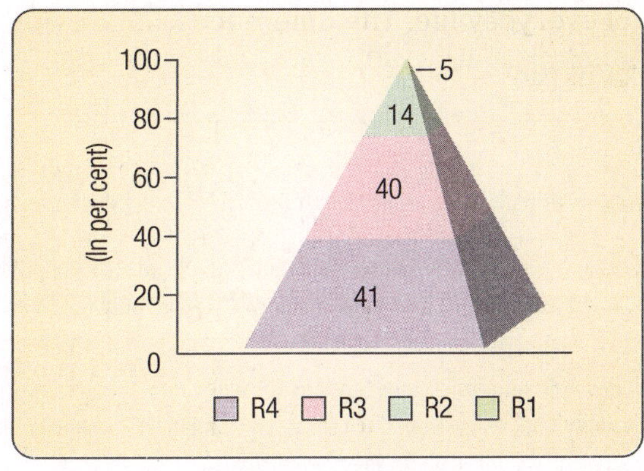

| FIG. **3.4** |
SEC Break-up in Rural
Source: Indian Readership Survey, 2010

Social Factors

The collective form of the decision-making process is highly prevalent in the rural segment due to the fact that they are reasonably isolated from other areas. Close-knit relationships therefore develop, and the affinity to formal or informal groups is prevalent in rural areas.

Rural SEC is the classification of Indian consumers on the basis of two parameters: type of house and education of the chief wage earner of the households. This classification is used by most media researchers and brand managers to understand the Indian consuming class.

REFERENCE GROUPS The groups may be primary where the influence is:

- ***Informational***. Trial of products used by others in the village
- ***Normative***. The need to belong

A consumer is also influenced by emerging social factors in the environment he lives and works in. These supplement the traditional reference groups, the role played by family, friends, and opinion leaders.

The emergence of new institutions in rural India, which have become part of the social fabric, have brought forward new reference points and influencers in the form of professional workers (see 'Rural Marketing Memo: Reference Groups in Rural' for more details).

An opinion leader in a village can be the sarpanch, teacher, bank manager, village development officer, doctor, youth extension officer, or social worker.

Opinion Leaders A person whose words and actions informally influence the action or attitude of others is an opinion leader. The influence is informal and usually verbal. However, the opinion leader's influence on opinion seekers could also be non-verbal, based on the observation of behaviour. This leadership comes from social status, power, or success in public life.

Rural India has traditionally had the gram pradhan or sarpanch, whose opinion leadership is universal by virtue of their knowledge, gained from exposure to, or interaction with, the external world through mass media and interaction with the government/administrative machinery. Villagers approach them for all matters, ranging from resolution of social and family conflicts, to introduction of new ideas about farming, to the purchase of technology products for farming or artisan work.

Post independence, as education facilities started reaching villages, teachers came to be respected as the owners and dispensers of knowledge. However, with more and more village children completing high school and pursuing higher education in urban centres, the influence of the schoolteacher is now largely restricted among school-going students.

The rural youth are now becoming opinion leaders in their families and neighbourhoods. Education and exposure to the media, to vocational training, new technology, new products, and urban life enables them to discern brand features and pronounce judgements. This power makes them important influencers and reference points for the recommendation and purchase of several high-involvement products like durables (TV, refrigerator, motorcycle, etc.). However, the male family head remains the exclusive decision-maker in the event that those high-involvement products directly impact traditional earning and livelihoods.

At the age of 20–22, the average rural youth is an additional 'bread earner' and a significant influencer in the family decision-making process. He is open to ideas regarding improving the family income and changing lifestyles, but continues to be strongly associated with his family and influenced by his community value systems.

RURAL MARKETING MEMO | REFERENCE GROUPS IN RURAL

Professional workers who form part of the reference group in rural areas are listed below:

- ***Anganwadi workers:*** Anganwadi workers are grassroots agents working on child-development programmes with a focus on nutrition, health and education. They are trained to communicate with and influence villagers. Besides influencing families, they are also pre-school teachers.
- ***Auxiliary nurses/Midwives:*** An auxiliary nurse/midwife visits homes for pre-natal check-ups and provides expectant mothers with recommendations on vaccination, nutrition and check-up schedules. Her services also extend to childbirth, post-natal check-ups and child care. She also supports the health centres.
- ***Self-Help groups:*** Self-help groups (SHGs) are thrift-and-saving groups promoted by government and non-government organizations to help the poor access low-cost finance. Ten to 20 women form an informal group and save on a regular basis. The group savings are parked in a bank account. Group members take loans from their group savings in case of emergencies, or for starting income-generating activities.
- ***Agri Cooperative societies:*** The cooperative society's model for agriculturists was started to provide farmers with access to funds for agricultural purposes. These thrift-and-saving societies changed over a period of time under government intervention, and are today known as Primary Agricultural Cooperative Societies. These societies channel programmes and funds from NABARD to their members.
- ***Non-Government organizations:*** Non-government organizations (NGOs) were encouraged by the government to help implement development programmes. The NGO workers belong to the local community, are sensitive to local needs, have greater access and are accountable to the community. They work in functional areas like agriculture, dairy, non-timber forest produce, health, education, drinking water and sanitation, shelter, etc.

In the evolving rural Indian market, the youth are driving the change in rural behaviour and practices.

SOCIABILITY People in rural India spend more time with family and friends, and they constitute the reference points for everyday life.

Rural families often drop in on other families socially, just to have a chat or exchange pleasantries. A man may drop in at the house of another to discuss some urgent matter, take his advice, or seek his opinion on a personal matter.

In rural areas, more time is spent on interaction within the community due to the availability of spare time.

For the male members, the village *choupal* or community meetings are the best places to meet. Women gossip with other women while performing daily chores such as fetching water, visiting the temple, and washing clothes at the pond. Packed household routines do not permit women in the village the luxury of the urban 'kitty party'.

A rural neighbour is not a polite (or unpleasant) stranger next door. Rather, they are an extension of the family, and at times even an active participant in the family decision-making process. Every new purchase is discussed, deliberated upon, and evaluated in the neighbourhood, thereby determining the acceptability, prospects of repeat purchase and/or adoption in other families.

SOCIABILITY

A soft drinks manufacturer approached MART for a research study through which to understand why its leading brand was losing market share among the youth, as the company could find no satisfactory reason for this. During the study, MART observed that consumers found nothing wrong with the brand attributes, but unfortunately the age for consuming hard drinks (a way to socialize in the rural context), which was 18 years earlier, had dropped to 16 years, thus shrinking the consumption of soft drinks.

FAMILY The traditional joint family is disintegrating due to factors like increased education and awareness of new opportunities and professions, which are driving the younger generation in rural areas away from agriculture.

Although individuals are branching off to form nuclear families (with separate cooking arrangements), they continue to live in the traditional family compound (under one roof). These hybrid families can be termed 'individualized joint families' (IJFs). The national Census records each *chulha* as a separate household. These IJFs live separately on a daily basis and take purchase decisions independently for FMCGs and consumer durables. But they bond with the 'parent' family on social occasions such as marriage, childbirth, death, and family disputes. On important decisions involving heavy investments or choice of a marriage partner for their children, they seek the advice of family elders.

Therefore, the nuclear family continues to live in the same realm as the 'parent family', with similar value systems; however, since the immediate family households are separate, purchase decisions and product choices could be quite disparate because of the different sets of influences. The chief wage earner becomes the head of the nuclear family for all household matters except in social matters, where the family elders from the 'parent' family continue to take decisions. In rural areas, the solidarity of the clan is symbolized by its coming together on social occasions.

ROLES AND STATUS In the rural sector, caste plays a very important role in defining social status. Individuals such as sarpanches, caste leaders, medical practitioners, retired military personnel and priests enjoy a higher status in the village. They constitute the upper level in society, regardless of their economic status, and represent role models of success.

People expect them to be exemplary and even their purchase decisions seem to have a significant influence on others.

Caste factors continue to impact the overall status within society. A person belonging to a higher caste continues to enjoy a higher status than one belonging to a lower caste, despite the former's inferior economic status and consequent inability to acquire status symbol products.

A progressive farmer is respected more now because he is viewed as a man of knowledge, a man ahead of his time. As innovators of technology and products, they have acquired a special status that makes them good role models to emulate in purchase decisions.

The Role of Rural Women Till a few decades ago, rural women used to remain in purdah or *ghungat*. They hardly left their homes except to attend social functions and festivals, always accompanied by male members of the family. Women were accompanied by male members of the family even while taking a sick child to a health centre or during pregnancy. Hence, their mobility was highly restricted. Few girls attended school regularly, as they were dragged into household activities. They were not aware of what was happening in the outside world and did not play any significant role in major family purchase decisions.

Now, however, the status of rural women is changing. They are more educated and more aware of the health and education needs of the family. The growing presence of the media also exerts a strong influence on their role and behaviour. They are no longer confined within their homes. They step out for several purposes—education, health services, social services, functions, and festivals. In short, women are more empowered today. Therefore, their involvement in the family buying-decision process is also increasing.

Personal Factors

Several personal factors influence consumer behaviour. These include age, occupation, economic situation in life, etc. These are examined in this section.

| TABLE 3.1 |
Consumption by Age and Lifecycle Stages

Age	Lifecycle Stage	Products and Services Consumed in Rural
Below 12	Childhood	Toys, snacks like Kurkure, local kulfi, cold drink, chocolate
13–19	Teenage	Mobile, television, cinema
20–40	Young	Motorcycle, mobile, LPG, readymade clothes, country/Local (*haath bhatti*) liquor, jeep, haat
40–60	Middle age	Tractor, playing cards, Kisan credit card, postal savings, *mela*
Above 60	Old age	Choupal, pilgrimage, hukka, social and political function

Source: MART Knowledge Centre

AGE AND STAGES OF THE LIFECYCLE The purchase of products and services and their forms and nature are influenced by age and the lifecycle stages of the consumer. This gives direction to the estimation of demand, segmentation, targeting of markets and product-mix decisions. Table 3.1 gives a fair idea of the products and services consumed at various stage of the lifecycle in rural areas.

India is a nation of the young, with 65 per cent of its population below 35 years of age, as seen in Table 3.2. Young adults, the group between 20 and 35 years, account for almost one-fourth of India's consumption base.

OCCUPATION AND INCOME In the rural sector, a range of goods and services beyond the very basic ones are bought by a consumer, influenced by the occupation and income of the individual. Fishermen buy a boat and large nets, whereas a farmer opts first for a tractor and pump-set. The same buying behaviour and choice of products cannot be expected from a cultivator, salary earner (teacher) and petty shopkeeper, all of whom may have identical incomes.

A farmer has to allow for variations in income during pre-harvest and post-harvest periods. The shopkeeper (*baniya*) behaves differently, as he is in a position to adjust his income according to demand in the village by adjusting his inventory and credit, without this affecting the purchase of goods. On the other hand, a salary earner has a fixed and assured income. Add to this the fact that the rural consumer has more than one source of income, supplementing the income from his main occupation (for example, agriculture and dairy). Truly, buying behaviour based on pure income parameters can cloud the understanding of priority and choice of purchase.

Apart from income, consumer behaviour is also guided by the working status of the earning member(s) of the family, especially the head of the household, as major purchase decisions are taken by him.

The occupation profile of owners of three key durables indicate that non-agricultural occupation groups (shopkeepers, salary earners) are high-consumption segments, and that this segment is growing rapidly, with reducing dependence on agriculture. Data on occupation patterns show a decline in farmers and an increase in other sectors.

| TABLE 3.2 |
Distribution of Indian Population by Age in Percentage (All India: Rural+Urban)

Year	Kids (0–4 years)	Children (5–14 years)	Adolescents (15–19 years)	Young Adults (20–34 years)	Mid Aged (35–65 years)	Aged (More than 65 years)
2001	11.8	23.7	10.1	24	25.8	4.4
2011	9.6	19.4	10.2	25.9	29.3	5.5
2026	7.5	15.9	8	24.8	35.3	8.4

Source: Census of India 2001, Population Projection

ECONOMIC SITUATION The purchasing power of an individual plays a significant role in the choice of products. People's economic circumstances are dictated by their disposable income, savings and debts, credit worthiness, and attitude towards spending and savings. The patterns of income of a farmer are linked to the harvest and stability of income from produce, and are also largely dependent on the monsoons.

The purchasing power of a daily wage earner, on the other hand, is redefined every day. The fact that a majority in the rural sector are self-employed increases the risk of stability of income. Agriculture being the main activity in rural areas, the purchasing power of the rural consumer is highly unpredictable, which may lead to high variations in the demand pattern of products.

Saving habits in the rural sector are more inclined towards fixed deposits and small savings in banks and post offices. The rural consumer is reluctant to go in for credit purchases as these are considered to dilute his status and reputation in the village.

LIFESTYLE Lifestyle deals with the everyday, behaviourally oriented facets of consumers, as well as their values, feelings, attitudes, interests, and opinions. It embodies the patterns that develop and emerge from the dynamics of living in a society.

The typical lifestyle dimensions are:

- ***Activities***. Allocation of time by the consumer/family (work, hobbies, social events, entertainment)
- ***Interests***. Consumer preferences and priorities (food, fashion, family, recreation)
- ***Opinions***. Consumer attitudes to events/issues (politics, education, social issues, future, culture)
- ***Demographics***. Age, education, income, occupation, family size, geography, dwelling

The lifestyle in rural areas is different because here the social and cultural environment, values and daily mode of living is different. Table 3.3 gives the various dimensions of a rural lifestyle.

Over the years, the rural consumers' attitudes and lifestyles have been changing, due to exposure through TV and awareness brought in by an increase in literacy levels. Growing industrialization is another factor effecting greater changes in the lifestyles of rural people. They are seen on stylish bikes with trendy mobile phones.

Lifestyle is a person's pattern of living. NCAER has classified it into different categories—destitutes, aspirants, climbers, well-offs, and affluents.

Products and Status Symbol The status of a consumer plays an important role in the choice of product in both urban and rural contexts. However, the rural consumer displays a marked difference in his criteria of evaluation. For instance, for television sets, the urban buyer shows a marked preference for 'add-ons' and fancy features. The rural buyer, however, looks at ease of operation rather than features.

In India, John Deere is the leader in the above-50-horsepower tractor segment. A farmer might not require such a powerful tractor for his work needs, but will purchase it to boost his status in society. In Maslow's need hierarchy theory, such a farmer features on the top of the pyramid, where his need is led more by aspiration than by basic existence.

Status symbols (see Table 3.4) in the rural context are linked more closely to the position enjoyed within a well-knit social fabric, clearly defined levels of status enjoyed in society, and the expectations people have of that status. In meeting these expectations, however, the relevance of symbols to their utility value in everyday life is a prime consideration in their acquisition.

| TABLE **3.3** |
Lifestyle in Rural India

Dimensions	Rural Lifestyle
Demographics	Government school, self-employed, joint/individualized family, small/scattered population, ordinary/spacious house
Activities	Agriculture being replaced by non-traditional occupations like shop/trade, skilled work, salaried job, physical sports, gossip, playing cards, cinema, religious congregation
Interests	'*Desi*' food, milk, readymade clothes, mobiles, jewellery, visiting towns, markets/mela.

| TABLE 3.4 |
Status Symbols in Rural India

Class	Product Owned
Affluents	Social and political status, four-wheeler, gold ornaments, DTH, pilgrimage
Well-offs	Bike, fridge, colour television, land, ready-made clothing
Climbers	Moped, audio system, television, mixer, pucca house, LPG
Aspirants	Bicycle, fan, iron
Destitutes	Wrist watch, pressure cooker, radio

Personality driven advertisements have good recall and a great impact on rural consumers.

PERSONALITY AND SELF-CONCEPT Personality is the sum total of the unique individual characteristics that determine and reflect how a person responds to their environment. It provides a framework within which consistent and long-lasting behaviour can be developed. Self-concept or self-image is the way we perceive ourselves in a social framework. There is a natural tendency to buy those products and services that we think fit or match with our personality.

In order to relate personality to the products people purchase, two aspects need to be considered: situation and person. When in social gatherings, rural youth prefer to buy *pan masala*, tea and *namkeen*, whereas while travelling they carry food items from their homes, or buy open food. A conservative villager may offer water or tea, whereas a person high on sociability may offer *lassi* or *thanda* to his friends.

Rural marketers are becoming increasingly concerned about giving a distinct image or personality to their products that adheres as closely as possible to that of the target customer.

Some marketers have learned from their mistakes (for instance, their earlier assumption that the same brand ambassador would appeal to rural and urban consumers alike) and have started using separate rural brand ambassadors for targeting rural markets.

A TV campaign for Bartan dish bar showed Hema Malini, the brand endorser, using the product to clean utensils. Rural/small-town audiences could not connect with the storyline as they could not imagine that a famous Bollywood personality would ever wash utensils in her house.

A few brand ambassadors—as shown in Table 3.5—are considered idealistic role models, and are perceived to have qualities considered most admirable by the rural audience in the relevant marketing territories.

When the iconic Amitabh Bachchan dons rural attire and promotes Navratan oil, rural consumers are convinced of its quality.

Psychological Factors

Motivation, perception, learning, and beliefs and attitudes comprise the psychological factors affecting consumer behaviour.

MOTIVATION The traditional rural consumer is quite content to satisfy his basic needs, relevant to his environment. He is less adventurous, averse to taking risks, and prefers to stay with the tried and tested. A lot of persuasion by an influencer whose achievements he respects is required to convince him to try new products. Opinion leaders also play a significant role in the case of products that are higher on the involvement scale (but not necessarily more expensive).

The rural consumer is not driven by 'status symbols' acquired by his neighbours in order to upgrade to a better lifestyle. Though high in self-esteem, he is quite content with his everyday life, resigned to adverse circumstances

| TABLE 3.5 |
Rural Brand Ambassadors

Brand Name	Rural Brand Ambassador	Brand Personality
Pulse Polio, Navratan Oil	Amitabh Bachchan	Rugged, conventional, self-confident
Coca-Cola, Tata Sky	Aamir Khan	Smart, simple
Aircel, TVS	Mahinder Singh Dhoni	Jovial, youthful, cool
Idea (What an idea Sirji!)	Abhishek Bachchan	Smart, colourful, modern
Kurkure	Juhi Chawla	Beautiful, homely

and less ambitious about comfort and material possessions, except those which seem to provide security.

Typically, through his lifecycle an urban consumer moves through five, or at least four, of the five segments of Maslow's model of the motivational pyramid,[2] that is, basic needs and needs of security, social needs, needs of self-esteem and needs of self-actualization (see Fig. 3.5). Most rural consumers, however, are mostly quite content to stay in the lower two sections of the pyramid all their life.

PERCEPTION Perception plays an important role in a consumer's selection of products. However, since perception is an individual concept, it acts more as a barrier to the trial and acceptance of products in the case of the rural consumer.

Perception plays a major role in the purchase behaviour of the rural consumer. Quality and price influence the perception of the consumer.

This perception is directly related to the level of acceptance of and satisfaction in the consumer's present way of life, and the role played by the existing products in that life. Awareness and exposure to the new media do not lead to impatience with the present and aspiration for trial and change in the rural consumer, fundamentally because of his perception of satisfaction, rather than that of dissatisfaction.

Quality and value, as attributes integral to a new product, are always related to the improvement they bring to consumer lives in terms of productivity and prices. Prices for such products are judged in the same manner, rather than on a comparative scale. For products that create the perception of providing comfort or improving the quality of everyday life, the price is not questioned or compared, and the role played by additional features as a differentiation is not significant in influencing choice.

Familiar and known sources, such as a retailer, for example, act as strong spokespersons for low-involvement FMCGs. In high-involvement products, however, an outlet

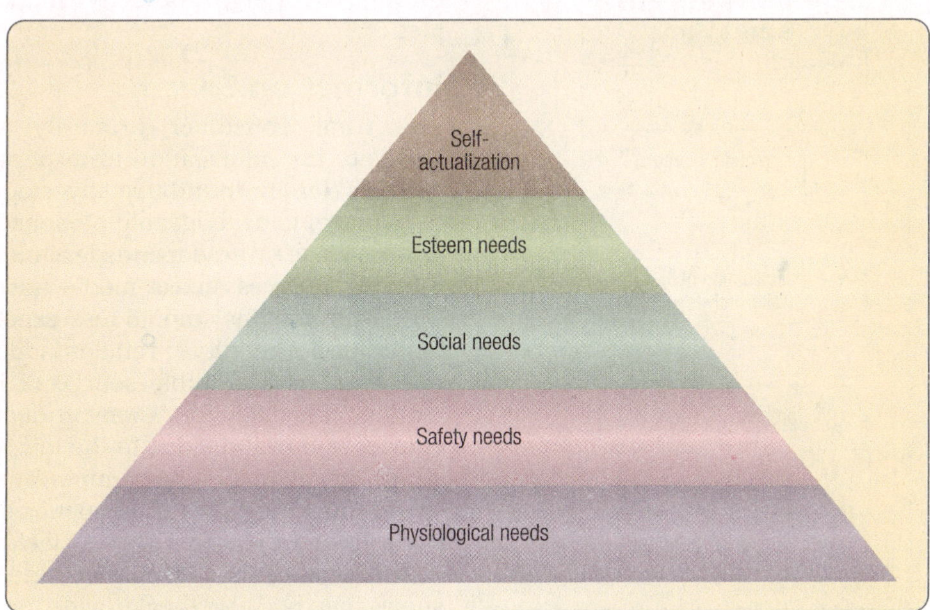

| FIG. 3.5 |
Maslow's Model of the Motivational Pyramid
Source: A. H. Maslow, *Motivation and Personality*, 3rd edition, Pearson Education, Inc., Upper Saddle River: NJ.

away from the rural environment and retailers and closely identified with the brand acts as strong reinforcement for that brand. For example, Aircel in its ad campaign used a bunch of upcoming cricketers like Suresh Raina, Praveen Kumar, and M. S. Dhoni, who hail from small towns and automatically establish a connect with the small town/rural audience.

Another example is of a leading agri-input company, Syngenta, which markets their international range of crop plant protection brands in India, and only targets the top-end farmer/grower segment it identifies as 'optimal farmers'.

LEARNING Consumer learning is a process that evolves as a result of newly acquired knowledge:

- Changes in an individual's behaviour based on experience
- Learning occurs through the interplay of:
  - ***Drive.*** Strong internal stimulus that call for action
  - ***Stimulus.*** Objects that convert drive to motive
  - ***Cues.*** Minor stimuli that determine when, where, and how the person responds
  - ***Responses***
  - ***Reinforcements*** through rewarding experiences

BELIEFS AND ATTITUDES Attitude describes a person's relatively consistent evaluations, feelings, and tendencies towards an idea or object.

- A belief is a descriptive thought that a person has about something.
- Beliefs impact brand image, which affects buying behaviour.

The Buyer Decision Process

Having reviewed the factors that affect rural buyers, we now need to look at how rural consumers make buying decisions. The buyer decision process consists of five stages, starting from need recognition and ending with post-purchase behaviour (see Fig. 3.6). Depending on the product, some of the stages may be skipped or even reversed.

Need Recognition

Need recognition is the first step in the decision-making process. In this stage, consumers recognize a need or respond to marketing stimuli. This need is mostly met through acquiring a product or a service. Marketers can stimulate need recognition through a variety of proactive marketing tactics.

| FIG. 3.6 | The Buyer Decision Process

Information Search

The rural consumer primarily seeks and gets his information from **personal sources** (family, friends, relatives outside the village, knowledgeable persons within the village), and depends less on **commercial sources** (mass media advertising, sales persons) due to less exposure. In addition, the village retailer is also an important and credible source of information, especially for newer product categories and brands, due to the low levels of awareness within the community.

The rural customer also depends on **experiential sources** (touch and feel, demonstrations, trials). Exhibitions and road shows help because they provide the rural customer with an opportunity to evaluate the product personally and absorb relevant information at their own leisurely pace. Haats, mandis, and melas facilitate informal consumer interactions, enabling consumers to seek and gather relevant information from each other. In the case of high-involvement products, this information search needs to be supplemented by an 'out-of-village' visit to a company outlet for an opportunity for personal interaction with sales persons/company representatives. The need to evaluate individual accessories of the product and their performance also becomes critical.

Buying behaviour is a five-step process that includes need recognition, information search, evaluation of alternatives, purchase, and post-purchase behaviour.

Marketers need to focus on reducing the information search time by inducing product trials and effectively reaching out to the consumer through preferred information channels.

The Evaluation of Alternatives

The process of evaluation depends on the kind of product, the type of buyer, and the buying situation. Buyers from the rural segment evaluate multiple attributes—price and quality being the major ones—of different brands, each of which is weighted differently. The purchase intent is ascertained after the evaluation is complete.

In the case of consumer durables, the evaluation is done more carefully and logically. The time taken is longer, as the product is evaluated on several parameters.

For convenience goods—grocery items, etc.—which are consumed within a short time, the evaluation process is very short. Sometimes these purchases are also impulse buys. The buyer is attracted towards a product, and buys it immediately without any evaluation.

The evaluation process and period is often longer for high-involvement products such as tractors, two-wheelers, and product categories new to rural markets, including mobile phones, personal computers, and DTH connections, as it takes time to gather adequate information about products and brands and evaluate them in the absence of other users in the village.

Marketers need to understand the product-specific evaluation process from primary research to mapping the progression of their brand from consideration set to choice set. This addresses the product deficiencies vis-à-vis competition, and improves its chances of selection during evaluation.

The Purchase Decision

After arriving at the choice set in the evaluation stage, all the selected brands are acceptable to the consumer. In this situation, the final choice is guided by the perceived risk associated with the product, as well as by the key influencers (opinion leaders, family, and friends).

Perceived risk is high among rural consumers as they find it difficult to gather and process the relevant information. Due to this reason, they make a collective decision for high-ticket items.

The role played by members of the family varies with demographics parameters, as well as with the type of products. For household products, the female member is also consulted, although the final decision is taken by the male head of the family.

Marketers need to address the perceived risk of rural buyers by showcasing the experience of users and ensuring service delivery close to the consumer's doorstep. 'Rural Marketing Snapshot: Key Opinion Leaders' captures the changes in profiles of the primary decision makers.

Post-purchase Behaviour

Post-purchase behaviour involves the buyer's activities, reactions, and evaluation after the purchase of a product. The buyer's expectation and product's performance are interrelated. This leads to satisfaction or dissatisfaction. If he is satisfied, he will engage in positive word of mouth.

Dissatisfaction results in complaint behaviour. The buyer may choose to return or exchange the product, or take action by spreading negativity about the product and the company. Bad word of mouth travels farther and faster than good word of mouth.

RURAL MARKETING **SNAPSHOT** KEY OPINION LEADERS

The traditional sarpanch

The modern, progressive farmer

The profile of the key opinion leader — the village sarpanch, the elders, etc. — has changed over the years. Key opinion leaders are now educated, aware of new technologies, and receptive to new concepts and ideas.

Many times it results not only in losing the trust of existing users, but also in endangering potential buyers' future purchase decisions.

Customer satisfaction is the key to building a profitable and sustainable relationship with customers. A satisfied customer develops trust in the brand and talks favourably about it to others, whereas a dissatisfied customer never tells the company about the problem. See 'Rural Marketing Insight: Aircel' for details on the factors that are critical to consumer satisfaction in the case of mobile phone services in rural areas. Therefore, it is critical for a company to measure customer satisfaction on a regular basis in order to track product performance and take corrective measures in time. Rural marketers need to focus more on retaining the existing customer by continuously meeting their expectations, as done by MNC players in the tractor and consumer durables market.

The Product Adoption Process

There are several products available in the market with similar features. Consumers select a particular product to fulfil their needs. The consumer carries out several observations, exercises, and trials before selecting a new product. This process is known as the product adoption process.

Adoption is a psychological process through which an individual takes a journey—from first hearing about an innovation to its final adoption.

Product adoption is concerned with the way new consumers learn about a new product and decide to become a regular user. The process by which one comes to a decision to use a certain new product regularly is a psychological one. Stages in the product adoption process:

1. ***Product awareness.*** Consumers become aware of a product, but lack information.
2. ***Product interest.*** Interest generated so information can be gathered on a new product.
3. ***Product evaluation.*** The information gathered is evaluated on various parameters (quality, features, utility, price, etc.).
4. ***Product trial.*** The customer tries the product to gain first-hand experience.
5. ***Product adoption.*** The customer adopts the product and decides to use it regularly.

RURAL MARKETING INSIGHT | AIRCEL

Aircel, a mobile phone service provider in India which offers both prepaid and postpaid GSM cellular phone coverage, commenced operations in 1999. It became the leading operator in Tamil Nadu within 18 months. It subsequently launched its services in 18 circles. The company decided to extend its operations to rural areas, and felt the need to understand the rural ecosystem with reference to present practices regarding mobile service delivery and customer expectation, mapping for the future practices of an elevated customer service delivery model. In 2009, it commissioned MART to study the usage, attitude, and behaviour towards different mobile phone services, identify the problems in the service delivery of different operators, identify future communication and information needs, and understand retailer behaviour.

The study was conducted in Uttar Pradesh, West Bengal, and Tamil Nadu, their focus markets. The respondent segments covered were consumers, key opinion leaders, and retailers. Participatory rural appraisal, mini focus group discussions, and in-depth interviews were used to understand the rural ecosystem.

The purchase process studied revealed that the need for a mobile connection was triggered by the chief wage earner or the youth in the household. Friends and relatives already using mobiles were contacted for information on different service providers. After collecting all the required information, the buyer would request some friends of his with an understanding of technology to accompany him to the nearby town, where he would get more product and brand choice, genuine products, and a warranty.

The SIM was bought from the village retailer who gave suggestions to the service provider on the best signal, and helped with the documentation.

Initially the phone was used like a landline as it always remained at home to be used by the entire family. But subsequently, when another mobile was purchased by the family, the first one became the personal phone of the chief wage earner, who carried it with him wherever he went.

After the study, Aircel learnt that coverage is the first criteria considered by the consumer while deciding upon a service provider. It is important to develop a last-mile reach so that the brand reaches the doorstep of the consumer. For the 'last-mile reach', Aircel needs to use the 'mobile retailer' format in addition to the regular distributor-retailer format. They also realized that simple schemes make for happy consumers.

The adoption process helps to turn a prospective buyer into a regular user of the product.

It is therefore important for marketers to understand rural hierarchies and tap into local opinion leaders to help brand adoption and diffusion within a rural community.

Winning over key opinion leaders is critical to penetrating rural communities. For example, doctors (for healthcare products) or progressive farmers (for farm inputs) could be tapped as opinion leaders. Colgate taps into school teachers to reach children (early adopters of more expensive toothpaste) through its 'Bright Smile. Bright Future' programme.

Being relatively closed societies, rural consumers are slower to adopt new brands and categories than their urban counterparts. Generating trial becomes more difficult than gaining loyalty.

Marketers therefore have to front-load their investment, and probably plan for longer lead times before their investment yields returns. However, the higher level of loyalty that can be expected (as rural consumers are slower to give up brands once they have adopted them) helps to justify the initial brand investment.

Many MNC brands that have long since vanished from shop shelves across urban markets can still be found in rural India, indicating the longevity of brands once they have been adopted. Newer brands will need a lot more on-the-ground effort to convince rural consumers to try them, as mass media input alone is seldom enough to get consumers to try new products.

::: Diffusion of Innovation

The flow of technology—from international boundaries to metros, to cities, to towns, to the *kasba* (feeder town), to the village, to the rural consumer—is a long chain. This long chain translates into less exposure to evolving products and services as far as the rural consumer is concerned. Here, the main way to create awareness is through

RURAL MARKETING INSIGHT | HPCL RASOI GHAR

To understand the adoption behaviour of rural habitants towards new products, a study was undertaken by MART in 2006 with respect to the adoption of the concept of HPCL-promoted community kitchens (HPCL Rasoi Ghar) by women in the villages of Uttar Pradesh. Cooking food using LPG was considered a new product innovation in this area.

The study was conducted among both early and late adopters (female population) of the community kitchen concept, and consumer insights were captured using the activities, interests, and opinions (AIO) framework.

Those who adopted Rasoi Ghar in the very first month of its inception were termed early adopters (innovators/early adopters), and the remaining population as late adopters. To map the behavioural and psychographic characteristics of these groups, in-depth interviews were conducted with the users.

The findings of the study revealed that those women who were opinion leaders and had more decision-making powers within their households emerged as early adopters. In addition, they were characterized as optimistic people with better education and reasonable influence within their families and society, who seek information on newer things. On the other hand, late adopters were pessimistic, low literates with little influence in family, unwilling to seek new information, and remaining confined.

Later, a user-centric communication strategy was designed taking cues from this study, which resulted in the diffusion of innovation and adoption of Rasoi Ghar in villages. Marketers of home appliances and other consumer durables can take a lesson from this study while developing rural marketing strategies.

Source: MART Knowledge Centre

word of mouth, especially for areas not covered by the mass media. Also, the reach of communication achieved here is often through word of mouth, especially in large areas not covered by the mass media.

While the external environment is restricting, the rural consumer is also limited in his ability or desire to adopt innovations due to low levels of literacy.

The theoretical concept of adoption of innovation remaining the same, the role played by different consumers in different stages varies.

Some customers try out products early, while some try them late. See 'Rural Marketing Insight: HPCL Rasoi Ghar' to understand how HPCL designed its communication strategy to popularize the use of LPG as the fuel of choice through community kitchens in rural areas. Based on the time taken for new product adoption, customers are categorized into five categories, as shown in Fig. 3.7. The profile and behaviour of the five segments in rural areas is summarized in Table 3.6.

Innovators and early adopters are generally highly demanding in the rural segment as they have high self-belief and put little trust in product claims unless they have experienced it themselves. Therefore, product demos and trials are critical to convincing them. However, once convinced with product promise and performance, they can be groomed as brand ambassadors to influence the other segments, and showcase the path of success for marketers in the hinterland.

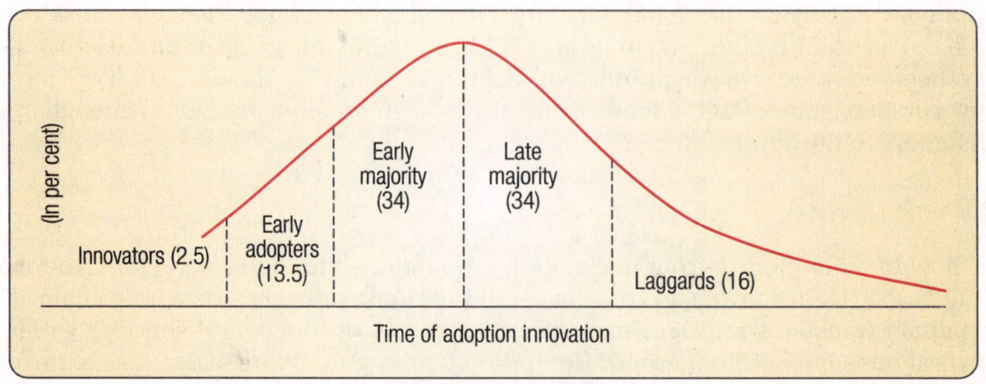

| FIG. **3.7** |
The Adoption and Innovation Curve
Source: Tungsten, http://en.wikipedia.ord/wiki/ Everett_Rogers. Based on Rogers, E. (1962) *Diffusion of Innovations.* Free Press, London, NY, USA.

| TABLE 3.6 |
Profile and Behaviour of Different Types of Consumer Segments

Type of Consumer	Profile	Behaviour
Innovator	Opinion leaders and trendsetters, well-educated, highly ambitious, high risk takers, high asset ownership, and high profitability	Explorers, goes extra mile to get new information, first to adopt, lead by example
Early Adopter	Rich farmer with large and medium holdings, high social status, conscious evaluator, risk takers, efficiency conscious, moderate asset ownership, and profitability	High on experimentation, willing to try new product/technology
Early Majority	Medium landholding farmers, takes calculated risks, opportunity seekers, middle path takers, moderate efficiency	Less open on experimentation, followers, deliberates, adopts before average person
Late Majority	Small and medium farmers, avoid risks, more knowledge receivers than seekers, less efficient with moderate resources	Low on experimentation, sceptical, tries out late, adopts only time-tested technology/product after approval of opinion leader
Laggard	Marginal farmers and labourers, using traditional forms of cultivation, subsistence farming, risk averse, unwilling to seek knowledge and receive opinions, pessimistic, conservative and traditionalists, least efficient with limited resources	Averse to trying new things, tradition-bound, suspicious of change

::: REVIEW OF OBJECTIVES

1. Describe the customer buying behaviour model in rural India in terms of cultural, social, personal, and psychological factors

Consumer behaviour is influenced by four main factors: cultural, social, personal, and psychological. These factors help marketers to identify buyers and serve them in a better way. The cultural factor is the most important determinant of a person's behaviour in rural India. It includes culture, social customs, and traditions.

People are highly influenced by the preferences of other people around them, like family, friends, neighbours, and by roles, and status. These play a big role in deciding both a product and a brand.

A buyer's decision is also influenced by personal characteristics like age and lifecycle stage, occupation, economic situation, lifestyle and personality, and self concept.

Every consumer has a set of perceptions, beliefs, and attitudes. So it is essential for the marketer to understand those psychological factors and motivate consumers to buy the product.

2. List and define the major types of buying decision behaviour and the stages in the buyer decision process

The buying process starts with need recognition. In this stage, the buyer recognizes a problem or need, or responds to a marketing stimulus. Next is the process of information search. The buyer decides how much information is required. He then obtains information from various sources, like family, friends, neighbours, retailers, newspapers, radio, television, etc. The usefulness and influence of these sources of information will vary by product and by buyer. In the evaluation stage, the alternative brands, products, and services are studied carefully. After evaluating the alternatives, the buyer finally selects and purchases a product. The final stage is the post-purchase evaluation of the decision. Post-purchase behaviour involves the buyer's activities, reactions, and evaluation after the purchase of a product. In some cases there is dissonance. The buyer experiences concern after making a purchase decision. The customer, having bought a product, may feel that an alternative would have been preferable. In these circumstances that customer will not repurchase the product immediately, but is likely to switch brands the next time.

3. Describe the adoption and diffusion process for new products

The consumer adoption process is one by which customers learn about new products, try them, and adopt or reject them. It comprises five stages—awareness, interest, evaluation, trial, and adoption. The diffusion of innovation occurs first with innovators and early adopters, and moves up to the laggards over a period of time, which varies for various products categories.

DISCUSSION AND APPLICATION

Discussion of Concepts

1. What are the main factors influencing consumer buyer behaviour?
2. Explain the differences between culture, subculture, and social class.
3. What is a reference group? Describe the different types of reference groups that can have an impact on a consumer's purchasing behaviour.
4. Define and explain the five stages of the consumer buying process.
5. Describe the adoption and diffusion process of new products in the rural context.
6. One of the frameworks for developing rural marketing strategies is the 4 A's approach. Do you know of frameworks that exist to understand the consumers at the BoP Segment before executing the 4 A's approach?
7. Do opinion leaders always influence purchase process in rural India?

Application of Concepts

1. Abraham Maslow sought to explain why people are driven by particular needs at particular times. How does Maslow's theory help marketers in rural areas?
2. Describe how the problem recognition process works in the model of the consumer buying process.
3. If a farmer wants to buy a tractor, what according to you would be the factors that will influence his decision? What will be the decision-making process followed by him?
4. Cite two examples of product adoption in the rural sector, explaining the diffusion for various consumer segments. What lessons can be taken by marketers for developing the entry strategy of products for rural markets?
5. Healthy Group is a chain of Wellness Company which continues to earn high revenues in western parts of the country. The CEO, Mr. Gogoi, wants to expand the business and want to start innovative clinics in the north eastern parts of the country. What aspects of culture, social customs, and traditions of the North East would you suggest the marketing manager that would aid him/her in the marketing planning process?
6. Describe the process of adoption and diffusion process of the following in the rural context:
   - RO drinking Water / Water Purifiers
   - CFL bulbs
   - Smart Phones

   Do you find differences in the adoption and diffusion process of each of the above ?

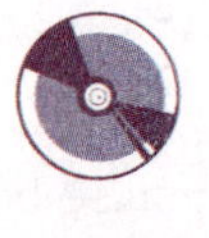

RURAL MARKETING CASE | HPCL RASOI GHAR

Liquefied Petroleum Gas (LPG) is marketed majorly by public sector undertakings (PSUs) in India. With nearly 60 per cent LPG penetration (NFHS survey 2005–06) in urban households, the companies necessarily needed new markets to grow. HP Gas, one of the PSUs, wanted to explore for new markets to grow. Rural markets were sighted as the new market since the LPG penetration was still around eight per cent in 2005.

The company, through one of its research studies, found that there were certain challenges in the adoption of LPG by rural consumers:

- Due to lack of product awareness, many rural consumers perceived LPG to be unsafe and difficult to handle (by illiterate women). Food cooked on gas stove was thought to affect digestion.
- The non-availability of LPG locally made it a difficult product to procure. The higher socio-economic consumer segments, which owned LPG as one of their multiple cooking mediums, used it more as an emergency cooking medium so that the LPG cylinder lasted longer.
- The purchase of the product necessarily included the purchase of a stove, a gas regulator, and an installation fee (under safety guidelines), making the total acquisition cost of the product around INR 1,600 and hence less affordable. The cost of refilling the cylinder was INR 270, which was a recurring cost.
- The product acceptability was low as consumers found it difficult to change their habit of cooking on the floor. LPG cooking required a raised platform for cooking.

Strategies were developed to remedy the 4As of the marketing mix. To address the affordability issue, HP Gas introduced a new product, a 5-kg cylinder at INR 95 for a refill and an initial connection cost of INR 800. Simultaneously, company dealers were advised to open extension counters in larger villages to make the product available closer to the villagers and the new product was promoted in haats to create awareness.

To improve product acceptability and lower the cost of access and use of LPG, HP Gas and MART co-created an innovative product concept of a community kitchen—Rasoi Ghar, where rural women could experience the benefits of safe, clean and convenient cooking on LPG without having to invest in a new LPG connection.

Rasoi Ghars were set up in participation with the village panchayat, HP Gas and the women self-help groups (low-income consumer segment) that managed the facility. The panchayat donated a small room accessible to the socially and economically backward classes, HPCL contributed gas stoves, LPG cylinders and cooking utensils and the SHG appointed a woman caretaker.

The product idea was to introduce rural households to this clean, efficient alternate fuel to firewood and expand its usage. Women brought their raw material, cooked on the gas stove and took back the cooked food, paying a small fee of INR 2. The money collected was used to refill cylinders and pay an honorarium to the caretaker. Thus, this new product concept became a huge success in more than 1,600 villages across four states where it was rolled out and implemented. As women understood the safety aspects of LPG, they got hooked to easy looking. SHGs also set up 'kitty' schemes to help women acquire their own 5-kg LPG cylinders. HPCL uproots its fixed assets and moves to the next village once all the women switch from firewood to LPG.

Discussion Questions

1. What challenges did HPCL face in getting rural women to adopt LPG? How were these challenges overcome?
2. What went wrong with the 50-kg gas cylinder? Which new approach was evolved? How were the issues of acceptability and affordability addressed?
3. What were the key success factors that brought about the desired behaviour change? How did HPCL benefit from this model? To which other product categories can this model be applied? How?

APPENDIX | THE NEW SEC SYSTEM

The widely preferred and accepted consumer classification in India, socio-economic classification (SEC) has been restructured by the Media Research Users Council (MRUC) and the Market Research Society of India (MRSI). The new SEC system, released in 2011, aims at a sharper classification of consumer households and reduces the heterogeneity within social grades. It uses the Lorenz curve and the associated Gini Index to measure discrimination or inequality.

In the new SEC system, the level of education of the chief wage earner and the number of assets owned by the family (from a predefined list of 11 assets) have been used as the two variables to categorize households into groups. The old SEC was based on the level of education of the chief wage earner and the type of household for rural areas, and on the occupation and the level of education in urban areas. The new SEC takes into account 11 assets as shown in Table 1.

Table 1 Assets Owned by the Household

	Items Owned/Have Access at Home	Circle	Tick
	Electricity connection	①	✓
	Ceiling fan	②	✓
1a	LPG stove	③	✓
	Two-wheeler	④	✓
	Colour TV	⑤	✓
	Refrigerator	⑥	✓
	Washing machine	7	
	Personal computer/Laptop	8	
	Car/Jeep/Van	⑨	✓
	Air conditioner	⑩	
1b	Agricultural land	11	✓
	NUMBER OF STANDARD 11 OWNED		8

The New Classification

Data drawn from various Indian Readership Surveys from 2005 to 2008 has been extensively analysed. Data was also drawn from MarketPlus, Indian Market Research Bureau's household panel, and special surveys.

On the basis of education and assets, Indian households are classified into 12 SEC groups: A1, A2, A3, B1, B2, C1, C2, D1, D2, E1, E2, and E3. These 12 groups are applicable to both urban and rural India. The LIFE score is used to decide the order of groups inside the grid defined. The LIFE score is weight in inverse proportion to the use/ownership of 34 products, ranging from the material of the wall and the roof, the mode of transport, the use of toilet soap, the use of ghee, the consumption of biscuits, etc.

Classifying Households into Groups

Let's assume a household owns eight of the 11 assets from the predefined list and the level of education of the chief wage earner is general graduate/post-graduate. In Table 2, the row corresponding to the number of assets owned and the column corresponding to the level of education intersect at A2. This indicates that the household falls in the A2 group. According to the new classification, the percentage of households in different groups is given in Table 3.

Advantages of the New SEC

The new classification system has the following advantages:

- It discriminates more between groups and less within groups, thereby ensuring a clearer distinction between groups.
- It uses a single system for both rural and urban India.
- The removal of 'occupation' as a classifying criterion has made the classification less subjective.
- It's simple, not very time consuming, easy to answer, classify and code, and the grade is easily arrived at.

Table 2 Classifying a Household

Number of Durables	Illiterate 1	Literate but no Formal Schooling/ School: For Up to 4 Years 2	School: For 5 to 9 Years 3	SSC/HSC 4	Some College (Including a Diploma) but not Graduation 5	Graduate/ Postgraduate: General 6	Graduate/ Postgraduate: Professional 7
None	E3	E2	E2	E2	E2	E1	D2
1	E2	E1	E1	E1	D2	D2	D2
2	E1	E1	D2	D2	D1	D1	D1
3	D2	D2	D1	D1	C2	C2	C2
4	D1	C2	C2	C1	C1	B2	B2
5	C2	C1	C1	B2	B1	B1	B1
6	C1	B2	B2	B1	A3	A3	A3
7	C1	B1	B1	A3	A3	A2	A2
8	B1	A3	A3	A3	A2	A2	A2
9+	B1	A3	A3	A2	A2	A1	A1

Table 3 The Percentage of Households in Each Category (in Rural India)

Groups	A1	A2	A3	B1	B2	C1	C2	D1	D2	E1	E2	E3
Rural Households (in per cent)	0.04	0.4	1.3	2.3	3.2	5.1	6.2	10.7	15.6	22.2	20.1	12.8

AFTER READING THIS CHAPTER, YOU WILL BE ABLE TO:

1. Understand the marketing research process and its application in rural areas
2. Identify special tools required for rural marketing research
3. Examine field procedures and rural realities
4. Understand the rural research business

CHAPTER 4 ::: RURAL MARKETING RESEARCH

four

In 2005, before implementing its water, sanitation, and hygiene programme for the rural folks of Rajasthan, UNICEF conducted a rural research study with the help of Rediffusion DY&R and MART to identify change agents within the rural community who would take forward its agenda and bring about a behaviour change in the community. This study saw an effective use of the 'chapati diagram' as the participatory rural appraisal tool for research.

Different sizes of chapatis or circles, depicting key persons related to health, sanitation, and hygiene in the village and their level of importance or influence on the community, were used during the participatory rural appraisal. The village community was then asked to pick and place these circles at different distances on a plain chart to show their accessibility to each key person.

With the help of this rural participatory research, UNICEF was able to identify the four most effective community change agents, based on the size and distance of each circle. (a) Auxiliary Nurse Midwives (ANMs) were the most accessible. ANMs were already dealing with this kind of activity in the village. (b) Anganwadi workers, who were socially sanctioned and had permission to enter rural households, were chosen as the second most influential. They dealt with sanitation and female health issues in the village, and had the social sanction to enter and communicate with the rural households. (c) The panchayat dealt with sanitation and hygiene issues, and any programme conducted in the village required its permission. (d) School teachers dealt with sanitation and hygiene issues related to children.

The researcher interacts with villagers to identify key persons and creates a 'chapati' diagram.

Research is the guidepost to laying the foundations of a successful marketing programme. Marketing research is essential to any strategic and operational decision-making. As the rural market is relatively new compared to its urban counterparts, there is a crying need to understand rural India, its beliefs and practices. It has become almost essential for companies who want to enter rural markets to understand and conduct research before taking appropriate decisions on their 4Ps—product, price, place, promotion—and also to keep abreast of the changing trends in rural consumer behaviour brought about by the advent of information technology, telecommunications, and media.

There are many challenges to designing and conducting rural marketing research. There is a lack of real-time information and data on rural markets; illiterate and semi-literate rural people cannot easily comprehend the 'written word'; and the lack of exposure to many concepts and practices of urban India also make their visual depiction incomprehensible. Further, there are not many appropriate marketing research tools to map rural consumer behaviour. Western ranking and rating tools often hold little relevance for a rural respondent as a framework of evaluation. Rural India is also highly scattered, remote, and inaccessible, making data collection difficult. Rural research therefore needs to be seen from a different perspective.

::: The Rural Marketing Research Process

The rural marketing research process consists of eight steps—defining objectives, budgeting, research design, sampling, developing research instruments, collecting and analysing data collection, and presenting findings.

The need for any marketing research arises on account of gaps in the existing information, based on which the problem is defined. The research leads to insights and a solution for that problem. Between these two stages of defining the problem and arriving at a solution are a number of steps that complete the marketing research process. Figure 4.1 describes a step-by-step approach to this process.

Defining the Objectives

Defining objectives is the first step in the marketing research process and involves two tasks—defining business objectives and defining research objectives.

BUSINESS OBJECTIVES Business objectives state the purpose for which the organization conducting the research will use the findings of that research. Normally it is stated in terms of a tangible benefit, for example, 'to design a new product catering to rural consumers'; 'to design a new distribution channel for a specific product for rural markets of India'.

RESEARCH OBJECTIVES Research objectives state the expected research output, which helps in taking decisions to achieve business objectives. Framing the research objectives calls for a clear understanding of the kind of information required to facilitate the decision-making process. For example, 'to map the buying behaviour of rural consumers for sub-35hp tractors'; 'to identify and profile the segments existing among rural consumer mass'.

Determining the Research Budget

Most marketing research projects involve a certain amount of cost incurred for collecting information and analysing data. Budget decisions depend on the research approach to be used for a particular study. Taking the budget decision involves two major steps:

- Specifying the approximate value of the information to be collected
- Determining the maximum amount that can be spent on the study

Once the budget is finalized, the research is designed accordingly.

Designing the Research

The third stage of marketing research involves developing an effective design for gathering the required information, which includes a decision on the research approach.

Research approaches are designed based on the purpose, nature, and sources of data. Using these three criteria, research can be classified as:

- ***Purpose***. Exploratory, descriptive, and causal
- ***Nature of data***. Quantitative and qualitative
- ***Sources of data***. Primary and secondary

We will discuss these in greater detail in this section.

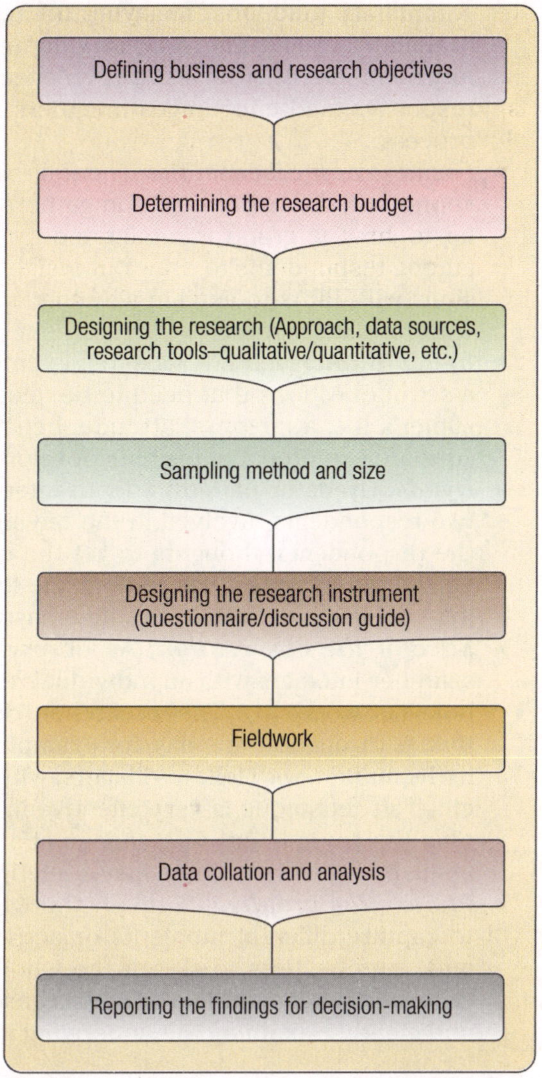

| FIG. **4.1** |
The Rural Marketing Research Process

EXPLORATORY, DESCRIPTIVE, AND CAUSAL RESEARCH When a manager is unaware of a phenomenon, they may initiate an **exploratory research** to gain a basic understanding of it. Next, they may take up **descriptive research** to obtain a thorough and analytical view of it. They may opt for experimentation before making huge investments on it.

For instance, if a company is interested in marketing its products in the rural market for the first time and the marketing manager is interested in knowing whether rural markets are attractive, they prefer a small-scale survey—a sort of pilot study to assess the attractiveness of the rural market. If the results are positive, they will go for descriptive research—a large-scale survey to assess the market potential and identify strategic options. In the final stage, they may undertake experimental research to test-market the product in a few select villages to predict its success. If the result is positive, they will implement this marketing plan for the entire rural market.

QUANTITATIVE AND QUALITATIVE RESEARCH Based on the nature of data, two broad research approaches are generally used in rural research—quantitative and qualitative.

Quantitative research is number driven and involves the use of structured interview questionnaires or other tools for data collection. The data thus gathered is in the form of numbers. It is analysed using various statistical techniques such as frequency and cross-tabulation.

On the other hand, **qualitative research** doesn't involve any fixed format or set of questions to be answered by the respondent; instead, the emphasis is on a free-flowing interview or discussion to aid an in-depth exploration of various issues or problems. The questions asked are open-ended and unstructured. For example, 'what problems do you face in the paddy cropping, describe'; 'who do you consult when taking decision on which seeds to purchase and why?'

The various qualitative research techniques in rural areas include PRA, FGD, In-depth interview, Dyads, SOLO, and Photo ethnography.

Qualitative research is mostly done face-to-face, using one or more of the following techniques:

- ***Participatory rural appraisals.*** A participatory rural appraisal (PRA) uses a set of approaches and methods that enable a group of respondents from the rural community to share, enhance, and analyse their knowledge of their own environment and life. The process adopted is pictorial and drawn by the community members themselves. It is an effective research tool for eliciting community responses, and encourages members to participate voluntarily in the research process.

- ***Focus group discussions.*** Focus groups usually involve six to 10 targeted respondents who are invited and gathered at a common place to discuss a particular topic. The group is moderated by a researcher who encourages discussion among respondents to draw out insights. Table 4.1 compares focus group discussions with PRAs to explain why the latter is the method of choice when dealing with rural consumers.
- ***In-depth interviews.*** A face-to-face interaction with an individual. This includes a set of questions that need to be deeply explored to gain insights into the consumer's life, awareness, attitude, behaviour, consumption, etc. The research issues are explored and insights developed.
- ***Dyads.*** Dyads or paired in-depth interviews are conducted simultaneously with two respondents involved in the buying decision process. It helps in stimulating the respondents' thoughts to get the complete information; for example, a rural household interview where both the female and male heads of the family take a joint decision to do with, say, the construction of the house.
- ***Slice of life observation.*** An observational research technique where the researcher interacts with an individual respondent in his natural setting, that is, his house or workplace. The researcher tries to observe the respondent's various activities throughout the day, for example, his interaction with his family members, in the market, with fellow villagers, with the products and brands, his influencers, etc. This technique is very effective in capturing the actual behaviour and mapping the true picture of a consumer's mind through non-verbal cues instead of going by his words, which may sometimes be misleading.
- ***Photo ethnography.*** A form of ethnographic research where the researcher tries to capture different moments or activities of the respondent through pictures, and, thereby, tries to sketch the whole story. The phrase 'a picture is worth a thousand words' holds true in this case as this tool is very effective in capturing and clearly explaining the underlying meanings.

In rural research, both qualitative and quantitative approaches may be used, either in isolation or in conjunction with each other. In many product categories, information is not available. Therefore, most researches start with the qualitative approach and then move on to the quantitative approach to validate the findings of qualitative research and capture variations among respondents. Rural research in sectors like

| TABLE **4.1** |
Differences between PRA and FGD

PRA	FGD
Large and heterogeneous in nature, ensuring participation from all walks of life.	Typically small and homogenous group
As expression is both verbal and non-verbal, even the less assertive people can express their views	A verbal channel—outspoken individuals often dominate the discussion
Moderator's role is limited, hence information flow is more natural	Moderator's intervention can be high in evoking a response from all sections
Attitude and behavioural change-oriented	Action-oriented
On-the-spot analysis by participants	Analysis done by moderators
Cross-checking and validation of data can be done on site by involving other members or groups	Findings be validated with more FGDs till a consensus is reached

energy, health, insurance, and banking, where not much prior information or knowledge exists, requires an exploratory or qualitative approach to start with. On the other hand, research in more matured sectors like FMCG, where a lot of rural research has already been done, can begin with quantitative research without any need for an exploratory approach.

Over the past five to six years, the rural research market has evolved quite a bit. Earlier, only exploratory studies were conducted in rural markets as these markets were nascent and companies wanted to understand the parameters that made them different from their urban counterparts. Gradually, as rural markets mature and rural consumers become aware and literate, companies are adopting quantitative research tools applicable to their product category/brand, leading to an increasing number of survey works being conducted by rural marketers in India. Some examples of the quantitative studies carried out in rural areas are customer satisfaction, brand tracking, market share measurement, forecasting, and segmentation studies.

PRIMARY AND SECONDARY RESEARCH Primary research involves collecting fresh data for specific research purposes through the methods mentioned above. Secondary research is based on data that has been collected in the past, been published, and exists in some repository. There are several secondary sources for rural data, but most of them revolve around demographic information and do not provide much on products or consumers. Table 4.2 lists some of the important repositories for secondary rural data.

Sampling

Once the research design has been developed, the next step in the marketing research process is sampling design, which involves deciding on the sampling method and sample size.

| TABLE **4.2** |
Important Repositories Providing Secondary Rural Data

Organization	Data Available
1. Census of India	Largest compilation of rural demographic data
2. NCAER (National Council for Applied Economic Research)	Largest sample surveyor in the country, compiles data on demographics, durables and non-durables
3. NSSO (National Sample Survey Organization)	Consumption and expenditure-related data on major products and services
4. CSO (Central Statistical Organization)	State-wise compilation of demographics, economic indicators, infrastructure, and welfare-related data up to the district level
5. State Statistical Abstract (available with State Statistical Officer)	Contains statistical records on demographics, welfare, economic indicators, and infrastructure of the state
6. District Statistical Handbook (available with District Statistical Officer)	Contains statistical records on demographics, welfare, economic indicators, and infrastructure of the district
7. ICDS (Integrated Child Development Scheme)	Compilation of village-level information, mainly on health, by Anganwadi workers
8. CMIE	Rural economy data and sector-wise information
9. Government of India (goidirectory.nic.in)	Official website of the Government of India providing data on state and district departments
10. AG Census (agcensus.nic.in)	Latest Indian agricultural data
11. Panchayat Office	Compilation of village-level information, household-wise on demographics, health, etc.
12. Marketing Research companies and Associations—MART, Rural Relations, Anugrah Madison, Sampark, Rural Marketing Association of India (RMAI)	Research reports, media statistics and rural consumer information

SAMPLING METHODS For qualitative studies in rural areas, a minimum sample which could saturate the information is covered. Here, largely purposive sampling (see Table 4.3) is done. In this case the respondent should be a very well-informed person so that the saturation level of information can be achieved with a small sample size. Wherever there is a possibility of variation in information among different types of respondents, some sample should be selected from each respondent type to avoid losing any possible information. As a rule of thumb, sampling is continued in qualitative research till a point is reached where the researcher ceases to gain any new insights or information.

The snowball sampling technique (see Table 4.3) is also commonly used in qualitative studies on rural markets. In this case, the researcher generally takes his first reference of the right-fit respondent from the Panchayat or through the Panchayat head, who also provides him with the social sanction to move freely within the village. He approaches and speaks to the referral, who is then asked to identify others in the population that the researcher might speak to and select for the interview. This method is also called 'recruitment of respondents' and is very commonly used for conducting focus groups, in-depth interviews, and dyads in a rural setting. It ensures that the respondent devotes quality time to sharing information.

In quantitative research a more exhaustive approach is followed through sampling. For instance, the use of multi-stage area sampling (see Table 4.3) is very common. It is a hierarchical method of sampling where the first step involves selecting different zones within a country (East, West, North, South), followed by the next step of selecting states, then districts and blocks within a state, and last, the selection of villages within blocks. Villages can be selected on the basis of parameters like population, proximity to the highway, occupation profile, religion, etc. The sampling method becomes all the more important since there is no readily available and complete list of all members of the population in rural areas, and the available lists are inappropriate for one reason or the other.

We now discuss the ways of selecting villages, households within villages, and the correct respondents within households. The selection of the correct respondent is critical in both qualitative and quantitative research.

Village Selection through Probability Proportion to Size Method When there is no relevant criteria available for the selection of either the village or the respondent, the probability proportion to size (PPS) method can be used.

| TABLE **4.3** |
Sampling Methods Used in a Rural Setting

Sampling Method	Description
Simple random sampling	Population elements are chosen by lottery method.
Systematic random sampling	A method of selecting sample members from a larger population according to a random starting point and a fixed, periodic interval. Typically, every '*n*th' member is selected from the total population for inclusion in the sample population.
Stratified sampling	Mini-reproduction of the population. The population is first divided into two or more mutually exclusive segments based on some categories of variables, and a sample drawn from each subset.
Purposive sampling	The researcher chooses the sample based on some specific purpose or who they think would be appropriate to the study. For example, some limited group of farmers or its subset, like marginal farmers.
Snowball sampling	The researcher identifies one member of some population of interest, speaks to him/her, and then asks that person to identify others in the population who the researcher might speak to.
Multi-stage area sampling	Multi-stage sampling is a kind of complex sample design in which two or more levels of units are embedded (one in the other) and at each stage, a sample of the corresponding units is selected.

| TABLE **4.4** |
An Example of the Probability Proportion to Size Method

Village Number	Size of Population	Cumulative Population	Sample Selection Number	Village Selected
1	2,000	2,000	905	X
2	3,000	5,000		
3	5,000	10,000	5,905	X
4	600	10,600		
5	4,000	14,600	10,905	X
6	900	15,500		
7	1,500	17,000	15,905	X
8	3,000	20,000		
9	1,000	21,000	20,905	X
10	4,500	25,500		

While using the PPS method, a list of all the villages in all the sample blocks as given in the census is prepared with their populations placed alongside, as shown in Table 4.4. The cumulative population is then worked out with the addition of each village. Further, the sampling interval is calculated by dividing the total cumulative population by the number of villages to be selected. For example, if the total population is 100,000 and the number of villages to be selected is 20, the sampling interval (S) will be 100,000/20 = 5,000.

A random number (R) between 1 and the sampling interval is selected, for example, 905, as shown in Table 4.4. The first village in the list against which the cumulative population equals or exceeds the random number selected will be taken as the first village. By adding the sampling interval to the number identified, subsequent villages are chosen. This procedure is followed till the list is exhausted. In this method, a large village has a greater probability of occurrence than small villages. On selecting an equal number of samples in each village through random sampling, the probability of the occurrence of each household in a large village is less compared to a small village. Thus it gets balanced out, and each household gets an equal probability of occurrence in the overall sample.

Household Selection through Listing Exercise and Right Hand Rule To select a household in rural areas, the probability sampling technique is adopted, which ensures an equal probability of occurrence of every household from the village in the sample. To achieve this, simple random sampling or systematic random sampling or stratified random sampling (see Table 4.3) is used. As rural areas do not have plot numbers of households or a list of households such as is found in a telephone directory, a listing of all eligible households is required in advance to carry out a simple random or systematic random sampling.

Since a listing exercise is quite expensive, it is not always possible. In such a scenario, sampling in a village is done by using four to five starting points, which could be north, south, east, west, and the centre of the village. At each point the 'right hand rule' is followed by selecting a household on the right side, maintaining an interval of households, depending on the sample size.

If information is likely to vary among households of different SECs, a quota for each SEC is maintained in the sample based on their ratio in the universe.

Respondent Selection through Kish Grid[1] If there is more than one respondent within the same target group in the selected household, the Kish grid is used to select a respondent randomly. The Kish grid, as shown in Table 4.5, is a widely

| TABLE **4.5** |
The Kish Grid

List of Males and Females between 15–50 years in a Household	Serial Number of Households Contacted									
	1	**2**	**3**	**4**	**5**	**6**	**7**	**8**	**9**	**10**
1	1	1	1	1	1	1	1	1	1	1
2	2	1	2	1	2	1	2	1	2	1
3	1	2	3	1	2	3	1	2	3	3
4	2	3	4	1	2	3	4	1	2	1
5	5	1	2	3	4	5	1	2	3	4
6	3	4	5	6	1	2	3	4	5	2
7	2	3	4	5	6	7	1	2	3	1
8	5	6	1	2	3	4	5	6	7	6
9	6	7	8	9	1	2	3	4	5	5
10	2	3	4	5	6	7	8	9	10	1

used technique in survey research, through which researchers/investigators issued with a list of households can then sample individuals on the doorstep by following simple and rigorous rules for selecting one person to interview from among the household residents.

If there is more than one respondent within the same target group in the selected household, the Kish grid is used to select the respondent randomly.

For example, the researcher is at the doorstep of household number 4 from among the list of households provided to him. He wants to interview any one person from the household who owns a mobile phone, and there are a total of five eligible members in this household. He will first list all the eligible respondents in the household in descending order of their age. He will match column number 4 (serial 4 household) with row 5 (as there is a total of five members listed) and then pick the number from the grid, in this case, three. Finally, the respondent who corresponds to the picked number is selected for interview within that household.

SAMPLE SIZE In rural qualitative research, sample size is important only to obtain complete information about the issue taken up for research. The size depends on the number of segments being studied and a representation of each such segment should be included. For example, while determining the sample size for a product usage study, a representation from user, aware but non-user, and drop-out user groups should be taken.

Also, while in the field the researcher can stop collecting data once information redundancy is achieved, that is, till they are saturated with information and start receiving repetitive responses. Thus, sample size determination in a rural qualitative research is not static but dynamic, and is more a matter of judgement on the part of the researcher as per the situation in the actual field.

In the case of quantitative research, while estimating the proportion of respondents who are regular users of some product, the following formula is used to determine sample size:

$$n = \frac{NZ^2\,(pq)}{Ne^2 + Z^2\,(pq)}$$

Where,
n = sample size;
N = size of the universe;
Z = the Z-score associated with the degree of confidence selected;

p = frequency of occurrence;
$q = (1 - p)$; and
e = the tolerable error.

The size of the universe is considered infinite if it exceeds 100,000. In that case the following formula is used:

$$n = pq \times \frac{z^2}{e^2}$$

Where,
p = probability of occurrence (for example, if the number of users in a sample is 30 per cent, then q would be 70 per cent (1–30 per cent) and pq will be 0.21 (0.3×0.7); when p cannot be guessed, it is taken as 50 per cent as at this value, pq is maximum—0.25—which ensures the highest sample size);
e = standard value at a specified margin of error (if it is 3 per cent, it becomes 0.03); and
z = standard value at a specified confidence level (the value is 1.645 for a 90 per cent confidence level and 1.96 at 95 per cent confidence level).

Using this formula, the sample size for any universe of infinite size (greater than 100,000) at 95 per cent confidence level at ±5 per cent error would be 384.

However, the above sample size needs to be selected through simple random sampling, adherence to which is very difficult in rural India due to the unavailability of a list of all the households or respondents. Therefore, to nullify the error arising from the non-application of simple random sampling, a higher sample size is taken in some cases.

Designing the Research Instrument

The research instrument can be of two types—**discussion guide** in the case of qualitative research, and **questionnaire** in the case of quantitative research. A discussion guide is an unstructured measurement form that permits a range of possible responses. It includes open-ended questions with a lot of points for probing a particular area. On the other hand, a questionnaire is a more structured research instrument. It mostly includes close-ended questions and seeks definitive responses in a particular format. For example—how satisfied are you with the usage of the new tractor? Please rate your satisfaction on the following scale: Completely Satisfied, Somewhat Satisfied, Neither Satisfied nor Dissatisfied, Somewhat Dissatisfied, Completely Dissatisfied. Figure 4.2 illustrates the process of preparing the questionnaire/discussion guide.

Certain points need to be kept in mind while designing the questionnaire or discussion guide for rural research:

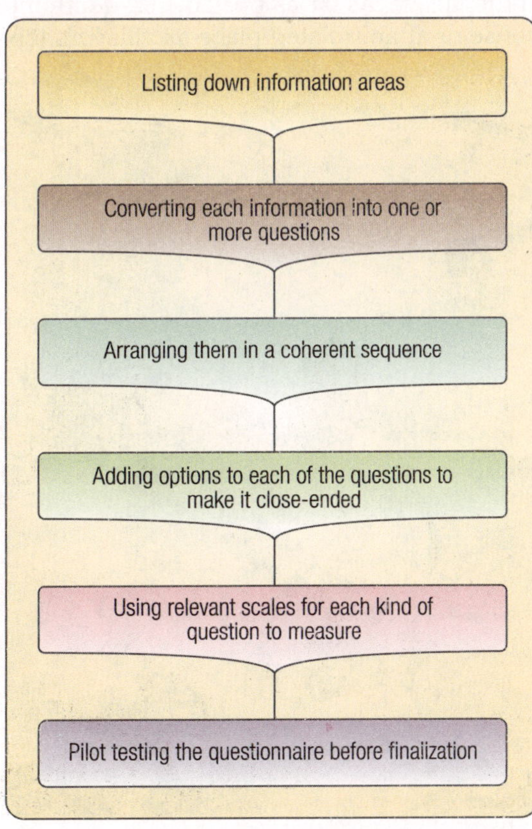

| FIG. 4.2 | Steps in the Preparation of a Research Questionnaire

There are five important steps to preparing a questionnaire—listing information areas, converting information areas to questions, arranging them in flow, putting options to questions, using relevant scales to measure responses, pilot testing the questionnaire.

- Questions in a discussion guide should contain probing points.
- Questions in a survey questionnaire should be close-ended.
- Questions should have a logical flow, and should progress from general to specific and from macro to micro.
- Questions should be simple and direct.
- Questions should not be repetitive as this might irritate the respondents.
- Negative questions should be avoided. It is better to say, 'Do you ever ...?' than 'Do you never ...?'
- Questions should be written in simple words. Translations should be in local language (colloquial).
- The accuracy of translations should be checked by persons from the same region to ensure that there is no shift in meaning or nuance.
- Clear instructions should be written for asking each question.
- In case any technical word or new concept is mentioned in any question, its meaning should be clearly explained through a visual in the questionnaire. This acts as a support for both the researcher and the respondent.
- For rating/ranking questions designed for rural respondents, one must use visual scales in the questionnaire (see section, 'Scaling Tools for Rural Quantitative Research'). A 'showcard' depicting the visual scale should be used for the respondent.
- For rating scale, either a three-point or five-point scale should be used.

Organizing the Field and Collecting the Data

In qualitative research, the researcher uses discussion guides to conduct focus groups, in-depth interviews or PRAs. Interviews in qualitative research in rural areas are always held within the natural setting of the village, rather than at a location that is central for the researcher and the respondent. Interactions with respondents are mostly audio recorded for the purpose of analysis. Focus groups are conducted at caste-neutral and common village points, such as the local village school, the panchayat bhawan, and the choupal, rather than at somebody's home, which might bias respondents of different communities in the village. As far as possible, in-depth interviews are conducted at the respondent's house or at an isolated place as villagers tend to crowd around strangers and also offer their views during the interview, making it difficult to capture the respondent's answers.

An in-depth interview being conducted at the respondent's house.

In rural quantitative research, data is collected using a structured questionnaire. Quality control measures are important in quantitative research since it is normally conducted by field investigators from field research agencies, who may not clearly understand the product category or the brand. In such a case, it is necessary to ensure that investigators involved in the fieldwork have prior experience of conducting research in rural areas. Briefing the field investigators on the questionnaire is important to aid their complete understanding. Each question needs to be explained to investigators and mock calls need to be organized before they can be sent to the field.

A day's handholding session is also organized for investigators, who are taken to the actual field to conduct interviews with rural respondents. This process is mostly adopted in rural research since there is limited understanding on the research subject, and investigators might face new problems during interviews. The researcher assists, clarifies, and solves any difficulties faced by the investigators. Following this, the actual fieldwork is rolled out.

Regular monitoring and surprise checks are also conducted to ensure that data collection is being carried out properly. Quality control measures in rural areas have to be very stringent at each stage of quantitative research, since carrying out corrections or repeating data collection is not feasible due to logistics and cost issues.

HUGHES NETWORK

As a crucial step in the process of rural quantitative research, the briefing of questionnaires and training of field investigators has been done through face-to-face classroom sessions. This process involves both time and high costs as both the field teams and the research trainer are required to be physically present at the same location. Looking at this, a new method of remote briefing and training for data collection is being explored in rural research. Options like video conferencing are being tried. An example is the Hughes Network, which has almost 9,000 centres across the country, and where field teams can gather and connect with the research trainer sitting at a remote location. This method is more cost effective as it does not require people to travel and be present physically at any one centre. Also, briefings for different locations can be done at the same time, and it would be the same as conducting face-to-face training.

Collating and Analysing the Data

In the case of qualitative research, the data collected in the form of notes, audio recordings, or PRA charts is transcribed and then collated in a set format. Further, content analysis is done using filters and specific colour codes to find similarities and variations in the data.

Based on the number of variables involved, three types of quantitative analysis can be done—univariate analysis, bivariate analysis and multivariate analysis.

In quantitative research, data input frames are prepared in Excel or SPSS software, where the data captured in the questionnaires is transferred for analysis. Broadly, three types of quantitative analysis can be done based on the number of variables involved:

- ***Univariate***. Analysis is done using one variable. For example, frequency calculation for nominal variable in terms of percentage.
- ***Bivariate***. Analysis is done using two variables. For example, cross-tabulation as well as bivariate regression can be done between two variables to ascertain the association.
- ***Multivariate***. Analysis is done using more than two variables. For example, factor analysis and cluster analysis can be done with multiple variables for measuring the interdependence level.

Reporting the Findings

As the last step in the marketing research process, the researcher presents the findings relevant to the marketing decision to the rural marketer. The report of the findings is prepared around the research objective of the study:

- **executive summary** provides the snapshot and key highlights of the research findings.
- **objectives** provide business and research objectives.
- **research methodology** describes the methodology used to conduct the research study.
- **findings** provide the detailed findings of the research.

- **conclusions** and **recommendations** sum up the findings and provide the way forward.
- **appendices** provide important additional and detailed information used in the analysis.

Special Tools Used in Rural Marketing Research

As conventional research tools have not been effective in rural markets due to the lower levels of exposure and literacy of rural inhabitants, rural researchers have come up with new solutions and special tools to capture the responses more accurately and effectively. Some of these qualitative and quantitative research tools are described below. See 'Rural Marketing Insight: New Age Innovation in Rural Research' for a brief discussion of how large corporations are reaching out to rural India.

Participatory Rural Appraisals

A PRA is an effective rural research tool for eliciting community responses. It empowers the community for voluntary participation in the research process.

A **participatory rural appraisal** (PRA) is a very successful tool for social research. This tool has been adapted to capture rural consumer insights and social behaviour. It is a set of approaches and methods that enable the rural community to share, enhance, and analyse the knowledge of their own environment and life. The process adopted is pictorial and drawn by the community members themselves, and hence cross-checking and validation of data is done automatically. Here, the role of the moderator is very low; s/he simply acts as a facilitator. The PRA approach empowers the community in such a manner that they voluntarily participate in the research process. Some of the **advantages of PRAs** are:

- It effectively captures both expressed and unexpressed behaviour and practices of the community members through diagrams, maps, association of features, and rationale for their beliefs.
- The large, heterogeneous group ensures participation of all classes of people.
- Relaxed rapport facilitates participation.
- Expression is both verbal and non-verbal.
- Participants cross-check and validate among themselves for accuracy.
- Information gathered is shared to check on acceptance.

RURAL MARKETING INSIGHT | NEW AGE INNOVATION IN RURAL RESEARCH

Rural markets are being seen as the next big thing by many national and global companies. These companies are gradually developing an appreciation of the huge opportunity that rural markets have to offer. In this scenario, it is crucial that managers in these multinational organizations, who are responsible for developing and managing products or services catering to rural markets, be well-versed in the environment and behaviour of rural inhabitants. This calls for a new and innovative research approach called the 'Rural Immersion Programme', which corporations have recently brought into focus.

The format of such programmes is largely practice-oriented and follows a 'go-to-market' strategy, where industry managers are taken to the actual rural settings to sensitize them to the rural environment and issues in rural marketing. Visits to villages, to various rural facilities like health, education, water facilities, houses, rural haats mandis, etc., are organized to provide them with an exposure to rural life. The participants interact with key stakeholders, including panchayat members and the village community, to learn more about their lifestyles and how they behave. Real-life exercises on sectors of interest—distribution, communication, etc.—are conducted to give participants a deeper and practical knowledge of the rural market.

Many world-class companies like Dupont, Pepsi, Ericsson, Nestlé, are taking this approach to immerse themselves in and explore rural markets in order to take their innovation agendas forward. These companies have realized the need for sensitization towards rural areas, their inhabitants, and their behaviour so as to clearly understand and feel their systems, processes, and needs, which can later be catered to through customized products and services.

Some important PRA tools are:

Some important PRA tools are market access or mobility maps, daily activity clocks, chapati diagrams, process maps, need assessment maps and wealth maps.

- A **market access or mobility map** allows us to understand the mobility of consumers in and around the village for accessing products and services. This helps to identify pain points and need gaps.
- A **daily activity clock** captures the economic and social activity in the daily life of a rural inhabitant. This helps to identify time windows for communicating with the community and potential consumers.
- A **chapati diagram** is used in consumer behaviour studies, specifically for capturing the importance of and access to any particular unit in the lives of rural people. The size of the chapati denotes its importance, and its distance from the centre denotes its accessibility by villagers. Examples are mapping different influencers and their importance in the lives of rural people; mapping the importance and accessibility of different agri input points for a farmer.
- A **process map** captures the step-by-step approach used for completing any activity; for example, the complete agricultural process from land preparation to the selling of produce. It captures current practices, pain points, and any need gaps at every stage. It is often used in innovation research and problem-solving research.
- A **need assessment map** is developed for any concept or new product and serves to identify issues associated with access, acceptability, or affordability. It also brings forth need gaps and helps to assess the perceived need of the product amongst the community.
- A **wealth map** is used to gather information on income flows and expenditure patterns for different communities and occupations. The objective is to gain insight into the variation in purchase and consumption behaviours.

Scaling Tools for Rural Quantitative Research

Visual tools that are more appropriate have been developed to capture rating and ranking responses from the less literate. Traditional rural practices of measurement have largely been a matter of approximation. Therefore, less literate populations find it difficult to fully comprehend and respond to numeric measures for rating. In fact, one MART study[2] revealed that a scale of more than five becomes almost impossible to administer amongst rural respondents.

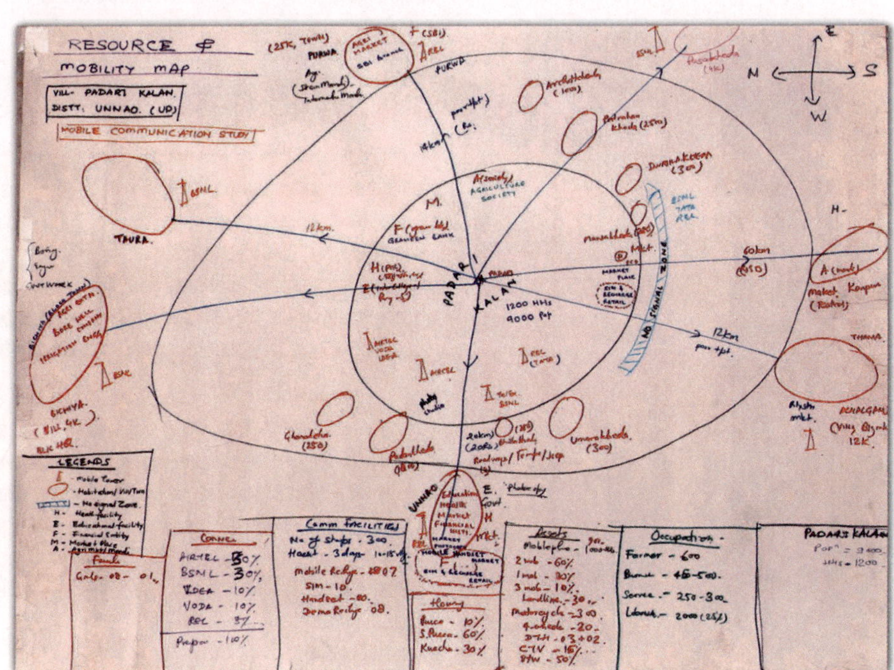

A resource and mobility map drawn with the help of a group of consumers during a PRA conducted in a village in Uttar Pradesh.

AIRCEL

In 2009, Aircel commissioned a research study through MART to understand the mobile calling pattern of rural inhabitants. The business objective of the study was to identify the appropriate time slot for making promotional and customized calls to different occupational groups in rural areas. The occupational groups identified were businessmen, farmers, students, the service class, and labourers. One of the effective PRA tools, 'activity clock', was used as the research tool to capture the appropriate information for the study. A representation of all five occupational groups was ensured during the PRA process in order to capture segment-wise information. A daily activity clock mapping the voice calling pattern of each group was drawn to find out their high, medium, and low voice calling, and mobile switch-off periods on a daily basis. This tool helped the company to identify the suitable time window for communicating with different sets of consumers during their low voice calling periods, when they would not be too engaged in other activities and hence could provide better attention and responses to the IVRs.

SATISFACTION SCALE A simple and creative way to capture the satisfaction of a rural respondent with a product or service has been developed. MART has used the images of faces with varying expressions (smiling to wailing) to measure satisfaction rating on a five-point scale (see Fig. 4.3). The highest scale is reflected with a very happy face and the lowest with a very sad face. These are developed into flashcards for field researchers to use during quantitative studies.

AGREEMENT SCALE Another new and simple tool has been recently[3] developed to capture the agreement–disagreement of the respondent on a five-point rating scale (see Fig. 4.4). It uses ticks to denote agreement and crosses to denote disagreement on any particular statement.

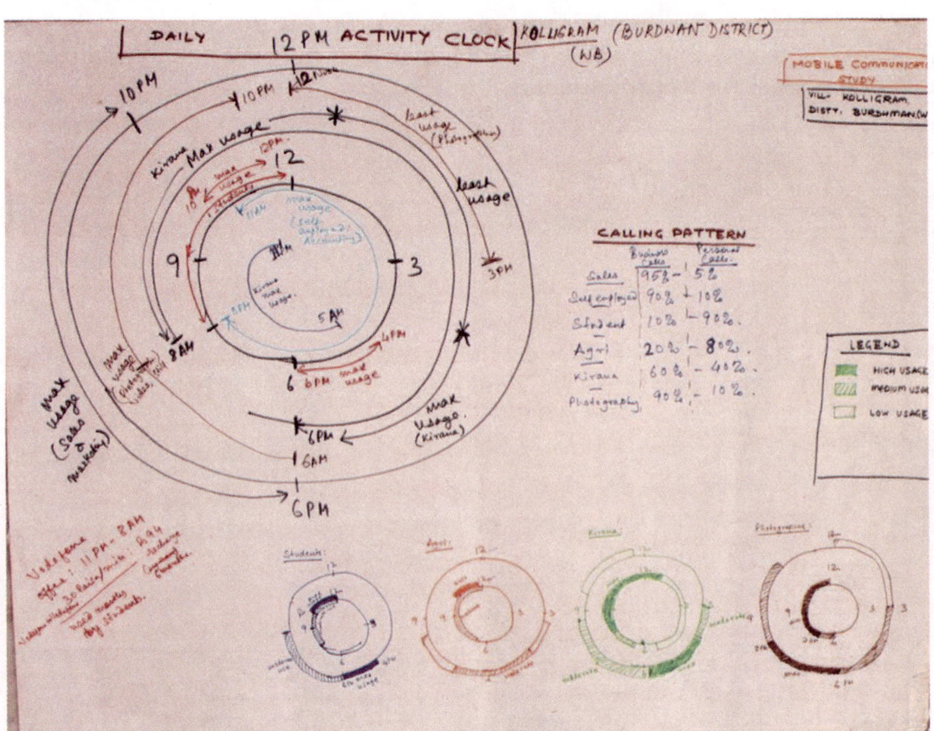

An activity clock showing variations in the mobile usage patterns of different occupational groups.

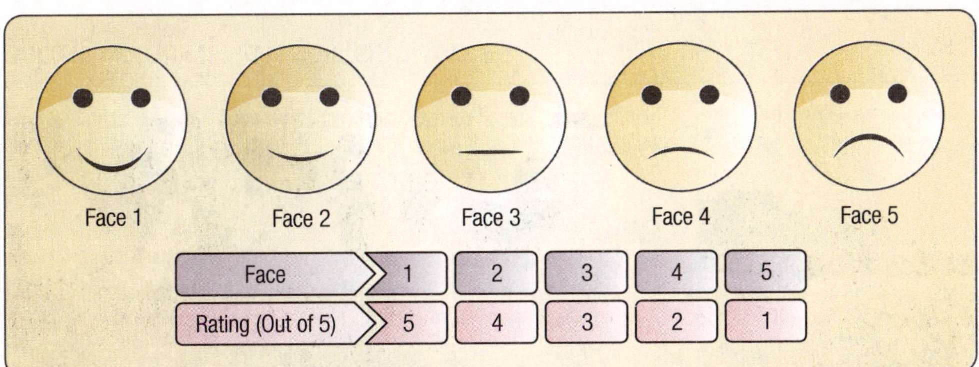

| FIG. **4.3** |
The MART Satisfaction Scale

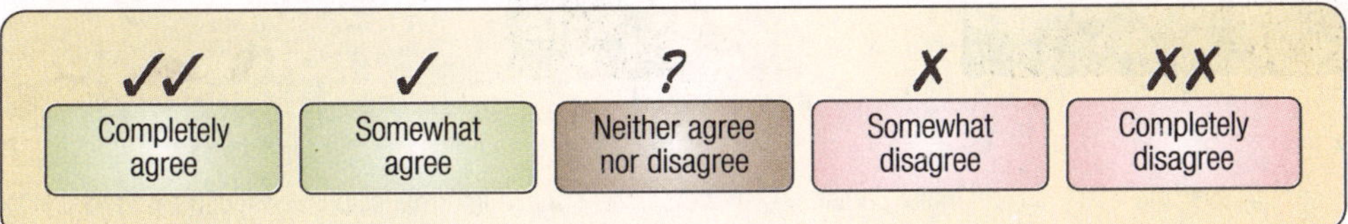

| FIG. **4.4** |
The Agreement Scale

RANKING LADDER A small bamboo ladder with the same number of rungs as the number of items to be compared is constructed or drawn. A higher rung implies a higher rank (see Fig. 4.5). It works well for a ranking scale in a questionnaire.

::: Field Procedures and Rural Realities

MART, on the basis of its experience, has developed a set of guidelines for conducting research in rural areas. These guidelines make the job of the researcher easier, and help to ensure higher degrees of accuracy and consistency in administering reach across different areas. 'Rural Marketing Snapshot: Data Collection in Rural India' depicts how primary data is collected in rural India.

Dos and Don'ts in Rural Marketing Research

Villagers have been historically exploited because of which they generally exhibit skepticism or suspicion. Thus, the biggest challenge of a rural researcher/investigator is to break through the inhibitions of rural respondents and build a rapport with them. 'Rural Marketing Memo: Attributes of a Good Researcher' provides an insight into the essential skills of successful researchers in the rural set-up.

| FIG. **4.5** |
The Ranking Ladder

- Rural people are very simple in their styles of living and communication. Thus, it is important to wear simple clothes so that villagers can feel comfortable in sharing and discussing. Villagers should be greeted very simply, in the same way they address their fellow villagers: '*Ram-Ram*', '*Namaste*

RURAL MARKETING SNAPSHOT | DATA COLLECTION IN RURAL INDIA

An informal discussion with a respondent

A PRA in progress

Data collection methods have improved rapidly over the years in rural India. Earlier, researchers used to have informal discussions with respondents to gather information. Now, participatory tools are being used to capture responses more accurately and effectively.

Bhaiyaji/Behenji' in the north, and similarly, in the local languages of other regions. A rural researcher should bear the following points in mind:

- The researcher should either be familiar with the local dialect or request an educated resident of the area to accompany them to explain issues/questions to the respondent, so as to avoid language problems and problems arising from a lack of understanding and misinterpretation.
- It is desirable to invest time in building a rapport with the respondent, by discussing issues that may not be directly related to the survey, but are of interest to them. This puts the villagers at ease regarding the researcher and helps in dispelling any doubts they might have.
- The conversation should be built up to gradually lead to the interview.
- Unless the purpose of the study is clear, the villagers do not share appropriate information. In order to gain their cooperation, the purpose of the research and its benefits should be explained every time at the outset of the interview.
- As far as possible, the respondent should be made a part of the research project. For example, the respondent could be told that his responses are very important for the company, and that they will help the company to bring out a better product.
- The respondent should be made to feel important by having his concerns listened actively to, even though they may not be related to the study.
- The respondent should be made to feel that he is the one leading the interview, since it has been observed that villagers like to be in control of situations.
- The researcher/investigator should talk a good deal about general topics, partly to show that he understands the conditions, and partly to show that he is interested in acquiring new knowledge.
- Occasional physical contact, such as touching the arm of a young male respondent, establishes kinship, but can be done only after building some rapport. However, a male researcher should never try to do this with a woman or elderly people, as the latter are held in high respect, and touching them would suggest an attempt to equal them in status.
- Sensitive issues related to the community should be managed carefully. For example, while asking about literacy levels, instead of asking '*aap padhe likhe hain kyaa*?' the researcher/investigator should ask, '*aap kitna padhe huye hain*'.

RURAL MARKETING **MEMO** | ATTRIBUTES OF A RURAL RESEARCHER

Conducting research in rural areas is difficult. The following attributes are desirable in a researcher working in rural areas.

1. *Mindset:* Since most researchers have an urban mindset, it is important for the rural market researcher to be able to think from a rural perspective, constantly evaluate responses, and mould his communication accordingly.
2. *Effective communication:* For more effective communication and eliciting accurate responses in rural research, a working knowledge of and familiarity with local dialects is desirable.
3. *Discerning ability:* Since information collection in rural research has to be in the form of general conversation, the researcher must know when to ask a specific question and put an end to the general discussion. He must also be able to discern between sensitive and non-sensitive issues/topics/questions and tackle them accordingly.
4. *Good memory:* Since the researcher is advised not to carry any writing material along, he is expected to memorize all the relevant information before putting it in the form of a written record.
5. *Patience:* The researcher needs to have a lot of patience to get specific responses from villagers, as they tend to get involved in their own rhetoric and repeat things, which the researcher may have to listen to patiently. However, he should have the ability to bring them back on track.

- Male researchers should always approach a woman respondent through her husband or some other male member from her family, or through a male known to her.
- Rural people can handle only limited information at a time. So a series of direct questions one after the other should be avoided, even when the respondent has shown a willingness to talk. It is therefore better to intersperse subject specific questions with some general questions to provide a mental break.
- Researchers/investigators may find it difficult to interact with villagers on a one-to-one basis, because villagers normally gather in a crowd before strangers. Moreover, the strong desire for social sanction in rural areas leads to interaction in the form of a group. It is therefore difficult to get a truly individual response. The researcher should request the persons accompanying the respondent to remain silent and allow the respondent to express his views and experiences. The respondent may be requested to choose a secluded place.
- Researchers/investigators should avoid being overfriendly, as respondents may give biased responses.
- Researchers/investigators should always carry food, water, and first-aid with them, and take necessary precautions to avoid health problems.

Limitations of Rural Research

There are certain limitations to conducting research in rural areas, which a researcher must keep in mind.

- ***Low literacy levels.*** The low level of literacy in rural India makes it difficult for villagers to understand questions, or respond to western ratings and ranking tools. This calls for continuous innovation in questionnaire design scales.
- ***Local language communication.*** There are 22 official languages in India, each with multiple dialects, making communication extremely difficult for researchers. It also means that a questionnaire needs multiple translations, and accordingly, separate training sessions for field investigators.
- ***Scattered and remote villages; inaccessible roads.*** Sampling remote, scattered and tiny villages is a really painful task for researchers. This also requires long durations of travel by the researcher and overnight stays.

- ***Social taboos; difficulty in interacting with women respondents.*** Women in some parts of the country like Rajasthan and parts of Uttar Pradesh remain behind purdah. If the respondents include women, it makes the job more difficult for the male researchers.
- ***Interview timing.*** Normally men go to work in fields or other areas in the morning and return only in the evening. Women are busy in the mornings and evenings with cooking and other household chores. Researchers need to plan their day as per the availability of the respondents.
- ***Rule out revalidation of data.*** Validation of data over the telephone in rural areas is difficult due to poor network coverage in the remote villages of India. Also, physical validation is not feasible as it is expensive to travel again to far-flung and scattered villages.

::: The Rural Research Business

In the past decade, the rural research business has grown by leaps and bounds. It started as a niche sector a few years ago, but is now taking centre stage as many Indian and global companies have begun focusing on the BoP (base of the pyramid) market, and want to understand its consumers and design innovative products and processes specifically for them. 'Rural' has become one of the main agendas for many companies, who are also setting up separate verticals to cater to this business. It is not just the corporations but also the advertising industry that is showing a keen interest in rural research.

All this has led to an increased demand for business rural research, and is sure to move ahead in a positive direction.

Some of the key players in this sector are:

- ***NCAER.*** The National Council for Applied Economic Research (NCAER) conducts large-scale national sample surveys on demographics, consumer durables, and non-durables in both urban and rural areas.
- ***MART.*** Established in 1993, MART is a pioneer in the rural domain. Over the years, it has also developed as the leading consultancy and knowledge-based organization in the emerging markets. MART's expertise lies in its understanding of the Base of Pyramid (BoP) segments, their environment, and behaviour, and it enjoys a unique position as an end-to-end solutions facilitator for both the corporate and the development sectors. It has utilized its experience and learning in the field of implementing income generation programmes and promoting social development in rural India to introduce successful innovations in the 4Ps of rural marketing. In rural research, it has conducted several path-breaking studies on haats and melas, spurious products, rural distribution, traditional media, the rural youth and women as buyers, among others.
- ***IMRB (SRI).*** The Social and Rural Research Institute (SRI) is the social research wing of IMRB (Indian Market Research Bureau), which was set up to conduct social research in and for rural markets. Social research deals with research on causes and issues that can contribute to action, which can then bring about social change.
- ***The Nielsen Company.*** The social research wing of the Nielsen Company has emerged as one of the largest social research consultancy organizations, offering its services in almost all fields of development, planning, and management, from conceptualization to final implementation.
- ***RMAI.*** The Rural Marketing Association of India (RMAI) is a premier industry body devoted to furthering the cause of rural marketing. Since its inception in 2005, the association has been helping marketers to plan and implement their rural marketing activities across the country. RMAI also undertakes research studies to spread and increase the knowledge base of rural marketers.

REVIEW OF OBJECTIVES

1. Understand the marketing research process and its application in rural areas

The rural marketing research process consists broadly of eight steps—defining business and research objectives, determining the research budget, designing the research (decision on research approach—exploratory/descriptive/causal; qualitative/quantitative; primary/secondary research), sampling method and size, designing the research instrument (questionnaire/discussion guide), collecting information from the field, collating and analysing the data, presenting the findings to make the right decision.

After the business and research objectives have been clearly defined and the budget finalized for the same, the researcher must decide on the research approach. Based on the nature of the data to be captured, the researcher can decide whether they want to go with the qualitative (PRA, focus group discussion, in-depth interview, dyads, slice of life observation, photo ethnography) or quantitative (face-to-face survey using structured questionnaires) approach. Most often in rural areas the research starts with the qualitative approach, and is followed by the quantitative approach to validate the findings and capture variations among respondents.

Further, the sampling plan is designed. Generally, in rural qualitative research, purposive and snowball sampling methods are used, and the sample size is dynamic rather than static, that is, the researcher continues to collect data from the field till they are saturated with information. In the case of quantitative sampling, more exhaustive techniques are used. Some of the sampling methods used are multi-stage area sampling, probability proportion to size method for village selection, household selection through the listing exercise, respondent selection through the Kish grid, etc.

Data collection in rural areas is generally done through face-to-face interviews with the respondent in their natural setting, that is, home or workplace. The researcher should be well-versed in the pros and cons of conducting research in rural areas, and should be comfortable with the same. Briefing, training, and handholding sessions are crucial in quantitative data collection. Lastly, data collation, analysis, and report writing are done to complete the process.

2. Identify special tools required for rural marketing research

As conventional research tools do not prove effective in rural markets due to the lower levels of exposure and literacy of rural inhabitants, rural researchers have come up with new solutions and special tools to capture responses more accurately and effectively. Some of these innovative rural qualitative research tools are participatory rural appraisal (PRA), which include the social and resource map, wealth map, the need assessment map, daily activity clock, process map, chapati diagram, and market access or mobility map.

In rural quantitative research, some visual scaling tools have been designed to capture ratings and ranking—the satisfaction scale using smiling and sad faces, agreement scale using ticks and crosses, ladder for ranking, etc.

3. Examine field procedures and rural realities

There are certain set guidelines for conducting research in rural areas, which make the job of the researcher easier and help to ensure higher degrees of accuracy and consistency in administering reach across different areas.

Some of these include dressing and greeting the respondent in a simple manner, knowing and speaking in the local language, building a rapport by talking on topics of general interest to the rural inhabitant, being patient and being slow in questioning and receiving responses, approaching a rural woman respondent through her husband or any other male member in her family, and exercising soft-control options for getting individual responses in a rural environment.

Researchers also have to take into account certain limitations of rural research, like the low literacy levels of respondents, the wide geographical dispersion of villages with inaccessible roads, difficulty in approaching women respondents, the prevalence of multiple languages and dialects, difficulty in getting individual responses, and the revalidation of data.

4. Understand the rural research business

Rural research began as a niche sector a few years ago, but is now taking centre stage as many Indian and global companies are focusing on the BoP (Base of Pyramid) market and want to understand its consumers and innovate products and processes specifically for them. The demand for and the business of rural research has increased drastically in recent years, and is sure to move ahead in a positive direction.

Some well-known and key players in this sector are NCAER, MART, IMRB (SRI), the Nielsen Company's social research wing, and the Rural Marketing Association of India (RMAI).

DISCUSSION AND APPLICATION

Discussion of Concepts

1. Briefly describe the rural marketing research process.
2. Describe the different qualitative research tools and techniques used in rural marketing research.
3. What is the probability proportion to size method (PPS) and why is it used in rural sampling? Explain with an example.
4. Briefly describe some innovative tools used in rural marketing research. Elaborate any one such tool with an example.
5. Understanding rural consumers has been a difficult task for marketers. IDIs, FGDs, and PRAs have been adopted by market research companies to understand rural consumers. What are the other methods adopted by market re-

search companies to understand rural consumers beyond these?

6. What are the limitations of conducting rural research?

Application of Concepts

1. Develop discussion guidelines for interviewing retailers in rural areas to understand the selection criteria employed for brand selection in any two product categories of your choice.
2. A leading hair oil company wants to launch its new product catering to rural women, and therefore wants to understand their current behaviour and practices related to the same. Prepare a research plan comprising the research approach, sampling plan (method and size), data collection method, and research tools.
3. A leading organization in the healthcare sector wants to know the average expenditure on health in a rural household in the southern market of India, covering three major states—Andhra Pradesh, Karnataka, and Tamil Nadu. Based on this, it will take a decision on whether to set up its private hospitals there or not. Decide on the research approach and develop a sampling plan, including the sampling method and size, for conducting the study in the area.

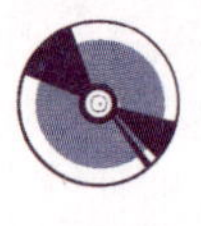

RURAL MARKETING **CASE** | PARTICIPATORY RURAL APPRAISAL

The participatory rural appraisal is an innovative research tool for eliciting community responses in rural research. It empowers the community for voluntary participation in the research process.

The video explains how PRA tools such as market access maps, process maps, and activity clocks enable the rural community to share, enhance, and analyse the knowledge of their own environment and life. It demonstrates how pictorials dilute the language and literacy barriers and bring forth deeper consumer insights.

The step-by-step process involves community mobilization for the PRA activity, moderation of the group, information collection from the respondents, and cross-validation. The PRA exercise lasts for two to three hours.

Discussion Questions

1. What advantages do PRA tools have over other research tools used in consumer research?
2. Explore new PRA tools that can be applied for understanding the brand adoption process in rural markets.

AFTER READING THIS CHAPTER, YOU WILL BE ABLE TO:

1. Describe the concepts of segmentation, target marketing, and market positioning, stressing the need to recognize heterogeneity amongst rural consumers
2. Understand the major bases for segmenting rural consumers and segmentation strategy
3. Understand how companies identify attractive market segments and choose target marketing strategy
4. Realize how companies position their products for maximum competitive advantage in the rural marketplace

CHAPTER 5 ::: SEGMENTING AND TARGETING RURAL MARKETS

five

For decades the Indian tractor industry has used a product-centric approach to reach its existing and potential customers. Tractor companies in India have always segmented the market on the basis of the power (measured in horsepower—hp) of the tractors, rather than segmenting consumers and marketing the right product that suits them.

A leading tractor company realized that it cannot connect with all customers in a large, broad and diverse market like India. The only way to reach out to all potential consumers was to divide the market into meaningful groups of consumers with distinct characteristics. An extensive research study was conducted by MART in 2009 to this end. Since this was the very first attempt at segmenting the Indian tractor market, the exploratory research looked at all possible variables that could define the underlying heterogeneity among consumers. Variables ranging from soil type, landholding, climate, age, family size, application of tractor, the horsepower of the tractor used were studied, but the most significant differentiating factor that emerged as the segmentation criteria for the Indian tractor market was the psychographics of tractor owners.

It was found that the psychographics of a person has a direct relation with the way they think and purchase high-value productive assets such as tractors. A total of five segments with distinct personality traits and attitudes towards life as a whole emerged from the study, which could later be tapped into by the company based on the brand–segment fit.

This customer-focused approach has helped the company to take another look at the Indian tractor market, and understand how its products are perceived by consumers. It is now working on changing the positioning of its products in view of the current scenario and the future target segment.

A new consumer-driven segmentation approach has helped a leading tractor company in improving brand positioning and marketing.

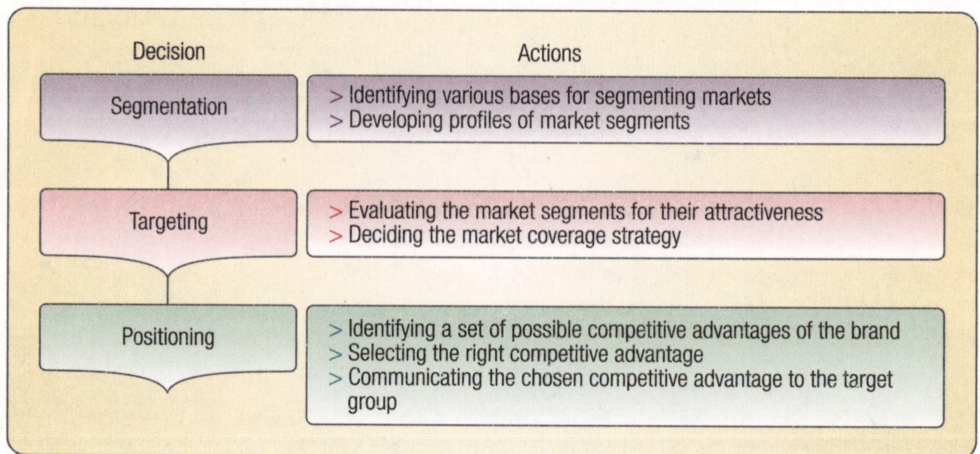

| FIG. **5.1** |
Segmenting, Targeting, and Positioning

The segmentation of rural consumers has gradually evolved with the evolution of rural markets in recent years. Marketers are progressing from the traditional descriptive geographic and demographic traits, largely used for segmenting nascent markets, to more evolved segmentation methods such as behaviour, psychographics and multiple attributes, which provide deeper insights and directly relate to consumers' purchases.

Segmenting markets and attracting consumers involves three key decisions—segmenting, targeting, and positioning (STP), as depicted in Fig. 5.1. Since rural markets have started growing rapidly, marketers need to evolve different targeting and positioning strategies for different customer groups if they want to penetrate rural markets effectively.

::: Segmentation

Segmentation is the process of dividing a heterogeneous market into several sub-markets or segments.

Segmentation is the sub-division of a market into homogenous subsets of customers where any subset may conceivably be selected as a target market to be reached with a distinct marketing mix. The power of this concept is that in an age of intense competition for the mass market, marketers venturing into rural markets may prosper through creatively serving specific market segments whose needs are imperfectly satisfied by the mass-market offerings.

For example, 50 per cent of rural people are engaged in agriculture, but they cannot be clubbed under one category of farmers. There are large farmers, medium farmers, small farmers, marginal farmers, and then agricultural labourers. Their incomes, lifestyles, and behaviour are different. There is, therefore, a need to classify farmers under different customer segments. Further, the remaining 50 per cent of rural people are engaged in non-farm activities. Therefore, rural customers could be segmented on the basis of self-employed farmers, daily wage labour, salaried employees, traders, micro-entrepreneurs, etc.

Families in rural areas with members residing in urban locales would have a different exposure level affecting their lifestyles. Access to mass media (TV or radio) also varies widely in rural areas, which would also affect consumer behaviour. So these factors can also be considered while segmenting rural customers.

Heterogeneity in Rural Markets

As discussed above, rural markets are heterogeneous in nature. There are a number of factors indicative of the heterogeneity of rural markets:

- Socio-cultural differences across regions (caste-based hamlets)
- Variation in population size and population density of villages
- Difference in the levels of infrastructural development (developed versus developing states)

- Media exposure levels (media dark, media grey, and media green regions)
- Variation in literacy levels (Bihar versus Kerala)
- Differences in income levels and patterns of income flow (farmers versus daily wage earners)
- Family structure (large joint families, individualized joint families, and nuclear families)

These factors play a significant role in consumer behaviour towards the purchase of products in rural markets. The heterogeneity is not only visible across different regions of the country, but is also observed within each region, each state, and also sometimes within a village. Therefore, it becomes imminent for a marketer to segment his market carefully so that the offering can address the needs of the target customer optimally.

Pre-requisites for Effective Segmentation

For any segmentation exercise to be effective, it should be measurable, accessible, differentiable, and substantial.

MEASURABLE The segmentation variables should be distinct, clear, and measurable. Only then can segments be described in exact terms and differences understood. Companies are unable to reach rural markets effectively due to a lack of comprehensive data related to markets and consumers. In the absence of information related to size, purchasing power, and profiles of rural consumers, they were considered similar to the urbanites. Also, factors measurable in urban (for example, monthly income) areas cannot be measured directly in rural areas due to a non-uniform income pattern and multiple sources of income. Today, rural markets are being studied by various companies to obtain valuable data that can be used for segmentation.

ACCESSIBLE Reach is important to serve the segments. Till recently, marketers preferred urban markets to rural ones because of the inaccessibility of the latter. Rural consumers were reached through vans and through village retailers visiting nearby town distributors and retail outlets. Now, while segmenting rural markets, it is important to ensure that the segmented market is conveniently reachable to the marketer to deliver products. With significant improvement in the connectivity of villages and increased interest among corporations in using traditional haats (weekly markets) and other new channels for distribution, rural markets are becoming increasingly accessible.

DIFFERENTIABLE Segments merit the consideration of marketers only when they have distinguishing features. Rural consumers are identified as a different segment as their responses may be different from urban customers, at least for some products. For instance, while buying a motor bike, rural consumers accord more importance to sturdiness, mileage, and the carrying capacity of the bike, whereas urban consumers look for style, power, and aesthetics.

SUBSTANTIAL A segment is attractive only when it is profitable. A segment should possess the following characteristics:

- ***Homogeneity.*** It should consist of people who are similar in perceptions, learning, preferences, attitudes, and actions. As such, covering them will be easy. For example, SEC R1 consumers will behave in a certain way that will generally be consistent across different geographies.
- ***Size.*** It should comprise either a large number of light users or a small number of heavy users so that marketing becomes beneficial to the company.

It is observed that rural areas are not homogenous. Region-wise differences are found in language, mindset, and behaviour. However, designing separate promotional programmes may have limitations as the size of consumers in each segment may not be large enough to make the effort viable.

| FIG. 5.2 |
Degrees of Segmentation

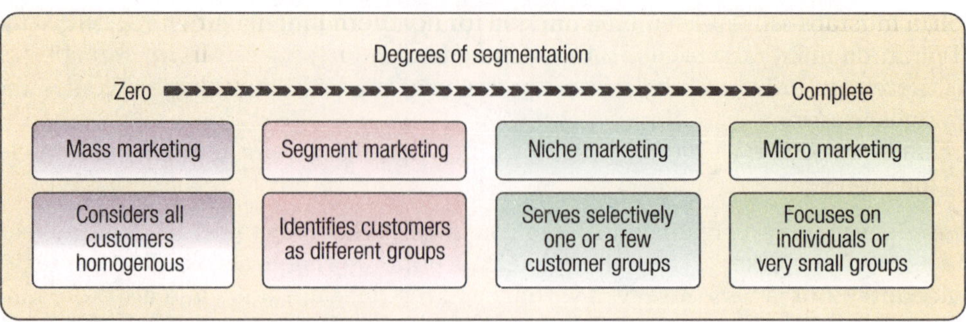

Degrees of Segmentation

There are four distinct segmentation approaches—mass marketing, segment marketing, niche marketing, and micro marketing.

If segmentation is considered a process with two polar points from zero to unity, four distinct segmentation approaches are identifiable, as depicted in Fig. 5.2.

MASS MARKETING A majority of companies have used the mass marketing approach in rural markets, not attempting any segmentation of consumers and treating all consumers as the same. A company can use this method to target the maximum number of consumers. This is the first step of marketing, when marketers do not have much knowledge of the market.

Initially, a majority of companies that entered the rural market treated it as an extension of the urban market. They followed the trickle-down theory and tried to sell urban products in rural markets. For example, Colgate-Palmolive successfully marketed the same Colgate toothpaste to all consumers in urban and rural markets till recently. However, as the rural market started to evolve and consumers became more demanding, Colgate introduced Cibaca.

SEGMENT MARKETING Segment marketing is still in its early stages in rural markets. It is only in recent years that marketers have realized the potential of different consumer segments that are substantial enough to target, and have designed and launched low-priced, innovative products for rural markets. Hindustan Unilever uses two different approaches to market its two different brands— Hamam and Lifebuoy. On the one hand it tries to reach the whole market in one go by using the mass marketing approach for its brand Hamam; on the other, it has introduced four variants of its brand Lifebuoy—Active Red, Active Orange, Plus, and Gold—to reach four different segments of the Indian market.

NICHE MARKETING Niche marketing caters to a very small group in a segment with some specific and distinct need, which the marketer satisfies through specific skills.

The GoldPlus brand of jewellery from the Tata Group is an interesting case in point. Targeted at meeting the requirements and aspirations of rural and semi-urban populations in south India, where jewellery is considered an investment, a reserve, this brand is hugely successful because of the Tata seal of good faith. Ghari detergent has used a unique parameter to segment the Indian market: the quality of water! On the basis of the quality of water in different regions, Ghari has introduced variants of its product, targeting different geographic segments. The 'Jeevan Sadhan' service of Nokia, launched in 2009, specifically targets rural Indian consumers. It is an ambitious programme that bundles the handset along with services like providing agricultural tips, market prices, weather forecasts, career information, and entertainment services like ringtones, news, astrology, and more.

MICRO MARKETING Micro marketing refers to the tailoring of products to satisfy a particular taste or need. One of the examples of micro marketing is Dabur's Anmol hair oil, a mustard–amla based oil launched for northern Indian markets at INR 10 for a 50-ml pack, targeted at rural consumers using loose mustard oil. Micro marketing can be further categorized into two—local marketing or individual marketing.

- ***Local marketing.*** Local marketing involves designing brands and promotions to suit the needs and wants of local customer groups on a geographical basis. As rural people do not have much exposure, local marketing has relevance in many cases. It helps in effective marketing in the face of differences in demographics and the lifestyles of communities in different regions. Regional and local brands are very good at local marketing since they operate in a limited geography, which helps them to develop a good understanding of local consumers and their specific needs. The vegetarian bathing soap sold in the Bundelkhand region (Jhansi belt) of India is targeted specifically at the local vegetarian population. The marketers focus on the products being *charbi rahit* while promoting them (soaps, washing powders, detergents, etc.).
- ***Individual marketing.*** Tailoring, forging, and carpentry are examples of individual marketing in a rural set-up. In this approach, an individual can get a product according to his specific need. To address the great diversity of rural markets, different segmentation approaches have been attempted by marketers to reach consumers effectively. Some of the concepts discussed above provide cues to marketers on how to segment rural customers.

Bases for Segmenting Rural Consumer Markets

A thoughtful approach is always required before selecting segmentation variables for rural markets. The variables generally used for urban segmentation may not necessarily fit into the scheme of rural consumer segmentation. For example, variables like income—as used for urban markets—are clearly inadequate for rural segmentation. Income in rural set-ups is seasonal for farmers, and daily wages to farm labour are often paid part in cash and part in kind (grain). Also, rural people do not file income tax returns, so it is difficult to capture the true income. Similar limitations are experienced with the other urban segmentation factors. Yet it is necessary to segment rural consumers in order to target them effectively. As shown in Table 5.1, there are four major segmentation variables used for rural consumer segmentation. These are geography, demography, psychography, and behaviour.

GEOGRAPHIC SEGMENTATION Rural customers can be segmented according to geographic factors like region, state, district, villages, and climate.

There are four bases of segmentation in rural markets—geographic, demographic, psychographic, and behavioural.

Regions The country is divided into four zones:

- ***North:*** UP, Rajasthan, J&K, Himachal Pradesh, Punjab, Haryana
- ***South:*** Tamil Nadu, Andhra, Kerala, Karnataka
- ***East:*** Bihar, West Bengal, Orissa, Assam, and Northeast states
- ***West:*** Maharashtra, MP, Gujarat

Regional diversity within rural India dictates that the real challenge lies in understanding the fragmented rural consumer if marketers want to succeed in convincing them to consume. Figure 5.3 presents a pictorial representation linking variations in the cultural and behavioural traits of consumers across the four regions of the country. It exemplifies the geographically determined traits that play an important role in determining consumer behaviour and product choice. Marketers need to evolve effective strategies around products that fulfil functional needs and the need gaps of different regions.

Village Population and Density The Census of India has categorized villages into different strata on the basis of their population. The rural lifestyle changes

| TABLE **5.1** |
The Major Segmentation Variables Used for Rural Consumer Segmentation

Bases of Segmentation	
Geographic	• Region: East, West, North, South • Village size: <1000, 1,000–2,000, 2,000–5,000, >5,000 • Density: Low, moderate, high • Climate: summer, rainy, winter • Culture: 56 socio-cultural regions (e.g., Avadh, Bundelkhand, Rohilkhand, Purvanchal, and Braj in UP)
Demographic	• Age and lifecycle: Children, teens, young adults, elders, seniors • Family structure: joint family, individualized joint family, nuclear family • Gender: Male, female • Income: Deprived, aspirers, seekers, strivers, global • Landownership: Landless, marginal, small, large farmers • Education: Illiterates, semi-literates, literates • House type: Pucca, semi-pucca, kuccha • Occupation: Self-employed farmers, daily wage labourers, salaried, traders • Religion: Hindu, Muslim, Christian, Sikh, Parsi • Caste: Upper caste, lower castes
Psychographic	• Social Class: Upper, lower, middle • Lifestyle: Trendsetters, followers/adopters, traditionalists • Personality: Authoritarian, ambitious
Behavioural	• Occasions: Festivals, melas, *jatras*, weekly haats • Benefits sought: Quality, convenience, value for money, service, etc. • User status: Non-user, ex-user, first time user, regular user, potential user • Usage rate: Light user, medium user, heavy user • Loyalty status: Strong, weak, non-loyal • Place of purchase: Village shop, haats, nearby town, melas, and jatras

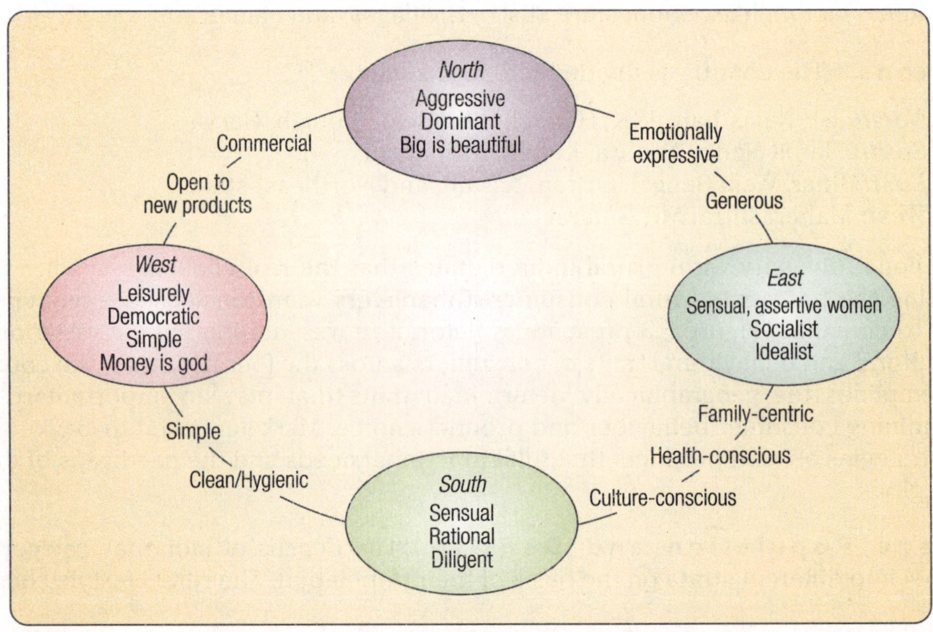

| FIG. **5.3** |
Regional Differences among Consumers

with the size (population) of the village due to a variation in the level of infrastructural and economic development. So far, most companies have targeted villages with a population of more than 2,000, which have better infrastructural facilities and high purchasing power. What marketers need to do is to segment the village markets on the basis of development indicators relevant to the product category, and target them accordingly.

Climate Climatic conditions also play a significant role in the consumption of specific products (agro-based technology companies segment India into eight geo-climatic regions based on the condition of soil and the climate).

Culture In the early 1970s, Rashiduddin Khan segmented the country into 56 socio-cultural regions (SCRs).[1] For example, Uttar Pradesh has five SCRs—Avadh, Bundelkhand, Rohilkhand, Purvanchal, and Braj. Each SCR has its own identity in terms of language, culture, dress, and location. The culture of a region provides a window into the attitudes of the people who live there, their relationships and power structures, and ultimately, their hierarchy of needs. Cultural identities have diluted to some extent in urban areas due to the influence of Western culture, but it is largely intact in rural areas. As discussed in Chapter 4, cultural factors play a significant role in consumer buying behaviour and also determine the dynamics of decision-making.

DEMOGRAPHIC SEGMENTATION Rural customers can be segmented on the basis of demographic factors like age and lifecycle, family structure, landownership, occupation, income, socio-economic class, religion, and caste.

Demographic segmentation can be done on the basis of age and lifecycle, family structure, landownership, occupation, income, socio-economic class, religion and caste.

Age and Lifecycle With the changing lifecycle stage, consumers' needs for products and brand preferences also change. This phenomenon is true for both urban and rural consumers. For example, in rural India, young adults exhibit a marked preference for mobile handsets with the latest features and technology, whereas elders are content with second-hand mobiles with simple and basic features.

Family Structure In rural areas, besides demographic characteristics such as age and gender, family size and structure are also important features. As the family size increases, so does the consumption of products. In such a case, the family pack or the economy refill pack works very well. Similarly, large families have more breadwinners, which translate into higher family income and, thus, greater consumption of products. This often leads to multi-brand consumption of a product category among different family members.

Rural India is gradually moving from the large joint family system to the individualized joint family system (families staying together but using separate kitchens) and the nuclear family system as discussed in Chapter 3. This is resulting in greater demands, particularly for consumer durables, as every new family unit living separately needs a refrigerator, pressure cooker, LPG connection, TV, DTH/cable connection, etc.

Landownership Rural livelihoods, security, prosperity, and sentiment are intrinsically linked to land. Urbanites tend to regard land as just another asset, and they fail to appreciate the emotional bond that farmers have with their land. Segmentation on the basis of land should include five factors—size of landholding (see Table 5.2), quality of land and area under cultivation, irrigation method (rain-fed, tube well, etc.), agricultural productivity and crop mix, and money realization.

Therefore, rural markets can also be segmented on the basis of landholding size into the following categories: large farmers, medium farmers, semi-medium farmers, small farmers, and marginal farmers.

Occupation The major occupations in rural India are—self-employment in agriculture, labourer (agriculture/non-agriculture), self-employment in non-agriculture, and regular salary/wages. The variation in the major occupational groups necessitates the segmenting of rural markets on a different basis. Both product categories and

| TABLE **5.2** |
Landholding Pattern

Size of Holding (in hectares)	Number of Landholdings (in per cent)
Marginal (up to 1)	67
Small (1–2)	18
Semi-medium (2–4)	10
Medium (4–8)	4.2
Large (over 8)	0.7

Source: Compiled from National Sample Survey Organization, 63rd Round Report, 'Household Consumer Expenditure in India', 2006–07, and MART Knowledge Centre

consumption patterns change among different occupation groups. Therefore, marketers should consider occupation patterns while segmenting the rural market for their product category.

Income Unlike urban India, where income for the majority of people is regular (on a monthly basis), in rural India the flow of income is mostly seasonal (post harvest for farmers) or weekly/daily (for wage earners). The salaried class with a regular monthly income constitutes a very small segment of rural consumers. Many urbanites pay income tax, whereas agricultural income is not taxable. Also, due to an irregular income pattern and multiple sources of income (for example agriculture, dairy, etc.), an assessment of rural income is difficult. Therefore, the urban income-based segmentation strategy is not entirely appropriate in the case of rural consumers. However, there have been some recent attempts to classify rural India on the basis of household income, as shown in Table 5.3.

Socio-economic Classification The level of education and type of dwelling are important indicators in understanding the profile of rural consumers. These

| TABLE **5.3** |
Rural Consumer Classification as per Household Income

Segment Name (Income in thousand INR)	Asset Owned	1995	2005	2015(E)	2025(E)
Global (> 1,000)	Household owning personal car/jeep with other products	0	0	0	1
Strivers (500–1,000)	Household owning any/all of these—air-conditioner, motorcycle, scooter, washing machine, refrigerator, colour TV with other durables, but not car/jeep	0	1	1	2
Seekers (200–500)	Household owning any/all of these—moped, VCR/VCP, mixer-grinder, sewing machine, audio equipment, B/W TV, geyser with other durables, but not those mentioned under the first two categories	1	3	6	20
Aspirers (90–200)	Household owning any/all of these—bicycle, electric fans, electric iron with other durables, but not mentioned under the first three categories	8	32	47	48
Deprived (< 90)	Households other than those classified under categories 1 to 4 above, owning any/all/none of these—wrist watches, pressure cooker, cassette recorder, and transistor/radio	91	64	46	29

Source: Compiled from McKinsey Global Institute (MGI), 'The Bird of Gold: The Rise of India's Consumer Market' Report, exhibit 4.3, p. 83, May 2007, and National Council for Applied Economic Research (NCAER), 'India Market Demographics Report', Box 8.1, p. 66, 2002

two variables have been used to segment rural consumers into four socio-economic groups—R1, R2, R3, and R4 (See Chapter 3 for more details on this.) This kind of segmentation is widely accepted. Income and occupation are not used as the bases for segmentation in this classification because they are not well defined and distinctive among rural people. In urban India, it is occupation and education that form the bases for defining social classes such as SEC A, B, and C.

As rural India is moving towards building pucca dwellings, the relevance of the socio-economic classification based on the type of house is reducing. This segmentation is currently being re-examined.

Religion and Caste Religion and caste play an important role in influencing the social, economic, political, and cultural behaviour of certain communities, particularly in rural areas. These differences are clearly visible in terms of the settlement pattern in villages, where hamlets of the upper and lower castes are kept separate. Village shops are also demarcated along similar lines in many cases. The settlement of villages has historically taken place on the basis of caste and religion, villages often having a predominance of people belonging to one particular caste or religion (for example, Rajput village, Bhumihar village, etc.). This peculiar phenomenon of caste dynamics cannot be ignored while segmenting rural markets. However, when it comes to trade and commerce, caste does not play a significant role.

PSYCHOGRAPHIC SEGMENTATION While geographic and demographic segmentation depict the visible characteristics of consumer markets, the true dynamics of purchase behaviour can be assessed only on the basis of the psychographics of the rural consumer. Psychographics include factors such as personality traits, lifestyle, and value systems.

Lifestyle Lifestyle is defined by the activities, interests, and opinions (AIO) of the person. It reflects the overall manner in which the person lives and spends his/her time and money. People within the same demographic group or social class can exhibit very different lifestyles, and hence, different psychographic profiles. This concept enables us to grasp and predict buyer behaviour. The segmentation approach adopted in rural areas to outline the lifestyles of all four socio-economic groups is shown in Table 5.4.

In some parts of Gujarat, it was found that farmers were buying big 50-hp tractors, when their actual need was for much smaller tractors, typically 25–30 hp. Further investigation revealed that the reason behind this was the compulsion 'to keep up with the neighbours'.

– A. P. Sonalkar,
Head of R&D,
Mahindra & Mahindra

| TABLE **5.4** |
Psychographic Segments in Rural India

Socio-economic Classification (SEC)	Rural Demographic Characteristics	Rural Lifestyle
R1	Landlord farmers, educated, exposed to an urban environment, children in schools/colleges in nearby towns, owns durables like tractor, two-wheeler, TV, music system, steel cupboard, LPG, refrigerator, mixer-grinders	Aspiring to match urban lifestyle, technology adopters, experiment with modern farming methods, eager for additional sources of income, socially and politically well-connected, high spender on social occasions
R2	Rich farmers with about 5 acres of land, may not be educated, friends and relatives living in urban areas, owns durables like tractor, two-wheeler, TV, LPG	Want children to get educated, consult friends and relatives in urban areas for technology adoption, conscious of status, aspire to be well known in social and political circles
R3	Average landholding 2–5 acres, manages small savings, children sent to village school, owns durables like TV, tractor (self and rental)	Opts for time-tested technology, low risk taker, desires more knowledge, followers, seekers
R4	Have little or no land, agricultural labour, living below poverty line, a major purchaser from public distribution system	Laggards, averse to latest technology, risk averse, uninformed

Source: MART Knowledge Centre

Behavioural segmentation can be done on the basis of parameters like purchase occasions, benefits sought, user status, user rate, loyalty status, and place of purchase.

BEHAVIOURAL SEGMENTATION Behavioural segmentation involves many parameters, such as purchasing occasions, benefits, user status, usage rate, loyalty status, and place of purchase.

Occasions Buyers can be segmented on the basis of the occasions on which they purchase a product. In rural areas, most durables are purchased during or after the harvest season because this is when farmers have cash after selling their agricultural produce. Like the Baisakhi season in Punjab, Onam and Ugadi in south India and Diwali and Dussehra in most parts of the country are important festival occasions when villagers prefer to buy new items. Similarly, melas which offer products at attractive prices are also important because bargaining is possible. Also, weekly haat days are the times to purchase daily use products, vegetables, and spices.

COCA-COLA

Through a research study done on Indian rural consumers, Coca-Cola India tried to map various occasions of purchase of its soft drinks, both 'at home' and 'out of home', linking it with the level of consumption (low, moderate, and high). It was found that the highest consumption of soft drinks at home is during festivals, functions, the newer rural phenomenon of birthday and anniversary celebrations, or as hospitality to urban visitors. Similarly, consumption is high when rural people are out of home for picnics/get-togethers, marriages and routine outings, or are having alcohol. It is comparatively lower during travel, along with fast food, after meals, or after school/college, as is maybe the case in urban areas. Also, a unique phenomenon of sharing a single bottle among rural youths was observed in the villages. This helped the company to identify the right occasions to promote its products and target the right customer segment.

Benefits Sought Benefit segmentation emerges from understanding the needs of consumers. The benefit sought from a product varies from consumer to consumer. Customer satisfaction depends upon product benefits such as economy, performance, durability, status, taste, flavour, etc. Rural consumers are more concerned with the utility of a product than with its appearance and sophistication. They give more importance to the core benefit of the product. Many marketers do the segmentation on the basis of the benefits sought by consumers to position their products in rural areas. For example, Fullerton India, a non-banking financial institution, segmented the rural consumer market based on their credit and investment needs and identified five segments, namely the salaried class, large businessmen (traders and producers), small businessmen (traders and producers), service providers, and farmers. The company designed a new financial product targeting the most potential segment for its business, 'small businessmen'.

User Status On the basis of the usage of a product, consumers may be categorized into different groups as first-time user and regular user (see Table 5.5 for details).

In rural markets, the majority of consumers fall within the categories of potential users or first-time users for most product categories. Therefore, a focus on product trials and demos is very crucial in rural areas, unlike for urban customers, who are already exposed to multiple brands and products through a number of channels (mass media, outdoor media, retail markets, shopping malls). The communication strategy of Ghari detergent is based on the line, '*pehle istemal karein phir vishwas karein*' (first try it and then believe in it), to induce customers to try out the product. This approach has helped the company covert non-users and users of other brands into regular users.

| TABLE 5.5 |
Categories of Consumers on the Basis of Usage

User Status	Description	Rural Marketer's Approach
Ex-user	• Stopped using • Using other brand	Explore reason for shift, address it, convince ex-user about merits of product over other brands
First-time user	• Trial buy	Assure benefits through demonstration
Regular user	• Repeat buy	Ensure regular availability, award with free coupons/gifts
Potential user	• User of other brand • Non-user	Induce free trials/samples, explain advantage of using brand/product over substitutes

Usage Rate Based on the amount or rate of consumption or usage, consumers can be categorized into light, medium, and heavy users. Taking this usage behaviour into account, marketers have introduced different pack sizes to meet the requirements of different users. Nowadays, most consumer goods are available in sachet packs for rural consumers, and family packs or economy packs for joint and large families.

Loyalty Status A market can be segmented on the basis of consumer loyalty to specific brands. Segmentation based on loyalty enables marketers to tailor the communication and product appeal to retain the loyal customers, or to attract new customers from rival brands or convert non-loyal customers into loyal buyers.

More than loyalty, the peculiar phenomenon of 'brand stickiness' works in rural areas, which helps marketers to retain customers for longer periods with minimal effort. However, it may be very difficult to do so in the case of urban consumers, who keep shifting to new brands.

Rural buyers take a long time to decide on a particular brand, but once they are convinced, they are generally more brand loyal than their urban counterparts. Also, the first mover advantage plays an important role in this case. That is why there are Nirma villages and Wheel villages; Escort villages and Mahindra & Mahindra villages.

The brand stickiness phenomenon works more in rural India than brand loyalty. It is a form of behaviour whereby the villager stays with a brand and doesn't experiment easily, since he is not aware of any better choice.

Place of Purchase Rural consumers buy different products and services at different marketplaces, as shown in Table 5.6. In rural markets, the place of purchase changes with the change in product categories, as shown in Table 5.6. This is unlike the situation in urban markets, where customers make most of their purchases from one place or even from one supermarket.

Taking advantage of this specific rural purchasing behaviour, marketers can promote their products by developing an understanding of the place where potential buyers congregate most often, and from where they prefer to buy specific products. Marketers

| TABLE 5.6 |
Place of Purchase for Different Products

Time	Place of Purchase	Products
Daily	Village shop	Tea, kerosene, edible oil, salt, cigarettes, match box, bidis
Weekly	Shandies (haat)	Food grain, pulses, chillies, vegetables, cosmetics, soaps, utensils, and agricultural tools
Monthly/Occasionally	Nearest town	Fertilizers, seeds, pesticides, consumer goods like radio, TV, electrical goods, motor-bike, tractor, entertainment, etc.
Occasionally	Melas and jatras	Clothes, cheap jewellery, cosmetics, agricultural tools, livestock, entertainment
	State capital	Legal matters or casual visits

like Tata Steel (Tata Shaktee roofing sheets), Colgate-Palmolive, and Marico Industries have already started using traditional retail spaces such as haats, realizing the potential that they offer in terms of sales and promotion of products.

Multi-attribute segmentation uses various variables together to effectively segment the consumer markets.

MULTI-ATTRIBUTE SEGMENTATION In practical terms, it is very difficult for a marketer to depend on a single variable for segmenting the market. Market segmentation is a complex function since it depends on multiple factors that define market dynamics. In order to identify smaller, well-defined, meaningful target groups, marketers use several variables. Some companies and research agencies have taken initiatives to develop multi-attribute segmentation so that marketers can use it as a market planning tool.

Some of these initiatives include R. K. Swamy BBDO's Index, where they came up with a prosperity index that classifies the districts and class I and II towns based on their **Market Potential Value (MPV).**[2] It uses five broad factors to define the MPV of any place—means or propensity, consumption pattern, awareness through media exposure, market support, and size of market or population.

Among other recent multi-attribute segmentation approaches is the **Household Potential Index (HPI)**[3] by Media Research Users Council-Hansa Research, which attempts to assign a 'premiumness' value to each household. Here, premiumness has been defined as something that is 'wanted by many' but 'consumed by few'. The concept of HPI allocates high scores for less penetrated products and services. On the other hand, lower scores are attached to higher penetrated or mass-consumed categories. A basket of 50 variables has been used for the calculation of HPI scores. These include durables, FMCG products, services, and demographic variables.

Household Potential Index scores have been used to construct a pyramid of Indian consumer classes, as shown in Fig. 5.4. The average HPI score of the first class needs to be (approximately) double that of the next class. In other words, as we move up the classes, the consumption potential doubles with every subsequent class.

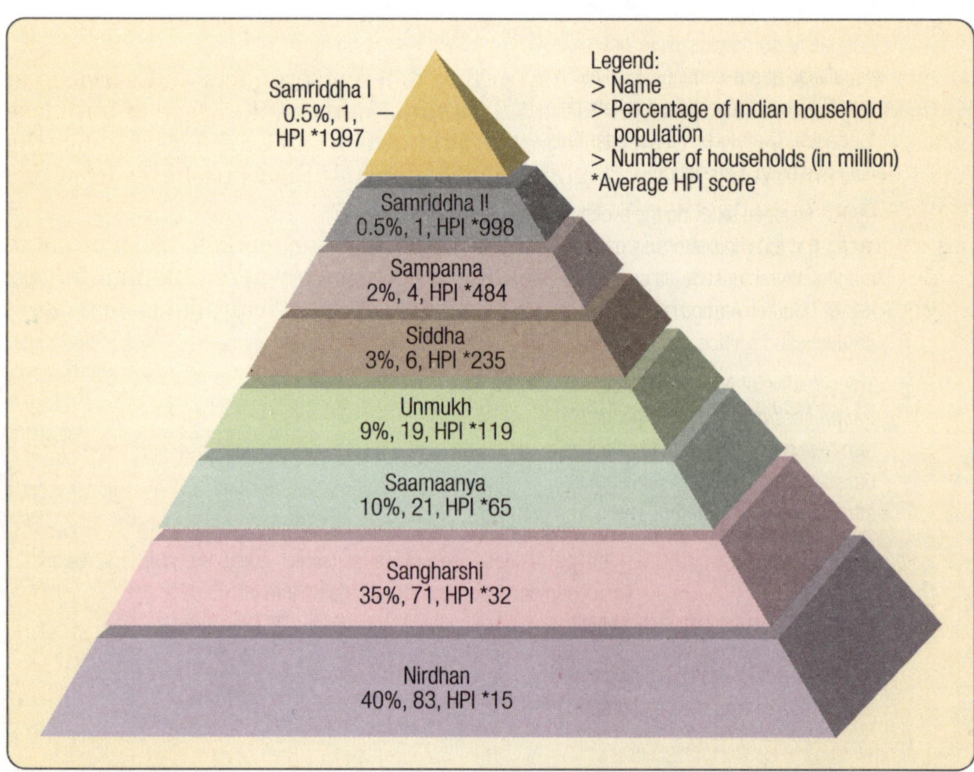

| FIG. **5.4** |
The Great Indian Pyramid
Source: MRUC

One of the most recent attempts on this front has been by MART, which has come up with the MART MAS (Market Attractiveness Score) Index. This index captures data as granular as below 5,000 population towns in India and tries to map their market attractiveness (see 'Rural Marketing Insight: MART MAS—Market Attractiveness Score Urban and Rural 'Prosperity Plus' Index').

Targeting

Targeting involves three steps—evaluating the segment attractiveness, selecting the segment for targeting, and choosing a coverage strategy.

Once segmentation has been done, one needs to evaluate each segment to decide which segment to target. Targeting involves evaluating various segments and selecting how many and which ones to target. The three aspects in targeting are evaluation, selection, and coverage.

Evaluation of Segments

While evaluating market segments, two broad factors are considered, the overall attractiveness of each segment, and the company's objectives and resource competencies.

OVERALL ATTRACTIVENESS The criteria for measuring the attractiveness of a segment are:

- Size
- Growth rate
- Accessibility

RURAL MARKETING INSIGHT — MART MARKET ATTRACTIVENESS SCORE: URBAN AND RURAL 'PROSPERITY PLUS' INDEX

India lives in nearly 8000 towns and 6,40,000 villages. The rural markets are dispersed and are not homogeneous. Physical Infrastructure is relatively poor compared to urban areas.

Not many corporates have been able to reach less than 50,000 population strata locations. Marketers have often felt dissuaded from venturing into these rural markets because of inadequate market information. Therefore, market prioritization and effective market planning has been a challenge.

MART has been studying the evolution of the rural markets and monitoring the data indicators to gain an in-depth understanding of the market characteristics. It developed a market planning tool called 'MART Market Attractiveness Score (MAS)' for different industries, products and service marketers alike.

The objective of MART MAS is to scientifically assess the market attractiveness/prosperity of a geography based on relevant indicators. It also allows the marketers to select assessment indicators themselves based on their business requirements. It allows the measurement of attractiveness at different levels from state, district, sub-district to small town.

KEY FEATURES OF THE MART *MAS*

- The MART MAS is a single index that measures attractiveness of a market area (geography).
- It has been derived by using scientific modelling (Principal Component Analysis) of different variables.
- Per Capita Prosperity can be assessed using the 'Market Intensity Score' (MIS) when a marketer wants to identify areas appropriate for high-value products.
- Market selection/prioritization can be done at different levels state, district, sub district, and towns. The indices can be derived for 35 states (State + UT), 640 districts, 6000 sub-districts and 8000 towns.
- The tool offers two options to the user:
  - Use it as Universal Prosperity Index, based on the 18 indicators which are applied. All indicators are weighted.
  - Customize by selecting indicators important for the business/product category. Further the user can give different weights to each indicator, as desired, to fully customize the tool to very specific business conditions.
- The tool has an 'Easy Interface' to process selection of markets and output tables. The outcomes can be exported to Excel tables if desired.
- Data used in the tool is from the latest Census 2011, RBI, Agriculture Census, etc.

(Continued)

(Continued)

THE MART-MAS MODEL

The **MART MAS**, or Market Attractiveness Score, provides a single index to aid marketers in selecting the 'Best Fit' locations across the range of India's population centres from Urban India to Rural India.

The **MART MAS** consists of a number of critical factors:

MAS = (Means + Consumption + Awareness + Infrastructure)* Population Size

The MART MAS is provided for administrative geographies as is defined in Census:

State Level	A. Overall State MAS (Urban + Rural)
	B. Urban State MAS
	C. Rural State MAS
District Level	D. Overall District MAS (Urban + Rural)
	E. Urban District MAS
	F. Rural District MAS
Town Level	G. Town MAS
Sub-district/ Block Level	H. Sub District MAS (Rural)

How the MART MAS Can Be Used

1. MAS—The tool is relevant for marketers to assess 'Relative importance' of the location in terms of its capacity to consume. The measurement mechanism is ranking of the locations based on weighted score of the variables. The population size of the location impacts the 'Market Attractiveness Score' (MAS). For example, an FMCG company may use MAS to discern the most attractive larger consumer aggregation locations. The same tool can be used by advertising agencies and research agencies to select appropriate geography for planning a communication or conducting market research.
2. MIS—The tool is relevant for marketers of products/services targeting consumers with high income. A higher 'Market Intensity Score' indicates higher per capita prosperity which can indicate potential for higher value products/services. For example, a two-wheeler/four-wheeler company may use MIS instead of MAS.
3. The Customized Index—The tool has a flexibility for marketers to select as many parameters from 18 identified variables to assign weights according to their product/service industry. The total weights assigned should add up to 100 for selected parameters. The tool processes customized MAS/MIS scores for the locations which is effective for the product/service.

Amplification and Scale

Weights for different factors were derived by Principal Component Analysis (factor analysis) onto overall prosperity. In the analysis process, for each factor, a factor loading was used as weight representing maximum variation.

Market Intensity Score (MIS) has been validated with the data of 'per capita income of states' as stated in 'Great Indian Middle Class Report, NCAER'; it has high correlation (0.89) with per capita income at state level.

The new version of MART MAS, the Dynamic MAS, offers features to customize the weights of variables to make it adaptable to product/service industry.

The tool is used for planning last mile distribution network, communication campaign, and market research or consumer research. The tool can also be used by development sector organizations or even corporate CSR teams to identify the low prosperity or poorly developed areas for their developmental activities.

| FIGURE | The MART-MAS Model

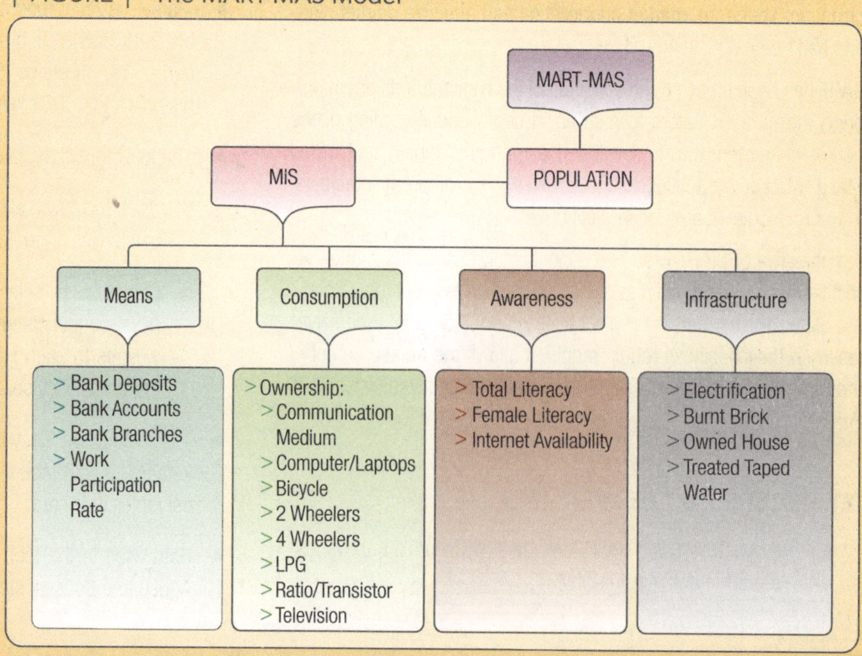

Source: MART Knowledge Centre

- Profitability
- Scale economics
- Low risk

While evaluating segments in rural areas, one should not be impressed by size alone because in rural India, the size may be large but purchasing power is limited. Therefore, the growth rate of rural markets for different product categories should also be considered while targeting the market.

COMPANY OBJECTIVES AND RESOURCE COMPETENCIES Marketers should evaluate the segment opportunity with reference to their short-term and long-term objectives. If a company's objective is to achieve long-term sustainable sales volume by expanding its consumer base, then it has to go to rural markets instead of expecting consumers to come to urban markets for products and services. This has been demonstrated by companies like Asian Paints, HUL, and Colgate-Palmolive, who are now reaching rural homes with their products.

At the same time, the company should also examine its compatibility with resources and capability to service rural markets. It should take calculated risks through small pilot projects, which will provide opportunities to evaluate the target segment behaviour towards products or services. Smart marketers in rural areas like HUL and ITC have initiated 'Project Shakti' and 'e-Choupal' pilots, which have been transformed into mega rural marketing models.

Selection of Segments

After evaluating segments according to the above-mentioned factors, segments can be selected by rating them on a pre-determined scale (low, medium, high) with respect to the evaluation factors. Finally, segments can be ranked based on the scores obtained, and those with the highest scores can be selected as target segments to enter the rural market.

Coverage of Segments

Coverage strategies for targeting can be of three types—undifferentiated, differentiated, and concentrated

Organizations have three alternative coverage strategies to suit their segmentation approaches, as shown in Fig. 5.5.

UNDIFFERENTIATED MARKETING Undifferentiated marketing takes into consideration what is common among consumers and tries to include it in the offer. Hence, it relies on mass distribution and mass advertising. Only one product line keeps down costs of research and development, production, inventory, transportation, marketing research, advertising, and product management. Due to the low cost incurred, the company can set its prices low.

For example, till date Ghari detergent has not come up with any variants for targeting different segments in rural India; rather, it has tried to appeal to all types of customers.

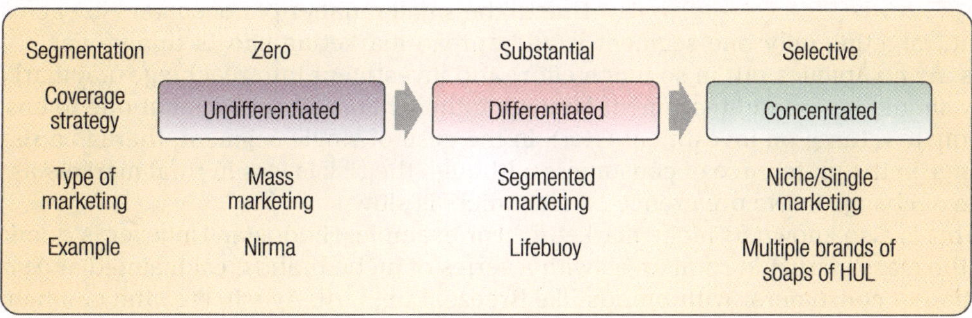

| FIG. 5.5 | Different Coverage Strategies

A majority of companies try to find a convergence between rural and urban lifestyles. Coca-Cola's campaign '*thanda matlab Coca-Cola*' is an example, as it targets both urban and rural markets.

DIFFERENTIATED/TARGETED MARKETING Differentiated market strategy investigates and identifies differences between segments, and tries to match the market offer to the desires and expectations of each segment. This strategy results in:

- Strong identification of the company with the product category
- More costs, but higher sales and profitability
- More loyal consumers

One of the examples of differentiated marketing strategy is Lifebuoy. After entering rural markets initially through the mass market strategy, Lifebuoy, through its four new variants—Active Red, Active Orange, Plus and Gold—is now eyeing a well-defined segment of customers instead of the faceless many.

Successful targeters thrive by securing the loyalty of their customers, who are often impervious even to price increase. Targeted marketing facilitates an intimate understanding of what the target customers value. Therefore, it is critical for marketers to recognize the need for differentiated marketing for differentiated consumer profiles.

WINNING MARKETS THROUGH EFFECTIVE SEGMENTATION AND TARGETING

In 2000, when one of the world's leading agri-business companies entered India, it segmented the consumer market for its hybrid seeds and crop protection products. A hybrid segmentation approach using variables like geography, adoption behaviour, crop economics, and usage pattern, and farmers' attitude and behaviour was used to come up with well-defined segments. The company identified three main segments in the Indian consumer market—optimal farmers, sub-optimal farmers, and marginal farmers. The optimal farmers comprise one-third of the total market, mainly in the agriculturally rich states of Punjab, Haryana, Tamil Nadu, and Maharashtra. These farmers were the first to have capitalized on the Green Revolution, are the early adopters of any new farming technology, use preventive rather than curative crop protection methods, are information seekers and self-dependent for knowledge on the latest products, have greater access to agricultural markets, and have a business outlook towards farming. The company found the best fit with this segment of optimal farmers and targeted them for its existing products. However, it has realized that the remaining two-thirds of the market is also crucial and has to be effectively tapped. Therefore, it is currently trying to profile the sub-optimal farmers, for whom new products can either be developed, or existing products marketed. This segmented approach will not only help the company to expand its market in India, but will also sell the right products to the right consumers.

CONCENTRATED MARKETING Due to the small number of consumers in each segment, targeting only one segment would spread marketing efforts thinly over a vast area. As companies put in so much effort and investment into reaching rural markets, they should have a multi-segment strategy rather than a single segment one to ensure adequate returns on investment (RoI). In the case of single segment, there is a risk of change in the preference of consumers, although the risk is less in rural markets as the pace of change in the preference of consumers is slow.

This is also known as niche marketing. For example, Hindustan Unilever is dominating the mass market in rural areas with a series of niche brands, each aimed at a small section of consumers. With brands like Breeze, Lux, Liril, Ayush, etc., the company is targeting different consumer segments in the rural market.

Profiling sub-optional farmers has helped organizations to understand the needs of this segment.

Choosing a Coverage Strategy

The marketer's approach towards strategy selection changes with reference to the state of four variables—company resources, product variability, product lifecycle stage, and market variability (see Table 5.7). For example, Mahindra & Mahindra as well as other tractor companies have adopted a differentiated strategy as these companies have large resources and more product variability. Also, the product is in the growth stage in the market, and has high market variability.

Positioning

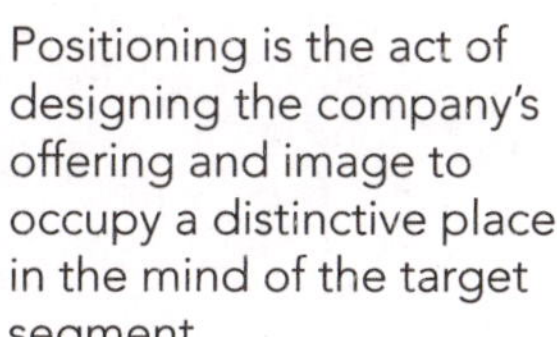

Positioning is the act of designing the company's offering and image to occupy a distinctive place in the mind of the target segment.

Positioning is the act of designing the company's offering and image to occupy a distinctive place in the mind of the target segment. It is typically defined by consumers on the basis of important attributes. Companies have to plan positions that give their products the necessary advantage in the target market. Positioning involves:

- identifying the unique feature of the product (USP), as well as differences between this offer vis-à-vis the competitor's offer;
- selecting the differences that have a greater competitive advantage; and
- communicating such advantages to the target audience.

Positioning begins with the construction of a visual map of the customer's mind. A mind-map is depicted as a flat space divided into four quadrants by two axes, each of which represents the continuum of a particular brand attribute such as cost—expensive/economical; features—traditional/modern; and quality—superior/inferior. For example, the Himani campaign for Sona Chandi Chyawanprash uses contrast to position the brand on two platforms—a healthy body and a sharp mind.

The position of a brand is determined by the spot it occupies on this mind-map. Each spot represents a unique combination of the attributes represented by the two axes. As mind-mapping exercises reveal, existing brands tend to be clustered around particular spots, which represents ideal value-points for the customer. And the line connecting the intersection of the two axes to each of these value-points represent the vectors along which brands tend to be grouped. Thus, a perceptual map summarizes the image in the customer's mind.

| TABLE **5.7** |
Variables for Choosing a Coverage Strategy

Variable	Coverage Strategy		
	Undifferentiated	**Differentiated**	**Concentrated**
Company resources	Moderate	Large	Limited
Product variability	Less	More	Less
Product lifecycle stage	Introduction	Growth	Introduction/Maturity
Market variability	Less	High	High

TATA ACE

TATA Motors launched its mini truck (commercial vehicle) Ace and positioned it as '*Chota Hathi*'. This positioning statement was a huge hit and helped the company to create a distinct place for itself in the minds of consumers. The company used four parameters—savings, service, performance, style, and comfort—to create a competitive positioning map for its new product. Tata used the following statements to position Tata Ace in the minds of consumers: India's first Mini Truck; Small is Big; Stability and Trust of big truck; Economic liberation; Feel good about the job; and Transportation at the last mile. The company successfully managed to position the Ace as high on savings, performance, style and comfort, and service. This strategy has paid off, and the Ace is currently one of the market leaders in its segment.

Smart marketers need to understand and analyse how competing brands are positioned in the minds of consumers so they can place their brands away from competing brands. For example, Ghari detergent identified the vacuum in the low-price–high-quality quadrant and positioned its brand accordingly. Today, Ghari has become a rural super brand in very little time, leaving behind a brand like Wheel.

In case every value-spot on the mind-map is occupied, a new entrant has to think outside the box by making effort to create a new vector.

Identifying the Positioning Concept

Positioning can be done on the basis of product differentiation, service differentiation, people differentiation, and image differentiation.

Marketers have to understand consumer motives behind purchasing a product. This will help in identifying the positioning theme. A marketer can adopt several approaches in positioning his product to develop or enhance its value to the customer. A marketing offer can be differentiated on the basis of product, services, people, channel, and image.

- ***Product differentiation.*** Products can be differentiated on attributes such as form, features, durability, and quality. Coca-Cola introduced the '*chota* Coke' at INR 5 for rural India. Hero Honda came out with the lower-priced Dawn model for the rural buyer. Colgate introduced a herbal version using the positioning of the natural feel preferred in rural areas. Meswak, Neem, and Babool toothpaste also followed a similar positioning strategy.
- ***Service differentiation.*** Services may be differentiated with respect to delivery, installation, and maintenance. Long warranty periods, free-service coupons, service at phone-call distance, 24 hours service, emergency care, etc., are some examples. Reliance, a private LPG company pitted against the three well-established public-sector undertakings (IOCL, BPCL, HPCL), differentiated its products on the basis of distribution and better refilling facility. It successfully differentiated its products despite the fact that they are priced higher.
- ***People differentiation.*** People or personalities (film and sports celebrities) that consumers respect and admire bring a differentiation to the image of products and services. Aamir Khan endorsing Coca-Cola in a villager's outfit or the endorsement of Sona Chandi Chyawanprash by Shahrukh Khan bring a huge differentiation to the product image and help in pushing its sales.
- ***Image differentiation.*** The image of a brand or a company may win the consumer over, despite the product being very similar to a competitive one. Image is built through advertisements, symbols, signs, colours, logos, and the atmosphere of organization.

Selecting the Positioning Concept

As there can be various parameters for positioning the product, the marketer has to select the best and most effective alternatives. A marketer has to select a positioning concept that serves as a bridge between the products and the target market.

Some of the critical factors that should be considered while positioning a brand are:

- ***Attractive.*** Does it provide value to the customer?
- ***Distinctive.*** Is it different from the products of its competitors?
- ***Pre-emptive.*** Is it very difficult for competitors to copy it?
- ***Affordable.*** Can buyers pay for it?
- ***Communicable.*** Can the difference be clearly expressed? Is it visible? Is it understandable?

Attributes that can offer a competitive advantage should be identified (for example, quality, service, technology).

Developing the Concept

Once the positioning strategy has been selected, the marketer needs to develop the concept in an effective manner so that it can be properly addressed to the target market. Then he has to select the appropriate media vehicle to reach the target market effectively. Marketers should strive towards linking the positioning platform closer to the target customer to ensure that it appeals to them.

Communicating the Concept

An effective communication is one that clarifies the target market, value proposition, and the supporting product differentiation.

- ***How many ideas/ differences to promote?*** There could be one idea, two ideas, or three ideas that could be promoted. Positioning two to three ideas would be better, as rural people would think that they were getting better value for money. The statements positioned should be consistent (should not be changed frequently). Otherwise, in the case of multiple statement positioning, there is a risk of buyers having a confused image of the brand, resulting from companies making too many claims.
- ***Which positioning to promote?*** For rural areas, the positioning statement should be the generic benefit of the product. *Sprite Bujhaye Only Pyaas Baki Sab Bakwas* and *Thanda Matlab Coca-Cola* are some of the suitable lines for rural markets.

::: REVIEW OF OBJECTIVES

1. Describe the concepts of segmentation, target marketing, and market positioning, stressing the need to recognize heterogeneity amongst rural consumers

The practice of marketing one undifferentiated product to an undifferentiated rural market died long ago. Marketers today have realized that the rural markets are heterogeneous and need to be segmented thoughtfully. Segmenting markets and attracting customers involves three key decisions—segmentation, targeting, and positioning.

Segmentation involves the identification of various bases for segmenting markets, and then developing profiles of market segments by dividing the heterogeneous market into several submarkets. However, the degree of segmentation varies from mass marketing to micro marketing. Further, the consumer segments are evaluated for their attractiveness, and a suitable coverage strategy for targeting is chosen. The third key decision involves identifying, selecting, and communicating the right USP (unique selling proposition) that provides a competitive advantage to the rural brand.

2. Understand the major bases for segmenting rural consumers and segmentation strategy

A thoughtful approach is required before selecting segmentation variables for rural markets, since the variables generally used for urban segmentation may not necessarily fit into the scheme of rural consumer segmentation.

The major bases for segmenting rural consumer markets are geographic, demographic, psychographic, behavioural, and multi-attribute. In geographic segmentation, consumers are segmented according to factors like region, state, district, village size and density, climate and regional culture. Regional diversity within rural India dictates the real challenge, and marketers need to evolve effective strategies around products that fulfil functional needs and the need gaps of different regions. In demographic segmentation, the market is divided into groups based on variables like age, family structure, landholding, occupation, income, socio-economic classification, religion, and caste. Psychographic segmentation involves factors like personality traits, lifestyle, and value systems, which provide deeper insights and directly relate to consumers' purchases. Behavioural segmentation involves parameters such as purchasing occasions, benefits, user status, usage rate, loyalty status, and place of purchase. In order to identify smaller, well-defined, meaningful target groups, marketers use a combination of several variables in multi-attribute segmentation.

Rural marketers are gradually moving forward from using the traditional descriptive geographic and demographic traits to more evolved segmentation methods like behaviour, psychographics, and multi-attribute segmentation.

3. Understand how companies identify attractive market segments and choose target marketing strategy

Once segmentation has been done, the marketer needs to evaluate each segment to decide which segment to target. Targeting involves three aspects—evaluation, selection, and coverage.

While evaluating market segments, two broad factors are considered, the overall attractiveness of each segment and the company's objectives and resource competencies. The attractiveness of a segment is measured on the bases of size, growth rate, accessibility, profitability, scale economics, and low risk. While evaluating segments in rural areas, one should not be impressed by size alone because here, the size may be large but purchasing power is limited. Therefore, the growth rate of rural markets for different product categories should also be considered while targeting the market. After evaluating, segments are selected by rating them on a predetermined scale with respect to evaluation factors. Post this, the marketer can choose any of the three alternative coverage strategies that suits his segmentation approach. It could range from a very broad to a very narrow targeting approach—undifferentiated, differentiated, and concentrated.

Undifferentiated marketing takes into consideration what is common among the consumers and tries to include it in the offer. A differentiated market strategy investigates and identifies differences between segments, and tries to match the market offer to the desires and expectations of each segment. Concentrated marketing involves focusing on only one or a few market segments. As companies put so much effort and investment into reaching rural markets, they should have a multi-segment strategy rather than a single segment one in order to receive adequate returns on investment.

4. Realize how companies position their products for maximum competitive advantage in the rural marketplace

Once a marketer decides which segments to target, he must then decide on its differentiation and positioning strategy. Positioning involves three major steps—identification of the unique feature of the product (USP) as well as differences between this offer and that of a competitor; selecting the differences that have greater competitive advantage; and communicating such advantages to the target audience.

An important aspect in identifying USP is constructing a visual map of the customer's mind, which depicts the exact position where his brand is placed. This helps the marketer to know the ideal value-point for the customer, and then design and communicate the right positioning concept.

DISCUSSION AND APPLICATION

Discussion of Concepts

1. Briefly describe the different bases for segmenting rural consumer markets.
2. Describe the importance of multi-attribute segmentation in rural markets. Explain one such approach used by companies for their market planning in detail.
3. What is the concept of 'brand stickiness'? How is it different from brand loyalty? Why is this concept more relevant in rural India? Cite some examples of the same.
4. What is product 'positioning', and how do marketers know what it is?
5. You are the marketing manager of 'Santosh Computer' Classes Pvt. Ltd – the only computer classes in Madhubani area of Bihar. Recently, a leading national computer education brand has started its centre and has started targeting the same set of customers as yours. You are afraid of losing the market and want to identify newer segments to target. What possible ways of segmenting the markets do you think would help you in the process?

Application of Concepts

1. Consider the mobile handset market in rural India. On what bases would you classify this market and why? How do you think the rural marketers in this industry would benefit from your segmentation scheme?
2. Build a case on a company that has moved from a mass marketing approach to a differentiated approach to make inroads into rural markets in India.
3. Think of the leading companies in the tractor industry in India. What would be the most appropriate dimensions on which these companies can be positioned? Discuss and come up with the two most critical dimensions and try to map each company on the perceptual map.
4. Identify three brands that have failed to create a unique positioning in rural markets in the last five years. What could/should have been done to position these brands more successfully in the minds of consumers from rural India?

RURAL MARKETING CASE | BRU INSTANT COFFEE CONNECT

Bru represents the coffee business of HUL and is the only brand to be present in all segments of the coffee category—instant, roast, and ground, and premixes. It is the volume leader in the roast and ground market. There are three different consumer segments based on their drink preferences in south India:

- Conventional filter coffee drinkers
- Tea drinkers
- Instant coffee drinkers

South India is a big market for coffee, filter coffee being the most prevalent, with a few pockets within the states of Andhra Pradesh and Karnataka also preferring tea. However, most people prefer conventional filter coffee for its taste and aroma. This segment when combined with the tea-drinking segment represents a huge, untapped market for instant coffee.

The Challenge

While people are aware of instant coffee, it is still a drink to be had on special occasions for many households. The marketing challenge, thus, was to convert these special occasions to Bru Instant Coffee occasions.

The company had to reach out to 1.3 million people spread across three segments for product trials.

As these households were a mix of tea drinkers/filter coffee and other coffee drinkers, conveying the right message across the segments was the key challenge for the company. Beverage preferences are difficult to change; it was not easy to get people to deviate from a beverage of their choice and sample instant coffee. The decision to leave samples with consumers significantly improved the impact of this trial campaign.

With multiple communicators of differing individual capabilities, delivering a *standardized yet customized* message *consistently* was an even bigger challenge for Bru. The fact that most housewives/target consumers have a *not-so-welcoming* attitude to a door-to-door salesman/communicator.

The brand, therefore, needed a breakthrough to overcome these hurdles and to communicate the benefits of Bru Instant to three different beverage drinkers.

The Solution

The accompanying video talks about how the communication strategy covered all three segments in one go using a door-to-door sampling strategy in a cost-effective manner for inducing trials. It talks about how innovative media vehicles were used during the campaign in the absence of effective mass media reach out to reach three sets of audiences.

During the campaign in 2009, 2.3 million households were sampled, resulting in the brand gaining a 70 per cent share of new category entrants.

Discussion Questions

1. What communication challenges did Bru face? Which innovative media vehicle was chosen for reaching the target group? Why? What else could have been used to improve the effectiveness of the campaign?
2. What kind of impact was generated by the campaign? How much rural growth was achieved as a result of this campaign?
3. Identify different consumer segments among health food drinkers in the rural sector. Suppose a new brand 'Health Plus' is entering this market . As the brand manager of the company, explain how you will enter this market and address the communication challenge for different segments.

AFTER READING THIS CHAPTER, YOU WILL BE ABLE TO:

1. Understand the concept, levels and classification of products in rural markets
2. Discuss relevant product decisions and product strategies at different stages of the product lifecycle as applicable to rural markets
3. Build and manage brands in rural markets
4. Understand the challenge of fakes and counterfeits and how to handle it
5. Understand the role and elements of packaging products for rural markets
6. Recognize the role and importance of after-sales service in the rural marketplace
7. Describe the theme of new product development for rural consumers and outline the relevant steps for it

Big on technology. Small in size.

Now, take pride in running your own business, at a low cost. Make the Tate ACE a partner in your success. With a more powerful twin-cylinder water-cooled diesel engine of 16 bhp © 3200 rpm, you can make daily trips of up to 500 km. Other car-like features and interiors give you maximum comfort which translates into more trips, more profits. Meeting BS II, BS III and all Indian safety norms, the eco-friendly ACE will go with you anywhere. Cities, villages, roads big and small.

TRUCKS & BUSES FROM
TATA MOTORS

CHAPTER 6 ::: PRODUCT STRATEGY

The launch of the Tata Ace in 2005 ushered in a new growth phase for Tata Motors. The Tata Ace, the country's first four-wheel mini truck, caught the fancy of many in the commercial vehicle category. It helped Tata to make inroads into a new segment of sub-one tonne category of commercial vehicles. It had many takers at the bottom of the pyramid segment, like the small-time transporters, poultry owners, laundry men, vegetable vendors, and scrap dealers across India. Within 18 months of being launched, it became the single largest brand for Tata Motors.

The Ace is one product from Tata Motors where product engineering, marketing strategy, and branding have worked perfectly well. Having identified an opportunity in the big gap in the market space between three-wheeler pick-ups and six-wheel light trucks such as the Tata 407, Tata Motors had worked intensely on the concept of a mini truck. The Ace proved to be flexible, comfortable, and fuel-efficient. The company initially wooed three-wheeler owners with the 'Rickshawaale se motor maalik' profile as the attraction. It also created a strong appeal in rural markets, where bullock carts and muddy paths gave way to small pick-ups. Many first-time users, particularly the unemployed youth, turned into owner-drivers. The Ace became the preferred vehicle for last mile transportation.

To reach out to potential buyers in interior India, Tata Motors opened 600 small sales outlets[1] at the district level, taking the total sales touch points to over 1,000. Another smart move was to facilitate vehicle financing through tie-ups with public-sector banks spread across rural India.

All along the amazing ride of the Ace, Tata Motors has shown savvy product diversification skills. Currently, the Ace family has its original base model mini truck, a passenger carrier in Magic, a CNG-run version, Ace Ex with fuel-efficient start–stop technology, and Super Ace with one-tonne payload. Product innovation continues as the Tatas come out with a four-seater people carrier, Magic Iris.

The Tata Ace has changed the face of rural transportation in India.

::: The Product Concept and the Classification of Rural Products

In the rural context, marketers have to use two frameworks—the 4 Ps (product, price, place, promotion) of the marketing mix and the evaluative rural marketing mix of 4As (acceptability, affordability, availability, awareness), concepts first introduced in Chapter 1. Product decision is the first and central decision in the marketing mix strategy and should be evaluated on the basis of the acceptability parameter to develop the right strategy for rural markets. Acceptability is one of the challenges a rural marketer has to face while developing products and services for rural areas. The challenge is to identify the tastes and preferences of rural consumers and then offer products that suit them.

The Product Concept

Product is the most vital element in the market offering. Marketing mix planning begins with formulating an offering to meet the needs and wants of the target customer. The rural customer judges the offering on the basis of three basic elements—product features and quality; services mix and quality (dealt with in Chapter 10); and the appropriateness of the offering's price (dealt with in Chapter 7).

The concept of a rural product may have to be unique since it has been observed that a rural consumer's needs and aspirations are often different from those of their urban counterparts, and what works for the latter may not work for the former. Most companies consider rural markets as an extension of their strategy to reach the low-income urban consumer. This approach does not yield results as the needs of the rural consumer are not met. Marketers can penetrate the rural market by designing innovative products, done successfully by companies such as LG, Philips, and HUL. In 1998, LG Electronics developed a customized television for rural markets called Sampoorna, which facilitated on-screen display in regional languages like Hindi, Tamil, and Bengali. The television was a runaway hit, selling 100,000 sets in the very first year. LG also devised a semi-automatic washing machine with double the capacity of its urban-based machines for the rural market, as there are still many joint families and the number of dirty clothes that need washing are many more. A memory back-up was also incorporated keeping in mind the frequent electricity breakdowns in rural areas.

Philips India launched its 'Free Power Radio' especially for rural India. This radio required neither batteries nor electricity for operation. A one-minute winding of the spring with a lever allowed the user 30 minutes of listening time. Priced at INR 995, this radio was ideal as it helped the rural consumer avoid a recurring battery cost.

A user-centric approach can provide marketers with insights that will aid them to develop appropriate products for these markets. For example, Cadbury launched ChocoBix, a chocolate-flavoured biscuit, based on the consumer insight that rural mothers opt for the more affordable biscuits rather than expensive chocolate bars for their children.

The acceptance of a product in rural markets is determined not only by consumer needs and wants, but also by the physical and social environment like the status of infrastructure facilities (the availability of electricity, condition of roads, etc). The product has to satisfy rural needs and should offer value for money. Rural consumers' decision to buy a product also depends on their attitude towards that product, and the cost–benefit analysis they would have done before buying it. Eveready Industries, which has an overwhelming share of dry cells and torches in the rural market, found that the plastic torches introduced by them received a very good response in urban markets, but had no takers in rural India. Farmers preferred heavy brass torches because of the salvage value the brass metal fetched when the discarded torch was sold to a scrap merchant.

Thus, in a nutshell, a marketer should keep the following aspects in mind while taking products to rural markets. The products should be:

- Appropriate for the rural environment
- Simple to operate
- Visually identifiable
- Affordable

Products marketed may include physical goods, services, places, ideas, persons, organizations, etc. In this chapter, we focus on physical goods as products.

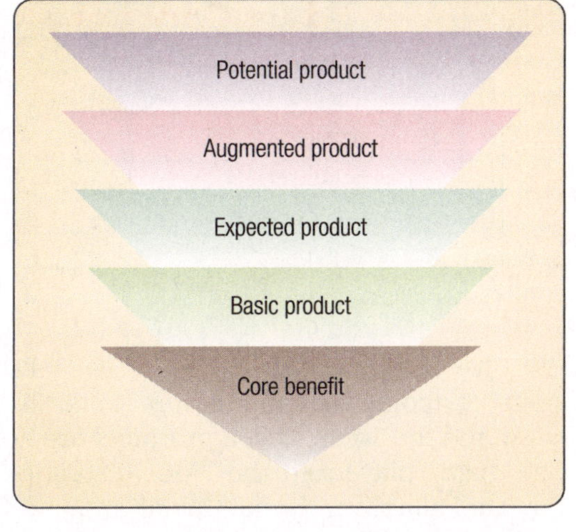

| FIG. **6.1** |
Five Product Levels

THE LEVELS OF A PRODUCT Based on the value proposition, marketers need to think of five levels of product offering—core benefit, basic product, expected product, augmented product, and finally, potential product.

The five levels of product offering include the core benefit, basic product, expected product, augmented product, and potential product.

Each level, as shown in Fig. 6.1, adds more customer value, and the five levels constitute a customer value hierarchy. For example, the core benefit of connectivity, or the experience of being in touch, is translated into a mobile phone as the basic product. At the third level, the marketer prepares an expected product, a set of attributes and conditions that a buyer normally expects when he purchases a product. Product differences start appearing from this level onwards. A mobile phone buyer in rural India expects voice clarity, good battery life, ease of operation, and durability. At the fourth level, the marketer prepares an augmented product that meets customers' desires beyond expectations and fulfils their latent needs, such as mobile phones with in-built radios, cameras, flashlights, additional 2GB memory cards, and localized language display modes. The real competition today in the rural market is at the product augmentation level. This leads marketers to look at the physical and socio-economic environment of consumers, and understand their consumption behaviour and the way they use the product. At the same time, rural marketers have to ensure that augmentation doesn't increase the cost significantly.

Finally, a potential product comes at the fifth level, which encompasses all the augmentations and transformations that the product might ultimately undergo in the future. Here, marketers search for new ways to satisfy their customers; for example, a mobile phone that runs on battery, which can be charged using solar light rather than electricity.

Thus, the products at the third, fourth, and fifth levels highlight the difference in consumer needs, and must be addressed effectively in order to make the products successful in rural markets.

MICROMAX MOBILE

Micromax Mobile, launched in 2008, targeted the rural Indian consumer with its feature-packed, economically priced handsets. The USP of Micromax X1i, the first handset to be launched, was the 30-day battery back-up, which made it extremely attractive to electricity-deprived rural consumers and frequent travellers. Priced at INR 1,250, this model was a huge success in rural India. Micromax has focused on providing value for money—more features at lower prices. This strategy has enabled it to endear the brand to the rural masses.

Rural Product Classification

Rural products can be classified into four broad categories—FMCGs, consumer durables, services, and agricultural goods.

Rural products can be classified into four broad categories—fast-moving consumer goods (FMCGs), consumer durables, services and agricultural goods, as shown in Fig. 6.2.

| FIG. **6.2** |
Rural Product Categories

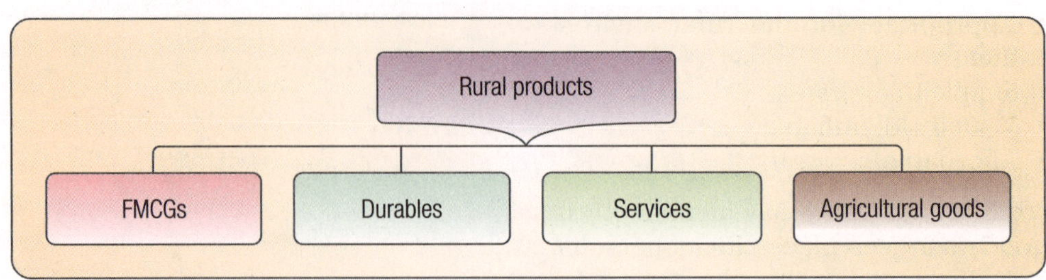

FAST-MOVING CONSUMER GOODS Fast-moving consumer goods (FMCGs) or consumables comprise all non-durable goods like toiletries, cosmetics, foods and beverages, and footwear. These products are consumed quickly and purchased frequently. The major players in the FMCG category in rural markets are HUL, Dabur, Marico, Colgate-Palmolive, Nirma, CavinKare, and Godrej.

Rural markets currently account for more than 50 per cent of the total FMCG consumption in the country, and the estimated size of the rural FMCG market is around INR 1,350 billion annually. The rural FMCG market has grown significantly in the last five years, outpacing urban consumption in 2009 (as can be seen in Fig. 6.3). This FMCG growth in rural India is mainly driven by the consumption of food categories, which reflects the acceptance of branded packaged and processed food by rural India.

To understand the overall FMCG market, it is important to assess the penetration of various categories of products within rural households. Rural penetration for products like edible oil, washing powders, tea, and biscuits is more than 75 per cent, but hovers around 50 per cent for commodities such as packaged tea, shampoo, and oral care products. Also, penetration remains low for products like milk powder, instant noodles, ketchup/sauces, and jams (see Table 6.1).

In the last decade, various categories of products have achieved significant recognition in rural households. As shown in Table 6.2, there has been an increase of 9 per cent points in the purchase of packaged edible oil, and an increase of 25 per cent points in packaged biscuits between 2000 and 2008. This indicates how fast the preferences of rural India are shifting from loose to packaged products. In this process, regional brands, local brands, and other unbranded offerings are being displaced by leading national brands. Again, the growth rate in rural markets has been astounding for shampoos, which has increased by 31 per cent within a span of eight years.

There is still a huge latent demand, both in terms of increasing consumption and penetration levels, which needs to be tapped by rural marketers. Growth in the sales of low-penetration categories will become a reality only when more consumers purchase these products and continue to use them regularly.

| FIG. **6.3** |
FMCG Growth in Rural and Urban India

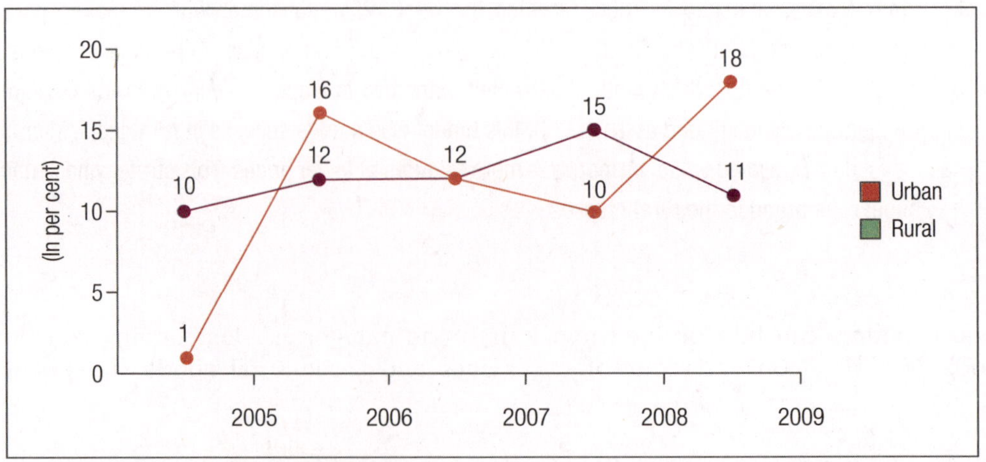

| TABLE **6.1** |
Household Penetration of FMCG Products in Rural India

Product	Penetration (in per cent)
Edible oil	96
Washing powders/liquids	90
Tea	89
Washing cakes/bars	85
Biscuits	76
Hair oil	70
Toothbrush	56
Toothpaste	51
Vanaspati	42
Toothpowder	29
Ghee/Desi ghee	18
Utensil cleaners	18
Toilet cleaner	8
Coffee—Instant or filter	8
Milk powder/Dairy whiteners	4
Instant noodles	3
Ketchup/Sauces	1
Jam	1

Source: Data taken from IRS, Q1-2010 published in 'Households—other product consumption' in *Media Market Guide India 2010* by R. K. Swamy Media Group.

CONSUMER DURABLES Consumer durables include products like home appliances, automobiles, watches, and furniture. Rural consumers generally purchase these goods from nearby small towns. The major durables players in rural markets are Usha, Bajaj, Philips, Titan, Godrej, Videocon, LG, Samsung, Hero Honda, Mahindra & Mahindra, Maruti, and Tata.

Rural markets currently account for more than 50 per cent of the total durables consumption in the country. Among the high-priced durables, televisions—with 37 per cent ownership in rural India—have penetrated rural markets with the highest degree of success. Other commodities such as pressure cookers, LPG stoves, and motorbikes are also quite popular, as can be seen from Table 6.3.

Although the penetration of durables is still low in rural India, its growth has been exciting. In the last decade, there has been almost a five-fold increase in the penetration of colour televisions in rural India, almost four-fold in motorcycles, and the penetration of refrigerators has doubled (see Table 6.4).

Rural India, with its increasing disposable income from non-farming sources, has a much higher potential for growth in the durables sector. Circumstances cannot be more favourable than they are now. See 'Rural Marketing Snapshot: Product Acceptability' to understand how value-conscious rural consumers have become.

| TABLE **6.2** |
Household Penetration of Fast-moving Consumer Goods in Rural India

	Packaged Edible Oil			Packaged Biscuits			Shampoo		
Year	2000	2005	2008	2000	2005	2008	2000	2005	2008
Penetration (in per cent)	9	14	18	39	54	64	13	32	44

Source: Data sourced from 'Penetration on Food and Beverages' and 'Penetration of Personal Care Products' in *The Marketing Whitebook 2010–11*, pp. 87, 88.

| TABLE **6.3** |
Household Penetration of Select Durables in Rural India

Product	Penetration (in per cent)
Television	37
Pressure cooker	25
LPG stove	20
Electric iron	14
Moped/Electric bike/Scooter/Motorcycle	11
Refrigerator	6
Telephone	6
DVD player	5
Air cooler	3
Washing machine	1
Still camera (non-digital)	1
Car/Jeep/Van/SUV	1

Source: Data taken from IRS, Q1-2010 published in 'Households—durables penetration' in *Media Market Guide India 2010* by R. K. Swamy Media Group.

SERVICES Major services in rural India include healthcare, telecommunication, information communication technology (ICT), banking, insurance, and education. This category is led by players like the Life Insurance Corporation, State Bank of India, Bharat Sanchar Nigam Ltd, and new entrants, including Airtel, Reliance Communications, ITC's e-Choupal, and ICICI. This category is dealt with in greater detail in Chapter 10.

AGRICULTURAL GOODS Agricultural products are tangible goods used in farm activities. These include agriculture inputs such as seeds, fertilizers, pesticides, insecticides, and implements (tractors, tillers, threshers, harvesters, pump sets, etc.). The products of allied sectors—livestock, poultry, and fishery—like animal feeds, dairy, poultry, and fishery equipments, are also included in this category. The agri-inputs market (including tractors) accounts for around INR 900 billion annually. The major players in this segment are Rallis India, Monsanto, DCM, Bayer, Indian Farmers Fertiliser Cooperative Limited (IFFCO), Mahindra & Mahindra, Tractors and Farm Equipment Limited (TAFE), and Escorts.

While developing products for rural markets, it is important for a marketer to take decisions on product attributes like quality, features, design, and style.

::: Product Decisions and Strategies

Marketers have to make product decisions at three levels—individual product decisions, product line decisions, and product mix decisions. They also have to strategize at each level of the product lifecycle. Each of these is discussed here.

| TABLE **6.4** |
Household Penetration of Consumer Durables in Rural (figures in per cent)

	Colour TV			Refrigerator			Motorcycle		
Year	2000	2005	2008	2000	2005	2010	2000	2005	2010
Penetration (in per cent)	4	11	18	3	4	6	3	5	11

Source: Data taken from IRS, Q1-2010 published in 'Households—Durables Penetration', R.K. Media Group and Swamy, *Media Market Guide*; 'Penetration of Consumer Durables', *The Marketing Whitebook 2010–11:* 87.

RURAL MARKETING SNAPSHOT — PRODUCT ACCEPTABILITY

Incandescent bulbs were used in the past

Modern rural households use CFLs

The rural consumer is a discerning buyer, always on the look out for newer products that offer better value for money. Thirty years ago, most villages in India lacked electricity leaving the rural folk dependent on lamps, lanterns, and the likes. With the electrification of villages, rural consumers started using incandescent bulbs. Frequent voltage spikes meant that these had to be replaced often. The CFL offered a cost-effective alternative which is why most rural consumers now prefer to use a CFL despite its high cost.

Individual Product Decisions

This involves decisions related to product attributes, branding, packaging, labelling, and product support services. While developing a product, it is important for a marketer to look into product attributes such as quality, features, design, and style.

QUALITY This signifies the ability of a product to meet the consumer's expectations related to durability, efficiency, economy, and reliability. This has a direct bearing on customer value and satisfaction. Before setting the quality parameters for a product, rural marketers must know how their target consumers evaluate a product's quality—whether consumers are dependent on technical specifications or whether they utilize their own norms, notions, and beliefs to sense quality. Most often in rural India, people set their own emotional specifications for judging the quality of a product: for example, a rural consumer views heavy watches as quality watches; he judges the quality of cement by its bitter taste; a tractor by the sound of its engine when started; and so on. Rural marketers must understand these emotional cues and translate them into physical signs in their products.

FEATURES These are the extra add-ons of a product that add value in the eyes of consumers. A marketer must carefully identify and select appropriate new features to be added to the basic product, based on customer value versus the company cost. Instead of offering stripped-down models of their products, many rural marketers have started adding features that enhance utility and convenience for rural consumers. For example, John Deere is the first company to have added power steering to its base model in the lower segment of 35-hp tractors to provide efficiency and convenience to farmers. Such features also act as competitive tools in differentiating a company's product from those of its competitors.

DESIGN AND STYLE The design and style of a product is yet another way of adding customer value. Style implies the appearance of a product, the way it looks and feels to the buyer. Design, however, is more than skin deep—it includes all those features that contribute to a product's usefulness and looks. While designing products for rural markets, one should take into account the environmental conditions in which the

AKASHTABLET(PRODUCT)

The cheapest tablet computer in 2011, which delivered modern technology to the countryside to help lift villagers out of poverty and get more of India's 220 million children online, is called Aakash or 'sky'.It was the latest in a series of 'world's cheapest' innovations in India. In comparison against the cheapest Apple iPad tablet which costs $499, this was developed by Developer Datawind who sold the tablets to the government at $45 each, and after subsidies, students and teachers had to pay $35 only. Aakash has a colour screenof 18cm (7in) and provides word processing, web browsing, and video conferencing. The Android 2.2-based device has two USB ports and 256 megabytes of RAM. It also planned for a solar-powered version of the same but it was not possible which would otherwise be an important feature for India's energy-starved hinterlands.But these low-cost Android tablets have enabled people with less resource to dream big.

MAX GAS

Rural consumers have been reluctant to switch to LPG for cooking because of concerns about quality, leakage of gas, and explosion of cylinders. Max Gas, a private player working in Punjab and parts of Uttar Pradesh, came up with a cylinder addressing these concerns. It designed a cylinder which had the following features:

- Auto cut-off regulator that shuts off gas supply immediately in case of leakage
- Double-sealed cylinder that ensured the correct weight
- Special three-layered, long-lasting, steel-braided hosepipe, which was rat resistant (unlike the rubber pipe) and did not crack on bending, eliminating the possibility of gas leakage
- Wider base of cylinders to ensure stability even on uneven rural kitchen floors
- Top ring open from one side for easy handling of the regulator

product will be used, its functionality, convenience of operation, and cost. For instance, cooking in rural areas, which is mostly done at the ground level, requires a pressure cooker with handles on both sides so that it can be lifted with ease. Also, the resale value of the product is an important factor in the case of durables. The popularity of metal/ alloy (aluminium/brass) torches over plastic torches is due to the high resale value of metal. Many dish-washing bar manufacturers like HUL use advanced technology to coat one side of the bar with plastic to prevent it from wearing out quickly, as most rural folk wash utensils in the open where the uncontrolled flow of water effaces the bar.

Intel has come up with a personal computer (PC) designed specifically for rural markets. This PC can withstand adverse weather conditions like heat, humidity, and dust, and can operate on alternative power sources such as truck or car batteries. Its removable dust filter keeps the dust at bay and the integrated air fan regulates the motherboard temperature, keeping it cool even at a temperature of 45°C.

The Nokia 1100 cell phone is yet another example of a product designed for rural markets. When Nokia developers watched field workers using mobile phones in India, they noticed that the intense humidity made the phones slick and hard to hold or dial. So they designed the Nokia 1100 with a non-slip silicon coating on its keypad and sides to resist the damage caused by the dust common in arid climates and some factory environments. The phones are otherwise basic: they can send and receive phone calls, and text messages. The screens are monochrome. Since the phones lack fancy software, they consume less power and the battery lasts longer between recharges. The only real extra is a tiny, energy-efficient flashlight that has proven popular in areas where power blackouts are common. At a reasonable price, the Nokia 1100 has become the best-selling cell phone ever.

Another classic example of product design for rural markets is the Godrej Chotu Kool refrigerator. This is an innovative and affordable product that not only caters to rural needs, but also aims at improving their living standards (see 'Rural Marketing Insight: Product Designing for Rural Needs—Godrej Chotu Kool').

Product Line and Mix Decisions

A product line is a group of closely related products priced within a certain range, targeted at the same customer group and distributed through the same channel. A product mix is the set of all product lines and items offered by a company.

After developing products, a company needs to create an appropriate product line and product mix for rural markets. A product line is a group of closely related products priced within a certain range, targeted at the same customer group and distributed through the same channel. A product line may consist of different brands or a single family brand with different variants from the same company. For example, HUL has soaps like Lux, Lifebuoy, Liril, Hamam, Breeze, Moti, etc., under its personal wash product line.

A product mix is a set of all product lines and items offered by a company. Table 6.5 shows the product mix of HUL. The product mix in rural markets is generally simple. Usually, only one product of a particular company is available on rural shelves (often in only one or two stock-keeping units). The limitations on investment in stocks, the slow movement and replenishment of stocks, and the dominance of the retailer in rural markets are some important factors responsible for the smaller range of products available in retail shops in rural markets. Consumers have little say in the choice of brands, and sometimes even the pack size. Retailers push those brands that bring them attractive margins.

Only a few companies like HUL and Dabur have more than one product available in their rural product basket. HUL has a good product width, with a presence in personal wash, laundry, oral care, hair care, foods and beverages, etc. Dabur has made its presence felt with Chyawanprash, over-the-counter remedies (Pudin Hara, Hajmola), hair oil, etc.

RURAL MARKETING INSIGHT | PRODUCT DESIGNING FOR RURAL NEEDS—GODREJ CHOTU KOOL

The changing consumption pattern in rural India has convinced marketers that rural markets can be significant revenue drivers. Now, companies design products and distribution channels keeping in mind the requirements of rural customers. One such specially designed product is the Chotu Kool refrigerator from Godrej. This product is designed to meet the daily cooling requirements of rural people at an affordable price. The larger vision behind this initiative was to better the lives of people at the bottom of the pyramid.

Godrej has done away with the traditional compressor in this product. Chotu Kool, operating on 12-volt battery power, uses advance solid-state technology to cool. A lightweight, fully plastic body makes it highly mobile. The unconventional top opening ensures that the cold air settles down in the cabinet to minimize heat loss and power consumption. Available in two variants of 30 litres and 43 litres, Chotu Kool keeps the basic goods—water, milk, vegetables and fruits—fresh and cool for a family of four or five. It works best in temperature conditions of up to 35°C. Priced at half the cost of an entry-level, conventional refrigerator, Chotu Kool is not a refrigerator. It is a new category in itself. It serves a distinctly different purpose and caters to a new segment of potential consumers. Hence, it needs personalized demonstrations through which to communicate and deliver its distinct value proposition. Godrej plans to reach out to potential consumers through a community network, which also improves the livelihoods of participating members as they canvass and demonstrate the product. Besides, the company believes that Chotu Kool has tremendous potential as an earning asset in the hands of small entrepreneurs in their business of selling products and offering services that need some cooling.

Currently, the initial model of Chotu Kool is being test marketed in Maharashtra. Over time, based on the market response, the company plans to come out with a range of sizes and models in the Chotu Kool category.

Source: Compiled from article on 'Godrej ChotuKool refrigerator—Product innovation, pricing and rural marketing at play', MART-Edelweiss Report on 'Rural India-Transcending Boundaries', p. 31, October 2010.

| TABLE **6.5** |
Product Mix and Product Line Length for Hindustan Unilever Limited

	Product Mix Width												
	Personal wash	**Laundry**	**Dish washer**	**Disin-fectant**	**Foods**	**Ice cream**	**Beverage**	**Water purifier**	**Beauty product**	**Hair care**	**Oral care**	**Deo spray**	**Health-care**
Product line length	Lux	Surf Excel	Vim	Domex	Kissan	Kwality	Brooke Bond	Pureit Water purifier	Fair& Lovely	Sunsilk	Pepsodent	Axe	Ayush
	Lifebuoy	Rin			Annapurna	Wall's	Lipton		Lakme	Clinic	Close-up	Rexona	
	Liril	Wheel			Modern Bread		Bru		Ponds	Dove			
	Hamam	Ala bleach							Vaseline				
	Breeze												
	Moti												
	Dove												
	Pears												
	Rexona												

Companies can take various product-mix decisions based on their strategies, like width extension (adding new product lines for diversification); length extension (adding new product items catering to different consumer segments); line pruning (reducing the number of product items to modernize the product portfolio); and depth extension (adding new product variants).

Product Lifecycle Strategies

A product passes through four stages in its lifecycle—introduction, growth, maturity, and decline. This fact holds true for products in rural markets as well.

It has been observed that the lifecycle of a product in rural markets is often longer than it is in urban markets. Each stage—of introduction, growth, maturity, and decline—lasts longer in rural markets due to the multiple challenges involved in the distribution, communication, and adoption of the product. However, the duration of the lifecycle from introduction to decline varies from one product category to another.

Many products launched in rural markets without serious planning die out rather quickly—either soon after introduction or during the growth stage. Examples include Aim toothpaste from HUL and Ruf-n-Tuf ready-to-stitch denims. Only companies that focus on brand-building and those that continue to innovate constantly can sustain themselves in rural markets. The length of each stage in the product lifecycle (PLC) depends on consumer acceptance, innovativeness, price proposition, and the nature of the product.

Marketers must also take into account the fact that rural markets are not homogenous; hence, it is not possible for a product to be in a particular lifecycle stage across the country. Rural markets can be categorized into three stages—developed, developing and under-developed. On the basis of this classification, it is evident how the same product could have reached maturity in a developed market while remaining in the introductory stage in an under-developed market. For example, Haryana is a more matured market for tractors than Bihar. Thus, rural marketers need to develop different product strategies for different markets, based on the stage of the market.

Most companies that have introduced products in rural markets are struggling to increase their penetration into this market. This is forcing companies to re-engineer their products or introduce low-price packs (sachets, 200-ml chota Pepsi, pricing white goods below the psychological barrier of INR 10,000). They are also trying to change consumption patterns through consumer education (increasing the frequency of soap usage from weekly to daily) and through the adoption of alternative channels to reach deeper (HUL's Project Shakti, haats, mobile vans, youth volunteers) and grow the market.

Pioneers in rural markets such as HUL, Eveready, and ITC, having achieved a high penetration with products at the maturity stage, are either extending their brands (Lifebuoy Regular to Lifebuoy Gold and Active; Eveready White to Red) or entering new segments (Dabur Hajmola initially targeted children, and was later promoted among adults). Companies like ITC are also creating new market systems (e-Choupal) to bypass the age-old mandi system and purchase agri-commodities directly from farmers.

The decline of products in rural markets is slow; it is hastened sometimes because of technological advancement (from VCR to VCD/DVD players; from analogue cameras to digital cameras).

A product lifecycle comprises four stages—introduction of the product, growth, maturity, and decline of the product.

::: Product Branding in Rural Markets

The concept of branding has been a late entrant in rural markets. It is only in the recent past that consumers have graduated from unbranded to branded products due to increased awareness and affordability of brands.

A quick study of the popular brands in rural markets reveals an unusual trend—rural consumers' brand association is mainly with colours, numbers, and visuals, and not necessarily with the name of the brand. For example:

- Colours—*Lal Dant Manjan*, *Lal sabun* (Lifebuoy), Red battery (Eveready), Brooke Bond Red Label tea
- Numbers—Godrej No.1 soap, 555 detergent bar, 502 *Pataka chai,* Brooke Bond A1 *karak chai*
- Visuals—*Ghari* detergent, *Rath vanaspati*, *Wagh Bakri* tea, 3 Roses Tea, *Katchua Chaap* mosquito coil and Cycle *Agarbatti*

In a rural set-up, the retailer plays a significant role in brand promotion. Retailers in rural markets have a strong bond with consumers. This, coupled with the consumers' low brand awareness, enables retailers to push any brand of their choice. Frequently, the customer will ask the retailer, '*Paanch rupaye waali chai dena*'. In other words, the customer trusts the retailer, and is okay with purchasing any brand of tea as long as it is priced at INR 5. Now it is up to the retailer to push the brand that he chooses. Thus, retailers are highly influential in rural markets.

The first-mover brands in rural markets have become generic brands. Detergent powder came to be identified with Surf, vegetable oil with Dalda, and mosquito coil with Katchua Chaap. Also, brands like Clinic Plus and Lifebuoy, which were first movers at the national level in rural India, have become the most successful brands despite being priced higher than the competition. As more products are identified with brands (thus becoming generic brands), converting consumers to a better brand in the same product category becomes a rather difficult proposition.

Building Brands in Rural Markets

Building a brand in rural markets involves three important decisions—developing a brand name, creating a brand identity, and building a brand image.

DEVELOPING A BRAND NAME A brand name in the rural context facilitates easy brand recall, and helps in drawing any colour, visual or numeric association. Some brands, however, are known by their names, such as Nirma and Colgate. The choice of 'Sampoorna' as the name for its rural television brand helped LG, as this is a Sanskrit word meaning *wholesome*, and hence can cut across all regional linguistic barriers. Names like 'Ajanta' (for toothpaste) and 'Bhoomiputra' (for tractor) were chosen for the same reason.

CREATING A BRAND IDENTITY The challenges in the creation of a brand identity in rural markets involve the need to relate the brand with the rural lifestyle, or with appropriate status symbols, or with the rural environment. As many brands are introduced first in urban markets and then move to rural markets, creating a brand identity in rural markets becomes a tough challenge. Tata Steel branded its galvanized corrugated sheets Tata Shaktee to create a brand identity that conveys the qualities of strength, durability, and toughness; Shree Ultra created a brand identity for its cement that said '*jung rodhak*' or rust retardant; Britannia Tiger biscuits created an identity of a smart, active, and sharp child.

BUILDING A BRAND IMAGE The brand should have a personality of its own. It should emote, empathize, and talk to its consumers. Such an ability helps in establishing a brand connect with rural audiences and contributes a great deal to brand equity and competitive advantage. Mahindra & Mahindra has maintained its sterling image in rural India. The *Bhoomiputra* (son of soil) series of tractors, with their rugged features and sarpanch (village head) series, have helped to improve sales. The sarpanch brand helped to draw a close brand recognition between the product and the head of the village. In this way, it provided an opportunity to the consumer to relate himself with the sarpanch, who commands high status and respect in the village.

Brand Loyalty Versus Brand Stickiness

Low levels of literacy and awareness make rural people less likely to switch brands, as they do not have the required knowledge or information to exercise a choice. They feel more comfortable purchasing tried-and-tested brands. They are therefore 'brand sticky' rather than 'brand loyal', as is often—but erroneously—believed by most marketers as discussed in Chapter 5. To establish a brand, the company needs to educate rural consumers, develop their interest through interactive communication, encourage their desire to own/use new products, and deepen their confidence in the brand through live demonstrations.

Companies should work towards building meaningful and long-term relationships with rural consumers. This will help consumers to identify and associate with the company brand and develop an emotional connect, leading to a positive brand perception. The Life Insurance Corporation introduced a village adoption scheme. Once the number of people in the village taking an LIC policy exceeded a certain percentage, LIC declared the place 'LIC Jeevan Bima Gram', and contributed INR 75,000 for the development of infrastructure facilities.

Another reason for brand stickiness is that many rural consumers are still discovering the core benefits of the product. Marketers have often observed that one brand seems to dominate a category in a particular village. This is a result of an early mover advantage. Whichever brand enters a village market first seems to gain acceptance in the community through 'word-of-mouth' communication (provided, of course, that the early users are satisfied with the core benefits). Thereafter, many prefer to 'stick' to this particular brand. A new brand then finds it difficult to gain entry into people's homes in that village.

In tractor marketing, it is not uncommon to find a 'Mahindra village' or an 'Escorts village', where most tractors in the village are from one company. The low levels of literacy and awareness limit the rural consumer's ability to understand technical benefits. They therefore tend to depend on the experience of an existing user—a progressive farmer whom they regard as knowledgeable and well-informed. If the progressive farmer is satisfied with his current brand of tractor, he recommends the same to the potential buyer. In this way, the same brand keeps getting recommended and bought in the same village. Rural consumers are averse to taking risks with something new and so expensive, and are ill-equipped to evaluate alternative brands. They feel more comfortable purchasing a tried-and-tested brand.

This phenomenon of stickiness is more visible among consumer groups of older people, who are low on literacy and exposure levels, whereas the more educated younger generation, which has considerable exposure to the media, is experimenting with new brands.

Due to the 'brand stickiness' exhibited by consumers in rural markets, the entry of new brands becomes difficult. This loyalty also varies according to product categories. Loyalty is low in low-involvement products such as toilet soaps and toothpaste, but is high in the case of *Chyawanprash*, skin creams, hair oil, and shaving creams. Brand loyalty is mostly lower in product categories where there are more product choices, and where not much brand building and brand differentiation has been attempted by companies.

Some common fakes found in rural markets.

To succeed in rural markets, companies must understand the preferences of different consumer segments rather than attempt a mass, pan-India marketing approach. Regional tea brands like Lamsa in Maharashtra and Kala Ghoda in Rajasthan are examples of successful regional brands that have flavoured their tea with spices to cater to local tastes. Such customization convinces local people that these brands care for them and creates a positive feeling towards the brand, the first step in building a strong relationship with customers. The emotional connect adds extra value to the product, resulting in regular purchase preference and creating enduring brand loyalty.

Fake Brands

Fakes are rampant in rural India, as a visit to the rural haat or marketplace, where many villagers purchase their daily needs products, would reveal. Major brands and products are facing huge problems with spurious products, for example Bond's (for Pond's) talc, Fair & Lonely (for Fair & Lovely), Likeboy (for Lifebuoy)—the list goes on.

Rural markets suffer from problems of low penetration and poor availability of branded products. Hence, although there exists a huge demand for branded products, there are no strong distribution channels to help the products reach the end consumer. This has led to the growth of spurious brands that fill this gap in the demand.

While exposure to electronic and print media has increased consumers' awareness about different brands, the lack of physical distribution has created a gap in the supply chain. This has led to the presence of spurious and me-too products in the hinterland. Pond's has been replaced with Bond's, Clinic shampoo with Clamic, and Tiger biscuits with Fighter. This has cast a shadow over the FMCG industry, resulting in the loss of business worth millions.

THE FAKES MARKET The entire range of products available in the spurious market can be divided into three distinct categories—look-alikes, spell-alikes, and duplicates.

Fake products in rural markets can be of three types—look-alikes, spell-alikes and duplicates.

- ***Look-alikes.*** Look-alikes are those products where the colour scheme on the packaging material closely resembles that of a popular brand, while the pack carries a different name. The overall appearance is similar to that of a popular brand in the same product category, for example, Shagun for Lifebuoy (150 g) and Lalita Amla for Dabur Amla.
- ***Spell-alikes.*** Spell-alikes are fakes of original brands packaged in colours and designs similar to those of the originals, but with names that are subtly and cleverly misspelt, for example, Paracute for Parachute, Fare & Lovely for Fair & Lovely, Pomes for Pond's.

| TABLE 6.6 |
Comparison of Different Categories of Fakes

Features	Duplicates	Spell-alikes	Look-alikes
Brand name	Original	Misspelt	Different
Pack appearance	Replica	Identical	Similar
Manufacturer's address	Original	Incomplete	Own name
Price	M.R.P	40% Less	10–15% Less
Margins	200–300%	100–150%	60–70%
Quality	Very poor	Poor	Reasonable
Intent	To cheat	To mislead	To freeload
Consumer mindset	Unaware	Unaware	Want cheaper products
Identify	None	Only literate	Majority
Offer	None	Discounts	Schemes

Source: MART Knowledge Centre

- ***Duplicates.*** Duplicates are exact replicas of original brands. The colour, design, and name on the package are the same as those of the original brand. All the details mentioned on the wrapper of the original brand, that is, ingredients, brand name, manufacturer's name, etc., are also present verbatim on the duplicate. Table 6.6 compares different categories of fakes on several parameters.

Brand awareness in rural India has gone up significantly because of the extended reach of television and the print media, coupled with the heavy advertising spending on the part of companies. This has created an unprecedented demand; however, genuine brands have not reached remote rural locations because of limitations in distribution reach. This has created a demand–supply gap which is being filled by manufacturers of spurious products, who pass off fakes against the demand for genuine brands.

STRATEGIES TO COUNTER FAKES While several companies have taken recourse to legal action, many have found that this strategy brings them negative publicity as well, with consumers avoiding the brand in question as it could be a fake. Even if raids are conducted and manufacturers nabbed, getting out of the problem is not difficult. Besides, the manufacturers are fly-by-night operators and can easily change the locations of their operations.

Companies have used several strategies to counter fakes. They are going in for upgraded packaging, making it difficult for manufacturers of counterfeits to copy their products. For example, Dabur replaced its plastic blow moulded container of Chyawanprash with a premium four-colour shrink sleeve packaging, which had a grainy texture and water bubbles. This packaging was difficult to replicate, and resulted in a sales growth of 12 per cent of the original product.

Some other companies have assigned the task of checking counterfeits to their sales force. For instance, Coca-Cola put in place 48 consumer response coordinators, who worked with their teams to redress consumer complaints about overcharging and spurious bottling. In addition, they had a large network of route salesmen, who had a one-to-one relationship with the retailers on their beat and hence were able to keep their ears to the ground.

However, the only sustainable strategy in the long run is to ensure deeper penetration, and continuous and regular availability of products through coverage of the markets and by forging strong relationships with local retailers. Rural marketers should also create awareness through local promotion and should highlight the harm that spurious products can cause the users (see 'Rural Marketing Insight: Dealing with Piracy').

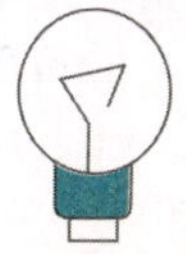

RURAL MARKETING **INSIGHT** | DEALING WITH PIRACY

The home video market in India was highly fragmented with no established market leader and rampant piracy. The 'legal' players used to price home VCDs/DVDs at a large premium and stress the quality difference between them and pirated videos. Moser Baer, the world's second largest producer of blank optical disks, charted out a strategy to combat piracy that had really not been followed anywhere. It came up with the innovative idea of adding content to its blank CDs/DVDs, and making home viewing of movies affordable for consumers. They cashed in on the fact that Indian consumers want good quality at a low price and priced their branded CDs at 80 per cent lower than those offered by established players. Aware that competitors and pirates will eventually catch up, they focused on building a strong distribution network; they took control over content by acquiring the rights to 10,000 titles in Hindi and 14 regional languages; and they tied up with regular content producers like UTV to release their productions on home videos after a certain period of theatrical release. With the plummeting of DVD prices in 2008, they created an extended offering with collections like the 'Shah Rukh Khan 6 pack', comprising six movies of the Bollywood superstar, priced at a premium and aimed at high-end customers. It also created a brand?—'Super DVD', priced in the range of INR 27 to INR 30, with three movies to cater to rural markets and take the pirates head on.

Source: 'Taking on Piracy, Profitably', *Business Today,* 19 (11) (30 May 2010): 58–60.

Packaging for Rural Markets

Packaging plays a significant role in the product offering for rural markets as it is associated with affordability, the ability to recognize (visibility, readability), convenience to users, and the appeal of the product. Packaging at the *primary level* involves protecting the product, whereas at the *secondary level*, it adds to the aesthetics and sales appeal of the product. Packaging for rural markets needs a special focus because of pro-blems like:

- Poor transport system (poor road conditions)
- Difficulties of safe storage (rats, moisture, heat, rainwater)
- Poor facilities (erratic power supply, leading to poor cold storage facilities for food products)

Therefore, the packaging of a product becomes a critical factor in its survival in rural markets. A product for rural markets should:

- Have a longer shelf life than products for urban markets
- Be able to withstand extreme weather conditions
- Be able to withstand sudden and jerky movements on dusty roads
- Have alternate storage arrangements (ice box for cold drinks)

Marketers need to consider three important factors for packaging—packaging material; pack size and convenience; and packaging aesthetics.

Packaging Material

Over the years, packaging materials have undergone a great deal of change. Tetra Pak has become ubiquitous. Traditional packaging material has been replaced by high- and low-density polyethylene films and plastics. The advantages of plastic are that it is waterproof, provides effective barriers to vaporous substances, is sunlight resistant and is lightweight. The majority of FMCG products (shampoos, tea, confectionaries, detergents, etc.) and agri-inputs (fertilizers, pesticides) now use plastic for packaging. One of the unique examples of packaging using plastic is that of Godfrey Philips, which has introduced its new Sona Bidi range and provides bundles of bidis in zip plastic pouches that protect them from being spoilt and damaged by moisture. Similarly, the introduction of Frooti in a 65-ml Tetra Pak at INR 3.50 helped Parle woo rural kids, making Frooti the bestselling beverage in a Tetra Pak. The use of Tetra Pak ensured longer shelf life even in the absence of refrigeration.

Pack Size and Convenience

A large section of rural consumers receives daily wages and, therefore, has a limited amount of money to spend. This factor influences the size of the pack preferred. One of the ways in which companies have addressed this issue of affordability in rural markets is through the introduction of small unit packs or sachets. The 'sachet revolution' was pioneered by Velvet shampoo, which introduced an INR 1 pouch of 20 ml of its shampoo in the late 1970s. With the focus on rural markets in the 1990s, a number of companies introduced sachets, leading to a boom in shampoo sales in rural areas. However, Chik shampoo, with its focus on low prices along with a small unit size, was able to transform shampoo usage in rural areas by increasing the penetration level from 13 per cent in 2000 to 32 per cent in 2005 (see 'Rural Marketing Insight: The Sachet Revolution').

This strategy of selling in smaller packs to include lower SECs was later followed by many companies. HUL introduced a 50-gram pack, priced at INR 2, of its largest selling soap brand, Lifebuoy. Coca-Cola developed small-sized bottles for tapping into rural markets. With aggressive pricing and effective communication, it was able to generate 80 per cent higher sales in 2003 in comparison to the previous year, and achieve the top position in rural markets. Similarly, Godrej introduced small pack sizes, priced at INR 4 to 5, of its three brands—Cinthol, Fair Glow, and Godrej No. 1—for the rural markets of Madhya Pradesh, Bihar, and Uttar Pradesh, where the consumption of its soaps was low. Nestlé too had come up with small packs of its Maggi noodles, Maggi Masala-ae-Magic and Maggi Rasile Chow, priced at INR 2 and INR 4, specifically targeted at rural markets. Glaxo SmithKline's (GSK) Horlicks Asha is another low-cost variant (40 per cent cheaper than Horlicks) for rural markets only. Asha tastes slightly different and is priced at INR 85 for a 500-gram pouch pack.

The success of the sachet is also attributed to the economical consumption of the product in addition to affordability. The consumer has control over the amount used at any one time (single-use packs). In the early 1990s, Rasna Industries introduced a

RURAL MARKETING **INSIGHT** | THE SACHET REVOLUTION

The success of the Velvet shampoo 'sachet' was the harbinger of a revolution in the shampoo industry, as conventional wisdom about it being an upper-class product was shattered. Realizing this potential, CavinKare entered the market way back in 1983, and grabbed the opportunity to provide the consumer with a 'good-quality shampoo with appealing perfume at a price that would delight consumers'. It launched the Chik brand in a sachet for exactly INR 1, and led the revolution known as the 'sachet revolution' in India.

Targeting the lower-middle class and rural women, the brand used innovative communication approaches. Feeling the pulse of its target audience, popular cinema dialogues were used in the advertisements, and film stars were roped in to endorse the brand. The concept of using shampoo to wash hair was new to many, and so people were apprehensive about its usage. CavinKare's team travelled extensively in rural pockets and demonstrated the product on schoolboys to make people more comfortable with the idea. At the same time, consumer schemes such as providing free sachets in exchange for four empty ones were also used. These experiments gave the brand its identity and consequent popularity.

Encouraged by the response, Chik shampoo turned national with a rural focus through innovative trade schemes and consumer offerings. By responding to consumers' needs by offering an attractive wrapping, for instance, Chik had become the second largest brand in its category by 1999. Later, the company realized that reducing its sachet price to 50 paise would convert many non-shampoo users to its use, and dramatic results were obtained as the market share increased from 6 per cent to 23 per cent after that.

'Products are made in the factory, but brands are created in the mind'. That's the mantra Chik shampoo has been chanting over the last 25 years, with excellent results. Today, with a 20 per cent share of India's INR 9.30-billion shampoo market, Chik is firmly rooted in the minds and heads of the Indian shampoo user.

Source: Compiled from the article 'Managing Rural Markets', contributed by Mr C. K. Ranganathan, CMD, CavinKare in *Praxis,* The Hindu Business Line, 4(2) (July 2003).

soft drink concentrate sachet priced at INR 5, which made six glasses (compared to the regular pack, costing INR 27.50, which made 32 glasses). This addressed the problem of cooling soft drinks in addition to the affordability factor. Several years later, Coca-Cola introduced its INR 1 single-use Sunfill pack for rural markets.

The sachet phase was followed by the coinage pack and see-through pack to grow the rural market successfully. Companies introduced soaps, cosmetics, cold drinks and toothpastes in smaller packs. Beauty soaps (Lux, Breeze), Pond's cold cream, Fair & Lovely cream, Chota Pepsi and Close-up toothpaste were made available at INR 5 in small packs. Tiger biscuits were introduced in transparent Oro packs specially designed for small outlets like *paanwalla* shops, which do not normally stock biscuits.

Convenience is another important factor in the decision to use a product. HUL launched its toothpaste in a sachet with a nozzle since it realized that the used sachet had to be folded after use, as there was no other way of closing and storing it for future use. Packs of Fair & Lovely cream also come with caps for convenience of use. Another innovation in packaging has been undertaken by Marico, which introduced its Parachute coconut oil in INR 1 plastic bottles that are easy to use at any time.

OPERATION BHARAT

HUL launched its Operation Bharat in 1997 to create awareness about its rural brands. The strategy also involved promoting the sales of its 'special packs' for rural areas. HUL provided hampers at discounted prices of INR 5, INR 10, INR 15, and INR 20, each comprising a Clinic shampoo bottle, a tube each of Pepsodent toothpaste, Fair & Lovely cream, and Pond's Dreamflower talc, in different sizes and combinations. The idea was to include a product each for hair care, dental care, skin care, and body care. Consumers were also made aware of the benefits of using HUL products and the affordability of the pack sizes on offer. The project hoped to address issues of awareness, attitudes, and habits. As consumers in rural areas became exposed to such value-added, value-for-money alternatives, it was hoped that they would continue to buy the different categories of products separately (once the scheme was withdrawn).

Packaging Aesthetics

The low literacy levels in rural India highlight the need to exercise care while making packaging decisions for rural markets. Rural consumers appreciate bright colours. Lifebuoy is identified as the red soap. Tiger biscuits have an attractive red pack with an image of a tiger. Distinct lettering, use of local languages on the pack, and images or symbols that convey the product's benefits influence consumer perception about the brand. The picture of a lightning bolt used on the Rin detergent pack is distinct, and communicates the brand benefits of whiteness easily and effectively to the illiterate consumer.

Texla drew a blank with its television sets with grey and black cabinets as rural consumers do not like dull and sober colours. These colours are more popular among urban consumers. It then introduced a new range in bright red and yellow, a wise decision that resulted in dramatically increased sales in rural markets.

The social and cultural differences in rural markets demand packaging variations for products. The significance of colours differs from region to region. This was seen in the case of ITC, which sold its Goldflake brand with a yellow cover in the south, where this colour is associated with prosperity and purity. In the north, the package colour was golden, as in this region yellow is often associated with jaundice and ill health.

The behaviour described above results from the lower levels of literacy in rural India. Consumers recognize and remember brands by colours, visuals, or numbers. This is an important behaviour trait and needs to be kept in mind while designing packaging for any rural brand.

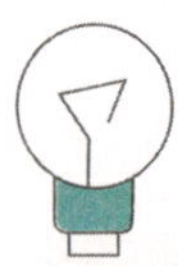

RURAL MARKETING INSIGHT | AFTER-SALES SERVICE INITIATIVES BY COMPANIES IN RURAL MARKETS

Of late, marketers have started realizing the importance of after-sales service in rural markets too. There are companies who have taken some solid steps in this direction:

Bharti Airtel: To increase its reach in rural India, Airtel, India's largest mobile service provider, created 25,000 Airtel Service Centres (ASCS) across rural India. This involved training a specific retailer in a village to handle service requirements, in addition to selling new connections and recharge coupons. Henceforth, these retailers would gain higher credibility leading to increased walk-ins, while Airtel provided a face to customer service interactions. In addition, the company set up a dedicated helpline or call centre in each circle, which acted as a real time back-up support to these ASCs.

Airtel also introduced SMS-based self-service systems in nine vernacular languages, and piloted call centres dedicated to rural consumers in Tier III and Tier IV towns with interactive voice response (IVRS) options in 16 local languages. The impact of these initiatives has been phenomenal. This localized service centre facility has not only helped Airtel to increase its penetration in rural areas, but also to create a strong brand loyalty and position among the rural folks.

Exide Battery: Exide Industries Limited is the market leader in lead acid storage battery. Exide batteries are fitted in almost all new tractors. Earlier, when the original battery of the tractor had run out, almost all the customers would fit a local-make battery supplied by the local '*Ustad*' auto electrician. As Exide dealers were located in bigger towns and did not have a local presence, they lost the opportunity to promote Exide for replacement sales. The Ustad provided round-the-clock doorstep service, and the price of his battery was also much lower.

To capitalize on this opportunity, Exide launched 'Project Kisan'. This project was a sales initiative targeting customers in rural markets, with the aim to convert users of low-cost, unbranded products into loyal customers of the company. The company introduced the 'Jai Kisan' battery to cater to the replacement market in this segment. This was a lower cost battery that would outlast the local battery, although it would not last as long as the regular brand. Exide made extensive use of kisan melas and dhabas to promote this product. The marketing division decided to price it aggressively, the rationale being that the replacement market was many times bigger than the original equipment fitment market, and hence large numbers could be sold, which would bring the costs down.

The north India regional sales team (this is where the highest population of tractors is concentrated) contacted the same Ustad and offered him the newly developed battery, along with a good margin and the added attraction of being appointed the 'authorized dealer'. In a small place, a company dealer enjoys a better status than the Ustad. In addition, Exide agreed to pay a small fee for every Exide battery the Ustad serviced at the farmers' premises. This generated extra income for the Ustad and created goodwill with the farmer.

As of 31 December 2009, the company had approximately 3,197 Kisan dealers across 14 states. The company intends to continue growing its dealer network, most notably in the under-served parts of rural India. Henceforth, it was seen that an increasing number of replacement batteries belonged to Exide brands. Project Kisan's initiative has significantly increased the penetration of the company in rural areas.

Source: Cover story, 'Bharti Airtel—Mobility for Rural Wallets', *Business Today,* (30 May 2010): 72–74; MART Knowledge Centre

::: Product Warranty and After-sales Service

When purchasing high-value durable products, rural consumers attach great value to the warranty offered on the products. The warranty cover is an effective selling plank in rural markets. For example, Polar fans offer a seven-year warranty on its products, which has helped to increase the company's rural market share.

With the increase in the usage of machinery, appliances, and equipments, there has been a continuous demand for after-sales services in rural areas. The consumer expects smooth, hassle-free maintenance and repairs at low charges, as well as the quick availability of spares and accessories at reasonable rates.

The subject of after-sales service to customers in rural markets has not been addressed seriously by most companies. The service centres of companies are generally located in towns and cities, which are not easily accessible to rural customers when the product requires attention. They usually end up getting it serviced locally, as the cost of taking the product to the service centre in a town is uneconomical.

A few tractor, motorcycle and auto component companies have started innovating service solutions in rural areas. Many tractor companies regularly organize service camps in big villages/small towns. They invite tyre, battery, fuel injection, and other component suppliers to participate. Advance notice is sent to tractor owners of the company brand with a request to come on the scheduled date for a free check-up. At the camp, company service engineers educate owners on maintenance and care of the engine, battery, etc. Spares like oil filters and engine oil are sold at discounted prices, and warranty complaints are attended to. Tractor companies have also started using mobile service vans, which move from village to village and provide door-step repairing services to tractor owners of the company's brand.

Some durables goods companies have also utilized their existing infrastructure in small towns to service rural consumers. For example, Godrej set up service centres in every small town that had a police station; Videocon focused on making its presence felt in villages and created a positive image by sending its company mechanics to villages twice a week to provide after-sales service (see 'Rural Marketing Insight: After-sales Service Initiatives by Companies in Rural Markets').

::: New Product Development in Rural Markets

Once a company has carefully segmented the market, chosen its target customer groups, identified their needs, and determined its desired market positioning, it is ready to develop and launch the appropriate new product.

Given the growing interest of companies in the rural market, developing new products suitable for the rural market has become an imperative. That is why companies like LG, Godrej, Philips, Tata, Mahindra & Mahindra, and GE are trying hard to innovate and develop products suitable to meet the requirements of rural conditions.

The new product development process involves four stages—idea generation, concept testing, product development, and market testing. Some examples of new products recently introduced in rural markets are the Pureit water purifier by Hindustan Unilever, Chotukool refrigerator by Godrej, Tata Swach water purifier and the Tata Nano car by Tata. GE is also developing low-cost ultrasound and ECG machines for India's base-of-pyramid market.

One important aspect of designing products for rural markets is the product fit with the rural lifestyle and environment. It is easier for marketers to relate the product to themselves in the urban context since they belong to urban areas and are familiar with the environment. Therefore, it is important to conceive a product idea and build a product concept in the rural environment by gaining a first-hand understanding of consumer lifestyles and behaviour patterns through consumer surveys. Companies like Dupont and Godrej have adopted the unique approach of rural immersion programmes (the concept introduced in Chapter 4), which provide a platform for new product **idea generation** through an exploration of and immersing within rural markets, thereby taking forward the product innovation agenda.

Based on this idea, once a concept is developed, it must be tested in the market. **Concept testing** in rural markets needs to be done in different regions, as needs change from area to area depending upon the characteristics of a particular region. The concept of a low-cost, dry toilet promoted by UNICEF (requiring little water) was appreciated in the water-scarce region of Rajasthan, but opposed in other regions where water availability is not a problem.

The new product development process involves four stages: idea generation, concept testing, product development and market testing.

After the concept testing, another crucial step is the final **product development**. Since the rural market is becoming the next big thing, many companies have started addressing it through a new approach vis-à-vis product development, that is, reverse innovation or frugal engineering.

A cell phone that makes phone calls and does little else (Nokia 1100); a portable refrigerator the size of a small cooler (Godrej ChotuKool); a car that sells for about INR 100,000 (Tata Nano)—these are some of the results of 'frugal engineering', a powerful and ultimately essential approach to developing products and services in emerging markets. Frugal engineering is not simply low-cost engineering or the latest take on the decades-long focus on cost cutting. Instead, frugal engineering is an overarching philosophy that enables a true 'clean sheet' approach to product development. Cost discipline is an intrinsic part of this process, but rather than simply cutting existing costs, frugal engineering seeks to avoid needless costs in the first place. It recognizes that merely removing features from existing products to sell them cheaper in rural markets is a losing game, because rural customers have unique needs that are usually not addressed by mature market products, and because the cost base of developed world products, even when stripped down, remains too high.

The central tenet behind every frugal engineering decision is maximizing value to the customer while minimizing non-essential costs. The term *frugal engineering* was coined in 2006 by Renault Chief Executive Carlos Ghosn to describe the competency of Indian engineers in developing products like Tata Motors' Nano, the pint-sized, low-cost automobile. The Nano is unlike so many other low-cost vehicles—a stripped-down version of a traditional, more expensive car design. Critical attention to low cost is always accompanied by a commitment to maximize customer value. The Tata Nano development team's decision to not include a radio in the standard model was not just a simple move to avoid cost. The team understood that the typical Nano customer places far more value on extra storage space. Using what would normally be the radio slot for storage not only avoided a major cost, but also added value for the customer.

When Tata Motors engineers began creating the Nano, they were inspired more by the three-wheeled vehicles known in India as auto-rickshaws than by any existing car models in Tata Motors' line-up. Building up from the bare minimum enabled the engineers to achieve their cost targets without compromising the essential functions of the car. The Nano uses not only just one wiper, but also just one side-view mirror, and the seats are not adjustable. Making these sorts of radical decisions is a form of innovation. Such choices are the answers to the approach of frugal engineering for emerging markets.

Market testing of any new product is the most important aspect, and it decides the failure or success of that product. It becomes critical in the rural context as the chances of failure are often high. Most companies ignore the fact that the cost of market tests is insignificant in comparison to the total project cost. Also, the product needs to be tested in different geographies as consumer responses could be different in different regions due to the socio-economic and physical characteristics of the place.

REVIEW OF OBJECTIVES

1. Understand the concept, levels, and classification of products in rural markets

The product is the most vital element in the market offering. The acceptance of a product in rural markets is determined not only by consumer needs and wants, but also by the physical and social environment. The product has to satisfy rural needs and should offer value for money. A marketer, while taking his products to rural markets, must keep in mind that the product should be appropriate for the rural environment, be simple to operate, visually identifiable, and affordable. Based on the value proposition, marketers need to think about the five levels of product offering, namely, core benefit, basic product, expected product, augmented product, and finally, potential product. Each of these levels adds more customer value. The real competition today in the rural market is at the product augmentation level. This leads marketers to look at the physical and socio-economic environment of consumers and understand their consumption pattern and the way they use the product. At the same time, rural marketers have to ensure that augmentation doesn't increase the cost significantly.

Rural products can be classified into four broad categories—FMCGs (fast moving consumer goods), consumer durables, services, and agricultural goods. Rural markets account for more than 50 per cent of the total FMCG and durables, and 100 per cent of the agricultural goods consumption in the country.

2. Discuss relevant product decisions and product strategies at different stages of the product lifecycle as applicable to rural markets

Marketers have to make product decisions at three levels—individual product decisions, product line decisions, and product mix decisions. While developing a product, it is important for a marketer to look into product attributes like quality, features, design, and style. Most often in rural areas, people set their own emotional specifications for judging the quality of a product. Rural marketers must understand these emotional cues and translate them into physical signs in their products. A marketer must carefully identify and select appropriate new features to be added to the basic product, based on the customer value versus the company cost. The design and style of a product are yet more ways of adding customer value. While designing products for rural markets, one should take into account the conditions of the product's use, its functionality, convenience of operation, and cost.

After developing products, a company needs to make appropriate product line and mix decisions for rural markets. A product line is a group of closely related products priced within a range, targeted at the same customer group and distributed through the same channel. A product mix is the set of all product lines and items offered by a company. The product mix in rural markets is generally simple. Usually only one product of a particular company registers its availability on rural shelves (often in only one or two SKUs).

A product passes through four stages in its lifecycle—introduction, growth, maturity, and decline. It has been observed that the PLC in rural markets is often longer than it is in the urban market. All the stages—of introduction, growth, maturity and decline—last for longer periods in rural markets due to the multiple challenges involved in the distribution, communication, and adoption of the product. Since rural markets are heterogeneous, the same product category may be in its maturity stage in a developed rural market segment, and in the introductory stage in the under-developed rural market segment. Thus, a rural marketer needs to develop different product strategies for different market segments.

3. Build and manage brands in rural markets

Consumers in rural markets have graduated from unbranded to branded products with the increased affordability as well as awareness in recent years. Brand association in rural areas is mainly with colours, numbers, and visuals, and not necessarily with the name of the brand. Building a brand in rural areas involves three important decisions—brand name development, creating a brand identity, and building a brand image. A brand name in the rural context facilitates easy brand recall and in drawing any colour, visual or numeric association. Many marketers use Indianized names for better association with their brands. The challenge in creating a brand identity in rural markets involves the need to relate the brand with the rural lifestyle, or with appropriate status symbols, or with the rural environment. The brand should have a personality of its own. It should emote, empathize with, and talk to its consumers. Such an ability helps facilitate a brand connect with rural audiences and contributes a great deal to brand equity and competitive advantage.

Low levels of literacy and awareness make rural people less likely to switch brands as they do not have the required knowledge or information to exercise a choice. They feel more comfortable purchasing tried and tested brands. They are therefore 'brand sticky', rather than 'brand loyal'. Another important aspect that a rural marketer must look into is the issue of fake products in rural India. This issue is largely due to the non-existence of strong distribution channels through which the products can reach the end consumer, and the gap is thus filled by fake products. Thus, the only sustainable strategy to counter fakes in rural markets is to ensure deeper penetration and continuous and regular availability of products through coverage of the markets, and by forging strong relationships with local retailers. Rural marketers should also create awareness through local promotion, and should aim at highlighting the harm the spurious products can cause.

4. Understand the role and elements of packaging products for rural markets

Packaging plays a significant role in product offering in rural markets as it is associated with the affordability, ability to recognize, convenience of use, and appeal of the product. Packaging for rural markets needs a special focus because of problems like the poor transport system, difficulties of safe storage, and poor facilities (erratic power supply leading to poor cold storage facilities for food products, for example). Marketers need to consider three important factors in packaging—packaging material; pack size and convenience; and packaging aesthetics. Over the years, a great deal of change has taken place in packaging materials. Plastics and TetraPak are the new packaging medium; low and high-density polyethylene films are used today in rural areas. The issue of affordability in rural markets is addressed by introducing small-unit packs or sachets. The success of the sachet revolution in rural markets is attributed to the economical consumption of the product, in addition to affordability. The consumer can control the amount used at any one time (single-use packs). The lower literacy levels in rural areas highlight the need to exercise care while making packaging decisions for rural markets. Rural consumers appreciate bright colours. Distinct lettering, use of local languages on the pack, and images or symbols that convey the product's benefits influence consumer perception about the brand.

5. Recognize the role and importance of after-sales service in the rural marketplace

When purchasing high-value durable products, rural consumers attach a great deal of value to the warranty offered on the products. The warranty cover is an effective selling plank in rural markets. With the increase in the usage of machinery, appliances, and equipments, there has been a continuous demand for after-sales service in rural areas too. The consumer expects smooth, hassle-free maintenance and repairs at low charges, as well as quick availability of spares and accessories at reasonable rates. A few tractor, motorcycle, auto component, and durable companies have started innovating service solutions in rural areas.

6. Describe the theme of new product development for rural consumers and outline the relevant steps for it

Given the growing interest of companies in the rural market, developing new products suitable for the rural market has become an imperative. The new product development process involves four stages, namely, (*i*) idea generation; (*ii*) concept testing; (*iii*) product development; and finally (*iv*) test marketing. Since rural markets are becoming the next big thing, many companies have also started addressing them with a new approach towards product development, that is, 'reverse innovation' or 'frugal engineering'. The central tenet behind every frugal engineering decision is maximizing value to the customer while minimizing non-essential costs. It is an overarching philosophy that enables a true 'clean sheet' approach to product development in emerging markets.

DISCUSSION AND APPLICATION

Discussion of Concepts

1. Explain the five levels of a product with examples.
2. Briefly describe various product decision strategies using relevant examples.
3. Critically analyse the issue of fake products in rural markets. What are the different strategies that a rural marketer should adopt to handle this issue?
4. What are the key elements in brand building in rural markets? Discuss.
5. Explain how packaging can make a product appealing in rural markets.

Application of Concepts

1. Imagine that you are the product development manager in a fairness cream manufacturing company. How would you augment the product and create its brand identity in rural markets?
2. Critically examine the product strategy of two regional washing soap brands, in comparison to one local (generic) brand in rural markets.
3. Identify two products each in the successful and failed categories in rural markets, and discuss the factors that contributed to their success and failure.
4. Discuss the innovation strategies adopted by any one MNC to penetrate into rural India.
5. I was flying from London to New Delhi where I met a scientist Ms. Smriti Singh. She has invented a new technology product—an engine which requires one start, and afterwards requires no energy input, and keeps on going. This engine can be put into any machine. She does not know how to make money out of it. You need to help her with the following:
   a) Is there any value proposition in such a kind of a product for rural markets?
   b) What are the possible forms in which the product can be made available?
   c) How would you market the product at each of the stages of product life cycle?
   d) What brand would you create for the product?
   e) Would packaging make a difference while marketing the product?
   f) Being a new product, how should she go about after-sales service?
   g) What is the next step that she needs to take?

RURAL MARKETING CASE | NEW PRODUCT DEVELOPMENT: IMPROVED BIOMASS STOVE BY SHELL FOUNDATION

The Shell Foundation, under its Breathing Space Programme, aimed at a significant long-term reduction in the incidence of indoor air pollution by deploying approaches that are market-oriented and commercially viable, associated with Enterprise Works Vita (EWV) and ARTI in India to develop environment-friendly, 'smokeless' cooking stoves for rural India. The two states of Karnataka and Tamil Nadu were identified as the target markets.

In collaboration with MART, a research study was conceived covering rural households for information on their knowledge, attitude, behaviour, and practices towards the biomass stoves in use, the improved biomass stoves being promoted by government agencies, and indoor air pollution. It also focused on understanding cultural and social behaviour in the kitchen environment. A technical study measuring cooking utensil sizes, stove sizes, and fuel wood was conducted to utilize them to develop a concept product. The shape and size of the cooking pot would determine the pot opening in the concept stove, while the size and shape of wood would determine the size of the mouth of the fuel space. The habit of cooking on the floor necessitated the need for an appropriate height while designing a concept stove.

The findings highlighted the fact that the black fumes blackened cooking utensils and kitchen walls, all of which have to be cleaned and maintained by the women in a household. Kerosene stoves were used whenever they needed to cook quickly. Women in Tamil Nadu cooked in open spaces outside their houses to avoid the inconveniences caused by the smoke. The mud stoves used in most homes were made in the kitchens by the women themselves, and were fixed. Terracotta stoves were available in the market for INR 50 and were portable. The Astra stoves (designed by the Indian Institute of Science (IISc), Bangalore, and promoted under a government scheme) were made by a mason in the kitchen and had a chimney. The stove was immovable and cost INR 125–150, including the mason's fee. While LPG was a much-desired stove and associated with status, it remained unaffordable for many. However, many of the households used it as a secondary stove. They were uncomfortable cooking on LPG while standing, and their cooking vessels were not appropriate either. Some of them were reluctant to use it regularly as it was not readily available.

The Big Idea

It was necessary that the new product design have the following features:

- It should be manufactured and be available commercially in the market. Quality has to be maintained.
- It should be designed in a way that ensured that households continued to use their old cooking vessels and continued to cook sitting on the floor.
- It should be able to use biomass as fuel, since that is most readily available.

Five different prototypes, three single-burner and two double-burner stoves, were designed and manufactured. The variations in the make had to do with mild steel and stainless steel. A study was conceived to test the prototypes in real situations in 110 households across both states. Feedback on cooking experiences with the stove and observations made were taken together to understand the acceptance of and intent of use for the concept.

Feedback on the features of the concept stove included:

- The height of the single-burner stove was high and inconvenient. The new stove should be at least 1–2 inches lower in height.
- The uneven size of the fuel wood used required that the fuel space be increased. This was a challenge because technically the burning chamber had to be of a height that enables all the wood to burn with maximum efficiency and allows all gases to get burnt. This had a bearing on the smoke emission from the stove.
- The pot support needed to be more stable to balance the utensils. This was important from the point of safety while cooking.

Two final stoves were developed based on this feedback, one single-burner and one double-burner. The new product reduced smoke emission by 75 per cent. The price of the single-burner stove ranged between INR 700 and 900, while the double-burner was priced at INR 1,400. The improved biomass stove was pilot launched in early 2008 and commercially launched later the same year.

The stove has also attracted the attention of semi-urban households that were using mud/terracotta stoves for everyday cooking. These had resulted in the blackening of both the kitchen and the vessels. Many of the households used to cook outdoors, in the open. The improved biomass stove has offered a solution whereby they can cook indoors, and is a great convenience during the rainy season. Thus, a product designed for rural households has also found acceptance in peri-urban households.

The Marketing Strategy

To promote the new concept, the Foundation launched a pilot project in Karnataka to raise social awareness about the dangers of smoke in the kitchen and promote simple measures to reduce smoke inside the house in 2008. The accompanying video shows how the programme called 'My Kitchen, My Pride' reached out to 112 villages in Karnataka through a combination of on-ground static and interactive activities like display of wall posters and wall paintings, mobile van campaigns, flipchart stories, interactive games, and street plays. The campaign was a part of a global effort to raise awareness about the dangers of kitchen smoke in rural India, especially villages with a population of 5,000–20,000.

The Shell Foundation has established new distribution and sales networks to reach rural homes at affordable costs. The Foundation has signed up a partnership with Envirofit International, a US not-for-profit organization to design and market a new range of improved stoves and to find commercial partners to manufacture and distribute stoves. Since unveiling its first line of clean cookstoves in May 2008, Envirofit has sold over 100,000 cookstoves in emerging markets around the world, with India as its primary focus. The objective of the programme is to sell 1,000,000 units in the next five years.

Discussion Questions

1. How did Envirofit implement its marketing plan to sell improved cookstoves in rural markets? What methods were used to create awareness and drive sales? What challenges were faced?
2. Find out details about other initiatives related to improved biomass stoves. What are the critical success factors of Envirofit stoves which differentiates it from others?

AFTER READING THIS CHAPTER, YOU WILL BE ABLE TO:

1. Discuss the fundamentals of pricing in the rural market
2. Describe the factors considered while setting the prices for rural products and services
3. Understand the various pricing strategies adopted in rural markets

seven

The price point of INR 5 has become a magic word for marketers across products. The 'paanch matlab Coca-Cola' advertising campaign featuring Aamir Khan may have become a marketing disaster, but the magic of the five-rupee price point continues to hold sway over marketers.[1]

Lower and middle-class consumers now buy packs of anything—from snacks, biscuits, chocolates, detergent bars, mobile calling cards to shaving blades—as long as it is available for five rupees. This price point allows first-time consumers to experience the category at an affordable price, and allows individual and one-time consumption. Another benefit is that of convenient coinage, which works both for consumers and retailers.

Most telecom players now offer INR 5 recharge plans. The Idea Cellular Daily Pack offers free local minutes, night calling minutes and SMS at just INR 5 per day. A multitude of brands across categories have used the magic five formula to drive trials, engage consumers, and demolish basic entry-level barriers.

However, unlike packaged foods, in personal care categories such as shampoo and skin creams, the INR 5 price point is not critical. Here, it is the 50 paise, INR 1, INR 2, and INR 3 packs that are preferred by consumers. HUL's INR 1 Clinic Plus, for example, is big at the mass end. And the INR 3 pack is important for top-end shampoos like Dove, Pantene, Head & Shoulders, etc. In creams, HUL's Fair & Lovely at INR 7 is a key price point.

The five-rupee price point has enabled companies to provide value to consumers, and make brands affordable and accessible.

Small packs are doing extremely well in the Indian market. Diverse products and brands, priced at INR 5 or below, can easily be found in the smallest of stores.

::: Pricing in Rural India

Price is the amount of money charged for a product or service. Pricing is a determinant of the market demand for the product.

Price is a major element in the marketing mix. It is defined as the exchange value of a product or service, and is the amount of money needed to acquire a product or service. Price is of fundamental importance as it is the only marketing-mix element that actually generates income. Pricing is an important strategic issue since it is related to product positioning. Further, it affects other marketing-mix elements such as product attributes, distribution channels, and promotion strategies.

The right price influences the quantities of various products or services that consumers will buy, which in turn determines the total revenues and hence the profit of the business.

In the 1980s, rural folks had low disposable income; hence, affordability was a major factor while purchasing any product. People also had a conservative approach, which made them wary of accepting a new product.

In 1983, C. K. Ranganathan started selling shampoo in a sachet with an investment of INR 15,000, and dared to take on the multinationals HUL and P&G, the unquestioned leaders in that segment. The 'sachet revolution' was a major event of this era. Most companies resorted to the low unit-price strategy, focusing on value-for-money products. All possible categories, like detergents, soaps, toothpaste, sauces, noodles, mineral water, toiletries, etc., were introduced in sachet packaging to ensure affordability of the product, and encourage the maximum number of people to try it.

Over the years, there has been a shift in rural consumers from farm to non-farm sectors, resulting in an increase in their purchasing power. Also, a series of good harvests backed by several good monsoons has boosted rural incomes in agricultural and allied activities. This is reflected in their living standards and possession of assets such as electrical gadgets and modern amenities at home.

Purchasing power in rural India is rising steadily, resulting in the growth of the rural market. Today, unlike in the past, price is not the only consideration in the purchase of a product. Also, with growing incomes, rural consumers aspire to live better, eat healthy, and have a better tomorrow. Hence, marketers have to find a way to cater to their changing aspirations, keeping in mind that rural consumers are value buyers (see 'Rural Marketing Insight: Rural Consumers Prefer Value for Money'). They expect great quality at affordable prices. The challenge for marketers is to make good quality aspirational products available to them at affordable prices.

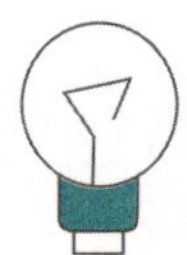

RURAL MARKETING INSIGHT | RURAL CONSUMERS PREFER VALUE FOR MONEY

Marketers often erroneously perceive price as their only weapon when targeting rural customers. In actuality, rural consumers are driven by value for money, not price alone. These consumers scrutinize products, raise real concerns, and eventually ask the marketer, 'Is your product worth buying?' If the consumers see value for money, they will buy the product. Their discerning and cautious approach does not stop them from upgrading to better products delivering higher value for money, as evidenced in the case of dish washing products and mosquito repellents. A few instances where consumers have adopted higher priced products in rural areas to get good value for money are:

1. **Dish Washing Products:** The shift to bars from local *mitti* cleaners and dish washing powder in rural India clearly indicates that rural consumers are willing to adopt higher priced products, provided that quality is superior. This is despite the fact that dish washing bars are priced at INR 50 per kg as against dish washing powders, which are priced at only INR 19 per kg. Today, the sale of bars is growing at 11 per cent annually, whereas that of cleaning powders is declining steadily (–13 per cent). This trend is reflected in the stocking pattern in rural stores, where the sales of powders is declining.
2. **Mosquito Repellents:** At 17 per cent, the rural mosquito repellent market is growing much faster than its urban counterpart, which is growing at a mere 8 per cent. Despite the fact that both vapourizers and mats require electricity, we see that the market share of liquid vapourizers is higher, and it continues to grow faster than the other available formats.

Source: FICCI Nielson Report, 2010.

High-value brands too are doing well in rural markets. Rural consumers across income segments are showing a marked propensity towards spending on premium high-quality products backed by strong brand values. For example, rural people have traditionally been '*bidi*' smokers; however, this is slowly changing, and the younger generation is shifting to cigarettes. Rural consumers are upgrading to aspirational products like face wash, deodorants, cream biscuits, and noodles.

How Do Companies Price?

For a company, it is crucial to decide how much to charge for a product. If it charges too much, the product will not sell; if the product is priced very low, the company may not be able to earn a significant revenue, and the product's market value will be diminished.

In rural markets, consumers look at the value for money. So companies have to price their products to meet consumer expectations and generate profits. Nowadays, companies also opt for target pricing in the rural segment. Target pricing involves setting a target price for the product prior to its production. For rural consumers, companies sometimes fix an ideal, affordable price, and then ensure that that price is met. A case in point is the Tata Nano, which holds the distinction of being the cheapest car on Indian roads. It is no secret that the Tatas fixed the price of the car and tweaked features and functionalities to deliver the end product at the pre-determined price point. The Nano uses just one wiper, one side-view mirror, and the seats are not adjustable.

Target pricing is a concept used throughout the product lifecycle, but is primarily used and is most effective at the product development and design stage.

GILLETTE

Gillette[2] commands about 70 per cent of the world's razor and blade sales, but it lags behind rivals in India mainly because rural consumers cannot afford to buy its flagship products. A mere 10 per cent use Gillette blades in India, against about 50 per cent worldwide. To attract and retain more consumers, Gillette has launched a new shaving system—Gillette Guard—comprising a blade and a light plastic handle at INR 15. The replaceable blades cost INR 5. P&G used target costing to develop this product particularly for rural customers. To cut costs, P&G started with a blank piece of paper for the new product, only including features that men in rural India valued and delivered benefits they were willing to pay for. Although most men in the USA and Western Europe prefer a heavy razor handle and lubrication strip, P&G found that men in rural India preferred a safe and affordable shave the most. To meet the key needs of safety and affordability, Gillette Guard was designed. The lighter handle and absence of lubrication strip ensured an efficient manufacturing process and lower product cost to meet the affordability parameter of men in rural India.

Gillette Guard was launched to provide high-quality shave at an affordable price and the feel of a premium brand for men in emerging markets.

Consumer Psychology and Pricing

A rural marketer should understand consumer psychology before setting the prices of their offerings. They need to keep the following points in mind:

- Rural consumers are very conscious of value for money. They do not always look for cheap products; instead, they want good quality for the money they spend.
- Rural consumers still do not perceive the premium value of brands. They are happy to deal with products, especially consumer durables, which offer basic functions. High-priced products

with difficult-to-handle features scare them off, which is why products with fancy features find no takers in rural India.

- Rural consumers generally compare a product's price to a reference price considered reasonable for a certain type of product. The reference price is based on either the memory of past prices, or on the price of other products on the same shelf, or the same product line. Based on the reference price, the consumer judges whether prices are too high, too low, or on target.

Setting the Price for Rural Products and Services

To set the price of any product, it is essential to understand the factors influencing price. Figure 7.1 summarizes the internal and external factors influencing rural pricing.

Internal Factors

The factors under the control of marketers are termed internal factors. Marketers are in a position to modify these factors to ensure compatibility with the external environment in order to achieve the desired results. The internal factors affecting price include cost and the pricing objectives of the company.

COST A company incurs two types of costs—fixed and variable. Fixed costs are those that do not fluctuate with changes in the production activity level or sales volume, such as rent, insurance, dues and subscriptions, equipment leases, payments on loans, depreciation, management salaries, etc.

Variable costs are those that respond directly and proportionately to changes in activity level or volume, like labour, materials, supplies, and certain utility costs. The company's total costs are a combination of fixed and variable costs. While pricing a product, a company sets a price that at least covers the total production cost of a product. In rural markets, huge resources are required for all elements of the marketing mix, and in many cases companies also need to invest in market development. In order to tap rural markets, marketers have to allocate sufficient funds under various heads, namely, packaging, setting up a number of SKUs, and promotion and distribution strategies suitable for these markets.

Promotional Cost Mass media is less effective in rural areas because television penetration is still low, and the press reach is limited. Also, rural people desire the 'touch and feel' experience before being convinced of the need to buy a particular durable that involves high costs. To bring down this promotion cost, companies make use of collective platforms like haats, melas, and mandis, places where large numbers of people turn out on their own.

Distribution Cost At the same time, extensive funds are required to establish an effective distribution system characterized by multiple intermediaries. Sometimes companies have to establish the entire distribution channel. For example, HUL has made sustained efforts to tap rural markets by investing in an innovative distribution channel (Project Shakti), and a customized promotion (Operation Bharat) and communication strategy. Such investments are viable for HUL because of the company's wide basket of goods, economies of scale due to the large market size, and the impressive dealer network at the district level.

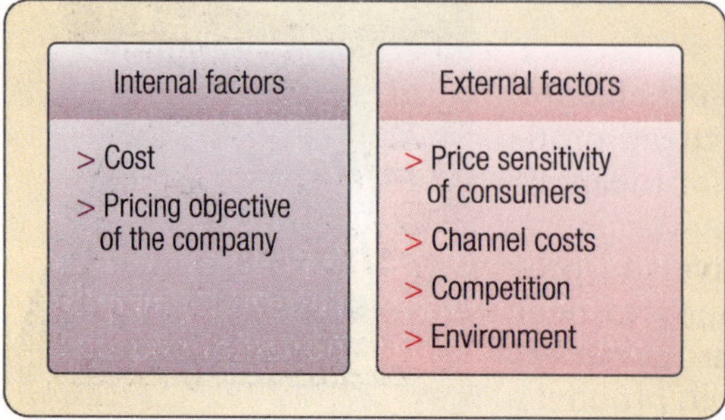

| FIG. 7.1 | Factors Considered in Setting Prices in Rural Markets

ITC has initiated an innovative model to procure farm produce for its business, which is simultaneously being used as a distribution channel to sell the products of other companies at competitive prices. At the same time, regional and local players, taking advantage of the low distribution costs and focused marketing efforts, offer their products at competitive prices. The regional media are more visible at the local level and media costs are lower, which in turn keeps the overall costs under control. Therefore, marketers have to take stock of variable and fixed costs and their impact on the pricing decision.

ITC's e-CHOUPAL

ITC has initiated an IT-based procurement system called *e*-Choupal for soya, tobacco, wheat, shrimp, and other crops. This system places computers with Internet access in rural farming villages. At harvest time, ITC offers to buy the crop at the previous day's closing price. The farmer then transports his crop to an ITC processing centre, where the crop is weighed electronically and assessed for quality. The farmer is then paid for the crop and is also given a transport fee. 'Bonus points', which are exchangeable for products that ITC sells, are given for crops of above-average quality. In this way, the e-Choupal system bypasses the government-mandated trading mandis. Farmers selling directly to ITC receive a 2.5 per cent higher price over the mandi rate. At the same time, ITC benefits from net procurement costs that are about 2.5 per cent lower (it saves the commission fee and part of the transport costs that it would otherwise have to pay to traders who serve as its buying agents at the mandi), and it has more direct control over the quality of the products it buys. The company reports that it recovers its equipment costs from an e-Choupal kiosk in the first year of operation, and that the venture as a whole is profitable. e-Choupals are also used for ordering seeds, fertilizers, and other products such as consumer goods from ITC or its partners, at prices lower than those available from village traders.

PRICING OBJECTIVES OF THE COMPANY Broadly, pricing objectives need to be compatible with the marketing strategy, including target market selection and the desired product positioning. There is usually a trade-off between the quality on offer and the price, so price is an important variable in positioning. Hence, the firm's pricing objectives must be clearly identified in order to determine the optimal pricing. The importance of pricing increases when the company focuses on price-based competition rather than on non-price-based factors such as promotion or availability. In the rural market, the level of consumer involvement with the product and the nature of competition in the particular industry play a significant role in the selection of the pricing objective.

Profit Maximization in the Long Run Companies should not expect short-term profits when entering the rural market. Initially, they should develop the market by introducing the product at a low price with low profit through penetration pricing of the product (setting the price lower than the eventual market price to attract new customers). The Tata Group launched a very low-cost water purifier, Tata Swach, in 2009 to provide affordable, safe drinking water to millions of rural households with no electricity or running water, using the ash from rice milling to filter out bacteria. It is aimed at 85 per cent Indians who do not currently filter their water. The cost of the purifier with 15 litre capacity is INR 1,200. It can filter 1500 litre of water. Its nearest competitor is the Hindustan Unilever Pureit Model with a capacity of 14 litre priced at INR 1575.

Tata Swach is a low-cost water purifier which operates without electricity and running water to meet the requirements of rural consumers.

Minimum Returns on Sales Turnover It is difficult to make instant profits in rural markets. Therefore, initially a company thinking of going rural should prepare its pricing objectives in such a way that it can recover the costs involved in distribution, production, and dealer margins.

Deeper Penetration of the Market Here, the objective is market expansion, so the company launches its product at a lower price. Britannia launched Tiger biscuits at INR 1, INR 2, and INR 4 price points, which are much lower than the price points of its other products like Glucon D and Marie Gold brands, to make it more affordable in the rural market. With the launch of Tiger biscuits, Britannia's share of the rural market increased.

Keeping Up with the Competition Firms whose objective is to meet the competition set a price to beat the leader's price. To be able to compete effectively, marketers are forced to become the lowest-cost producers, and manage with only a few channel intermediaries to minimize distribution costs.

- Due to the cut-throat competition, companies must study the pricing strategies of their competitors and try to price their products accordingly in order to maintain parity.

In the rural market, companies face major competition from regional and local brands. Due to their low production and distribution costs, regional players are able to offer lower prices and take a significant market share away from national players. Products like Ghari detergent, Wagh Bakri tea, Anchor toothpaste, Priyagold biscuits, Emami cosmetics, Parakh foods, and Maxo mosquito repellant are pegging their prices in competition with the price leader in their respective regions, and managing to attract huge business away from their competitors.

To gain a foothold in semi-urban and rural markets, several regional and some national brands enter with the objective of taking on the competition. They fight their marketing battles by selecting a particular brand—often the market leader! They then deploy their entire marketing arsenal against this selected competitor. Even the advertising and distribution strategies are designed with an eye on the company's opponent. This hurts the big companies badly.

Ujala, Fairever, Ghari, and Chik have used this strategy against their competitors Robin Blue, Fair & Lovely, Nirma, and Clinic Plus respectively.

Increasing Sales Volume and Market Share In sales maximization, the management sets an acceptable level of profitability and then tries to maximize sales. To accomplish this objective, the firm needs to not only keep its prices low, but also make investments in R&D, distribution, and other elements of the marketing mix. In other words, it must adopt a cost-intensive strategy. With large-sized rural markets, marketers are assured of the availing economies of scale. This objective fits well with product categories high on price sensitivity and at the growth stage of PLC, for example CavinKare's Chik shampoo in 50-paise sachets. Generally, it is FMCG companies that adopt this pricing objective. Britannia's Tiger biscuits and Nirma soap are also examples of products whose marketing strategy follows the objective of increasing the sales volume. This strategy allows national companies to effectively meet the low-priced competition from regional or local players.

Other objectives include social and ethical considerations, status quo objectives, and image goals. Non-profit organizations and government agencies use social and ethical objectives to cover their costs wherever possible, and to raise money for their activities. Non-profit organizations use pricing to achieve social goals. Government agencies use pricing to recoup some or all of their operating costs while delivering needed services. Status quo objectives maintain the market share by meeting competitors' prices, achieving price stability, or maintaining the public image. This is common in industries where the product is highly standardized. Prestige pricing objectives establish a relatively high price to develop and maintain an image of quality and exclusiveness. Companies usually go for a blend of pricing objectives along with other elements of the marketing strategy to ensure their success in business.

External Factors

The price elasticity of customers, channel costs, competitors, and the environment are the external factors determining pricing. Marketers have no control over these factors.

CHIK SHAMPOO

CavinKare realized that for a family of five members, at INR 2 per sachet and a minimum of four hair washes per person per month, it would mean an INR 40 expenditure on shampoo alone. Many rural families cannot afford this expense. The feedback was that if the cost of hair wash could be reduced to INR 2 per person per month, villagers would not be averse to trying a shampoo, that is, a 50-paise pack. It was a challenge for the company to develop a formula and packaging to bring down the cost so radically. When the 50-paise sachet was launched, the Chik market share grew suddenly. Out of the total sale of Chik today, 65 per cent comes from rural markets.

PRICE SENSITIVITY OF CUSTOMERS The most obvious external factors influencing price setting are the expectations of customers. When it comes to making a purchase decision, customers assess the overall 'value' of a product and then assess the price. When deciding on a price, marketers need to conduct customer research to determine what 'price points' are acceptable. Pricing beyond these price points could discourage customers from purchasing.

Price sensitivity is the consumers' awareness of what they perceive as the window of cost, within which they will buy a particular product or service.

It is imperative that marketers understand the price sensitivity of customers who form the target segment of the products they are trying to sell.

Consumers in rural markets look for 'value for money', and are reluctant to try new products or brands. They pick the brand or SKU that offers the best volume for money.

The price sensitivity of customers presents a major challenge for marketers while setting a price. It is based on various personal, social, economic, and geographical factors. Income in rural areas is not high, and is seasonal for many. This clearly indicates the limited and fluctuating purchasing power of rural consumers. Therefore, marketers need to build the pricing strategy of the company keeping in mind not only the customers' limited ability to pay, but also the modes and timing of payments that the rural consumer usually adopts.

THE SELF-MANAGED INSTALMENT SCHEME

Small towns suffer from long power cuts lasting eight to 12 hours a day. Shopkeepers in these '*kasba*' towns find it difficult to invest large sums of money to buy a generator as even the lowest-capacity Honda genset is priced at INR 20,000. Banks are not willing to give unsecured loans to small retailers. A Honda distributor in Uttar Pradesh conceived a novel scheme. He encouraged 20 shopkeepers to come together and contribute INR 1,000 each every month into a common pool. One name was drawn each month through a lottery system, and the lucky shopkeeper got his genset that month. This scheme was repeated every month till all the members of the pool had got their gensets. This easy, interest-free, self-managed instalment scheme has become quite popular.

Many regional and local players armed with such an understanding have made significant inroads in rural India; for example, Chik shampoo, by offering 50-paise sachets targeting daily and weekly wage earners, and Ghari and Fena washing soaps by offering smaller SKUs at low price points. Many national players have adopted similar strategies in rural markets. Some durable goods giants such as Samsung and LG promote their products during the harvest season, which also coincides with the marriage season. Others offer extended instalment payment facilities to push their sales during the lean period by roping in banks and private finance companies.

Rural consumers are deeply involved in the purchase of agri-inputs and wedding items. Here, price plays a role, but not at the cost of quality. A certain level of family prestige and social reputation is associated with the giving of dowry gifts (motorcycle, CTV). Marketers need to understand this psychology of rural consumers, and can set high prices for wedding items.

COCA-COLA

Coca-Cola[3] attracted rural consumers by halving the price of a 200-ml bottle to INR 5. INR 5 is a psychological price point. A price greater than INR 5 means that a consumer has to break a INR 10 note. Once he has spent INR 7–8 on something, he ends up spending the entire 10 rupee note. At the time, Coca-Cola claimed that the low price spurred sales, and that the real thought behind the 200-ml bottle was to get people in rural India used to this packaged beverage. When Coca-Cola India came up with this concept, a price war erupted, as its rival PepsiCo matched the INR 5 price. Both firms have since dropped the strategy, however, and let prices for their 200-ml sodas rise up to around INR 8, although the rivalry remains as intense as ever: PepsiCo India's beverage business grew more than 32 per cent in 2009, its highest volume growth in recent years, making it the fastest growing beverage company in the country for the second consecutive year. A price war can be an effective business strategy, but it must be managed well. It works best in fragmented markets in which consumers are price sensitive.

CHANNEL COSTS Distribution is perhaps the most difficult task in rural areas because of approximately 600,000 village locations. Marketers have to consider the compatibility of the company's target customers with a particular retail format, and their preferred mode of payment for a particular product category. For example, the retailer in a village is compelled to extend credit to his customers, while the retailer in a haat sells only on cash as his customers come from many surrounding villages. Similarly, mobile traders extend credit facilities to their regular customers.

To extend distribution, a sub-stockist may be required in the small town in addition to the existing channel. This would entail an additional margin, increasing the company's channel costs. To counter this added expense, some companies are experimenting with more direct distribution models such as mobile traders, haats, and self-help groups. Such models not only minimize the number of intermediaries and their roles, but also help in extending the reach in rural markets.

Retailers in rural markets have small sums to invest in their business, and are therefore compelled to stock brands on which they get a credit facility to set off the credit they have to offer to their customers. It is mostly regional brands that are available on credit; these also offer higher margins. Since 'credit' consumers do not have much say in the choice of brands offered, retailers do not find it difficult to push popular regional brands. To displace the regional brand on the retailer's shelf with a national brand, the sub-stockist will have to extend credit. This may in turn force the company to extend credit, which would push up the product cost.

Firms within the marketer's channels of distribution also must be considered when determining price. Distribution partners expect financial compensation for their efforts, which usually means that they will receive a percentage of the final selling price. This percentage or margin between what they pay the marketer to acquire the product and the price they charge their customers must be sufficient for the distributor to cover their costs and also earn a desired profit.

COMPETITION While setting the price of a product, the competitor costs, prices, and market offerings should be taken into consideration. Consumers in rural areas compare the price charged by one manufacturer with the price offered by competitors.

For a company entering the rural market, the competitor's pricing will influence the pricing of its products. The company with the maximum share (market leader) often creates a 'pricing standard' against which other product/service prices are compared.

If the marketer has the ability to price lower than the competition and still be profitable, he can capture a greater market share which can benefit him in the long run. In such a situation, there is a chance that the competitor would perceive that low pricing has the potential of reducing their market share or impacting their influence in the industry, and may respond with an even lower price.

Earlier, when there were few large companies, the competition was mainly from lower priced regional brands (and not so much from other national players). But lately, with the arrival of multiple national and international players in the rural market, these players are also defining competition in the majority of product categories.

ENVIRONMENT Within the environment, government policies, change in the economy, and new technology are the main factors affecting price.

Government policies provide a cost advantage to small-scale units under the priority sector (agriculture and allied activities) by providing tax benefits, subsidies on inputs, low bank interest rates, and ensuring a market for goods. Manufacturers benefit from such assistance, which in turn introduces price competitiveness in the market.

Changes in the economy, like poor monsoons and crop failures, affect the pricing of products. A poor monsoon destroys crops, which decreases the purchasing power of rural consumers. This forces companies to lower the prices of their products in rural markets, especially companies like HUL and Dabur, which earn a significant share of revenue from rural areas.

NIRMA

Nirma's[4] USP in the market is price. Nirma's strategy, directed at providing quality at an affordable price, enabled it to establish the brand in the market quickly. It started retailing its washing powder at a price significantly lower than the market rate to take on HUL's Surf. Operating in the small-scale sector, Nirma saved an enormous amount of excise duty which MNCs—including HUL—had to pay. Working to be the lowest-cost detergent manufacturer in the world, it adopted a backward-integration strategy which reduced its costs by 25 per cent. Self-sufficiency in key raw materials protects it against commodity cycles besides yielding substantial savings in raw material cost. Following the completion of backward integration, it focused on building large volumes and gaining from economies of scale. Also, till 1985 the ingredients for the detergent were simply mixed by hand, requiring neither machinery nor capital investment. The scale of the product combined with the simple non-mechanized production process enabled Nirma to gain a number of tax and excise benefits for not using electricity. Further, Nirma, being a cottage industry, was not compelled to abide by minimum wage rules and saved millions in labour costs. These cost-effective product offerings have resulted in an impressive growth in the market share of Nirma in rural India.

Nirma's USP in the rural market is good quality at an affordable price.

New technology helps to reduce the cost of the product. However, this takes time as the cost of using new technology is initially high. Subsequently, though, the price goes down.

There have been many innovative products targeting rural consumers in India over the last few years. One such product is Chotukool refrigerator from Godrej & Boyce, the world's cheapest refrigerator with a price tag of INR 3,250. This portable, top-opening unit weighs only 7.8 kg, uses high-end insulation to stay cool for hours without power, and consumes half the energy used by regular refrigerators. This is a product that has crossed several technological barriers and is designed to cross several social barriers as well. The top-opening fridge is 1.5-feet tall and 2-feet wide and has a capacity of only six litres. It has no compressor; instead, it uses a cooling chip and fan similar to the ones that keep desktop computers from overheating. It can run on battery during the power outages that are inevitable in villages.

Market leader Dish TV is working on low-cost set top boxes and cheaper monthly subscription schemes (tailor-made packages that suit rural consumers' interests) to tap the non-cable and satellite TV homes in India. The company is planning to consolidate their market share from the bottom of the pyramid in future.

Nokia 1100, one of the best-selling cell phones, has a long battery life and features targeted at the rural segment.

Nokia introduced simple handsets that became a smash hit. Nokia's 1100 model is a classic case study of a customized model at an affordable price for rural consumers. At a price of INR 690 to INR 920, the Nokia 1100 is the best-selling cell phone ever. It has a radio, alarm, and flashlight, which are of great use to rural people.

GE Healthcare has announced a global partnership with Embrace to distribute a low-cost infant warmer that looks like a small sleeping bag, and can help to keep an infant warm for hours. This product will be distributed initially in India to improve rural infant care, and as an alternative to more expensive warmers. It will cost under INR 10,000.

Videocon introduced a washing machine without a drier for around INR 2,500; Philips launched a low-cost smokeless *chulha* (stove); DCM Shriram developed a low-cost water purifier especially for rural areas.

Price Setting Strategies

One of the four major elements of the marketing mix is price. Pricing is an important strategic issue because it is related to product positioning. Furthermore, the pricing strategy affects other marketing-mix elements such as product features, channel decisions, and promotion campaigns. Depending on the company's business objectives, the influence of internal and external factors, and the stage of the product lifecycle, marketers can follow a particular pricing strategy or a bundle of pricing strategies. The different pricing strategies adopted by marketers at various stages of the product lifecycle are discussed below.

Market Entry Strategies

The pricing strategy generally adopted by companies at the entry stage of launching new products or entering new markets is skimming pricing or penetration pricing.

SKIMMING PRICING A pricing strategy wherein a company charges the highest initial price that customers will pay for a product. As the demand of the first customers is satisfied, the company lowers the price to attract another, more price-sensitive segment. For example, Procter & Gamble introduced Ariel and Tide at high prices and then later reduced them. They did this basically to create the image of a superior product.

Penetration pricing is initially setting a low price for a product in order to penetrate the market quickly and deeply. This attracts many consumers and wins a large market share.

PENETRATION PRICING A penetration-pricing strategy involves setting the prices of products relatively low compared to those of similar products in the hope that they will secure wide market acceptance, which will allow the company to raise the prices at a later date. Such a policy is often adopted when the firm expects competition from similar products within a short time, and when large-scale production and marketing will produce substantial reductions in overall costs. The low price is adopted with the aim of keeping out the competition, and it is essential that the company maintain its low-price position since the market is highly price sensitive. Production and distribution costs are expected to fall as sales volumes increase. A penetration pricing policy is appropriate when demand is elastic. For example, Anchor White and Ajanta toothpastes used penetration pricing to enter the crowded dental cream market. The marketers obtained as many customers as possible through a low price, and established a position for their product in the market.

Product Mix Pricing Strategies

The pricing strategies adopted by a product when it becomes a part of the product mix are optional pricing, captive pricing, and bundle pricing.

OPTIONAL-PRODUCT PRICING Optional-product pricing is the pricing of optional or accessory products along with the main product. This strategy helps to bring in customers who are not inclined to buy high-value products, despite having sufficient resources to make the purchase. Consumer durables giants such as LG, Samsung, Onida, and Videocon are using this pricing strategy to penetrate into villages and small towns. An example would be a company selling tractors for a lower sticker price, but charging high prices for servicing and spare parts.

CAPTIVE-PRODUCT PRICING Captive-product pricing is setting a price for products that must be used along with the main product, such as blades for a razor and film for a camera. It is the product characteristics rather than the type of market that drives this strategy. In the case of services, this strategy is called two-part pricing, where there is a fixed fee and variable usage rates. A few marketers have devised pricing strategies where they initially reduced or abolished fixed fees to rope in customers in rural markets, and later on charged prices in accordance with usage rates. For example, BSNL, the government-run telecommunication services company, offered free telephone connections to rural consumers. At the same time, ITC's e-Choupal has levied no charges for extending Internet facilities to rural consumers, but charges high rates for other transactions.

PRODUCT-BUNDLE PRICING Product-bundle pricing involves combining several products and offering the bundle at a reduced price. Companies commonly use this pricing strategy during periods of inflation. It helps to generate sales and attract consumers in a highly competitive market. It is extensively used by companies during festival and marriage seasons to sell various goods bundled together at reduced prices.

Bundle-pricing Strategy HUL launched a combo pack comprising a Clinic shampoo bottle, a tube each of Pepsodent and Fair & Lovely, and a Pond's Dreamflower talc for rural areas. They provided hampers at discounted prices of INR 5, INR 10, INR 15, and INR 20, in different sizes and combinations. The project was aimed at addressing issues of consumers' awareness, attitudes, and habits. As consumers in rural areas were exposed to and became familiar with such value-added, value-for-money alternatives, HUL hoped that they would continue to buy the different categories of products separately (once the scheme was withdrawn). Overall, the operation generated 70 per cent trials. In each case, dipstick surveys before and after the operation suggest a substantial increase in key parameters like brand awareness, trial during the operation, and repeat purchase subsequently.

In bundle pricing, several products are combined in the same package. This can be used to sell the old stock or sell those products that are not sold as a single piece.

Reliance Mobile created a revolution in India by launching a combo pack of handset and SIM card at INR 500, a very affordable price for the common man.

Vodafone has already launched its ultra low-cost bundled handsets to get a bigger share of the rural Indian market and increase its market share. Vodafone has launched the 'Magic Box', which consists of either a monochrome or a colour handset and a connection, available at INR 1,199 and INR 1,599 respectively. The Magic Box comes with some added benefits just to make the whole package attractive. It includes free talk time of INR 50 and a cheap tariff.

Price Adjustment Strategies

Basic prices are adjusted to account for various customer differences and changing situations. Companies offer various price adjustments of all types to buyers who satisfy some criteria that reduce their selling costs. The different price adjustment strategies adopted by marketers are examined below.

DISCOUNTS AND ALLOWANCE PRICING Discount and allowance pricing has the effect of reducing prices to reward customer responses—such as paying early—as well as promoting the product. As discussed earlier, rural people are price sensitive, and hence, discounts play an effective role in giving rural customers a psychological justification or rationale to purchase goods.

- ***Cash discount.*** Cash discounts are price-reduction offers to buyers who pay their bills promptly. For instance, rural consumers buying on cash would ask for a reduction in prices and retailers would agree to extend such a benefit. This practice is very common in periodic markets or feeder centres, as most transactions take place in cash. In these markets, customers usually avail quantity discounts from retailers. Therefore, marketers need to extend sufficient incentives to their channel partners to attract customers who are in a position to purchase large quantities, and on cash. See 'Rural Marketing Memo: Caution for Marketers Giving Discounts to Rural Consumers' for the risks involved in offering discounts to rural consumers.
- ***Quantity discount.*** Providing more quantity for the same price, for example, offering 125 g of toothpaste at the price of the standard 100-g pack. Many companies—such as Good Night mosquito coils—also offer the 1+1 scheme.

FREEBIES Offering a free gift with the purchase of a product has been found to be the most effective price-adjustment strategy in rural India. Marketers need to ensure the compatibility of the free gift with the core offering; for example, toothbrush with toothpaste, cup with tea, etc.

Regional and local brands have used this strategy to great advantage as they have a better understanding of their customers' needs, and also because their delivery system is geared to ensure that the free gift reaches the consumer.

With national companies, consumer schemes often do not reach the end consumers. The retailer or stockist generally does not pass on the free gift to the end consumer. As rural consumers are less educated and ill informed, they often do not demand the free gift associated with the product at the time of purchase. The poor reach of the media in rural areas adds to the problem. In many cases, the retailer replaces the

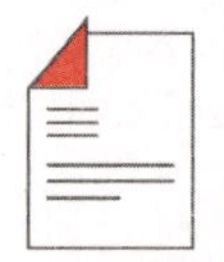

RURAL MARKETING MEMO | **CAUTION FOR MARKETERS GIVING DISCOUNTS TO RURAL CONSUMERS**

Rural consumers are very keen to buy products at discounted prices. However, marketers need to be very cautious while giving them discounts. The risks involved in giving discounts are:

- If a quantity discount is given in the case of commodities such as flour and salt, the discount strategy is often not very successful, as most people do not like to buy larger quantities of such goods even at lower prices. Many customers will tell the retailer to keep the extra quantity and instead give them the regular quantity after adjusting the price.
- A perception is created among consumers that the reduced price is the actual price of the product, and that the company had been charging a higher price earlier.
- Once a company gives a discount on a product, consumers start buying it; however, the moment the discount is withdrawn, they start exploring other brands.

promotional item with a sub-standard item, which harms the image of the company among its customers. An example would be detergent companies that give a good-quality bucket free with the purchase of their product; but what the dealer does is substitute the promotional gift with a low-quality bucket and sell the original high-quality bucket in the market.

To overcome such constraints, marketers should use the following delivery strategy while offering the free-gift scheme:

- Use the local media to announce the schemes
- Insert the gift in the main pack (if size permits)
- Print a picture of the free gift on the pack of the core product

For example, Colgate Palmolive gave a toothbrush free with a 150-gram pack of toothpaste, and inserted the toothbrush inside the pack to ensure that it reached consumers.

SPECIAL-EVENT PRICING Companies offer products at reduced prices in rural markets at certain times of the year such as the harvest season, the wedding season, and during festivals like Diwali, Pongal, and Durga Puja to draw more customers.

Hero Honda ran a van campaign before the harvest season in rural areas, took bookings against a token deposit of INR 500, and gave a watch free in return. At harvest time (which also coincides with the wedding season), customers surrendered their booking coupons to purchase bikes at discounted rates.

ECONOMY PRICING This is a no-frills low price. In this case, the non-essential features of a product are removed to keep the price low. The production cost of such products is reduced by using less sophisticated technology and emphasizing the physical strength and utility of the product.

SARVAJAL

Clean water for all is one of the country's most urgent needs, 720 million still lack access to it. Diseases such as diarrhoea, caused by water unfit for drinking, claim thousands of lives annually. Piramal Water Pvt Ltd, supplies drinking water, under the brand Sarvajal in 154 cities, towns, and villages across Rajasthan, Gujarat, Uttar Pradesh, Madhya Pradesh, Haryana, Delhi, and Maharashtra. The purified water is sold at rupees 0.33 per litre. Sarvajal was started by Ajay G. Piramal Foundation in August 2008 as a charitable initiative in the Piramals' native village of Bagar in the Jhunjhunu district of Rajasthan. To achieve scale, 154 franchisees in 2012 have been appointed across the seven states, who pay INR 50,000 as initial charges and thereafter share 40 per cent of their revenue

'No-frills' is a term used to describe any service or product for which the non-essential features have been removed to keep the price low.

with Sarvajal. Sarvajal has also installed 17 'water ATMs' (automated teller machines) in Gujarat, Rajasthan, Maharashtra, and Delhi. Customers can buy prepaid water cards and use these at the ATMs.

The real challenge for the company was to make purified potable water affordable for the people of hinterland at such a low price The water undergoes reverse osmosis and ultraviolet treatment before it is supplied. To keep the cost low Piramal Water and its franchisees do not use the ozonization process for purifying water that big companies do. The ozonization process as well as some other purification methods, along with advertising and distribution expenses, are among the reasons why big companies sell bottled water at a much higher price.

Maharaja Appliances Limited (MAL) has launched a range of no-frills home appliances, Bonus, especially for the rural and semi-urban markets. MAL realizes that the rural demand for home appliances is mushrooming. Since branded and quality products are not affordable, rural folk have to make do with sub-standard or illegal products. The difference between the price of grey products and legal branded ones is high, and so they are generally unable to buy the branded ones. Maharaja counters this by selling a sturdy Bonus Washing Machine, priced at INR 2,990. This machine does not have a drier, which is not of much use to the rural folk as they dry their clothes in the open, under the sun. Removing the drier has reduced the cost of the product.

LG Electronics has come up with products at prices that can address the rural market. Earlier they had television sets priced at INR 20,000, but today they cost INR 8,000. LG knows that rural markets operate on a price-value proposition. So they have knocked off some of the frills in their products. They want to provide features that are absolutely indispensable. For example, rural customers do not need the Golden Eye Feature, and hence their base model does not have it. Similarly, they do not require 200 channels, and so the number of channels has been reduced to 100 in their base model. This is just to bring down the cost of the product.

The government has asked banks in rural areas to give no-frills credit cards to their customers. The credit limit offered on these cards will be relatively low.

VALUE PRICING This approach is used in cases where external factors such as economic recession or increased competition forces a company to provide 'value' products and services to retain sales. For example, Godrej No. 1 soap placed their offering containing rose, sandalwood, and neem ingredients at a very economical price. Similarly, Ajanta offered its 'vegetarian' toothpaste at a low price.

PSYCHOLOGICAL PRICING The price–quality relationship refers to the idea that consumers tend to equate product quality with the price charged. Cases have been documented where retailers experienced difficulty in selling a product until they raised its price to the same level as that charged by competitive offerings. This is known as the good, old-fashioned snob appeal.

DISCRIMINATORY PRICING Discriminatory pricing is selling the same product or service at different prices. The types of discriminatory pricing are related to different sets of customers, different versions of the products, and different locations.

- ***Customer-segment pricing.*** A type of price discrimination where different sets of consumers are charged differently for the same product or service. For example, a hospital targeting the rural masses could charge lower fees for women and senior citizens. Rural retailers sell products at different prices to different consumer segments. They sell products at the MRP to people who buy on credit, whereas they will offer the same products at lower prices to people who purchase on cash to earn their goodwill.
- ***Product form pricing.*** Different versions of the product are charged at different rates. For example, in rural markets certain items like cigarettes and mosquito-repellent coils are sold loose by the piece at a higher unit price compared to the pack price.

RURAL MARKETING **SNAPSHOT** | RISING CONSUMPTION OF BRANDED PRODUCTS

Low-cost, unbranded products

Highly visible, branded products

Rural India is shifting from loose, non-branded products to well-packaged branded products. The growing affluence of the rural consumer and small pack sizes have brought about this transition.

- ***Location pricing.*** The same product is sold at different prices at different locations, although the cost of offering at each location is the same. For example, a product will cost a rural buyer differently at nearby towns, at the village retailer's and in haats. At the nearby town, the product is available at a price that is much lower than the MRP due to the high competition in the market. The village retailer charges a price very close to the MRP as the cost of distribution is higher, and there is low competition and a low sales volume. In haats, there is lot of bargaining, and so one gets the product at a cheaper price.

Rural-specific Pricing Strategies

There are some specific pricing strategies adopted by marketers in rural markets. These strategies have helped shift consumers from unbranded, loose products to branded, packaged in low-unit packs. 'Rural Marketing Snapshot: Rising Consumption of Branded Products' showcases how the increased affordability of branded products has changed the face of rural shelves.

LOW PRICE POINTS As the majority of the rural people are daily wage earners, they never have sufficient money on any given day to invest in large SKUs, as they have to purchase a variety of daily-need items with their limited earnings. Therefore, companies need to introduce low-point price packs so that their product is included in the daily basket of purchases of the wage earner. The advantages of low price packs are:

- It helps to penetrate markets that one would otherwise not have penetrated due to the high price tag of larger packs.
- As these low price packs are small in size, they also help to maintain the freshness of what is on offer. Instead of opening a large pack where the freshness of the contents can be compromised, opening smaller packs keeps things factory fresh.
- Small packs offer 'variety' options. Take for example biscuits. Instead of getting stuck with just one type of biscuit that costs INR 25, small packs of INR 5 will give the consumer the ability to buy five different variants of biscuits.

Chik Shampoo was the trendsetter in the sachet market many years ago, when it introduced shampoo sachets at INR 1 to penetrate the rural market. This gave the company an edge, and the low price point helped in better market penetration. Other fast-moving consumer goods (FMCG) players like HUL, Godrej, and Dabur have also tried this route for different products, at different price points. Today, HUL sells the maximum number of its products (ranging from shampoo to hair oil) in sachet packs in rural areas.

Low price points in India continue to be magical in providing affordability and accessibility across a wide variety of foods. Small packs help to attract new users into a category.

Bharat Petroleum has introduced 5-kg 'mini' gas cylinders, priced at INR 100, to reduce the initial deposits and refill costs for rural consumers. Targeted at the fixed, low monthly income group, the oil company has entered the kitchens of rural folks, persuading them to move to a cleaner LPG fuel from kerosene and wooden chulahs.

Several companies are offering products at low-unit price points to increase their sales volume and for deeper market penetration.

- Godrej is selling its Expert hair colour and Nupur henna at INR 5 and INR 10 price points. It has recently introduced three brands of Cinthol, Fair Glow, and Godrej in 50-gram packs, priced at INR 4–5, meant specifically for Madhya Pradesh, Bihar, and Uttar Pradesh.
- Nestlé has introduced Nestea, its pre-mixed iced tea, in refill packs of INR 2 and INR 10. It is also promoting Maggi noodles at INR 4 and Maggi seasoning at INR 2 for low-income group consumers, beginning with Mumbai's Dharavi slum.
- CavinKare sells Nyle and Chik shampoos in 50 paise and INR 1 packs.
- HUL's Pepsodent toothpaste is available in a sachet for INR 4.
- Dabur has rolled out Hajmola in 50 paise packets and Amla hair oil in INR 1 sachets.
- PEPSICO'S snack foods arm, Frito-Lay, has launched its Kurkure brand in packs of INR 3 and INR 5.
- Britannia Industries recently introduced Good Day and Cream Treat biscuits in INR 5 packs.
- Cadbury has launched an INR 2 version of its flagship brand Cadbury Dairy Milk, called CDM Shots. A few other candy and chocolate brands are priced at INR 2 per unit.
- Premium brands like Taj Mahal tea are also available in paise packs in rural areas, with a sub-brand, 'Janata Blend', printed below the brand name of the pack.
- Tata DoCoMo, Airtel, and Vodafone have hopped on to INR 5 bandwagon with recharge options at that price point.
- GlaxoSmithKline is rolling out Asha—a milk food drink from Horlicks for rural consumers in Andhra Pradesh.
- Coca-Cola has begun selling a powder-based beverage called Vitingo at INR 2 per sachet across villages in Orissa; and PepsiCo has announced that the company is working on a beverage or snack priced between INR 1 and INR 5 for people suffering from malnutrition and deficiencies.
- Emami Group is launching low-unit packs of Zandu Balm at INR 2.

LOW-COST PACKAGING The cost of a product can be brought down by using low-cost packaging materials that are durable and aesthetic. The packaging need not be very sophisticated as rural people may not be willing to pay higher prices for fancy external appearances. Since they are more interested in the sturdiness and utility of the product, simple packaging can be adopted. A good example is of Britannia's Tiger biscuit, which is doing good business in rural markets because of its small affordable packaging especially designed for rural consumers.

REFILLABLE/REUSABLE PACKS Products are made available in refill packs so that marketers can add value pricing to it. Products like edible oils, health drinks, and coffee are available in refill packs.

Reusable packs are those where empties can be used for some purpose. An ideal example is the packing of fertilizers. Companies have started packing fertilizers in low-density / high-density polyethylene (LDPE/HDPE) sacks, which are not only tamper proof, but also reusable. These can be used later as sturdy shopping bags by stitching handles on to them. The Shell brand of lubrication oil has introduced a 10-litre pack in an attractive, high-quality reusable container for truck owners who need 6.5 litre of engine oil at a time. Asian Paints has also introduced emulsion in 10-litre and 20-litre reusable bucket packs.

HIGHLIGHT VALUE, NOT PRICE Although the rural consumer is price sensitive, he is willing to pay more if he sees value in a product. Hero Honda motorcycles are popular in rural areas as the company highlights features such as more mileage, lower maintenance costs, and higher resale value for the vehicle.

COINAGE PRICING The coinage pricing strategy is mostly used in rural markets for FMCG brands. For the convenience of retailers and consumers, companies adopt this kind of pricing in order to avoid the problems caused by a shortage of change. Prices are set at a coin value. Coinage price is directly proportionate to the package size. These packs are small in size and are normally meant for one-time consumption (shampoo sachet), or a day's consumption (tea bag), or a week's consumption (bathing or washing soap). Coinage pricing has been found to be easy to communicate to consumers. For example, Coca-Cola has effectively used the communicated price point (INR 5) of their small bottle to attract new segments. Some of the brands that HUL sells for INR 5 are Pepsodent, Pond's Dreamflower, Pond's Cold Cream, Rin, Taaza, Fair & Lovely, Clinic Plus, and Lux.

PRODUCT-SHARING SERVICES Many rural consumers cannot afford high-value products even if they need them. Enterprising customers cooperate to purchase the product, and then share the benefits with each other. Companies have themselves developed another alternative to this problem of affordability by setting up ventures for shared services of their products.

A good example of this is the HPCL Rasoi Ghar model. A community kitchen is set up in smaller villages where women come and cook. The local Panchayat contributes a room (10 ×10 or bigger) for the kitchen; HPCL contributes cooking stoves, LPG cylinders, utensils, a cooking counter, and water connection. One SHG member is appointed the caretaker. Women bring raw materials and take cooked food home. They pay INR 2 per half hour of gas usage. The caretaker collects the money, which is used to order refill cylinders, and she keeps the premises clean. Her monthly stipend is also paid out of this collection. The model is self-sustaining and scalable. Non-users (the BOP segment) experience the advantages of a clean, convenient, safe, and healthy LPG without having to buy a connection. Once they are satisfied, many decide to buy individual connections. It is a win-win model for all. Poor women get to cook food under clean, convenient, and safe conditions, HPCL gets new consumers as and when these women decide to buy their own connections, and the panchayat gets a good name in the community.

::: REVIEW OF OBJECTIVES

1. Introduce and discuss the fundamentals of pricing in rural markets

Price is a critical element in the marketing mix. It is the exchange value of a product. Pricing is a determinant of the market demand for the product.

Purchasing power in rural India is steadily rising, and has resulted in the growth of the rural market. Today, price is not the only consideration as it was a few years ago, when price played a major role in purchasing. Also, with growing incomes, rural consumers are becoming aspirational. Expensive brands too are doing well in the rural markets. Rural consumers across income segments are showing a marked propensity towards spending on premium high-quality products, which are backed by strong brand values. Companies in rural markets should sell products at affordable prices that still generate profits as consumers look for value for money. Nowadays companies also go in for target costing in rural markets.

2. Examine the factors considered while setting the prices for rural products and services

While setting the price of a product, a company needs to consider several factors that have been discussed under two heads—internal and external factors. Pricing decisions are influenced significantly by internal and external factors. Marketers have sufficient control over internal factors. The internal factors affecting price include cost and the pricing objectives of companies. The external factors affecting price are the price sensitivity of customers, channel costs, competition, and the environment.

In short, marketers need to have an understanding of the internal and external factors in order to determine the optimal pricing strategy in accordance with customers' tastes and preferences, and other entities in the value chain.

3. Understand the various pricing strategies adopted in rural markets

Different pricing strategies are adopted by marketers at various stages of the product lifecycle—market entry strategies, product mix strategies, and price adjustment strategies. The pricing strategy adopted by companies at the entry stage for launching new products or entering new markets is skimming pricing or penetration pricing. The pricing strategies adopted by a product when it becomes a part of the product mix are optional pricing, captive pricing, and bundle pricing. Companies offer various price adjustments of all types to buyers. Price adjustment strategies are discounts and allowances, freebies, special event pricing, economy pricing, value pricing, psychological pricing, and discriminatory pricing.

Commonly used pricing strategies in rural markets are low price points, low packaging cost, refill packs/reusable packs, coinage pricing, and product-sharing services.

DISCUSSION AND APPLICATION

Discussion of Concepts

1. Explain the fundamentals of pricing in the rural context.
2. What is target pricing? Explain by giving examples of a few companies who have done target pricing of their products for the rural market.
3. Discuss the internal and external factors considered while setting the price of a product.
4. What is the difference between skimming and penetration pricing strategy?
5. Elaborate on the pricing strategies specific to the rural market.

Application of Concepts

1. Devise the pricing strategy of a consumer durable company planning to enter rural areas.
2. Analyse the pricing strategy of a national, regional, and local player in any FMCG category of your choice, and also identify the impact of industry and product characteristics on the pricing strategy.

RURAL MARKETING **CASE** | COCA-COLA'S STRATEGY FOR RURAL MARKETS

Coca-Cola India adopted an innovative two-pronged approach in 2002 to gain a foothold in rural markets. It devised an innovative pricing strategy to attract price-sensitive rural consumers, which was backed by the rural-centric '*thanda matlab* Coca-Cola' marketing campaign featuring the Bollywood star, Aamir Khan.

Adopting an aggressive pricing strategy, the company reduced the price of a 200-ml bottle by half to INR 5—a psychological price point which worked in favour of the brand. A higher price than this means a consumer has to shell out a 10-rupee note which they tend to spend entirely, already having spent INR 7–8 on the bottle of Coca-Cola. This is why most rural consumers refrained from buying a cold drink in the past. Coinage pricing (at INR 5) addresses this psychological barrier. The use of the Hindi word *thanda*—meaning cold— in the marketing slogan clearly established that Coca-Cola was actively wooing the rural consumer. The combination of clever pricing and astute marketing worked to Coca-Cola's advantage in rural markets.

The accompanying video shows how Coca-Cola used its pricing strategy effectively to gain impressive growth in rural markets. It also describes how the products were distributed in remote rural markets to meet the consumer demand generated through the campaign. The low price spurred sales and the 200-ml bottle created a new market by driving adoption of packaged beverages in rural India.

Discussion Questions

1. What were the critical success factors for Coca-Cola in rural markets? How did the competition respond to this strategy?
2. Identify two major brands which adopted a similar pricing strategy to crack rural markets.

AFTER READING THIS CHAPTER, YOU WILL BE ABLE TO:

1. Understand the challenges and dilemmas in rural distribution
2. Describe the channels of distribution
3. Understand the rural retail environment
4. Explain channel behaviour in rural areas
5. Identify the prevalent distribution models of different product categories
6. Describe innovations in rural distribution and rural-centric distribution models
7. Discuss the logistics challenges in rural India

CHAPTER 8 ::: DISTRIBUTION IN RURAL MARKETS

eight

Moser Baer, currently the world's second largest producer of blank optical disks, took on piracy by adding content to its blank CDs/DVDs to make home viewing profitable. Its key challenge was diversifying into branded home video—an impulse purchase with customers displaying no brand loyalty. It used the technology and pricing in blank disks to create low-price, high-quality products that revolutionized the industry from a high-margin, low-volume one to a low-margin, high-volume one. The first to implement successful FMCG tactics in this industry, it formed relationships with content providers across regions/languages to establish a network, and leveraged technical capabilities in manufacturing to radically reduce the cost. Additionally, it adopted a low-cost FMCG-type distribution model, complete with regional offices, sales teams, and a right mix of FMCG and entertainment trade distributors, and activated cycle carts in cities. It partnered with regular content producers like UTV to release their productions on home videos after a certain period had elapsed post theatrical release. It created an extended offering with collections priced at a premium and aimed at high-end customers. The Super DVD brand priced at INR 27–30 with three movies caters to rural markets and counters piracy head on. The average cost of a movie VCD/DVD has come down from INR125/250 to INR 25/50 respectively. Even the share of home entertainment to the film industry's revenues has gone up from eight per cent to 20 per cent. It is now moving into new content generation, with plans to produce content specifically for DVDs in direct-to-home educational and devotional categories. Moser Baer's home entertainment business now accounts for 10 per cent of group revenues of INR 234.4 billion.[1] It has become a household brand with 50,000 sales outlets and over 400 distributors.

Moser Baer adopted an FMCG-type distribution model to take on piracy and reach rural consumers.

Availability: The Challenge and the Dilemma

Generating awareness about products yields dividends only when steps are taken to ensure constant availability, particularly in rural India, where availability determines volume and market share because the consumer, influenced largely by the retailer, purchases what is available at the outlet.

The physical distribution of products continues to pose an immense challenge to marketers because reaching 7.8 million retail outlets spread across 600,000 villages and feeding a retail network of village shops is a distribution nightmare. With the rising aspirations and incomes of rural consumers, companies have to get the distribution in place to tap the deep rural markets.

Despite the growing number of consuming-class households and increasing disposable income, small and remote villages (85 per cent of the total villages house a population of less than 2,000) largely remain untapped as it is economically not viable to reach these villages. Even the largest player in rural markets (HUL) reaches only 100,000 villages (each with a population exceeding 2,000) directly through various channels.

The rural market now offers a big attraction to marketers. However, it is not possible to transplant urban strategies to rural markets because the urban strategy of deep and intensive retailing and continuous customer-pull generation through advertising and promotion cannot work in rural markets. The main problems in rural distribution are:

- Large number of small markets
- Dispersed population and trade
- Poor road connectivity to smaller villages (lack of all-weather roads as well as adequate transport facilities)
- Multiple tiers (a large number of intermediaries), leading to higher distribution costs
- Poor availability of suitable dealers
- Low density of shops per village and high variation in their concentration
- Inadequate bank and credit facilities to rural retailer, leading to poor viability of retail outlets
- Poor storage system, leading to inadequate stocking of products
- Highly credit-driven market and low investment capacity of retailers
- Poor visibility of product on rural shelves
- Poor communication of offers and schemes due to the poor reach of the media
- Inadequate power supply (for example, a lack of refrigeration leading to spoilage)

Reaching rural consumers economically across 600,000 villages is the single biggest challenge in rural marketing.

Most organizations have leveraged traditional wholesale models to get their products across rural shelves. However, with the increasing consumer pull in rural markets with exposure to the media, more and more retailers want a full assortment of products, not a limited range; regular frequency of service and convenience of door delivery; credit to fund their cash flow needs; promotions, fair prices, merchandising, and activation support for their shoppers. In many ways, they want an urban model of servicing, and not compromised servicing just because they are in rural areas.

The challenge for suppliers is the small size of each village with low throughput per outlet, coupled with the high cost of distribution since these villages are some distance away from the distributors. These factors make high quality distribution unviable.

According to a recent study done by the Nielsen Company, acceptability among consumers has grown twice as much as availability in rural India, as shown in Fig. 8.1. On the one hand, dealer off-take has grown rapidly due to consumer pull; on the other, however, companies have been unable to fulfil their demand because of poor distribution growth and portfolio expansion as they are struggling to address distribution challenges.

To address the availability challenge, some major players like HUL, ITC, Colgate, Coca-Cola, and Bharti Telecom have ventured into rural markets with innovative distribution approaches, which have yielded reasonable success.

To understand and address the problems, one needs to understand where rural consumers buy, what retail behaviour is, and the logistic management and stocking

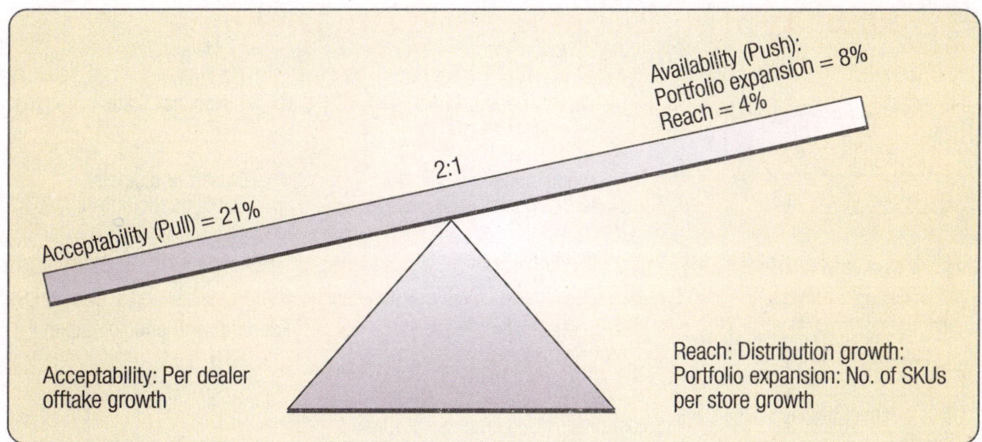

| FIG. **8.1** |
The Acceptability Versus Availability Dilemma
Source: Nielsen Consumer 360 India 2010, presented in New Delhi, 24 November 2010.

pattern of retailers. Marketers also need to sensitize themselves to the rural retailer's economic capabilities, his education level, and physical environment.

::: Distribution Channels

In this section, we discuss how distribution channels evolved in rural markets. We also examine the key channels members and channel dynamics.

The Evolution of Rural Distribution Channels

Distribution is the most important variable in the marketing plans of most consumer goods manufacturers in the country, because managing such a massive sales and distribution network is a huge task. It is estimated that there are over 18 million market intermediaries—wholesalers, stockists, transporters, and retailers—involved in the distribution of a variety of consumer goods all over the country. Marketers use this network to access more than 5,000 cities and towns, and over half a million villages.

The distribution network in India is characterized by a predominance of family-owned proprietary concerns. Although urban areas have a range of distribution outlets, from large supermarkets and superstores to the smaller neighbourhood retail stores, villages have only small shops that are part of the local supply network.

Traditional channels have several advantages for marketers as they perform the basic marketing task efficiently because of their experience, specialization, knowledge of local conditions, contacts, and scale. In fact, they offer services that manufacturers could hardly come up with on their own. Also, being family-owned outfits, they enjoy a huge cost advantage in terms of low operations costs and lower overheads.

There are five layers of distribution channels (as shown in Fig. 8.2) used by all major companies for the movement of a product from the company depot to the interior village markets.

Most companies have direct representation up to level 3 in the form of redistribution stockists. High outlet density and a large consumer base ensure economies of scale in servicing these markets through regular workings of sales-cum-distribution vans. However, large FMCG majors like HUL, Dabur, Colgate, and ITC are extending their reach to levels 4 and 5 in feeder towns and villages as the next growth is coming from these markets, using conventional as well as innovative low-cost distribution channels.

To achieve sustainable growth in rural markets, marketers need to maximize the direct reach of stocks from level 3 to 5 and fuel retail activation till the last mile. Entering level 4 requires market planning for small towns (also referred to as feeder towns as they serve as the feeder points for rural consumers) based on their market potential, and the catchment population in rural areas dependent on these towns. The last mile distribution (level 5) is the most crucial as well as the most challenging link, where existing

| FIG. **8.2** |
Rural Distribution Channels

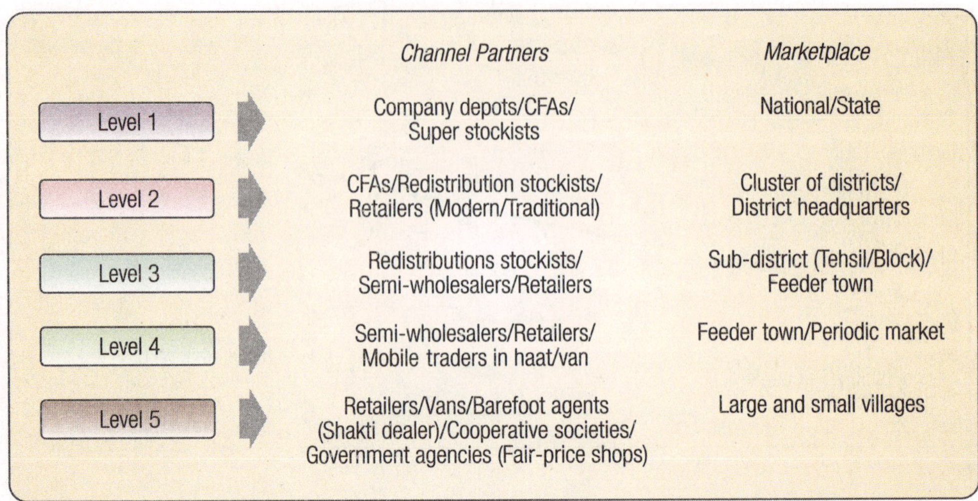

distribution models fail to provide an economically sustainable distribution of products to villages. However, at the same time these villages form the bulk of consumption in rural areas. Only a few players like HUL, ITC, and Colgate have been able to reach this level directly, using out-of-the-box and innovative distribution channels.

Channel Dynamics

Channels play a pivotal role in marketing by performing a number of vital distribution functions. Firms mostly rely on their marketing channels to generate customer satisfaction and achieve differentiation over competition.

Although branded majors may fare better in the more brand-conscious urban markets, it is the small-town markets with smaller populations that are worrying marketers. Today, most of the growth is seen in the lesser penetrated semi-urban and rural markets. Rising consumerism with rapidly rising incomes and urban exposure has shown that the rural markets will determine future consumption growth for marketers, as market penetration in urban areas reaches saturation levels. Lower penetration levels for most product categories in these markets offer a great opportunity to nurture future growth. (Rural penetration levels are still very low for soft drinks—10 per cent, candies—14 per cent, and skin creams—25 per cent.)

Under the current circumstances, the major area of concern for companies is making their products available in the remotest of the 600,000 villages. This does not come easily and companies are incurring huge costs to make their products available in 7.8 million rural outlets. Designing a cost-effective distribution model capable of meeting the growing demand from the rural market is a challenge for any company. For effective reach in rural markets, players operating in different product categories use appropriate channels, as depicted in Table 8.1.

Channels of distribution have the maximum channel partners in FMCG distribution, and the minimum in the case of the distribution of a durable product due to differences in place and frequency of purchase.

Rural Channel Members

A marketing channel performs the work of moving goods from producers and sellers to the consumers. It overcomes the time, place, and possession gaps that separate products and services from those who need or want them. The conventional distribution channel members servicing rural markets primarily include four participants: carrying and forwarding agents (CFAs), redistribution stockists, wholesalers, and retailers.

CFAs CFAs are the first link with the company depot for supplying products to channel members, generally engaged by FMCG and consumer goods companies to

| TABLE 8.1 |
Channels of Distribution for Major Product Categories

FMCG	Durables	PDS - Government	Fake Goods	Cement	Bulbs and Tubes
Company manufacturing plant	Company manufacturing plant	FCI	Manufacturers	Company manufacturing plant	Company manufacturing plant
Company depot			Wholesalers (City)		Depots
CFAs	CFAs	Zonal offices	Wholesalers (Small town)	CFAs	
Redistribution stockists		District office		Distributors	Distributors
Sub-stockists		Depot			
Retail outlets	Exclusive dealers/Dealers	Fair price shop	Retailer (Village, haat, mobile trader)	Outlets	Exclusive dealers/ retail outlets
Consumer	Consumer	Consumer	Consumer	Consumer	Consumer

supplement their own depot. They usually cater to one region or state, depending on the stock handled. They are of two types: one with investment, investing in stocks and transporting it to the next level, and the other without investment (also known as the forwarding agent), acting as the transporter for the company. The majority of CFAs fall in the second category, providing godown space for stock-keeping and supplying stocks to redistribution stockists in larger cities and district centres servicing urban and rural markets. The orders are booked by company representatives and passed on to the CFA for execution.

The conventional distribution channel members servicing rural markets primarily include CFAs, redistribution stockists, wholesalers, and retailers.

REDISTRIBUTION STOCKISTS Redistribution stockists are the critical link between a company and its rural channels as they are responsible for supplying stocks to both the rural and the urban retail networks. They generally cover about 30 per cent of rural retailers and are located at district headquarters. Unlike CFAs, they are the first customers for the company, investing in stock and employing a sales force to cover rural and urban retailers as per the permanent journey plan (PJP).

Some companies with large product portfolios like HUL also have separate stockists, termed rural distributors, for covering rural markets.

WHOLESALERS Wholesalers, one of the oldest channel members servicing rural markets, continue to control half the rural supplies and consumption in the absence of the direct reach of companies to rural retailers.

More than 70 per cent of the rural market is still beyond the reach of direct distribution. In rural areas, there is seldom a clear-cut distinction between wholesalers and retailers. Particularly in the feeder markets, all retailers act as wholesalers and vice versa, because small retailers from surrounding villages buy from these retailers.

The Indian wholesaler is principally a *galla kirana* (foodgrain merchant) who strongly believes that business is speculative rather than distributive in character. He is a trader rather than a distributor, and therefore tends to support a brand during a boom and withdraws support during a slump. Within a distribution channel, their behaviour is similar to that of a retailer as they also receive the stocks from a stockist and sell it to the small rural retailers from surrounding villages who come to feeder towns to replenish their stocks.

The Indian market has largely been a seller's market. In spite of the wholesaler's importance as the most critical rural interface for distribution, marketers have not felt the need for their activation and integration as a formal channel member. Companies have focused more on retailers in urban areas, who are numerous. This has resulted in the consolidation of retail-based distribution and a deterioration of wholesale-based distribution.

Rural markets were neglected by many. The low density of rural retail outlets forced companies to depend heavily on wholesalers, who exploited the companies on account of their ability to take products to the smallest of rural retailers. This resulted in trade malpractices, such as undercutting and distribution of fakes in the channel.

The need of the hour is to activate and develop wholesalers of adjoining markets (small towns and large villages) as distributors of products to rural retail outlets and build their loyalties to companies.

RETAILERS They are the last link in the distribution chain and the first interface for rural consumers. They mostly procure stocks from wholesales in nearby feeder towns, and in a few cases supplies reach them from stockists through van supplies.

In addition to regular retailers with permanent shops, there is another set of retailers comprising mobile traders. These traders do not have a fixed shop or place of selling, and go from door to door. Traders selling in haats also fall under this category of retailers. We discuss this in more detail in the following section.

::: The Rural Retail Environment

The rural retail environment primarily comprises traditional mom-and-pop stores and a few modern retail stores that have emerged in recent years in some pockets of the rural markets. In this section, we will cover these two retail systems in detail.

Traditional Retail

With the spread of consumers across various population categories, marketers face the problem of accessing these markets. Apart from ensuring the reach of their products to retail outlets, marketers also need to motivate retailers to stock their product or brand. An RMAI study on 'Rural Retailing in India 2008' reveals that retail infrastructure improves as we move from smaller to larger villages.

It is an easy proposition to distribute a truckload of soaps in an urban market covering a small geographical area. However, to sell the same truckload in a rural market, one has to cover hundreds of small and large villages, which increases the distribution and promotion costs.

Table 8.2 depicts the spread of rural retail across villages in India. A close examination of the data shows that 54 per cent of the rural population resides in the 100,000-odd large villages (population exceeding 2,000). These villages are connected by all-weather roads and they account for 60 per cent of rural wealth. At the other end are 390,000 small villages (population less than 1,000), which have hardly any shops. HUL, Eveready, ITC, and other companies that have the most deeply penetrated rural distribution system just cover the retail network in the larger villages (with population exceeding 2,000).

| TABLE **8.2** |
Spread of Rural Retail

Village Population	Percentage of Total Villages	Percentage of Population	Percentage of Retail Outlets	Number of Outlets Per Village
> 5,000	3	22	14	28
2,001–5,000	14	32	32	16
1,001–2,000	22	25	33	9
< 1,000	61	21	21	2
Total	**100**	**100**	**100**	**6**

Represents 17% of villages, 54% of rural population and 60% of rural wealth

Hardly any shops in 60% small villages

Source: Census of India 2001, and 'Rural Retailing in India 2008', Rural Marketing Association of India.

A close examination of Table 8.2 reveals that the number of retail outlets increases as we move from smaller to larger villages. However, their proportion corresponding to population is highest among the 1,000–2,000 population villages. These players may look at expanding their retail coverage in the 1,000–2,000 population villages, which account for one-fourth of the population and have 33 per cent retail outlets. The importance of direct coverage of village outlets cannot be overlooked, as daily need products —like 70 per cent of groceries and toiletries—are bought here as per the RMAI study.

For distribution purposes, most durables companies define *rural* as any location with a population of less than 50,000. The RMAI study mentioned earlier found that 80 per cent of durables and 70 per cent of clothes and footwear are purchased from small towns in the 20,000 to 1,00,000 population, numbering 1,900.

National players need to ensure distribution reach to these small town locations for effective coverage of rural areas. Below the 20,000 population level, the returns diminish and it becomes uneconomical as distribution moves to still smaller towns. The key dilemma for MNCs eager to tap the large and fast-growing rural market is to determine whether they can do so without hurting the company's profit margins.

THE RURAL RETAIL SPREAD Rural retailing in India accounts for INR 1.9 trillion, with about 7.8 million retail shops (R. K. Swamy BBDO Market Media Guide 2010) out of 18.5 million retail shops in India. The number of retail outlets in rural areas has more than doubled in the last decade (3.5 million in 2002, according to ORG). Rural retail is growing rapidly and is projected to dominate the retail industry landscape in India by 2012, with a total market share of above 50 per cent. However, the logistics of feeding the small retail outlets spread over 600,000 villages is a daunting task indeed. The high distribution costs due to geographical spread and low volumes per outlet act as a deterrent to the entry of products in rural markets. However, to build volume companies need to invest in distribution infrastructure. They should consider this expense an investment because rural markets need to be viewed from a long-term perspective rather than from one of short-term gain.

The number of rural retail outlets has more than doubled in the last decade, from 3.5 million in 2002 to 7.8 million in 2010. Today, more than 40 per cent of retail outlets are present in rural areas.

As per the RMAI Rural Retail Report[2] mentioned earlier, the average monthly turnover of rural outlets is INR 12,000, which is INR 7,000 more than the average turnover reported in 1990 (Rural Market Probe, IMRB). Also, an average annual increase of 5 per cent in turnover was reported by retailers. This change has led to an increase in the variety and range of products stocked. However, the range and variety is still very limited in medium and small villages. Moreover, since a significant portion of the sale is on credit, it puts most village shops in a self-limiting sales cycle. A recent study, 'Haats as Marketing Hubs' by RMAI[3] also confirms the fact that despite the same products being available in the village shop, 60 per cent of villagers prefer to buy these from a haat because of the lower price, better choice, and wide range of products available at one place.

Given the limited availability of stocks and variety in village outlets, companies would need to appoint distributors up to the 10,000–20,000 population Class IV towns (taking the total supply of locations to more than 2,000). Many of the channel partners in these feeder towns already have a supply network covering around 150 outlets in 40–50 locations. In this way, these distributors can cover most of the larger 2,000+ population villages, numbering around 100,000.

Marketers also need to design cost-effective systems of distribution to ensure that products reach rural markets, and to build volumes.

RETAIL PREMISES As shown in Fig. 8.3, with rising rural incomes and consumption, the rural marketplace is also changing fast in terms of shop size, category of outlet, and product categories, and brands stocked. The average size of rural outlets has increased to 140 sq. ft, with the maximum growth witnessed among medium and large-sized shops in the last decade, as shown in Table 8.3. Also, two-thirds of the shops in rural areas have permanent structures today, as reported in the RMAI study.

The shops in small towns are located on rented premises and make use of electricity, while only a few shops in feeder villages have this facility. Normally, rural shops are

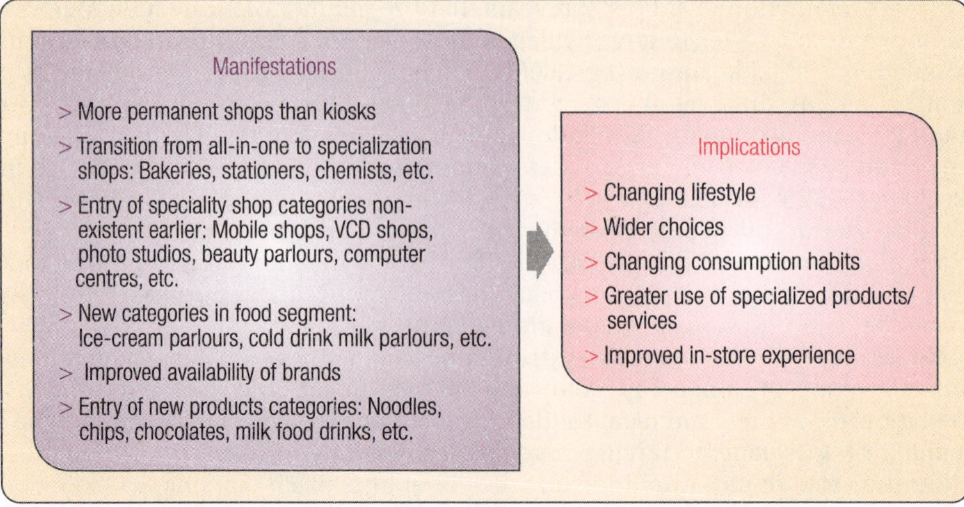

| FIG. **8.3** |
The Rural Marketplace
Source: MART Knowledge Centre

| TABLE **8.3** |
Rural Shop Size

Size (in sq. ft)	Year	
	1999–2000	2008
Up to 100	71	53
101–250	25	37
> 250	4	10

Source: A. C. Nielsen Shop Census 1999/2000; RMAI 2008

an extension of the house in which the family resides. In interior villages, retailing is part-time activity due to fewer customers, unlike the case of a town retailer.

A village shopkeeper generally operates under a number of infrastructural (lack of sufficient space, inadequate power supply, no proper storage system) and financial constraints (inadequate credit and bank facilities). However, with the emergence of microfinance institutions and improving physical infrastructure, as discussed in Chapter 2, the face of rural retail is improving. Some companies like Coca-Cola India are also offering rural-specific, non-electricity based cooling solutions—like ice boxes—to address infrastructural bottlenecks.

COCA-COLA INDIA

Coca-Cola's first India foray faltered because of insufficient attention to refrigeration—a critical criterion in the purchase of a cold drink. In rural markets, refrigeration is even more important as both electricity and refrigerators continue to be scarce in rural India. Upon its return to India in 1993, Coca-Cola India overhauled its supply chain and ramped up its route-to-market strategy to win over rural consumers. Greater focus on refrigeration was a key component of this new strategy. In electricity-deficient areas, such as some of the hinterland in Uttar Pradesh, it now provides shops with brine coolers so products can stay chilled for up to 12 hours without electricity. In other places, it has trade agreements with local ice makers to address this bottleneck. These strategies have enabled Coca-Cola to tap the hard-to-reach rural consumers. In 2009, its sales grew by over 30 per cent[4] and it reported a profit for the first time since 1993.

| TABLE **8.4** |
Rural Shop Categories

Type of Shop	Shops (in per cent)
Chemists	4
General stores	13
Grocery stores	62
Paan plus	21
Total	**100**

Source: Nielsen MAT 2009, Presentation by Partha Rakshit at RMAI workshop, 20–21 January 2010

The maintenance cost of retail outlets in interior villages is low, with most of the cost spent on travelling and transportation. This suggests that the retailer in the interior village would prefer a product or brand that can be delivered to the outlet, or one that can compensate the travelling or transportation costs.

THE RURAL RETAIL SHELF With changing consumption habits and rising demand for new products and services, the profile of rural outlets and stocks on rural shelves are changing rapidly. Earlier, rural markets used to have shops stocking groceries and tobacco products. Over the last decade, new shop categories like general stores and chemists' shops have emerged in rural areas, as evident from Table 8.4. In addition, existing shop categories like paan shops have diversified into more product categories, like confectionaries and toiletries. See 'Rural Marketing Snapshot: The Changing Face of Rural Retail'.

The grocery and paan plus shops are present in all categories of villages and primarily sell consumer products like soap, washing powder, biscuits, and tobacco products. However, the emergence of specialized stores, like general stores dealing in cosmetics, stationery, and electrical goods, and chemists has been visible more in villages

RURAL MARKETING **SNAPSHOT** | THE CHANGING FACE OF RURAL RETAIL

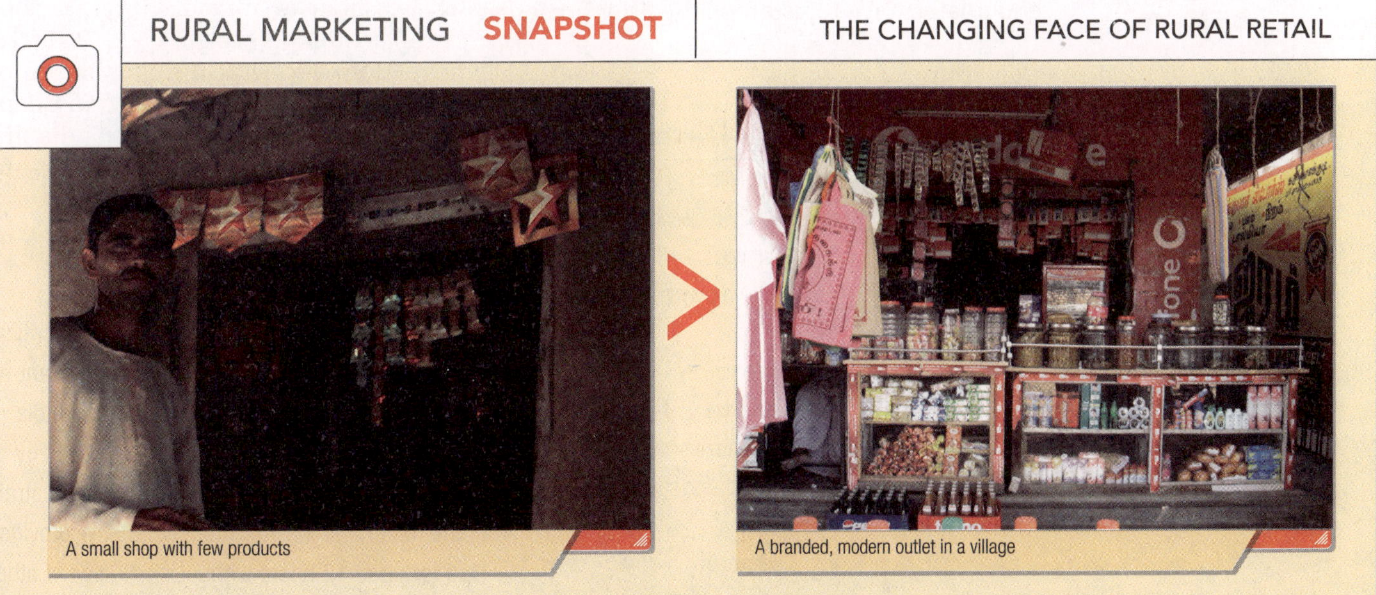

A small shop with few products

A branded, modern outlet in a village

The rural retail landscape has changed rapidly from small kiosks selling loose and unbranded products to modern retail outlets stocking national brands in various product categories. This offers opportunity to marketers to occupy the rural retail shelf space.

| TABLE **8.5** |
Product Categories Stocked

Product Category	Shops (in per cent)
Food articles	75
Tobacco products	69
Cosmetics/toiletries	68
Groceries	53
Stationery	39
Electricals	31
Fruits and vegetables	14
Clothes/Footwear	6
Construction material	4
Agri-inputs	4
Durables	3
Kitchen appliances	2

Source: RMAI Rural Retail Report, 2008

close to highways, or in very large feeder villages. In addition, shops stocking garments and footwear, construction material and agricultural inputs are also registering their presence in the rural marketplace, as shown in Table 8.5. As consumer durables and jewellery are bought once in a while on special occasions like weddings, festivals, or after the harvest, rural consumers prefer to buy these from a nearby town or city, as the bigger shops offer a wider variety and a better choice of products.

New and urban-oriented products like shampoos, ready-to-eat snacks, and chocolates have registered a healthy presence on rural shelves in recent years.

Table 8.6 lists the products available on rural retail shelves across the product categories mentioned in Table 8.5, showing the easy availability of toiletries, food products like packaged biscuits, tea and confectionaries. It is interesting to note that today, relatively new and urban-oriented products like shampoos, ready-to-eat snacks, and chocolates have registered a healthy presence on rural shelves.

| TABLE **8.6** |
Rural Retail Penetration

Product Stocked	Penetration (in per cent)
Cigarettes	62
Packaged biscuits	58
Shampoos	56
Washing powder	55
Tea	52
Confectionary	48
Toilet soap	47
Blades/razors	46
Ready-to-eat snacks	45
Toothpaste	44
Chocolates	40
Pens	34

Source: RMAI Rural Retail Report, 2008

On an average, the number of product categories stocked by rural and urban stores does not vary significantly (19 versus 27). But what does vary is the number of companies/brands (42 versus 92). This difference in stocking patterns is because of the poor reach and difficulty in servicing rural stores. The number of brands per product category decreases as we move deeper towards smaller villages.

The first task is making brands available. However, marketers simultaneously need to make efforts to ensure their visibility on rural retail shelves. Products are stocked in a cluttered and disorganized way. Slow-moving products, covered with dust accumulated over a period of time, are a common sight. The visibility of brands is very poor due to the absence of proper racks and display boxes and stands. Brands advantageous to the retailer's business are displayed prominently. Therefore, marketers need to devise strategies to occupy rural retail shelf space by providing display and storage systems (wall-mounted display strips for fairness creams and ice boxes and vizi-coolers for soft drinks).

STOCK TURNOVER As per a MART study on rural distribution (2004), the average value of stocks per product category in the interior villages is about a third of that in feeder villages. The average value of stocks of all packaged goods in the interior villages[5] is about a fourth of that in the feeder villages. The monthly off-take of packaged products is similar in interior and feeder villages; however, there is a variation in composition. The off-take of packaged foodstuffs and tobacco products is higher in interior villages, whereas toiletries have a higher off-take in feeder villages in comparison to other products. Some retail outlets in feeder villages with a high turnover are acting as semi-wholesalers.

The cash outlay for the rural retail outlet is extremely low, coupled with the fact that the retailer only purchases the fast-moving and high margin commodities. The low off-take, less stocks, and lower stock turnover ratio poses challenges for a marketer of a new product looking to occupy retail shelf space. The marketer has to ensure that their product and brand is on that shelf, otherwise competitors' brands will be occupying the shelf instead. This would require a combination of margin, credit, and servicing that is superior to that of the competition.

RURAL RETAIL HABITS With improving connectivity, increasing brand awareness, and rising rural aspirations, rural retail habits are also changing fast.

As per the RMAI retail study[6] 2008, the tendency to shop from the nearby town or city is high among consumers residing within a 25-km periphery, or in villages close to the highway. Seventy per cent of groceries, toiletries, and other daily need products are bought from villages, whereas 80 per cent of durables and 70 per cent of clothes/footwear are purchased from the nearby towns and cities. Therefore, marketers need to ensure product availability at the right places to generate rural sales.

ITC's Choupal Saagar, Aadhaar, and Tata Kisan Sansar are the key players in modern retail in rural India.

The Emergence of Modern Retail in Rural Areas

An overwhelming proportion of the INR 15-trillion Indian retail market is unorganized. In fact, the share of organized retail is very low (merely 5 per cent) at present. Approximately, only 10,000 out of 600,000 villages in India have access to organized retail services. Given the size and diversity—geographical, cultural and socio-economic—there is no role model for Indian retailers to follow or adapt in their attempts to expand into rural markets. In such conditions, marketers have largely taken the agri-input and agri-output routes, through initiatives like ITC's Choupal Saagar, Aadhaar, and Tata Kisan Sansar to serve end consumers in rural markets.

ITC became the first organized player in rural retail space by launching the country's first rural mall, 'Choupal Saagar', and offering a diverse product range, from FMCGs to electronic appliances to automobiles, attempting to provide farmers with a one-stop destination for all of their needs. We discuss the following major initiatives in this section:

- ITC Choupal Saagar
- DSCL Hariyali Kisaan Bazaar
- Tata Kisan Sansar
- Godrej Aadhaar
- 3A Bazaar

Each initiative uses a different business model to reach out to the target group.

ITC CHOUPAL SAAGAR ITC's Choupal Saagar was the first rural mall in India to offer multiple services under one roof. It opened in 2004 and stands on an 8-acre plot with a shopping area of 7,000 sq. ft. It offers a self-service facility, with attractive merchandise displayed on open shelves. The mall is located near the stock points of ITC's e-Choupals, making it an integrated model. Choupal Saagar acts as a marketing hub by supplementing the farmgate presence of e-Choupal (since most Choupal Saagar outlets are positioned within tractorable distance of 30 e-Choupal centres and their user communities). It offered a place where farmers could bypass intermediaries and sell directly to the parent company, serving as the core infrastructure to support ITC's rural distribution strategy. Farmers can come and sell their produce here, thereby providing themselves with cash, which they can spend to purchase products. The footfall is between 400–450 on an average per day, and 900 during the season. It is targeting customers using consumer goods, as well as those using agriculture products.

Product and Service Offerings The product mix at Choupal Saagar covers a wide range of categories, including apparel and footwear, toys, games and music, and horticulture products, fertilizers and pesticides, and motor pumps. Farmers can buy food items, groceries, white goods, toiletries, and almost everything they need for the family, including automobiles, watches, mobile phones, garments, footwear, and stationery items, all belonging to leading national brands. The highest product sale is usually consumer and agricultural products, with the ratio being 2:1.

This landmark infrastructure, which has set new benchmarks for rural consumers, also incorporates farmer facilitation centres, with services such as sourcing, training, soil testing, health clinic, cafeteria, product quality certification banking and investment services, fuel station, etc. The company is also marketing a new range of clothing and shoes for rural customers. In addition, ITC agri-sourcing centres also provide farmers a transparent, best-price sales window at Choupal Saagar.

Customer Profile The customer profile consists of farmers (mostly with medium and large landholdings), villagers (shop-owners, service-class people, and others, all with a family income of more than INR 10,000), and semi-urban consumers (family income more than INR 10,000). The customers generally come here from a distance of 8–10 km. As ITC malls are located just outside the city and close to the highway, semi-urban customers usually visit this mall, because of which the consumer goods product sale is high. If the malls had been closer to villages and farmers, the sale of agriculture products would have been high compared to consumer goods.

Some strategies used to attract customers are: neighbourhood walks, posters, hoardings, pamphlets and wall paintings, melas, LPG from BPCL provided to village houses.

Expansion At present, there are 24 outlets of Choupal Saagar in Madhya Pradesh, Uttar Pradesh, and Maharashtra. ITC planned to expand to 700 outlets by 2013. To complete the supply chain, ITC planned to set up 140 retail stores called Choupal Fresh in 54 towns across the country to sell fresh fruits and vegetables by 2009. The first Choupal Fresh store opened in Hyderabad in August 2006, and in 2007 there were four stores operating in Hyderabad and Pune.

Hariyali Kisaan Bazaar, the largest rural retail chain in India, caters primarily to the household and agricultural needs of shoppers.

DSCL HARIYALI KISAAN BAZAAR Based on its experience in the sugar and seed business, DCM Shriram Consolidated Limited (DSCL) set up Hariyali Kisaan Bazaar (HKB), a rural business initiative, in 2002. The aim was to create a long-term relationship with farmers through 'all-under-one-roof' retailing and direct sourcing of quality farm produce, thereby increasing rural incomes through improvement in agricultural practices. HKB emerged as India's largest rural retail chain in terms of the product categories stocked and the volume of business, targeted at farmers, however, HKB is not operational now. It evolved as a hub and spoke format model, depending on the market potential of the location.

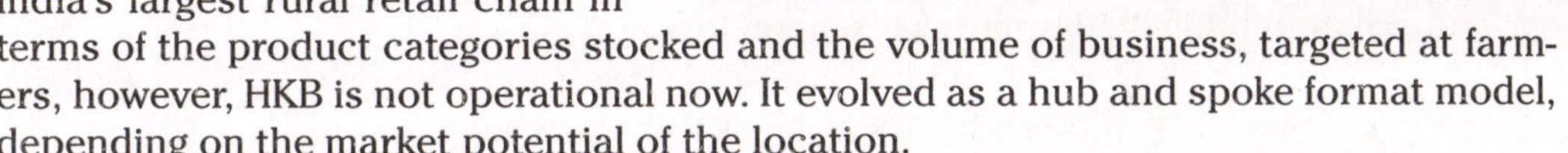

- The hub format comprises large centres located in large rural agglomerations or on highways spread over a 4-acre campus containing banking services, a fuel station and recreation areas, encompassing agri-services, one-stop retail shop, and sourcing.
- The spoke format essentially comprises small convenience stores in 4,000–5,000 sq. ft areas located in small towns, encompassing agri-services and retail of select categories.

Products and Service Offerings The range of goods and services at HKB included retailing of consumer products, agri-inputs, fuel, financial services, agri-advisory services, and output linkages.

Hariyali Kisaan Bazaar offered 50 per cent agricultural products along with 50 per cent consumer goods (FMCGs, households and durables, food items, grocery and apparel, personal care items). Among agricultural products, it stocked multi-brand agri-inputs (seeds, fertilizers, pesticides, etc.), farm implements, veterinary products, and irrigation items. Agriculture products were sold more as compared to consumer products. The HKB is envisioned as an instrumental link in the retail value chain, able to supply large urban retailers with fresh fruits, vegetables and grains procured directly from the farming communities with which DSCL had built relationships. Generally, an HKB outlet stocked around 400 categories and 5,000 SKUs of agri and non-agri products.

The average year-on-year growth for the average outlet from year one to year two was 40 per cent, and from the second year on, 25 per cent. DSCL estimated revenues of INR 50 million per year from each outlet once it had been running for two to three years.

Customer Profile and In-store Experience Most of the customers were farmers from nearby villages and service-class people and shop owners. Customers from a catchment area of 15–30 km visited the centre. The average footfall ranged from 800 to 900. The racks were a key feature, allowing farmers to touch, feel, and examine the products before making a choice, in contrast to the over-the-counter format of competing mom-and-pop shops. Products on the shelves were all clearly labelled in Hindi and English with price tags, another novelty. According to one HKB outlet manager, the transparent pricing of products gave farmers a sense of trust. Each centre had four to five agronomists who give farmers free advice on how to increase productivity.

Some strategies used to attract customers were banners, pamphlets, neighbourhood walks by the agronomists for the farmers, posters, and word-of-mouth publicity. Customer service employees involved themselves in the neighbourhood walks and made the customers aware of the consumer goods, thereby promoting sales.

Expansion DSCL had its presence primarily in the states of Rajasthan, Uttar Pradesh, Haryana, Punjab, Uttaranchal, and Madhya Pradesh. DSCL had the largest rural retail network with more than 300 outlets throughout northern India.

Tie-ups The cellular phone manufacturer, Motorola had struck a deal with DSCL for the sales and distribution of its medium and low-end handsets through HKB outlets. In its effort to provide more services to farmers (besides quality agri-inputs, financial services, farm output services, fuels, FMCGs, consumer goods, durables, apparels), the company tied up with Bharat Petroleum and opened 13 petrol pumps on its various store premises. HKB also partnered with ICICI Bank, which provided services such as agricultural credit, life insurance, and general insurance.

TATA KISAN SANSAR Tata Kisan Sansar (TKS) is an initiative of Tata Chemicals, which has had a long association with farmers through its supply of high quality agri-inputs. In 1998, the company started Tata Kisan Kendra (renamed TKS in 2002); however, realizing the need of the hour, it moved its proposition from a 'one-stop agri-input shop' to a 'one-stop farmer solution shop', with the clear objective of empowering farmers through offering an entire range of agri services, including quality agri-inputs.

The TKS is a network of nearly 600 farmer resource centres catering to more than 3.5 million farmers in 22,000 villages in the northern and eastern parts of India, in the states of Punjab, Haryana, and Uttar Pradesh. In terms of numbers, this is the largest network providing agricultural services to farmers. The centres are one-stop solution shops that provide farmers with access to a wide range of agricultural inputs, such as vital fertilizers, seeds, and pesticides, pulses, cattle feed, and farm implements, along with agricultural services such as soil testing and crop advisory services.

In order to support the activities of TKS (which are basically franchisee outlets), the supply chain model that evolved is a hub-and-spoke model.

- The hub acts as a resource centre to cater to the needs of the TKS outlets in the vicinity.
- Each resource centre supports primarily 20–25 TKS franchisee outlets within a radius of 50–60 km, whereas each TKS centre caters to 30–40 villages covering approximately 13 million acres overall.

New services being explored include financial services and IT-enabled market information. In the fertilizers segment, TKS, through Tata Chemicals, offers the services of agri-inputs and service solutions focused on improving farm income.

Tata Kisan Sansar has recently expanded its basket of products to include lifestyle items like Sonata watches, Tata Indicom telecom services, and Tata BP solar power products.

GODREJ AADHAAR Godrej Aadhaar is a joint venture between The Future Group and Godrej Agrovet, started with a vision to emerge as a complete solution provider to Indian farmers. Aadhaar is positioned as a rural supermarket.

Product and Services Offerings Aadhaar offers consumer durables, food and grocery, apparel, footwear, etc., thus catering to every requirement of the rural household. In addition, it provides farm advisory services, a supply of agri-inputs and animal feeds, financial services, the latest information on weather, price, soil, and water testing facility.

Expansion Plans At present there are 66 Aadhaar outlets across the country. They reach out to 50,000 farmers every month, catering to 2,000 villages across the states of Punjab, Haryana, Maharashtra, and Gujarat. The rural retail initiative of Godrej Agrovet Ltd is planning to set up at least 1,000 stores across rural India in the next five years. The new format Aadhaars provide a very conducive retail atmosphere and a women-friendly interface. Aadhaar's objective is to improve productivity, ensure higher returns, and provide an improved cost-benefit ratio.

Tie-ups Aadhaar has tied up with Eicher Motors to provide commercial vehicles and HDFC Bank for delivering financial services to rural consumers. The company is in discussions with Apollo Hospitals to set up pharmacies/polyclinics at the large format stores, as well as with BPCL for launching petro-outlets in semi-urban and rural areas.

3A BAZAAR 3A Bazaar is the first mobile retailing initiative launched by a leading export house in north India. The initiative aims to uplift and empower rural India by enhancing the reach of information and quality products. 3A Bazaar is a unique strategy aimed at providing the first chain of rural retailing in India through mobile vans.

3A Bazaar is in operation only in the villages of J. P. Nagar in Uttar Pradesh. It visits 700-odd villages in the district. In its first phase, the company began its operations with five mobile vans in J. P. Nagar. Each van operates in villages with populations less than 10,000 people.

Every day, each van is stuffed with 1,300 items worth between INR 200,000–250,000, ranging from groceries to FMCGs, cosmetics, garments, and stationery, covers three to five villages. Each van is visited by 150–200 customers. The daily sales are between INR15,000 to 20,000 per van. The company targets lower-middle class customers, whose family incomes are around INR 10,000 per month,

3A Bazaar helps consumers to buy authentic and quality products at cheaper prices from their own doorsteps. From the consumer's point of view, it enhances their savings by minimizing their transit costs, which is a regular expenditure while purchasing the basic necessary products. It makes life convenient for consumers who have to travel 20–30 km and spend INR 30–40 on travel to buy petty products.

As far as marketers are concerned, 3A Bazaar helps these companies to reach the interior villages, where consumers have access to communications media, but not the products.

The company plans to add another 20 vans and set up fixed stores in the near future. 3A Bazaar is also working towards rural development by educating consumers in, and exposing them to, new and genuine products.

::: Channel Behaviour in Rural Areas

The retailer is a crucial link in reaching rural consumers, and hence it is necessary to examine the rural retailer's behaviour and its impact on marketing strategies. The dimensions of channel behaviour examined here include:

Rural channel behaviour entails understanding sourcing and stocking behaviour, credit behaviour, pricing by channel, relevance of trade promotion schemes, and the role of the retailer as influence.

- Sourcing of stocks and purchase cycle
- Stocking behaviour and seasonality
- Credit pattern
- Transfer of capital
- Pricing by the channel
- Channel promotion
- Retailer–consumer dynamics

Sourcing of Stocks and Purchase Cycles

For the retailer, the wholesaler is the most important source of information as well as stocks. The wholesaler is also the most important influence on the retailer. Retailers in interior areas are not serviced by agents of distributors; they go to nearby towns/large feeder villages once or twice a month to buy their stock. Retailers in feeder villages purchase items like cosmetics, toiletries, detergents, and packaged foodstuff from agents of distributors, who visit their shops at regular intervals and deliver these items.

What is the retailer's purchasing cycle? In high-turnover feeder villages, rural shopkeepers visit the neighbouring urban wholesale market as often as three to four times a week for their purchases. In other areas, where rural shopkeepers depend only on counter sales and not on wholesale sales, they may buy once a week or a fortnight. In the case of brands which they buy from the company salesman, they may buy once a month or even only when the company salesman visits. In such cases, when the stocks run out for one brand, they may substitute it with another brand or product. Rural retailers prefer to make their purchases on their terms or for better margins. In other cases, they like to go from wholesaler to wholesaler and buy from the one who gives them the best terms. For grains and other produce, they often depend on the regular mandis held for these items.

It is worthwhile to find out from the larger retailers—whose frequency of purchasing is high—which towns they buy their stocks from, and guide the retailer to buy from the company's stockist in that town, briefing the stockist to give him good service. Alternatively, if the retailer has his own preference for a particular wholesaler, this wholesaler could be provided with extra benefits—such as additional stocks under deals/schemes—on the understanding that this benefit will be passed on to the rural retailer.

This means that the marketer would do well to motivate the wholesaler to get the retailer in the rural market to stock his company's products, particularly the newer products. This is the approach followed by Nirma.

Stocking Behaviour and Seasonality

There is a definite seasonal pattern in the stockholding of retail trade. This is probably because the main buying season for consumers is during the harvest, and so the retail stocking also follows this pattern. Retailer investment goes up by three to four times during the harvest, and the retailer tends to stock a large variety of consumer novelty items like toiletries, cosmetics, ribbons, bangles, clothes, footwear, etc., during this period. The stocking of novelties and consumer items is followed by the stocking of fertilizers and seeds. This is probably because after the harvest is over, the rural consumer starts buying the requirements for the next crop. Shortly thereafter, consumer purchases taper off as consumers settle down to the planting of the next crop, and retailers in turn curtail the inventories in their retail shop.

Also, rural retailers usually stock a particular item because the consumers demand it, and to a lesser extent because of the wholesaler's push or because a competitor stocks the item too.

This implies that the marketer has to direct his efforts to promoting the brand both to the consumer and to the wholesaler, keeping the seasonality factor in mind. This supports the inference based on the observation of the rural consumer's loyalty to both the brand and the retailer. Motivating dealers to promote the brand requires restricting their numbers. Limiting the number of dealers prevents undercutting and improves their margin.

HAFTA VASOOL_WHOLESALE ACTIVATION

Dabur has a line of seasonal products which has specific trade uplifts. Dabur did a year-long activation which kept the trade flowing as per the consumption demand. The objectives behind this was shrinking space for competitive brands, make programme result oriented, ensure bulk buying by the retailers, and redesign programme to make it sustainable.

In the initial formative stage, the retail incentive programme was built with high decibel activity structure with branded van announcing Hafta Vasool arrival to ensure retailers visit to the wholesale markets. Head on visibility at entry in the market, having bannering to maximize the contact with retailers and drive them to explore the offers from the brand. Phase two of Hafta Vasool took a fresh approach to study its results of past two years' execution. It ensued intelligent data mining and applying strong analytics to drive pattern to get desired reach and results .

The trends clearly reflected the pattern to arrive on ideal buying cycle, preferred bundle offers, best schemes and gifts and database to target retailers stocking Dabur products for participation. From activity calendar to offers to prioritization of wholesaler shops in Mandi everything was based on analytics. A leaner model of one promoter was followed. The rural retailer procured stocks on weekly basis from the nearest feeder towns. Retailers came to wholesale markets with a pre-decided list of products. Apt planning backed by strong analytics incentive programme helped them prioritize Dabur products within the retailers limited purchase budget.

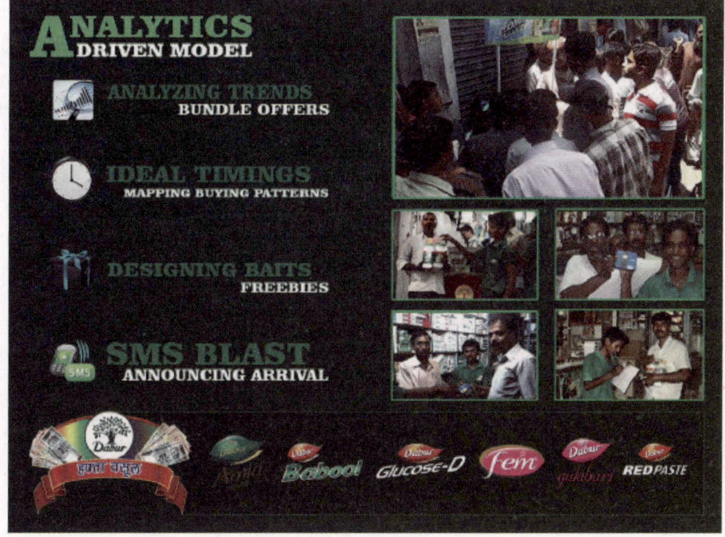

These retailers also have a huge influence on their neighbourhood's rural consumers and thus delivering the programme successfully with respect to brand availability and ensuring retailer's push to shelve the products. In order to reach out to maximum audience, they employed various tools to amplify the activity. Pre-event information blasts were sent through SMS. Also SMS blast during the activity was done to highlight the mega prize winners. It resulted in wholesale activities across 140 cities in 7 states; 60,000 SKUs were picked up by wholesalers and 10 lakh by rural and urban retailers.

Credit Patterns

The credit offered by retailers to consumers differs from area to area. In some villages and districts, credit sales account for as much as 60 per cent to 70 per cent of the total business, while in others it is only 15 to 20 per cent. The reasons for this variation are as yet unclear. Consumers normally have a running credit with part of the outstanding amount being paid off every month and settled only at the time of harvest. In other cases, the bulk of the outstanding amount is settled only at the time of the harvest. The outstanding amount is settled in cash or (very often) in kind, that is, with the produce of the land. At this time, when retailers have a lot of liquid cash, promotions aimed at them could be mounted to stock up the retailer and create pressure on him to push the products on the consumers. Credit is extended mostly on essential commodities such as rice, wheat, and cooking oil, but not on packaged goods. In some cases, it was observed that retailers offer national brands to cash customers, but push local/regional brands to credit customers because retailers buy national brands on a cash-and-carry basis.

Transfer of Capital

This pattern conveniently follows the retailers' own need to transfer capital from the store to their own cultivation, since most retailers themselves have landholdings; when the harvest is over and cash from their crops is realized, they invest it in building inventories in the retail shop. After the harvest, fresh investments in seeds and fertilizers have to be made on the farm, and their investments shift from the store to the farm. Marketers in rural areas could use this pattern to time their promotions. Although daily need products are more or less in constant demand, their consumption seems to increase during the selling season. Hence, new introductions and promotions could be timed to catch consumers when they are most amenable to buying.

Pricing by Channel

Sometimes retailers in interior villages sell at a price higher than the maximum retail price. They justify this on the grounds that they spend time and money to fetch the products from town wholesalers. This in turn suggests that channel members in rural markets may seek higher margins. Festival discounts announced by companies and routed through wholesalers and retailers only result in higher stocking up by them; most of the time, these concessions are not passed on to consumers. However, with increasing media exposure and consumer education the retailer's malpractices are diminishing.

A town wholesaler may deliberately cut the price of a fast-moving brand to increase his business. When this happens, other wholesalers often retaliate by dropping their prices. This price war results in a lower margin for the wholesaler, resulting in a lack of interest in the brand. It is very difficult to maintain price discipline once wholesalers come into the channel.

Channel Promotion

Retailers in interior villages prefer to limit the quantity purchased and therefore do not qualify for discount schemes, whereas retailers in feeder markets buy in bulk and get the benefit of such schemes.

Discount schemes should be targeted at retailers in feeder markets, as they can buy additional stock to sell not only to consumers, but also to retailers from interior villages.

Retailer–Consumer Dynamics

Understanding the consumer–retailer interface is critical for a marketer to service rural markets.

Consumer loyalty to the retailer is very high in rural markets as consumers are dependent on retailers for various needs. The retailers stock brands that rural consumers are habituated to buying; they are reluctant to stock new items.

In spite of increasing brand awareness and media exposure, the retailer continues to be the key influencer in rural markets. They are considered trustworthy by villagers, and their opinions and recommendations are highly valued. They also play the key role in brand choice as the product in question is not visible on rural shelves, but is chosen largely by the retailer. This is also an important factor facilitating the selling of spurious brands to consumers with low literacy levels. Realizing the importance of retailers in small towns and rural markets, Coca-Cola has launched customized training programmes for retailers to enhance their marketing skills.

COCA-COLA'S UNIVERSITY ON WHEELS

In late 2008, Coca-Cola's University on Wheels launched a nation-wide training programme called Parivartan (a positive change) on 20-seater buses for mom-and-pop retailers in Tier II and III towns across India. The objective was to help these retailers develop skills to survive, compete, sustain, and grow in a fast-changing retail scenario in the country. Around 20 small retailers who typically own small 300-sq. ft kirana shops are taught the tricks of the trade with the help of audiovisual aids in a two-hour session. The training content is structured around the four pillars of retail—customer, shop, stock, and finance. The results show that after having undergone the programme, most of the retailers have adopted the best practices taught to them. Based on their feedback, the company is developing 'Advanced Parivartan', which will cover issues like shop layout and location, display, the basics of finance, knowledge of credit card transactions, and people management skills. The programme has helped over 1 lakh retailers learn the tricks of the trade.[7]

Village retailers, who are also residents of the village, generally have a very strong bond with their customers. The relationship is often guided by family relationships. It is important to note that retailer loyalty is greater than brand loyalty in rural markets. Gillette, for instance, ensures that their products are well distributed all over the country. They expect this marketing and distribution effort to result in their products reaching rural areas through rural retailers.

The consumer loyalty pattern also suggests that promotion by the retailer is more important in rural markets. Studies suggest that retailer promotion supplements the efforts at creating brand knowledge in rural markets. A promotion announcing the benefits of a product or brand, coupled with distribution efforts, can be observed in rural markets in the FMCG category.

However, with the changing rural retail landscape, the marketer should look for newer ways to promote a new brand beyond the traditional retail channel. This innovation requires breaking through the hurdles created by the high costs and low volumes of the marketer, the limited shelf space available with rural retailers, and the limited opportunities available to consumers to try out new brands. The haat (refer to rural-centric distribution models) is perhaps one option that allows marketers to overcome these barriers.

::: Distribution Models in Rural Markets

Companies engaged in different product categories often use varying distribution models, depending on how optimally they can reach and service those markets. That is why Ghari detergent uses fewer channel members as against HUL in rural distribution.

The Distribution Models for FMCGs

As per the MART study on rural distribution conducted in 2004,[8] the rural distribution models of all major FMCG companies can be divided into two universal models, with minor variations from one company to another. These two models will henceforth be

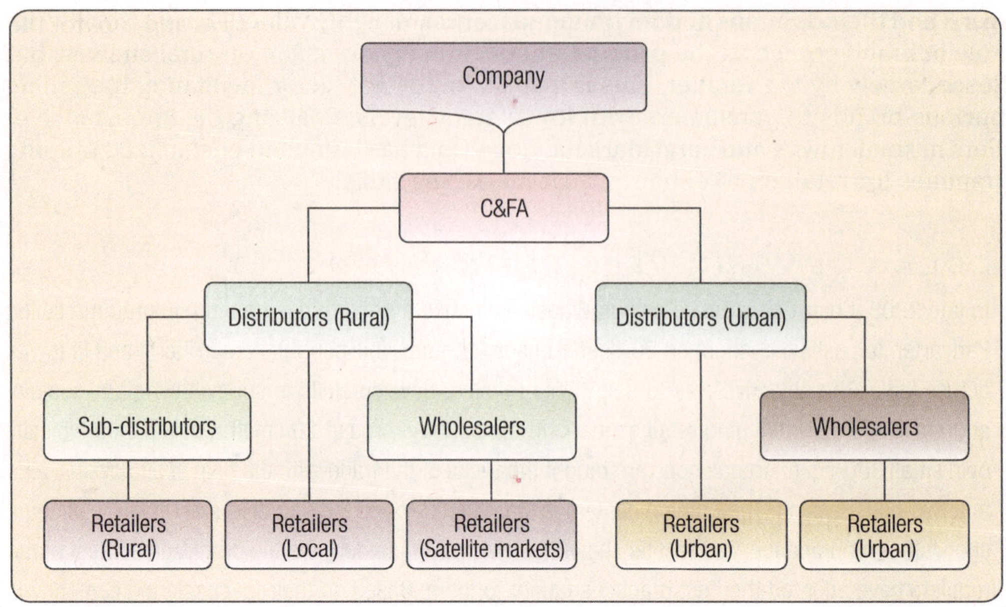

| FIG. **8.4** |
Distribution Model 1

referred to as Distribution Model 1 (DM1) and Distribution Model 2 (DM2). They are described below.

DISTRIBUTION MODEL 1 The DM1 is an advanced model in which separate channels are used for product distribution in urban and rural markets, as depicted in Fig. 8.4. This model is mostly adopted by established players who have a deeper penetration in rural markets.

Channel Structure In this model, rural distribution has been separated from urban distribution to create a specific focus on the rural market. The coverage area of rural distributors (RDs) is clearly defined. The company appoints a sub-distributor (SD) under the RD to penetrate deeper into rural areas, up to the 5,000 population villages. The RD covers a large area with poor road networks and a low volume per outlet, which makes it unprofitable for him to cover small locations. The RD services the wholesale market in his area. The wholesaler becomes important because of the assortment of goods that he keeps, the volume that he generates, and the customers to whom he caters from the satellite markets, where the company distribution has not yet penetrated. The generalized model DM1 has a larger number of points appointed in rural areas, because the locations are many and scattered. This ensures that the company's products reach the maximum number of rural locations.

The distributor has to supply smaller quantities at a higher frequency. The DM1 model focuses more on distributors and sub-distributors rather than the wholesale channel. The wholesale channel continues to play a role, but its importance is considerably reduced. This model ensures better monitoring, price discipline, and control over the sale and distribution of products. The distribution model of HUL is an example of DM1: HUL appoints rural distributors at the district level. The company appoints star sellers for every 20–25 villages. The star sellers invest money and stock all lines. Usually a big wholesaler in the area is selected as the star seller as he has the capacity to invest in the company business, and has an existing retail network and links with satellite markets in nearby areas. To reach the remotest villages (with a population of less than 2,000) directly, HUL introduced Project Shakti, under which individual women members of SHGs are appointed as dealers, to sell in their own villages as well as in four or five neighbouring villages. Refer to rural-centric distribution models for more details.

Transportation Stock from the production units to the CFA and up to the distributor's point is moved at company expense. The stock is first transferred to the CFA, and then sent to the distributor on freight-paid basis. The transfer from the production units to the CFA and to the distributor is mostly done on heavy transport vehicles, with an annual contract executed with transporters on fixed freight rates. The RDs cover their market using a light commercial vehicle, while urban distributors generally use three-wheelers. The SDs cover the market using a van or a pick-up truck. The higher transportation costs in rural areas are due to the poor road network; the cost of the longer distances to be covered is compensated by the company, through higher margins or a small percentage of the SD's sales. The cost of coverage for the distributor generally comes to an average of 1–1.5 per cent of the volume of business that they do. This includes the salaries of four or five employees and the maintenance cost of vehicles.

Coverage While the objective of a company is to improve reach, care needs to be taken while devising the route plan (permanent journey plan—PJP), which should be done in consultation with the distributor and the sales team so as to optimize effort and reduce expenses. The factors to be taken into account are haat days, distance, and the number of outlets to be covered, and the type of vehicle required. The PJP is prepared for six working days a week. Outlets are covered only fortnightly (mostly weekly in urban areas) because of the geographical spread and the small volume of business generated per outlet. In general, the number of outlets covered in a day is 30–40 (depending on the number of SKUs), of which 15–20 are productive. The typical distributor area is around a 50-km radius, depending on the market potential.

DISTRIBUTION MODEL 2 The DM1 is an advanced model in which product distribution in urban and rural markets happens through separate channels, as depicted in Fig. 8.4. In contrast, the DM2 is primarily a traditional model of distribution in which rural markets are serviced through the same channel servicing urban markets (see Fig. 8.5). This model is mostly adopted by some regional and national players with limited SKUs who generally do not adopt a separate rural strategy.

Channel Structure This is a simpler model compared to DM1. There is no separate channel for rural distribution. This model minimizes distribution costs, allowing the company to offer better margins to the distributors and other channel partners, who then push the sales of such products. Wholesaler locations work as feeder markets, from where the company caters to the requirements of nearby villages, places not covered by the distributor.

It is mostly companies with a limited number of SKUs and high sales volumes that adopt this model. Channel partners are few, and the distributor is given a large territory. In addition to higher margins, distributors and other channel partners also sell large volumes and earn good money. Ghari detergent, Priyagold biscuits, and other regional companies with high sales volumes follow this model. This model is preferred by new entrants who lack the infrastructure required for a wide distribution network. Also, companies using this model generally do not have a separate strategy for the rural market.

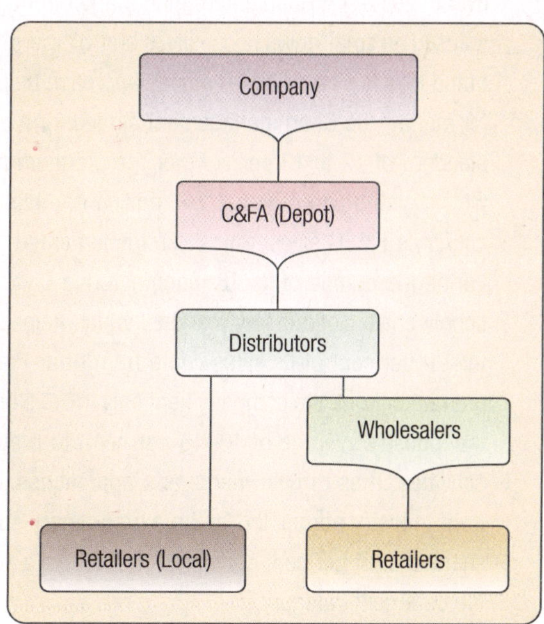

| FIG. 8.5 | Distribution Model 2

Transportation The stock is sent to the company depot on a transfer basis, and then on to the distributor on a freight-paid basis, using a heavy vehicle.

Distributors cover their areas using their own vehicles, mostly Matadors or tempos. Companies do not reimburse the transport expenses of distributors. The distributor employs three or four persons for the work, depending on the market to be covered.

Coverage The area covered by the distributor in DM2 is bigger than it is in DM1. Therefore, coverage becomes an issue, and the problem is further compounded by the fact that there is no SD to cover the more interior parts. Most of the time it is the wholesaler market that is responsible for the availability of these products in the interior-most parts of the country. The coverage for companies following this model is mostly done on a ready-stock basis, especially because of the lower number of SKUs as well as the high volumes. In the case of Priyagold biscuits, the number of assortments is high and so the company follows an order booking policy, which is an exception to the generalized model.

Nirma, which has been following this model for its limited SKUs, is now beginning to face problems as the number of SKUs has increased with the introduction of beauty soaps, the Nirma range of products, and other products like salt and edible oil in its basket of offerings. This model is not very effective for launching new products as wholesalers prefer products that already have a high demand. The company is now adopting a variant of DM1 to distribute the newer products. For the Nirma range of products, a parallel distribution and sales channel consisting of 2,000 distributors and an independent sales force has been set up (see Fig. 8.6).

The structure followed by Nirma consists of minimum channel partners. Direct distributors receive supplies from the depot. Market coverage is mainly through the wholesalers' network, and hence few distributors are required to handle bulk despatches. In some cases, a big wholesaler plays the role of a sub-distributor, supplying to the retailers and wholesalers in his area.

Distributors are appointed, and are the only channel partner recognized by the company. The distributor's area is one or more districts, depending on the market potential. The depot is company owned. The company supplies goods on a ready stock basis.

The following caselet describes how a small regional brand like Ghari successfully competed with MNC giants like HUL and P&G by using the traditional distribution model (DM2) to service rural markets effectively.

GHARI

Ghari, the second largest-selling detergent brand in India with an INR 3 billion turnover in 2012–13. Ghari entered the market through the economy segment where real volumes lie. It focused on small-town housewives and villagers, who are extremely value-conscious buyers with no brand loyalty. The value for money approach helped Ghari to differentiate its product. To offer value for money, the Ghari management settled for a net profit margin of 9 per cent against the industry standard of 12 to 13 per cent for the premium brands. Further, it restricted itself to Uttar Pradesh which, with a population of 167 million (the highest in India), accounts for over 12 per cent of the country's FMCG sales. Ghari also implemented an extensive dealer network throughout the state. Furthermore, nine of its 18 manufacturing units are in Uttar Pradesh. Thus, the company kept its supply chain close to key markets, which helped in controlling the transportation costs. Even now, 60–70 per cent of its sales come from Uttar Pradesh, Madhya Pradesh, and Maharashtra. On the promotion front, the company kept only INR 3.5 billion (or less than 2 per cent of the turnover against the industry average of 13–15 per cent) to promote the brand through above and below-the-line activities. These frugal marketer's approaches, combined with the daring to do things differently from industry norms, led to the extraordinary success of Ghari. In 2012, Ghari occupied a market share of 17.4 per cent compared with Wheel's 16.9 per cent making it the overall market leader in the detergent category.

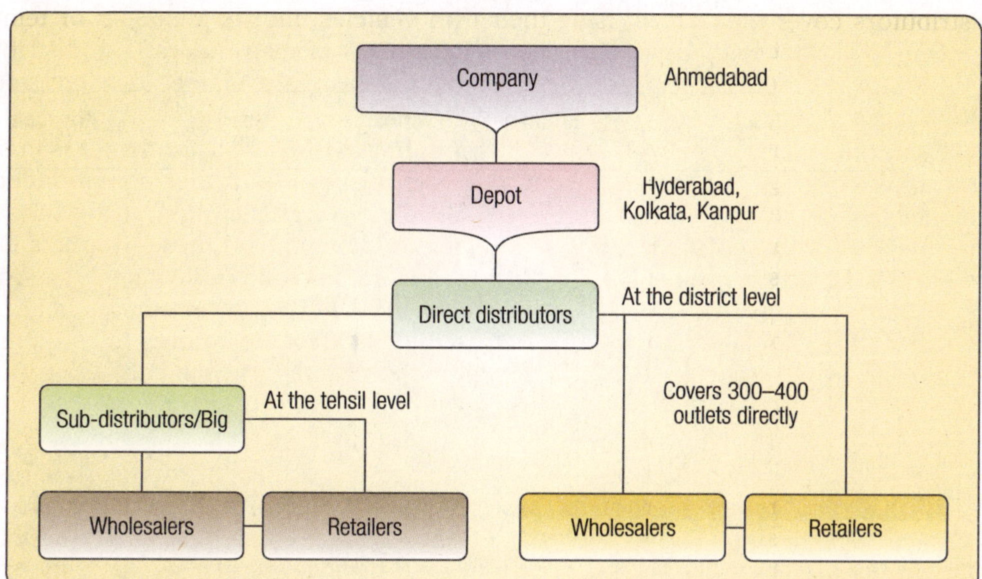

| FIG. 8.6 |
The Nirma Distribution System

Table 8.7 compares the distribution system of various FMCG companies. Colums II–V, i.e., CavinKare, Eveready, HUL, and Britannia represent the first group. Nirma, Ghari, and Priyagold (columns VI–VIII) comprise the second group. Two distribution models, namely, Distribution Model 1 (DM1) and Distribution Model 2 (DM2) broadly represent these two groups.

Ghari adopted the frugal marketer's approach to become the second largest detergent brand in India.

The Distribution Model for Durables

Since durables are purchased largely from small and large towns, the number of locations for distribution is only a few thousand, and these can be managed by a few channel partners. Two types of models similar to FMCG distribution models have evolved in durables goods. The first is the traditional model using an undifferentiated approach, in which rural markets are serviced through existing urban distribution channels as distribution is mostly restricted to town and cities. The first model is used by most companies, for example, by Usha International and Bajaj Electricals. On the other hand, the second model uses a separate distribution and service network to service rural markets efficiently. This model has been adopted by a few companies like Philips and LG, who have dared to set up dedicated sales and service channels for rural markets.

Philips Lighting has been in India for more than 70 years. The company makes incandescent bulbs. Over 75 per cent of the sales in this category are from rural markets. Philips has put in place a distribution system (see Fig. 8.7) to service this market efficiently. The product moves from the Philips manufacturing plant, which is located in Gujarat, to the company-owned depots.

| TABLE 8.7 |
Comparison of Distribution Systems

Parameters I	CavinKare II	Eveready III	HUL IV	Britannia V	Nirma VI	Ghari VII	Priyagold VIII
Number of channel partners in distribution system	6	7	7	6	3	3	3
Different channels for rural and urban areas	Yes	Yes	Yes	Yes	No	No	No
Margin structures different for rural and urban areas (in per cent)	Urban—6 Rural—3+5	Urban—5 Rural—5+1+ Van subsidy	Urban—4.75 Rural—6 to 7	Urban—5 Rural—6	Not applicable	Not applicable	Not applicable
Coverage pattern	Order booking	Ready stock	Order booking	Order booking	Ready stock	Ready stock	Order booking
Mode of payment	Advance cheques	Advance cheques	Advance cheques	Advance draft	Advance cheques	Cash/Draft on delivery	Advance cheques
Number of distributors per district	2–3 distributors in a district but also depends on the market size.	1 van operator in a district and 2–3 retail stockists covering the larger local markets in the district.	2–3 for urban markets and 1–2 for rural markets in each district	2–3 distributors in each district, including the rural distributor	1 distributor in a district	1 distributor in a district and sometimes 1 distributor in 2 districts if the market size is small	1 distributor in a district
Number of outlets covered per distributor	160–80 outlets directly covered by distributors in <50,000 population areas. The rest by the sub distributor. 180–250 outlets covered in <50,000 population areas by distributors.	The distributor covers 1,500–1,600 outlets directly through double van operation. The remaining 800–900 outlets in the local markets is covered by the 2–3 retail stockists	350–400 for the urban distributor with 30–40 wholesalers. The rural distributor covers 25–30 SS where each SS covers 60–100 outlets. He also supplies 70–80 Shakti dealers	250–300 outlets covered by the distributor.	400–500 outlets covered directly and the rest through wholesalers and sub-distributors appointed by the distributor	350–450 outlets covered by the distributors, the rest is covered by the wholesalers	Not available
Number of assortments	High	Low	Very high	High	Medium	Low	High
Regional/National operation	National	National	National	National	National	Regional	Regional

Source: Study of Rural Distribution Channels, MART

Each depot is in charge of catering to at least one state. The depot directly services both urban and rural distributors as per the orders placed by them. The distributor in urban areas is usually allocated a city, servicing roughly 900–1,200 retail outlets on a fixed-journey plan basis. Rural coverage is also done in a similar manner. The rural distribution network of Philips covers a population strata of 15,000–20,000. Locations of below 15,000 population are usually catered to by the electrical wholesale outlets in rural locations.

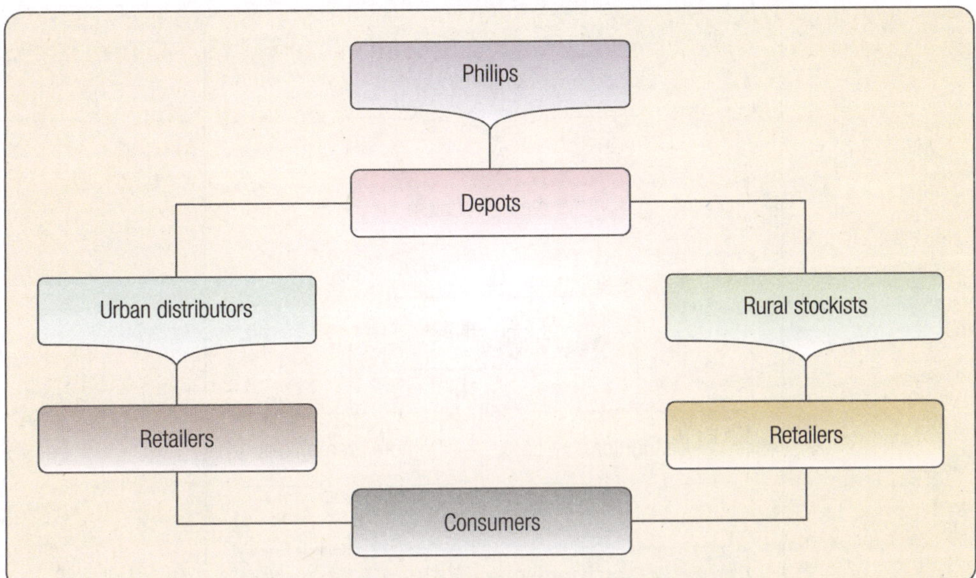

| FIG. **8.7** |
The Philips Lighting Distribution Model

The LG Electronics distribution model depicted in Fig. 8.8 is another example of the recently evolved second distribution model which has helped LG make in roads into rural markets and establish it as the market leader.

Today, LG is the market leader in the white goods segment. This distinction has been achieved through building a rural-focused service and distribution network. Between 2004 to 2008, the company has tripled its retail and distributor outlets in rural areas. This has led to an increase in sales from the hinterland. To cater efficiently to the growing market of rural India, LG introduced a new set-up within the existing channel—the introduction of the company's rural office at the district level. A separate stocking point was created to manage the logistics of deeper penetration. LG also appointed dealers and one exclusive dealer to cater specifically to the rural audience, who are directly serviced by the rural district offices.

Rural markets account for 75 per cent of the total sales of Philips incandescent bulbs.

Today, LG reaches the rural market through a network of 40 branch offices and 65 remote area offices, 230 service centres and 2,600 mobile authorized service personnel for villages with less than 10,000 residents. This increased service network has resulted in an increased rural market service reach. It also tapped local forms of entertainment like annual fairs, weekly haats, mobile vans, exhibitions, cookery classes, road shows, and in-store demonstrators, and made huge investments in infrastructure for distribution and marketing. As a result of these efforts, the rural market for LG grew at 25 per cent over 2009–2010, against a 15 per cent growth in urban areas. Sampoorna TVs, sold in the Indian heartland and the semi-urban belts, enforced a strong connection with India for LG.

| FIG. **8.8** |
The Distribution Model of LG Electronics

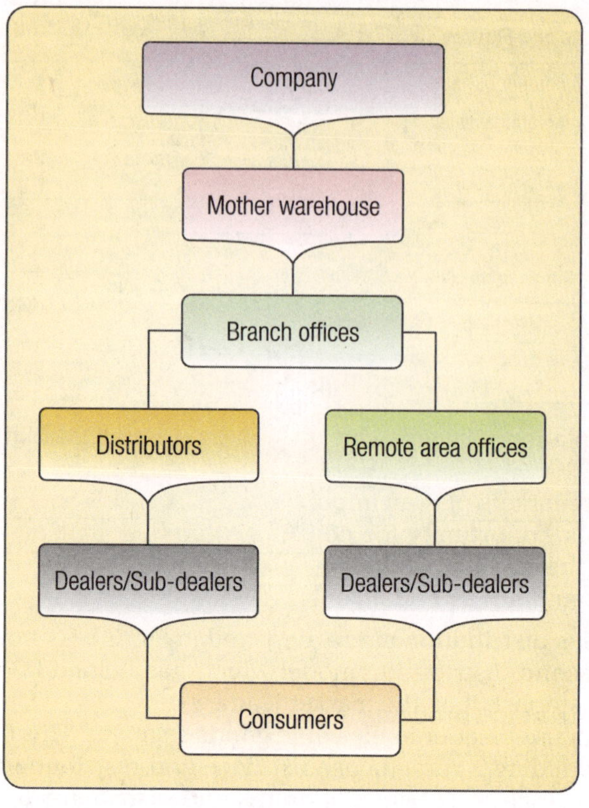

Rural-centric Distribution Models

Rural-centric distribution models are those that optimize the existing infrastructure and human resources available in rural markets to create innovative and cost-effective sustainable business to service rural consumer needs.

With the entry of new players in rural markets, marketers are innovating new cost-effective approaches to reach these markets. Given the bottlenecks of rural distribution, the solution has to be derived from learning from old rural distribution systems (haats, mobile traders, PDS) and optimizing the existing physical and social infrastructure (SHG, cooperatives, NGOs, youth groups, petrol pumps) and ensuring the participation and economic sustainability of all stakeholders. These approaches are leading to the emergence of rural-centric distribution models in recent years. Among rural-centric models, both traditional (haats/shandies, cooperatives, PDS) and modern approaches (SHG model, youth entrepreneurship model) have been adopted by corporations to reach the last mile. Also, other unconventional channels of distribution (like petrol pumps and NGOs) are recent initiatives in this direction to reach the rural consumer. These cost-effective initiatives, aimed at establishing sustainable distribution models, are based on a 'wheel of collaboration' between different stakeholders to reach the rural consumers.

Haats/Shandies

Haats are rural bazaars that spring up every week across India's heartland. Rural haats are the nerve centres for the rural marketing system in India, and a readymade distribution network embedded in the fabric of rural society.

A new study by the Rural Marketing Association of India, conducted in 2010,[9] allows a better understanding of rural markets for corporate India as it tries to sell more and more of its wares to a humongous mass of people rapidly climbing the consumption ladder. At 43,000, the number of haats outnumbers the number of stores of the world's biggest retailer, Wal-Mart, at five to one. And even though sales are dominated by low-value, small-ticket items, they still add a sizeable INR 5,000 billion annually (see Table 8.8). Every week, on an average 545 stalls appear in a large haat (located in a 10,000+ population place), while around 327 stalls are set up in a small haat (located in

| TABLE **8.8** |
Facts and Figures About Haats

Facts and Figures		
Total number of haats	43,000	
Average annual sales	INR 5,000 billion	
	Large Haat	**Small Haat**
Total number of stalls	545	327
Average number of visitors	12,000	5,600
Catchment area (Number of villages)	57	21

Source: RMAI, Haats As Marketing Hubs, 2010

5,000–10,000 population villages). Out of the total footfall, around two-fifth belongs to female visitors.

These periodic markets play an important role in the Indian rural economy and provide a tremendous opportunity for consumer goods companies to promote and sell their products to the rural populace. Haats are generally located in places that are well connected, and could act as nodal centres of the region and possibly cater to a large rural population.

PROFILE OF OUTLETS AND PRODUCT SOLD Although haats were started for the distribution of agricultural products, manufactured products are gaining a lot of importance in these periodic markets (see Table 8.9). This is a good sign for companies who want to use haats as marketing hubs for their products.

The sale of FMCG products is increasing in haats, and customers now prefer to buy certain products like soaps, shampoos, detergents, tea, groceries, etc., particularly from haats. Some of the well-known FMCG brands like Clinic Plus, Lifebuoy, Colgate, Ponds, and Fair & Lovely have already gained dominance and preference among rural buyers at haats across states. This is because of the availability of a wide variety and better choice of goods, and the comparatively lower prices at haats.

CORPORATE PRESENCE IN HAATS Companies like Mahindra, Hero Honda, Bajaj, TVS, Tata (Ace), Ape tyres, Ceat tyres, Emami (Navratan Oil), Nippo Batteries, Parle Products (Parle G), Hindustan Unilever (Wheel, Bru, etc.) Coca-Cola (Thums Up), Nestlé (Nescafé), Dabur, and Samsung, followed by mobile service providers like Airtel, Tata Docomo, Idea, Reliance, Vodafone, BSNL, and Aircel are taking the maximum advantage of this huge potential by using haats as awareness generation mediums. However, the leaders here are Mahindra and Airtel.

HAAT SELLERS: AS POINT OF SALES AND REDISTRIBUTION The haat seller generally buys his wares from the nearby city wholesaler, and preferably on credit. Most

| TABLE **8.9** |
Profile of Products Sold at Rural Retail Outlets

Category of Outlets	Percentage of Outlets
Agri products	53
Manufactured goods	19
Processed food	6
Handicrafts	5
Forest products	5
Services	4
Meat/Poultry	3
Others	5

Source: RMAI, Haats As Marketing Hubs, 2010

A haat selling branded FMCG products.

sellers feel that the longer they sell in a haat, the larger would be their loyal customer base. To increase their sales, a seller usually tries to visit a large number of haats. These sellers usually make weekly purchases (from wholesalers or retailers), mainly on non-haat days. Although 42 per cent of the FMCG sellers buy goods on credit, not many sell it the same way to their customers at haats.

The average amount of sale of branded products—especially by an FMCG seller—is around INR 2,224 per haat day, while his total sale (including unbranded FMCG products) adds up to around INR 7,521 per haat day. Therefore, the sale of branded FMCG products in a haat is one-third of the total sale of FMCG products.

Rural folk are regular visitors at haats, with women accounting for two of every five haat visitors. They prefer to buy branded consumer expendables at the haat rather than from the permanent village shop because of the variety on offer at these weekly markets. Lower prices, better choices, and a wide range of product availability at one place are the key triggers for purchase. Impulse buying does take place in high numbers. On an average, a buyer spends around INR 40 on purchase of FMCG products.

IMPLICATION FOR MARKETERS With growing rural incomes and rising brand awareness, big brand marketers can look at converting huge unbranded and copycat goods consumption at these haats into sales for their value-priced brands. The future is very promising for those who can understand the dynamics of haats and exploit them to their best advantage.

| FIG. **8.9** |
Profile of Buyers and Buying Behaviour
Source: RMAI, Haats As Marketing Hubs, 2010.

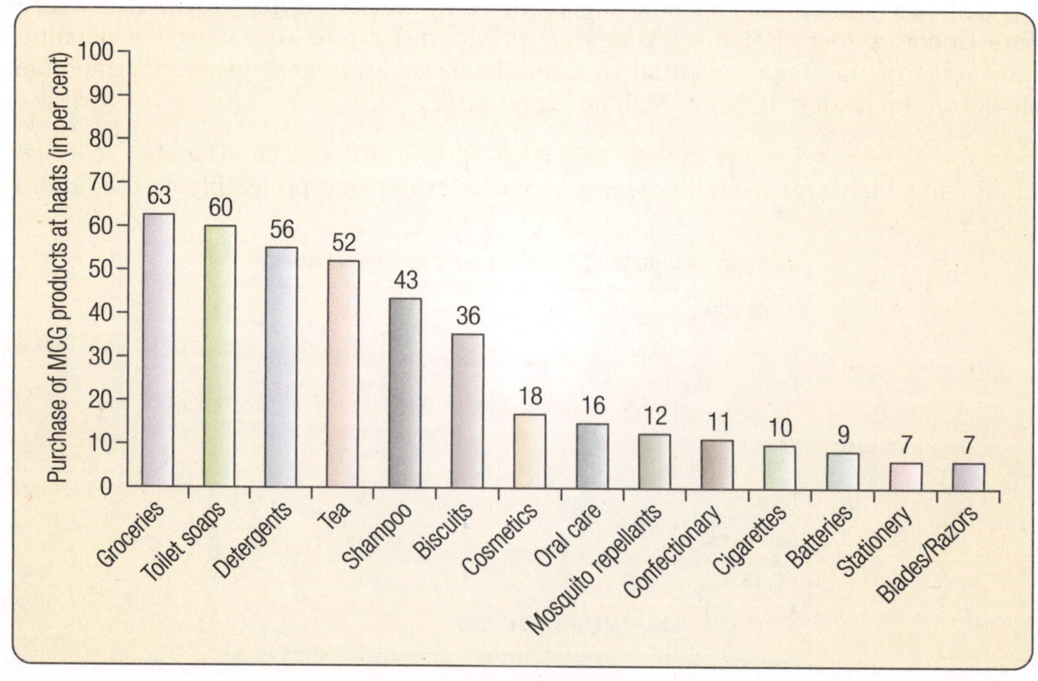

Modern Distribution Models

With the increasing need to take products and services to rural markets, companies that are seriously interested have invested in rural markets to develop new distribution channels to service rural markets effectively. Two types of distribution models have evolved in the last decade, namely the SHG model and the youth entrepreneurship model.

THE SHG MODEL A self-help group (SHG) is a group of 10–15 women organized by government bodies or NGOs, who come together to form a mutual thrift group, to inculcate savings discipline, and boost feelings of self-worth among women. Members of SHGs get matching loans from rural banks to set up income-generating enterprises. SHGs were originally formed to support poverty-alleviation programmes in rural areas after the success of this model in Bangladesh, where this concept originated.

The rapid growth of the SHG movement in India has provided marketers with an opportunity to establish a path-breaking distribution model through linking these groups. With over seven million SHGs across India, this holds a great potential to develop a low-cost distribution model to reach rural homes in the remotest parts of the country. The initiative taken by HUL (with strategic and implementation support from MART) in this direction has achieved phenomenal success. See 'Rural Marketing Insight: Project Shakti' for more details on this.

RURAL MARKETING INSIGHT | PROJECT SHAKTI

As Hindustan Unilever (formerly Hindustan Lever Limited) was contemplating how to increase its rural reach, self-help groups based on the Grameen model of microfinance were springing up and flourishing across India. Shakti started out by tapping into these groups in one part of rural Andhra Pradesh in 2000. The idea was to create low-risk, profitable micro-enterprise opportunities for women, who become direct-to-home distributors of Hindustan Unilever's products. Under Project Shakti, SHG women in remote areas were appointed as local dealers of HUL products, providing them with a sustainable micro-enterprise opportunity while HUL gained access to previously untapped remote rural markets.

The new initiative through SHG women makes products available in the sub-2,000 population villages. Under Project Shakti, distribution has been organized through a comprehensive, three-tier network: first by a CFA at the state level, then by the Rural Distributors (RDs) at the district level, who delivers the stocks at the doorsteps of Shakti Dealers (SDs) in remote villages. The Shakti dealers then distribute not only in their own village, but also in three to four surrounding villages. Through this tiered system, distribution spreads through an extensive network covering outlying villages with poor accessibility, and sometimes with populations of less than 1,000 people. The products are packaged in quantities small enough to be affordable to rural buyers, and often cost as little as half a rupee each.

Project Shakti was piloted by HUL–MART in December 2000, in the southern state of Andhra Pradesh. There are over seven million groups in existence today. Andhra Pradesh has by far the largest number of SHGs in the country, with over 400,000 SHGs mobilizing close to six million village women. Based on the local data provided by the state's District Rural Development Agency, a total of 50 SHGs were chosen from the district of Nalgonda to participate in the pilot venture. Three one-day training programmes were organized specifically to build the capacities of these SHG women, with particular focus on the issues of entrepreneurship and marketing. Once an SD has been nominated, she invests in at least INR 10,000 worth of stock, which is secured through the means of a group loan, or otherwise. The SD is then provided with basic training before being linked with her Rural Distributor (RD), who will ensure that all her subsequent stock orders are delivered directly to her door within seven days of her placing an order. The responsibility of supporting and monitoring the distribution and sales of the SDs is taken over by the HUL Rural Sales Promoters (RSPs). Since expansion began in February 2002, Project Shakti has been satisfactorily rolled out across the country with strategic and implementation support from MART. A total of 65,000 Shakti dealers have been appointed so far in 135,000 villages. They operate like a 'Rural Direct to Home' distributor (access, awareness, changing attitudes, selling) and cover more than three million rural homes in India.

The monthly earnings of an SD vary between INR 700 to 2,000. To begin with, an SD may choose to sell her stock either to local retailers for a limited profit margin of 3 per cent, or directly to private consumers at a higher profit margin of 11–13 per cent. SDs are strongly encouraged to seek a wider consumer base by taking their business from door to door. Much of the additional income goes towards educating children, and also towards purchasing consumer durables such as television sets or motor scooters (which allow them to go into more villages), further expanding the rural market for such products. HUL also embraced other novel distribution strategies

| FIGURE | The Project Shakti Model

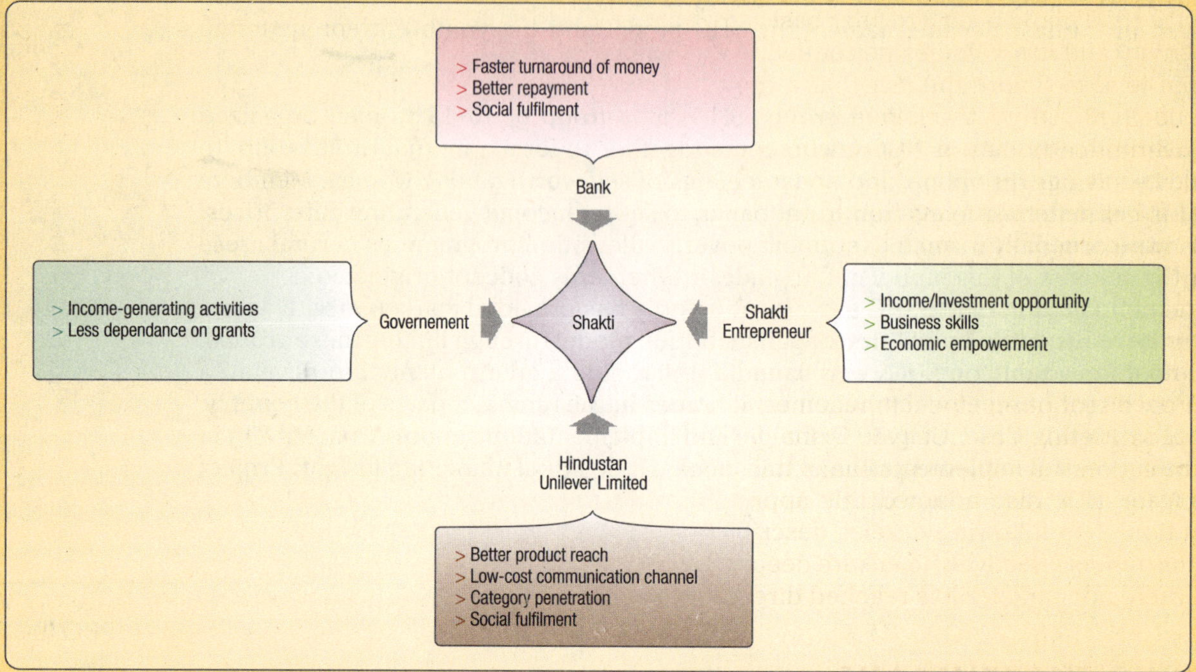

such as selling products like Sunsilk and Clinic shampoos in small, inexpensive packets for low-income consumers in the hinterland with spare cash.

Additional strategies and information for marketers

1. **Shakti Day** was conceived as a regular promotional event. This would centre round an SD stall within the village itself, from which customers could purchase a range of HUL products as well as redeem special offers. Publicity would be carried out both on the preceding day and throughout the day in question, via a public announcement system. The Janata Accidental Insurance Policy (New India Assurance Company) was selected as the most appropriate, offering insurance coverage of up to INR 25,000 for a period of one year. Given that the sale of insurance policy would not require any initial outlay from the SD, she could diversify her range of products and widen her customer base without requiring any diversion or increase in her overall level of investment.
2. **I-Shakti unit,** an IT-based rural information service that seeks to provide online solutions to common problems in the areas of agriculture, education, vocational training, health, and hygiene is operated from within the village itself, ensuring its accessibility and also allowing content to be monitored and updated for continued relevance. Piloted once again within the Nalgonda district of Andhra Pradesh, the project is now facilitating empowerment-through-information in a total of eight villages across the state. Hindustan Unilever has also tied up with partners such as Tata Consultancy Services, which is actively involved with the iShakti portal, and ICICI, a financial services institution involved with providing micro-credit loans.
3. **Shakti Vani Programme**. Under this programme, trained communicators visit schools and village congregations to drive home messages on sanitation, good hygiene practices and women's empowerment. This serves as a rural communication vehicle and helps the SD in their sales.

Project Shakti is a live example of a public–private community partnership model as depicted in the figure. As for the bank, there is a faster turnaround of money, better repayment, and social fulfilment. For the government, it provides income-generating activities and less dependence on grants. For HUL, there is better product reach, a low-cost communication channel, category penetration and social fulfilment. For the Shakti entrepreneur, it is an income/investment opportunity, providing business skills and economic empowerment.

Future Direction

The project has been tailored and implemented in South-East Asian, African, and Latin American markets. The project has been named as 'Joyeeta' in Bangladesh and 'Saubhagya' in Sri Lanka. Unilever also plans to increase the number of Shakti entrepreneurs from 45,000 in 2010 to 75,000 in 2015, globally.

THE YOUTH ENTREPRENEURSHIP MODEL It has been observed that most companies employ a centrally recruited sales force to venture into rural markets. This approach has had limited success as company representatives failed to service rural markets on a regular basis due to poor road connectivity and low volumes per outlet. However, marketers often tend to ignore the fact that a huge force of educated, unemployed youth resides in remote villages, with the potential to become entrepreneurs if proper orientation and training are imparted. Tapping into this segment to expand the distribution reach led to the emergence of the 'youth entrepreneurship' model in rural markets, pioneered by MART.

In recent years, companies like Colgate, Heinz, and Novartis have used this model developed by MART to gain entry into unreachable rural markets using the rural youth, an approach that has met with phenomenal success. (Refer to 'Rural Marketing Case: Colgate Disha' for more details.) After the successful implementation of this model by MNCs like Colgate, HUL also adopted this approach for deeper penetration. The following caselet describes how HUL is using this model effectively to ensure deeper penetration in areas where no marketer has reached directly.

Youth entrepreneurs, used by Heinz for last mile distribution, sell Nycil, Glucon D and Complan in rural areas.

HUL'S SHAKTIMAANS

Shaktimaans—distributors on bicycles—have been recruited by Hindustan Unilever Limited in 150,000 remote villages with populations of less than 2,000 (which are beyond the reach of the company's redistribution stockists) to distribute their products in remote villages. There is a demand for such products in these villages, but they do not have a distribution network. Every day these entrepreneurs set out on company-owned bicycles to distribute products and sachets of popular brands like Wheel, Lifebuoy, Pond's, and Brooke Bond, among others, to aspiring consumers. Earlier, these consumers had to satisfy their needs by purchasing products from the nearby villages where the company had direct distribution. Now their needs will be met in their own villages by the visiting Shaktimaans. A Shaktimaan is a male member of a Shakti entrepreneur family. Roughly one in two Shakti households would provide a Shaktimaan, who is chosen on the basis of his locational advantage and his proximity to the villages to be covered. A Shakti entrepreneur typically earns an average of INR 1,000 per month. It is estimated that the Shaktimaan would earn INR 2,500 and HUL would treble its revenues. There are over 50,000 Shaktimaans across India.

Vans

Mobile vans have an important place in the distribution and promotion of products in villages. A few companies like Eveready use vans for distribution in rural areas. In this system, the salesman loads the van with stocks from the nearest stockist or company stock point and works the surrounding markets. Once they have covered all such markets, they move to the next stock point and starts covering the villages surrounding that particular stock point. In this manner, they move from one stock point to the other and returns to the original stock point to complete their journey cycle. The van can be used for both sales and promotions. Although this is an effective method, it can be expensive if the company has to invest in all the vans. Eveready is the only company that is successfully operating its own fleet of 1,000+ vans across the country.

EVEREADY

Eveready, the market leader in batteries and torches, aimed to be the lowest-cost producer of the highest-quality products with better customer reach. Availability in all markets and retail outlets was the major hurdle. To solve this problem, it established an extensive distribution network comprising 44 warehouses supplying the products to over 4,000 distributors using 1,000 vans.[10] This is the largest company-owned van distribution system in the country, consisting of city vans for metro cities, major cities, and smaller towns, and upcountry vans for rural areas. Retail stockists cater to the small towns, while wholesale distributors cover the major wholesale markets in cities and big towns. These vans reach 3.3 million retail outlets directly, with each van making 50 to 60 calls per day. The distribution structure extends coverage out to 5,000-population villages. Eveready ensures that the van revisits a retailer every fortnight. The stock for these vans is supplied by small-town distributors. For every territory there are approximately three city vans and four upcountry vans. Eveready avoids conflict between channel partners by allotting exclusive territories to van operators, wholesalers, and retail stockists.

The Public Distribution System

The public distribution system (PDS) is a system of distribution of essential commodities to a large number of people through a network of FPS (fair price shops, often referred to as 'ration shops'). The commodities are wheat, rice, sugar, edible oil, and kerosene. The PDS has been evolved to reach both the urban and the rural population in order to protect consumers from the fluctuating and escalating price syndrome.

RURAL MALLS—THE NEW FACE OF FAIR PRICE SHOPS

Model fair price shops, grandly described by the government as micro rural malls, are springing up all over Gujarat, where village people can shop for all their needs 24 × 7. The scheme was launched as a pilot project in mid-2007 in two blocks of Vadodara district, as the government planned to convert 500 FPS into such rural malls. Already 512 such 'malls' have sprouted and another 508 are on the anvil. The state government plans to have 1,000 such malls every year. The 'malls' are, in effect, model fair price shops, under a programme launched to deregulate the scope of the services of fair price shops by allowing them to deal in all kinds of goods and services. The revamping of the public distribution system undertaken by the state's department of civil supply is a first of its kind initiative in India. There are about 15,000 fair price shops all over Gujarat. At the rural malls, people can not only buy grains, fortified flour, edible oils, and other essential commodities, but also get gas cylinders, cosmetic items, recharge vouchers, fertilizers, seeds, and packaged goods. These malls were proving to be viable commercial centres, meeting the diverse needs of villagers. The concept seeks to make the model fair price shops meet retail needs on the lines of the modern market, while at the same time controlling the practice of leakages and diversion of the essential goods meant for vulnerable sections of society, who are eligible holders of ration cards. Initially, the owners of the shops used to earn not more than INR 1,500–2,000 as commission from sales. They can now hope to earn INR 5,000 a month. Following the initiative, companies like ITC, HUL, major oil companies, Videocon, and telephone service providers like Tata, BSNL, and Hutch are selling their products through these shops. Other products include Life Insurance Corporation (LIC) policies and ice-cream parlours. Both state-run and private banks are trying to position themselves in rural areas by making the malls a sale link for their financial products. The proliferation of malls has cut down the time and money people from rural and semi-urban areas used to spend to go to urban centres.

The PDS, with a network of about 476,000 FPS, is perhaps the largest distribution network of its type in the world. Out of the total number, 380,000 FPS (80 per cent) are in rural areas. As per the norms prescribed by the Government of India, one FPS caters to 1,000 population in rural areas. India's Planning Commission estimates that 160 million families purchase commodities at ration shops every year.

PDS has a huge infrastructure base that could be utilized for the distribution of consumer products by marketers. Realizing the potential of this old distribution system the state government in Gujarat is transforming fair price shops into micro rural malls established to distribute essential commodities in rural areas.

Cooperative Societies

Cooperatives occupy an important place in India's rural economy in terms of their coverage of the population and their share in the total supply of agricultural inputs, including credit. India has the largest network of cooperatives in the world, comprising more than 500,000 cooperatives spread across the country, even in the remotest villages. Cooperatives account for 34 per cent of the total quantity of fertilizers distributed in the country. There are 4,398 primary marketing societies and 2,933 large multipurpose primary marketing services (LAMPS) in India. The cooperatives interface closely with the rural masses as they play a key role in the economic value chain, from production to marketing, and procurement to distribution and credit in both the agriculture and non-agriculture sectors.

Warana Bazar and Farmers' Services Cooperative Societies (FSCS) are some of the cooperative networks which function like mini supermarkets for rural consumers, where consumables, household durables, and agricultural products are sold at economical and reasonable prices.

WARANA BAZAR

Warana Bazar, a milk and sugar cooperative society in the Kolhapur district of Maharashtra, opened the first departmental store in 1978. Today it has two big departmental stores and 50 branches in the rural areas of Sangli and Kolhapur districts. Warana Bazar has become a one-stop shop for rural consumers looking to purchase all kinds of items of rural need, ranging from FMCGs, durables, auto components, and agricultural products. Consumers come to Warana Bazar accompanied by several members of their family, and carry the purchased items home in their tractor-trolleys.

Petrol Pumps and Extension Counters

In India, there are over 12,000 petrol pumps spread across the country, 60 per cent of which are located on highways close to villages. These pumps, in addition to selling petroleum products, have also started selling consumables like food products and

INDIAN OIL CORPORATION'S KISAN SEVA KENDRA

Kisan Seva Kendras, IOC's rural retail initiative, are retail outlets catering to the requirements of rural customers. Besides fuel, these outlets sell a variety of consumer goods, agricultural and banking products. These outlets—typically 150–175 sq. ft in size—are set up on the dealers' land, with the dealer retaining the entire revenue from the non-fuel sales, in addition to the standard margin they earn on the sale of petrol and diesel. Each outlet witnesses a daily footfall of 20–25 customers and earns an average daily sale of INR 4,000–5,000. It has also entered into alliances with companies like Dabur, Airtel, Tata Chemicals, Godavari Fertilisers, Gokulam Fertilisers, Hindustan Unilever, and Godrej Agrovet to market their products. More than 6000 outlets out of total 24,000 outlets in the country have been automated and the company also plans to automate 7500 more outlets by 2014–15.

toiletries. Oil companies are exploring the possibility of selling agri-inputs, LPG cylinders, and other rural-based items from these outlets. In the past, oil companies had operated on the concept of multipurpose distribution centres in rural areas, which is what is now being planned in a modified way. The recent rural retail initiative, Kisan Seva Kendra, of the Indian Oil Corporation is an excellent example of how to harness this platform.

Non-government Organizations

Non-government Organizations (NGOs), which have been present in rural areas for a long time, also offer an alternative platform to reach rural markets. There are more than 3.3 million NGOs operating in various sectors in India today. A large number of NGOs are focusing on rural development and income-generation activities through SHG and community-based organizations. Some marketers are joining hands with them, as it is a win-win situation for both stakeholders. While NGOs facilitate reach to the rural masses through infrastructure and grassroots-level networking, the company provides employment opportunities to the rural residents. Tata Tea's project 'Gaon Chalo' is a successful example. See 'Rural Marketing Insight: Gaon Chalo: A Tata Tea Initiative' for more details on this.

Rural Mobile Traders: Last Mile Distribution

Mobile trading is one of the age-old unorganized distribution systems of rural India, in which traders travel through dusty villages selling products home-to-home. Mobile traders visit village houses to fulfil the daily needs of rural consumers. They sell detergent, cosmetics, and personal care products, as well as garments and footwear. They carry their products on bicycles, mopeds, push carts, or on foot. They cover one to two villages and visit almost 30–40 households per day. They mainly sell non-branded products or local brands. Most mobile traders buy and then sell the product, earning the retail margin as profit. A few are employed on a salaried basis and some receive commissions on sales.

Mobile traders have a deep reach as they mainly target small villages (less than 2,000 population). Their selling technique involves the consumer in the process, and they have a fixed, committed consumer base and share a long-term relationship with them.

These traders could emerge as a cost-effective way of direct selling. However, the barriers to using this sales force are: they are not organized, they sell local brands and non-branded products/fakes, they have a limited investment capability, and a lack of credibility.

Due to media exposure, rural consumers now want to use genuine products and good brands. A MART study shows that some mobile traders have begun to carry a few genuine brands (5–7 per cent of their sales), and in recent times some trading communities (like Manihaars) have been organizing themselves to improve their credibility and effectiveness. Helping them to initiate the business by providing them with the initial capital or bicycles can induce them to sell genuine products. Properly printed (with the company logo or name) promotional material (like caps, T-shirts, badges, etc.) can improve their credibility.

Tata Tea has successfully developed an unconventional, sustainable distribution network across 10,000 villages in UP, using NGOs to service rural consumers.

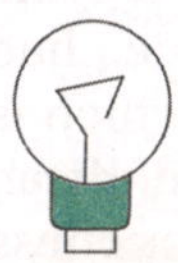

RURAL MARKETING INSIGHT | GAON CHALO: A TATA TEA INITIATIVE

Launched in December 2005, the Tata Tea initiative ***Gaon Chalo***, meaning 'let's go to the villages', saw Tata Tea joining hands with 12 NGOs to spread its reach across rural Uttar Pradesh. By the end of 2006, Tata Tea had added more than 20,000 retailers, including 500 new rural distributors, in 10,000 villages across UP to its distribution network. As part of the initiative, agreements were signed with NGOs (Rural Dealer-1) to act as the main distributors at the district level, collecting various products from Tata Tea (that is, only tea variants) on credit before giving them out to rural distributors.

An NGO in Raebareli has been the principle partner for Tata Tea since 2006, launching Project Gaon Chalo for eight districts in Uttar Pradesh. Today, it has over 3,200 people working for project Gaon Chalo across the eight districts, with 52 permanent employees on its payrolls. Let us understand the structure of Project Gaon Chalo through this diagrammatic hierarchy.

| FIGURE | The Hierarchy in Project Gaon Chalo

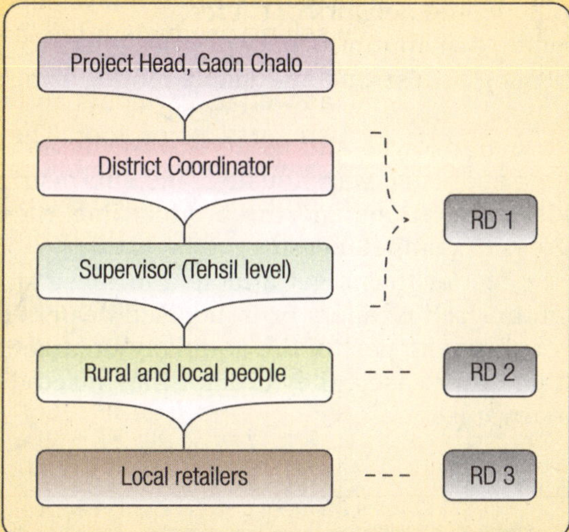

- The Project Head is in charge of the project in eight districts of UP, and coordinates with the District Coordinators and the Client.
- The District Coordinator appoints Supervisors at the Tehsil level, who in turn appoint RD2 at the village level. Generally an RD2 is in charge of one village, but he may at times be in charge of more than one, depending on the size of the village. A village with about 2,000 populace has only one RD2.
- The stock of Tata Tea is placed at the doors of the District Coordinator as soon as the requisition for fresh stock is updated. Transportation costs are born by the company. Generally, the Distributor at the district level of Tata is responsible for this task.
- The District Coordinator distributes the stock to Supervisors according to their requisition (demand). The transportation cost here is born by the Supervisors.
- The Supervisors then distribute the stock to the RD2, who is generally a local person from a particular village. The selection of RD2 is done on the basis of some parameters like previous sales experience, convincing demeanour, etc. Fresher(s) are generally the last choice. Accountability and experience are the two key parameters in their selection.
- The RD2 then convinces the local retailers and small shopkeepers (that is, RD3) to sell the products in their villages. The margin for these retailers is very high since there is no sharing of margins between the District Distributor and local retailers. All the middle layers are completely removed.
- The margin for the local retailer is the same as that of the super stockist in cities.
- The District Coordinator and Supervisors are employed on a salary basis, and share no margins.
- RD2 shares a very minimal margin, and so now s/he has begun selling the product directly to end consumers in the village, thereby benefiting from the margins that RD3 was achieving. Sometimes s/he also sells the stock to RD3, but includes his margin (RD3 readily agrees to it as he still earns a huge margin).
- The stock is procured on a credit basis and payments are made within 15 days with a credit limit of INR 150,000–200,000 for Supervisors.

In the beginning, this was a pilot project and all initial expenses were supported by Tata. But as the project grew, Tata adopted the policy of caution deposit for NGOs.

Tata has only been selling its tea brands through this project as of date. The three brands are Tata Tea Premium, Tata Tea Agni, and Tata Tea Gold. Tata Tea Life was launched. but later withdrawn from this market due to non-popularity among rural customers. The SKU has been from INR 1 packs to 1 kg. It had tried to sell Tata Salt, but that did not prove a viable option as RD1 and RD2 had rejected the proposal due to transportation issues. Tea is generally lightweight and easy to transport as against salt.

The Tata team has efficiently taken over the network and has addressed major operational issues. For instance, the sales force has mapped each and every retail outlet to track the sales and performance of front line teams. Further, they run more like a traditional channel set-up.

::: Rural Logistics

The Indian logistics industry is characterized by a dominance of unorganized players. Most transporters own three to four transport vehicles. As a result of the underdeveloped trade and logistics infrastructure, the logistics cost of the Indian economy is 13 per cent of the GDP, which is much higher than developed nations.

The logistic challenges increase and the costs multiply once we move to remote rural areas to deliver products and services. With rising disposable income, changing lifestyles, the government's focus on rural infrastructure, and private-sector initiatives to ensure the growth of rural markets, rural logistics have received special attention in the past two to three years. Rural logistics, though lucrative, have a number of challenges which makes it difficult to tap the opportunity. The development of cold chain/ warehousing infrastructure thus remains at the core of the government's plan to enable the growth of rural areas.

The method of handling logistics largely depends on the nature of the product category, the number of outlets, and their locations. Most FMCG players employ the 'hub and spoke' system to address the logistics challenge. Some players have also entered into syndicated distribution to connect the last mile in a cost-effective manner.

The Hub and Spoke System

The hub and spoke model of distribution comprises a system of connections arranged like a chariot wheel, in which all traffic moves along spokes connected to the hub at the centre.

This is a system of connections arranged like a chariot wheel, in which all the traffic moves along spokes connected to the hub at the centre, as depicted in Fig. 8.10. This increases efficiency by simplifying the network of routes.

Also known as the satellite distribution concept—designed to penetrate rural markets—this system is emerging as a strong and viable model. The system works as follows:

Stockists are appointed in major towns and feeder towns. By and large, they discharge the following functions: financing, warehousing, and sub-distribution. Depending on the size of the stockist's operations and the product line, these functions are performed with varying degrees of competence.

Retailers in and around the feeder towns get attached to these stockists. In some cases they function as the authorized retailers or franchised dealers of the company, and are recognized officially as forming part of the company's marketing network, operating through the stockist. In other cases, they are not franchised dealers, but form part of the stockist's network by custom.

| FIG. **8.10** |
The Hub and Spoke Model

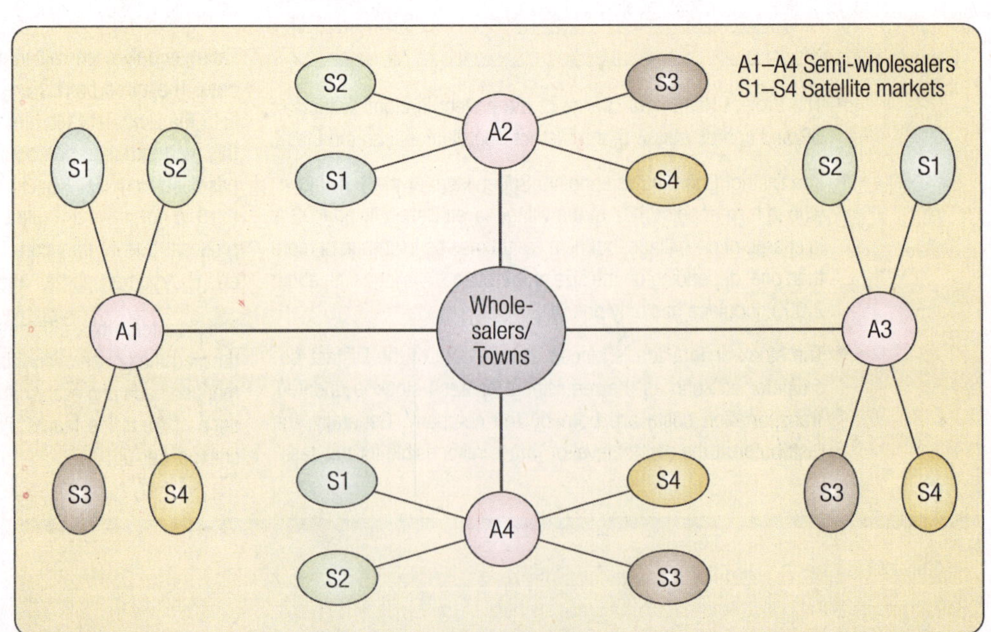

The manufacturer supplies goods to the stockists, who take care of sub-distribution. Often, the stockists operate their own delivery vans to take care of secondary transport and local delivery jobs. They are fully responsible for their own financial arrangements.

The volume of the business done by retailers varies, partly because of their location and partly because of their own capacity for doing business. Over a period of time, some retailers have grown in stature and importance. If such retail points coincide with centres of demand and transportation within the feeder town area, they are elevated to stockist points. Of course, the area of operations of the original stockists shrinks on account of this, but care is taken to see that their business volumes do not shrink. This is easily achieved because of the ever-growing demand for products, as well as through increased market penetration. If 15–20 retailers were operating as part of the original stockist's network, five or six are elevated over a period of time to the position of stockists. Fresh retail points are established simultaneously, out of which some retailers get attached to the original stockist and others to new stockists, depending on location, service convenience, and other factors.

The process continues as long as market size increases, consumption levels keep expanding, and supply catches up with the demand. Just like the second-generation stockists, sets of third-generation stockists also become established with the passage of time. At any point in time, a certain number of retail points always stay close to a particular stockist. Hence, the system is called the **satellite distribution system**.

The main advantage of this system is that market penetration takes place right into the interiors of rural markets, without the manufacturer having to expand his direct stock point network. If care is taken to ensure that the motivation of stockists is not destroyed due to the overzealous and premature expansion of the network, the system will indeed bring ample rewards in terms of increased sales and lower distribution costs.

With the growing rural demand, there is a need to move the hubs from district headquarters and cities to smaller towns closer to the villages to service markets effectively, as demonstrated by players like Coke and Pepsico.

PIONEERS OF THE HUB AND SPOKE MODEL

The per capita annual consumption of carbonated soft drinks in rural areas is only 0.40 litre, as against the national annual average consumption of 2 litre. Also, the rural contribution to total consumption is limited to 20 per cent. The cola majors are trying new ways to reach rural consumers. Although India's rural population is thrice the urban population, the rural market is not three times the urban market. Neither is it homogenous. To reach out to rural markets, companies have to cover large areas, resulting in disproportionately high logistics costs. Availability continues to be the biggest challenge in rural markets. Traditionally sold in returnable glass bottles, soft drinks cannot be sold through conventional FMCG channels. Therefore, Pepsi has chosen a hub and spoke distribution format. Typically, the spoke is closest to the retail outlets and is serviced by a hub distributor supplied directly from the manufacturing plant or the company's warehouse. This format allows for large loads travelling longer distances and short loads doing short distances, an arrangement that is cost-effective. A similar strategy has been adopted by Coca-Cola India as well. Rather than transporting beverages directly from bottling plants to retailers, it is first transported to a hub, and then to nearby spoke centres for order filling. This approach reduces costs because fewer long-haul journeys in large, uneconomical vehicles are needed, and increases efficiency through more timely, tailored fulfilment. The company has increased its village penetration from 9 per cent in 2000 to 28 per cent in 2004, and covers approximately 175,000 villages today. Rural India now accounts for 30 per cent of Coca-Cola's sales volumes.[11]

Syndicated Distribution

Syndicated Distribution is a system in which two or more companies come together to form a syndicated trading organization, to jointly distribute a collective group of products or services by sharing distribution costs.

Distribution poses a major problem for a new company targeting the rural market. It requires too many levels in the channel (multiple tiers), and setting up a distribution channel for rural markets is a costly proposition. Coca-Cola India purchased the Parle brands (Thums Up, Limca, etc.) for INR 5.5 billion in 1993, mainly to use Parle's existing distribution network. However, unlike Coca-Cola, small companies cannot afford to buy another company for the purpose of using its distribution network. In such a situation, syndicated distribution is a viable and novel approach to gain entry into rural markets. Under this approach, two or more companies come together to form a syndicated trading organization, to jointly distribute a collective group of household products in rural markets by sharing distribution costs.

The solution for small companies is to tie up with a leading company that already has a presence in the rural market, in order to distribute products through its distribution network. The golden rule is that the small company should not deal in the same products that the leading company sells.

Also, this type of joint collaboration can help both companies to reduce distribution costs, and can convert operations that seem unviable into financially viable ones.

See 'Rural Marketing Insight: Syndicated Distribution for Rural Dominance' to understand how the syndicated approach can help an organization to establish itself as a market leader in rural markets.

Some problems with the syndicated model of distribution are:

- Markets for the coverage of both companies are different.
- Terms of payment are different; it could be cash in the case of one company and credit in the case of another.
- As a salesman of only one company accompanies the van, he pushes his own products and is lax about booking orders for the other company.
- The salesman does not make serious efforts to collect payments for the other company.

RURAL MARKETING INSIGHT | SYNDICATED DISTRIBUTION FOR RURAL DOMINANCE

Bharti Airtel was faced with the challenge of profitably serving the rural areas of India due to the poor infrastructure, widely dispersed populations, and low incomes. To address these challenges, it decided to piggyback on distributors for consumer product companies such as Godrej and HUL, which had been operating in India for more than half a century. The enterprise gave around 10,000 distributors specific territories, and barred them from selling other carriers' products there. The distributors paid the company up front, but provided credit to retailers, who could sell products from competing carriers. More than one million shopkeepers in India sold Airtel pre-paid and post-paid telecom cards in 2009, and that number will double by 2012. To penetrate rural India, Bharti Airtel teamed up with India's largest microfinance institution, SKS. This partnership enables customers to take out a loan for the Nokia 1650 and pay for it through 25 instalments of INR 85 a month. Bharti Airtel also works with a fertilizer manufacturer, IFFCO (Indian Farmers Fertiliser Cooperative), which sells co-branded subscriber identity module cards through its retail outlets. Every day, farmers get three free voice updates on market prices, farming techniques, weather forecasts, and fertilizer availability.

Bharti Airtel even collaborates with competitors in order to save capital. As it expanded into rural India, putting up passive infrastructure such as towers, air-conditioning and generators became a large expense, especially in sparsely populated areas. This was not going to be a differentiating factor, so the company mooted the idea of merging its infrastructure unit with those of two other cellular service providers, Vodafone and Idea. By December 2007, the companies had struck a deal to set up Indus Towers, in which Bharti Airtel and Vodafone each own approximately 42 per cent of the equity and Idea owns the remaining 16 per cent. This structure allows the three companies to share the cost of setting up passive infrastructure and reduces the investment that each of them must make to expand operations in India.

With its innovative strategies, it has networked 440,000 villages covering 84 per cent of India's total population By April 2010, it had more than 27 per cent share in rural areas.

Source: 'Bharti Airtel Rural Strategy—Conneceted Life Experiences on the Move,' Cisco, October 2010, http://www.cisco.com/en/US/solutions/collateral/ns341/ns525/ns537/ns705/ns1058/Cisco_BhartiAirtel_CS.html (accessed 17 February 2011).

REVIEW OF OBJECTIVES :::

1. Understand the challenges and dilemmas in rural distribution

Availability is the biggest challenge among the four As. Reaching rural consumers is the most difficult as it requires the maximum time and resources to service these markets, spread across 600,000 villages and a 3.3 million sq. km area, economically. However, the saturation of urban markets and the growing potential of rural markets in terms of buying power and increasing acceptance of national brands and new product categories have forced marketers to adopt out-of-the-box thinking and come up with innovative solutions to ensure that their products reach remote locations.

2. Describe the channels of distribution

There are five layers of distribution channels used by all major companies to move their products from the company depot to the interior village markets. Most companies have direct representation up to level 3 in the form of redistribution stockists, but marketers face the real challenge in creating the last mile reach by taking products to levels 4 and 5 in the villages. Only a few players like HUL, ITC, and Colgate, who dared to think out of the box and designed innovative distribution channels to reach rural doorsteps, have a direct reach to this level.

The conventional distribution channel members servicing rural markets primarily include four participants: CFAs, redistribution stockists, wholesalers, and retailers.

3. Understand the rural retail environment

The rural retail environment primarily comprises traditional mom-and-pop stores and a few modern retail stores that have emerged in recent years in some pockets of the rural markets.

In traditional retail space, the number of rural retail outlets has more than doubled in the last decade, from 3.5 million in 2002 to 7.9 million in 2010, which is more than 40 per cent of the total outlets in India. The rural marketplace is also changing fast in terms of shop size, category of outlet, turnover, product categories, and brands stocked. The average size of the rural outlet has increased to 140 sq. ft and the average monthly turnover of rural outlets stands at INR 12,000. Relatively new and urban-oriented products like shampoos, ready-to-eat snacks, and chocolates register a healthy presence on rural shelves today.

On the other hand, modern retail has emerged only in the last decade with the entry of players like ITC's Choupal Saagar, DSCL Hariyali Kisaan Bazaar, Godrej Aadhaar, and Tata Kisan Sansar, who are experimenting with different approaches to attract rural consumers.

4. Describe channel behaviour in rural areas

The retailer is a crucial link in reaching rural consumers. Rural channel behaviour is characterized by frequent sourcing of stocks from wholesalers in feeder towns due to low investment capacity, seasonal stocking of products based on the harvest cycle, and the mostly credit purchase of stocks. They also enjoy high loyalty among their customers and command great influence in purchase decisions.

5. Identify the prevalent distribution models of different product categories

Companies engaged in different product categories often use varying distribution models depending on how optimally they can reach and service those markets. FMCG players primarily follow two types of distribution models, DM1 and DM2, depending on their rural coverage strategy.

Some companies like HUL and Britannia follow DM1, in which they have different channels for rural and urban coverage, involving a large number of intermediaries. On the other hand, DM2 is characterized by a single channel of distribution for both rural and urban areas, in order to minimize channel cost through using fewer intermediaries successfully. This is practised by companies like Nirma and Ghari detergent.

In the case of durables, too, most companies service rural markets through the existing urban distribution channel, as distribution is mostly restricted to towns and cities. The exceptions here are a few players like LG and Philips, who have established separate distribution and service networks for servicing rural markets efficiently.

6. Describe innovations in rural distribution and rural-centric distribution models

With the entry of new players in rural markets, marketers are innovating new cost-effective approaches to reach these markets. Given the bottlenecks of rural distribution, the solution has to be derived from learnings from old rural distribution systems (haats, mobile traders, etc.) and optimizing the existing physical and social infrastructure (PDS, petrol pumps, SHGs, cooperatives, haats and youth groups) and ensuring the participation and economic sustainability of all the stakeholders. The SHG distribution model (Project Shakti), youth entrepreneurship model, Public Distribution System, cooperatives, petrol pumps, and other unconventional channels of distribution are the recent cost-effective, sustainable initiatives based on a 'wheel of collaboration' between different stakeholders to reach the rural consumer. We are likely to see more such initiatives in coming years to achieve the last mile connect.

7. Discuss the logistics challenges in rural areas

Rural logistics in India are characterized by poor road connectivity and an inefficient transport system, which pose huge challenges to marketers trying to reach the hinterland in a cost-effective manner. To address this challenge, most FMCG players employ the 'hub and spoke' system. Some players have also entered into syndicated distribution to connect the last mile in a cost-effective manner.

DISCUSSION AND APPLICATION

Discussion of Concepts

1. What are the key challenges in reaching rural markets? How can companies address these bottlenecks?
2. Why has modern retailing not expanded beyond a few initiatives in rural areas? Discuss the challenges faced by modern retailers. What can be done to improve their sustainability?
3. Discuss the key changes that have taken place in the rural retail environment. What lessons can a new FMCG marketer venturing into rural markets learn?
4. Debate the merits and demerits of the DM1 and DM2 models. Find two players each for these models in rural markets. Describe their models and explain how they have helped them to succeed in rural markets.
5. Discuss three successful rural-centric distribution models. How have these models benefited companies? Debate the barriers faced by companies experimenting with these models.
6. 'Live Long Health Insurance' has enjoyed the special status as India's leading healthcare Insurance Provider. They want to penetrate into the rural markets and have already tried the conventional methods of distribution including (Banks, Post Offices etc.) and other prominent methods of rural distributions (e.g., Youth Entrepreneurs, Women's' Self Help Group, Bank Correspondents). What are the other innovative distribution models spanning across other industries that you think could prove beneficial to 'Long Live Health Insurance' and why ?

Application of Concepts

1. The retail environment is fast changing in rural India. How can a durables marketer plan his entry into rural markets to optimize this opportunity?
2. A durables company wants to sell its products in rural markets. Which distribution approach should it apply to achieve success? Draw out the distribution model and service network for the company.
3. A new company is planning to enter the rural retailing business in north India. Please develop a three-year plan for the company, defining the geography, retail format, product, and service offerings.
4. Develop a last mile distribution model for an FMCG company using rural haats as a platform. Present the business model for the company and explain the advantage it holds over traditional models.
5. Develop a retail activation strategy for a company planning to introduce ready-to-eat snacks in rural markets. How should the company motivate the retailer to stock products? Sketch the activation plan.
6. Evaluate the differences between village retail shops and retail outlets in periodic markets. What are the key lessons that they derive from each other to optimize their efficiency?.
7. Develop a rural-centric distribution model for a chocolates and confectionary company using a rural platform. Explain why you chose a particular platform. How it will improve the sustainability of the model?
8. Your client 'Healthy Chocolates' is a leading distributor and manufacturer of chocolates. According to Mr. Kuldeep Singh, CEO of the company, the traditional strength of selling chocolates in rural India has been with grocery stores, which still account for the majority chocolate sales of Healthy Chocolates. But, 'Kids Baazar', a kid's food chain startup, has been growing at a healthy rate of almost 15 per cent per year and has now become 'Healthy Chocolates' largest customer. Mr. Kuldeep Singh is not sure how to react on this as a distribution strategy. Being a rural market distribution consultant, he has asked you to advice on this.

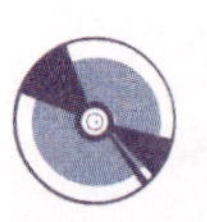

RURAL MARKETING **CASE** | COLGATE DISHA: THE EVOLUTION OF A SUSTAINABLE PPP MODEL IN THE BOP MARKET

Colgate-Palmolive, the world's leading manufacturer of oral care products, dominates the Indian oral care industry with a market share of more than 62 per cent. The word *Colgate* has become synonymous with toothpaste for most consumers in India, especially those in rural India.

As the leader, Colgate was faced the challenge of expanding the market which would ultimately result in increased business for all players. The urban market is more or less saturated with most consumers in this segment already using oral hygiene products in one form or the other. In the rural context, however, there was scope for growth, as over 30 per cent of the population of 800 million still used traditional methods of oral care. Colgate's rural coverage reached only large villages which had a population of more than 5,000 through direct distribution channels. Colgate was unable to penetrate any deeper into the rural market. The competition was steadily increasing, putting further pressure on Colgate. Powerful MNCs such as HUL had also entered the market with Pepsodent, while smaller regional players like Anchor, Ajanta, and Amar were cashing in on religious sentiments with vegetarian toothpaste, increasingly segmenting the market further, and in the deep interiors the fight against spurious products had already made a heavy dent in Colgate's market share.

The big challenge was reaching out to the medium and small villages (of population less than 5,000) which accounted for 85 per cent of the rural population of India. These medium and smaller villages would have little economic development, with a small proportion being affluent and the majority at the bottom of the pyramid. In this stratum, people would typically have to travel out of the village for the purchase of many necessities; periodically visiting haats, shops at nearby larger villages or the block town. Low per capita usage in these medium and small villages fosters an environment where there is inadequate scale for return on investment and which makes regular access untenable for existing direct distribution channels. Colgate was looking for a solution to these issues.

Deliberation

MART prepared a report in an attempt to gain a holistic understanding of the oral care industry, the levels of market penetration (summarized in Table 1) and other issues dogging the industry as a whole. Figure 1 shows the market penetration of the prominent brands. MART also analysed the existing distribution structure, as depicted in Fig. 2. It found that the existing structure allowed direct access only to the inhabitants of village with a population of more than 5,000.

Table 1 Oral Care Penetration Figures in India

Particulars	India			Zones			
	All	Urban	Rural	North	South	East	West
Toothpaste	48.6	74.9	37.6	47.8	61.8	40.0	44.4
Toothpowder	34.7	30.6	36.5	37.1	35.7	30.0	36.1

| FIG. 1 | The Market Penetration of Colgate (in per cent)

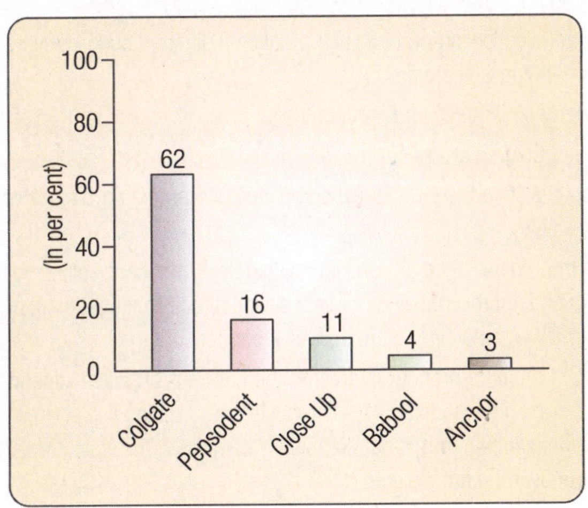

| FIG. 2 | The Existing Distribution Structure of Colgate

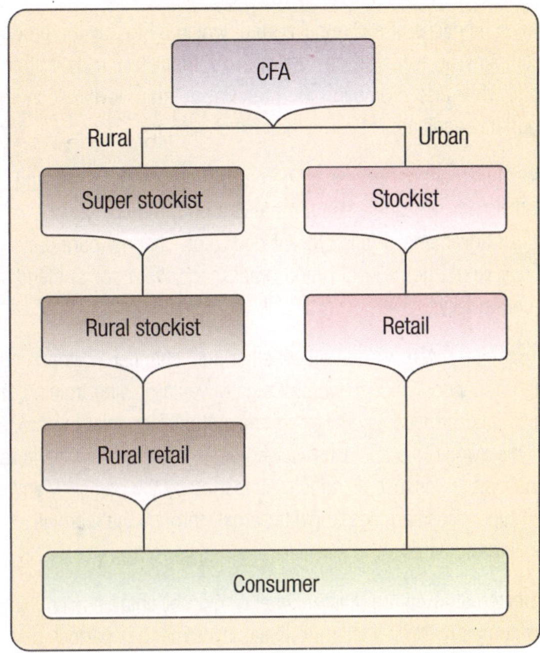

Buying Behaviour

The BoP population, which accounts for a substantial proportion of the rural market, depicts unique buying behaviour. Their main interest is in value-for-money offerings. They also shop more frequently than their urban counterparts, but fewer items on each occasion. As there are limited shops in villages of this population stratum, the BoP segment usually conducts most of its purchases from the nearby haat.

From the overview of the oral care sector and understanding on the BoP segment buying behaviour, it became evident that the solution needed to focus on three main factors:

- Distribution enhancement to expand beyond current coverage levels to access the BoP segment
- Provision of strong communication on identification of fakes and use of the genuine article
- Ensuring sustainability and scalability of the developed model

Issues and Strategic Perspective on a BoP Access Model

After much deliberation within the MART team, several issues emerged to be addressed while conceptualizing a model:

- As the traditional retailer-driven/sales-force model had not proven to be cost effective at lower population strata, a lower-cost model would have to be developed. This would not necessarily be a low-opportunity model, but it would be unlikely to meet traditional margin expectations. Further, the proposition of overcoming physical coverage issues in the vast remote areas of rural India would be unattractive to a distributor. These factors called for a channel partner who would be rural in residence and orientation, as well as having low economic expectations.

- The main functions of a channel partner would be to buy the products from the company at an approved rate and sell them to the next channel/consumers, while also promoting the brand at different levels. Identification of appropriate candidates became the next challenge.
- The ideal channel partner would be one who promoted the brand, communicated brand messages, sell the product and, thereby, earn a reasonable living. An advantage of this type of dedicated channel partners is that the company would get a loyal brand ambassador with social standing in the local community.
- The team at MART wondered whether the channel partner could work through a 'support' model, where Colgate would provide training, products, margins, and promotions while the channel partner sells the products and earns his living. This could be viewed as a new business venture for the channel partner, despite being fully supported by the company and provided a fixed stipend, as earnings would be largely through the margins earned and the business created.
- Being external in nature, this channel would not entail any ongoing liability to the company. However, some initial investment in partner development would be required and these costs would be spread across the total personnel deployed over the duration of the initiative. Being from a social sector organization, rural youth channel partners would have the capability to act as 'brand ambassadors' independently in the rural environment, reducing risk for the company.
- In this scenario, the company would gain with deeper brand penetration and access to unreached markets, allowing the brand to strike back at fakes and duplicates. At the same time, the partner would be able to start his own business selling company products, earning his livelihood while being respected as the company man in the area. A win-win situation; creating value for all.
- In the Indian, and even global, context, presence in the BoP sector is the single largest remaining market opportunity which any company can address today.

Model Development

After extensive internal deliberation by the MART team, the following model emerged:

- Identify educated, unemployed youth in villages as potential channel partners for Colgate products
- Selected youth to act as entrepreneurs, paying cash for stock and earning from sale of products
- To keep costs low, youth will travel by bicycle with a stock box attached for product storage.
- Makeshift stall, using a branded umbrella, erected at venue to attract buyers.
- Branding of channel partner through company logos on T-shirt, bicycle and box will increase visibility and ensure authenticity.

The Entity of Entrepreneur

| FIG. 3 | The Reach of the Entrepreneur

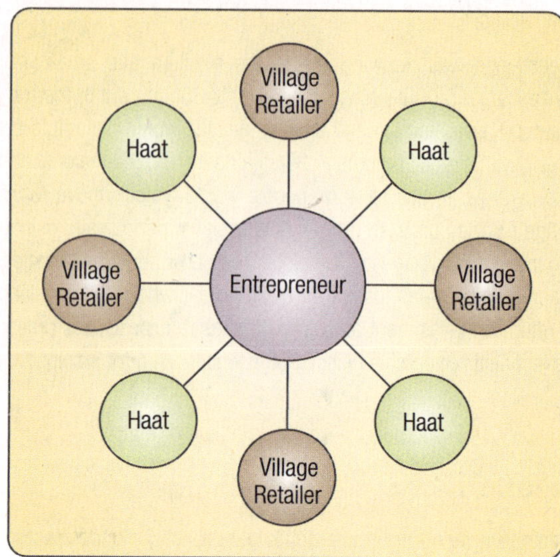

To reach the BoP market in sub-5,000-population villages, MART decided to hire local youth from different sources including the Nehru Yuva Kendra Sanghathan. The process used is as follows:

- Map the uncovered territory of the rural Colgate stockists. Select a cluster of 20–30 uncovered villages within a 10-km radius. Ensure haats are present.
- Identify, select, recruit, and train youth.
- Allocate territories and develop a permanent journey cycle plan to cover these markets. In one day, the entrepreneur covers two village retailers and one haat (see Fig. 3.) On 'non-haat' days, the entrepreneur covers four villages.
- At the village retailer, activities are:
  - Introduction of the entrepreneur as a Colgate last mile channel partner
  - Sharing journey plan and visiting on fixed day
  - Promotion of Colgate products
  - Placing posters at shops
- At the haat, activities include:
  - Ensuring an optimal vantage point for location of stand
  - Setting up branded umbrella on cycle and display of stock
  - Communication on oral hygiene practices, differentiating between fakes and genuine Colgate products.
  - Offering of samples and product trials
  - Sale of Colgate products
- The youth is linked to the nearest company stockist and buys stock on cash, usually weekly.
- The entrepreneur margins are approximately 3 per cent selling to village retailers and approximately 8 per cent selling directly to consumers at haats, creating a weighted average margin of 7 per cent.
- To sustain the entrepreneur interest in the business an initial stipend of INR 1,500 per month was fixed. This is reduced, on a sliding scale, over time as the business grows, but is not completely eliminated to retain some degree of control over the entrepreneur.

Roadblock and the Way Out

Post roll out, first-time hiccups and ground realities had to be taken into account while refining the model. The pilot implementation phase had encountered three major roadblocks:

- Channel partner motivation and retention was an issue over time. During the initial phase of operations, earnings rise very slowly and reducing the stipend before the business is established would lead to exit by the channel partner. In order to maintain a sustainable earning potential and to keep the partner motivated, MART introduced the concept of a monthly stipend payable on reducing scale. As business volumes build to attractive levels, the stipend is reduced in a calibrated manner to INR 1,200 but not withdrawn totally. This continued payment ensures control over the channel partner is retained.
- Correct identification of youth is required to ensure that their income expectations are consistent with the lower earnings available as a channel partner. The profile to be targeted to avoid duplication of efforts and resources are from needy lower-middle-income homes, who have a small family to support, earn less than INR 1,000 a month currently and have an education of up to 12th standard.
- A major challenge will be to retain channel partner 'buy in' over time as demonstrated through increasing investments as the business grows and observing total loyalty to Colgate only. The continued stipend will work to prevent the shifting of loyalties.

Size and Scale of Model

The model was implemented across 28 districts with 240 entrepreneurs working full time for Colgate. It took roughly 18 months for MART to operationalize this model in the field.

Impact of Model: Characteristics Enhancing Viable Access of the BOP Market

This model addresses the following issues:

1. Distribution
   - The model created a viable distribution structure for Colgate in the below 5,000 population villages to access BoP segment as desired.
   - The new distribution set-up could be integrated into regular channels without any alteration of margin structures.
   - The 'cash-and-carry' system ensured a no-risk business for Colgate.
2. Rural Orientation
   - The model recruited manpower from local areas providing livelihood opportunity to villagers through a sustained corporate partnership.
   - Increased entrepreneurship possibilities were created by setting an example, without displacing the rural youth.
3. Promotion of Genuine Products
   - The promotion of the genuine brand by an authorized partner to village consumers created an advantage for Colgate over fakes.
   - Communication at haats to the target audience on how to identify the genuine brand impacted sales positively.
4. Other Benefits
   - This is a self-sustaining, entrepreneurial model based on sales earnings rather than a typical salary outflow employee mode.
   - It is a low-cost model targeted at high sales volumes through access to large concentrated crowds at haats and by serving the larger requirements of village retailers rather than addressing individual consumers.

These benefits would allow any company with a brand to gain a strategic foothold in the BOP market in below 5,000 population villages provided that it is ready to partner a new entrepreneurial channel with an open mind, has a readiness to support the livelihood of the partner and be willing to provide long-term growth prospects. In 2005, the initial year of implementation, the 28 identified districts contributed to a total of 2 per cent of rural sales for the state. By 2006, this figure had grown to 6 per cent and, by 2008, it had jumped to 9 per cent of the state's rural sales. The accompanying video shows how project DISHA has taken shape.

Discussion Questions

1. Why do you think the youth entrepreneur was chosen as a channel partner? Who else could have been chosen in their place. Why?
2. What were the key success factors of project DISHA?
3. Do you think this model in sustainable and scalable? Can it be replicated by other players? Give arguments to support your choice.
4. Which product categories and players can replicate this model for rural distribution? Why?

AFTER READING THIS CHAPTER, YOU WILL BE ABLE TO:

1. Understand the major challenges in rural communication: rural heterogeneity and spread, and the need to understand the rural audience
2. Outline the process of rural communication
3. Detail the process of developing effective rural communication
4. Highlight the need for distinct advertisements for rural audiences and the factors to be kept in mind
5. Examine and discuss various media vehicles of the conventional mass media and the non-conventional, rural-centric media
6. Describe other relevant rural communication tools, such as sales promotion and events and experiences

CHAPTER 9 ::: COMMUNICATION STRATEGIES FOR RURAL MARKETS

nine

Tata Shaktee, the market leader in branded galvanized corrugated sheets with a market share of 30 per cent, faces competition from regional brands which lure consumers (mostly from the R2, R3, and R4 categories) with similar sounding brand names. Although consumers are concerned about product quality, lack of education and awareness makes them susceptible to retailer push/influence. Till 2003, Tata invested in minimum brand-building activities and used communication media like wall paintings, shutter/shop paintings, video on wheels, and point of purchase displays. These media could not reach the target consumer (the male head of the family) effectively. Wall paintings could serve as effective reminders at best. Shutter paintings, POP displays, etc., were restricted to dealer shops in feeder towns, and their impact was felt only when consumers visited these shops. Tata consulted MART to develop more effective forms of rural communication, educate the target segment on product/brand benefits, and create an experiential opportunity. MART (in partnership with Rediffusion DY&R) designed the Haat Hungama campaign centred on the theme: sardi garmi ya barsaat tata shaktee hardam saath. *Interactive brand games in the form of a set of flash cards created an edutainment (education + entertainment) platform for the audience. Moreover, the active participation of local Tata Shaktee dealers added authenticity to the whole campaign. Haats, traditional business centres in rural India, attract males from the R3 and R4 segments. They are the decision makers and have reasonable purchasing power. Thus haats, especially the bigger ones catering to 20–50 villages, enabled Tata Shaktee to reach the target customer at the right time and the right place, resulting in a 37 per cent increase in sales.*

The Haat Hungama campaign helped Tata Shaktee reach out to rural consumers.

::: Challenges in Rural Communication

There are many challenges to communication in rural markets. Low literacy levels, poor media reach and exposure, and the vast, heterogeneous and diverse rural audiences characterized by variations in language, culture, and lifestyle—all these factors pose multiple challenges to marketers looking to take their messages to the largely media-dark or media-grey areas of rural markets.

Heterogeneity and Spread

The communication pattern in any society is a part of its culture. No communication medium can exist in a cultural vacuum. Communicating the message to rural consumers has posed enormous challenges to the rural marketer because of the large numbers of consumers scattered across the country. Due to the widespread geographical dispersion (638,000 villages in India), many of them are still beyond the reach of conventional media. Even the use of unconventional media makes it almost unviable for the marketer to touch base with the widely scattered rural audience.

This problem is further compounded by the heterogeneous nature of the consumers in terms of their languages. There are 22 scheduled languages and 114 local vernaculars in India, which are further dialect-specific. For example, the dialect used in the Vidarbha region of Maharashtra is different from that used in the Marathwada region of the state, which in turn is different from the dialect spoken in the Konkan region in coastal Maharashtra. Thus, communicating the message in the right manner and language becomes a huge challenge in rural markets.

Low Literacy and Varying Comprehension Abilities

There are vast variations in the levels of literacy among rural citizens. Around two-fifths of the rural population is illiterate and only one-fifth holds a matriculate or higher degree. Also, literacy levels vary hugely among different states. For instance, the literacy level in Kerala is 94 per cent, whereas in Bihar it is only 64 per cent. These variations pose a challenge to easy and clear comprehension of the message by all sets of rural audience. To communicate effectively with the less educated, it becomes necessary to focus on creating a simple communication message using self-explanatory visuals comprising storyboards, role plays, and flip charts, rather than text.

Different Media Reach and Habits

The limited reach of mass media in rural areas (see Table 9.1) and its regional and state variations pose limitations on a universal approach to communication for rural consumers. Television has the maximum reach in Goa (83 per cent) and the least in Bihar (11 per cent); the press reaches 62 per cent people in Kerala but only 4 per cent in Madhya Pradesh; the penetration of radio is 40 per cent in Tamil Nadu, whereas it is a minimal 3 per cent in Andhra Pradesh where cinema has the highest reach at 20 per cent.

| TABLE **9.1** |
Media Penetration in Rural Areas

Medium	Penetration (in per cent)
Television	47
Cable and satellite	31
Radio	18
Press	13
Cinema	6
Internet	1

Source: Indian Readership Survey Q3, 2010

Also, different perceptions, traditions, and values across states—and in some cases within a state—have to be kept in mind while developing a communication package. This necessitates understanding the mindset of the target audience for every product category in every region. Correct use of visuals and attire, and correct depiction of the culture and beliefs of the target audience become important while designing communication for a specific region. Dabur's choice of the Bhojpuri film star, Ravi Kishan, to endorse its Chyawanprash brand exclusively for localized promotional activities through direct interaction with consumers, dealers, and stockists, particularly in Bihar, and Uttar Pradesh, is an apt example of this. Looking at the above challenges, there are three requirements for a rural marketer:

- To identify the most suitable medium to ensure maximum spatial reach across the country.
- To develop region-specific consumer profiles to understand the characteristics of the target market.
- To design the most effective and persuasive communication and promotional strategies to induce the target audience to buy the product.

::: The Communication Process: An Overview

It is necessary for rural marketers to understand the fundamental elements of the communication process, which are crucial for taking decisions pertaining to the actual message and the media. The information seeking and processing behaviour of rural consumers influences the choice of media and the message.

Figure 9.1 shows the communication process model. As seen in the model, the sender's task is to communicate the message to the receiver. How the sender encodes the message and passes it to the receiver and how the receiver perceives or decodes that message is crucial, especially in the case of rural markets, where the environment exercises considerable influence on the receiver. This might lead to the receiver not receiving the intended message for any one of the following three reasons:

- ***Selective attention.*** The consumer may not notice the stimulus provided.
- ***Selective distortion.*** The message is deliberately twisted so that the consumer hears what they want to hear.
- ***Selective retention.*** The consumer retains only a small fraction of the message that reaches them.

The comprehension of a message is therefore a critical problem in Indian rural markets. This is shown in a study that tested the responses of rural and urban consumers to television advertising (see 'Rural Marketing Insight: Rural and Urban Responses to Television Advertisements'). The distortion in the study indicates the gravity of the problem.

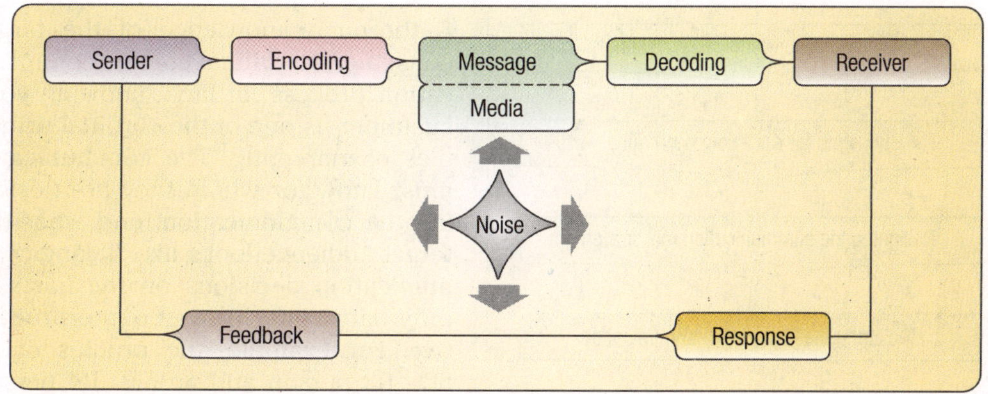

| FIG. **9.1** |
The Communication Process Model (Based on the Shanon–Weaver Model published in The Mathematical Theory of Communication, Urbana,IL: University of Illinois Press, 1945: 5.)

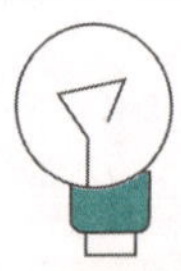

RURAL MARKETING **INSIGHT** | RURAL AND URBAN RESPONSES TO TELEVISION ADVERTISEMENTS

A study was undertaken jointly by MART and Anugrah Madison in South and North India, covering both urban, and rural areas, to assess the comprehension, association, credibility, and acceptability of television commercials for Babool (featuring a young man undertaking a series of activities, yet looking fresh through the day) and Navaratna hair oil (featuring the film actors Govinda and Rambha in a group dance) in the FMCG category, and Samsung Plano Digital Flat TV (an estranged young couple being united because of the rays emanating from the TV) and Asian Paints exterior emulsion paint (featuring the average joe Sunil Babu) in the consumer durables category.

Respondents included 60 regular TV viewers (40 from rural areas and 20 from urban areas, equally distributed over both regions) in the age group of 18–50 years, both male and female, from SEC A and SEC B (for urban) and SEC R1, SEC R2, and SEC R3 (for rural). These were the primary findings:

- **Babool:** Rural people had a problem comprehending the message as they perceived it to be too quick. In the north, some respondents thought the advertisement was for a toothbrush/shaving cream.
- **Navratan:** Rural people questioned why Govinda was dancing in the advertisement despite the so-called headache. Most rural respondents from the south could not recognize Govinda. Similarly, in the north the recognition of Rambha was very low.
- **Samsung:** The advertisement went over the heads of rural respondents and most felt that the ad was meant only for the educated and rich people. Urban viewers seemed to have comprehended the message of the advertisement. People in the south loved the mood and the graphics, but urbanites in the north found it 'boring'.
- **Asian Paints:** The advertisement scored very well on the 'believability' factor among the urban audience. Rural consumers were sceptical as they thought the paint would last for only a couple of years, which, according to them, was not value for money. Some rural respondents thought it was an advertisement for a housing company.

From these findings, it is evident that what works in the south may not work in the north. Quickies, gimmicks, or slick advertisements cannot seduce rural people. They expect the message to be rational.

Source: MART Knowledge Centre

Developing Effective Rural Communication

Developing any communication programme targeted at rural consumers involves the seven steps specified in Fig. 9.2: identifying and profiling the target audience, determining communication objectives, designing the message, selecting communication channels, budgeting for rural communication, designing the marketing communication mix strategy, and integrating the communication process and measuring impact and results.

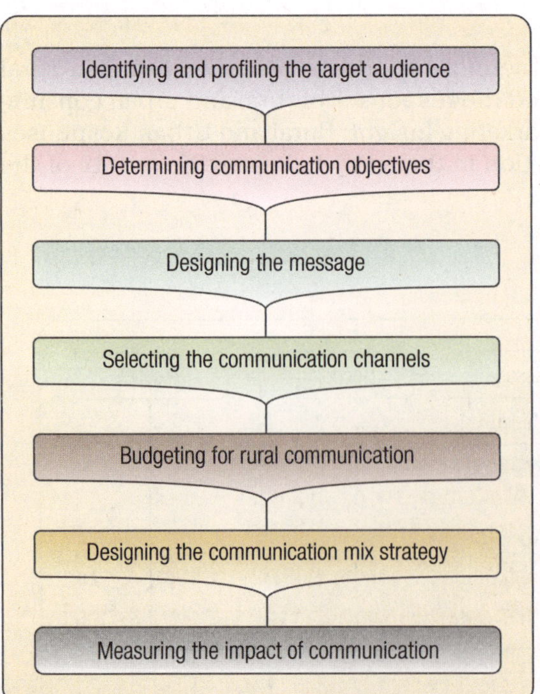

| FIG. 9.2 | Steps for Developing Effective Rural Communication Programme

Identifying and Profiling the Target Audience

A thorough knowledge of the target consumer is critical to the communication process. In fact, 'knowing your customer' is one of the cardinal principles of marketing. The communicator must know for whom they are designing the communication, and what the target audience looks like. Taking communication decisions on the basis of only data could prove counterproductive. For example, the profiles of an SEC R3 person and an SEC R4 person in rural Punjab could be in sharp contrast to the profiles of people from similar socio-economic classes in Bihar. It would be dangerous to design the same communication programmes for both without understanding the difference between the two.

Probing the environment and behaviour and profiling the target audience can be done in terms of any of the segmentation parameters identified in Chapter 5. These could be demographic variables like age, gender, religion, etc., or behavioural and psychographic parameters like buying roles, purchase needs and value propositions, and lifestyles of people.

Many companies conduct such probing and profiling exercises before they come up with their rural communication idea and design. To market its baby gripe water Dabur Janam Ghutti, Dabur India profiled rural consumers at haats and melas. The exercise helped the company to debunk the myth that the rural consumer will opt for tried-and-tested home recipes when it comes to baby-care products. In addition, it was discovered that while it is the housewife who decides on the product category, the man does the brand selection and purchase. These insights helped Dabur India to redesign its communication strategy. See 'Rural Marketing Insight: Religion—A Key Profiling Factor for Designing Communication' to understand how HUL profiled customers on the basis of religion and customs.

Profiling of the target audience for communication can be done in terms of any of the segmentation parameters, like geographic, demographic, behavioural, and psychographic parameters.

Determining Communication Objectives

Once the target market/audience and its characteristics have been identified, the marketer and the communicator must decide on the desired audience response. The ultimate response, of course, is purchase and satisfaction. The communicator needs to know how to move the target audience to higher states of readiness to buy.

Communicators make efforts to put something into the consumer's mind, to change their attitude, and get them to act. The AICDA model of communication, the oldest and best-known response-hierarchy model, as shown in Fig. 9.3, best summarizes this communication strategy.

One of the most common communication models used in rural markets is AICDA—awareness, interest, conviction, desire, and action.

The model shows how the consumer passes through the state of being unaware of a product to actual purchase behaviour. Any communication should get

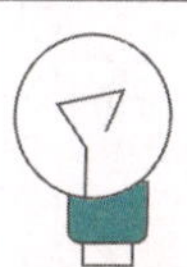

RURAL MARKETING INSIGHT | RELIGION: A KEY PROFILING FACTOR FOR DESIGNING COMMUNICATION

Religion and its associated customs have been used as key profiling factors for the target audience of Lifebuoy, one of the leading brands of Hindustan Unilever, for designing its rural communication programme.

Realizing that conventional media could not effectively communicate the underlying hygiene issues and create brand awareness among rural consumers, HUL wanted to use a cost-effective and powerful medium to promote this programme. It chose religion—one of the strongest emotional platforms—to stress the need to use soap each time people washed their hands. To this end, it segmented and profiled people based on their religion, analysed their rituals and customs, and designed a suitable awareness programme.

HUL initiated this programme in gurdwaras (the Sikh place of worship) in Punjab, an important place for congregation. Upon entering a gurdwara, devotees are required to take off their shoes, and wash their hands and feet at designated locations before they can go inside the prayer room. Conducting this activity within gurdwaras enabled HUL to capture the moment of truth (washing hands before offering prayers) and subtly work on creating brand awareness among rural consumers. The format was standardized for replication elsewhere during the course of this programme.

With the permission of the governing bodies of gurdwaras, relevant hygiene messages were created and integrated with the religious sentiment and environment. Messages were placed alongside soap dishes containing Lifebuoy soap cakes at the water points, and tokens handed out in exchange for placing shoes in safe custody carried messages on the importance of washing hands. Lifebuoy soaps were also distributed as gifts. HUL covered 156 gurdwaras across 138 small towns in Punjab, and reached out to over 35,000 people with the Lifebuoy health and hygiene message.

Similarly, in the southern part of the country, devotees have to take a bath before entering the temple or doing '*darshan*'. Most devotees go barefoot to famous temples, many of which are situated on the top of hills. Lifebuoy has found an apt opportunity here and has placed its branded mobile bathing units for devotees to take a bath with Lifebuoy for free. This has created a huge visibility for the brand among rural folks.

| FIG. 9.3 |
The AICDA Model

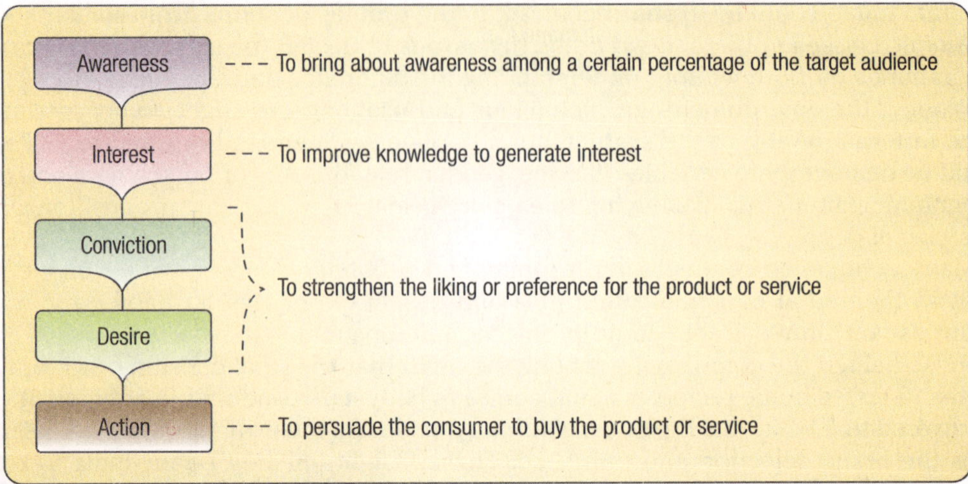

The LG Batteria campaign created interest and excitement among rural consumers.

the prospect's *attention*, foster the consumer's *interest* in the offer, build a *desire* for the product or service, and generate a favourable *action* by the customer. Thus, the marketer may seek to achieve any one or more of these communication objectives.

Marketers can use different static or dynamic promotional elements, as suggested in Table 9.2, based on their communication objectives or AICDA level, to communicate with the rural audience. Although in urban markets the emphasis during communication is more on the last AICDA level, that is, action or promoting usage among the target audience, in the case of rural markets the need is to focus more on awareness generation objectives since media and product exposures are low.

LG'S BATTERIA CAMPAIGN[1]

Low battery back-up is the primary concern of rural consumers, due to their habit of listening to music on their mobile phones. To tackle this complaint, LG launched the All Rounder with improved battery life, which they promoted using the Batteria campaign designed by RC&M. The aim of this campaign was to make rural consumers aware of the practices that reduced the overall battery life. Under the Batteria or battery-ka-bacteria concept, brief events such as role plays and skits were conducted in villages and video vans, posters and danglers were displayed at retail outlets to create awareness, interest and excitement about the new product among the rural audience. This campaign helped LG generate sales worth INR 23 million, out of which INR 15 million were on-spot sales.

Designing the Message

Having defined the desired audience response, the communicator moves to the next step of developing an effective message. Formulating the message requires solving five problems: what to say (message content); how to say it logically (message structure); how to say it symbolically (message format); in what context to say it (context association); and who should say it (message source).

| TABLE 9.2 |
Choice of Promotional Elements Based on Communication Objective or AICDA Level

Promotional Element	Communication Objective or AICDA Level	Expected Results
Dynamic		
Haat demonstrations	A, I	Awareness, Interest, Questions, Doubts, Prospect Identification
Short campaigns	A, I	Awareness, Interest, TOMA,* Excitement, Announcement
Video shows	A, I	Awareness, Interest, Excitement, Large-scale impact, Doubts, Questions
Farmers' meetings and village demonstrations	I, C, D, A	Awareness, Interest, Queries, Argument, Desire
Opinion leaders	I, C, D, A	Positive word of mouth
Personal selling	C, D, A	Argument, Desire, Action
Static		
Handbills	A, I	Awareness, Information, Interest, Questions, Doubts
Wall paintings	A, I	Awareness, TOMA, Information
Dealer signboards	A, I	Awareness, TOMA, Information, Excitement
Audio jingles	A, I	Awareness, TOMA, Information, Excitement
Caps, T-shirts, bags, calendars	A, I	Awareness, TOMA, Recall, Information

**TOMA: Top of the Mind Awareness*
Source: MART Knowledge Centre

While designing the message content, the rural communicator can look at three kinds of appeals—rational, emotional, and moral.

THE MESSAGE CONTENT The communicator has to figure out what to say to the target audience in order to produce the desired response. This process has been variously called the appeal, theme, idea or unique selling proposition. Three types of appeals can be distinguished:

Rational Appeal A message could appeal to the audience's self-interest. Examples would be messages demonstrating product quality (nylon cord-breaking contest for *pahelwans* [muscleman] in the audience, held to demonstrate the strength of nylon-made MRF bullock cart tyres called '*Pahelwan Chaap Baggi Gadi Tyres*'); economy (theme of the Babool toothpaste advertisement, '*Babool Babool, paise wasool*'); performance (Tata Shaktee GC sheet punch line, '*Sardi garmi ya barsaat, Tata Shaktee hardam saath*').

Emotional Appeal A message often plays on qualities like heroism, love of family, pride in achievement and humour, and has universal appeal. It attempts to stir up negative or positive emotions that will motivate purchase. For instance, the television advertisement for Kayam Churna shows a forest ranger who fails to shoot the three evils depicting '*kabz*' (constipation), 'acidity', and 'gas', and exclaims, '*Goliyon ka bhi asar nahin*'.

Communicators have also based appeals on guilt and shame to get people to buy products. For example, Birla White Cement targeted small-town consumers with its television advertisement showing a grandmother who initially refused a marriage proposal for her granddaughter, saying, '*Chuna lagane walon ka hamare ghar mein kya kaam.*' But she later accepted the prospective groom when he shifted to Birla White Cement.

For rural consumers, functional elements have a stronger influence than emotional appeal. Quality and value-for-money propositions attract many rural consumers. Companies that have understood the interests and aspirations of rural customers are more successful today.

Moral Appeal A message appeals to the audience's sense of what is right and proper. It is often used to exhort people to support social causes such as childbirth spacing. One such advertisement featured a farmer who suggests that just like a distance of at least three feet should be maintained between two plants for their proper nourishment and growth, there should be a similar difference of at least three years between two children.

In one of its social communication campaigns focusing on improving maternal and new-born health in rural India, the international funding organization Program for Appropriate Technology in Health (PATH) came up with an innovative punch line for its communication programme—'*Pehla Ek Ghanta*'. The brand was called that as most of the communication focus for behaviour change was on the first one hour after childbirth. It also developed a jingle for its video van, which moved from village to village using these words: '*Pehla ek ghanta maa bachhe ki zindagi badal sakta hai*', where it informed rural women about the right practices during the first hour of childbirth, since this would determine the health of both mother and child in the coming days.

PEHLA EK GHANTA

The level of maternal and new-born mortality and morbidity is quite high in India. About one-fifth of the world's maternal deaths and one-quarter of all new born deaths take place in India. To reduce this PATH launched Sure Start Project in India in 2006 and began connecting with the target population in Uttar Pradesh. Sure Start is funded by the Bill and Melinda Gates Foundation as part of its Health Solutions Initiatives. It tried to understand the realities of maternal and newborn heath. The health supervisors of the programme shared many simple things that could prevent the death of many new-borns with just simple acts at home––such as cutting umbilical cords with sterile blades, using skin-to-skin contact to keep babies warm, or recognizing danger signs that require hospital care. It informed rural women about the right practices during the first one hour of childbirths since this would determine the health of both mother and child in the coming days.

Despite its efforts and implementation till 2009 the behaviour change did not see much of acceptability in the household. The propagated healthy practices around pregnancy, delivery, and new born care had no significant recall, however understood by mothers and family members.

The captivating concept was carried on ground in target villages through a well-crafted day long community level programme in the village comprising a mother-meet, influencer felicitation, and community evening show. Mother-meet intercepted the pregnant woman and her female family members especially her mother-in-law to make her feel important and win her acceptability. Anganwadi centres and Panchayat grounds were the venue for the mother meetings and community show. The community show marked the grand finale of Pehla Ek Ghanta programme. Engagement of fathers around the messages and support by Pradhans/Health and sanitation committee members, ceremonial felicitation with branded name plates of all stakeholders gave a larger than life image of the programme in the village. Simultaneously, for recall purposes, messages were crafted on the walls with the referral numbers and address for institution care. The tin plating at the stakeholder's home was intelligent footprints of the activity left behind for visibility and reminders. Also street plays were enacted cashing on the Anti-natal day traffic of new-borns and pregnant mothers.

The project has reached 24 million people in 7 districts, 115 blocks, and 12000 villages in 2 years 2009-10 and 2011. In 2012, the Pehle Ek Ghanta initiative was adopted by child fund India for addressing infant morbidity issues in tribal districts of Rajasthan and Madhya Pradesh. Focus group discussions showed that mothers who had been to the Sure Start meetings had a strong sense of confidence about managing their pregnancies and their new-born babies. This initiative has helped changing the mindset of husbands through new learnings and attitude of mother-in-laws have also changed. The initiative has been well recognized and has won many awards across the healthcare and rural development platforms.

While designing the message content for rural markets, the language of communication plays a very important role, as it is not universal across different geographies. The language needs to be simple and direct for better receptivity. A word can have different meanings in different regions, and hence may cause distortion. Therefore, the message needs to be designed in the local language/dialect as far as possible. Traditional and cultural considerations and other area-wise and region-wise peculiarities should also be considered. For example, Tata Shaktee GC sheet is known by different names in different parts of India—*chaddar* in Uttar Pradesh, *nalidar chaddar* in Madhya Pradesh, patra in Maharashtra, *tina* in Bihar, and *tadag* in Tamil Nadu.

THE MESSAGE STRUCTURE AND FORMAT The effectiveness of a message depends on both its structure and content. For the rural audience, the message structure has to be simple, short, and self-explanatory. Simple logic, sequential ordering of thoughts, easy-to-understand arguments, and clearly drawn conclusions are helpful in making rural communication effective. In case of audiovisuals, components of the message like dramatic voices, attractive expressions, and strong colours also play an important role.

Considering that literacy levels in rural India are low, and also that the rural audience have low levels of comprehension, pictorial representations have a better impact and recall than verbal descriptions. The use of 'symbols' (the 'tortoise' symbol of Tortoise [*Kachua Chaap*] mosquito coil, the 'plus' symbol of Clinic Plus shampoo) in promoting the brand helps rural customers to easily identify the brands at the point of purchase.

Rural consumers prefer messages that link benefits to product attributes. The use of narrative messages like those featuring short stories for the promotion of products, and exhibiting demonstration effects are effective communication strategies for rural markets. Many rural marketers have developed rural, story-based commercials with rural mascots to promote their products, which help in increasing retention through involvement.

A television commercial for Pril, a dish-washing soap targeted at small-town consumers, features a mother-in-law who tells her daughter-in-law, '*Bahu, doodhwala bartan lana*'. The *bahu* smells two or three utensils that all look apparently clean, and then chooses a utensil that smells of milk. This communication is followed by the introduction of the Pril bar, which boasts of a mix of lemon and vinegar; the lemon cleans the utensils and the vinegar removes the smell of cooked food.

CONTEXT ASSOCIATION The rural audience is influenced by the context of the communication. Communications with urban settings, or those that are far removed from the everyday reality of rural life, do not find favour with rural consumers, as they are unable to relate to such a context. Rural consumers are therefore not influenced by advertisements that depict a different or alien world, as they find it difficult to relate to.

Marketers, therefore, need to pay attention to the rural environment, dress styles, food habits, and other cultural preferences in order to create a close association/identification with rural audiences. Ignoring these aspects can result in the failure of the communication.

THE MESSAGE SOURCE Message source is again an important element to look at while designing the communication. The source can be categorized into three groups:

- ***Likeable source.*** The use of a likeable source to communicate the message increases its acceptance among the target audience. Testimonial advertising using film stars has been quite successful. For example, *Thanda matlab Coca-Cola* featuring Aamir Khan and *Jaandaar sawaari, sabse shandaar sawaari* for Rajdoot motorcycles featuring Dharmendra.

LIFEBUOY SE HAATH DHOYA KYA

One of the world's largest religious gatherings, with over 80 million people in 2013, the Allahabad Maha Kumbh mela is a dazzling spectacle of spiritual fervour. The Maha Kumbh provides a unique opportunity to communicate messages to a large, predominantly small-town and rural population. Companies like HUL took this opportunity to make it conversation points where one can interact with the audience. HUL using public health concept of washing hands before a meal, used their marquee brand Lifebuoy. By partnering with major caterers at the mela, and using a heat press HUL marked rotis with the message 'Lifebuoy se haath dhoya kya' (Have you washed your hands with Lifebuoy?). The idea, medium, and message made a brilliant use of the context, manipulating the same to get the marketing message across. In effect, this simple, clutter-breaking idea helped HUL to reach out to a massive audience, at a very low cost.

- ***Trustworthy source.*** Word-of-mouth communication works to a large extent in rural markets. Villagers prefer to use a source that they can trust; these are generally friends, relatives, neighbours, etc. A television commercial for Markfed-branded pesticides and insecticides shows a farmer who is unhappy because of the low crop yields caused by pest infestation. His fellow farmers advise him to use Markfed-branded pesticides and insecticides to ensure a better output in the future.
- ***Expert source.*** For the purchase of big-ticket, high-involvement items like durables, opinion leaders are consulted for more information about the product. Opinion leaders are defined according to the product category. For example, a *mistri* (mason) is consulted for the purchase of building and construction-related products like cement and roofing sheets. An auto mechanic is generally consulted during the purchase of a tractor or motorcycle. Some of the other expert sources whom villagers look up to are school teachers/headmasters, social health workers, retired army persons, the village sarpanch or pradhan, etc.

Asian Paints promoted its Utsav brand of paint by painting the village sarpanch's house a few months prior to the launch, to demonstrate that the paint does not peel off and is an ideal replacement for *chuna*.

A television commercial for Birla Plus cement features a young small-town man who says to the *mukhiya*/sarpanch, '*Jidhar dekho, Birla Plus hi istemal ho raha hai*'. The sarpanch replies, '*Is cement mein jaan hai*', thus establishing the credibility of the cement in the eyes of the villagers.

Messages delivered by attractive sources achieve higher levels of attention and recall. However, equally important in rural markets is credibility: the spokesperson must be credible. Messages delivered by highly credible sources are more persuasive. See

DOCTORS AS OPINION LEADERS

Glaxo Smithkline promoted a range of its over-the-counter brands through a pilot in the top five haats in western Uttar Pradesh. It employed the services of two doctors—one from the city and the other from the local haat village—while organizing health check-up camps at the haats. Company products were prescribed and free samples were also given out to a select few. Despite not being paid for participating in this campaign, the doctors participated with a view to practising medicine in the long run. The company presented each of them with a token of appreciation for their services as opinion leaders, and enrolled them on the company panel.

'Rural Marketing Memo: Developing an Effective Rural Communication Message' to understand the various myths associated with rural consumers and how Coca-Cola's '*Thanda Matlab Coca-Cola*' campaign shattered these myths.

Selecting the Communication Channels

The communicator must select efficient channels of communication to carry the message. Communication media channels are of two broad types—personal and non-personal.

Designing the right message for rural markets involves five essential elements—message content, message structure, message format, context association, and message source.

PERSONAL COMMUNICATION CHANNELS Personal communication channels involve two or more persons communicating directly with each other. They might communicate face to face, person to audience, over the telephone, or through mail. Personal communication channels are further divided into:

- ***Advocate channels,*** consisting of company salespeople who contact buyers in the target market. Dalmia Consumer Care assembled a team of rural sales promoters (RSPs) to promote their non-tobacco bidi brand Vardaan in rural areas. In addition to performing their routine sales jobs, the RSPs also used to target consumers directly at haats. ACC Cement representatives visit each house and provide information about stability of the product.
- ***Expert channels,*** consisting of independent experts who make statements to target buyers. Marketers of building/construction products like cement and GC sheets target masons to promote their brands. Village and town retailers act as experts for agri-input companies. Expert communication channels command more credibility in rural markets as they are considered insiders who possess the required technical knowledge.
- ***Social channels,*** consisting of neighbours, friends, family members, and associates who talk to the target buyers. In the rural context, the social channel is the first to which potential consumers automatically turn, before they solicit views

RURAL MARKETING MEMO | DEVELOPING AN EFFECTIVE RURAL COMMUNICATION MESSAGE

In 2003, the rural market contributed 28 per cent to the total sale of carbonated soft drinks in India.[2] It was also the fastest growing segment of the Indian market, with an annual growth rate of 15 per cent. To grow the market, Coca-Cola India decided to introduce an INR 5 returnable glass bottle. It partnered with McCann Erickson, its advertising agency, to design a campaign focusing on positioning the product offering within the context of the existing reality, emphasizing the universal appeal of the drink through the use of the word *thanda*.

The '*Thanda Matlab Coca-Cola*' campaign depicting the film actor Aamir Khan in different situations—as a Punjabi farmer, as a rural icon, as a Hyderabadi pan shopkeeper, as a Nepali guide, as a Bengali babu—was a runaway success. This campaign shattered several myths associated with rural consumers and clearly established the following:

- It is possible to speak to rural India without grossly stereotyping the people.
- It is important to understand the rural psyche.
- It is important to speak to motivations without patronizing rural consumers.
- It is important to develop the skill to speak in many languages.
- It is important to understand the different communication forms.
- It is important to track changes in the mindsets and aspirations of rural consumers.

The success of the campaign emphasized the need to invest much more than we are doing at present in understanding the rural consumer and 'owning' rural India.

Source: Compiled from a presentation, 'Communicating to Rural India', by Santosh Desai at the FICCI Rural Marketing Conference, New Delhi, April 2003.

and opinions from the outside world. A fellow progressive farmer acts as a social channel for agricultural and allied products like seeds, pesticides, tractors, etc.

In rural areas, personal communication channels are more effective since they provide a platform for first-hand experience and feedback from the end consumer.

Communicators can select different channels of communication to carry the message. Communication channels are of two types—personal channels (advocate, expert, social channel); and non-personal channels (mass media, atmospherics, events).

NON-PERSONAL COMMUNICATION CHANNELS Non-personal communication channels carry messages without personal contact or interaction. They include the mass media, atmospherics, and events.

The **mass media** consists of the print media (newspapers, magazines, direct mail), broadcast media (radio, television), electronic media (audio tape, videotape), and display media (billboards, signs, posters). Most non-personal messages come through paid media.

An **'atmosphere'** is a 'packaged environment' that creates or reinforces the buyer's leanings towards product purchase.

Events are occurrences designed to communicate particular messages to target audiences. A major goal of HUL's Project Shakti was to spread the word across the village about the appointment of the Shakti dealer, and in turn make the business proposition more viable for the latter. Thus was born the concept of 'Shakti Day', a monthly promotional event where the woman dealer puts up a stall in the village to offer/sell special pro-

GREENPEACE'S OORJA KRANTI

Greenpeace, a non-government environmental organization, aimed to create awareness regarding the use of renewable sources of energy. To that end, they designed a campaign called 'Oorja Kranti', through which they created the complete atmosphere required to sensitize key opinion leaders and stakeholders in the villages of Bihar to this concept. They tied up with local NGOs, collaborated with eminent personalities to promote the concept and reach out to the audience, held debates and panel discussions to build an opinion among the audience, held '*Yatras*' or van campaigns, engaged people to sign and take the pledge to use environment-friendly products, held a lighting the lamp ceremony, and conducted street plays. All these activities helped in creating an engaging atmosphere to introduce the audience to, and convince them about, the concept of renewable energy. The programme helped to engage 1,500 key opinion leaders across 10 districts of Bihar.

The Greenpeace 'Oorja Kranti' *Yatra* in Bihar sensitized key opinion leaders and stakeholders on the benefits of decentralized renewable energy.

motional schemes. The event was publicized on the preceding day, as well as throughout the day itself, via a public announcement system. Shakti Day has now become an integral part of Project Shakti. It continues to be held periodically across several villages, drawing crowds and serving as an effective medium for marketing and communication.

Budgeting for Rural Communication

After deciding on the channels of communication, the next step for the rural marketer is fixing a communication budget. The allocation of a budget for different planned media like advertising, sales promotion, campaigns at haats and melas, road shows, wall paintings, etc., is done. There should be an objective analysis of the goals and tasks of communication to determine the size and allocation of the budget. An estimate is generally prepared based on the different activities one plans to conduct and the results in terms of the exposure levels, trails, and usage one expects.

Designing the Communication Mix Strategy

Companies face the task of distributing the total communication budget across different communication tools—advertising, sales promotion, direct marketing, publicity and image-building tools, personal selling, etc. They generally utilize one or more tools to design a complete communication package. Each communication tool has its own unique characteristics and costs. Marketers have to understand these characteristics in order to select the most appropriate and useful tool. We will briefly review each of these tools and discuss them in more detail later in the chapter.

ADVERTISING Advertising is a highly public mode of communication. Its public nature confers a kind of legitimacy on the product and also suggests a standardized offering. Advertising can be used to build and enhance a long-term image for a company/product. ITC's advertisement 'Putting India First' cleverly wove the company's rural initiatives of e-choupals and large-format rural retail stores to position ITC as a fairly Indianized company, concerned about the uplift of rural people and also with triggering quick sales.

SALES PROMOTION Sales promotion tools include incentives like coupons, contests, discounts, demonstrations, and sampling. Although diverse, the tools have three distinctive characteristics:

- ***Communication.*** They gain the consumer's attention and usually provide information that may lead the consumer to the product.
- ***Incentive.*** They incorporate some concessions, inducements, or contributions that offer value to the customer.
- ***Invitation.*** They include a distinct invitation to the consumer to engage in the transaction now, for example, through demonstration and sampling.

The propensity to try new products is less pronounced among rural consumers. In such a case, sampling acts as an effective tool to achieve conviction about the brand. It registers the brand in the consumer's mind and reaps benefits for it in the long run. It plays a vital and unique role in brand conversion in rural markets. Godrej hair dye targeted small-town consumers (both male and female) in Punjab with the help of demonstrations and free sample distributions at beauty parlours and salons. Beauticians and barbers were also used as opinion leaders, who instructed consumers in the use and benefits of hair dye and encouraged them to maintain clean and healthy hair.

In 2010, Cadbury, a leading confectionary company in India, conducted a retail activation programme through which it planned to seed its low-entry products of INR 5/2/1 across uncovered retail outlets in rural markets, and also create the retention of these newly acquired outlets.[3] Through this programme, the company touched base with 200,000 village retail outlets, and energized and created excitement among them by offering redemption coupons and merchandizing their outlets with the new product, hence creating spot and repeat purchases among them.

Other FMCG companies like Wrigleys have also conducted similar sales promotion programmes in rural UP, where they offered immediate cash discounts to the newly joined retailers on each candy jar that they purchased.

DIRECT MARKETING Direct marketing is one of the most powerful ways to meet the target audience on their turf and build product awareness as well as sales promotion. Direct marketing helps the marketer to bypass the middlemen and directly reach and communicate with the customer. Mobile marketing, vending machines, and direct mailers are some of the direct marketing tools used in rural areas. However, the success of any direct marketing campaign in rural areas depends on the marketer's sensitivity and emotional connectivity to the rural audience.

A few examples of direct marketing in rural India include organizations like Indian Railways, NACO, and HLL Lifecare Limited, which effectively communicate with the rural audience directly by using postcards as their branding platform; of the 20 million Rediffmail sign-ups, 60 per cent are from the small towns of India. Fifty per cent of the transactions from the Rediffmail shopping website are also from small-town people; Reuters Market Light (RML), through its paid service, provides the latest information on agricultural mandi rates, weather conditions, and insurance and loan facilities to farmers on their mobiles.

PUBLICITY AND IMAGE BUILDING Public relations and publicity creates high credibility. News stories and features seem more authentic and credible to readers than do advertisements, as the message appears to buyers in the form of news rather than as sales-directed communication.

When TVS planned to introduce and sell its Scooty to small-town and rural women, it started by teaching these young women how to ride a scooter through a woman trainer. This was a good PR exercise to build their brand image among its target audience. Cookery classes for rural women were conducted by LG at different locations to promote its new range of microwave ovens targeted at rural markets.

PERSONAL SELLING Personal selling is the most cost-effective tool at the later stages of the buying process, particularly in building the buyer's preferences, convictions, and actions. Personal selling, when compared with advertising, has the following advantages:

- ***Personal confrontation.*** It involves an alive, immediate, and interactive relationship between two or more persons.
- ***Response.*** Personal selling makes the buyer feel that they are under some obligation for having listened to the sales talk. The buyer has a greater need to attend and respond to the salesperson, even if the response is only a polite 'thank you'.

Right Concept Marketing (RCM) is a multi-level marketing company in Bhilwara, Rajasthan, which offers a wide range of products including FMCGs, eatables, stationery,

LIFEBUOY SWASTHA CHETNA

HUL's popular brand, Lifebuoy, created an innovative communication package called the '*Swastha Chetna*' for rural India to facilitate behavioural change in favour of soap usage among school-going children. They targeted children in the age group of 5–13 years, studying in primary and middle schools. A range of activities for children—quizzes, games, songs, pictorial storytelling through flip charts, and the popular 'GLO-GERM' demonstration kit, which showed the germs present when they rinsed their hands only with water—was organized as part of the programme. This was a multi-phased activity during which Lifebuoy representatives initiated contact with students and influencers (key opinion leaders) in the rural community, like the Panchayat bodies, Anganwadi workers, medical practitioners, and school teachers, to further promote this initiative and gain a larger acceptance within the community. This campaign helped in long-term brand image-building for Lifebuoy in rural India.

computers and electronics, ready-made garments, accessories and footwear, plastic ware, and agri-inputs. It operates through an innovative communication and distribution model where the rural consumers themselves become sales agents and promoters for its products, and earn a commission from every sale that they make in their area.

Similarly, many Life Insurance Corporation (LIC) agents personally visit houses in rural areas to promote and sell insurance schemes. This approach has been quite successful in rich rural areas.

THE COMMUNICATION MIX DECISION While deciding on the communication mix, companies should keep in mind certain factors like the type of product market, consumer readiness to make a purchase, and the stage in the product lifecycle.

A rural communication programme can be a mix of various communication tools like advertising, sales promotion, direct marketing, publicity and image-building tools, personal selling.

Type of Product Market The communication mix is heavily influenced by whether the company chooses a push or a pull strategy to create sales. A push strategy calls for using the sales force and trade promotion to push the product through the channels to the end consumer. A pull strategy calls for spending a lot of money on advertising and consumer promotion to build consumer demand. Consumer goods companies rank advertising, sales promotion, personal selling and public relations, in that order. For example, established players with deep pockets and a national presence—like HUL and Britannia—rely heavily on the pull strategy, whereas small, regional players with limited promotion and advertising budgets—like Ghari and Anchor—prefer the push strategy.

Buyer Readiness Stage Promotional tools vary in their cost-effectiveness at different stages of buyer readiness. Advertising and publicity play the most important role during the awareness stage, being far more significant than the roles played by either 'cold calls' from sales representatives or sales promotion. Personal selling influences customer comprehension and conviction to a larger degree. Personal selling and strong sales promotion predominantly influence the closing of the sale.

When combine harvesters were launched to expedite the process of harvesting and threshing of wheat and rice in Punjab and Haryana, the initial communication efforts were aimed at creating awareness, then interest, followed by knowledge among potential consumers. Agricultural officers who educated the farmers about the combine harvesters and their benefits carried out the process of education. A conviction among consumers was created and reinforced through field demonstrations.

Product Lifecycle Stage Promotional tools also vary in their cost-effectiveness at different stages of the product lifecycle. In the introduction stage, advertising, publicity, events, and experiences have high cost-effectiveness, followed by sales promotion to induce trial and personal selling to gain distribution coverage. In the growth stage, the focus on all tools can be toned down because the demand will have built up its own momentum through word of mouth. In the maturity stage, the order of preference should be sales promotion, advertising and personal selling, and during the decline stage, sales promotion continues to be strong, while advertising and publicity are reduced.

Since the maturity stage of any product is yet to be reached in rural areas, the communication focus is more on generating 'awareness', 'interest', and 'conviction' among the audience through appropriate media usage.

Measuring the Impact of Communication

After implementing the communication plan, the communicator must measure its impact on the target audience. In rural areas, where mostly non-conventional communication media (as discussed later) are used, the effectiveness and impact of the communication plan are measured using controlled and non-controlled situations and areas. The controlled area includes those places where the rural activation or communication programmes have been implemented over a given period of time, and non-controlled areas are those where activation has not been done by the marketer. The impact in terms of the total footfall at retail outlets or haat/mela stalls, enquiries and sales generated over a given period of time is measured for both areas and then compared to find the effectiveness of the rural non-conventional communication mediums.

::: Creating Advertisements for Rural Audiences

Advertising is any paid form of non-personal presentation and promotion of products, services or concepts by an identified sponsor. Before developing an advertising programme, marketers must be clear about the objective or purpose of advertising, that is, what it is that they are seeking to achieve out of the advertisement. The communicator must know whether their aim is to inform, persuade, remind, or reinforce their message vis-à-vis the target audience.

The main advertising objective of most companies wanting to reach rural markets is creating awareness about their offerings. Therefore, they go in for informative advertising. For companies like HUL and Dabur, which have already made a strong mark in rural markets, the focus is more on reminder advertisements, through which they aim to stimulate a repeat purchase of their products and services (see 'Rural Marketing Insight: Hitting the Bull's Eye').

Communication experts need to keep the following factors in mind when creating advertisements for a rural audience:

- Understand the mindset of potential customers, including their hopes, fears, aspirations, and apprehensions. Conducting qualitative research with the target audience would help in a better understanding of the consumer mindset.
- Pick up 'gems' in the form of idioms, expressions, words, etc., in relation to the product category for later use in the creative aspect.
- Tricky, clever, gimmicky, or even suggestive advertising does not work with rural

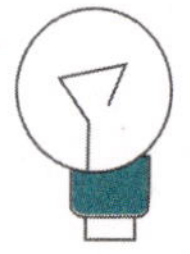

RURAL MARKETING **INSIGHT** | HITTING THE BULL'S EYE

The Shriram Group, a pioneer in the area of chit funds, has been involved in the truck finance business for over three decades. Aided by its excellent infrastructure, innovative products and effective promotional strategies, the company has been able to take on big players like Sundaram Finance and Ashok Leyland. In order to enter the southern markets with its loan products, the company hired Anugrah Madison, which first conducted a qualitative study among the potential target audience—small fleet owners and drivers—to design a targeted campaign.

In the first phase, the communication strategy targeted small fleet owners by appealing to their business sense and played on the theme of 'Shriram, your friend'. Pop-up invitations to the Shriram Prosperity show were delivered personally to the fleet owners; these contained lucky dip numbers to encourage participation. During the show, a three-fold communication package was unveiled. This consisted of a motivational video film (based on popular film songs on the theme of friendship) to establish the image of Shriram as a 'best friend'; a special tele-film highlighting the product features; and a testimonial film based on the real-life experiences of truck drivers. Gift kits, prizes and bumper prizes (two-wheelers, refrigerators, etc.), promotional brochures, and refreshments were also given out; this was accompanied by participation in interactive games like 'guess how much money is in the briefcase'. A popular anchor hosted the show, which the participants greatly enjoyed. The show produced excellent results.

In the second phase, the communication strategy targeted the drivers through an emotional appeal to their dream of becoming vehicle owners. A specially decorated video on wheels carrying promotional material visited various sites along a predetermined route. At each location, the drivers were identified and given invitations for a road show, thus making them feel important. At the road show, the audience participated in a lucky-dip draw and had to identify the film star hidden behind the company logo; the winners were then requested to voice the campaign message. A tele-film featuring popular film stars was screened, and a quiz conducted to assess and reinforce the message comprehension. Bumper prizes, gift kits and promotional brochures were handed out; participant response was highly encouraging.

Target-oriented communication strategies via unconventional and through-the-line media, as opposed to mass media marketing, seem to work well in campaigns aimed at reaching out to semi-urban and rural consumers.

The campaign was rolled out in six states. The success of this two-fold strategy was reflected in a 20-fold growth in loan disbursals, thereby establishing the Shriram Group as the undisputed leader in truck financing.

Source: R. V. Rajan (CMD, Anugrah Madison), Hitting the Bull's Eye, *Praxis*, 4(2—'Managing Rural Markets'), 2003, pp. 28–31.

audiences. 'Flicks' using very expensive computer graphics without any human presence go over the heads of rural audiences.

- Combining education with 'entertainment' is a good route to take when targeting rural audiences. Using locally popular film stars or even featuring religious events (melas) popular in the region helps to strike a chord with rural audiences. According to a study, it is Govinda and not Shah Rukh Khan who is most popular among rural folk in north India. In the south, it is the superstars of the Tamil and Telugu film industry who are immensely popular among the masses, but they are not easily available to endorse products. Hence, in a state like Tamil Nadu, popular comedians are used to promote products and services, and the new generation of stars—like Vijay and Vikram—has now begun endorsing products (Coca-Cola).
- 'Quickies' (short television commercials) do not register well with rural audiences. Advertising agencies need to provide for ample time and space to communicate a message properly and effectively to the intended audience. This is seen, for instance, in the popularity of the two-minute theatre commercials screened in rural cinemas. Pond's Two-minute Advertisement Capsule—the two-minute Pond's Talc film produced to launch the product in sachet packs in rural Tamil Nadu—was based on a story with a rural setting, and included song and dance, romance, and demonstration. On the whole, it was entertaining and educative. It was so effective that it helped to establish Pond's Talc as the leading brand in rural Tamil Nadu.
- While developing audiovisual communication employing the 'slice of life' approach, it helps to bring in an aspirational element. For example, showing a rural youth who has moved out of the village and made his mark even in urban areas. Such people act as role models for the rural audience. However, it is important to keep the communication at a simple, uncomplicated, and direct level, so that rural audiences can understand the message. Documentaries should sustain audience interest from beginning to end.

While designing advertisements for the rural audience, one must understand the mindset of the rural audience, keep the message simple and logical, and avoid making it gimmicky. The use of 'education with entertainment' and 'slice of life' observations are good ideas.

Rural Media

Rural media can be classified broadly into conventional mass media and non-conventional rural-centric media. Figure 9.4 shows the various media vehicles under these two categories, which have been covered in detail in this section.

Conventional Media

Conventional media consists of mass media—radio, television, press/print, cinema; outdoor media—wall painting, hoarding; and personalized media, like point of purchase, direct mailers, etc.

MASS MEDIA A medium is termed a mass medium when it reaches millions of people. However, poor exposure to the mass media and the ineffectiveness of universalized communication aimed at a heterogeneous rural audience make it difficult for the mass media to address the communication needs in rural markets in an effective manner.

Radio Irrespective of literacy levels, topography, geographical location, or area of residence, radio reaches people

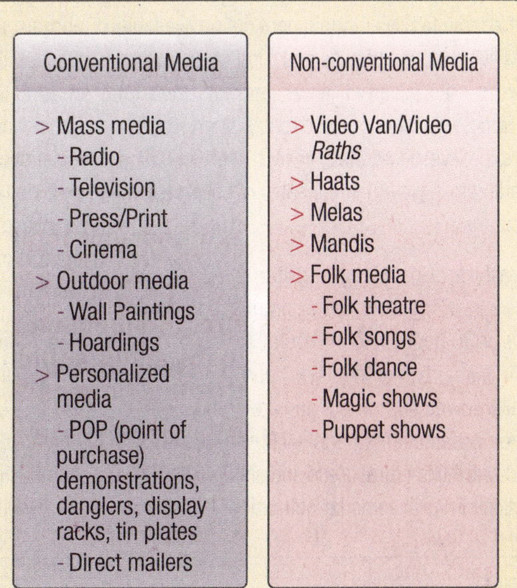

| FIG. 9.4 | Media Vehicles

KAN KHAJURA TESAN

Kan Khajura Tesan, which means 'earworm radio channel' in English, was used by HUL to engage its brands with their rural consumers in media dark areas of Bihar where power outages are for several hours, resulting in limited or no access to television and no radio frequency. TV and print media reaches only 20 per cent of the population. Kan Khajura Tesan, an on-mobile entertainment radio channel in which the content is interspersed with HUL brand communication. Consumers have to dial 1800 3000 0123 and give a missed call. They would then receive a call from the channel to enjoy 18 minutes of pre-recorded popular local music, and HUL advertising spots, jokes, and an RJ to host the show advertisements.

The essence of the campaign is in the promotional message making the process of connecting with rural consumers quite easy '*Missed call lagao, muft manoranjan pao*' (Give us a missed call and get free entertainment).It has reached out to more than 11 million subscribers. In all, HUL has had engaged consumers for 180 million minutes of engagement with consumers and the company's ads have been heard 100 million times. The advertising done on the radio channel resulted in 'significant increases in spontaneous awareness for Ponds White Beauty (56 per cent), Close Up (39 per cent), and Wheel (20 per cent)'. The tesan is run on Telco's cloud communications platform, so it had to make no capital investment to maintain, manage, or upgrade any technology. This led to a 40 per cent reduction of in operation cost by 40 per cent and a 15 per cent increase in brands' awareness among the target audience by 15 per cent. On 14 April 2014 the radio station rolled out a contest rewarding 1,000 consumers everyday with mobile recharges of INR 10 to increase engagement of rural folks.

RURAL MARKETING INSIGHT | INCREASING ROLE OF DTH IN RURAL INDIA

From the black-and-white TV sets of the 1970s to the colour revolution of the 1980s and multi-channel satellite cable TV in the 1990s, television viewing in India has come a long way. Today, the direct-to-home (DTH) technology is set to do to television viewing in rural India what the mobile phone did to communication. Launched in 2003, DTH has revitalized India's journey towards media digitization.

The Wireless Revolution in Home Entertainment

Television is the only affordable family entertainment option available for middle-class Indians living in small towns and rural areas across the country. DTH provides entertainment, news, and lots more to viewers in even those remote pockets of the country where neither public television nor cable have penetrated. In fact, the increasing popularity of DTH is leading to a growth in the sales of colour television sets across the country.

The states of Maharashtra, Goa, Punjab, Uttar Pradesh, and Rajasthan are the leaders in DTH subscription, contributing over 6.4 million DTH connections or 30 per cent to the overall DTH subscriber base. The myth that DTH is an urban product has been proved wrong as people living in smaller towns and rural areas are demonstrating far more usage than their urban counterparts—70 per cent of DTH connections in India today are from rural areas and small towns. The 14 million DTH connections in rural areas far outnumber the six million in urban India. Dish TV and DD's Direct Plus DTH service are the market leaders in rural India, while Tata Sky, Dish TV, and Sun Direct DTH services are the preferred brands in the top metros.

DTH in Rural India

Being a wireless service, DTH has truly brought the power of affordable home entertainment to rural households. Rural households are finding value in the entertainment, service and picture quality that DTH offers, and are purchasing their first colour televisions. Today, rural households with a monthly income of less than INR 3,000 are also purchasing DTH. For the growing rural customer base, the value lies not only in the availability of a high-quality viewing and customer service experience, but also in the value-added services such as pay per view, which offers rural consumers the chance to watch the latest Bollywood movies immediately after their release in the metros, or sometimes on the day of their theatrical release. In 2012, of the total 22 million DTH subscribers, 60 per cent reside in rural areas and small towns.

The Future

DTH is undoubtedly the future of home entertainment in India. With its huge bouquet of channels and value-added services, it has grown from a niche delivery mechanism for a few thousand households to a mainstream business that is expected to reach over 100 million households.

Source: www.dthnews.mediadir.in, 7 February 2011

easily. It continues to be an important source of information for many rural people, either through habit or through choice. Earlier, the Indian radio industry was limited to the state broadcaster—All India Radio (AIR); today, with the rise in the number of FM radio stations, the radio has truly matured as a medium of rural communication. The total reach through radio in rural India today is pegged at 18 per cent.[4]

Mass media options in rural areas include communicating through radio, television, press/print, and cinema.

However, listening is generally limited to news, songs, and plays. In addition, involvement with advertisements on the radio is lower than with television advertisements, as they lack any visual content. Fertilizer and tractor companies and FMCG companies largely use this medium for advertising.

Television Television is the fastest growing, most powerful and most popular mass medium in rural India. With the increasing ownership of television (36 per cent) and the influx of cable and satellite (C&S) in addition to terrestrial TV, this medium is gaining new ground in rural areas. The total rural reach of television is 47 per cent, and that of cable and satellite is 31 per cent[5] (see 'Rural Marketing Insight: Increasing Role of DTH in Rural India'). Community viewing of television or watching it at a neighbour's house also increases the viewership percentage in rural areas. In spite of these advantages, this medium has the following limitations:

- Low electrification among rural households: Currently, only 60 per cent of rural households have electricity connections. Also, electricity is available mostly for agricultural activities, that is, at those times of the day when the decision-maker of the household is busy working in his fields and has no time to watch television programmes, and hence expose himself to the influence of advertising. After the harvest season, when he has sufficient free time to watch television, electricity is diverted to meet the needs of industry.
- Women who have televisions in their homes do not watch much TV during the day as they are busy with household chores; at night, they don't usually watch TV in the presence of the elder male family members.
- Indian society is tradition-bound, and the clash of value systems between the older and the younger generations is manifested in a particular resistance to the blandishments of television advertising.

Press/Print Media Press includes newspapers, magazines, and other publications; however, newspapers form an important part of print media in rural areas. Some interesting facts about newspapers in rural areas are:

- They carry useful and detailed information about a product or service.
- A marketer can choose region-specific newspapers to communicate his message in different languages to the target audience in different states. Some of the well-known regional newspapers include *Eenadu* (Andhra Pradesh), *Daily Thanthi* (Tamil Nadu), *Punjab Kesari* (Punjab and other states of north India), *Loksatta* (Maharashtra), *Anandabazar Patrika* (West Bengal), *Dainik Bhaskar* (Uttar Pradesh, and other Hindi-speaking states of north India).
- People are generally more interested in reading regional news focusing on sensational topics involving politics, crime, etc., rather than national or international news.
- Newspapers contain a variety of pages catering to the needs of different reader segments—children, youth, and adults—covering topics on development, sports, cinema, health, education, religion, etc. The rural youth is emerging as an important class of news readers owing to their interest in the daily sports columns and weekly special supplements that provide useful information on career, communication skills, competitive examinations, general knowledge, etc.

However, in rural areas the print medium still faces problems of both reach and access, coupled with low literacy levels. The current reach of the press in rural areas is only 13 per cent.[6] Newspapers do not reach rural areas in the morning due to poor infrastructural facilities. The print medium is mainly restricted to the educated classes. Community reading is popular, and very few households individually subscribe to a newspaper; community/public places like *panchayat bhawans*, STD phone booths, tea stalls, and barber shops generally subscribe to newspapers for the villagers.

Cinema Cinema is an important communication media in many parts of the country, due to its universal appeal that cuts across the barriers of geography and language. Films in theatres (especially in the southern states of India) attract large rural audiences, and provide an opportunity to disseminate product information by way of short advertisement films and cinema slides. Life Insurance Corporation (LIC) and other private insurance companies have been showing short movies in rural theatres to create awareness about life insurance.

However, there are a number of limitations in the reach and impact of cinema as a medium of communication:

- Cinema is experiencing a downward trend in viewership with the increasing popularity of television and video compact disc (VCD) players in rural areas. It is a comparatively costly medium because of its limited reach (6 per cent).[7]
- Cinemas in rural areas are generally located in feeder towns. The rural youth frequent these towns; hence, watching movies is most popular among them.
- Cinema is not free, as one has to pay to buy tickets.
- Advertising through cinema is done on a very limited scale, at the start of the movie and during the interval.

OUTDOOR MEDIA: WALL PAINTINGS This medium is a widespread form of advertising and is the favourite of the Indian rural masses, as they can view it at their leisure. Wall paintings are important because they constantly remind rural people about the brand name and logos, in addition to highlighting the key brand promise. They also reflect the vibrant economic and social life of the area. Brightly painted walls near the village bus stop, cinema halls, banks, post office, big retail outlets or *panchayat bhawan* generate lot of visibility among the rural audience. Lafarge Cement India has used this format in a unique way by painting its brand logo on the gate arches in villages during one of its rural activation campaigns. Some key characteristics of wall paintings are:

- They are economical as compared to other traditional media forms, as the manpower and infrastructure requirements are low.
- They can be easily customized in accordance with regional language variations without this impacting their artistic content.
- Audience recall rates are high.

Wall paintings, the most widespread form of advertising for rural masses, create brand awareness and enhances top-of-mind recall.

There are also certain limitations to using this communication medium:

- Lack of available wall space at prominent locations is an issue.
- The quality of the wall space available is not always satisfactory. The base of rural wall structures is generally not smooth, and this impacts the final output.
- No exclusive wall rights are given to the company. It may happen that a company gets a wall painted, and after sometime when the company executive passes through, he finds that the painting has been replaced with the advertisement of some other company.
- The quality of the painters available is also poor. Companies prefer to hire painters locally as they are familiar with the area, and the cost of hiring them is lower when compared to the cost of hiring painters from outside.
- Wall paintings are generally an outsourced operation. While the job often appears to have been completed on paper, in reality this is sometimes not the case.

The rural marketer's rules for advertising through wall painting are:

- Wall sites around public gathering places like haats, mandis and melas should be selected in order to maximize the impact and reach of the advertised message.
- Wall paintings should be made at eye level, so that they are easily visible; the height also ensures that villagers will not spoil them by urinating against the wall.
- Active monitoring is required. The company should make the dealer/distributor responsible for the quality and maintenance of wall paintings, and ensure that they are spread uniformly in order to increase visibility.

PERSONALIZED MEDIA: POINT OF PURCHASE DISPLAYS AND DEMONSTRATIONS

Point of Purchase (POP) displays and demonstrations are a part of consumer sales promotion and take place at the point of purchase or sale. They may include danglers, display signs and boards, tin plates, display racks and dispensers. Retailers in rural areas find it difficult to handle the hundreds of displays, signs and posters that they receive from companies as the physical size of their shops is small, and the wide variety

There are various point of purchase options that a rural communicator can use. They include danglers, display signs and boards, tin plates, display racks, and dispensers.

POP displays at an STD booth for the promotion of video telephony in villages.

of product categories they stock causes congestion. In addition, since many retailers prefer to push local/spurious products on which they get better margins, they avoid hanging POP displays of products/brands from standard companies.

Rural-centric Non-conventional Media

India's multilingual and multicultural identity limits the role of mass media activities, particularly in rural areas. This gap is filled to a great extent through non-conventional, rural-centric media, like video vans, haat/mela/mandi campaigns, and folk media.

VIDEO VAN/VIDEO RATH The use of video vans has been of prime significance in conducting promotional activities in rural areas. Companies including Tata Tea, HUL, LG, Marico, Colgate, TVS, and virtually all agri-input companies have used this communication tool to successfully deliver their customized messages through audio and video media, in any language, to a specific audience. See 'Rural Marketing Snapshot: Changing Means of Rural Communication' to understand how audiovisual media have been used in rural areas to reach out to consumers.

Generally, a video van is fitted with audiovisual equipment and a large LCD screen for film shows. The van in fabricated to provide space for stocking samples, products for sale, and collaterals like banners and posters, and is manned by trained personnel. The vehicles commonly used for this purpose are Tata 407/207, Eicher, Swaraj Mazda, Tata Ace, Tata Magic, Mahindra, and the smaller versions of the Matador/Omni/Trax, depending on the vehicle's capacity to carry the specified goods, or its ability to conduct the selected communication programme. A typical van cycle is 26 days to a month, during which it moves from village to village as per its pre-arranged journey plan. There are various advantages of a video van:

- The van can double as a mobile exhibition vehicle to perform demonstrations and carry product samples to induce trials. Van promoters can undertake retail

RURAL MARKETING **SNAPSHOT** | CHANGING MEANS OF RURAL COMMUNICATION

The traditional way of communication

Branded mobile vans

India's multilingual and multicultural identity limits the role of mass media activities, particularly in rural areas. This gap is filled to a great extent through non-conventional, rural-centric media like video vans, haat/mela/mandi campaigns and folk media. Earlier sales promotion and communication happened mainly through traditional means like *Munadi* (oral communication). Nowadays, companies have started using audiovisual media to capture and hold the attention of the audience and create a long-lasting impact.

merchandizing and conduct door-to-door campaigns. Activities organized around the van can be used to achieve multiple marketing objectives, including product demonstration, trial/sampling, merchandizing/retailing (spot sales), establishing direct contact and rapport with consumers, and educating consumers about the product.

- Vans have the potential to be used at weekly markets, fairs and festivals; events like interactive games can be organized around them.
- The van acts as a point of attraction or focus of attention, around which people gather in large numbers. This is particularly useful in those areas where it may not otherwise be possible to reach out through conventional media and communicate to a large gathering.

There are also a few limitations to using a video van, which a rural marketer must keep in mind.

- The van generally arrives in the morning for promotions (except for film shows, which are held during the evening) when the head of the family, who not only holds the decision-making power but also controls the purse strings, is away in his fields.
- The cost per person contact works out to be high.
- The number of children who gather for film shows is generally much higher than the number of people from the actual targeted segment.

GOOGLE[8]

In 2009, Google India launched a unique initiative to educate the offline population in India about the benefits of the Internet. Called 'The Internet Bus', the project was designed to extend web access to different small towns and rural areas across India, giving people an opportunity to experience the Internet first-hand. The bus took off from Chennai, headed to Vellore, and covered most small towns in the state of Tamil Nadu in a span of six weeks. The bus showcased popular Internet services including search, email, social networking, maps, and others. The Internet-enabled bus focused on four themes—education, information, communication, and entertainment. It was loaded with useful and informative content in English and Tamil. Google's aim here was to showcase how the Internet could make everyday life simple. Updates of the bus' travel plans were regularly posted on the website created to showcase the initiative.

HAATS The haat—better known as the mobile supermarket of rural India—is the oldest marketing channel in the country. It plays a vital role in the lives of villagers as it provides a first-contact point with the market. It is a place for exchanging rural surplus, for buying daily necessities as well as farm supplies and equipment, and a place for socio-political and cultural contact. Some important facts about haats are:

- There are around 43,000 haats in India, which are held every week across different parts of the country.
- A large haat in a 10,000 plus population location caters to 57 villages and attracts 12,000 visitors on the haat day; and a small haat, located in a 5,000 plus population village, caters to 21 villages with an average footfall of 5,600 a day.[9]
- Villagers prefer to buy from haats because these markets offer better variety and lower prices.
- Almost every villager is a regular haat visitor, with over three-fourths visiting one every week. Out of the total visitors, around two-fifths are females.

Haats thus provide a good opportunity for any big bang communication aimed at rural consumers. The haat is where consumers are in a buying mode, and the average time spent visiting each haat stall is less when compared to melas. People visiting haats look for discounts and bargains, and organizations should have this strategy built into their haat campaigns. Marketing efforts for FMCG products should include on-the-spot offers (discounts or price-offs should be direct and clearly mentioned on the pack itself). Consumer durables and high-involvement products can have tear-off coupons that are distributed at haats, with the scheme details, validity period, and contact details of the nearest dealer clearly mentioned on the coupons. Live demonstrations or product samples are essential to convert consumers at haats as their attitude is utilitarian; they like to touch and feel the product before making any purchase decision.

Any FMCG haat campaign should plan three consecutive outings, the first focusing on creating awareness, the second looking at sales promotion and conversion, and the third concentrating on entering into a long-term business relationship with haat sellers. A consumer durables campaign can plan a single outing, as the primary focus is on brand promotion.

MELAS Melas or fairs are an important feature of Indian rural life, held periodically (seasonally or annually) to commemorate important events, or to honour a deity. In addition to the religious, social, and cultural significance of melas, they also have a strong commercial aspect. Around 25,000 melas are held annually, but 90 per cent of these last only a day, usually in conjunction with a religious festival, and thus have limited commercial value.

Corporations with a pan-India presence, who are looking at melas as a potential platform from which to communicate with rural audiences, should start by targeting the top 100 commercial melas and then focus on micro melas, which have a limited but focused reach. Clutter-free compared to their larger counterparts, micro melas cater to a homogenous audience, enabling specific marketing activities to be created and offering greater opportunities for mileage-building activities. For companies with a regional base, this would work the other way round: they should start by focusing their energies and inputs on micro melas and then slowly enlarge their activities to reach the top 100 melas.

The focus should be on melas that last for a longer duration; otherwise, the resources would be spread too thin.

Sales alone is not the best indicator for assessing the relative commercial importance of each mela, since the duration of the mela varies from one to 45 days. The sales per day offer a better idea of the commercial importance of a mela. A large number of corporations are engaged in targeting the major fairs of national repute, and this may lead to communication clutter, as the same target audience is being bombarded with different brand messages (see 'Rural Marketing Insight: Clutter-free Communication at the Mela').

There are a few key differences between a haat and a mela, which one must keep in mind while planning communication at these locations:

- The haat primarily caters to the essential needs of local people, whereas the mela caters to a much larger population, both rural and urban, supplying goods not only for their basic needs, but also offering more sophisticated products for sale.
- The haat is where consumers are in a buying mode, where business-like communications are registered easily. In a mela, the same brand of communication needs to be more extravagant and interspersed with entertainment to register any impact.
- Unlike a haat, which is largely frequented by males, a mela can target brand messages towards the entire family. Women have social sanction to visit the mela. Marketers can take advantage of this tradition to establish face-to-face communication with females.

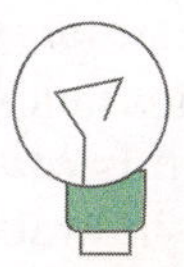

RURAL MARKETING INSIGHT | CLUTTER-FREE COMMUNICATION AT THE MELA

Bihar contributes 15 per cent to the national market share in the mosquito repellent coil segment. As Bihar is a priority market for Mortein, the company decided to participate in the local Sonepur Mela. Sonepur Mela is held for 25 days and attracts approximately a million people.

The Plan

Mortein had to devise a communication plan distinct from the run-of-the-mill mela campaigns, which would act as a stand-out exercise for it. Also, the plan was to enable the designed activity to gradually grow into an eagerly anticipated annual affair. The objective was to create a high visual impact and buzz around the brand, generate curiosity, and involve the maximum number of visitors to the mela. The challenge was to think out of the box and design a campaign that would be in sync with the spirit of the Sonepur Mela. Thus emerged the innovative concept of Lui *dahan*, designed on the lines of the popular cultural event of burning the effigy of Ravan. The two characters—Lui the mosquito and Mortein coil—were made to arrive and emerge at the mela through a skit. Gigantic, inflatable figures of Lui and Mortein helped to communicate the power of mosquito coils to keep diseases like malaria and dengue at bay. The underlying mythological context proved to be one of the most relevant associations that still clicks with the rural audience.

An 80-ft high, Ravan-shaped dummy of Lui was displayed at a main entry road leading to the mela. The size of the dummy ensured visibility across the entire mela area. A skit using the inflatables of Lui and Mortein coil was held every day to communicate the brand message and the story. Fliers were distributed announcing the date of 'Lui *Dahan*'. A lot of hype was created across the mela area and nearby villages on the D-day, which led to over 50,000 people participating in the evening event.

The Tools

A combination of different communication tools was used to reach out to the million visitors to the mela.

- Banners and arches were displayed at important points across the mela and nearby villages in order to generate curiosity and publicize the event details. Event fliers were also distributed among visitors and onlookers.
- A stall was set up at a strategic location for interacting with the target audience.
- Skit shows were held six times a day to communicate the hazards of the mosquito and the brand propositions.
- A brand *baraat* was organized to create the desired hype and participation of the audience. Visitors danced to the popular jingle all across the baraat route in large numbers.
- A local popular celebrity was invited on the *Dahan* day to ensure media coverage.

The Outcome

The results of this campaign were enormous. Around 250,000 people visited the site during the 25 days of the mela (an average of 10,000 per day). The event day turnout was over 50,000. Awareness about the brand was created not only among the mela visitors, but also among people in 15 surrounding villages. Almost all local newspapers and networks covered the event. 'Lui Dahan' is now a proprietary event of Reckitt Benckiser, and is being held for the last five years.

Source: Impact Communication 'Lui Dahan', available at http://www.impactcomm.org/mar.html

MANDIS Like haats and melas, mandis also offer great potential (especially for companies targeting large and medium farmers) as a communication platform for marketers. In states like Punjab and Haryana, where haat markets do not exist, the network of mandis is very strong; these provide an opportunity to interact with about 200 farmers a day during the harvest season. Marketers of tractors, fertilizers, and durables goods use this platform.

With a large network of over 7,600 mandis spread across the country, this channel offers great potential to marketers to tap cash-rich consumers who are in the mood to spend.

An innovative, out-of-the box communication approach rooted in rural customs and traditions helped Mortein find a place in the minds of rural consumers.

Folk media is a good form of non-conventional, rural-centric media, and may include folk theatre, magic shows, puppet shows and interactive games.

FOLK MEDIA Folk media consists of folk songs, folk dances, and other theatrical forms, including puppetry, street theatre and magic shows, which are an intrinsic part of the culture and heritage of the land. They are capable of communicating messages about contemporary issues, topics, and concerns as per the needs and demands of a changing society. The essential characteristics of folk media are that they are interactive, repetitive, and narrative. The characters and situations are woven into a storyline so that a brand message can be sneaked in. It also offers the advantage of using local language and talent so that receptivity and interest level remains high. There are different kinds of folk media:

- Folk theatre
- Folk songs
- Folk dances
- Magic shows
- Puppet shows
- Interactive games

Folk Theatre Folk theatre, interspersed with folk song and dance, is a simple and entertaining form of communication. It can also be informative and educational. In the past, folk theatre had been used to arouse public opinion against the British Raj, draw attention to atrocities against the girl child, and raise public consciousness about other socially relevant issues.

The Escorts Tractors' folk media campaign at Nauchandi Mela, Meerut, was designed to increase awareness about its Farmtrac 35 Champion model. The theme of the *nautanki* revolved around the benefits of buying an Escorts tractor. Towards the end of the play, the attributes of the Escorts tractor were repeated.

Hindustan Latex's '*Swasth Gram Pariyojana*' at Gwalior involved the social marketing of contraceptives. The decision to use folk media was triggered by the observed trend of the decreasing efficacy of video van campaigns. The nautanki style was used to propagate the theme of problems resulting from population increase. To convert this awareness into action, the play projected the grassroots-level worker as an adviser and confidant of the villagers in matters of family planning.

Folk Songs Folk songs are basically simple and direct compositions that are usually transmitted orally from one generation to the next, and not through the written word. The structure of the folk song is characterized by simplicity and uniformity in rhythm. The songs consist of many stanzas sung in more or less the same tune. Each region and state has its own particular traditions of folk songs and ballads. *Alha, birha,* and *qawwali* are popular forms in Uttar Pradesh.

Folk Dances Folk dances are basically simple and rhythmic, and mostly religious in nature. Communication takes place through dramatic gestures and the accompanying music. Folk dances are visually very arresting, attracting audiences with their elaborate costumes and stage settings.

Magic Shows Magic shows are another very entertaining form of folk entertainment and draw large crowds, particularly because of the high curiosity factor and the use of hypnotic effects. A case in point is the marketing campaign of Britannia Tiger biscuits. Britannia launched a campaign aimed at increasing the visibility of its Tiger brand of biscuits, as well as the Coconut Tiger and Chai biscuit variants. Magicians were hired to perform at local melas using the ribbon flowing trick. The communication to the audience was: 'after eating Tiger biscuits, the heart beat moves as fast as the ribbon'.

Puppet Shows The puppet (*kathputli*) performance is the most common form in folk tradition. The origin of puppet theatre is closely linked to the performance of religious ceremonies. The connection between rituals and the use of puppets is found in almost all states in India.

Traditional puppeteers were mostly itinerant performers who depended on royal patronage for their survival. Even today, tales of chivalrous kings like Prithviraj Chauhan and Amar Singh Rathore are narrated through puppet performances in the villages and towns of Rajasthan.

The different forms of traditional puppetry are glove, rod, string, string-rod, and shadow puppets. Differences between these exist not only in name, but also in form, structure, manipulation techniques, and geographical origin and spread.

The Life Insurance Corporation of India used puppets to educate the rural masses about life insurance. These plays were shown to audiences in villages in Uttar Pradesh, Bihar, and Madhya Pradesh. The number of inquires at local life insurance companies during the period immediately following the performance was compared with the normal frequency, and found to be considerably higher.

Thums Up has also used puppetry to promote its soft drink. The shows comprised of puppets of Thums Up and other rival soft drinks. The Thums Up puppet comes and strikes down the other soft drinks, thus reinforcing its slogan 'Taste the Thunder'.

Interactive Games Although interactive games do not constitute a folk form, they are a very popular device used by advertisers to draw large crowds. Games have also been used to induce trials and spot sales of products. They are sometimes chosen to exploit or coincide with prevailing trends in a particular region. For example, arm wrestling competitions can be used in Punjab and Haryana where public displays of physical strength attract considerable crowds; however, this form is not popular in West Bengal. Dabur designed a pinball game in which the ball was in the shape of the Dabur Chyavanprash container and the pins represented germs, which would be destroyed upon taking the health tonic. People were invited to slip the ball in and see how many pins were punctured.

Despite the major benefits that folk media campaigns offer advertisers, this form does suffer from a few shortcomings.

- Folk media campaigns involve high costs.
- The visible costs are due to the intensive preparations that go into the making of a successful campaign. Research into the socio-cultural characteristics of the region, the appropriate form of folk media to be used, tracking down and training the troupes available—all these steps involve considerable time, effort and expense.
- The invisible costs of handling contingencies also need to be factored in. These could be due to natural causes (rainstorms, unexpected death of a key person in the village) or man-made causes (the sudden disappearance of an artist in the middle of the campaign, unruly and rowdy crowds, inter-caste clashes).
- Implementation costs are also high. Costs are incurred during the campaign in attempts to penetrate deep into the rural markets.
- The availability of the right kind of troupe and the talent and skills of its members and crew can dramatically affect the implementation of a campaign.

The rural marketer's rules for using folk media as a communication medium are:

- Folk media is a useful channel to promote/propagate generic issues that can be woven easily into the script. A campaign is not likely to be very successful if its focus is solely on brand promotion. This is because the people are clever enough to understand that it is merely a promotion for a product; they do not mind it as long as they can derive their share of entertainment along with it. The campaign will lose its impact and the audience will melt away if it adopts a preaching mode.
- Non-conventional media are effective tools for raising hype about new products, or for re-launching existing products. This is particularly true in the case of FMCG products, where the hype generated can propel sales volumes, provided the advertising campaign is backed by a good distribution system.

- The timing of the performances is very crucial. Certain factors need to be considered. First, shows should be held during that time of year when farmers are relatively free. If the shows are held during the harvest season, farmers are likely to be too busy in their fields to pay any attention. Second, performances should be held at that time of the day when they are free and relaxed.
- Campaign coordinators should choose the venue of the performance with care, keeping in mind the caste and religious differences in the village. For example, if the show is held in a largely Muslim part of the village, Hindus may not attend it, and vice versa. Similarly, the quality of the relationship between the upper and lower classes/castes in the village will also determine the choice of venue.
- The selection of both the script and the actors/artistes, both male and female, should be done carefully so as not to hurt the sentiments of any community, or give cause for offence.
- The folk troupe chosen should not be alien to the audience. If the audience cannot relate to or identify with the troupe and the actors, the campaign is not likely to be very effective.
- Apart from providing entertainment to promote technically sophisticated products like tractors, the marketing campaign also needs to provide substantial information to villagers about the benefits of the product, the correct method of its use, the cost, and the place where the product will be available. Subsequently, the choice of media also needs to be in accordance with the product type. FMCG products like soft drinks and biscuits can be advertised through light media like magic shows or interactive games, but this avenue may not work for technically advanced products involving product detailing.
- The medium used should also gel with the culture of the region. For example, the *kalbelia* dance is popular in Rajasthan, but it will not draw an audience in West Bengal.
- The appropriate level of media exposure should also be kept in mind. People living in villages located close to a highway are relatively more exposed to the electronic media than people living in the interiors. Hence, traditional media campaigns in such villages should be more lively and extravagant.

Sales Promotion and Events and Experiences

This section details other relevant communication tools extensively used in rural areas—sales promotion and events and experiences.

Sales Promotion

Sales promotion consists of incentive tools that are mostly short term and are designed to stimulate and induce trial and make the offer attractive for early conversion by consumers or trade. It may include tools for *consumer promotion*—samples, coupons, discounts, free gifts, reward for loyal customers, POP displays and demonstrations; *trade promotion*—price offs, advertising and display allowances, free goods.

This section largely covers different types of consumer promotion as conducted by companies in rural areas.

The consumer sales promotion tools include samples, discounts, free gifts, rewards for loyal customers, POP displays, and demonstrations.

DISCOUNTS Discounts are deductions from the usual cost of a product, typically given either for prompt or advance payment or to a special category of buyers. Envirofit International is an entrepreneurial, non-profit organization working on a sustainable approach to tackling the global indoor air pollution/cooking-stove problem. It relies on market mechanisms to guide product development and drive consumer demand for 'bottom of the pyramid' markets. Although the cost of the standalone stove was INR 849, it launched an offer in which a biomass stove was bundled with an MTS mobile phone for INR 1,299. This was done to induce trials and generate quick sales from the consumers.

TVS offered discount coupons to rural consumers to induce quick sales during the wedding season.

COUPONS Coupons are tickets or documents that can be exchanged for a financial discount or rebate when purchasing a product. During the wedding season in India, the sale of motorbikes generally goes up, especially in the rural areas and small towns of north India. This is largely because motorbikes are purchased as a gift for the groom from the bride's side. To cash in on this trend and to induce quick sales, TVS offered a discount coupon of INR 501 on the purchase of the TVS Star brand to all prospective buyers (wedding families) in the four northern states of India during one of its rural activation campaigns.

SAMPLING Sampling is a promotion tool that acts as a double-edged sword and creates both brand awareness and conviction. There are two forms of prominent sampling:

- ***Dry sampling.*** Distribution of product samples like soaps and toothpastes to consumers for trial at their own discretion.
- ***Wet sampling.*** Application trial to consumers in real time to demonstrate utility.

Bru representatives visiting houses to generate product preference through sampling.

Marketers prefer the second option in rural areas as they fear samples reaching the wrong target group and a long gestation period. Thorough planning and detailing can overcome these shortcomings and act as a boon for rural marketers. Emami has used rural haats for promoting its Navratan brand oil, and giving the consumer a live experience of '*Thanda Thanda* Cool Cool'.

INSTALMENT SCHEMES Traditionally, rural consumers do not fit into the EMI (equated monthly instalment) framework as their income is seasonal and is realized during the harvesting season. However, this can be used as a strategic tool to market products. To popularize the use of 5-kg LPG cylinders among the base-of-the-pyramid consumers, MART designed a unique chit fund scheme wherein eight interested consumers were grouped together. Each consumer was required to deposit INR 100 per month. One consumer, selected through a lucky draw, received a 5-kg LPG cylinder each month. Thus, all the eight consumers were converted to LPG users within eight months.

BRU INSTANT CONNECT[10]

Bru instant coffee wanted to increase its market penetration in rural south India, where the penetration of instant coffee is as low as 27 per cent despite the fact that it is a big market for coffee. Most rural consumers prefer the conventional filter coffee for its taste and aroma. In certain pockets within Andhra Pradesh and Karnataka, people prefer tea. For some, instant coffee is reserved for visitors and special occasions. Bru, desirous of addressing the diverse consumption patterns, appointed communicators to go from door to door and show a short film on the basis of the beverage preference of the household. Following the completion of the film, consumers were posed a question and presented with a free sachet of Bru instant coffee. This process created an awareness and interest in the product among rural consumers, and enabled Bru to complete a trial in 38 districts in Andhra Pradesh and Karnataka. A lot of buzz was generated through this activity, enabling Bru to reach out to more than a million rural households.

DEMONSTRATION/EXPERIENTIAL MARKETING Rural consumers generally know that branded companies charge a premium, but are unable to comprehend the utilitarian advantage achieved by spending the extra money. Physical demonstration or experiential marketing offers rural consumers an opportunity to experience the product and make an informed choice. Advertising expenditure on experiential marketing for rural areas is about INR 7–8 billion.

RC&M created a platform, 'Cash Flow with Air Flow', to promote 235 DI Mahindra, an entry level tractor with special air flow technology. It was targeted at small and medium farmers who could use the 235 DI not just for farming, but could also earn extra income from haulage. The tractor was cost-effective because high maintenance items were replaced with technology that cooled the engine with air flow. Therefore, to communicate the advantages of air flow, the target group was made to experience this technology in a chamber fitted with an exhaust fan. The event was publicized through hoardings, tin boards, dealer boards, etc. The activity generated an overwhelming response as around 20,000 enquiries were generated, 10,000 test rides were held and 400 tractors were sold on the spot.

Events and Experiences

Some prominent forms of rural events are sports events, consumer/farmer meets, channel partner meets and key opinion leader meets.

In the rural context, one of the best ways to capture the attention of the audience is through events. Since rural areas have limited venues for entertainment, conducting a well-planned event draws a good response and gets the brand good mileage through strong visual impact and long-term brand recall. Some prominent forms of rural events are sports events, consumer/farmer meets, and channel partner meets.

The experiential air chamber, where farmers could know about the tractor's features and experience the air-flow technology firsthand, was used to promote Mahindra tractors.

SPORTS EVENTS The Kila Raipur Sports Festival is a well-known example of a rural sports event. Originally organized as an annual recreational meet where farmers from areas surrounding Kila Raipur in Punjab—located 15 km south of Ludhiana and well-connected by air, rail, and road with Delhi—got together to test their corporal endurance, this festival has metamorphosed over the years into an energetic youthful annual sports event, popularly known as 'Rural Olympics'. The event, organized during the first weekend in February, attracts participation from more than 4,000 sportspersons representing both recognized and traditional sports over a three-day period. In 2011, the scheduled events included athletics, hockey, junior and senior kabaddi, tug of war, bullock and mule cart race, cycle race, weightlifting, archery, events for the disabled, clay-pigeon shooting, air pistol, paragliding and aero modelling, paddy trolley loading and offloading, sack lifting (in pairs), tractor race, tent pegging, *gatka* (martial arts), etc. The *Nihang*s displayed their riding skills, while others exhibited *Bazigar* feats of strength at the event. Cultural events like *gidda, bhangra*, and other folk dances were also organized. Over a million viewers witnessed this sports extravaganza. Prominent corporations have begun to express interest in this event. Ambuja Cements was the main sponsor of the event in 2011, with Maruti India and Idea Cellular as the co-sponsors.

RURAL BRAND EXPERIENCE EXTRAVAGANZA *Grameeno ke Beech* is a village fair for rural India. It targets people of all categories—from school children to farmers and even rural women. The event aims to reach out to the complete family; therefore, it brings about a feeling of oneness. The idea behind this fair is to bring customers of all categories under one roof and allow them to experience, enjoy, interact, understand, and engage with the displayed products for higher trails and brand recall. Several interactive games and product demonstrations are organized to highlight product features. *Grameeno Ke Beech* is publicized through multimedia like mobile miking, handbill-cum-ticket to fair distribution, merchandizing, and stock replenishment.

CHANNEL PARTNER MEETS Channel partner meets may include dealer/retailer meets. The primary objectives of these meets is to build a relationship with local traders; impress upon them the advantages of associating with a big company; sensitize traders about quality norms; and build the image as a quality-conscious outlet and how it will add to driving consumer footfalls.

Grameenon ke Beech in a village fair that brings customers of all categories under one roof to create the right sales and promotion mix.

In order to improve the skills of trade partners and keep their motivation levels high, Tata Shaktee has designed a platform called 'Learn & Lead', which comprises training programmes conducted by professional agencies and the Indian Institutes of Management. The company also organizes regular relationship programmes and meets to encourage stronger distributor–dealer bonding.

KEY OPINION LEADER MEETS (MASON/MECHANIC/CARPENTER/PAINTER) The primary objective of key opinion leader meets is to promote brands among the key opinion leaders in the village, and create a database for building a relationship and future meets. The meets are generally held at the district/block/town level. A few guidelines need to be followed while organizing such meets:

- A comprehensive database should be compiled for future use with the help of dealers and hardware/spare part retailers.
- Personalized invitation cards should be sent out to participants to boost their esteem.
- The presence of the local dealer is recommended.
- The presence of company personnel—such as the local sales officer—is recommended.

The Mason Meet, an initiative organized by JK Lakshmi Cement, to promote the brand and update consumer on the latest happenings in the area of construction.

- An interactive discussion session explaining the technical specifications of the product and apprising participants on the best practices followed in trade should be included in the programme.
- Towards the end of the proceedings, a short quiz can be followed by a lucky draw.
- Customized slab schemes can be announced to retain interest and gain the confidence of the participants.

REVIEW OF OBJECTIVES

1. To understand the major challenges in rural communication: rural heterogeneity and spread and the need to understand the rural audience

Rural communication calls for understanding the key challenges at hand—rural heterogeneity and spread, low literacy and varying comprehension abilities of rural folks, and difference in media reach and the habits of people. Communicating the message to rural consumers has posed enormous challenges to rural marketers because of the large numbers of consumers scattered across the country. This problem is further compounded by the heterogeneous nature of consumers, in terms of their languages.

Around two-fifths of the rural population is illiterate and literacy levels vary hugely among different states. To communicate effectively with the less educated, it becomes necessary that the focus be on creating a simple communication message. The limited reach of mass media in rural areas and its regional and state variations also pose limitations on a universal approach to communication for rural consumers.

In the light of these challenges, a rural marketer should identify the most suitable medium to ensure the maximum spatial reach across the country; develop region-specific consumer profiles to understand the characteristics of the target market; and design the most effective and persuasive communication and promotional strategies to induce the target audience to buy his product or service.

2. To outline the process of rural communication

The communication process consists of nine elements: sender, receiver, message, media, encoding, decoding, response, feedback, and noise. To get their messages through, marketers must encode their message in a way that takes into account how the target audience usually decodes messages. They must also transmit the message through efficient media that reaches the target audience, and develop feedback channels to monitor the response to the message.

How the sender encodes the message and passes it to the receiver and how the receiver perceives or decodes that message becomes especially crucial in the case of a rural setting, where the environment exercises considerable influence on the receiver, as a result of which he/she may not receive the intended message in a correct manner. The comprehension of a message is therefore a critical problem in Indian rural markets, something that needs to be kept in mind while designing the communication plan.

3. Detailing the process of developing effective rural communication

Developing an effective rural communication involves eight steps: (*i*) identifying and profiling a target audience; (*ii*) determining the communication objectives; (*iii*) designing the message; (*iv*) selecting the communication channels; (*v*) budgeting for rural communication; (*vi*) designing a marketing communication mix strategy; and (*vii*) integrating the communication process; and (*viii*) measuring the impact and results.

The first step in designing an effective communication is 'knowing your customer'. The communicator must know who to design the communication for, and what the target audience looks like. Once the target market/audience and its characteristics have been identified, the communicator the must decide on the desired audience response. The ultimate response, of course, is purchase and satisfaction. The communicator needs to know how to move the target audience to higher states of readiness to buy. Marketers have the option of using different static or dynamic promotional elements based on their communication objectives.

Having defined the desired audience response, the communicator moves to the next step—developing an effective message. Formulating the message requires solving five problems: what to say (message content); how to say it logically (message structure); how to say it symbolically (message format); in what context to say it (context association); and who should say it (message source). Further, the communicator can select different channels of communication to carry his message. Communication channels are of two types—personal channels (advocate, expert, social channel); and non-personal channels (mass media, atmospherics, events).

The allocation of a budget for different planned media is the next step. Here, an estimate is generally prepared based on the different activities one plans to conduct and the results—in terms of exposure levels, trials and usage—that one expects. Companies face the task of distributing the total communication budget over different communication tools—advertising, sales promotion, direct marketing, publicity, and image-building tools, personal selling, etc. They generally utilize one or more tools to design a complete communication package.

Each communication tool has its own unique characteristics and costs. Marketers have to understand these characteristics in order to select the most appropriate and useful tool. They must also consider factors like the type of product market in which they are selling, how ready consumers are to make a purchase, and the product's stage in the product lifecycle while deciding the marketing communication mix.

After implementing the communication plan, the communicator must measure its impact on the target audience. In rural areas, the effectiveness and impact of the communication plan is measured in terms of the total footfall at retail outlets or haat/mela stalls, and enquiries and sales generated in a given period of time in the area where the rural activation was done as against the area where the activities were not conducted to see the difference.

4. Highlight the need for distinct advertisements for rural audiences and the factors to be kept in mind

Advertising is any paid form of non-personal presentation and promotion of products, services, or concepts by an identified sponsor. Before developing an advertising programme, marketers must be clear of the objective or purpose of advertising, that is, what it is that they are seeking to achieve from the advertisement. The communicator must know whether their aim is to inform, persuade, remind, or reinforce their message on the minds of the target audience. For most companies that want to reach rural areas, their main advertising objective is creating awareness about their offerings; hence, they go in for informative advertising.

While designing advertisements for the rural audience, one must understand the mindset of the rural audience and keep the message simple and logical. One should avoid making it gimmicky, tricky, or clever, and also avoid 'quickies' as these do not register well with the rural audience. The use of 'education with entertainment' and 'slice of life' are good ideas.

5. Examine and discuss various media vehicles of conventional mass media and non-conventional, rural-centric media

Rural media can be classified broadly into conventional mass media and non-conventional, rural-centric media. Conventional media consists of mass media—radio, television, press/print, cinema; outdoor media—wall painting, hoarding; and personalized media—point of purchase and direct mailers, etc. On the other hand, non-conventional media includes rural-centric media like video vans/video raths, haats, melas, and mandis as the platforms for communication, as well as the folk media.

Irrespective of literacy levels, topography, geographical location, or area of residence, radio reaches people easily. The rise in the number of FM radio stations has truly matured radio as a medium of rural communication. Television is the fastest growing, most powerful and most popular mass medium in rural India. Rural India has also witnessed a rapid growth in DTH (Direct-To-Home) connections in recent years. Press includes newspapers, magazines and other publications; however, newspapers form an important part of print media in rural areas. The print medium continues to face problems of both reach and access, coupled with the low literacy levels in rural areas. Cinema is another form of mass media that provides an opportunity to disseminate product information by way of short advertisement films and cinema slides.

Other conventional outdoor media includes wall paintings, a widespread form of advertising in rural areas. Wall paintings are important as they remind rural people constantly of the brand name and logos, in addition to highlighting the key brand promise. POP displays and demonstrations form a part of personalized media and consumer sales promotion, and take place at the point of purchase or sale. They include danglers, display signs and boards, tin plates, display racks, and dispensers.

India's multilingual and multicultural identity limits the role of mass media activities, particularly in rural areas. This gap is filled to a great extent through non-conventional, rural-centric media like video vans, haat/mela/mandi campaigns and folk media. A video van is fitted with audiovisual equipment and a large screen for film shows. It also provides space for putting up banners and posters. It is a successful communication tool for delivering customized messages through audio and video media in any language, to a specific audience in even the interiors of the country. Haats, the weekly markets held across the country, also provide marketers with a great opportunity to communicate their message to a large audience who gather at a single point week after week. Melas or fairs are also an important feature of Indian rural life, and are held periodically to commemorate important events or to honour a deity. In addition to the religious, social, and cultural significance of melas, they also have a strong commercial aspect. Folk media consists of folk songs, folk dances and other theatrical forms, including puppetry, street theatre and magic shows, which are an intrinsic part of the culture and heritage of the land. They are capable of communicating messages about contemporary issues as per the needs and demands of a changing society. The essential characteristics of folk media are that they are interactive, repetitive, and narrative.

6. Detailing and understanding other relevant rural communication tools like sales promotion and events and experiences

Sales promotion consists of various incentive tools, which are mostly short term and are designed to stimulate and induce trial and make the offer attractive for early conversion by consumers or trade. It includes tools for consumer promotion—samples, coupons, discounts, free gifts, rewards for loyal customers, POP displays and demonstrations; trade promotion—price-offs, advertising and display allowances, free goods.

In the rural context, one of the best ways to capture the attention of the audience is through events. Since rural areas have limited venues for entertainment, conducting a good, well-planned event in rural areas elicits a good response, and gets the brand the right mileage through a visually strong impact and long-term brand recall. Some prominent forms of rural events are sports events, consumer/farmer meets, and channel partner meets.

DISCUSSION AND APPLICATION

Discussion of Concepts

1. Explain the steps involved in message design. Develop a communication message for promoting hybrid seeds and pesticides.
2. Briefly describe the various communication tools that can form a part of the rural communication mix strategy.
3. Describe different forms of folk media. What are the benefits of using folk media? What are the critical points to be kept in mind while using folk media as the communication platform?
4. Explain the different sales promotion tools used in rural communication with examples.
5. How similar or different is humour in rural India compared to that of urban India? Develop imaginary humour based conversation caselets for (a) Consumer durable company (b) National Health Mission for any of their product/ programme to effectively promote their messages to rural populations.
6. Visual Communication (specifically symbols) are a powerful tool amongst marketers. With the help of internet and interactions with designers, find out whether the commons symbols used by marketers to communicate message in rural India and whether any variations in interpretations of symbols has proved disadvantageous to corporates in rural India.
7. Sixty per cent Indians work as farmers but many face difficulties in sustaining this livelihood. Lack of knowledge about locally relevant agricultural practices is one of the major reasons. What medium of communication would you as an entrepreneur use to tap this opportunity and create a common platform for farmers to share these practices with one another?

Application of Concepts

1. Devise a comprehensive communication strategy for a regional brand of toothpaste in any two Indian states. Identify the dimensions that will help to distinguish the communication strategy.
2. Critically examine the communication strategy of a national and regional player in the durables category in rural markets.
3. An international processed food manufacturing company has come up with its new fortified products (biscuits and snacks) which it wants to promote in iron-deficient rural areas of India. Devise a communication plan for the company to help it to effectively communicate its message.
4. The Government of India has launched the 'Digital India Programme' which aims to connect 2.5 lakh panchayats using the fibre optic cables to provide high speed broadband by 2017. What role would social media play in attracting more rural customers for corporates and possible customizations compared to current social media strategies?

RURAL MARKETING **CASE** | TATA SHAKTEE GC SHEETS

Galvanized Corrugated (GC) sheets are a part of the product portfolio of Flat Products Division. The Flat Products team at Tata Steel, managing the Tata Shaktee brand of GC sheets, was contemplating the brand communications budget.

The TATA Shaktee Brand over the years

Galvanized corrugated sheets are mainly used for roofing in rural houses. They are also used for making sidewalls and shop extensions, and for sheds for cattle, storage, etc. Competing products include thatched roofs, and tile and asbestos cement sheets, which have a distinct price advantage; and to a small extent reinforced concrete cement or RCC, which is relatively very expensive. RCC is preferred by rural consumers for roofing.

Tata Steel was the third largest producer of GC sheets in the country, and had a market share of 9 per cent in 2000. The Flat Products team had set the objective of becoming market leaders in the Indian steel roofing market. The focus was on rural housing, and on segments detailed in Table 1.

Table 1 Consumers of GC sheets

Consumer	Characteristics
R2, R3, R4 sections of rural society Internet	Lower literacy levels, very cost conscious farmers, shopkeepers, and labourers Concerned about product quality, but lack sophistication and technical knowledge Susceptible to retailer push/influence High involvement purchase Purchase usually happens from feeder towns

The Tata team had identified an opportunity to differentiate and establish their brand by focusing on delivering more value to their target consumers. This was based on brand differentiation on some major consumer concerns and needs, which were unfulfilled, namely:

1. Need for more durable and cost-saving roofing products

In rural territories, word of mouth and dealers' recommendation plays a role, and knowledge is less technically sound. Consumer evaluation of the product is based on product parameters like weight, size, etc.

2. Need for assurance on fair price and good quality

The performance of the sheets depended on many factors including the usage purpose, as well as the quality of the product and method of using and storing sheets.

3. Need to buy from a reliable outlet

Consumers' concerns if they invested in a costlier brand of GC sheets were to ensure that the retailer was trustworthy, was not only delivering the right services and dispensing the correct usage advise, but was also quoting them the right price/brand.

In a market seeking assurance and fair play, brand identity would play a major role if a brand took up the opportunity and challenges. The category audit revealed strong challenges at four levels: the consumer connect, market dynamics, immediate competition, and the channel structure and trade practices and norms.

The strategy adopted to tap into this opportunity rested on strengthening their branding of GC sheets, the Tata Shaktee. It was positioned as a high value option for GC sheet users in rural India, especially for roofing needs. Tata Shaktee was re-launched in 2000 in the retail construction segment. The strategy was to create consumer intimacy, and establish a unique identity and robust distribution network that enveloped the customer till the last mile. The key implementation challenges were to communicate the brand meaning, and identity and create the right distribution channel, which would create access to a trusted source of GC sheets for consumers, a source that would be transparent, accessible, and fair in pricing. Providing peace of mind to the consumer was a driving factor, through pricing, quality, and brand assurance. Credibility would be a major pillar of the Shaktee brand, and would drive the commodity market to recognize value in brands. It would also impart a unique differentiator to the brand.

Distribution Channel for Tata Shaktee

Retailers of hardware, paint, cement, plywood, etc. are located mainly in feeder towns (those towns with a population greater than 20,000). Most retailers sell multiple brands.

Coupled with the strengths of the Tata Shaktee GC sheet brand itself, this was expected to bring about the re-shaping of the market towards a brand versus commodity competition.

Brand Communications

Tata Shaktee became a market leader in branded GC sheets, ranked first in the country by share and unit weight. The company's approach was to create consumer intimacy through various means. One was through creating a unique identity for the Tata Shaktee brand, such that the value proposition to consumer was clearly established as a higher value than the competition. This higher value was based on the pillars of brand differentiation, and a unique identity was proposed to be established in consumer perception around these four dimensions. The challenge was to create awareness and establish the brand identity and proposition.

The Tata Shaktee Brief

The brand communication requirements were spelled out with the above scenario in mind, and the following objectives were crystallized. Customer intimacy was to be established through communicating the unique brand identity and advantages through various communication channels, including direct communication to the end consumer.

Communication Objectives:

1. Creating brand awareness of Tata Shaktee GC Sheets brand proposition
2. Product demonstration
3. Building a relationship with the customer and creating brand loyalty through a burst of below the line promotional activities

The Communication Challenge

The challenge was to promote the brand's consumer value-add through effective communication directly to the rural-end consumer and decision maker. The first objective of the campaign was to communicate the benefits of Tata Shaktee vis-à-vis other brands.

Since this was the only company to launch extra width GC Sheets, the benefits of the much wider GC sheet—like the significantly lower cost of construction (attributed to the less number of sheets and accessories required to cover the same area)—was to be communicated to customers, and linked to the brand name. The brand also had many other features that would position a clear point of differentiation: RCP, zinc coating benefits, 120 GSM, etc. These features were technical in nature and difficult to explain to consumers who were less literate, and often not aware of technical issues of the building trade.

The other communication challenge was to create direct communication opportunities that allowed product demonstrations. It had to be an opportunity where something as cumbersome as a GC sheet could be wielded and put up for a demonstration.

Critical issues identified during the client-agency interactions were as follows:

- The buyer, mostly the head of the family, who makes decisions relating to purchase/financials spends the maximum time in his fields during the day.
- Tata Shaktee charges an INR 10–15 premium per sheet over other brands.

- Technological superiority like RCP, 120 GSM Zinc coating are difficult to comprehend, and is to be communicated in simple language and in terms of utility to consumer.
- Variations within Hindi as a language of communication.
- Being a durable product, opinion leaders like mistris (technicians incharge of placing roofs) play a role because of the rational decision-making process.
- Communication needs to focus on demonstration and touch and feel for greater impact.

Solution (Efforts Made by the Agency)

Phase I (2001–3)

In the first phase, the communication medium chosen by Tata Shaktee were wall painting, shutter/shop painting, VOW (Video on Wheels), POP (Point of Purchase) displays, but these did not yield the desired result.
Learnings from Preliminary Field Visit:

Product/Brand point of view: Favour

- GC sheets are lighter than asbestos sheets/tallis/thatch, and require a lighter understructure
- GC sheets are easy to re-locate compared to asbestos sheets/tallis/thatch
- GC sheets have a longer life (15–20) years as compared to other co-categories
- GC sheets are fire-resistant
- Tata sheets enjoy good brand equity in the market
- Tata is the only GC sheet with product specification printed on it

Product/Brand point of view: Against

- GC sheets are more expensive than asbestos sheets/thatch roof/tallis as a product, but when the total cost of roofing (understructure, cladding material and labour) is considered, GC roofs are cheaper
- A house with a roof made of GC sheets is hotter compared to those with roofs made of other materials
- Consumers are shifting to thinner GC sheets since prices have increased by about 30 per cent. Tata Shaktee does not have any product offering in thinner sheets.
- Competition (Jindal National) product range starts from 0.14 mm thick, whereas Tata starts from 0.25 mm
- The price of Tata sheets is about 5 per cent higher than the nearest significant competitor

Consumer point of view: Favour

- Consumers shifting to GC sheets from thatch/tallis as it lasts longer
- The usage of asbestos sheets is declining rapidly due to health hazards
- Consumers are concerned about the safety and security of their families and prefer fire-resistant GC sheets
- The rural consumer feels that the quality of Tata sheets is better than the competitors

Consumer point of view: Against

- The target segment for GC sheets is R3 and R4, who are very price-sensitive
- The low literacy level of the consumer means that he can be easily duped by the retailer
- Less knowledge about the product specification printed on Tata sheets and its implications

The visit also brought out the fact that in this customer segment, buyers have low literacy levels, are susceptible to duping, have limited purchasing power, and are multilingual even within this segment, across states and regions.

Therefore, the challenge from a communication point of view was to establish a communication channel with the consumer, and propagate awareness and value of the brand.

MART's Strategy for Direct Customer Contact

The possible alternate channels of communication and below the line tools considered by MART were:

- Use below the line media
- Public platforms to engage with rural customers
  - Agricultural mandis
  - Sugar mills
  - Kisan Mela organized by Agricultural Universities
  - Special meets
  - Live demonstrations in rural large format retail stores
  - National fairs

It was thus decided to focus primarily on utilizing rural congregation platforms like haats and melas to reach out and educate the rural masses on product/brand benefits, and possibly create an experiential opportunity. The haat is the business nerve centre, where visitors are in a buying mode.

Learning from the Pilot Project

After the pilot, Tata Steel decided to put a hold on roll out in melas, as it was the less appropriate platform from which to start off. The category purchase behaviour is such that the entire family does not play a major role; it is usually the head of the family or the chief wage earner who needs to be targeted. Melas are occasions for the entire family, and involve both purchases of essential and non-essential items, and are sources of entertainment. As melas are seen more as an entertainment/family outing, it was jointly decided to drop them as a promotional platform.

Campaign Roll Out in 2004

The agency embarked on its roll-out plan with the help of local field implementation partners. Due to this, the dealer could not participate, and the consumer's technical queries about the product remained unanswered. Also, a sample sheet could not be displayed because the company dealer was responsible for the physical transportation of the GC sheet. A mismatch in the location of haat and dealer also inconvenienced consumers, as they had to travel long distances to purchase the Tata Shaktee GC sheet after learning about it at the haat from the promotional team. It was felt that the company would have to ensure the availability of consumer price lists and a scheme with a fixed validity period, as well as the presence of a dealer and sample sheets at the haat promotion. The company should also ensure the availability of both the normal and the wider GC sheet samples at the haat.

Haat Hungama Campaign—2005

Additional promotional material was planned for 2005 over the previous year's campaign.

- A Haat Hungama welcome stand (to greet visitors coming to the stall)
- Set of flash cards (five famous Indian monuments and three hit filmi jodis, brand game)
- Tata Shaktee flip chart (for uniformity in communicating with consumers)

Campaign Roll Out in 2006

During the activation phase, the team was instructed to take a sample sheet from the distributor/dealer and place it on a carrier mounted on the travelling vehicle. This ensured the availability of sample sheets at all haat/mandi locations. Haat Hungama 2006 was also spread over 2,000 haats/mandis, and was a major success in further strengthening the Tata Shaktee brand and its attributes and increasing brand salience and patronage among rural consumers.

Tata Shaktee Haat Hungama Campaign from the Communicator's Viewpoint

The AIDA model of communication (Baldwin and Ross, 1992), although possibly the oldest, is an effective response–hierarchy model, and was chosen as the basis for the first-level brand communication objectives. Tata Shaktee Haat Campaign 2004 started off as a basic-level campaign with the sole objective of registering its brand in the consumer's mind and increasing his awareness, comprehension, and knowledge of the brand. Therefore, it was limited to fulfilling the first two elements in the AIDA model, that is, Awareness and Interest. In 2005 and 2006, the branding of the campaign was done as Tata Shaktee Haat Hungama and the specific brand theme was christened: 'Sardi garmi ya barsaat Tata Shaktee hardam saath', that is, Tata Shaktee promised to be with the consumer in any and every season, be it summer, winter, or the monsoons. Interactive brand games centred round this broad campaign theme were designed like a set of flash cards (five famous Indian monuments and three hit jodis from Bollywood/cricket).

Consumers were asked to identify the monuments and the faces of the hit pairs of actors (the card showed a face that was half male and half female), and the winner walked away with a gift. Consumers were also explained the logic of designing these games and how, with the usage of Tata Shaktee GC sheets, their homes would last longer, just as the monuments had survived the travails of time and like the hit pairs of actors, who have had an association that has strengthened over the years. In brief, the 2005 and 2006 campaign focused not only on awareness, but also convinced the consumer and aroused desire for/interest in the brand, finally motivating the consumer to take the next step of visiting the nearby dealer's place for more specific enquiries and conversion to sales.

Impact of the Tata Shaktee Haat Hungama Campaign

There was a 40 per cent increase in footfalls at the Tata Shaktee haat stall (year on year basis), an average footfall of 600 visitors per haat stall, a total of 3.5 million potential consumers contacted over five years and a 37 per cent upswing in sales. The Haat hungama campaign started off with less involvement from the distributor/dealer, but slowly caught up by the third year. During the campaign, the Tata Shaktee Distributor ASO was present in 92 per cent of the cases, the product displayed in 93 per cent, and the dealer present in 84 per cent of the haats. The campaign seemed effective from this point of view.

The Brand Communication Options

The communication media being used currently rested on interactive media directly reaching the rural audience. Video on wheels, innovative media like bullock and camel cart displays, the mobile vans in haats (van with GC sheet display), the Bollywood road show and street plays were all being used along with dealer-based stalls at haats, and games and displays to bolster the involvement of consumers at haats. The agency also suggested a communication-cum-sales lead generation system—an enhanced effort that went beyond the haats by using teams of youths who would visit haats, mandis, as well as conduct direct consumer visits during the haat/mandi off-days. These would be local youths who might even be personally known to consumers.

The Shaktee stores also used point of purchase materials and structures to create the Shaktee Sansar (World), meant for both loyal and multi-brand stores, and enhanced the consumers' experience of the brand.

Discussion Questions

1. What is your assessment as a marketer of the opportunities shared by Tata Steel, especially when looking at rural markets?
2. What do you feel about the brand features? Is this relevant to the context we are talking about?
3. What do you propose as a strategy for Tata Steel? Describe each step that you wish to take in detail.

AFTER READING THIS CHAPTER, YOU WILL BE ABLE TO:

1. Trace the growth of the services sector and its relevance for rural markets
2. Understand the growth of telecommunication services and the role of M-VAS services in the marketing of products and services in rural markets
3. Identify the role of ICT (information communication technology) in rural India and its relevance to the marketing of products and services
4. Understand the marketing of financial services in rural India, including banking and insurance
5. Describe the improvement of healthcare services and the emergence of new delivery models in rural markets

CHAPTER 10 ::: RURAL SERVICES MARKETING

ten

The Byrraju Foundation provides a promising pay-per-use operation in water purification in rural Andhra Pradesh and Rajasthan using community filtration plants. Water is sold in 12-litre containers for INR 1.5—about half the price of individual, activated-carbon water filters, and about a third of the cost of boiled water, which covers the daily clean-water needs of an average household.

Byrraju has built 57 water filtration plants, serving 850,000 people in six districts of Andhra Pradesh. The facilities are operated and maintained by a local gram vikas samiti *(GVS) or village development committee. The GVS begins with a short marketing campaign, raising villagers' awareness of the benefits of clean water. Residents are then asked to contribute an amount equal to about three-quarters of the total cost of setting up the plant and installing the equipment (approximately USD 15,000).*

Byrraju provides high-level support, including fortnightly laboratory-based water-quality analysis to ensure a consistent quality of water. At the prices charged by Byrraju, the water meets the critical 'low-price' criterion. More consumers are willing to adopt the Byrraju-type pay-per-use model than individual filters. The model is self-sustaining, and thus commercially viable. Even if some 500 households buy one 12-litre container per day, the plant covers its costs.

More than 75 per cent of Byrraju's existing plants are already operationally profitable. As penetration levels vary between 20 to 45 per cent—purified water is often a push product that requires a substantial marketing investment—each Byrraju plant serves the needs of two or three neighbouring villages in addition to the village it is situated in. The filtration technology is also proven, low-cost, easy to acquire and replicate, and is thus easily scalable.

The Byrraju Foundation provides clean water at a nominal fees to people in rural Andhra Pradesh and Rajasthan.

The services sector is the lifeline for the socio-economic growth of a country. Today, it is the largest and fastest growing sector, at 11 per cent per annum in 2010–11. This sector has witnessed a major boom and has been one of the major contributors to both employment and national income in recent times. Today, it contributes 57 per cent of the GDP and employs 34 per cent of the workforce.

This growth is also reflected in the rural economy, which has moved from farm to non-farm, led by services like retail trade, transport, and communication. As per the NSSO report of 2006–07, 60 per cent of the country's 16. 5 million services sector enterprises are in rural areas, which employ 76 per cent of the total workforce in the sector.

In rural markets, services primarily comprise retail trading, transportation and communication, financial services, healthcare, housing and construction, education, and community and social services. Among services, sectors like telecommunication, finance, healthcare, and entertainment have witnessed an impressive growth in rural markets as marketers have used innovative ways to take these services to rural markets, encouraged by the government's pro-rural programmes and policies. We examine four major rural services in this chapter—telecommunications, ICT (information communication technology) services, financial services, and healthcare.

::: Telecommunications in Rural India

Today, India is the fastest growing telecommunications market and the second largest in the world with more than 940 million subscribers. A huge chunk of this growth is contributed by rural markets, which have witnessed exponential growth, adding more than 300 million subscribers in the last five years. 'Rural Market Snapshot: The Telecom Revolution in Rural India' shows the change mobile telephony has brought about in rural areas.

Subscription in rural India has registered a multi-fold growth, with the subscriber base crossing 383 million in 2014.

By June 2014, rural markets had reached a user base of 383 million, with the growth coming from both small and large villages. In spite of the challenges of distribution, service, product knowledge, and affordability, marketers have successfully devised ways to reach the hinterland. Where marketers of consumer durables had failed to overcome the infrastructural bottlenecks to penetrate deeper, the mobile telecommunications industry redefined the rules of rural marketing by converting a perceived luxury product into a utility product through relevant and attractive schemes, such as removing entry barriers by introducing free lifetime validity SIM, INR

An STD booth – a common sight in villages in the past

Youths talking leisurely on their mobile phones

Mobile telephony has almost wiped out STD booths and public call offices (PCOs) in rural India. The number of rural subscribers has exploded in the last five years. Mobile phones offer convenience at an affordable price to rural consumers across all SECs.

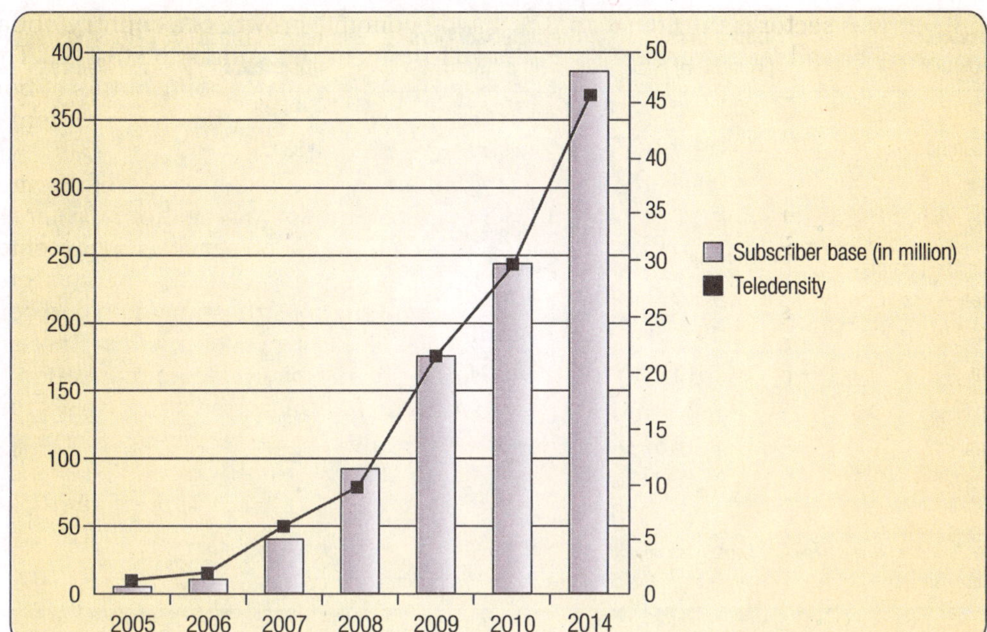

| FIG. **10.1** |
Rural Subscriber Growth

5 recharge vouchers, and coupling the cheapest call rates with the cheapest handsets in the world on an instalment basis. Also, infrastructure sharing (for example, mobile towers) by major players, which is not seen in other sectors, has helped in lowering costs and created an enabling environment for players to cover widely scattered rural markets profitably.

In the four-year period between 2006 and 2014, rural India outpaced urban India as the rural subscription base grew multi-fold, versus the three-fold growth (see Fig. 10.1) in urban India. The availability of content in vernacular languages has led the growth of rural markets, with strong prospects for M-VAS services like IKSL, RML, and Nokia Life Tools, which offer informational services to rural consumers.

Besides the mobile telephony subscriber base, the Internet user base has also grown in recent years in rural India. In 2013, there were 68 million Internet users versus 7.5 million online users in 2009 in rural India. Rural India witnessed a y-o-y growth of 58 per cent of active Internet users since June 2012, facilitated by the focus on user concentrated touch points like e-Choupal, common service kiosks, n-Logue, and other ICT initiatives in rural markets.

The rural mobile space has become very competitive in the last few years with the entry of all the major players, who jumped into this market owing to the cut-throat competition and saturation of urban markets, to ride the next growth wave. Among these, Bharti is the market leader with a 25 per cent share in the rural market. Vodafone and IDEA are at the second and third positions, as can be seen from Table 10.1.

Rural telecom marketers have been trying to promote educational, financial, and informational services through the ICT (Information Communication Technology) platform. Mobile players are introducing customized value-added services (VAS) for rural consumers to increase the average revenue per user (ARPU). Nowadays, cellular companies are

Airtel, the largest mobile services provider in the country, has successfully wooed rural consumers with affordable, world-class services.

| TABLE **10.1** |
Rural Subscribers and Market Share

Service Provider	Subscribers (in million)	Rural Subscribers (in million)	Per cent of Rural Subscribers	Rural Market Share
Bharti	208.75	93.76	44.92	24.82
Vodafone	166.62	89.39	53.65	23.66
IDEA	135.79	74.72	55.02	19.78
BSNL	113.14	38.42	33.96	10.17
Reliance Communication Group	112.13	27.32	24.36	7.23
Aircel	70.15	25.51	36.37	6.75
Tata	64.55	15.24	23.61	4.04
Telewings	35.61	11.2	31.46	2.97
Other*	26.28	2.17	25.61	0.57
Total	933.01	377.73	40.49	100

Note: *Includes Sistema, Quadrant, Loop, Videocon, and MTNL

Source: January – March, 2014 TRAI Report on The Indian Telecom Services Performance Indicators

BHARTI AIRTEL

Bharti Airtel, India's largest mobile telephony player, has got to where it is today largely on the back of its rural growth. It has kept its leadership position intact since 2005. Initially, Airtel faced several hurdles. The biggest problem, however, was the negligible presence of handset manufacturers in rural markets. Airtel entered into a crucial partnership with Nokia to bundle handsets with connections and other alliances for distribution. It helped that both Airtel and Nokia had the same, immensely popular brand ambassador, Shah Rukh Khan. The right mix of product and pricing, strengthened by a vast and unique network of over 25,000 centres to serve customers, formed the backbone of the Airtel strategy. Airtel's recharge rates came down, eventually culminating in 'lifetime validity' connections for as little as INR 99 and micro-recharges where consumers could top up as required, in multiples of INR 10. To increase reach and distribution (not just for initial consumer acquisition, but for recharge and service requirements), Airtel created a two-tiered structure with rural super-stockists and distributors under them. Airtel service centres helped to widen service, and a roaming distributor helped to acquire consumers. Airtel also created service options targeted at rural consumers, such as service in the village, SMS-based systems, vernacular IVR systems, etc., through effectively outsourced systems like the Airtel service centres. It created a cost-effective, young entrepreneur-led distribution channel. It effectively worked around the issue of handset manufacturers not having the relevant distribution networks. In addition to the freedom to communicate, rural consumers are also provided with support to their livelihood through job alerts, weather, and price-related information. Rural distributors were effectively young entrepreneurs (around 30,000 at last count), who were allocated territories around a few mobile towers and were responsible for consumer acquisition. Airtel also entered into alliances with IFFCO, which helped it to sell connections through 35,000 agricultural societies. It built an enabling system that allowed 700,000 rural retail outlets to sell recharges through a mobile device. The penetration in rural India has increased manifold, given that two out of three net subscriber additions in India today come from its villages. ■

tying up with various players to provide rural-specific, real-time, customized informational services on mandi prices, weather, and other needs and transactional services, such as banking and ticket reservations.

The real-time information helps farmers to optimize their returns, and encourages rural consumers to pay for the services, as demonstrated by VAS providers like Reuters Market Light (RML). Some of the key initiatives for VAS in rural markets are Reuters Market Light, IFFCO Kisaan Sanchar Ltd, and Nokia life tools.

Idea Cellular, in partnership with RML, launched Krishi vouchers which provide agriculture-related informational services.

Reuters Market Light

Reuters Market Light (RML) is the first highly personalized, professional mobile phone-based information service for farmers in India. It was started in Maharashtra in April 2007 on a trial basis; by 2009, the company had sold subscriptions to over 1.4 million farmers in 50,000 villages across 17 states in India. RML helps farmers to achieve better yields and secure better prices by allowing them to receive accurate weather forecasts and local price information direct to their mobile phones, in their own language. In addition, it also provides information on produce arrivals, tips for the best practices based on stage of crop cycle, and agri-news updates on regional and crop-specific events.

Prior to the launch of RML, farmers had limited access to information pertaining to current and local market prices for their crops, knowledge about when to harvest their crops, etc. This hindered market efficiency, reduced yields, increased wastage, and adversely affected a farmer's earnings and livelihood. By providing accurate and timely information, RML has helped farmers to tackle these problems successfully. Above all, it has reduced crop wastage and increased the average farmer's productivity and profitability.

RML charges INR 175 for three months, INR 350 for six months, and INR 650 for one year. RML has partnered with Idea Cellular Ltd. to increase the reach of its crop information service in Maharashtra and Goa. Idea Cellular Ltd. is distributing Krishi Vouchers, pre-paid cards with a value of INR 75, which will provide informational services through SMS alerts in Marathi, English, and Hindi.

RML

Manikrao Gawade, an onion farmer in Maharastra, held back 70 quintals of onions following RML news. In the next 20 days, he realized a 70 per cent gain and made an extra profit of INR 25,000. Another RML customer who tracks rainfall information does not engage field labour whenever he gets a rainfall alert. In this way, he has managed to save INR 70 per head for three labourers in three instances totalling INR 630. At an average saving of INR 650 a day, his return on investment is 100 per cent in three days.

IFFCO Kisaan Sanchar Limited

IFFCO Kisaan Sanchar Limited (IKSL) is a joint venture between Bharti Airtel and IFFCO to provide rural-specific telecom services to rural households. It aims to empower people living in villages by fulfilling their communication requirements and disseminating relevant and pertinent information through value-added services. Under this model, the telecom products of Airtel are made available to farmers and people living in villages through cooperative societies.

It was launched in 2007 in eastern UP and has since rolled out across the country in 18 states. These connections are sold under the name Green SIM to farmers, who receive at least five SMSes every day advising them on various agriculture-related issues to do with crops, horticulture, aquaculture, government programmes, etc. These services are provided free of cost with the connection. A toll-free service number has also been introduced, where farmers can have their queries answered by agriculture

RML was the first entrant in the M-VAS market in rural areas with highly personalized priced agri-information services.

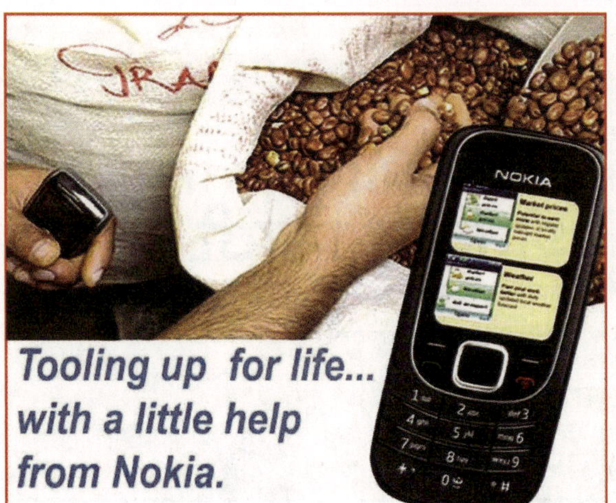

Nokia Life Tools offers a range of services aimed at emerging markets.

experts. The company had a subscriber base of more than 30 million individual farmers and 39,000 cooperative societies across the country on December 2010.

Nokia Life Tools

Launched in Maharashtra in 2008, Nokia Life Tools aim to provide users with direct access to information that can change how they do business. It delivers agricultural information, educational resources, and entertainment to users over SMS. The agricultural part of the service is provided in conjunction with Reuters Market Light. Localized information provided includes weather conditions, advice about crop cycles, and general tips and techniques, as well as market prices for crops, seeds, fertilizers, and pesticides.

Nokia is collaborating with Tata DoCoMo to provide value-added services in rural and semi-urban markets. This service is being provided across 18 states in 11 regional languages. It provides consumers with two choices: a basic plan at INR 30 per month which includes daily updates on the weather, agriculture, and other relevant news, and useful advice and tips; and a premium plan at INR 60 per month, which provides information on the closest market prices of any three crops selected by the subscriber, in addition to the services offered in the basic plan. Users can subscribe to their chosen educational service like English, GK, or a few tips on exams at a cost of INR 30 per month.

M-VAS refers to the value-added informational (weather, price, etc.) and transactional (banking, ticket reservations, etc.) services provided on mobile phones.

See 'Rural Marketing Insight: M-VAS Initiatives in Rural India' for details on other M-VAS initiatives, such as the Fisher Friend Project, Mandi on Mobile, and Grameen VAS. These examples in the rural telecom space demonstrate how M-VAS players have addressed the challenge of the 4As to gain success in rural markets. Table 10.2 summarizes the different marketing mix strategies adopted by these players.

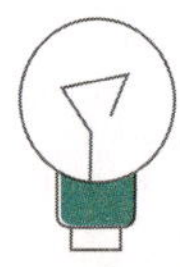

RURAL MARKETING INSIGHT | M-VAS INITIATIVES IN RURAL INDIA

The arrival of mobile phones in rural India has spurred the demand for informational services to improve incomes and livelihood. The real-time information provided through such a service is helping rural consumers, especially farmers, to optimize their returns. Some unique initiatives on this front in rural India are:

- **Fisher Friend Project:** Launched as a pilot project in 2007 in Tamil Nadu and Pondicherry, the Fisher Friend project is aimed at the fishing community. QUALCOMM, MSSRF, and Tata Teleservices have collaborated to provide information on opportunities, risks, and market prices. Apart from important safety and weather information, fishermen also receive information on the locations of fishing areas and real-time market prices of fish. The project directly involves 450 participating fishermen along with members of the project team, who visit the fishermen on a regular basis for training and research purposes. Foggy conditions are common and force fishermen to return to shore since they rely on line-of-sight navigation. GPS can potentially enable fishermen to venture farther out in their boats to higher-yielding sea depths, and allow them to fish for longer periods of time more efficiently. *Fisher Friend* is commercially available on Tata's CDMA network at an affordable monthly charge of about INR 25–30.
- **Mandi on Mobile:** BSNL has launched a 'Mandi on Mobile' service in UP in association with the state government. The service enables farmers to call up the BSNL number and ask for the rate of any vegetable, grain, pulse, or fruit in any mandi across the state. The farmer is required to simply name the product and the district, and he will be told the tehsil-wise rates. There are 108 items, ranging from grains, pulses, and fruit to vegetables, for which the daily rates of 247 mandis can be availed by farmers.
- **Grameen VAS:** Grameen VAS is a Reliance Communications initiative launched in collaboration with Krishak Bharati Cooperative Limited (Kribhco) to provide Internet and mobile services in rural markets in September 2009. It will cover 500,000 villages, and offer education, health, and travel services, and facilitate commerce and transactions. Services will include *mandi bhav* (commodity prices), agriculture and animal husbandry updates, weather forecasts, local information, *samachar* (news), as well as community messaging. Most importantly, these will be available in multiple Indic languages, and accessible via voice portals, SMS, and data. At a monthly charge of INR 15, it is positioned as a low-priced service.

The success of M-VAS players demonstrates that rural consumers can pay for informational services if they experience tangible benefits from it.

| TABLE **10.2** |
Rural Marketing Strategy in Telecommunications

Marketing Mix	Rural Strategies
Acceptability	Ultra low-cost handsets with easy-to-pay instalment option, lifetime-free prepaid service, bundled product
Affordability	Low call rates, INR 5 recharge coupon, electronic recharge for small amount, group subscription without SIM
Availability	Agri-cooperatives, village retailer, syndicated distribution with FMCG companies, MFIs
Awareness	Mass media, BTL activities (sponsoring rural events, van campaign, haats, and melas)

Information and Communications Technology (ICT) in Rural Areas

ICT is emerging as a potential catalyst for economic and social development, leading to a transformation of rural markets and improving access to information, products and services through rural kiosks, and creating new employment opportunities through rural BPOs.

Mobile telephony has ushered in sweeping changes in rural markets by offering a convenient, affordable, and versatile platform to marketers and consumers alike. Similarly, ICT is on the brink of revolutionizing informational and transactional services in rural India. In this section, we examine the factors that have rendered ICT an attractive and sustainable platform for rural marketers in the absence of reliable physical delivery systems. We also discuss the vital role of ICT in various sectors, including agribusiness, finance, healthcare, and education, in rural areas.

Encouraged by the phenomenal success of ICT in urban India, rural markets became the test bed for innovation in ICT for marketers desirous of taking their products and services to rural consumers. Be it e-choupals (call centres for farmers) or e-services provided through common service centres (CSCs) across the country, the saga of ICT in rural India is on the upswing.

The ICT platform came as a saviour for marketers looking to reach the last mile in widely scattered rural markets in the absence of reliable infrastructure and cost-effective distribution channels. This drive was manifested in the form of rural ICT kiosks and rural BPOs, initiated by both government and private players, who used a multi-pronged approach to provide access to information, working simultaneously on content digitization, and increasing the penetration of own kiosks and PPP/collaborative kiosks.

Today, more than 65,000 ICT kiosks are operational in the country, led by the government-sponsored CSCs and the corporation-initiated ITC e-Choupal initiative (see Table 10.3). We discuss the prominent initiatives in this section.

ITC's e-Choupal

e-Choupal, initiated by the tobacco giant ITC's agribusiness division in 2000, was aimed at creating a direct procurement channel to buy agricultural produce from farmers rather than from mandis. What began as an effort to re-engineer the procurement

| TABLE **10.3** |
Major ICT initiatives in Rural India

ICT Initiative	Number of Kiosks
CSC	55, 979
ITC e-Choupal	6,500
n-Logue	1,700
Drishtee	700
NICT (Gyandoot and others)	400
DA-TaraHaat	40
Datamation	35
Total	**65,354**

Source: Mukesh Hajela at the Regional workshop for Knowledge hub's and Networks Next Step, 11–12 December 2009, UN ESCAP, Bangkok

e-Choupal provides Internet access to rural farmers for accessing the daily prices of crops, weather forecasts, the latest farming techniques, crop insurance, etc.

process for soya, tobacco, wheat, shrimp, and other crops in rural India has now created a highly profitable distribution and product design channel for the company—an e-commerce platform that is also a low-cost fulfilment system focused on the needs of rural India.

e-Choupal was conceptualized as a chain of Internet kiosks connected through VSATs to facilitate the procurement of specific commodities. Each kiosk is part of a hub and spoke model, with the ITC procurement centre as the hub and the e-Choupals as the spokes. As a direct-marketing channel virtually linked to the mandi system for price discovery, the e-Choupal aims to eliminate wasteful intermediation and multiple handling.

By providing farming know-how and services, timely and relevant weather information, transparent price discovery and access to wider markets, e-Choupal enables economic capacity to proliferate at the base of the rural economy. At present, four million farmers use e-Choupal to their advantage and the network of 6,500 e-Choupal centres spread across 40,000 villages has emerged as the gateway to an expanding spectrum of commodities leaving farms. The reverse flow carries FMCGs, durables, automotives, and banking services back to villages. This model has led to a 4–7 per cent reduction in the true cost of contract for different buyers in the commodities business, and for ITC, there has been a 40 per cent reduction in transaction costs of procurement.

The company is planning to roll out version 3.0 in collaboration with Nokia Life Tools, in which it will offer personalized crop management advisory services to individual farmers, integrating mobile phones into the digital and physical network of e-Choupal. It will enable a farmer to provide information on the type of soil, crop variety, the date of sowing, and details about crop condition on an ongoing basis to the company. This will provide ITC with an additional reach of 16 million farmers in its area of operation.

Common Service Centres

CSCs are emerging as a potential catalyst for economic and social development, leading to a transformation of rural markets and improving access to information, products and services though rural kiosks, and creating new employment opportunities through rural BPOs.

The CSC Scheme has been formulated as a public–private partnership (PPP) model and is bringing about an unprecedented movement across the country with its ownership being accepted at every level of the governance structure. The idea is to develop a platform that can enable the government, private, and social-sector organizations to integrate their social and commercial goals for the benefit of rural populations in the remotest corners of the country, through a combination of both IT and non-IT services. Within each state, the CSC scheme follows a three-tier hierarchy

(*i*) The first level comprises village-level entrepreneurs (VLEs) who service rural consumers in a focused cluster of five to six villages. Loosely, the functioning of these VLEs is similar to that of franchisees in an urban distribution network.

(*ii*) The second level comprises service centre agencies that train, manage, and expand the business of VLEs. Srei Sahaj e-Village Limited, a subsidiary of Srei Infrastructure Finance Limited, is such an agency. It has set up over 28,000 ICT-enabled e-kiosks across six states, which together form the largest chain of centres among the 55,979 CSCs present across the country as shown in Table 10.3.

(*iii*) The third level comprises state-designated agencies (SDAs) that facilitate implementation of the scheme within the state, and provide policy, content, and financial support to the SCAs.

An operational CSC.

Under this initiative, the government has planned to establish 100,000 ICT-enabled access points across the country, covering all villages. The plan is to have one CSC for six census villages, catering to 6,000 citizens. At present, around 56,000 CSCs are operational across 13 states in the country. Information services and products ranging from e-governance services, utility services, payments, deposits, insurance, and other financial services to a host of e-information and e-learning facilities are delivered through these CSCs at economical prices. CSCs not only save resources and improve the quality of life of rural inhabitants, but also provide employment to the rural youth. These centres are paving the way for new channels of distribution in rural India for products and services. Over a period of time, CSCs will lead to increased savings and income, which will enable the rural population to spend a sizable portion of their income on the consumption of services and products, thereby boosting rural retail.

n-Logue Village Internet Kiosks

n-Logue Communications was set up by the Telecommunications and Computer Networks (TeNet) of IIT Madras. It is in the business of providing Internet, voice, e-governance, and other rural services through a network of local service providers (LSPs) and kiosks by establishing and maintaining corDECT (wireless access)-based communication systems. corDECT is particularly well suited for use in rural areas due to its affordable costs, low maintenance requirements, and ease of deployment.

n-Logue has developed a scalable for-profit business model for establishing rural connectivity based on demand. At the top tier, n-Logue has the responsibility for managing the overall operations; at the second tier, local service providers (LSPs) set up the infrastructure providing connectivity; and at the third tier is the village, where local kiosk owners supply the rural population with information-based services. By building local capacity and utilizing local resources, this business model aims to reduce the costs presently associated with providing both telephony and Internet access to rural India.

The services delivered by the n-Logue kiosks include basic communication services, computer training, desktop publishing, word processing, school curriculum-based tutorial classes using multimedia applications, and astrological predictions. In addition, the kiosks offer online consultancy through agricultural and veterinary experts;

doctors and student counsellors are given access to online land records through the Bhoomi projects, and access to online medical databases in collaboration with Web healthcare.

At present, n-Logue has about 1,700 kiosks in the states of Tamil Nadu, Karnataka, Maharashtra, Rajasthan, Andhra Pradesh, and Gujarat, and it intends to expand steadily, connecting at least a million subscribers.

Drishtee

Drishtee started operations in 2000 through ICT information kiosks with the aim of delivering services and related information to the village community. Currently, it has a network of 700 kiosks spread over three states—Assam, Bihar, and Uttar Pradesh—servicing 1.5 million villagers. The kiosks are run by local entrepreneurs who provide a range of services to the village community.

Marketers of various products and services like health, agribusiness, finance and consumer products are leveraging ICT platforms to take their services to rural markets.

Broadly, two types of services are provided—**local** services and **centralized** services. The local services can be offered at the kiosk level itself, whereas centralized services are offered through Drishtee. Centralized services include computer and English education, selling of services and products such as insurance, recharge coupons, Scojo reading glasses, and Amaron batteries. Local services include an operational digital photo studio, entertainment services, and various Internet-based information services such as information on agricultural products like mandi rates, or weather information, and exam results. In addition, it has also introduced rural BPO services to provide training and employment opportunities to the rural youth. The rural BPO model follows a hub arrangement responsible for the quality assurance of the deliverable, with a large number of kiosks functioning as spokes. The key customer base includes large private organizations such as banks and libraries, or the government, both of which require digitization services. It also targets the customer service/customer acquisition market, particularly where the local language/dialect and knowledge of local communities is important.

DABUR: DEPLOYING TECHNOLOGY TO EXTEND REACH

Dabur is the world's largest Ayurveda and natural healthcare company with annual sales revenue in excess of US$1 billion and market capitalization of US$4 billion. Dabur's offerings are very popular in rural markets' products like Chyawanprash, Amla hair oil, and Hajmola digestives. In fact, about 47 per cent of its sales in terms of consumption comes from rural markets with populations smaller than 50,000. Although the company ranks third among rural players, only 31 per cent of its rural sales come through direct distributor networks. Dabur needed to increase its direct reach to boost rural market revenue and build distribution for higher margin categories including fruit, juice, oral care, and home care. To expand its reach, Dabur launched Project Double in 2010.

Project Double was divided into two phases. Phase 1 was launched in UP and Maharashtra to validate the sustainability of the idea. Phase2-focussed on the remaining eight states it had targeted. A GIS tool was used to select 287 districts based on characteristics such as presence of a bank, per capita income, and population. Each month the distribution network received a fresh cluster of new targets and route planning software optimized work across geographics. To structure its distribution and avoid multiple company contacts at a single outlet, Dabur decided to use one umbrella for all its categories and developed two-layer distribution structure. Super-stockists operated from the key towns in a district and feeder sub-stockists covered small areas. Super-stockists received inventory directly from Dabur and did not carry out any local distribution. Local distribution was done by sub-stockists who reached villages with a population up to 3000. To avoid parallel distribution, super-stockists worked only through the use of transaction software provided by the company. Dabur also recruited a large number of rural sales representatives at the front end to generate incremental sales. They covered villages within the 60 mile radius and were responsible for taking orders and ensuring fulfilment by stockists. The RSRs were given tablets that track activity on a daily basis. The variable pay structure was dependent on RSRs' updates. The tablet also provided information on van routes, work schedules, and order status. The apps also offer access to sales history and inventory at the sub-stockist level.

To generate sales for categories with less penetration, Dabur needed to increase village demand. After conducting consumer insight research the company discovered that rural customers wanted quality-value messages that stress functionality. The messages needed to address benefits, solve issues, and most important involve people. Symbols, colours, and logos were the most common form of brand identification. Dabur piloted rural customer connection programmes across haats and melas to provide consumers with the opportunity to experience Dabur products first hand. Company also turned to opinion leaders such as healthcare camps that provide medical examinations and advice.

With a year and a half, Project Double has reached 24,000 of the targeted 33,000 in the top 10 states. Planned sales revenue has more than doubled and gross margins have improved through a significantly better product mix.

The Relevance of ICT Services in Rural India

Apart from services, ICT also assists all elements of the value chain in bringing about a more efficient exchange of goods and services. For example:

- It enables marketers to access wider areas more effectively, thereby leading to better economies of scale.
- It enables retailers and other intermediaries to exchange relevant information with suppliers speedily, thereby minimizing stockholding costs and wastage in distribution, and avoiding stock-outs for a particular brand or product.
- It enables consumers to gather sufficient information in order to arrive at an optimum choice.

ICT allows information to be integrated, packaged, and shared in customized ways in accordance with the needs, ability, and convenience of rural consumers. For example, the e-governance service extended by the Andhra Pradesh government incorporates information in the five languages most commonly used by residents of the state. ICT has enabled rural consumers to easily gather, compare, and share information about brands and products. ICT gives marketers the mechanism to collect and analyse more complete information on individual consumer purchasing patterns and preferences.

Retailers and intermediaries in rural areas have used ICT to their advantage in particular, and to enhance the overall efficiency of the value chain in general. Today, retailers prefer to place orders or gather information from distributors or wholesalers directly over the telephone rather than visiting them personally in the nearby town(s). This has smoothened the supply chain and reduced investment in stocks. Such benefits help retailers to invest in a comprehensive length and breadth of merchandise and extend quality service to their end customers.

Therefore, to meet the infrastructural challenges in rural markets, marketers are building their distribution channels around the ICT medium. The 'anytime-anywhere' advantage of e-marketing leads to efficient price discovery and offers economy of transaction for trading, and a more transparent and competitive setting. This attracts many rural developmental agencies and marketers to deploy web sites for the marketing of agricultural and non-agricultural products. Finally, many corporations have experienced how ICT has increased bottom-up participation in the processes, and how it can expand the reach and accessibility of a company's offerings. In short, ICT has direct implications in enhancing the affordability, awareness, acceptability, and accessibility of offerings and services in rural markets.

::: Financial Services in Rural India

The financial services sector contributed 18 per cent to India's GDP in the financial year ending in 2013. Currently, it is the second-largest sub-sector in the services economy. The financial market in rural India, comprising microfinance, banking, and insurance services, is expanding and offering customized products and services to meet the increasing demand and rising incomes. Favourable demographics in terms of rising literacy and a younger population are driving the demand for financial services.

As of March 2013, rural India has a financial infrastructure comprising 37,953 rural branches of commercial and regional rural banks, 46,000 rural and semi-urban branches of microfinance institutions, more than 96,000 cooperative institutions, and over 135,000 post offices.

The financial market in rural areas primarily comprises microfinance, banking, and insurance services, which have demonstrated tremendous growth potential in recent years.

The financial needs of rural customers are linked to their lifecycle needs, ranging from savings to credit to insurance to remittances. As per an Edelweiss-MART survey, as many as 78 per cent households save small amounts from their incomes, mostly for emergencies and future needs. Also, the average annual household savings stood at INR 22,960 in 2010. Rural households use both formal and informal savings instruments. Informal instruments continue to dominate as 85 per cent households save cash at home and 25 per cent invest in gold (see Fig. 10.2). Among formal channels, bank deposits, insurance, and postal savings are the preferred financial instruments in rural India. Access to savings and investment facilities is critical for the rural consumer. The two critical needs are **micro-savings** and **frequent withdrawals**. These needs facilitate a customer in building capital over the long term, as well as in coping with emergencies. However, banks do not offer adequate services to address these needs. The lack of services therefore leaves the rural poor with little option than to transact with the informal banking market.

We examine the three components of rural financial services in this section: banking, microfinance, and credit, and insurance services.

Banking Services

The low penetration of banking services in rural India presents a huge opportunity for marketers. Due to the poor presence of the banking system, moneylenders are the major providers of financial services in rural India.

Access to banking services is influenced by issues such as the basic economic state of the rural population, lack of physical infrastructure facilities, regulatory constraints, and the economics of rural banking. On the other hand, usage is constrained by social issues such as illiteracy, incomplete service offerings by banks, and high transaction costs in the formal banking system.

Today, only 7 per cent of Indian villages have banks, and more than 80 per cent villages do not have a bank branch within a 2 km radius. Moreover, low deposit and credit penetration and low average values pose huge challenges to marketers looking to service the rural markets profitably.

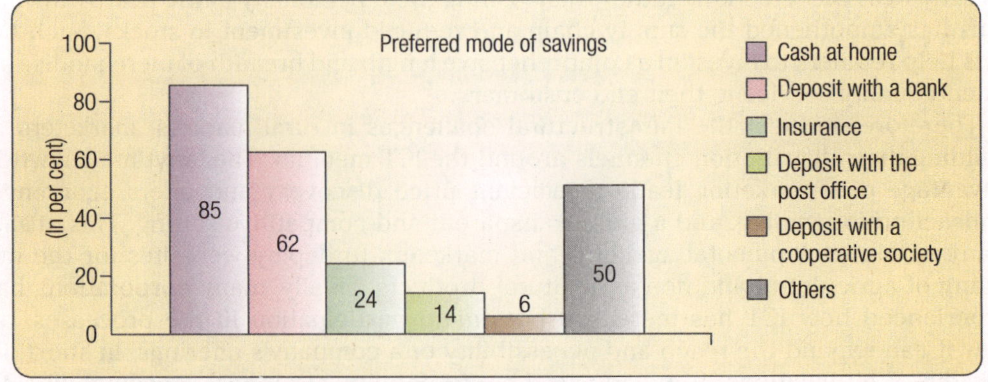

| FIG. **10.2** |
How Rural India Saves
Others include savings in gold, land/property, chit fund, money lender, bonds shares/mutual funds
Source: NCAER.

The cost of opening and operating an account using the formal banking system is rather high for rural consumers on account of the additional costs incurred in reaching the bank, and the opportunity cost of lost wages. This is why, despite the financial security offered by the formal banking system, rural consumers lean towards the informal system. Informal systems involve a lower transaction cost, but are risky and, in some cases, may result in the loss of one's entire capital. To address these challenges, bankers are experimenting with new delivery models like the no-frills account, business correspondent model, cloud computing, smart card, etc.

There are 185 million 'potentially bankable' people in rural India who do not use formal banking services because of reasons like poor access or usage of services.

A good mix of public and private-sector banks provides stability and growth to the economy. In addition, non-banking financial institutions, cooperative banks, primary agricultural societies, etc., are spread across the country to meet local needs.

Today, there are close to 37,953 bank branches in rural India (around 40 per cent of the entire branch network). In addition to bank branches, a huge network of cooperative credit institutions is also present for the disbursement of credit products (see Fig. 10.3). In the second phase of financial inclusion, remaining unbanked villages, close to 4,90,000 have been identified in villages with less than 2000 population and have been allocated to banks, for opening of banking outlets by March 2016.

Primarily, financial products are distributed through two systems—branch and non-branch delivery. However, due to the limited reach and poor viability of the branch system in rural areas, a large number of initiatives have been taken to reach the last mile through the non-branch route. Some of the initiatives have been mobile ATMs, smart cards and mobile banking, use of intermediaries including SHGs, MFIs, post offices, and the business correspondent/facilitators model (see Fig. 10.4).

BANKING DISTRIBUTION CHANNELS IN RURAL The business correspondent (BC) model is one of the most effective initiatives that is now being replicated by many players to register rural footprints. Under this model, the intermediaries chosen to spread banking services are called business facilitators and business correspondents. Facilitators identify borrowers, process loan applications, and create awareness about savings and banking products. Correspondents handle money directly, collecting deposits, disbursing loans, accepting loan repayments, and also selling mutual funds, pension and insurance products.

Under the BF model, banks utilize the network of intermediaries such as not-for-profit organizations, microfinance institutions, post offices, non-banking finance companies, and retired bank employees to promote and sell financial services to rural households. Recently, however, petrol pumps, provision stores, pharmacies, and fair-price shops, and other business entities have been included to improve viability through cost reduction. These new intermediaries will not be required to reach out to customers because consumers visit them regularly.

Since the inception of the banking correspondent model in January 2006, the entire focus seems to have been on opening no-frills accounts that require very low or zero minimum balance. The number of these accounts has risen from 0.48 million to 182.06

| FIG. **10.3** | Banking Services in Rural India
Source: www.rbi.org.in, 2011

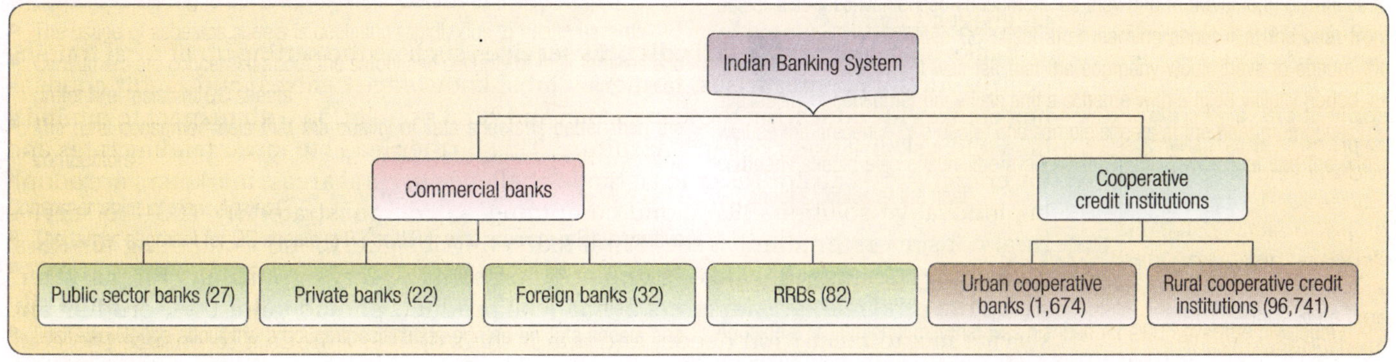

| FIG. **10.4** | Banking Distribution Channels in Rural India.
Source: www.rbi.org.in, 2011

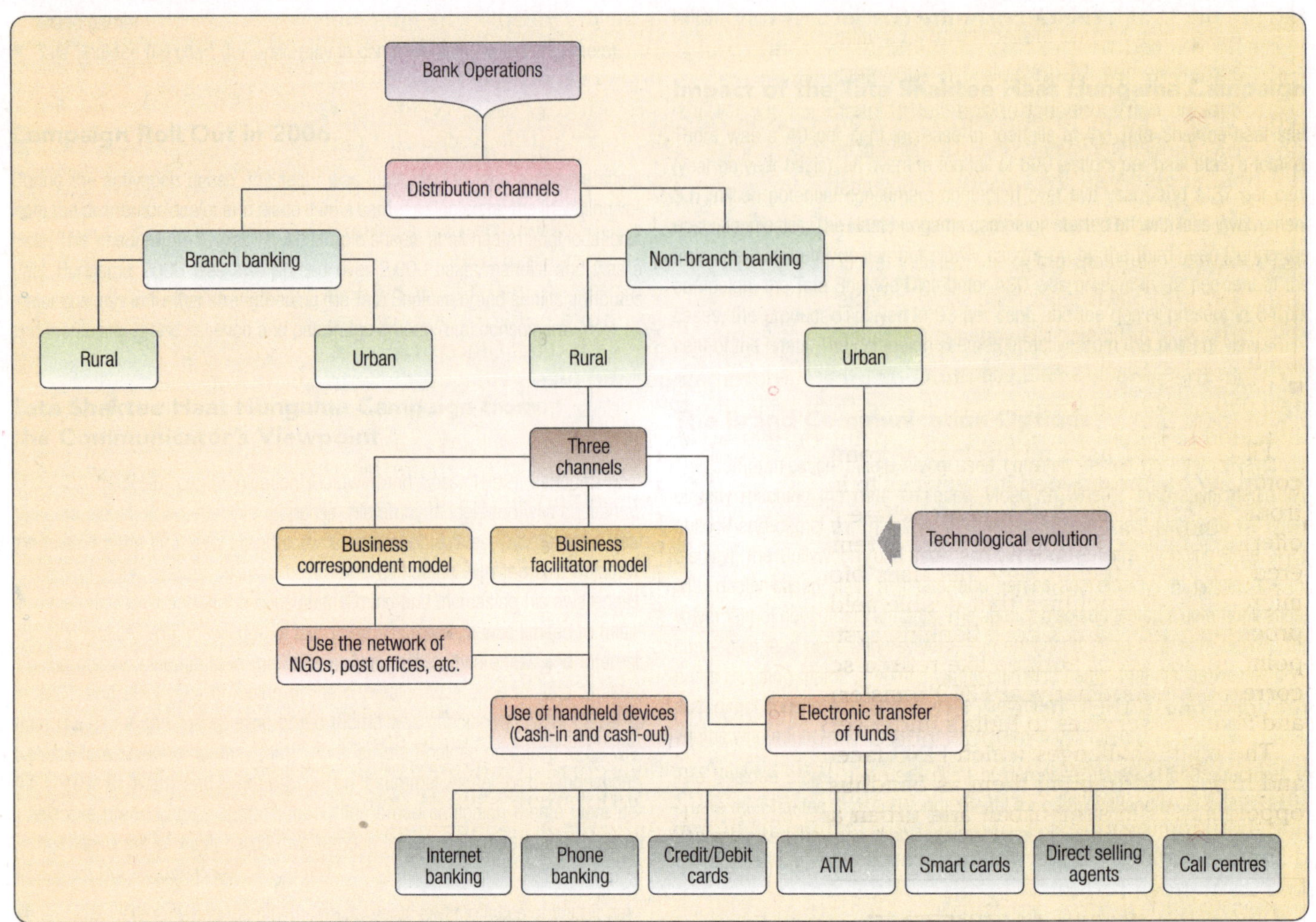

million in the last five years, primarily driven by public-sector banks. Intermediaries under these models have knowledge about the local population and provide feedback about their requirements. As the local population trusts these intermediaries, it is possible to cross-sell various products. The usage of such non-branching delivery channels has been very low. However, with the rising incomes in semi-urban and rural areas, there is further scope for private banks to adopt such non-branching delivery models.

Business facilitators and business correspondents are the intermediaries chosen to spread banking services. Facilitators identify borrowers, process loan applications, and create awareness about savings and banking products. Correspondents handle money directly, collecting deposits, disbursing loans, accepting loan repayments, and also selling mutual funds, pension, and insurance products.

In addition to the branch and non-branch delivery systems adopted by public and private-sector banks respectively, banks also use simple-to-use **cash dispensing and collecting machines** similar to ATMs, which have operating instructions in vernacular languages as well.

Banks have also initiated **credit plus** services such as the setting up of rural training centres for small enterprises, farmers' clubs, knowledge centres, and credit counselling centres for educating the semi-urban and rural population with respect to minimizing yield risk and price risk in agriculture. This further leads to lower lending rates and lower credit risk. To address the last-mile challenge in rural areas, marketers are adopting innovative solutions like cloud computing—as demonstrated by TCS—to service rural consumers profitably (see 'Rural Marketing Insight: Cloud Computing for Rural Banking'). The huge un-banked population presents a great opportunity for marketers to tap the rural market. Marketers of financial products should tailor their product and service mix to meet rural needs, and adapt their delivery models to ensure the commercial viability of their rural banking operations.

FINO PAYTECH: ENGAGING DIRECTLY WITH CONSUMERS

A year ago, Karuna muqaddam was a village homemaker in a one-wage earner family. Today she earns between INR 2000 to INR 3000 per month as a FINO bandhu. In this role , she serves as a banking correspondent or agent who takes over bank's front end for a fee and does the due diligence in lending money and opening accounts for customers for a leading nationalized bank. She serves more than 300 account holders mostly women who work for daily wages. She values providing banking services to villagers who previously had no access to them. Karuna also recently started her own self-help group for her women customers helping them to learn skills that will improve their lives. The fi nancial and social impacts she brings in is the result of being FINO's bandhu. FINO (Financial In-clusion Network and Operations) was founded in 2006 to deliver banking and fi nancial products to India's rural population.

FINO started as a technological company to serve microfinance institutions, the company has broadened its services to include banks, insurance companies, and electronic transfers for government welfare programmes and social security pensions. Its offerings include savings, insurance, remittance, and credit. These services are delivered through a technology that uses biometric smart cards, hand-held devices, and micro-deposit machines that enable field operations and safe integration of front-end processes with bank's core banking systems. In 2006, the RBI permitted banks to appoint not-for profit entities like retired school teachers, etc. to act as bank's business correspondents. That year FINO transferred itself from pure technology to technology and financial services to India's under-served areas.

The main challenges which FINO faced are like difficulty in finding the right talent and hiring and training them as bandhus because educated rural youth found better opportunities in semi-urban and urban areas. Lack of appropriate products for rural

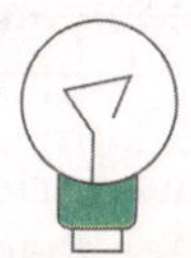

RURAL MARKETING INSIGHT | CLOUD COMPUTING FOR RURAL BANKING

For banks, reaching rural India through the traditional branch-banking model is not viable because of the low value of transaction per customer and a dispersed population. There is little experience in managing remote information technology (IT) infrastructure and guaranteeing security and services. From the consumer's perspective, the time spent in banking transactions set off against the opportunity cost of employment posed challenges to the adoption of banking services in rural areas, as did the habit of storing money at home.

Branchless banking uses cloud computing to take banking services to the un-banked. (Cloud computing refers to Internet-based computing where the delivery of services is through servers; storage and other resources are served from the Web rather than on-premise assets.) It was the TCS financial solutions business unit that pioneered banking automation and branchless banking in India. The State Bank of India was its biggest success story.

Today, it has 60–70 rural banks using its offerings, connecting more than 1,000 branches. Typically, a bank would be able to connect 20–30 branches in a 200-mile radius. Shared resources, software and information were provided to computers and other devices on demand. A bank's operational data could be transferred to a cloud (a server that customers and branches can connect to through the net), enabling banks to offer basic banking facilities on mobiles, Internet- enabled computers, and other devices.

The branchless solution has a smart card or a debit card that is given to the account holder, containing his personal information, and a biometric handheld device operated by the bank's agents. The handheld device is small enough to be carried around and has the memory and battery power to capture a full day's work. This enables electronic financial transactions as well as full integration, and a seamless experience of using the mobile phone as a device for business transactions. TCS Innovation Labs is also testing banking via a television set-top box so that TV users (and the penetration of TVs is significantly higher than that of computers in rural India) will get the experience of Internet banking without access to computers, but with the help of a more familiar user interface that does not require Internet fluency.

customers made it hard for conventional banks to target the market. Furthermore, the financial literacy. Lack of financial viability—low value , high-volume transactions in rural markets make the economies unviable for traditional banks.

FINO directly engaged with customers by establishing teams of financial product experts responsible for designing, developing, and bringing retail products to market with partner banks. Currently, FINO's revenue comes from banking partners and is derived from individual transactions or as a percentage of the amounts disbursed through bandhus. This year, FINO estimates that some 60 per cent revenue will come from recurring income streams such as rentals and transaction charges. FINO is focusing on remittances as its main product offering. One remittances in these areas is complete. FINO will bring new product to the same target segments. Leveraging biometric technology and integration with banks has become a cornerstone of FINO's approach. The company uses it to integrate field operations with back-end banking systems. Biometric and smartcard authentication is easy to use and perceived as secure by consumers. Hand-held systems work on and offline and reach remote areas where mobile and GPRS connections are not available. Internet transaction receipts ensure trust. FINO has also established a 65-member channel skills development team responsible for agent training. There is also a separate team responsible for driving customer financial literacy. In addition, the organization has also conducted financial literacy programmes in many states in partnership with the World Bank, etc. FINO also offers zone-level, mobile-based knowledge management systems and mobile training so that agents and employees can keep abreast of knowledge and refresh their skills. FINO has given a lot of effort in finding the right bandhu. To ensure that customers continue to transact with FINO requires trust and as women are viewed as more trustworthy than men, they have chosen women as bandhus. To ensure the right mix of skills, FINO and bank officers interview each candidate to evaluate their technical skills, financial literacy , social standing, and trainability. The Smartcard biometric system ensures that daily visits are centrally reported at all levels including agents, blocks, and district coordinators. Samvaad, an SMS and Internet-based dashboard, monitors performance and identifies both high and low performers in the field. Today, FINO is the market leader among banking correspondents who have brought banking services to rural India. It employs more than 38,000 agents and has 56 million customers. The company currently operates in 25 states and works with more than 30 of the country's largest financial institutions. Its model is profitable and is scaling for further growth in future.

Microfinance and Credit Services

Rural customers need credit not only for productive purposes, but also for their consumption needs. As shown in Fig. 10.5, apart from agricultural support, rural customers need micro-credit for consumption, healthcare, education, and emergencies. With changing lifestyles, credit is required for buying durables and meeting the expenses of social ceremonies such as weddings and festivals. However, the access to personal loans for consumption needs is limited, which forces them to raise these loans through informal sources at higher interest rates. In addition, larger households need occasional high-value, micro-enterprise loans for business needs. Although banks offer these loans, they require excessive documentation and time-consuming processes, which discourage consumers from approaching them.

Credit is availed from both formal and informal sources in rural India. Local moneylenders, traders, and commission agents are the major informal sources of credit, whereas banks, cooperatives, and microfinance institutions (MFIs) are the formal sources available.

Dependence on informal sources of credit has declined from more than 90 per cent in the 1950s to about 40 per cent now. However, access to formal credit is limited to only 28 per cent of all farmers as formal banking has failed to deliver. The private sector-led microfinance initiatives have improved this situation in recent years, which is discussed in the next section.

CREDIT INSTRUMENTS To meet the credit needs of rural people, MFI loans and kisan credit cards have evolved as effective instruments.

Microfinance Microfinance is defined as the provision of thrift, credit, and other loan products of very small amounts to poor people to enable them to improve their quality of life. It is aimed at providing banking services to the population that does not use banks, primarily comprising those residing in rural areas as they have poor access to formal banks.

The limited reach and poor access of formal financial institutions in rural areas has created the scope for microfinance services to cater to the credit needs of this population. The microfinance segment in India has witnessed a rapid growth in recent years, and has become the world's largest microfinance programme today. In India, microfinance lending operates using two models.

- ***SHG–Bank linkage model.*** This model involves the SHGs, financed directly by commercial banks (both public and private), regional rural banks and cooperative banks.
- ***MFI–Bank linkage model.*** This model covers the financing of MFIs by banking agencies for on-lending to SHGs and other small borrowers covered under the microfinance sector.

The SHG–bank linkage model has been the most successful microfinance approach. As on March 2011, there were around 7.46 million saving linked SHGs with aggregate savings of INR 70.16 billion and 1.19 million credit linked SHGs with credit of INR 145.57 billion. The MFI–bank linkage model has also grown rapidly in recent years. With a network of around 70,000 branches, of which around 46,000 are in rural and semi-urban areas, microfinance has emerged as one of the largest credit institutions in rural India. The deeper reach and low default rate in comparison to commercial banks has led the growth of these institutions.

Microfinance is defined as the provision of thrift, credit, and other financial services and products of very small amounts to poor people to enable them to improve their quality of life.

The MFI Industry currently serves 25 million clients and has been growing by an impressive 30per cent to 50 per cent per year. According to CRISIL, MFIs are set to report a buoyant growth over the medium term, their loan assets are likely to reach INR 35,000 crore by March 2015. At present, there are more than 230 MFIs with a 22.6 million customer base. SKS microfinance is the largest player in this market (see Table 10.4).

The growth of non-government organizations (NGOs) and SHGs and their linkages with banks offer ample scope to facilitate microfinance activities in rural areas. In order to develop into sustainable and profitable microfinance enterprises, NGOs and SHGs have started focusing on alternate revenue streams besides their income from core microfinance operations. This includes services such as micro-insurance, money transfer, procurement, and supply chain financing for agriculture and allied activities.

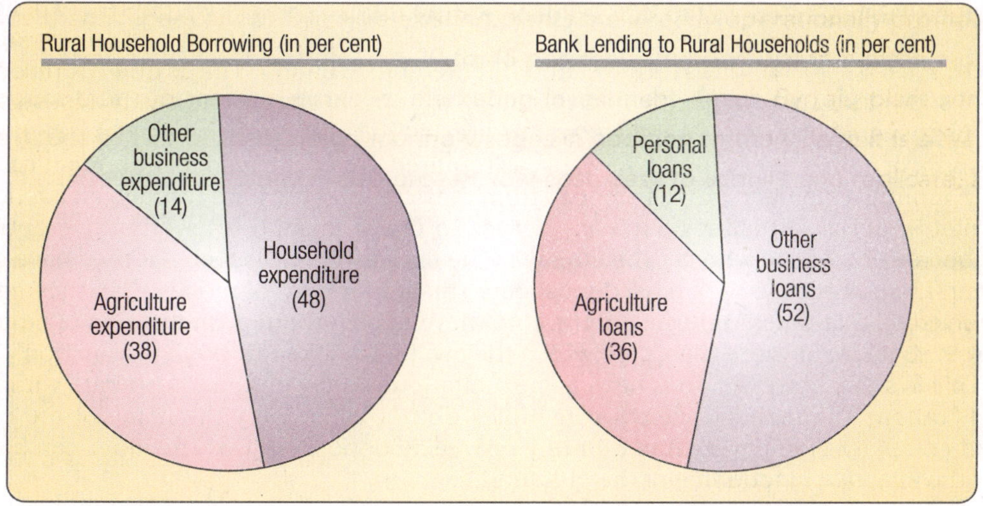

| FIG. **10.5** |
Credit Needs and Purpose of Borrowing
Source: Vinod Nair, Andrew Safield, and Vijay Mulbagal. 'Building a More Inclusive Financial System in India,' *Diamond Report*, 2006.

| TABLE **10.4** |
Major MFI Players

Major Players	No of Branches
SKS Microfinance	2,029
Share Microfin	1,117
Bhandhan Financial	1,551
Spandana	1,533

Source: India Brand Equity Foundation

Marketers can use the microfinance platform to market products and services in rural markets, as is done by some companies like HUL and Bharti.

SKS MICROFINANCE

SKS Microfinance Ltd,[1] India's largest MFI with more than 2,000 branches spread over 19 states in the country, reaches over 100,000 villages in 379 districts The company's cumulative loan disbursements stand at INR 198.41 billion. SKS loans are designed for convenience, with small weekly repayments corresponding to cash flows. Small first loans inculcate credit discipline and collective responsibility. It lends to individual women, utilizing five-member groups where the groups serve as the ultimate guarantor for each member. SKS has entered into strategic partnerships with various technology leaders and innovators like Microsoft, Wipro, Reliance, HCL, and Sify to establish an agile and scalable technology architecture that is capable of handling the challenges specific to the microfinance sector.

Kisan Credit Card The Kisan Credit Card (KCC) Scheme, introduced by the Government of India in 1998–99, aims to provide adequate and timely financial support from the banking system to farmers for their short-term credit needs, primarily for agriculture. It has now become a widely accepted mechanism for the delivery of credit to farmers. In order to make it more user friendly, a reasonable component for consumption needs has also been included in the KCC scheme. By August 2010, 96 million KCCs had been issued by commercial banks, cooperatives, and RRBs, and an amount of INR 437 billion had been sanctioned under this scheme.

The kisan credit card is a revolving cash credit facility with unlimited withdrawals and repayments, with the credit limit based on operational landholding, cropping pattern, and scale of finance. Unlike the plastic credit cards in urban areas, it is in the form of a bank savings passbook.

As per KCC norms, up to 20 per cent of the credit limit under KCC can be used for the purchase of non-agricultural products. This means that on an average credit limit of INR 50,000 that a farmer enjoys, up to INR 10,000 can be used for the purchase of durable products (CTV, mixer-grinder, music system, etc.). This provides a great opportunity to marketers to tap KCC holders in rural markets.

Chit Funds Chit funds form yet another credit instrument. This is quite popular in rural south India, where people find this financing option simple and easily accessible. People become members of registered or unregistered chit fund groups and pay a certain sum of money every month or week, as required under the fund management rules. Each month, a member can take money from the accumulated fund through an auction. Limited process formalities and easy access to credit make this an attractive option for borrowers. Those who get the money in the first few months feel that they have got cheap funds, because they have deposited a smaller amount of money than they have received till that time. At the end of the chit, they would have deposited a sum of money that is equal to, or more than, that which they will have taken through the auction.

This system, however, does have some limitations. Many chit funds operate without registration. The money receipts sometimes do not even carry the name of the chit fund company. Non-payment of monthly or weekly deposits by any member can hamper the effective functioning of the chit fund.

The following example demonstrates how chit funds can be utilized for promoting consumer financing of durables. Some villagers in Paravakottai in Tanjore district of Tamil Nadu wanted to purchase mixer-grinders for their homes, but lacked the funds to make an immediate purchase. The representatives of the mixer-grinder company tried to finance the purchase from local banks, but consumer loans were denied. Doubts were raised about the repayment capacities of the potential consumers. The interested villagers eventually joined a local chit fund group in order to access funds and purchase the mixer-grinders.

Insurance

The insurance industry in India is at an early stage with low penetration and high potential. The total premium of the insurance industry has grown at a compound annual growth rate (CAGR) of 24.6 per cent from 2002–03 to 2008–09 to reach USD 52.6 billion in 2008–09. The insurance sector can be classified into life and non-life insurance companies (see Fig. 10.6).

Low penetration (25 per cent) and high awareness (73 per cent) offers a great opportunity to grow the life insurance market in rural India.

Life Insurance

India's life insurance sector is the biggest in the world with about 36 crore policies and is expected to increase at a compound annual growth rate (CAGR) of 12–15 per cent over the next five years.

Post liberalization in 2000, the sector has witnessed tremendous growth, both in rural and urban business. The rural and social obligation set up by the IRDA has ensured that new players would service rural markets to improve insurance penetration in rural India. According to the McKinsey Global Institute, rural penetration will increase from about 25 per cent at present to 35–42 per cent by 2012. This presents new players with a great opportunity to tap this market. According to the Max-NCAER study (2005–06), 73 per cent of rural households are aware of life insurance and 19 per cent households are policy owners. The average sum assured stands at INR 99,000 with an annual premium of INR 3,560.

| FIG. **10.6** | The Insurance Sector in India
Source: Indian Brand Equity Foundation, www.ibef.org.

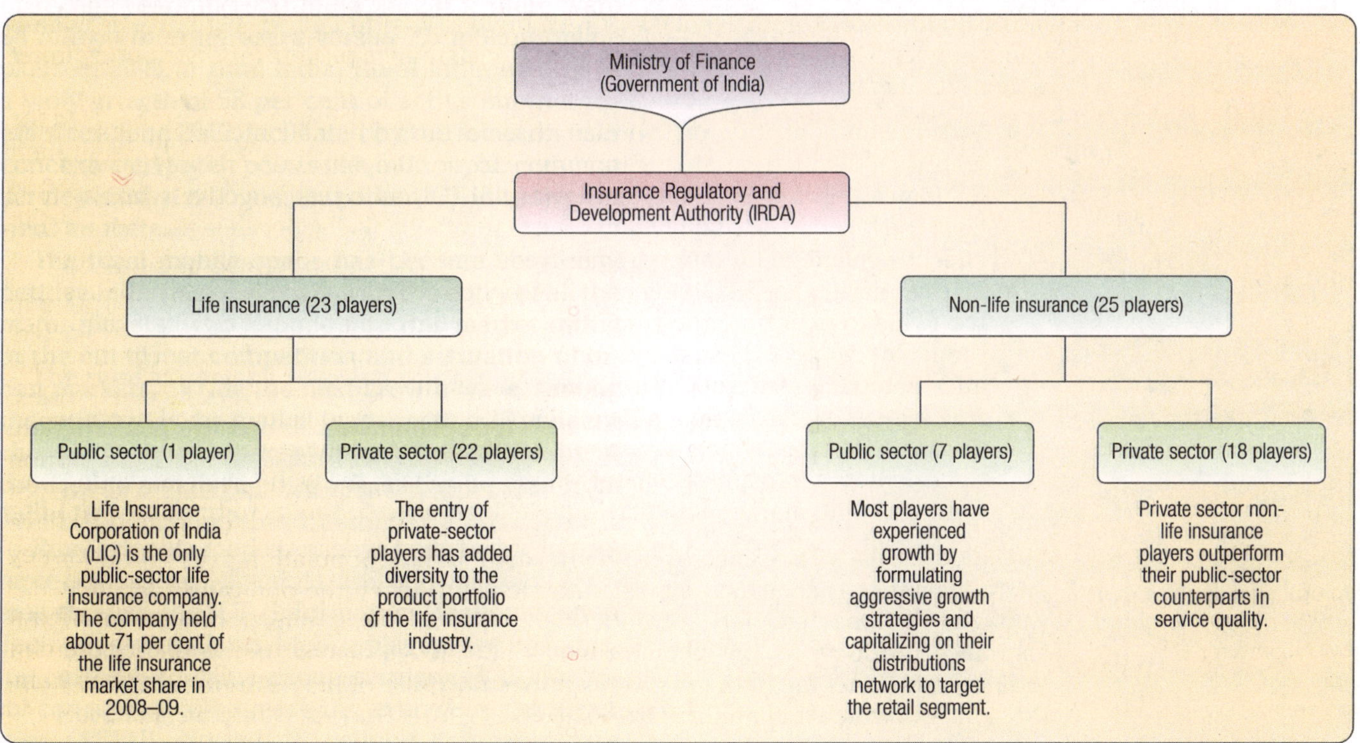

There has been increased insurance penetration due to a growing consumer class, rising insurance awareness, and increasing domestic savings and investments. Premium income as a percentage of GDP has increased from 3.3 per cent in 2002–03 to 7.6 per cent in 2008–09. The entry of private-sector players has added diversity to the product portfolio of the life insurance industry. At present there are 24 players, one from the public sector (LIC) and 23 from the private sector. The Life Insurance Corporation of India (LIC) is the market leader with 71 per cent market share. Amongst private players, ICICI Prudential, Bajaj Allianz, and SBI Life are the leading players. According to the IRDA report, all players have fulfilled the prescribed obligation of 25 per cent policies for the rural sector in 2009–10. The Insurance Regulatory and Development Authority has mandated a tie-up between CSCs and life insurance companies, which will help the latter reach customers in rural areas.

Apart from rural obligation, the introduction of a micro-insurance policy by IRDA and the emergence of new distribution channels have transformed the rural insurance market, which will be discussed in the following section.

NON-LIFE INSURANCE Non-life insurance primarily comprises health, automobile, accidental, house, and property insurance. Today, in this sector, there are 28 players, out of which seven are public-sector players and 21 are from the private-sector. The non-life sector growth was 19 per cent in 2012–13. Public-sector players lead this segment. In the recent past, rural market, auto and health insurance have been an opportunity for general insurers. Among private players, ICICI Lombard and Bajaj Allianz are the market leaders. Auto insurance has the largest share (44 per cent), followed by health (21 per cent).

DISTRIBUTION OF INSURANCE PRODUCTS IN RURAL MARKETS Non-life insurance companies utilize distribution channels such as direct mail, direct sales force, insurance agents, agreements with the corporations, banks, real-estate companies, etc. In life insurance companies, distribution is mainly through agents, as personal interaction is necessary to persuade the customer. As on 31 March 2010, there were three million life insurance agents in the country. LIC has the largest network of agents (1.4 million). Of these, 74,000 are present in rural areas.

In addition to individual agents, there has been an emergence of new distribution channels such as bancassurance, brokers, direct selling agents, and corporate agents such as non-banking financial companies (NBFCs) and tie-ups of para-banking companies with local corporate agencies (for example NGOs) to deliver insurance service in remote areas. The new approaches adopted by insurance players for distributing insurance in rural markets are as follows

- MFIs are an important distribution channel for many insurance companies. MFIs lend to SHGs in rural areas. Many insurance companies are selling group term-insurance policies to members of those SHGs that have collectively taken credit from the MFI. SHGs willingly buy such insurance policies because they act as cost-effective collateral for them to avail credit from MFIs or other financial institutions.
- Private players are also tying up with public-sector banks, cooperative banks, and the RRBs to penetrate the rural market. The large rural customer base and wide branch network of these banks offer an effective distribution channel to the insurance companies, thereby promoting bancassurance.
- A few insurance companies have also tied up with consumer goods companies like HUL, ITC, etc., which have a well set-up distribution network. For example, ICICI has entered into an agreement with e- Choupals, the web-based marketing platform of ITC, to market and distribute its insurance products to rural households.

Micro-insurance is a low premium, affordable insurance product targeted at low-income rural people as a hedge against unforeseen risks.

MICRO-INSURANCE Since over two-thirds of India's population lives in rural areas, micro-insurance is seen as the most suitable aid to reach the poor and socially disadvantaged sections of society. Introduced by IRDA in 2005, it aims to provide affordable insurance products to low-income people as a hedge against unforeseen risks. The total premium income in the micro-insurance portfolio of life insurers for 2009-10 was INR 4 billion, which had doubled from the year before. Fourteen life insurers have so far launched 28 micro-insurance products, and by the end of March 2010, there were 8,676 individual micro-insurance agents in India.

The industry is also promoting micro-insurance as a viable business opportunity and integrating the same with the poverty alleviation programmes of various state governments. Low insurance literacy and awareness, high transaction costs, limited regulations, and a narrow understanding of client needs and expectations have restricted the demand for micro-insurance products. However, with the development of rural health insurance regulations and growing awareness about micro-insurance products, the focus of many private players has shifted to these areas.

::: Rural Healthcare Services

Rural healthcare has assumed greater importance in recent years. In this section, we examine the challenges, the status of rural health infrastructure, the healthcare market, growth drivers, and key initiatives in the rural healthcare space.

An Overview of Rural Healthcare in India

The Indian healthcare sector is expected to become a USD 280 billion industry by 2020 with spending on health estimated to grow at 14 per cent annually, according to an industry report. Healthcare has emerged as one of the most progressive and largest service sectors in India with an expected GDP spend of 8 per cent by 2012 from 5.5 per cent in 2009.

Healthcare expenditure in India is expected to increase by 15 per cent per annum. According to an Ernst and Young report, India has the potential to add nearly 1.74 million beds between 2008 and 2025, with an investment of about USD 104 billion during the same period, to fulfil the unmet needs.

In recent years, the healthy growth of the rural economy, increased purchasing power, higher literacy rate, and increased awareness and education about preventive and curative healthcare has led to a growth in the healthcare demand. According to a McKinsey Global Institute report, rural health spending will multiply five times from INR 700 billion in 2005 to 3,494 billion in 2025 (see Fig. 10.7). In the same period, the share of the wallet on health spending will double from 7 to 13 per cent.

This presents a huge opportunity for marketers to tap into the rural segment, which had been the exclusive domain of the government in the past.

Rural health spending will multiply five times to become an INR 3.4 trillion market with the doubling of healthcare spending by 2025.

The Challenges in Rural Healthcare

The state of rural healthcare has remained poor due to inadequate physical infrastructure and an acute shortage of skilled manpower in rural areas. According to an NCAER study, only 25 per cent healthcare centres located in rural India service 75 per cent of India's population. As many as one-third of the rural population travels 30 km for

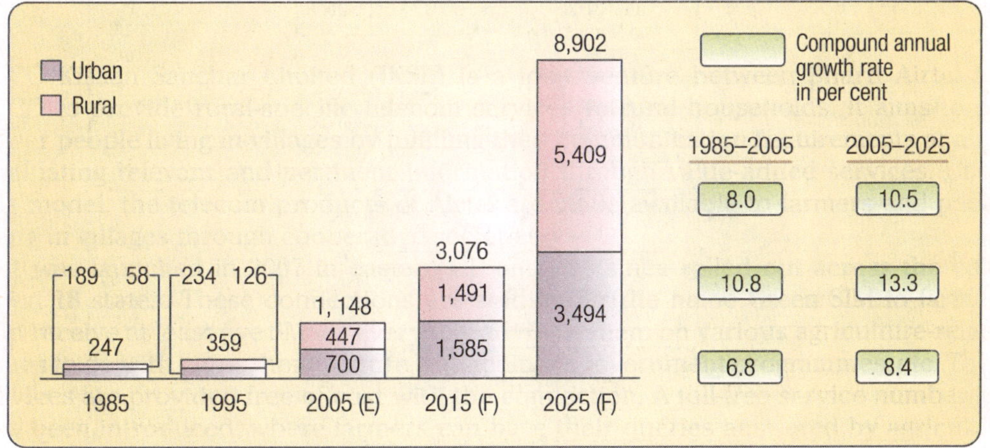

| FIG. **10.7** |
Growing Healthcare Consumption in Rural India
Reproduced with permission from the McKinsey Global Institute.

health services and spends 25 per cent of the healthcare cost on transport. Also, two-thirds of rural Indians do not have access to critical medicine.

Healthcare has been a neglected sector for decades, with minimal spending by the government. Healthcare in India is driven largely by private spending, which is as high as 50–80 per cent. The private consumption of healthcare services accounts for 80 per cent of the total healthcare spending in India, although it is more expensive than public healthcare services. The preference for private healthcare can be attributed to its better perceived quality and accessibility.

Given the poor state of public health infrastructure, recent years have seen the growth of private players in healthcare, attempting to meet the pent-up demand. Infrastructural bottlenecks in the public system have made the central and state governments invite private players to deliver critical healthcare. There is a big opportunity for private healthcare to fill this gap.

The Healthcare Infrastructure

As shown in Fig. 10.8, the government has a three-tier public health infrastructure, comprising community health centres (CHCs), primary health centres (PHCs), and sub-centres (SCs) spread across rural and semi-urban areas, and tertiary medical care providing multi-specialty hospitals and medical colleges located almost exclusively in urban areas.

The sub-centre is the first contact point between the community and the primary healthcare system. It employs one male and one female health worker, with the latter being an auxiliary nurse midwife (ANM). It is responsible for tasks relating to maternal and child health, nutrition, immunization, diarrhoea control, and communicable diseases.

A sub-centre at the village level caters to a population of 5,000, whereas PHCs and CHCs (at larger locations) service approximately 30,000 and 120,000 people, respectively, providing secondary healthcare. Rural India has a network of approximately 152,000 sub-centres and more than 25,000 PHCs, as depicted in Table 10.5.

Despite this elaborate network of facilities, only 20 per cent of those seeking outpatient services and 45 per cent of those seeking indoor treatment avail of public services. Figure 10.9 shows the demand and supply of rural healthcare. While the

| FIG. **10.8** |
The Rural Healthcare System

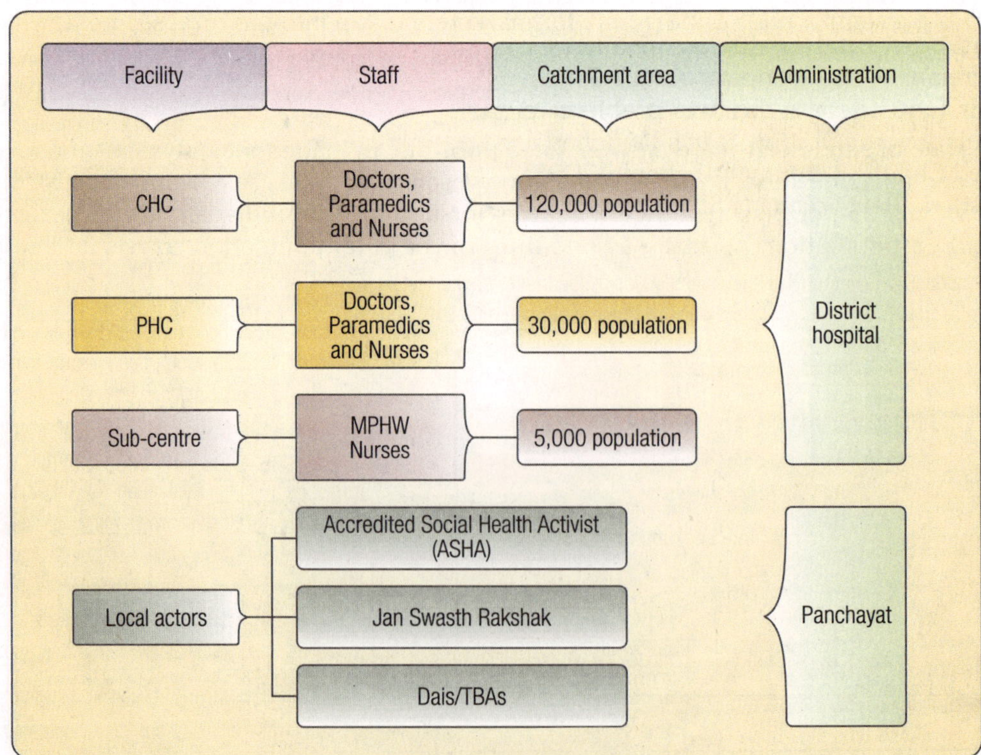

| TABLE **10.5** |
Healthcare Infrastructure in India

Facilities	Number
Sub-centres	146,036
Primary Health Centres (PHCs)	23,458
Community Health centres (CHCs)	4,276
Dispensaries and Hospitals	35,071
Doctors (2009)	757,377
Beds	540,328

Source: Rural Health Statistics in India, 2009 and National Health Profile, 2009

dilapidated state of infrastructure and the poor supply of drugs and equipment are partly to blame, the primary culprit is the rampant employee absenteeism. The nation-wide average absentee rate is 40 per cent. In order to bridge this gap and provide accessible, affordable, equitable healthcare, the government has launched a large number of programmes and schemes. The NRHM is one of the major government initiatives in this direction.

The healthcare market primarily comprises medical services, pharmaceuticals, medical equipment, and the health insurance market, of which services and pharma account for two-thirds of the market.

The Healthcare Market

The healthcare market (see Fig. 10.10) primarily comprises medical services, pharmaceuticals, and the medical equipment market. According to the McKinsey Global Institute, the size of the Indian healthcare market in 2005 was INR 1.1 trillion. This is estimated to grow nine-fold to become INR 8.9 trillion by 2025. During the same period, the size of rural healthcare will multiply five-fold at 8.4 per cent CAGR to become an INR 3.5 trillion market, unleashing a huge latent demand. Healthcare delivery and pharmaceuticals together account for nearly 75 per cent of the total healthcare market. Medical services (driven by the private sector) will be the largest market, fuelled by the demand from rural areas. India will become 10th largest pharma market by 2015, with 27 per cent growth contribution from rural India.

Government Initiatives in Rural India

To address rural healthcare challenges, the government has launched a flagship programme—the National Rural Health Mission (NRHM)—to meet the healthcare needs (and address the twin problems of accessibility and affordability) of the rural population. In addition, it has launched a number of other initiatives such as the Integrated Child Development Scheme (ICDS), Janani Suraksha Yojna (JSY), and Rashtriya Swasthya Bima Yojana (RSBY). We scrutinize the NRHM and the ICDS here.

NRHM is the flagship programme in rural healthcare, aimed at strengthening and promoting access to improved healthcare through accredited social health activists (ASHA).

| FIG. **10.9** | Demand and Supply of Rural Healthcare

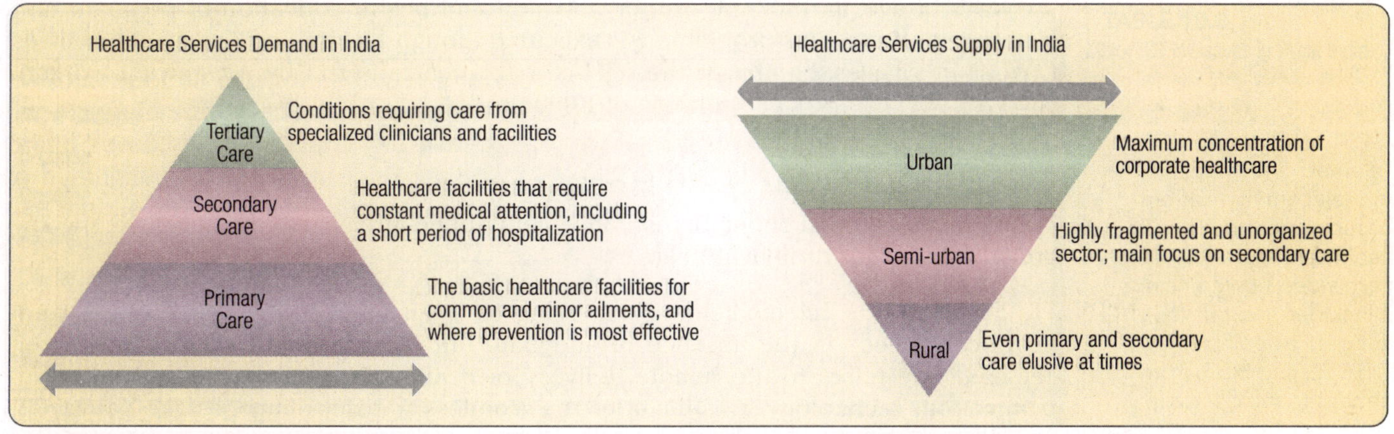

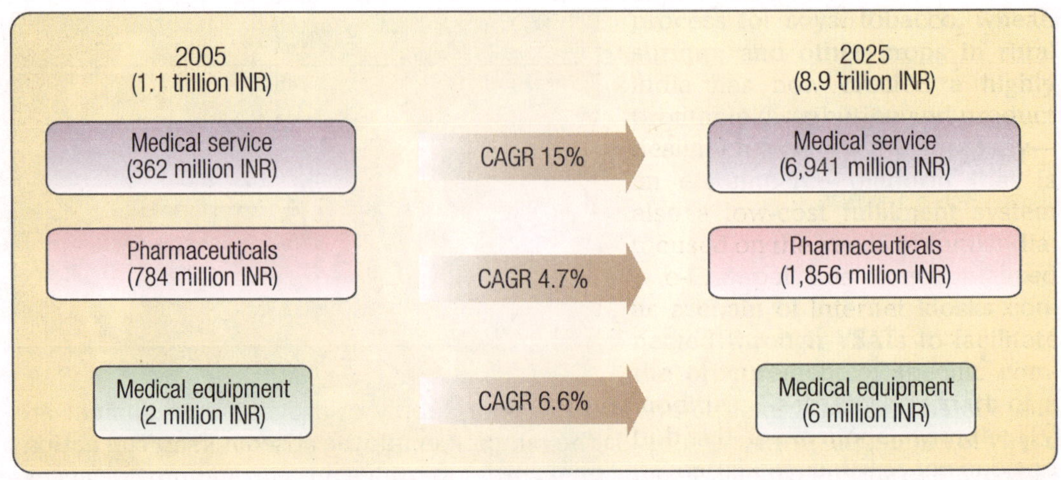

| FIG. **10.10** |
The Healthcare Market
Reporduced with permission from the McKinsey Global Institute.

THE NATIONAL RURAL HEALTH MISSION The National Rural Health Mission, initiated in 2005, aims to provide quality healthcare for all and increase the expenditure on healthcare from 0.9 per cent of the GDP to 2–3 per cent of the GDP by 2012. The mission's objective is to strengthen and promote access to improved healthcare through accredited social health activists (ASHA). In addition, the programme strengthens the state rural healthcare system through the provision of physical infrastructure, human resource, equipment, emergency transport, drugs, diagnostics, and other support. The NRHM has emerged as a successful programme by further providing an overarching umbrella to the existing programmes, including the Reproductive Child Health Project (RCH-II) and other programmes for the treatment of major diseases such as malaria and tuberculosis. Under the NRHM, ASHA has been added as a new functionary at the village level for every 1,000 individuals to improve the last mile delivery (see Fig. 10.11).

Some key achievements under the NRHM programme are as follows:

- As on 31 March 2012, 8.66 lakh ASHAs were engaged.
- Over 1.4 lakh Human Resources have been engaged across the country on contractual basis under National Rural Health Mission. These include ANMs, staff nurses, paramedics, doctors, specialists, and AYUSH specialists.
- As per the Health Management Information System (HMIS) under the National Rural Health Mission, the total institutional deliveries increased from 1.62 crore in the year 2009–10 to 1.68 crore in the year 2010–11 at public and private accredited health facilities.

THE INTEGRATED CHILD DEVELOPMENT SERVICES (ICDS) SCHEME Launched in 1975, ICDS aims to provide support for the holistic development of children below six years of age, and for the proper nutrition and health education of pregnant and lactating mothers. This programme is executed though 1.24 million Anganwadi centres (AWCs) in villages. Similar to the ASHAs, each centre is run by Anganwadi workers (AWWs), who cater to a population of 1,000 people.

Growth Drivers of Rural Healthcare

Telemedicine refers to the telecommunications-based remote delivery of healthcare services. Apart from video-conferencing, it includes the transfer of images, including X-rays, CT, MRI, and ECG, from the patient to the doctor in real time.

Telemedicine, growth of health insurance, and public–private partnerships are the key growth drivers for rural healthcare.

TELEMEDICINE Telemedicine is emerging as a sustainable solution to meet rural healthcare needs in the absence of adequate infrastructure and skilled manpower. Telemedicine refers to the remote delivery of healthcare services through telecommunications technology. This includes the seamless transfer of images like X-rays, CT,

| FIG. **10.11** | The Revised Rural Healthcare System (NRHM)

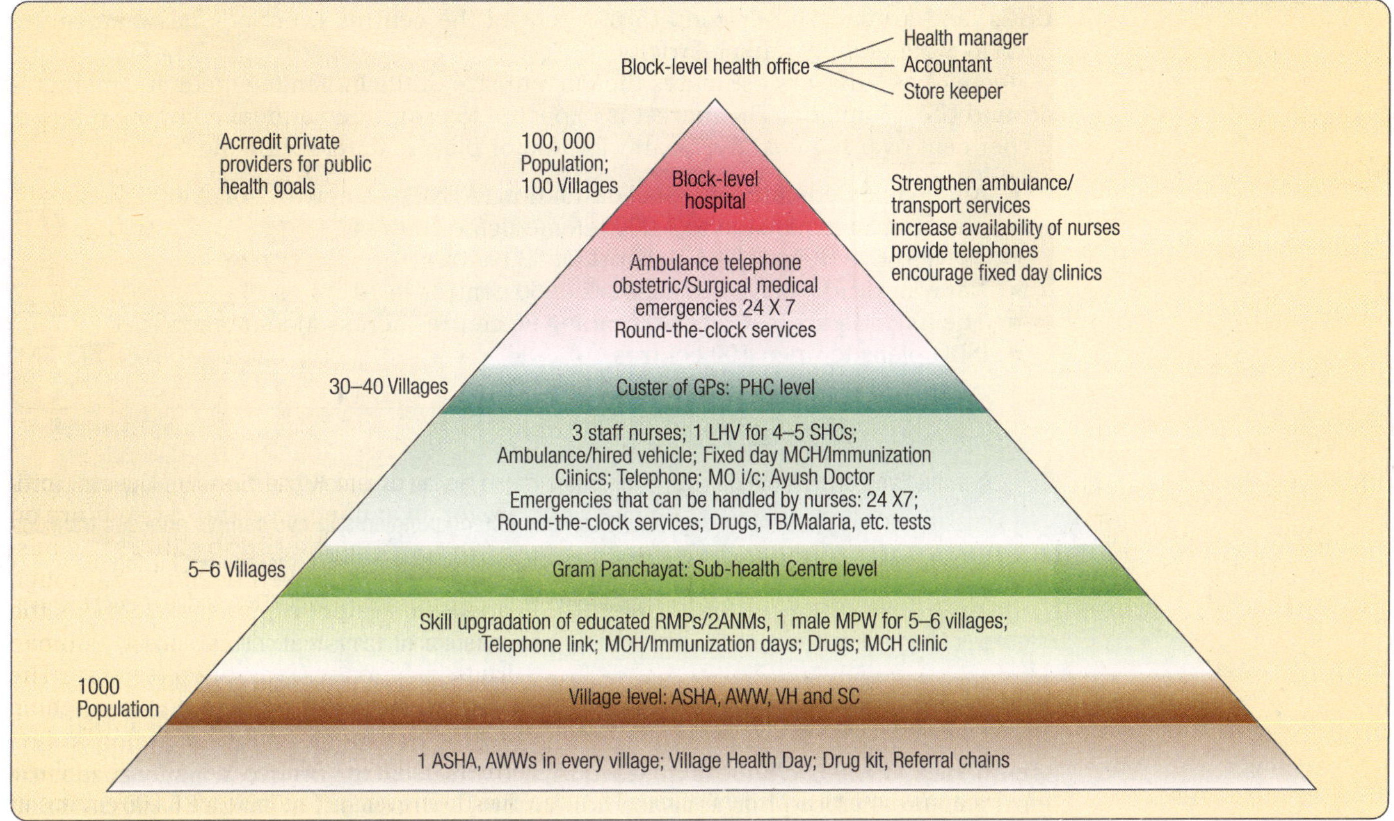

MRI, and ECG from patients to medical experts, apart from live video-conferencing between the patient at a remote hospital with specialists at the super-speciality hospital for consultation and treatment.

Telemedicine is most relevant to rural India as it faces a scarcity of both hospitals and medical specialists for secondary and tertiary care. Despite the launch of the National Rural Health Mission in 2005, India continues to grapple with a 33% shortage of rural hospitals, which are called Community Health Centres (CHCs). In the hospitals

NRHM is a key driver of government-led rural healthcare programmes.

which are present, there is an acute shortage of staff. As per the Ministry of Health and Family Welfare, there is a shortage of 50 per cent–70 per cent technical staff at the CHCs, and around 10 per cent–15 per cent of the centres even lack basic amenities such as water supply and electricity.

Technopak Advisors estimates the current size of the Indian telemedicine market is around US$7.5 million. The market is expected to grow at an annual compound rate of 20 per cent over the next five years. The major players in telemedicine include:

- Apollo telemedicine Network Foundation (ATNF)—A network of over 60 hospitals, planning an expansion to 1,000 telemedicine centres
- Aravind Eye Hospital—A network of 32 centres
- Narayan Hrudayalaya—A network of 60 centres in 10 states
- The Asian Heart Institute is planning 60 centres across Maharashtra
- ISRO plans to open 100 centres

ARAVIND EYE CARE

Aravind Eye Care, founded in 1976, operates much like an assembly line to ensure low-cost, high-quality, and high patient throughput. It screens potential patients in eye camps, provides transport to its hospitals, and deploys para-skilled professionals at each stage, thereby optimizing the use of skilled resources—doctors. It uses emerging technologies such as Wifi PDAs and low-cost technology for imaging to reduce the response time to patient complaints and ensure a quality assurance process. It has a model called *Vision Centres* to reach out to a population of 50,000—a challenge since each community cannot afford an ophthalmologist. Telemedicine proved to be a viable solution. Working on the hub and spoke model, each of the 32 centres (spokes) is connected to the hub (the base hospital at Madurai) through telemedicine. On an average day, there are 6,000 outpatients in the hospitals, four to five outreach screening eye camps examining 1,500 people and 850–1,000 surgeries. Twenty-five centres are planned for villages with a population of less than 5,000 in Madurai and a scale-up plan in UP, Orissa, and Bihar is also in the pipeline.

Rural health insurance services will grow from 14 per cent to 20 per cent by 2015, fuelled by PPP initiatives and customized product offerings.

HEALTH INSURANCE The Indian health insurance market has emerged as a new and lucrative growth avenue for both the existing players and the new entrants. Today, only 14 per cent of the Indian population (approximately 100–110 million people) is covered by health insurance. According to a 2010 research RNCOS report, the health insurance market represents one of the fastest growing—and the second largest non-life insurance—segments in the country. It has grown at a CAGR of 34 per cent in the last five years. As per IBEF report in 2014, the total market size of India's insurance sector is projected to touch US$ 350–400 billion by 2020 from US$ 66.4 billion in FY13.

The growth of health insurance in rural India will be primarily driven by social and community insurance programmes due to the low affordability of insurance plans in rural markets and the focus of the government on providing insurance cover to rural households. With the launch of the Rashtriya Swasthya Bima Yojana (RSBY) in 2008, the Indian government is currently providing annual medical care to 36 million families across 27 states, which has enhanced the market presence of health insurance. Community insurance is likely to grow from 2–3 million to 8–10 million by 2015, primarily through the attempts of NGOs and SHGs. According to a McKinsey Report, 20 per cent of the population will be covered by 2015, driven by the social and community insurance programme. It is estimated that 300 million poor people will get government health insurance cover by 2014. Sensing this opportunity for community health insurance, some initiatives—like the **Yeshasvini** scheme (Karnataka) and the Arogya Raksha (Andhra Pradesh)—have also been undertaken through PPP routes, which have yielded positive results.

YESHASVINI

Initiated by the Karnataka government and Narayan Hridayalaya as a PPP initiative in 2002, the Yeshasvini scheme aims to provide quality healthcare facilities to cooperative farmers across the state of Karnataka. This is the world's largest self-funded healthcare scheme to access quality healthcare at the nominal amount of INR 5 per month, covering over 1,700 surgical procedures for the farmer and his dependent family members. This is a contributory scheme where the beneficiaries are offered cashless treatment in over 135 hospitals across Karnataka. Within the first seven months of being launched, 5,000 farmers underwent various types of operations and 23,500 farmers had out-patient medical consultations for just INR 5 per month. Yashaswini Cooperative Farmers Healthcare Scheme, which presently has over six lakh enrolled members from rural cooperative societies will soon be extended to the entire state's population of 6.5 crore.

PUBLIC–PRIVATE PARTNERSHIPS With increasing opportunities in the rural healthcare space for private players, and the government's willingness to improve healthcare services in rural markets, public–private partnerships (PPPs) are emerging as a win-win solution to provide cost-effective, quality healthcare to rural consumers (see Fig. 10.12).

CHIRANJEEVI YOJNA

Chiranjeevi Yojna was undertaken in 2005 by the Gujarat government as a PPP initiative, in collaboration with private healthcare providers to provide delivery care to the poor in rural India. The pilot was launched in five backward districts of the state, with a total population of 11 million. Under the scheme, the health department empanelled and contracted private, practising obstetricians and gynaecologists who ran their own small hospitals in rural areas to provide adequate care and treatment, if necessary, to the women in these districts for USD 4,500 (for 100 deliveries) This scheme was promoted via meetings with the community leaders, obsterical and gynecological societies, district health offices and rural auxiliary nurse midwives (ANMs). To allay the fears of private doctors that the government does not pay on time, the empanelled doctors were given an advance payment of about USD 625 on signing the contract with the government. As deliveries took place in private hospitals, they were reimbursed rapidly by the district health office. Paperwork was also kept to a bare minimum. Based on the successful experience of the first year, the scheme was extended to the entire BPL population. The scheme was extended in January 2007 to the whole state, where there are about 282,000 deliveries of poor women per year, or 23,500 deliveries per month. Under the scheme, the coverage of deliveries among the poor in the state increased from 27 per cent in April 2007 to 48 per cent in December 2007. By 2012, approximately 800 private-sector hospitals were participating and the programme had helped pay for more than 800,000 deliveries.

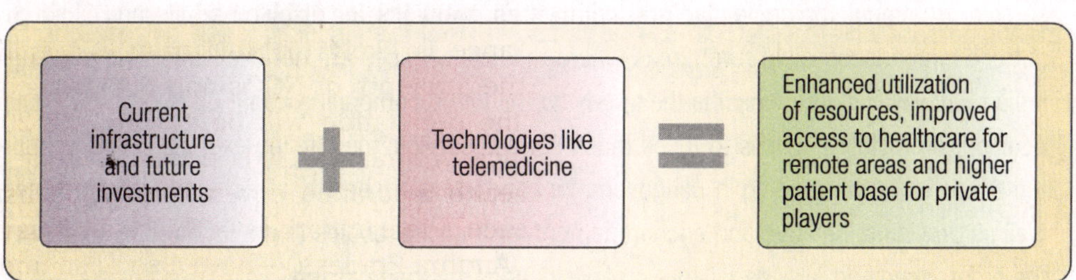

| FIG. 10.12 | Advantage PPP

PPP is bringing about cost-effectiveness and higher productivity, leading to an accelerated delivery of services with a clear customer focus. Thus, it is delivering the promise of enhanced social service along with ensuring the recovery of user charges. Various state governments are collaborating with the private sector through PPPs to address the inefficiency and inequity in the health system. Partnership initiatives range from super-speciality, tertiary-care hospitals (for example, Apollo Hospital, Raichur, and SMS hospital, Jaipur) to primary care hospitals (for example, Karuna Trust in Karnataka). **Chiranjeevi Yojna** is an excellent example of how public–private partnership for maternity care has dramatically reduced maternal and infant mortality in the state of Gujarat.

INNOVATIVE APPROACHES TO RURAL HEALTHCARE PRODUCTS AND SERVICES With rising incomes and the increasing demand for quality health products and services, a number of players have entered this market in recent years with innovative product and service offerings. While companies such as Novartis are taking healthcare services to the hinterland and setting up the last mile network, others, including DSM, Coca-Cola, and Pespsico, have come up with fortified food products in rural India to address malnutrition. In addition, some players such as the Byrraju Foundation and Water Health International, sensing the latent demand for potable drinking water in villages, are targeting the safe-drinking-water market with innovative, community-centric approaches. These initiatives depict how success can be achieved and scaled up in rural markets.

JEEVAN REKHA EXPRESS

The Lifeline Express or Jeevan Rekha Express is a mobile hospital train which travels all over rural India to provide free medical treatment to the neglected poor. It is the first free service of its kind in the world.

Lifeline Express takes up each project which will continue for three to four weeks. During this time, at least five thousand patients are provided with medical treatments in that particular area. Till now, 20 projects have been taken up in madhya Pradesh; 18 in UP and Orissa; 15 in maharashtra, and 11 in Andhra Pradesh.

The train has two operating theatres, recovery rooms, offices, and accommodation. The first service was started on 16 July 16 1991, with the help of Impact India, a non-profit organization, based in seven countries around the world, with its Indian head-quarters in mumbai. Impact India still helps in running these trains along with Indian Railways and funds from donors.

It was developed in collaboration with the Indian Railways and Health ministry and has been funded by Impact UK, international charitable sources, Indian corporate houses, and individuals. So far the service has benefitted 400,000 Indians in the remot-est rural parts of the country over the course of approximately 93 projects.

The Lifeline express was started to provide on-the-spot diagnostic, medical, and ad-vanced surgical treatment for preventive and curative interventions for disabled adults and children for outreach into inaccessible rural areas where medical services are not available; offered using the Indian Railway Network which is the largest in the world comprising about 63,500 km of tracks. In addition to providing access to these much needed service, the Lifeline express seeks to improve the efficiency of the existing lo-cal government and voluntary health infrastructure and services, as well as providing initiative and encouragement for the local bodies to get involved in all aspects of the programme and provide follow-up services after the train has left.

REVIEW OF OBJECTIVES

1. To trace the growth of the services sector and its relevance for rural markets

The services sector is the lifeline of socio-economic growth. It makes the maximum contribution towards GDP and employs 34 per cent of the workforce. Among services, sectors like telecommunication, financial services, healthcare, and entertainment have witnessed an impressive growth in rural markets as marketers have used innovative ways to take these services to the rural markets, encouraged by the government's pro-rural programmes and policies.

2. Understand the growth of telecommunication services and the role of M-VAS services in the marketing of products and services in rural markets

Today, India is the fastest growing telecommunication market and the second largest in the world, with more than 723 million subscribers. A huge chunk of this growth has been contributed by rural markets, which have witnessed an exponential growth, adding up more than 200 million subscribers in the last five years. In spite of the challenges of distribution, service, product knowledge, and affordability, marketers have successfully devised ways to reach the hinterland.

The arrival of mobile phones in rural areas has led to a growth in the demand for informational services to improve incomes and livelihood, which are offered in the form of M-VAS services by players like RML, IKSL, and Nokia life tools to the farmers. The real-time information is helping farmers to optimize their returns and encouraging rural consumers to pay for the services, as demonstrated by Reuter's Market Light (RML).

3. Identify the role of ICT (Information Communication Technology) in rural India and its relevance to the marketing of products and services

Inspired by the success of mobile communication, the information and communication platform is also increasingly becoming an attractive and sustainable platform for rural marketers to deliver informational and transactional services through ICT kiosks in the absence of reliable physical delivery systems.

Today, more than 65,000 ICT kiosks are operational in the country, led by government-sponsored CSCs and the corporate-initiated ITC's e-Choupal initiative. These kiosks provide informational and transactional services on agriculture, education, e-governance, banking and finance training, health and hygiene. Many providers are using this platform to sell insurance and consumer products in rural areas.

4. Understand the marketing of financial services in rural India, including banking and insurance

The financial market in rural India, comprising microfinance, banking and insurance services, is expanding and offering customized products and services to meet the increasing demand and rising incomes. At present, rural India's financial infrastructure comprises 32,000 rural bank branches, 46,000 rural and semi-urban branches of microfinance institutions, more than 96,000 cooperative institutions, and over 135,000 post offices. In spite of this, informal channels like moneylenders play a dominant role in providing financial services as formal channels fail to offer adequate services to meet rural needs.

Thus, there are 185 million potentially bankable people currently not using formal banking services, a fact that offers a great opportunity to marketers. Sensing this opportunity, service providers are using innovative non-branch banking channels like the business correspondent facilitators model, smart cards, mobile ATMs, and applying cloud computing technology to service rural markets, as demonstrated by players like SBI and ICICI.

Among credit services, microfinance service in rural areas has emerged as the largest programme in the world, given its rapid growth in recent years. The programme has successfully met the micro-credit needs of the rural poor through the SHG-bank linkage and the MFI-bank linkage models, benefiting 120 million customers. Riding on this success, MFIs are entering other services such as micro-insurance, money transfer, and procurement and supply chain financing for agriculture and allied activities.

Besides savings and credit services, micro-insurance is emerging as a high growth market due to the high affordability among low-income people in rural India, given the high awareness and low penetration of insurance products.

Similar to the distribution of banking services, insurance players are experimenting with non-agent routes such as bancassurance, brokers, direct selling agents, corporate agents such as non-banking financial companies (NBFCs), and tie-ups of para-banking companies with local corporate agencies (for example, NGOs) to deliver insurance service in remote areas.

5. Describe the improvement of healthcare services and the emergence of new delivery models in rural markets

Healthcare has emerged as one of the most progressive and largest service sectors in India with an expected GDP spend of 8 per cent by 2012 from 5.5 per cent in 2009.

Similar growth is expected in rural healthcare spending, which is likely to multiply five-fold in the next two decades. The healthcare market is estimated to grow nine-fold to become an INR 8.9 trillion by 2025 (INR 3.5 trillion from rural areas).

The three-tier public healthcare system has not succeeded in delivering quality healthcare, plagued as it is by poor infrastructure and a shortage of drug supply, and the rampant absenteeism of health professionals. The government has made serious efforts though its flagship NRHM programme to rejuvenate this system, which is now showing positive results.

However, given the poor state of public health infrastructure, recent years have seen the strong growth of private players in the health space, attempting to meet the pent-up demand. Infrastructural bottlenecks in the public system have made the state and central governments invite private players to deliver critical healthcare through a public-private partnership approach.

Today, telemedicine, growth of health insurance, and public–private partnerships are the key growth drivers for rural healthcare. The success of the Aravind eye telemedicine model, the Yeshasvini health insurance scheme and Chiranjeevi Yojna testify to the growth potential of healthcare service, provided the right marketing mix is offered.

DISCUSSION AND APPLICATION

Discussion of Concepts

1. To what do you attribute the unexpected success of mobile communication in rural India, cutting across all segments in a short span of four years? Why have other household products like televisions and refrigerators failed to penetrate rural markets in a similar fashion, despite being present for decades? What lessons can they learn from the success of the telecommunications industry?
2. How can the rural customer be encouraged to pay for informational services, given the fact that information shared with one customer is likely to be shared with the entire community? Suggest a specific pricing strategy.
3. How do you think corporations can optimally realize the potential of the ICT platform for the marketing of products and services? What is the future of ICT initiatives in rural India?
4. Discuss the key changes that have taken place in the rural financial environment in recent years. How have they improved the accessibility and affordability of financial products for low-income consumers?
5. What are the key growth drivers of rural healthcare markets? How are government efforts catalysing the growth of this sector?
6. Research on the future business potential of the following service industries in rural India :
   (i) Rural Tourism
   (ii) Real Estate
   (iii) Recreation

Application of Concepts

1. Design an M-VAS appropriate to meet the healthcare needs of the rural population. Develop the marketing mix for this product along with the STP strategy.
2. Evaluate various distribution models of financial services in terms of sustainability and scalability. Also suggest a new distribution model that marketers can profitably use in the near future.
3. Evaluate various healthcare initiatives in rural India and develop a SWOT framework.
4. Suggest an effective business model for delivering diagnostic healthcare services in rural India.

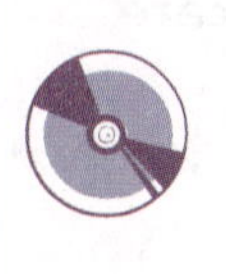

RURAL MARKETING CASE | AROGYA PARIVAR: A RURAL HEALTHCARE DELIVERY BUSINESS MODEL

For the first time in India, a global pharmaceutical company went beyond the traditional medical representative route by addressing the unmet health needs of rural India, thereby dramatically improving access to medicine while at the same time providing opportunities to expand business in an innovative and socially responsible way. Novartis is the first pharmaceutical multinational to use a social business model to reach India's rural markets.

For some 800 million men, women, and children in more than 600,000 villages across India, the idea of accessible, affordable, and high-quality medicines is often as remote as their rural homes. Institutional healthcare in rural India is limited to the government structure. Private healthcare services are individual-driven and unstructured. The government offers health services free of cost but over 70 per cent rural people pay for health services.

Novartis commissioned MART to understand the heath needs, behaviour, and attitude towards medicine in rural areas. MART found that the awareness of health issues was poor, and people accessed health services after trying various home remedies. The delay in treatment and the ensuing emergency were considered natural. Ailments related to nutrition, allergies, and infections were not differentiated, leading to the patient not approaching the relevant health service provider. This leads to a significant waste of money and no relief from ailments. Many of these people stayed undiagnosed because they either did not understand their symptoms, or the doctors were too far away, or they were afraid of the costs involved or of social prejudice. Women and children were particularly vulnerable. Tuberculosis (TB) was identified as a key ailment in rural areas and this case focuses on TB treatment.

Problems

The main problem in healthcare for rural people was related to the 4 As, which is discussed below.

- Affordability
  - Perceived or experienced cost of treatment for TB, if the patient has to be taken to a nearby town for treatment (treatment period is from six to nine months) is estimated to be more than INR 10,000 in government health centres, against INR 15,000 through private treatment. In government centres, patients had to go to private diagnostics centres and buy medicines.
  - For simple infections or skin allergies, the cost of private treatment was between INR 250–1,000.
- Availability
  - Access to health services and medicines has been the major problem. Qualified doctors, private or government, or licensed drug stores are not available in villages. Therefore, there is the cost of travelling to the block town, where the PHC (public health centre) or a private doctor is located.
- Awareness
  - Patients have poor discerning capabilities and cannot identify the appropriate doctor for their ailment.
  - They have no idea if the medicines prescribed by the doctor are the same as those given by the chemist.
  - Patients have no idea if the 'medicines' are preventive, curative, or for maintenance.
- Acceptance
  - Patients have their own perceptions about ailments. Only those ailments that affect their work productivity are attended to.
  - Treatment of children gets priority over that of adults.

Hence, Novartis felt the need for reliable health services and medicines at a reasonable cost.

MART's Strategic Suggestions

- To create awareness among the local population, establish a network of 'foot soldiers' recruited from villages to work as 'health educators'. They would support patients for all health services and follow up to complete the treatment process.
- To improve the availability of health service, qualified doctors need to be identified either from a medical institution or individual practitioners in towns with populations greater than 50,000 (block towns or below).
- To make health services affordable. Patients were often misinformed about the total treatment cost and believed it to be much higher than the actual cost, because of which they avoided seeking treatment. This wrong perception was corrected, after which patients realized that the treatment was affordable.
- To make health service acceptable, the programme identified critical health issues related to infection, nutrition, and allergies. The Arogya programme addressed these identified issues, delivering good results, and thereby building trust within the community.

The Solution

To address the health issues in rural India, Novartis designed an *arogya* (meaning good health) programme, the winner of the best long-term rural marketing initiative (RMAI 2008 Silver Award, WOW 2008 Silver Award and Golden Peacock Awards 2008), which offered pharmaceutical solutions and also integrated the need to network with local doctors, educate potential customers (patients), and link patients to specialized doctors. The Novartis team addressed the challenges by using an innovative direct approach to make villagers aware of prevalent diseases and encourage them to seek treatment. By late 2006, the Arogya Parivar initiative was launched with the help of MART as a pilot programme in Uttar Pradesh and Maharashtra.

Arogya Parivar follows a decentralized model where the field force is in autonomous cells (250 cells in 2011), each covering a radius of approximately 35 km or 20 miles. Each cell is managed by a supervisor, assisted by a few health educators who collaborate with local health professionals, pharmacy chains, and NGOs to address the whole 'patient flow', including education, diagnosis, treatment, delivery, and availability and accessibility of medicines.

A key differentiator is offering patients integrated solutions to health problems rather than mainly selling products to health professionals. Products selected for the initiative are simple to use and packages are reduced in size to keep out-of-pocket costs low. The initiative aims to build a sustainable, profitable business that improves access to healthcare among the underserved millions in rural India by creating awareness, enhancing local availability, and designing appealing and affordable health solutions. This social business approach represents a mix of corporate citizenship and creative entrepreneurship.

An Arogya brand was created for the unique health services offered by the company. The umbrella brand helped to overcome brand-related issues and became easy recall for the illiterate and semi-literate villagers. The Arogya Parivar brand is supported by consistent graphics of leaflets, banners, education programmes, uniforms for health educators, and decorations for bicycles. All collaterals are designed keeping in mind the nature of the audience, particularly in terms of literacy and comprehension levels. Effort is made to focus on specific disease/s on respective World Disease Days through active doctor participation.

To create awareness among the local population, Novartis established a network of 'Health Educators' (HE) recruited from villages to provide patients with support and follow-up to complete the treatment process. The HEs were provided with branded T-shirts, caps, and bags. Novartis used branded audiovisual vans, community meetings, and advisory leaflets to communicate the benefits to the rural masses. The 'HE' moves from village to village on a permanent journey plan (PJP). They conduct group meetings, identify patients in different households, educate the family, and convince them of the need for treatment. They also ensure that patients have their support when they decide to visit the doctor. It is also important that the medicine is consumed as prescribed. One-on-one communication is necessary to convince the patient and their family. An informed patient is more positively oriented towards completing the treatment (there is a tendency to discontinue treatment as soon as the patient feels some relief). The HE serves two blocks and 30 active patients and is paid INR 1,500 per month (commission of 10 per cent from sale of medicines), and new products are being added by Novartis to supplement income. The Novartis expense on communication and promotion is compensated through the margin from increased sales of their medicine.

The initiative is structured as a 'social business' and is a perfect opportunity to expand the reach of healthcare to those people who fall out of the current system simply because they do not live in urban or semi-urban India.

Arogya Parivar builds on a 'bottom-of-the-pyramid' business approach meant to sell products and services to low-income populations in emerging countries.

Arogya Parivar is targeted at all age groups, especially women and children. The target was selected on the basis of published data and market research. This population was effectively disfranchized from the right to quality health.

Arogya Parivar uses a unique business model, combining techniques used by pharmaceutical and consumer goods companies. Its fundamental innovation rests on applying a marketing mix based on the 4 As—awareness, acceptability, affordability, and availability—adapted to low-income markets.

The communication tools used for the Arogya Parivar are detailed in Table 1. The communication strategy included:

- One-on-one interaction at the community level (SHGs)
- Branded van using audiovisuals on the various health issues and the need to seek treatment
- Branded T-shirts, caps, branded bicycles, handbills, flip charts, patient cards.

Impact

Table 1 Communication Tools

Tools	Communication
Leaflets	Communication about the ailments and their symptoms
Flip charts	To communicate the methods of identifying symptoms for ailments, causes of ailments, and necessary treatment procedures
T-shirts and caps	To identify the HEs with the Arogya Programme
Branded vans	Use communication to create a high decibel
Branded bicycles	Used by HEs. Brand recall for the audience exposed to the high decibel brand promotion
Patient cards	For identified patients to carry as reference to the concerned doctor

Arogya Parivar sales have jumped 25 per cent since its launch in 2007, and the programme broke even in the first 30 months. Novartis now provides access to medicine to more than 42 million people in 33,000 villages within India. The initiative includes 250 cells in 10 states and has 530 educators and supervisors. It also serves almost 39,000 doctors and just over 29,000 pharmacies. The product portfolio covers 11 therapeutic areas with a portfolio of 80 stock-keeping units (SKUs) that include over-the-counter treatments and vaccines.

Arogya Parivar has built a healthy network of doctors, paramedics, and pharmacists, who share a similar mission and support the initiative. It has also established strong alliances with pharmacy and hospital chains that serve as a good complement to Novartis.

The competitive advantage of Arogya Parivar is that it makes every actor win. Patients are educated and avoid health complications. Health professionals see more people than they might otherwise, and are also trained. Health educators who work for the company are locally based, receive extensive training, and gain additional status within their communities. As for Novartis, they are improving healthcare and changing the lives of people in need.

A holistic model, Arogya Parivar has ensured that areas that were hitherto relatively untouched by traditional medical representatives are now on the road map. The initiative has succeeded in bringing in additional revenue, thus adding to the bottom line of the company.

| FIG. 1 | The Arogya Model

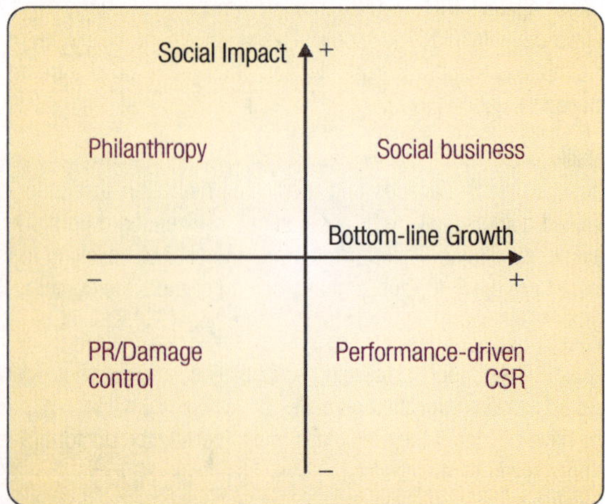

Since its business model is not based on pure donations, Arogya Parivar is an economically sustainable 'social business', scalable to more people in India and abroad that aims to:

- Provide health education (hygiene, nutrition, disease awareness) and improve the quality of life for local populations
- Improve public health without the need for costly government intervention or limited-duration NGO projects
- Create a revenue stream for local persons associated with Arogya Parivar
- Increase footfall at local health providers and business partners (encouraging their support to rural markets)
- Generate income for Novartis and build brand equity with an upwardly mobile population
- Highlighted by Novartis in internal and external communication (in the same manner as CSR)
- Fulfil former President Abdul Kalam's vision of PURA, that is, providing urban remedies to rural India

Learning

- The poor are willing to pay for quality and effective treatment.
- Earlier, male patients were reluctant to consult ANMs (females); however, the Arogya HE is male and able to gain acceptance, convince patients, and support them.
- Chemists began stocking Novartis products once doctors began prescribing them.
- Doctors are motivated due to the increase in income, and are therefore willing to participate in the programme.
- Doctors are professionally satisfied that patients now complete treatment and get cured.

The Way Forward

The Arogya programme is cognizant of the importance of working with NGOs, especially in awareness programmes via community-level meetings and health camps. In 2011, the Arogya programme planned to form a consortium of at least 20 NGOs in India to provide targeted intervention in the causes of diabetes, tuberculosis, diarrhoea, and also for the provision of clean water.

Encouraged by the programme's success in India, Novartis is now expanding it to other emerging markets including Kenya, Indonesia, and Vietnam.

Mother and child nutrition, skin allergy, and diabetes are being added to the list of treatments. Novartis also plans to add allied products like sanitary napkins, water purification products, and clean delivery kits to supplement the income of the HE. The accompanying video explains how this project has been initiated and implemented in Uttar Pradesh.

Discussion Questions

1. What problems of the rural community were addressed through this model?
2. List the key reasons for the sustainability of this model.
3. Do you think this model can be replicated in other countries? If yes, how and in which countries?

AFTER READING THIS CHAPTER, YOU WILL BE ABLE TO:

1. Define small towns, their potential, and relevance.
2. Understand the behaviour of small-town consumers.
3. Understand the strategic importance of small towns for rural marketers.

CHAPTER 11 ::: MARKETING IN SMALL TOWNS

eleven

Ten years ago, one could not have imagined a day when Amritsar would have a higher mall penetration than Delhi, and a small-town boy would rewrite history by leading India to victory in the cricket World Cup. Small towns have come of age. It is very interesting to watch people entering the Adidas shop on the Delhi road in Rohtak, a small town 70 km from Delhi; several middle-aged farmers from nearby kasbas *and villages are seen coming in their SUVs to buy the most expensive white sneakers which match their white kurta pyjamas and pagris. Some also pick deodorants, a substitute for the traditional* ittar. *Earlier there was just one big shoe store in Rohtak; today, however, one can find separate stores for Adidas, Puma, Lotto, Reebok, Woodland, and Liberty. One can now see at least 100 super luxury cars—Mercedes, Audis, and BMWs—parading the narrow roads of Rohtak.*

Earlier the people of Rohtak would go to Delhi for a slice of the 'good life'. Now things have changed completely. One can find malls, multiplexes, management institutes, air-conditioned preparatory schools, and outlets like Dominos and Baskin Robbins in this small town.

Towns like Allahabad and Kota are now saying 'I'm loving it' to new McDonalds outlets. Jalandhar and Patiala are feasting on aloo da tikki burgers. Similarly, Nagpur, which once boasted of only Soaji (Nagpuri cuisine) joints and highway dhabas, is now biting into Subway sandwiches and sipping cappuccinos at Café Coffee Day.[1]

Malls, found only in the metros till a few years ago, are becoming commonplace in small towns. Small-town folk don't need go beyond the city limits for a 'slice of the good life'.

::: Small Towns: A Definition

Small towns are those towns that have a population of less than one million. There are 5,127 small towns in India.

Small towns have been defined as towns with populations of less than one million. According to the tier classification, Tier III and IV towns are considered small towns. There are a total of 5,127 small towns with more than 50 per cent share of urban households, as depicted in Fig. 11.1. Tier III comprises 33 towns and Tier IV 5,094 towns. Traditional marketers have always focused on cities. However, as these markets are getting saturated, companies have started targeting small towns and rural markets, which have emerged as novel and gigantic markets. Population and income details of Tier I to Tier IV towns are given in Table 11.1.

Most of us have a stereotyped image of small-town India—pitted roads, loads of garbage, open drains, stagnant pools of water, overhead electric wires, long power cuts, and acute water shortage. However, this image is now changing with the emergence of success stories from small towns—Olympic medal winners, talented young people who win television reality shows, and many of our cricket stars come from these small towns. It is seen that Tier III towns resemble the urban mindset, whereas the Tier IV mindset is similar to that of rural areas. See 'Rural Marketing Snapshot: The Changing Face of Small-town India' to see how small towns have changed into dynamic, thriving centres of activity.

The Potential of Small Towns

Small towns are growing at a very fast pace and are becoming hubs for marketing activities. With the economy growing consistently, the purchasing power of people in

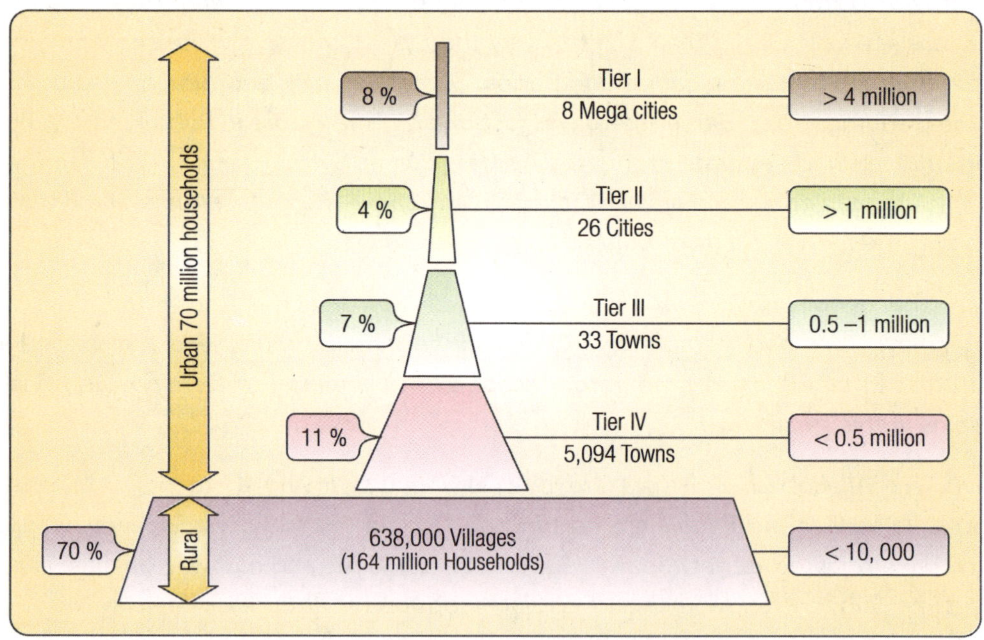

| FIG. 11.1 |
Classification of Towns in India
Source: Census projections, 2010 and MART Knowledge Centre.

| TABLE 11.1 |
Distribution of India's Urban Population by City Tier

	Number of Cities	Share of Households (in per cent)	Income per Household	Share of Total Disposable Income (in per cent)
Tier I	8	29	186,000	39
Tier II	26	15	129,000	14
Tier III	33	9	136,000	9
Tier IV	5,094	47	114,000	39
Total	5,160	100		100

Source: The Great Indian Middle Class, NCAER; Mckinsey Global Institute (MGI) India Consumer Demand Model; MGI Analysis

RURAL MARKETING SNAPSHOT | THE CHANGING FACE OF SMALL-TOWN INDIA

Small-town India then

Small-town India now

The small towns of the past—categorized by the absence of roads, pucca houses, motor vehicles, and prominent brands—are evolving. Rising income, better education, and increased exposure have brought about this change.

these towns is showing a rising trend. The rush towards smaller towns is triggered mainly by the availability of adequate land at a reasonable price. These towns have the advantage of low construction costs and lower rentals. Hence, it would not be wise for marketers to neglect these towns. As per the McKinsey Urbanization Report (2010), small towns hold much importance[2] because:

- There has been a significant and impressive economic growth in these smaller towns in the last 15 years despite the low municipal spending (see Figs 11.2 and 11.3).
- It is assumed that Tier III and IV towns will account for 50 per cent of the urban GDP and add 70 million consumers by 2030 (see Figs 11.4 and 11.5).
- Small towns will become self-sufficient in times to come, with the provision of basic services. This will reduce the migration load on larger cities.

The main reasons for the high potential of small towns are:

- ***Own (small towns) population.*** The population of small towns alone makes them attractive to marketers. Tier III and IV towns

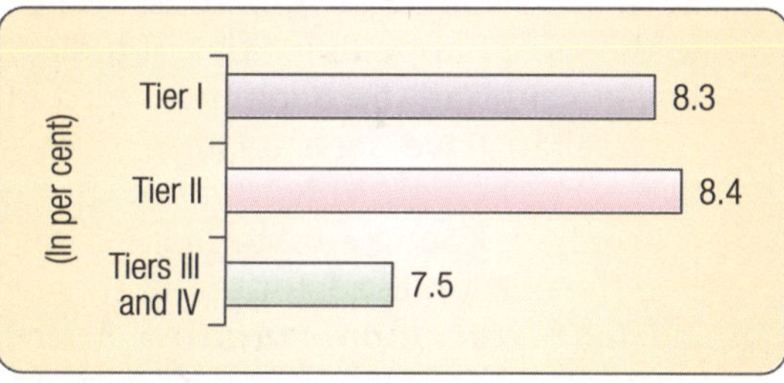

| FIG. 11.2 |
Tier I to Tier IV Growth Rates (1999–2006)
Source: McKinsey Global Institute.

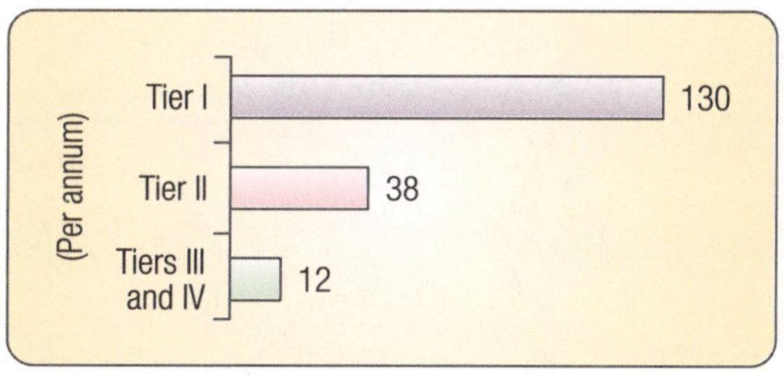

| FIG. 11.3 |
Municipal Spending (USD per capita per annum)
Source: McKinsey Global Institute.

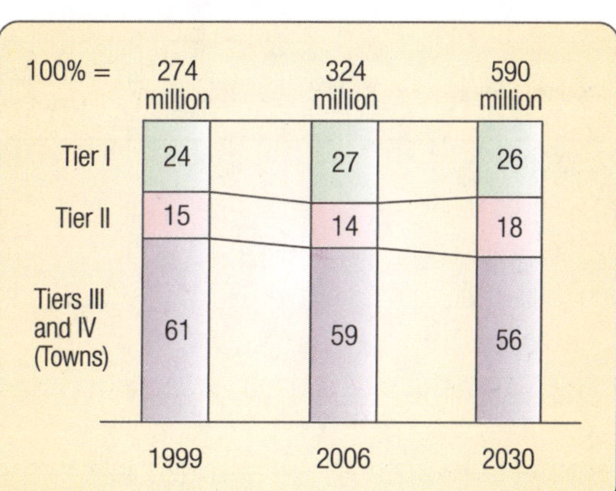

| FIG. 11.4 |
Town Population (in per cent)
Source: McKinsey Global Institute.

| FIG. 11.5 |
Town GDP (in per cent)
Source: McKinsey Global Institute.

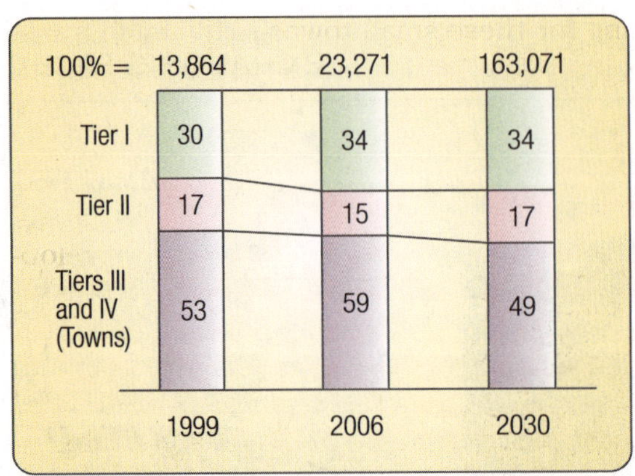

together constitute 59 per cent of the total urban population as seen in Fig. 11.4, and so marketers cannot afford to overlook this huge consumer mass and its potential.

- ***Proximity to villages.*** Most small towns are close to villages, with each town catering to the requirements of as many as 200 adjoining villages. These towns act as hubs in the distribution channel, with villages as the spokes. These small towns have become the preferred destination for rural masses to buy products and access major services.

Marketers are aggressively targeting small towns, which has resulted in a focus shift in media spends from the metros to the non-metros. This trend is likely to continue with the changing consumption pattern of consumers, fuelled by greater purchasing power.

- ***Income levels and buying power.*** It is a proven fact that these Tier III and IV towns have high income levels, as shown in Table 11.1. The disposable income in smaller towns has risen significantly in the recent past because they were largely unaffected by the slowdown. This has also led to an increase in their buying power. A distribution of households by income and size of town is shown in Table 11.2.
- ***Bridge between urban and rural.*** Small towns are windows to bigger cities (see Fig. 11.6). They portray images of urban and bigger cities to the people residing in small towns and rural areas. Some of the Tier III towns are in close proximity to the most happening cities of India, and it will not be a mistake to call them extension cities of the booming metros. Of late, Tier II cities like Pune, Kolkata, and Hyderabad have seen business opportunities and infrastructural development like never before. Now it is the turn of the Tier III or smaller towns like Jaipur, Ghaziabad, Kochi, etc., to make it big in the realty business as the government and the corporate sector target them as 'India's Next Destination Cities'.
- ***Infrastructure opportunities.*** There lies a huge opportunity for emerging infrastructural growth in the small towns and everyone today is heading towards it. One of the basic reasons for investments flocking into the smaller cities is the available properties and affordable prices. Moreover, special initiatives taken by the respective state governments to provide the infrastructural facilities and create special economic zones (SEZs) have played a vital role in promoting these small towns as cities of the future. Keeping in mind all the congenial factors necessary for setting up corporate infrastructure, investing companies, ranging from pharmaceuticals to financial institutions, automobiles to the IT and ITeS sectors, as well as the

| FIG. 11.6 |
Small Towns as Bridges between Urban and Rural India

Cities
Small towns
Rural areas

| TABLE 11.2 |
Distribution of Households by Income and Size of Town (in per cent)

Income Class	Tier III Towns (Population: 0.5–1 million)	Tier IV Towns (Population: Less than 0.5 million)
< 90,000	48	58
90,000–200,000	39	34
200,000–500,000	10	6
500,000–1,000,000	2	1
> 1,000,000	1	1

Source: NCAER, 'The Great Indian Middle Class' report (2001–02), p. 105

retail and real-estate sectors are opting for these small towns, and hence transforming them into India's fastest growing cities. Gurgaon is a perfect example to understand the impact that infrastructure investments have had on the economic growth of a region. Till the 1980s, Gurgaon was simply a small town located at the borders of Delhi. The establishment of the Maruti manufacturing plant in 1981 and the Hero Honda plant in 1997 changed the face of the town and also attracted many auto-ancillary players. The economic growth and infrastructural development projects—road, railways, and airports—in Delhi also had a ripple effect on this satellite town. The increasing urbanization and congestion in Delhi, coupled with improved road connectivity, have also come to the attention of investors and attracted investments in multiple sectors, ranging from the automotive, IT and ITeS, real estate, retail, and hospitality, to education and healthcare in Gurgaon. Today, Gurgaon is called the 'Manhattan of India'. A huge number of multinational companies have located their operations here. In just about a decade, it has become the industrial and financial hub of Haryana, and has the third highest per capita income in India after Chandigarh and Mumbai.

IT, ITeS, and the BPO companies are vying for small towns because of better infrastructure, state-of-the-art office spaces, and skilled manpower.

- ***Penetration of durables and FMCG products.*** As shown in Table 11.3, there is a huge scope of increase in the penetration of refrigerators, two-wheelers, and

| TABLE **11.3** |

Household Penetration of Durables and FMCG Products (in per cent)

Products	All India	Tier III Towns (Population: 0.5–1.0 million)	Tier IV Towns (Population: 0.1–0.5 million)	Tier V Towns (Population: 0.5–0.05 million)	Tier VI Towns (Population < 0.05 million)
Durables					
Pressure cookers	35	74	64	56	49
Television sets	42	77	70	66	59
Refrigerators	12	32	25	20	15
Two-wheelers	14	34	25	21	18
Washing machines	4	12	8	6	4
Air conditioners	1	1	1	1	0
Computers	1	3	2	1	1
Food & Beverages					
Biscuits	69	80	75	71	72
Edible oil	95	99	98	98	98
Instant noodles	6	18	12	10	7
Ketchups/Sauces	4	13	9	5	4
Tea	84	93	91	90	87
Personal Care					
Toothpastes	49	79	73	69	61
Tooth powders	35	29	33	36	40
Household Care					
Mosquito repellents	27	61	58	49	40
Utensil cleaners	28	65	52	47	39
Detergent cakes	89	95	92	94	93
Washing powders/Liquids	86	91	91	88	87

Source: MRUC–Hansa Research Guide to Indian Markets, 2006. Data taken from Table 7.2, p. 154; Table 8.3, p. 178; Table 9.2, p. 206; and Table 10.2, p. 234.

| TABLE **11.4** |
Household Penetration of High-end Durables in Towns with Less than 100,000 Population

Product Name	Towns Contribution (in per cent)	Product Category Growth (in per cent)
Flat TVs	33	214
Frost-free refrigerators	28	31
Fully automatic washing machines	20	54

Source: Data from ORG-GFK estimates quoted by Kala Vijaraghavan, 'High-end Durables Catch Small Towns' Fancy,' *The Economic Times*, 16 March 2005.

washing machines in small-town households. Penetration of air conditioners and computers is negligible as of now; hence, these can be treated as virgin markets for durables companies. On the other hand, FMCG penetration in Tier III and IV towns is comparatively better and much higher when compared to the all-India penetration.

Consumer durables companies are sharpening their presence in small towns due to an increase in the demand for products like flat-screen TVs, frost-free refrigerators, and fully automatic washing machines. The penetration of these high-end durables in towns with a population of less than 100,000 can be seen in Table 11.4 (also see 'Rural Marketing Insight: The Dhoni Effect').

Small-town Consumer Behaviour

It is of utmost importance to understand the behaviour of consumers living in small towns. Although these places are small, the masses residing in these towns have big dreams and aspirations; they have good disposable incomes; aspire for a better standard of living; and are more brand aware and exposed through good media penetration. Understanding the demographic, behavioural, and psychographic characteristics of this set of target audience is crucial for any marketer who wants to gradually make it big in the emerging market space.

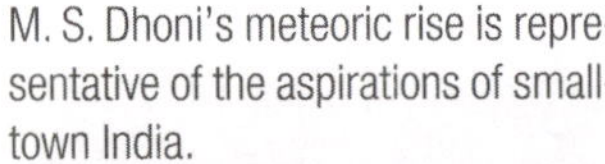

M. S. Dhoni's meteoric rise is representative of the aspirations of small-town India.

The characteristics of a typical small-town consumer are explained here.

1. ***Growing affluence, leading to a better standard of living.*** As mentioned earlier, the disposable income of people living in Tier III and Tier IV towns together comprise 48 per cent of the total disposable income in urban India. This rising affluence is a result of multiple factors like less overheads, minimum loan traps unlike the village folks, low transportation cost, and low cost of living when compared to bigger cities, greater job opportunities for multiple members of the family, and to top it all, the influx of repatriated money that comes from the family members who have moved to bigger cities for jobs and are earning handsomely. These towns are much smaller than the top metros, but many have per capita incomes that are higher than those in the top metros and have also been able to sustain a double-digit growth. A rise in disposable incomes has steered the urge for a better standard of living. Table 11.5 shows that the expenditure pattern of small-town people matches that of those in bigger urban cities. Some facts, like the Gitanjali Group's (a diamond jewellery company) maximum growth in jewellery coming from places like Berhampur and Bhubaneswar in Orissa, and basically from all across India's

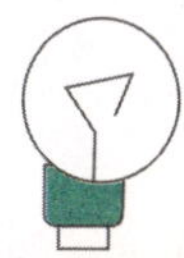

RURAL MARKETING INSIGHT | THE DHONI EFFECT

The rise of Mahendra Singh Dhoni, a small-town boy from Ranchi, to his current iconic status is no surprise in a country where cricket is a religion. His success is representative of the aspirations and abilities of small Indian towns—a segment that was neglected by companies for a very long time. That it is these very towns which have the highest growth potential can no longer be ignored. In fact, the 2008 Ernst & Young report on developments and trends in marketing spend across the Indian market and how marketing decisions are impacting media spend vis-à-vis actual ground realities which directly indicate market growth for India held him up as representative of the quintessential small-town India that is taking centre stage in marketing activities.

For the study, E&Y divided the country into three sections—the six metros (Mumbai, Delhi, Bangalore, Hyderabad, Chennai, and Kolkata); the key urban towns (KUTs) which includes 22 cities; and the rest of urban India (ROUI) which comprises urban cities other than the KUTs. Some of the key findings of the study were:

- Increasing affluence has led to increased consumption growth in key urban towns and rural markets, which have been relatively untapped until now.
- The relevant consumer base is large and growing, as are affluence levels. Towns such as Chandigarh, Ahmedabad, Jaipur, Lucknow, Indore, and Pune have three-quarters or more of the affluence levels of Mumbai. The small-town urban India is attractive in terms of purchasing power, time spent on media, and product consumption comes across clearly.
- Recent investments and developments in infrastructure and connectivity have increased the physical reach to small towns. The movement of organized retail into smaller towns has made things easier and more cost-effective for marketers.
- Rising disposable incomes, easier access to credit and improved retail reach have helped push television, satellite, and radio in the key urban towns in absolute terms.
- The low penetration level of products and services in the KUTs and the ROUI presents a unique opportunity for growth for marketers.

These findings were further analysed in the 2010 E&Y report titled 'The New Market Shehers: Tapping the Potential of Emerging Markets'. This report reveals that the number of malls has grown by 55 per cent in the KUTs between 2006 and 2008 as against a mere 24 per cent in the metros. Similarly, in 2008–09, the growth rate of the sales of refrigerators and washing machines in the KUTs and the ROUI was almost twice of that in the metros. These trends clearly indicate that it is the KUTs and the ROUI that present potential for growth to companies. In the recent past, companies have started focusing on these townships. Samsung's dealership network has increased from 20 towns in 2007 to 50 towns in 2008. Skoda has increased its marketing budget for non-metros from 25 per cent in 2006 to 40 per cent in 2009.

An increasing number of companies and marketers are being compelled to take notice of the needs of the small town consumers and devise new ways of exploiting this emerging opportunity.

Source: Ernst & Young, Press Release, available at http://www.ey.com/Publication/vwLUAssets/New_market_shehers:_tapping_potential_beyond_metros/$FILE/The%20New%20Market%20Shehers%20Press%20Summary_11%20May,2010.pdf ; India Knowledge@Wharton, An Increasingly Affluent Middle India Is Harder to Ignore, 10 July, 2008, available at http://knowledge.wharton.upenn.edu/india/article.cfm?articleid=4303; and Priyanka Mehra, 'Dhoni Effect: Urban Growth Story Spreads To Smaller Cities, *Live Mint.com*, 20 March, 2008.

| TABLE **11.5** |
Distribution of Routine Expenditure by Size of Town (in per cent)

Categories	Tier I and II	Tier III	Tier IV
Food	44.9	44.8	46.4
Housing	6.4	5.5	5.4
Health	4.2	4.4	5.2
Transport	11.3	10.6	10.9
Education	8.4	10.8	8.4
Clothing	6.9	6.6	6.7
Durables	4.9	5.0	5.2
Others	13.0	12.2	11.9

Source: Rajesh Shukla, 2007, *How India Earns, Spends and Saves: Results from the Max New York Life–NCAER India Financial Protection Survey*, (New Delhi: 2007), Chapter 3.

TATA NANO

Tata Motors, India's leading auto manufacturer, launched the first television commercial of its car Nano in 2010. The commercial portrays the Nano as a roomy and sturdy car, an enviable car by virtue of its looks and performance, and apt for small-town people. The advertisement plays on the touch-and-feel concept, a very important aspect in purchase decisions for its target audience. The commercial shows a little girl asking her grandmother when the Tata Nano will come home. The Tata Nano finally arrives, getting admiring glances all the way. The yellow Tata Nano truly stands out as it drives through rough terrains to reach the house situated on a hilltop. The small-town neighbourhood gathers to see the brand new Tata Nano car. The little girl hugs the car and the family prepares a traditional welcome. The girl applies kohl from her eye on the car as protection against the ill-will caused by prying eyes. This innovative commercial perfectly captures the essence of an Indian small town and its natives, and conveys the simple message that two-wheeler and three-wheeler owners in these towns may easily shift to the affordable car—the Tata Nano.

small towns; General Motors India's compact car, Chevrolet Spark, driving into small towns quite aggressively; and nearly 40 per cent of Hyundai's sales coming from small towns and rural areas are a perfect reflection of the high disposable incomes and purchasing power of these small-town habitants.

2. ***Increasing awareness and importance of education.*** Today, consumers in small towns are more aware because of increased media penetration. Be it the Internet, DTH (Direct-to-home) or C&S (Cable and Satellite), the off-take of all of these is growing faster in small towns. Contrary to the perception that DTH television technology is an urban or a metro phenomenon, 70 per cent of its subscribers today reside in small towns and rural areas. It is specifically towns with a population under one million that contribute to the two million DTH subscribers. Also, as per a study[3] conducted in 2009 on Internet usage in India, it was found that around 36 per cent of the total Internet users in India are from towns with a population of less than 500,000, like Kolhapur, Thrissur, and Panipat. This high media penetration is opening mass media communication options for marketers, which in turn is making these consumers more aware and exposed to a wide variety of products. As small-town inhabitants become more aware, they have also started giving considerable importance to education. Although the middle-aged people do not have separate dreams for themselves, they hope their children will study and make it big in their lives. It is through the children and youth that the dreams and desires of small-town India is being expressed. It is because of this that one can observe a phenomenal amount of money being spent by small-town parents to aid their children's dream careers as doctors, engineers, IT specialists, or in the IAS. Knowledge of English is seen as a symbol of status and upward mobility, and a means to end the social and economic apartheid among small-town youths. This has led to the sprouting of spoken English coaching centres at every nook and corner in small towns. Taking a cue from this consumer psyche, a number of companies have started wooing small-town consumers along this axis of ambition and achievement, some of them being Fair & Lovely Woman's Emancipation, the Colgate Scholarship, Hero Honda Career Programme, and ICICI Prudential Life Insurance's 'Pragati Ki Anokhi Paathshaala' programme.

The Tata Nano targets small-town consumers who aspire to upgrade from two-wheelers to four-wheelers.

Brand ambassadors and icons for this consumer segment are changing, and it is the small-town achievers who are becoming the hot role models.

3. ***Aspirations and Lifestyle.*** This growing awareness and exposure has led to changes in the aspiration levels of small-town inhabitants, especially its youth. Young people from small towns are today aspiring for urban jobs like those of air hostesses, pilots, flight stewards, newsreaders, and radio jockeys. Such jobs are not only high paying, but also provide a high-flying lifestyle to the ambitious youth. With an increasing number of youngsters opting for this field, training institutes are taking off in a big way, and even companies are hiring people from these small towns. It is not just urban jobs, but also self-grooming that has become a very important part of the lifestyle of small-town inhabitants. Their aspiration levels have gone up, to the extent that today, one can see a number of beauty parlours, salons, and gyms coming up in every nook and corner of the towns. Small-town women have surprised retailers and manufacturers with their willingness to try new things and pay large amounts for beauty treatments and products. Beauty treatments such as age correction, removal of skin imperfections, and products for hair streaking have become increasingly popular there. The psyche of these small-town consumers can be described as: 'they are ambitious and they are happy'. Since they are still below the urban metros, their ambition leads them to look at the people above them and adapt their lifestyle; at the same time, they are happy to look at those below them (the rural folks) and enjoy their economic freedom.

Growing affluence, increasing awareness through mass media, rising aspiration levels and lifestyle, and increasing brand awareness characterize a typical small-town consumer.

THE AVIATION INDUSTRY

Young people from small towns are aspiring to become pilots, air hostesses, and flight stewards, and are also taking up various ground duties. The pay package here is high compared to other industries. Initially, people were apprehensive of sending their children to the aviation industry, but now the mindset has changed considerably. With more and more youngsters from small towns opting for this field, training institutes are expanding their operations. The Frankfinn Institute of Air Hostess Training now has 61 centres in 45 towns. The number of girls and boys enrolling in these institutes has also gone up steadily. Airlines are increasing their number of flights and targeting small towns as new airport hubs. They are also encouraging young people from small towns to join them, and are holding interviews for cabin crew in non-metros as well. Emirates, for example, has been holding interviews in Lucknow, besides Delhi and other metros. Earlier, people in small towns used to perceive this as a glamorous profession meant for the metro-bred youth. Now, however, this perception has changed, and young girls and boys from places like Kanpur, Siliguri, Coimbatore, Jamshedpur, Guwahati, Karnal, Rishikesh, Haridwar, Ludhiana, Raipur, Kochi, Mangalore, Salem, and Belgaum are entering this profession. They are leading a high-flying lifestyle and getting a handsome pay package. They also get to travel and meet celebrities. The starting salary is INR 25,000 plus per month in the domestic sector.

4. ***Increasing brand awareness and preference for premium products and services.*** Today's small-town consumers have become more brand aware and brand conscious. Many of them prefer to buy premium products and avail of the high-quality and best services in their towns. This is the reason why multinational brand names can be seen scrawled on the walls and billboards in these towns. Out of the many product categories, it is in the food products category that a brand name commands the maximum respect in a small town. There is practically no mention of unpackaged or unbranded purchase of cereals, oils and sugar. Brands like Priyagold biscuits, Wagh Bakri and Parivar Tea, Bournvita, Horlicks, and Complan can be seen in small-town households. A well-planned strategy of many

CANON

Canon, a Japanese imaging equipment maker, launched a special campaign named *Image Express* in 2010 to push its sales in smaller towns. This campaign was launched to create awareness about its products. As part of this campaign, trucks with the Canon brand would travel for a year and touch 37 towns across the country. Display trucks will be parked in various towns and will create a 1,500 sq. ft showroom displaying all the products. People can come in, touch, and feel the products. The company has made a total investment of around INR 150 million on this campaign. The company currently derives 60 per cent of its revenue from small towns and cities, and expects it to increase to 90 per cent in the next five years.

CARVAAN—MELA KHUSHIYO KA

The exposure to mass media and increasing disposable income of the evolving rural and semi-urban consumer class has shaped up their aspirational values. They strive for latest trends and offerings. But there is absence of shopping avenues to meet these aspirations. Also the population in small towns is entertainment starved. Cities for their sheer competitive presence of brands, and villages owing to their vast untapped landscape get marketers' focus, and between the two huge markets, small town as a potential market remains surprisingly ignored. And this led to the conceptualization of a unique project 'Caarvan-Mela Khushiyon Ka' for small towns, a syndicated model, to leverage these potential markets.

Caarvan was a two-day event. It was a unique consumer connect event for brands built on the planks of entertainment, shopping, and engagement. The event was given a carnival feel so that people could relate to it as a festival. Caarvan had an advantage over others. Brands conventionally use van-based activities to penetrate and engage consumers in small towns and villages which has low engagement quotient. To gain mindshare and to give higher brand experience it followed a unique format on wheels

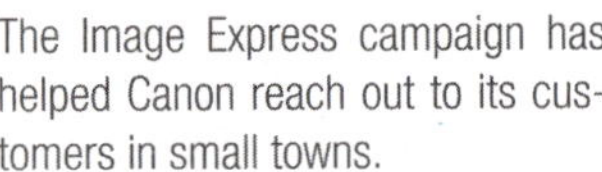
The Image Express campaign has helped Canon reach out to its customers in small towns.

with huge visual impact, high on entertainment and engagement quotient. Thus, giving the organizers the opportunity for mapping consumer insights, buying patterns, and mindshare. Caarvan was crafted to provide non-competing brands an opportunity of coming together in a syndicated event, each one of them pooling their bit and achieving the least value for their bucks both in terms of experience delivered and cost per contact. Participating brands were Honda, Idea, Vaseline, Eveready, Taaza, and Joe Soap. Caarvan incorporated strong mela flavour with experimental zones like 3D movie theatre, video gaming zones, and beauty zones, etc., a special take away for each member of the family.

Consumers were living brands for an entire day. Also print ads were given in local newspapers, publicity vans were deloyed for announcement and over 1,00,000 door-to-door invites were given to increase the footfalls. The whole event had a huge impact as more than 6 lakh consumer footfalls were registered, 300 villages and 50 towns were covered, 25000 consumer data was captured and analysed. The Caarvan journey continues and the second phase is scheduled to take off from eastern UP and extended Bihar.

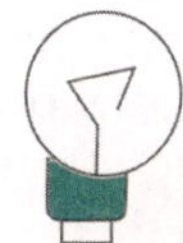

RURAL MARKETING INSIGHT — CONSUMER BEHAVIOUR IN SMALL TOWNS OF INDIA

MART conducted a research study in 2010 to understand the psychographics, brand preference, and purchase behaviour of small-town consumers in India. The study was conducted in four zones across four states—Uttar Pradesh, West Bengal, Andhra Pradesh, and Maharashtra—covering a total of 12 towns. The findings of the study revealed that:

- Watching television is the most preferred indoor entertainment activity and travelling the most preferred outdoor activity for small-town inhabitants.
- Family, money, and status are the top three priorities in life for them.
- Owning a big house, an all-India tour, and a foreign trip are their main aspirations.
- Mobile phones and good food emerge as the biggest necessities in their lives.
- Family's prestige, the money that one has made, and the education level of the family are the three attributes that define social status for small-town consumers.
- Among the media, television and the print media have good exposure. 8 PM to 10 PM, which falls in the prime time category, is the most convenient slot for watching television for the majority of small-town consumers.
- Economy and mid-segment brands are preferred in most product categories, as shown in the table.
- While making purchase decisions, small-town consumers are mainly influenced by advertisements, friends, and relatives. The father is the main decision-maker in the family.
- The majority of them purchase FMCG products from nearby *kirana* stores, mainly because of proximity and trust. They purchase consumer durables from either a nearby local store or unorganized retail outlets.

Product Category	Preferred Brand
Toilet soaps	Lux
Skin care	Pond's, Fair & Lovely
Biscuits	Britannia
Tea	Tata, Taj Mahal
Edible oil	Gemini, Saloni
Aerated drinks	Thums Up
Detergent powders	Wheel, Sunlight, Surf Excel
Ceiling fans	Usha, Orient
Colour TVs	Akai, Sansui, LG
Two-wheelers	Hero Honda, Bajaj

Since there is a lot of potential in these small towns, marketers have started devising specific strategies to tap these markets. To do so, marketers need to understand consumer behaviour, for which this study would be very useful.

Source: Compiled from the report on 'Consumer Behaviour and Distribution Channels of Small Towns' June 2010, MART Knowledge Centre

regional companies like Surya Foods, Wagh Bakri, and Sapat has been to enter these markets first before making a mark in the hinterlands, thereby avoiding competition with the national players. However, of late, many companies have started recognizing the potential of these small-town markets and are fast moving into this space. A company like S. Kumars, known for its premium brands such as Reid & Taylor and Belmonte, is launching a mass brand for the Tier III and IV towns at very reasonable rates. The Arvind Group, which is already getting 30 per cent of its revenue from these towns, is planning to locate a noteworthy share of 30 outlets and more in Tier III towns. Welspun Retail, which has more than 200 stores under its Welhome brand that targets budget customers in the home furnishing category, plans to add 70–80 stores in the financial year 2011, with 30 per cent of them focused on such small towns.

5. ***Consumer buying behaviour.*** The buying behaviour of consumers in small towns is a reflection and mix of the behaviour of people in urban cities and rural villages. For consumers in small towns, similar to those in urban cities, the occasions for purchase are festivals like Holi, Deepawali, Baisakhi, etc., and not really the harvest or wedding season, as is typically the case in villages. Also, the place of purchase is a mix of small traditional mom-and-pop stores, convenience stores, and malls. In smaller towns, the traditional trade still holds strong, especially due to the relationship between the retailer and the consumer, but for a brand that wants to use the last mile for experiential marketing, malls have become a very good option for displaying and selling their products. This is the reason why stores like Vishal Mega Mart, Nilgiris, 6Ten, and BestPrice have come up in a big way in these towns. Also, with the advent of such stores, the traditional mom-and-pop stores have become more innovative in their offerings and services and have started giving discounts, credit, and even free home delivery facilities to retain their old customers. For a small-town consumer, friends and relatives act as the main influencers during the purchase of a product. They are also influenced to a large extent by the advertisements. The male head of the family (usually the father) is the main decision-maker (see 'Rural Marketing Insight: Consumer Behaviour in Small Towns of India').

Small-town India offers a sizeable floating consumer mass for marketers, provided their value system can be leveraged. The success of tomorrow's marketers lies in understanding the needs of this heterogeneous mass. Those who can read these behavioural signs properly will be rewarded with exponential growth.

The Strategic Importance of Small Towns for Rural Marketers

Small towns are important for rural masses as they act as selling and redistribution points for products, hubs for servicing and services, provide agricultural linkage, and also act as entertainment hubs for rural inhabitants.

We have seen that small towns act as a critical link between urban cities and rural villages. They are the urban windows to small-town and rural consumers, and their strategic importance, especially for the rural masses, should be understood by marketers. The importance of small towns for rural folks is described in the following points:

As Selling and Redistribution Centres

Small towns act as redistribution points for many FMCG companies. Since directly reaching thousands of villages is an unviable option for these companies, they distribute their products to the wholesalers or stockists located in these strategically placed towns, who further redistribute it to the village retailers (see Fig. 11.7). Again, durables companies also place their products in these towns since rural folks generally access them directly for purchasing the white goods.

In addition to this, garments, construction material, hardware, furniture, kitchen appliances, and automobiles are also purchased by rural people from these towns because of the better choice and price advantage (see Table 11.6).

As Servicing Centres

Small towns have also developed as service centres for many automobile and durables companies. Although rural people go to local repairing shops within their own villages for small repairs, they access service centres located in small towns for a complete servicing or check. Seeing this, companies like LG have set up around 230 service centres in such small towns, which can cater to remote villages.

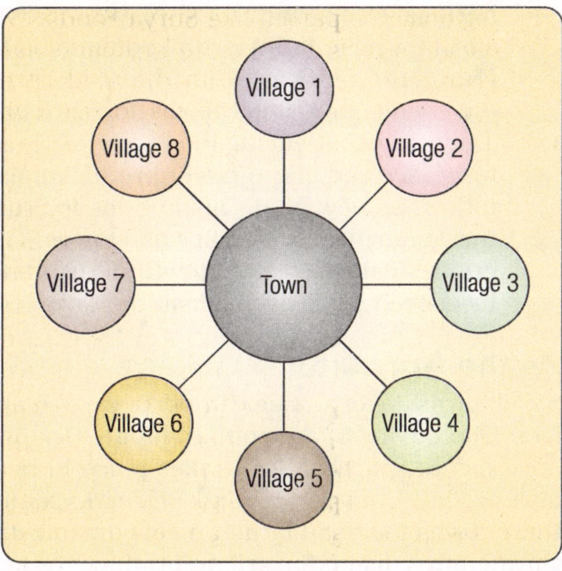

| FIG. **11.7** | Small Towns as Hubs for the Purchase of Products for Villagers

As a Hub for Availing Services

Small towns act as hubs for rural people wanting to avail of services like health, education, banking, and insurance.

- ***Health.*** Due to the lack of qualified professionals and 24 × 7 health facilities in rural areas, villagers frequently travel to small towns. In spite of the presence of PHCs and sub-centres in rural areas, the majority prefer to visit nursing homes and hospitals in small towns for the more hygienic and better health services. Sensing this opportunity, the Gujarat government has tied up with private nursing homes under the *Chiranjeevi* project to encourage institutional deliveries. This has also yielded good results. Thus, marketers can also look at similar public-private partnerships (PPP) to provide healthcare services to the rural masses through these small towns.
- ***Education.*** Providing children with a good education has emerged as the key priority for rural parents. To this end, rural families have started sending their children to nearby small towns for an English education rather than enrolling them in government schools, where the quality of education is inadequate. Also, rural parents are aspiring to provide vocational training, like computer education, to their children. The rural youth is aspiring for new careers in BPOs, and the retail and energy sectors.

Small towns act as hubs for rural people wanting to avail of three important services—health, education, and financial services.

| TABLE **11.6** | Products Purchased from Different Locations by Rural Consumers (in per cent)

Products	Village	Nearby Shandy/Mela	Larger Village Close by	Nearest Town	Larger Town Close by	City
Groceries	79	8	7	18	7	7
Food articles	82	12	8	18	8	6
Tobacco	84	5	6	9	3	3
Cosmetic and toiletries	73	12	13	29	11	11
Fruits and vegetables	47	26	9	22	9	7
Stationery	48	7	11	27	13	11
Electricals	41	11	14	30	16	14
Agri-inputs	16	9	12	34	20	20
Kitchen appliances	12	11	8	35	20	24
Construction materials	13	6	9	33	23	28
Clothes/Footwear	8	11	9	35	22	28
Durables	6	7	7	37	25	35

Source: Compiled from Francis Kanoi-Rural Marketing Association of India Report on 'A Study on Rural Retail Stores and Retail Habits', 15 May 2008

National-level educational players like NIIT and APTECH are focusing on such small towns to tap the rural potential in this sector.

- ***Financial services.*** With the modernization of banking services, rural people are frequenting small towns for agricultural and non-agricultural credit needs. They are experiencing the use of ATMs and becoming first-time buyers of micro-insurance and micro-credit products. Also, with the arrival of microfinance institutions as new credit institutions for rural masses, people are regularly visiting their branches located in small towns. This awareness generation by private players has catalysed the growth of insurance, credit, and banking services, which have been made available at the town level.

As the Agricultural Linkage

Small towns are of strategic importance to marketers of agricultural products and services. The buying of agricultural inputs (fertilizers, seeds, pesticides) and agricultural implements (tractors, etc.) takes place in nearby towns. Agri-extension services are also availed from agricultural offices located in the block towns. Farmers also visit these towns to attend farmer meets organized by the government and private players. On the other hand, for selling produce, farmers visit mandis located in these feeder towns. There are more than 7,000 mandis present in these towns across the country. Companies like ITC and DSCL are setting up their retail outlets close to these towns to attract rural buyers.

As a Place for Leisure and Entertainment

With increasing disposable income and the rising consumerism and aspirations among rural people, small towns are becoming the preferred destination for leisure and entertainment. Rural youth and families frequent these small towns for picnics, family get-togethers, watching movies, and dining out, as cinema halls and restaurants are located here. With the arrival of multiplexes and malls in towns, they have become the new attraction points for rural folks, in addition to fairs and festivals as the outing occasions. Many companies are also utilizing communication platforms like in-mall displays and road shows to create awareness and hype about their brands among the visitors.

REVIEW OF OBJECTIVES

1. Define small towns, their potential and relevance.

Small towns in India have been defined as towns with population of less than one million. In other words, Tier III and IV towns are considered small towns. The potential of these towns lies in their own residing population; their proximity to villages, because of which they act as hubs for the purchase of many products; the increasing income levels and buying power of small-town inhabitants; as an important linkage between urban and rural India; and their vast infrastructural opportunities, leading to an increase in food joints, branded retail outlets, and malls.

2. Understand the behaviour of small-town consumers.

Understanding the behaviour of small-town consumers is of prime importance to marketers who plan to enter these lucrative markets and stay there for a long time. This is possible only when these marketers become well-versed with the behaviour of the inhabitants staying in these small towns. The behaviour of these small-town consumers is characterized by their growing affluence leading to better standards of living; increasing awareness through media and higher importance accorded to education; higher aspiration levels for urban jobs and lifestyles; increasing brand awareness and preference for more premium brands; and shopping from a mix of mom-and-pop stores to convenience stores to malls.

3. Understand the strategic importance of small towns for rural marketers.

The significance of small-town markets for the rural masses lies in the fact that they are the selling and redistribution points for durable and FMCG products; act as servicing points for electronic items and automobiles; are the hubs for rural people wishing to avail of services like health, education, banking, and insurance; are an important linkage in the agricultural space; and last but not the least, have emerged as the leisure and entertainment hubs for the rural inhabitants.

DISCUSSION AND APPLICATION :::

Discussion of Concepts

1. How do you define a small town? Give three examples of small towns in India which have seen a fast-paced progression in the last five years.
2. 'Small towns have huge potential.' Explain this statement with examples.
3. What are the characteristics of a small-town consumer?
4. Explain the strategic importance of small towns for marketers of financial services with the help of the 4 As.

Application of Concepts

1. Imagine you are a marketing manager of a national level durables company (refrigerator). Devise a comprehensive marketing strategy to enter the Tier III and IV towns of Uttar Pradesh.
2. If you were to communicate and make your target consumers aware of your newly launched 'small town car', how would you do so? Devise a complete communication plan for the small-town audience.
3. 'European Eat' is a chain of restaurant which serves European food. The USP of the restaurant is its bland food, which is mostly preferred by the expats and the higher SECs in India. Recently, due to job opportunities, a number of expats have landed in India. Also, a number of NRIs are returning back to India and have their residences in smaller towns. This led to expansion of chain in smaller towns of India. But the restaurant is not yielding profits due to lesser number of customers. Customizing as per the Indian taste (generally spicy) to encourage more customers would mean the loss of the USP for the restaurant. Help devise a marketing strategy to attract greater number of takers for 'Bland Food' category for 'European Eat'.

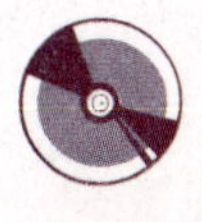

RURAL MARKETING **CASE** | PHILIPS LIGHTING: BULB *KA BADSHAH*

Philips, despite being a well-known brand in the incandescent light bulbs segment, was facing a huge threat from regional players in small towns and villages in India in the early 2000s. The low brand loyalty of consumers was at the heart of this problem. Consumers bought light bulbs by wattage instead of brand name, which resulted in low brand association and negligible brand loyalty.

Philips was losing its market share to competition, including local players. In addition to luring consumers with low prices, the local players were offering attractive margins to retailers. Retailers play a critical role in popularizing and pushing products in semi-urban/rural markets. In this case, retailers pushed local brands by offering personal guarantees and assuring replacement. Hence, the market share of Philips, an established brand, was declining steadily. This forced Philips to focus on brand reinforcement among consumers and to develop new points of sales, besides strengthening the existing retail channel.

The Campaign

Philips partnered with MART to design and implement a campaign that would help it to regain the lost market share. In the beginning of 2004, MART launched an activation campaign in the states of Gujarat, Madhya Pradesh, and Uttar Pradesh. The campaign was rolled out in 480 small towns (with the population ranging from 15,000 to 50,000) for a period of one-and-a-half years. To promote brand recall, branded vans were used to carry out the campaign in small towns for consumer and retail contacts. Consumer contacts were made in marketplaces and residential areas, and engaged through interactive games and lucky draws. Innovative POPs at retail points, retailer get-togethers, and one-to-one contact with regular follow-ups were used for retail activation. Apart from traditional retailers, non-electrical shops were also included in the campaign as new selling points.

The Result

The campaign resulted in an annual sales growth of 120 per cent, with stronger and sustainable channel partnership and the welcome addition of non-traditional sales channels. The presence of a company distributor at retail outlets, the use of catchy, innovative POPs such as long-lasting inflated bulb-shaped balloons, and the focus on establishing a rapport with retailers were the key factors responsible for the success of the campaign.

Discussion Questions

1. Give examples of two leading brands that have faced a similar problem of commodification in small-town markets. Explain how they responded to this challenge.
2. Why do you think that this campaign achieved phenomenal success?

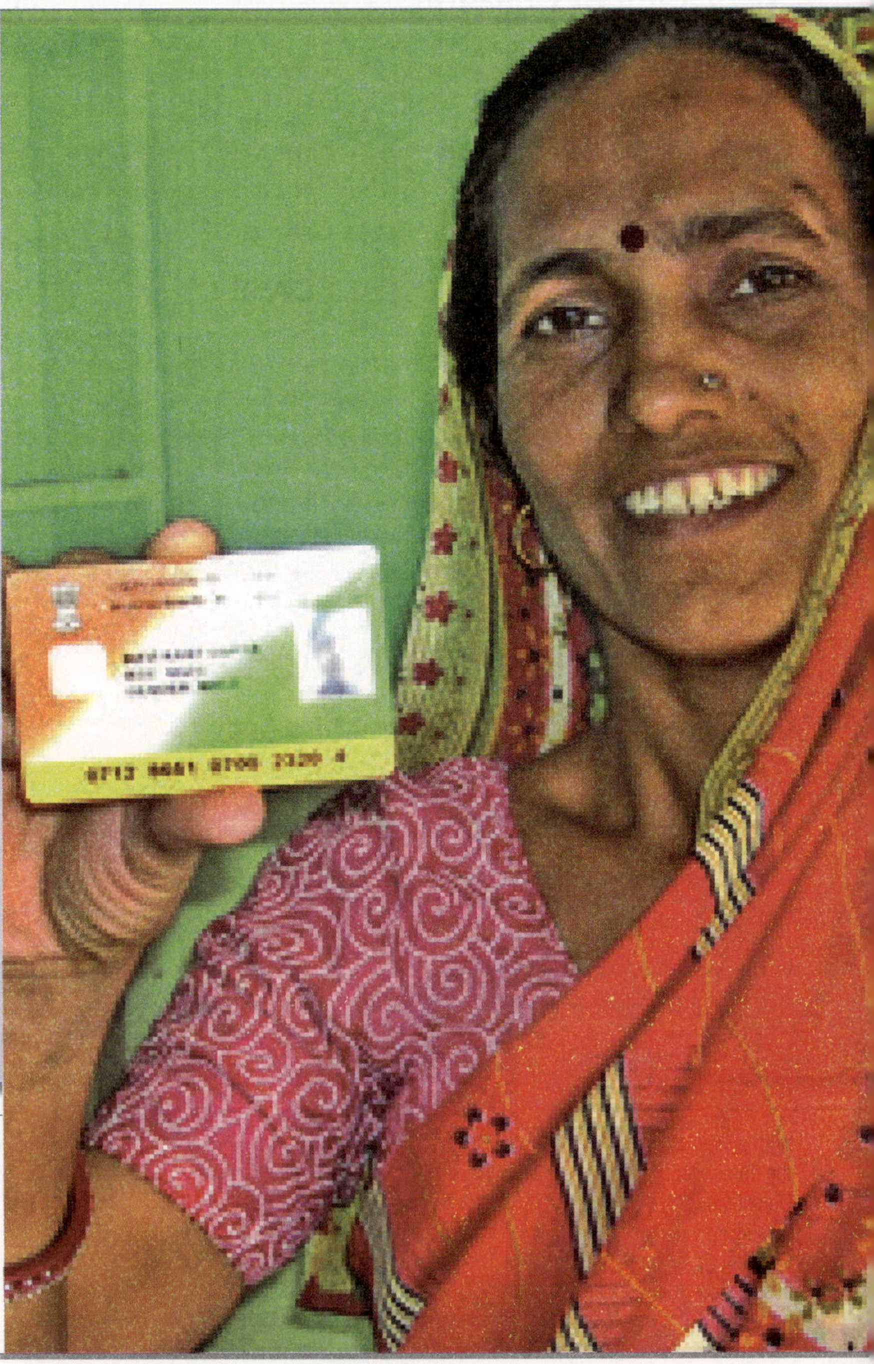

AFTER READING THIS CHAPTER, YOU WILL BE ABLE TO:

1. Understand the significance of role of government in developing rural India
2. Describe various schemes laid out by the government for the development of rural infrastructure including health, education, skill building, and sanitation, schemes for the provision of employment, financial inclusion, and growth of agriculture in the country
3. Understand how government schemes can lead to development of the market alongside providing social benefits

CHAPTER 12 ::: ROLE OF GOVERNMENT IN RURAL INDIA

twelve

Shiv Kumar Pandey is just counting his days, when he will be working inside his office. At present, he is doing duty of a security guard outside the office of a BPO company. He earns only INR 7000 per month which is a petty amount to meet even the basic necessities of the family.

One day he got an offer from one of his senior, working in office, for back office customer service executive. He needs to have only a basic knowledge of computer with Internet for that position, and can earn a handsome remuneration of INR 11,000.

To be able to upgrade his job from security guard to customer executive, he has started taking computer classes. He is also taking help of his son to learn using the Internet. He will soon join after the completion of his course. He says, 'mujhe vishwaas hi nai hua ki internet seekh kar main, itna zaada kama saktaa hun' *(I did not believe that I can earn so much more after learning the Internet).*

With a view to generating employment opportunities in rural areas, the Tamil Nadu government has unveiled Rural Business Process Outsourcing (BPO) Policy 2010 providing capital and training subsidies to BPO units setting shop in village panchayats.
Opening up of rural BPO has enhanced reach of computer and access to Internet connectivity which has in turn changed the way households earn their livelihood in rural India.

Why Is Government's Intervention Important for Rural Development?

Rural development is an important pillar for the development of the country. It is the responsibility of the government to provide basic amenities, good infrastructure, and better quality of life to our rural population. For providing basic infrastructure including connecting roads, housing facilities or provision of health and education facilities in every nook and corner of the country, the government's intervention is essential as the scale of investment required is huge.

It is equally important that the rural economy grows at a healthy pace and create the much required jobs in our country.

What is the Government doing?

The government has initiated various schemes and programmes in different domains to develop rural India in a holistic manner.

::: Rural Infrastructure

Connecting the Rural

The **Pradhan Mantri Gram Sadak Yojana (PMGSY)** is a centrally sponsored Scheme that aims to provide all-weather road connectivity to all unconnected rural areas of the country. PMGSY-II has been launched aiming to upgrade the existing selected rural roads to make the road-network vibrant. The routes would be selected with the objective of identification of rural growth centres and rural places of importance. Development of rural hubs and growth centres are crucial to the overall strategy of facilitating poverty reduction through creating rural infrastructure.

All villages with population of 500 and more, have been connected under the scheme, thereby ensuring that 90 per cent population has easy access to nearby towns. Figure 12.1 shows the increase in habitations due to increase in connectivity of villages.

This has transformed the rural economy. Farmers can now transport their produce fresh to the agri-markets, which has facilitated crop diversification. As a result, more farmers are growing vegetables which fetch a better price. Increase in road connectivity has enabled marginal or landless farmers to experiment with poultry farming; 3.2 million jobs were created in poultry industry between 2005 and 2010. Similarly, retail shops now receive stocks against orders placed on town stockists without delay. As the ordering cycle has reduced, retailers can now make quick orders for their products and need not store huge inventories. This has led to unlocking of funds from reduced inventories and retailers invest in newer product categories. The increase in product variety has helped in achieving higher sales and better incomes for the 10 million retailer community. Road connectivity has also reduced the land price difference between locations, and also allows land to be put to more productive uses such as horticulture, floriculture, and poultry.

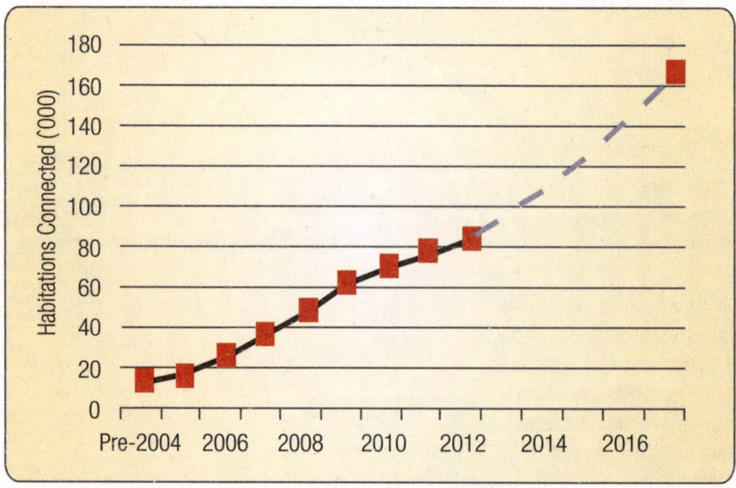

| FIG. **12.1** |
Increase in new habitations connected by road
Source: PM Gram Sadak Yojana, Ministry of Road Transport

Good connectivity and the need for fast transportation has inspired companies to launch low-cost utility vehicles. Tata Motors launched Tata Ace (Chhota Hathi), a mini truck at an economical cost, Mahindra & Mahindra derives 60 per cent of volume sales of utility vehicles from rural India.

Better roads have created a huge market for the two-wheeler segment of automobile companies like Hero MotoCorp. Suzuki Motorcycle India also launched a mass market motorcycle Hayate, at an aggressive price of about INR 40,000 (US$ 650 approx.). The company is doubling its manufacturing capacity by setting up another plant at Rohtak.

Housing in Rural

With a view to meeting the housing needs of the rural poor, Indira Awaas Yojana (IAY) was launched in May 1985 as a sub-scheme of Jawahar Rozgar Yojana. The scheme aims at helping rural people below the poverty-line (BPL) in construction of houses and upgradation of existing kutcha houses by providing full grant. Currently, the government is working on converging the two big schemes—MNREGA and IAY, wherein the government will provide the amount as labour component from MGNREGA to the poor who work on building their homes under the grant from IAY.

Emphasis on creating housing facilities in rural India has pushed up the construction industry as there is an increase in demand for cement, bricks, and paints. Thirty per cent of the total cement demand comes from rural housing. Companies, including Holcim Cement, ACC, Ultratech, Binani, and Shree Cement are planning to expand their reach to the vast untapped rural market.

SHUBH GRIHA

Tata launched a concept of ready-made Nano homes to provide housing facilities to rural India, under the name Shubh Griha, priced between INR 3.9 lakh and INR 6.7 lakh. 'The opportunity lies at the bottom of the pyramid as there is a huge shortage at this end of the market,' Tata Housing MD Brotin Banerjee said. Shubh Griha is in line with the Tata group's philosophy of contributing and having a positive involvement with the society at large.

Electrifying the Rural Houses

In addition to the Rajeev Gandhi Grameen Vidyutikaran Yojana (RGGVY), the government is also trying to electrify the villages by investing heavily in bio-gas, solar as well as wind energy. Programmes such as Jawaharlal Nehru National solar mission have been launched to fasten the pace of electrification with a goal of providing complete electrification by 2025.

For a rural household, a light bulb is 60 per cent–80 per cent cheaper than kerosene lamp. If one assumes one light bulb equals two kerosene lamps, the cost saving becomes INR 1,400/

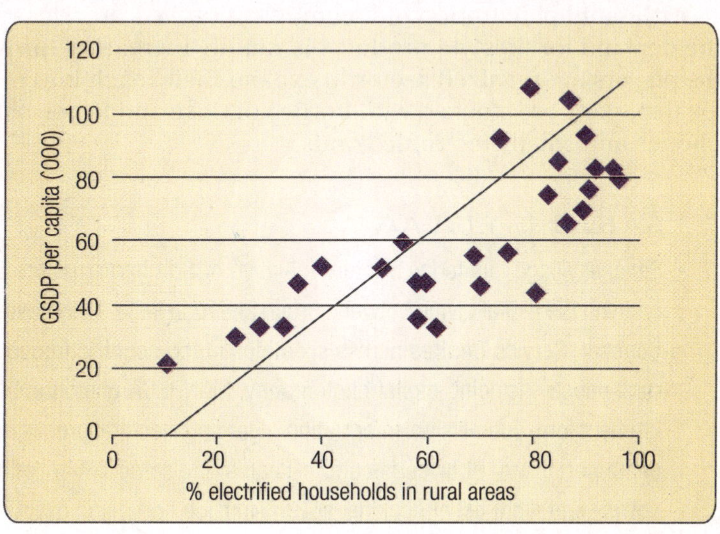

| FIG. **12.2** |
State GDP increases with electrified rural households
Source: Census of India, RBI, Planning Commission, Credit Suisse estimates

year. The result is an increased usage and demand for electrical appliances and electronics. Availability of electricity has also led to an increase in the daily productivity of rural households (the usage of the simplest of consumer appliances can help save several hours a week), leading to rise in productivity of the state (see figure).

Urbanizing the Rural

The central government has been running Provision of Urban Amenities to Rural Areas (PURA) programmes in several states since 2004. Shyama Prasad Mukherjee Rurban Mission was also launched in 2014 to provide urban amenities in rural areas through public private partnership (PPP) model. The Rurban mission is expected to help reduce migration from rural to urban areas as modern infrastructure is being created in villages. Urbanization of rural areas will help rural people find opportunities in their surroundings and will help decongest cities.

In order to build infrastructure in rural India, various programmes to build model villages have been started since 1990s. With an objective to provide adequate physical and institutional infrastructure, the Prime Minister's Adarsh Gram Yojana (PMAGY) was launched in 2009 for the development of villages with a majority of scheduled caste population. On similar lines, Sansad Adarsh Gram Yojana (SAGY) was launched in 2014 wherein all the Members of Parliament (MP) are required to develop a village of their choice for all-round development. The scheme requires every MP to identify and develop one village with population ranging from 3,000 to 5,000 in the plains and 1,000 to 3,000 in the hills into a model village, by utilizing the resources available under the various running developmental government programmes.

To transform India into a digitally connected economy, the government launched the Digital India Programme, with a target to digitally literate 10 lakh people by 2015 and provide broadband connectivity to 2.5 gram panchayats by 2019. Part of the programme is eKranti which is about providing every citizen with the access of services through electronic delivery system such as e-Health, e-Education, e-Banking, and real time price information to farmers. The programme will make available all government services on Internet and mobile platforms.

The Digital India campaign is expected to boost the IT sector in the country. Google has already become a part of the initiative and is developing various mobile applications, including the one for the Prime Minister's office. Likewise, many Indian companies are going to be involved which will bring about the required push to IT literacy and jobs in the sector.

Access to online service of the government through the Internet on mobile phones will raise the demand for smart phones, hence, a great opportunity for telecom companies. The aim of expanding broadband to rural and unreachable regions in the country will boost the broadband and fibre optic companies.

A Credit Suisse report points out that 76 per cent of all men in rural India own a cellphone, compared to only 29 per cent of the women. With an aim to increase women's access to cellphones, Uninor and GSMA plan to invest 11million rupees within the period of six months.

With rapid penetration of communication and broadcasting services in rural areas, the demand for lifestyle products is rapidly increasing, providing huge opportunity to the players in organized sector to expand their reach into rural India. Tiny shops in the local markets are stocked with bottles of Coke and Pepsi, shampoos and soaps, mobile phones and small electronic goods.

SAHAJ E-VILLAGE

Sahaj e-Village Limited, a venture initiative of Srei Infrastructure Finance Limited, has delved into bridging the digital divide between urban and rural India. They have set up and are managing 28,006 Common Service Centres across six states in the country, through which they provide services to rural people including digital photography, MGNREGA photograph, MGNREGA data collection, government form submission, information regarding electoral processes, addition and deletion, Internet, death certificate, birth certificate, e-Learning, electric bill collection (WBSEDCL), mobile top ups, railway and flight ticket booking, advertising, job portal and examination results, etc.

e-Governance in Rural India

Department of Electronics and information technology (DeitY) is the nodal ministry for the purpose of promoting e-Governance in the country. Its main role has been to formulate an e-governance plan for the country. Infrastructure created by DeitY include creation of State Wide Area Networks (SWAN) and State Data Centres across the country, Common Service Centres (CSC) in the rural areas and State Service Delivery Gateways (SSDGs) across the states. The Mobile Seva initiative of the ministry has provided services to over 1,000 central and state government departments and agencies across the country to provide mobile-based services to the citizens and businesses.

The Government of India launched the Direct Benefit Transfer Programme in January 2013 in selected districts, to transfer subsidies directly to the people through their bank accounts. The primary aim of this programme is to bring transparency and terminate pilferage from distribution of funds sponsored by the Central Government of India, including subsidies for LPG, kerosene, fertilizer, food, student scholarships. These payments are being transferred through Aadhaar payment bridge.[1]

Direct cash transfer can be a boon to migrant workers as they can have access to Government benefits from anywhere in India.

The kerosene pilot in Alwar district of Rajasthan revealed that kerosene consumption and subsidies fell up to 80 per cent with the introduction of direct benefit transfer.

Education

With an aim to universalize elementary education in a time bound manner, Sarva Shiksha Abhiyan was launched by the Government of India in 2001. The programme makes attaining free and compulsory education a fundamental right for children in the age group of 6 to 14 years. Similarly, with an objective to universalize secondary education, the Government has initiated the Rashtriya Madhyamik Shiksha Abhiyan.

To enhance enrolment and attendance in schools, cooked nutritious food is provided to all children studying in primary and upper primary level under the Mid-Day Meal scheme, launched in September 2004 by the Ministry of Human Resource Development. For the year 2014–15, the government has allocated an amount of INR 13,215 crore.

104.5 million children were covered and benefitted from the scheme in 1.16 million schools during 2013–14.

Apart from these schemes, emphasis has been laid on building basic infrastructure in schools including separate toilet and drinking water facility for girls and even setting up of virtual class rooms.

To cater to the quality of education imparted, the government has attached special importance to the training and education of teachers and quality assessment for schools.

In addition to finding better livelihood opportunities, education also helps the rural households to make better choices, expand their product basket, leading to market development and improvement in the village economy.

- Better education is directly proportional to better awareness about health and hygiene related aspects. This has opened up opportunities for FMCG companies like HUL (Lifebuoy is the no. 1 soap used in rural), Johnson & Johnson, Colgate (no. 1 tooth paste used in rural), Dabur and many others.
- Better education has led to households switching from traditional stoves to improved cook stoves, owing to health problems of family members. The country has seen an increase in improved cook stove manufacturers, distributors, non-governmental organizations working in the space. This has led to creation in livelihood opportunities for many people.

[1] Aadhaar card is a unique identity card being issued to every citizen of the country and bank accounts of every citizen are being linked to the unique Aadhaar numbers. Nandan Nilekani was quoted as saying that the implementation of this service would show how easy it is to transfer money to people across India.

Health

The **National Health Mission** (NHM) was launched in 2013 to enable universal access to equitable, affordable, and quality health care services. The NHM subsumes the National Rural Health Mission (NRHM) (discussed in Chapter 10) and National Urban Health Mission (NUHM) as sub-missions, initiated in 2013 to expand the primary healthcare service coverage in the country. The NUHM covers slum dwellers and other marginalized groups of all cities/towns with a population of more than 50,000, while the towns below 50,000 population are already covered under the NRHM.

Reproductive and Child Health (RCH): Two RCH programmes, namely, Janani Suraksha Yojna (JSY) and Janani Shishu Suraksha Karyakram (JSSK), aim to bring about a change in three critical health indicators, maternal mortality rate (MMR), infant mortality rate (IMR), and total fertility rate (TFR). In order to meet the increased demand for delivery care services, the initiative to introduce 100-bedded maternal and child health wings in 158 district hospitals and medical colleges has been taken up. Mother and child tracking system (MCTS) has been introduced to track every pregnant woman for timely pre-natal care, institutional delivery, and post-natal care, with immunization of the children. The registration of pregnant women and children has reached about 2.08 crore and 1.67 crore respectively during 2013–14. Under the JSY, institutional deliveries conducted by skilled birth attendants have increased from 7.38 lakh in 2005–06 to more than 1.06 crore in 2012–13. The number of institutional deliveries during 2013–14 (up to September 2013) was 80.94 lakh. Under the JSSK, all pregnant women delivering in public health institutions are entitled to absolutely no expense deliveries including caesarean, free drugs, diagnostics, blood and diet, and free transport from home to institution, including during referrals. Of the many schemes being implemented for the welfare of women and children, the Integrated Child Development Services Scheme is an important one (discussed in Chapter 10).

The women and child department, Government of Maharashtra, initiated a pioneer programme - Rajmata Jijau-Mother Child Health and Nutrition Mission in 2005, with an aim to eliminate child malnutrition in a mission mode. The programme is completely funded by UNICEF and is implemented through the existing ICDS and health machinery in the state. The mission focuses on the health requirements of a child in the first 1000 days of conception. As per the Nutrition Survey in Maharashtra—CNSM 2012, all indictors of malnutrition have reduced substantially in the last 6 years, including stunting and wasting.

Rashtriya Bal Swasthya Karyakram (RBSK) was launched in 2013, with an aim to provide comprehensive healthcare and improve the quality of life of 25 crore children across the country, through early identification and early intervention for children from birth to 18 years to cover defects at birth, deficiencies, diseases, development delays, including disability.

Emphasis on health infrastructure in rural India leads to enhanced access to healthcare for rural people. This results in increase in productivity of the work force, more number of work days, more earnings and less expenses on illness. Private companies such as GE and Biocon are exploring the rural market potential by developing innovative products and services for the rural markets.

GE HEALTHCARE

GE Healthcare created the 'Lullaby baby-warmer', to help save lives in a country that has the highest rate of pre-term baby deaths in the world. It is a low cost product which was 70 per cent cheaper than the traditional models. The Lullaby warmer consumes less power than most incubators, which means cost savings for the healthcare centre. The design includes pictorial warnings and colour coding, so that even semi-literate rural healthcare workers can operate the machine. The Lullaby warmers work in combination with Lullaby phototherapy systems, which were also re-engineered by GE. Doctors use them to treat infants with neonatal jaundice, a common illness caused by their immature livers.

Canara bank has extended its support to Biocon Foundation and Orissa Trust of Technical education and Training (OTTET) for a public private partnership with the Odisha Government, with regard to an e-healthcare programme that seek to improve rural regions in the state. Under this partnership, Biocon Foundation and OTTET will establish an e-health centre emanaged by local entrepreneurs, at all primary health centres in the state.

Social enterprises such as e-health point (telemedicine), Glocal healthcare (rural health clinics) are trying to make quality rural healthcare available and affordable through innovative experiments.

Though existing infrastructural set-up for providing health care in rural India is on track, yet the qualitative and quantitative availability of primary health care facilities is far less than the defined norms by the World Health Organization. This leads the rural people accessing facilities of private health care practitioners, usually unregistered at affordable charges in their villages. Number of people impoverished due to spending on medicines was 34 million in 2011–12. Rashtriya Swasthya Bima Yojana (RSBY) was launched by the Ministry of Labour and Employment, Government of India, to provide health insurance coverage for Below Poverty Line (BPL) families. Beneficiaries under RSBY are entitled to hospitalization coverage up to INR 30,000 for most of the diseases that require hospitalization. Coverage extends to five members of the family which includes the head of household, spouse and up to three dependents. Beneficiaries only need to pay INR 30 as registration fee.

RASHTRIYA SWASTHYA BIMA YOJNA

Rashtriya Swwasthya Bima Yojna (RSBY), which was implemented through biometric smart card based delivery system spearheaded by FINO, has brought a turnaround by unlocking the business potential of around INR 45 billion for health insurance companies.

Another indirect benefit of the efficient delivery of the RSBY is the evolution of the Public Health Delivery System. Under RSBY, both public and private hospitals can be empanelled and public hospitals are given incentives to treat beneficiaries as the money would flow directly from an insurer to the public hospitals which can be used for purposes like improving health infrastructure and bringing modern technologies in hospitals.

Skill Development

Recognizing the urgent need to upgrade the skills of working population of India and to bring more people in the employability net, the Government of India adopted the Prime Minister's National Mission on Skill Development as part of the Eleventh Five Year Plan with a vision to skill 500 million people by 2022. A three-tier skill development institutional structure was formulated comprising the Prime Minister's National Council on Skill Development, the National Skill Development Coordination Board, and the National Skill Development Corporation. While the Council is responsible for setting up the basic principles governing the overall strategy of skill development, the Board is responsible to integrate the efforts being made by various government ministries and departments in the area of skill development.

The National Skill Development Corporation (NSDC) is a PPP enterprise responsible to facilitate the setting-up of vocational training institutions in the country, with the help of private sector participation and providing low-cost funding for training capacity. The corporation is expected to provide vocational skills to 150 million people by the year 2022. As of 31 March 2014, a total of 10,05,074 persons have been trained by NSDC through 2856 active training centres, with 64 per cent as the placement ratio.

In addition to the national skill development mission, various states and Union Territories have established their own skill development missions.

In addition to this, under the new scheme Apprentices Protsahan Yojana (Apprenticeship Training Scheme), the labour ministry, Government of India, plans to partly finance the cost of first two years of apprenticeship/training of one lakh youth by 2017 (started from October 2014). With a budget of INR 346 crore, the focus of the scheme will be on imparting skills related to the manufacturing sector, in sync with the BJP-led NDA government's 'Make in India' campaign.

Skill development of rural people helps in raising their employability as well as the income levels. An unskilled laborer earning INR 100–INR 150 for a day's work, after undergoing skill development training becomes a mason and gets higher wages up to INR 300 per day. A mere one per cent increase in India's rural income translates to a large buying power of INR 10,000 crore (US$ 1.79 billion).

NIS SPARTA

Skill Development initiative of the government has given a boost to companies like NIS Sparta. NIS Sparta is a Reliance ADA group company. It provides training and placement opportunities to central and state-initiated employability programmes under PPP strategy, apart from other programmes across the nation.

::: Employment

National Rural Employment Guarantee Act (NREGA)

A total of 632 districts have been covered under NREGA as of 31 December 2012.

With an annual allocation of INR 34,000 crore for the year 2014–15, special emphasis has been laid on development of backward districts which are covered under the Integrated Action Plan (IAP).[2] Construction of playgrounds and Anganwadi Centres has also been allowed as a part of the programme.

An increase in wage rates of manual labour employed under NREGA has helped in benchmarking the market wages of manual labor at a higher rate. There is an increase up to 50 per cent, over a five-year period from the start of NREGA, as compared to a 5 per cent rise in wages in pre NREGA five-year period. As a result, the BoP population has benefited in two ways, more number of days of work in their own village and much higher wages. This is driving demand for consumer products and other product categories at the BoP. Fig. 12.3 shows the increase in wage rates of rural population.

The MGNREGA Advantage:

- Due to improvement in incomes of people, child labour has reduced as many households are now sending their children to schools.
- As people have been given employment within their own villages or nearby, migration to work in other cities has reduced. As a result, states like Punjab are facing scarcity of labour.
- Nearly 8.6 crore bank/post office accounts have been opened for the rural populace under MNREGA and around 80 per cent of MNREGA payments are made through this route. The opening of accounts has brought the poor into the organized sector and in some cases, provided them with better access to credit.
- Work undertaken under MNREGA has led to creation of important infrastructure for the country including development of roads, development of water irrigation facilities, water harvesting facilities amongst others. This has improved connectivity of rural villages and has also improved agriculture productivity in the country.

Other than employment programmes such as MNREGA and Ajeevika (refer Chapter 2), the government is also promoting rural entrepreneurship as an engine of growth and job creation.

[2] The Integrated Action Plan (IAP) was formulated to provide additional assistance to address the development of Left Wing Extremism (LWE) affected districts. The plan involves central assistance for development of public infrastructure and services such as school buildings, anganwadi centres, primary health centres, drinking water supply, village roads, electric lights in public places such as primary health centres (PHCs) and schools.

| FIG. **12.3** |
Rural wage growth
Source: Labour Bureau, NSSO, Credit Suisse estimates, 2014

Financial Inclusion

115 million banks accounts have been opened in rural India as of January 2015.

In addition to RBI's previous efforts for financial inclusion, the Pradhan Mantri Jan Dhan Yojana was launched on 15 August 2014, aiming to bring poor people, rural or urban, under the banking net. With simpler know your customer (KYC) rules, people are encouraged to open zero balance accounts in public or private banks along with which they can avail an over-draft facility, accidental insurance of INR 1 lakh, RuPay debit card, and basic access to mobile banking facility. These accounts will also be used for transfer payments and subsidy deposits of government schemes like NREGA.

Similar to Kissan Credit Cards (discussed in Chapter 10), banks provide General Purpose Credit Card (GCC) to the rural households, which is a revolving credit facility up to INR 25,000 to banks' customers based on the assessment of cash flow, with no strict requirements of security, purpose, or end use of the credit.

Clear land titles and increasing awareness has sharply increased the number of Kisan Credit Cards. This has not only boosted rural consumption (marriages, education, motorcycle purchases), but also in cases where this is put to agricultural use; it allows inventory holding by farmers, thereby improving realizations (a report by Credit Suisse, 2013).

Further to the Business Correspondent model of operation (discussed in Chapter 10), banks have been mandated in the 2014 to open at least 25 per cent of the total number of branches to be opened during a year in unbanked rural areas.

HDFC BANK

HDFC Bank is rapidly transforming its business model. From being primarily urban focused (80 per cent branches were urban till 2005), it is now rapidly growing (opening 80 per cent new branches) in non-urban locations. 47 per cent of its 2,800 branches are now non-urban (will reach 55 per cent by FY15). The bank mostly offers products that are secured in nature such as pre-/post-harvest loans, kisan gold loans and tractor loans in non-urban centres. Also, the share of saving deposit for non-urban branches is much higher at (42–50 per cent) vs 15–30% in urban branches.

Sanitation

Rural sanitation came into focus for the Government of India in the World Water Decade of 1980s. Government launched the Central Rural Sanitation Program (CRSP) in 1986 with an aim to improve the quality of life of rural people, eradicating associated diseases and enhancing social security for women.

The programme was revised to Total Sanitation Campaign in 1999 which was later known as Nirmal Bharat Abhiyan. Focusing on demand-driven approach to eradicate

2000 gram panchayats in Maharashtra were given open defecation free status.

the practice of open defecation by 2017, the programme involved construction of school toilet units, Anganwadi toilets, individual household latrines, and Community Sanitary Complexes along with Solid and Liquid Waste Management activities. Gram panchayats attaining complete sanitation coverage were given Nirmal status and were awarded Nirmal Gram Puraskar along with monetary rewards. With the initiative of the Department of Drinking water and Sanitation, Ministry of Rural Development, Government of India, it was implemented in close coordination of the central and state governments, involving participation from Panchayati raj institutions, NGOs and SHGs.

Taking forward the sanitation campaign, Swachh Bharat Abhiyan was launched in the year 2014 to cover 100 per cent rural households with sanitation facility by the year 2022. With a provision of INR 4,260 crore earmarked for the year 2014–15, the programme has widened the inclusivity of 'Above Poverty Line' households along with 'Below the Poverty Line' households. The government is also encouraging the corporate sector to collaborate in the sanitation campaign as a part of their corporate social responsibility initiatives.

This campaign is expected to create employment opportunities for a large pool of workforce. It takes four days for one mason and one helper to construct a toilet. Assuming a time frame of five years to construct the 100 million toilets needed in rural households, it can provide continuous employment to 2,50,000 masons and helpers for 5 years.

Aligning with the sanitation programmes of the government, JSW launched pre-fabricated toilet structures which only need to be installed and used. Similarly, large companies are contributing to rural sanitation through their CSR funds. Indian Oil Corporation assigned a total of INR 235 crore for construction of toilets, Tata Consultancy Services and Bharti Airtel both plan to spend INR 100 crores for the cause.

Agriculture

The National Development Council launched the National Food Security Mission in 2007 with an objective to raise the yield of rice, wheat, and pulses. The mission addressed the major productivity constraints through farm management techniques and promotion of agricultural technologies to meet the desired objectives. With the help of the mission, there was a total productivity increase of 40 million tons during the Eleventh Five Year Plan, against the targeted increase of 20 million tons. The mission has been extended to Twelfth Five Year Plan, aiming at raising the yield of wheat, rice, pulses, and coarse cereals.

Agriculture sector is the most significant and broadest economic sector in India. The variation in production is directly affected by many unfavourable conditions such as pest attacks, variations in weather conditions such as rainfall, temperature, humidity, etc. To protect the farmers from the vagaries of nature, the government also launched the National Crop Insurance Scheme in 2013, for insuring farmers from drought, floods, and disease-struck crops. Under the scheme, agricultural insurance company along with 10 other private insurers with adequate infrastructure are providing insurance to the farmers.

HDFC ERGO is offering a comprehensive Yield-based Crop Insurance Policy which is aimed at covering the production risks faced by the agricultural sector. This policy covers any shortfall in yield resulting due to natural phenomena such as natural fire and lightning, storm, hailstorm, cyclone, drought, dry spells, pests/diseases, etc.

To help farmers improve their productivity through an informed application of nutrients to the soil, the government launched a scheme to provide a Soil Health Card to every farmer in the country. A Soil Health Card is used to assess the current status of soil health and to determine changes in soil health that are affected by land management over time. The card carries crop-wise recommendations of nutrients/fertilizers required for farms, making it possible for farmers to improve productivity by using appropriate inputs.

As of March 2012, over 48 crore soil health cards have been issued to farmers in states including Tamil Nadu, Gujarat, Andhra Pradesh, and Haryana. The centre plans to make the provision of soil health card pan India.

The Agricultural Department, Government of India, launched the Integrated Scheme for Agricultural Marketing to promote creation of agricultural marketing infrastructure—physical and ICT-based infrastructure including nation-wide information network for speedy exchange for market information on prices. With the total budget of INR 4548 crore for the Twelfth Five Year Plan, the scheme aims to help farmers realize better prices, connect with processors, extension of cold storage capacity, and benefit from other consultancy and upgradation facilities for farmers.

Apart from these, the government has rolled out various funds including National Adaptation Fund, Price Stabilization Fund, fund for financing landless farmers, rural credit fund to boost the agriculture sector of the country.

MAHARASHTRA AGRICULTURAL COMPETITIVENESS PROJECT

Maharashtra Agricultural Competitiveness Project (MACP) funded by the World Bank and the Government of Maharashtra, was launched to increase the productivity, profitability, and market access of the farming community in Maharashtra. This was proposed to be achieved by providing farmers with technical knowledge, market intelligence, and market networks to support diversification and intensification of agriculture production aimed at responding to market demand. Farmers will also be assisted in establishing farmer organizations, developing alternative market channels outside of the regulated markets and in supporting the modernization of promising traditional wholesale markets.

Growth in agriculture is opening up opportunities for private entrepreneurs as it promises them big returns.

ZAMINDARA FARMSOLUTIONS

Fazilka-based (Punjab) entrepreneur-cum-farmer Vikram Aditya Ahuja, started Zamindara Farmsolutions which rents out high-priced farm equipment to farmers at affordable prices. The venture aims at keeping small-scale farmers motivated by helping them yield good crops with the help of high-tech farm equipment and also to make farmers debt-free. The venture has made a difference in the lives of thousands of farmers, nearly 800 small-scale farmers and boys from economically weaker backgrounds directly or indirectly have been given employment. Nearly 10,000 to 15,000 farmers have benefited though rental scheme.

Conclusion

Two-thirds of Indians still live in villages which represents untapped captive population. The government schemes and initiatives have transformed the face of rural India, through the provision of elementary infrastructure. The government is even targeting to digitize the villages to enable rural population to easily access the government schemes as one of the objectives.

As the government continues to spend on rural infrastructure, especially the construction of roads, it has become easier for the corporate sector to reach out to the masses. The corporate sector is now considering rural markets as their target markets where they find tremendous growth opportunities.

REVIEW OF OBJECTIVES :::

1. Understand the significance of role of government in developing rural India

The role of government is essential for the provision of basic infrastructure in villages such as connecting roads, health centres and hospitals, schools, toilet and drinking water facilities, access to banks and micro finance for the rural poor, and other key infrastructure.

2. Describe various schemes laid out by the government for the development of rural infrastructure including health, education, skill building and sanitation, schemes for the provision of employment, financial inclusion, and growth of agriculture in the country

Three flagship programmes of the government for rural development and upliftment have been Bharat Nirman, MGNREGA, and National Rural Health Mission.

For Infrastructure development, some of the prime schemes under Bharat Nirman include Pradhan Mantri Gram Sadak Yojana, Indira Awas Yojana for rural housing, Rajeev Gandhi Grameen Vidyutikaran Yojana, National Rural Drinking water programme, Rural Telephony programme.

National Health Mission which covers National rural and urban health missions is the flagship scheme for healthcare followed by Rashtriya Swasthya Bima Yojana. Many other healthcare schemes are also in operation.

Rurban Mission, Sansad Adarsh Gram Yojana are schemes introduced for village development and modernization.

Sarva Shiksha Abhiyan and Mid-Day Meal schemes are the key schemes for promoting education.

Some of the schemes for agricultural development include National Food Security Mission, National Crop Insurance Scheme, Soil Health Card, Integrated Scheme for Agricultural Marketing.

Some of the recently launched schemes are Swachh Bharat Abhiyan, Pradhan Mantri Jan Dhan Yojana.

3. Understand how government schemes can lead to development of the market alongside providing social benefits

With the help of the above-mentioned schemes, there has been an improvement in the standard of living of rural population.

Schooling facilities and incentives for promoting child education through free stationary, free meal during school hours, provision of drinking and sanitation facilities for girls and boys, enables rural youth find better livelihood opportunities. It also helps them make more informed choices as well as understand health and hygiene aspects better, opening up opportunities for FMCG companies.

Access to good health infrastructure and provision of free services through the rural health machinery comprising of primary health centres, ASHA workers, etc., helps rural people live a healthy and productive life.

Basic infrastructure such as roads enhances the connectivity of rural people, they can access local markets, sell agriculture produce, buy products which are hardly available in their village premises. This in turn leads to increased opportunities for farmers, companies, retailers etc.

Financial inclusion programmes help rural people access to formal saving mechanisms such as savings account and access to micro credit facilities. Banks and other financial institutions also benefit as opening of more accounts implies more money in circulation.

::: DISCUSSION AND APPLICATION

Discussion of Concepts

1. How do you think the schemes pertaining to agriculture lead to development of manufacturing and service sectors in the economy?
2. Which schemes do you think are more important—skill development schemes or employment generation schemes? Why?
3. Identify the government programmes which have been implemented through public private partnership model. Discuss how that model can be applied to other government schemes.

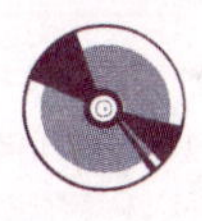

RURAL MARKETING CASE | RURAL MARKETS

In its ongoing race with Flipkart and Amazon India for e-commerce supremacy, Snapdeal is set to tap into the rural areas in India. In partnership with FINO Pay-Tech, Snapdeal will reach out to people living in slums like Dharavi in Mumbai, and villages in Rajasthan and Haryana, among many others, as *Times of India* reports.

The e-commerce company plans to set up as many as 5,000 e-commerce kiosks across 70,000 rural areas in India. These kiosks will include PCs and tablets for people to go online and shop, and will also act as collection points for packages. A FINO agent at the kiosk will login and help people shop for products across a wide range of categories including speakers, juicers, solar lanterns, diner sets, cameras, and mobile phones among others. Snapdeal's Kunal Bahl believes that by tapping into the rural market, the company will be able to reach around 5–10 crore new customers in the next three years.

Snapdeal isn't the only company looking to tap into the Indian rural market. Amazon India is reported to be in talks with the government to improve the Indian postal service, and also use to ramp up its delivery mechanism to within 24 hours anywhere within the country. Flipkart's Sachin Bansal too was recently quoted as saying that the company was in talks with the government to roll out better connectivity in rural areas, which would boost e-commerce in these areas.

Discussion Questions

1. According to you, what has prompted e-commerce companies to go rural?
2. What could be the role of government in promoting e-commerce in rural India? Which government policy could have prompted e-commerce in rural India?
3. What would be the success and failure factors for an e-commerce company operating in rural India?

AFTER READING THIS CHAPTER, YOU WILL BE ABLE TO:

1. Understand the rural boom
2. Identify the way forward for rural marketing
3. Understand the rural dividend and new opportunities

बात करने की खुशी
दिखाई दे अब फोन पर

PCO से कीजिये अपनों से मुलाकात,
बी एस एन एल/एम टी एन एल की कॉल दरों पर।

नज़र आये वो, बात जिससे हो

एरिकसन की प

CHAPTER 13 ::: THE FUTURE OF RURAL MARKETING

thirteen

The 3G technology has the potential to be used for various applications in form of voice and data, one of which is video telephony. However, the cost of acquiring this technology is very high, since it requires a 3G mobile phone connection in a 3G-capable handset, which is not affordable for the low-income segment. Service providers in India were therefore looking for solutions in terms of business models that could bring this technology within the reach of the masses.

Ericsson, in consultation with MART, came up with Aamne Saamne—an innovative shared-access model that could lower the costs for the base of pyramid segment. Its studies showed that there was a significant migration of people from rural areas to urban locations to earn a living, to gain skills, or for education. These migrants stayed in slums or in unauthorized colonies in the cities/towns, and remained connected with their families in the village through telephone/mobile. This migrant segment presented Ericsson with an opportunity to bring in the 3G video telephony model. Having identified the declining PCO industry as the appropriate channel for this technology, Ericsson converted virtually dying PCOs into public video telephony booths. This way the consumer paid only for the minutes used, while the actual investment was made by PCO owners. A marketing communication campaign was designed and implemented to make people more aware and act, which caused a behaviour change in terms of people communicating with each other. They switched from mobile communication to video communication. This model, initiated in the Delhi–Bihar circles, is planned to be replicated in other parts of the country and in other emerging economies of the world.

Aamne Saamne, a shared-access model initiated by Ericsson, connects low-income migrants from rural areas to their near and dear ones through shared video telephony.

As exemplified by the opening vignette, even high-end technologies like 3G have a lot of scope and are being successfully implemented in rural areas, which are fast progressing. Rural India is moving from a static agrarian economy to a more vibrant and diverse one. The time for rural India has arrived, and the future only looks better. The day is not far when rural India will have access to all the facilities currently only seen as appropriate for the upwardly mobile classes in urban areas. It is just that companies have to look beyond the obvious and seek new opportunities for growth; and rural India will be there to accept it whole-heartedly.

::: The Rural Boom

Rural India is now a one trillion USD economy, equal to the current size of the Canadian or South Korean economies. Over the past decade, the rural economy has registered an impressive growth, driven by eight good monsoons, a 100 per cent increase in the minimum support price for primary crops, and a booming non-farm sector driven by improvements in infrastructure and growing exports of handicrafts, gems and jewellery, and carpets. In fact, the non-farm output now constitutes 60 per cent of rural income, and the economy is far less dependent on agriculture, which contributes only 40 per cent of the total rural income (this is expected to come down to 30 per cent by 2020). In fact, there are now more non-agricultural enterprises operating in rural (20 million) India than in urban (16 million) India. Most households have multiple sources of income, both from farm and non-farm sources, and one member from most families earns a regular salary in a government or private job. This is good news for marketers as they no longer have to wait till the harvest to sell high-ticket durables to villagers. With a regular income, rural people are in a position to buy at any time of the year. The rate of increase in rural consumption has jumped from an average of 3–4 per cent per annum in the early part of the last decade to a whopping 13.5 per cent in 2009–10.

Of the total 600,000 plus villages, 67 per cent are now connected by an all-weather road, leaving only the tiny, below 500 population villages unconnected. The 67 per cent connected villages provide access to 90 per cent of the rural population and rural wealth, which is good news for marketers. Almost all villages—and over 60 per cent of households—have electricity connections. This 60 per cent accounts for over 80 per cent of rural wealth, which is good news for the durables industry, although uninterrupted electric supply is still a problem. Hopefully, the quality of supply will improve soon. There are more than 317 million mobile connections in rural India, which translates to an average of more than one connection per household—as there are a total of 175 million families in the rural sector—suggesting that all consuming households are already connected.

Literacy levels have been rising rapidly and today there are more graduates in rural India than in urban India. The educated youth are employed in nearby towns in banks, government offices, schools, and in the private sector. They earn urban salaries, but because they continue to live in self-owned homes in the village, they have the highest purchasing power. In fact, in 2006, a village retailer in rural Tamil Nadu explained that most of his customers for Horlicks were from salaried households. This educated, salaried population—fully aware of and exposed to urban influences—is a powerful force and an early adopter of new products and services.

Rural consumption and penetration levels for most FMCGs are significantly lower than those in urban India. However, with rapidly rising incomes and a growing middle class, the demand for most categories is expected to explode. A recent McKinsey report[1] estimates that by 2017, the per capita consumption of FMCGs in rural India will equal current urban levels. With a population that is three times the urban population, marketers can look forward to a bonanza from rural markets in the coming decade. The trend is already visible. Although the rural and urban market shares were nearly equal for both FMCGs and durables last year, rural sales grew at twice the level of urban sales for FMCGs and thrice for durables! In 2009, for the first time since the introduction of sachets, the volume of Clinic Plus shampoo sold in bottles is growing rapidly, indicative of the growing middle class who buy 'value for money'. This trend is visible in other categories as well. Another emerging trend in rural India is the use of multiple brands in the same household, again reflecting the growing rural prosperity.

Almost all villages are expected to be connected by an all-weather road, every panchayat village to have Internet connectivity, and almost every home in the 500 plus population villages to have electricity and be the proud owner of a mobile phone. With this significant improvement in rural infrastructure, coupled with the agriculture reforms already underway, rural markets have reached an inflexion point by 2013. This will lead to an explosion in demand, in much the same way that it happened in the urban auto sector in the mid-1990s as a result of easy consumer finance, a boom in the IT sector, and a steep increase in corporate salaries. Companies are not anticipating this boom and many will be taken by surprise when it happens.

::: The Way Forward

The future of the rural market is bright, but to exploit its potential, companies will have to take a dedicated look at this market, have innovative rural distribution strategies, work on approaches like forward innovation and inclusive marketing, etc. These approaches are clearly explained in this section.

Forward Innovation

The approach concerned with designing and manufacturing products in emerging economies for the local, emerging consumers is called forward innovation.

Ever since the BoP concept was introduced at the turn of the century, many companies have tried to transform their business models through single-serve sachets, low-cost production, extended mom-and-pop distribution and NGO partnerships. But in the rush to capture the fortune at the base of the pyramid, something may have been lost—the perspective of the poor themselves. Most such initiatives have failed to hit the mark. Pushing the company's reformulated or repackaged products into villages may indeed produce incremental sales in the short term. But in the long term, this strategy will almost certainly fail because the business remains alien to the communities it intends to serve.

Some MNCs have even set up innovation centres in emerging markets to take advantage of lower-cost scientists and engineers to develop low-cost options and produce more from less. These more affordable products developed in such centres are then marketed in developed economies. This approach, popularly referred to as **reverse innovation**, is useful for selling to the 'affordable' middle-income segment, which is relatively small in size in these affluent economies. However, it is in the emerging economies that the 'affordable' segment is growing at a phenomenal rate, and offers a huge market opportunity. It is estimated that by 2020, rural India alone will have 500 million middle-income consumers, perhaps more than in the entire continent of Europe! Companies would be well advised to take advantage of the low-cost design and production capabilities in India to develop acceptable products specifically for the rapidly expanding, huge rural consumer segment. This approach of designing and manufacturing products in emerging economies for the local emerging consumers is called **forward innovation**. It benefits our country as it creates more manufacturing jobs locally, and contributes excise and sales tax revenues to our exchequer.

A New Price–Performance Paradigm

Some very successful products in rural markets are those that deliver on the core benefit with no frills at a lower price point than the established competition. Nirma or Ghari washing powders are excellent lower performance–lower cost products, as compared to the global Surf and Ariel brands. They may not offer softeners or whiteners, but they do deliver on cleanliness—the core requirement of a washing powder. A company should aim at providing 75 per cent of the performance at 50 per cent of the cost to create a definite impact in rural consumers' mindsets.

Innovative Rural Distribution

The biggest challenge in rural areas remains availability, or reaching your product to a massive 600,000 villages, compared to the 5,000-odd towns in urban areas. A few new rural distribution and procurement models have been innovated by ITC e-Choupal and

HUL Project Shakti, but much more needs to be done in this area. Companies need to explore the possibility of using the social infrastructure being created by the government. For example, there are over 7 million women's microfinance groups in existence, with a combined membership of 70 million. This means that nearly one in every two rural households is a member of a self-help group. Most groups are linked to some large microfinance institution. As several of these women and their families run mom-and-pop stores out of their homes, can the MFI–SHG channel be used innovatively to reach products and services to rural homes? The Future Group is piloted an experiment to service such retail stores by buying products in bulk and routing supply through SKS Finance.

Inclusive Marketing

The concept of inclusive marketing looks at the poor not only as consumers, but also as producers/suppliers of goods and services.

Companies need to go way beyond simply selling to the BoP. They should look at the poor not only as consumers, but also as producers/suppliers of goods and services. Such an approach offers the promise of adding economic value to the goods and services contributed by the poor, and can therefore impact poverty positively. This approach is called **inclusive marketing**. ITC's e-Choupal is a perfect example of inclusive marketing. The business model ensures that farmers as producers get better value for their produce. Once their incomes are enhanced, the model then uses the same channel created for procuring produce to push the relevant goods and services needed by the farmers as consumers. The government and the private sector need to come together to promote inclusive marketing and grow the size of the rural pie through the development of reverse distribution channels, instead of companies fighting with each other to grab a share of a limited pie.

Dedicated Rural Teams

Although companies have begun to look at the rural market as a high-potential market, very few have created separate rural teams to cater to the specific needs of this market. It is recommended that companies shift power to where the growth is by creating dedicated, empowered teams for rural markets. Such a team would be more responsive to market needs and changes, and would allow strategies and products to evolve based on the ground realities, a bottom-up approach rather than a top-down one. This would also counteract the resistance that a typical urban-based sales team would have in covering the more difficult and smaller off-take rural markets. In most such cases, sales executives dump the rural quota onto their urban distributors, thereby avoiding the hardship of travelling to remote locations. This results in an under-serving of rural markets. MBAs from B-grade small-town institutes should be hired. Not only will they work at much lower salaries, they will also stick around as they belong to the local areas and will prefer to continue there rather than being forced to relocate from urban centres. This new team will be sensitized to rural conditions and rural consumers, increasing the availability of acceptable products and services in rural locations.

::: Rural Dividend

While most nations have ageing populations, India is a young country with half its population under 25 years. We will continue to remain young for a long time. This offers a huge demographic dividend because this young population has their whole working life ahead of them, and they will continue to be consumers for all these years.

We know that the penetration and consumption of most products are much lower in rural areas than in urban areas. For example, while urban markets are nearing saturation levels, only about half the rural population uses toothpaste. If we could persuade non-users to use toothpaste through consumer education, the market for toothpaste would double in size. Further, if we could get them to brush their teeth both in the morning and the evening instead of just once a day, the market has the potential to grow four times the size of the current rural market.

Seventy per cent of India's young population lives in the under-served rural India. The example of toothpaste is illustrative of how companies can derive a huge **rural dividend** if they get their focus and strategies right. So the demographic dividend we

RURAL MARKETING **MEMO** | SOME STARTLING FACTS

- **Healthcare:** The total rural spending on healthcare is currently INR 700 billion and is expected to reach INR 3.5 trillion by 2025, an impressive five-fold increase. Despite the launch of the National Rural Health Mission, 80 per cent of health spending will be in the private sector.
- **Durables consumer financing:** In the 1990s, consumer finance became easily available in urban India, which led to a high growth in the sale of automobiles and durables. With the rapid rate of rural electrification, rural consumer finance has only now become a big opportunity, and could have a multiplier effect on rural growth.
- **Banking:** According to a World Bank study,[2] the bankable population of rural India is 185 million.
- **Construction and housing:** Currently, there is a shortage of 20 million houses in rural India.

talk about is largely a rural dividend. See 'Rural Marketing Memo: Some Startling Facts' for more details.

With 70 per cent of its young population living in the under-served rural areas, India offers a huge rural dividend for companies who plan to increase the consumption of their products in the Indian market.

New Opportunities

Rural markets now offer a number of new growth opportunities that are expected to reach their potential in the coming years. Agriculture offers huge opportunity for growth. Public and private investments are coming for mechanization, introduction of best practices, modernizing the supply chain, making price mechanisms more transparent and reducing post harvest losses. India can become the Food Basket to the world because we have all the agro-climatic regions and can grow variety of food that is available on planet.

Take durables. A study conducted at MART concluded that if the industry makes consumer finance available, one can witness the same growth that we did in the 1990s in the auto sector in urban India. With a shortage of 22 million homes, the construction industry can prosper, provided it can design affordable homes for low-income families. The banking sector offers a huge opportunity with 185 million bankable but unbanked people, provided it can use IT effectively to reach out to customers in remote locations. IT and IT enabled services will ensure 'democratization of information' as it reaches millions in rural India. On the other hand, Government is committed to skilling 500 million people by 2022 when we have a surplus of 57 million employable youth against a global shortage of 46 million. Thus we can become the skills capital of the world

The real challenge is to develop business models that address accessibility, affordability, and availability in an appropriate manner. For this, companies will have to get over their bias against the rural sector and realize that the next big growth will come from this sector. The first thing they must do is understand the rural consumer and the ecosystem, so they can then be able to develop elegant solutions to the unique rural needs. However, winners in the rural segment will be companies that bring a 'business mind, social heart' approach. Passion, combined with compassion, will help connect better with rural consumers. Let the race begin.

To sum up, the next growth will come from the rural market and companies that ignore this segment will do so at their own peril. A recent visit to Hamira—a 5,000 population village in Kapurthala district of Punjab—was an eye-opener. All the houses were pucca, almost all homes had a TV and refrigerator, and 50 per cent even had an inverter! The local market boasted a glass front, open format, 400-sq. ft store with an electronic cash register at the counter! The scene was not much different from an urban colony store. We know that Punjab is the most prosperous state, and this scene is far from representative of the rest of rural India today. But with the rural economy set to double in the next seven years and many states—including laggards like Bihar and Chattisgarh—trying hard to catch up, what is a reality in Punjab today will be a reality in many states in the coming years.

REVIEW OF OBJECTIVES

1. Understand the rural boom

Over the past decade, the rural economy has registered an impressive growth. The factors driving this boom are the eight good monsoons, a 100 per cent increase in the minimum support price for primary crops, and the growing non-farm sector. Better infrastructure in terms of roads and electricity, and rising mobile connections, literacy levels, and purchasing power are all indicative of this rural boom. With rapidly rising incomes and a growing middle class, the demand for most categories is expected to explode. Another emerging trend in rural India is the use of multiple brands in the same household, again reflecting the growing rural prosperity. With this significant improvement in rural infrastructure, coupled with the agriculture reforms already underway, rural markets are expected to reach an inflexion point by 2013.

2. Identify the way forward for rural marketing

The way forward for companies who want to exploit the potential of rural markets to the fullest is: they should have separate rural teams that can cater to the specific needs of this market; the companies should look at 'forward innovation' (designing and manufacturing products in emerging economies for the emerging consumers) as a way of innovating new products; they need to look at the poor not only as consumers, but also as producers/suppliers of goods and services (inclusive marketing); they should create innovative rural distribution channels like the MFI–SHG linkage to reach their products and services to rural homes; and should aim at providing 75 per cent of the performance of their product at 50 per cent of the cost to create a definite impact in rural consumers' mindsets.

3. Understand the rural dividend and new opportunities

India, with its young consumer base, offers a huge demographic dividend for companies who plan to increase the consumption of their products, and hence the growth potential. This demographic dividend is nothing but the rural dividend, since 70 per cent of India's young population lives in the under-served rural India. Companies can derive this dividend if they get their focus and strategies right. Rural markets now offer a number of new growth opportunities that are expected to reach their potential in the coming years. The real challenge, however, is to develop business models that address accessibility, affordability, and availability in an appropriate manner. The companies that bring a 'Business mind, social heart' approach will be able to connect better with rural consumers and win this rural race.

DISCUSSION AND APPLICATION

Discussion of Concepts

1. What do you understand by the 'rural boom'? Explain.
2. 'India's growth lies in the rural dividend.' Discuss.
3. Is the future of rural India bright? What are some of the important approaches that a company should keep in mind while going forward in this direction?

Application of Concepts

1. Imagine you are into the education business. Design an inclusive marketing model for your company and provide a rationale for why it qualifies for the same.
2. Explore any two products that have used the concept of forward innovation in rural India. Discuss their complete strategies.

RURAL MARKETING CASE | 3G VIDEO TELEPHONY

There are several over-the-top applications on the Internet like video chat that are used by millions of people globally for long-distance visual communication today that connects emotionally. A computer with a high-speed broadband connection is a necessary tool to use this application.

Background

With the introduction of 3G and 4G telephony—that gives broadband access and mobility—in India, there is great potential to bridge the prevailing digital divide in this country. The most optimistic forecasts predict a subscription base of about 350 million wireless broadband subscribers by 2015. This still leaves about a billion people with no access to high-speed Internet services.

Research indicated a need for long-distance, social communication channels amongst the people at the base of the pyramid. There is significant migration of people from rural areas to urban locations for livelihood, skill enhancement or education. For such people, continuous electricity supply, maintenance, of computers, space, and the minimum level of competence needed to manage these assets are barriers to the adoption of web-based applications. So far, these people have had to rely on long-distance telephone calls as the sole means of communication.

3G technology, deployed for years around the world, has the potential to meet this requirement of visual communications. Currently, its global uptake is being driven by the need for mobile broadband. Currently, there are no 'killer applications' for base of pyramid segment (BoP) due to computer literacy, language, and cultural barriers. 3G has the potential to be used for various applications in the form of both voice and data. Despite the launch of 3G services, the acquisition cost of this technology by the BoP consumer is very high as:

- Both persons using this technology need to have 3G devices.
- Both persons need to activate 3G services on their phone, which have high tariffs.

Hence, all equipment manufacturers and telecom service providers have been working on developing a viable business model that would put this technology within the reach of the masses. Ericsson India Pvt. Ltd. approached MART in 2010 to conceive and develop a new business model around shared video telephony using the existing Public Call Office (PCO) foot print in the country for taking 3G services to rural markets.

Marketing Challenges

The following were the marketing challenges faced with respect to implementation of 3G services in rural markets:

- ***Affordability.*** Very high perceived and experienced acquisition cost of 3G technology.
- ***Awareness.*** Low level of awareness about applications of 3G and its benefits.
- ***Availability.*** The necessary equipment may not be easily available.
- ***Accessibility.*** At the time of the initiation of the study, only BSNL/MTNL had the licence to provide 3G services and their new networks being deployed were available only up to district towns.

The MART Approach

MART followed a three-step approach to overcome these challenges and achieve the business objectives:

1. ***Research.*** It studied the profile of PCO users and analysed their telecom usage behaviour.
2. ***Strategy.*** It designed a pilot for testing and assessing video telephony for the low-income masses.
3. ***Pilot implementation.*** It demonstrated the relevance and utility of video telephony to meet the emotional needs of masses and, in the process, generate a new business opportunity for PCO owners.

The Business Model

There is a definite need for a visual communication channel in the BoP market. The PCO which heralded the telecom revolution in India 30 years ago is now a sunset industry. This is due to the high penetration of mobile communication, which is slowly wiping out PCOs. Most PCOs have started diversifying into photocopying, mobile sales and/or repair, sale of recharge coupons, etc. to survive. It is only the low-income group that still uses PCOs to make calls. The business is not booming, but is still relevant. PCO owners were willing to experiment with new technology, hoping for a new opportunity to draw back customers.

MART's research reinforced two insights—the need for visual communications in the BoP segment and the adoptability of the PCO booth as a platform for shared usage. Ericsson India Pvt. Ltd. gave the go ahead to project Aamne Saamne. Figure 1 shows the steps MART used to convert PCO shops into Aamne Saamne video booths.

| Fig. 1 | Converting PCOs to Aamne Saamne Video Booths

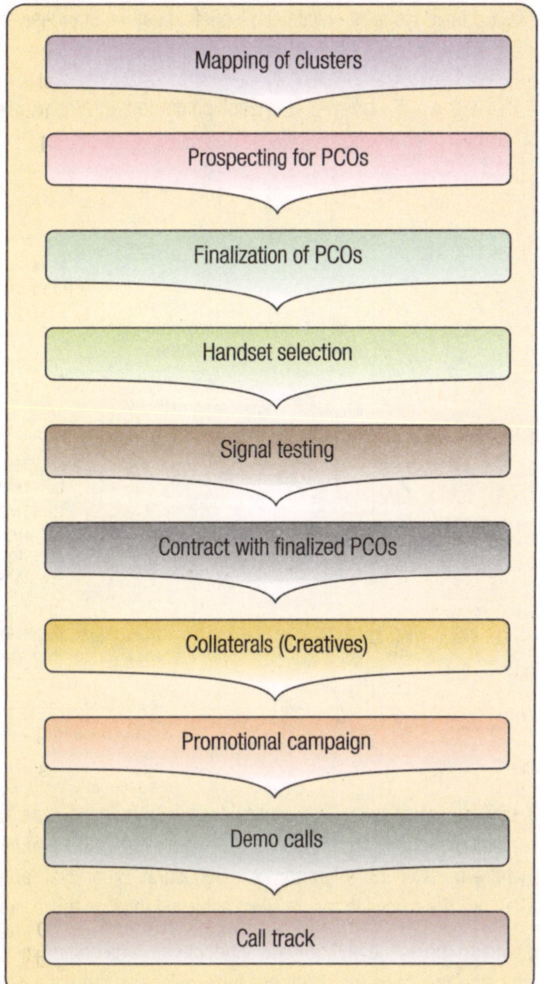

The Communication Campaign

The marketing communication campaign was crucial in making this concept a success. MART used a three-pronged strategy for this communication:

1. ***Category need awareness.*** Create an emotional connect for the migrant men who often miss their families and loved ones
2. ***Giving video telephony as one of the solution for that need.*** Demonstrate the technology as a means to fill up their emotional vacuum
3. ***Brand introduction.*** Visual and reminder medium to induce migrants to try the technology

The accompanying video shows how MART used its learning from the target audience to develop the communication strategy and implement this pilot project to bring the desired behaviour change.

- Launching the PCO for Video Telephony
  - Merchandizing the PCO to raise existing customer's inquisitiveness. Create 'talk of town' among the target audience
  - For communication at the PCO (PCO backdrops, danglers, standees, posters)
- Educating the PCO customers and target population
  - Posters with different themes (two types one showing wife from village talking to his husband in metro and other parents from village to son in metro and third poster having all addresses of video booths, i.e., call of action to make call)
  - Leaflets with addresses of booths and benefits of video telephone application as takeaways which people can keep in their shirt's pocket

MART developed five types of collaterals: leaflets, posters, standees, banners, and danglers. The message/punch lines were developed to:

- introduce a solution to the need, i.e., to be able to see the person they are talking on phone—*Pehle Sirf Baat, Ab Phone Par Hi Mulaqaat*;
- detail the benefits of the application in a simple and easy-to-understand manner—*Baat Karne Ki Khushi Dikhayi De Ab Phone Par*, and
- avoid people misunderstanding this service from mobile instead of from PCO booths and counter villagers' perceptions about new technology being costly and unaffordable—PCO *Se Kijiye apnon Se Mulaqaat* BSNL/MTNL *Ke* call *Daron Par*.

MART used other communication programmes as well (see Fig. 2). These included:

- Promotion using a mobile public address system
- Cycle-rickshaw promotion
- Community meetings
- One-to-one household meetings

| Fig. 2 | Reaching out to the Target Audience

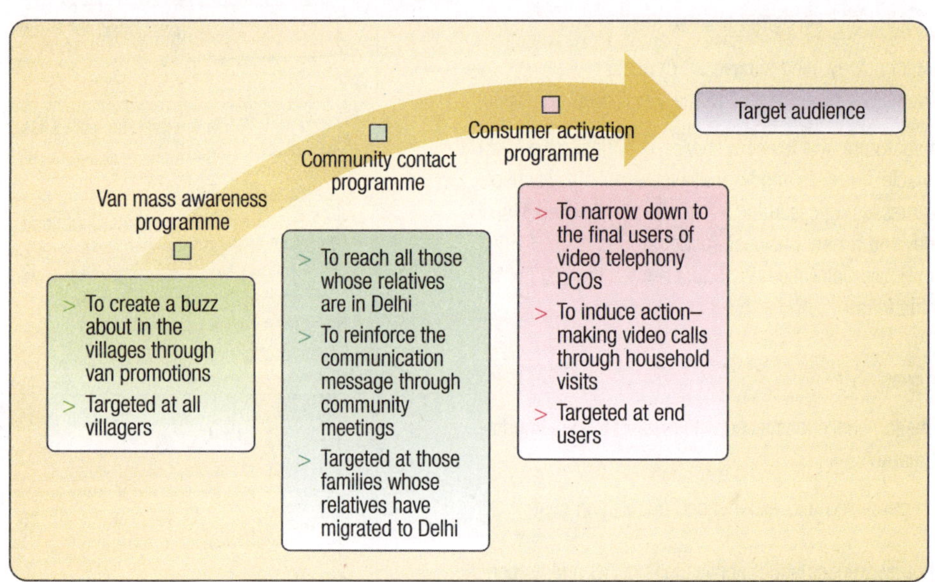

Scale and Result

The total duration of pilot implementation was four months, from research to pilot implementation. The scale of the pilot was eight PCOs—four in Delhi (clusters where most of the migrants from Begusarai, Bihar live), and four in Begusarai, Bihar. The following results were achieved through this project:

- Understanding the usage and attitude of people towards communication
- Understanding the need for social communications at the base of pyramid and its potential market
- Demonstrating the use of video telephony booths as viable business model

Table 1 captures the relevant statistics regarding the outcomes of the project.

Above all else, with the help of 3G technology, this pilot brought about a change in the behaviour of migrants from Bihar in terms of communication modes. This project won the national rural marketing award in 2010 from Rural Marketing Association of India in the ICT category.

In conclusion, video telephony is the lowest hanging opportunity for 3G service providers across the globe to improve the penetration of technology in the BoP segment, thus, rendering it a potential service for adoption by the masses. The business model will continue to revolve around shared usage. This pilot showcases a proof point for all stakeholders involved—policy makers, service providers, rural entrepreneurs, and the ecosystem at large.

| Table 1 | The Reach of the Aamne Saamne Pilot

Reach	Number
People contacted through the promotional campaign	2,355
Total demo calls made	392
Calls made (Behaviour change)	127
Total calls made	519

Discussion Questions

1. What were the key barriers to the adoption of 3G services? How did this project achieve the acceptance of a new concept?
2. Why were PCOs targeted in this model as the delivery channel? 'The rollout of 3G services can revive the PCO business in rural India.' Give arguments in favour of and against this statement.
3. What triggered the actual behaviour change? Which communication approaches were effective in bringing about this change? Why?
4. What could be the other possible rural delivery channels that could be used for delivering video telephony services?

ENDNOTES

Chapter 1

1. Compiled from the case 'Promoting Women's Economic Empowerment: The learning journey of Hindustan Unilever', May 2010, from http://pslforum.worldbankgroup.org/casestudies/unilever/.

Chapter 3

1. Rama Bijapurkar, *We Are Like That Only: Understanding the Logic of Consumer India*, Penguin, New Delhi, p. 130.
2. Abraham Maslow, *Motivation and Personality*, Second Edition, Prentice-Hall, Upper Saddle River:NJ, 1970.

Chapter 4

1. L. Kish, 'A Procedure for Objective Respondent Selection within the Household', *Journal of the American Statistical Association*, 44 (247) (September 1949): 380–387.
2. MART, 'To Identify and Develop Specific Set of Tools and Techniques that can be Universally Applied to Conduct Market Research in Rural Areas', June 2000.
3. MART, 'A Study on Sub-Optimal Farmers in India', January 2011.

Chapter 5

1. Rashiduddin Khan, 'Regional Dimension', *Seminar*, 164 (April 1973): 38.
2. Available at: http://www.rkswamybbdo.com/guide/about/index.html, last retrieved on 5 July, 2011.
3. MRUC-Hansa Research, 'Guide to Indian Markets', 2006, p. 10.

Chapter 6

1. Manu P. Toms, 'The Ace that Tata Served', *The Hindu Business Line*, 9 September 2010.

Chapter 7

1. Ratna Bhushan and Bhanu Pande, 'INR 5 price point becomes a magic word for marketers across products', *The Economic Times*, 24 December 2010.
2. Article published in *The Wall Street Journal*, 1 October 2010. Available at http://online.wsj.com/article/SB10001424052748704789404575524273890970954.html.
3. Article published in India Knowledge@Wharton, 6 May 2010. Available at http://knowledge.wharton.upenn.edu/india/article.cfm?articleid=4471.
4. Profile of Karsanbhai Patel in indiaprofile.com. Available at http://www.indiaprofile.com/people/karsanbhaipatel.htm.

Chapter 8

1. 'Taking on Piracy Profitably', *Business Today*, 30 May 2010, pp. 58–60.
2. RMAI, 'Rural Retailing in India', 2008, p. 21.
3. RMAI, 'Haats as Marketing Hubs', 2010, p. 38.
4. 'Coca-Cola India: Winning Hearts, Minds ... and Taste Buds in the Hinterland', *India Knowledge @Wharton*, 6 May 2010. Available online at: http://knowledge.wharton.upenn.edu/india/article.cfm?articleid=4471).
5. 'Rural Distribution Channels', MART Study, 2004.
6. 'Rural Retailing in India', RMAI, 2008, p. 21.
7. 'Coca-Cola India: Winning Hearts, Minds ... and Taste Buds in the Hinterland', India Knowledge@Wharton, 6 May 2010, *http://knowledge.wharton.upenn.edu/india/article.cfm?articleid=4471* (accessed 17 February 2011).
8. 'Rural Distribution Channels', MART Study, 2004.
9. RMAI, 'Haats as Marketing Hubs', 2010.
10. http://www.evereadyindustries.com/about-us/distribution.asp (accessed 16 February 2011). Compiled from a presentation made by Roshan Joseph, Marketing Director, Eveready Industries, at a rural marketing conference, April 2003, Mumbai, organized by The Rural Network.
11. 'Coca-Cola India: Winning Hearts, Minds ... and Taste Buds in the Hinterland', India Knowledge@Wharton, 6 May 2010, http://knowledge.wharton.upenn.edu/india/article.cfm?articleid=4471 (accessed 17 February 2011).

Chapter 9

1. Lintas Media Guide, 2008.
2. Presented by RC&M at the Third RMAI (Rural Marketing Association of India) Rural Marketing Awards, 26 November 2010.

ENDNOTES

3. Presented by Impact Communications at the Third RMAI Rural Marketing Awards, 26 November 2010.
4. Indian Readership Survey, Q3, 2010.
5. Indian Readership Survey, Q3, 2010.
6. Indian Readership Survey, Q3, 2010.
7. Indian Readership Survey, Q3, 2010.
8. RMAI, '*The Rural Marketing Journal*', 5 (2), August 2010, p. 21.
9. RMAI, '*Haats* as Marketing Hubs', Report, November 2010, pp. 15–16.
10. Presented by Ogilvy at the Third RMAI Rural Marketing Awards, 26 November 2010.

Chapter 10

1. Vikram Akula, 'Business Basics at the Bottom of the Pyramid', *Harvard Business Review*, June 2008. Available online at http://hbr.org/2008/06/business-basics-at-the-base-of-the-pyramid.

Chapter 11

1. Avijit Ghosh, 'Small Towns, Big Leap', *Crest, The Times of India*, 4 December 2010, http://www.timescrest.com/coverstory/small-towns-big-leap-4186.
2. McKinsey Urbanization Report, 'India's Urban Awakening: Building Inclusive Cities, Sustaining Economic Growth', April 2010. Available online at http://www.mckinsey.com/mgi/reports/freepass_pdfs/india_urbanization/MGI_india_urbanization_fullreport.pdf.
3. 'Internet in India', Report, Internet and Mobile Association of India (IAMAI) and Indian Market Research Bureau (IMRB), April 2010.

Chapter 13

1. 'The Bird of Gold: The Rise of India's Consumer Market', Report, McKinsey Global Institute, May 2007.
2. 'Building a More Inclusive Financial System in India', Report, Diamond Management and Technology Consultants, 2006.

PHOTO CREDITS

Chapter 1

2 Courtesy of MART; 8 'Rural Marketing Snapshot' Courtesy of MART; 10 Courtesy of RMAI.

Chapter 2

12 Courtesy of MART; 17 Courtesy of MART; 20 Courtesy of MART; 24 Courtesy of MART; 34 'Rural Marketing Snapshot' Courtesy of MART; 35 Courtesy of MART; 37 Courtesy of MART.

Chapter 3

42 Courtesy of MART; 45 Courtesy of MART; 52 Courtesy of Emami Group of Companies; 56 'Rural Marketing Snapshot' Courtesy of MART.

Chapter 4

64 Courtesy of MART; 74 Courtesy of MART; 77 Courtesy of MART; 78 Courtesy of MART; 80 'Rural Marketing Snapshot' Courtesy of MART.

Chapter 5

86 Courtesy of MART S. D. Ali; 96 Courtesy of Ccca-Cola India Private Limited; 103 Courtesy of MART.

Chapter 6

108 Courtesy of Tata Motors; 115 'Rural Marketing Snapshot' Courtesy of MART; 121 Courtesy of MART; 125 2 Courtesy of CavinKare; 127 Courtesy of Exide.

Chapter 7

134 Courtesy of MART; 137 Courtesy of Gillette; 139 Courtesy of Tata Chemicals; 143 Courtesy of Nirma; 144 Courtesy of MART/Insiya Poonawala; 149 'Rural Marketing Snapshot' Courtesy of RMAI and MART.

Chapter 8

154 Courtesy of Moserbaer; 163 'Rural Marketing Snapshot' Courtesy of MART; 166 Courtesy of MART; 167 Courtesy of MART; 176 Courtesy of Ghari Industry Private Limited; 178 Courtesy of MART; 181 Courtesy of RMAI; 184 Courtesy of MART; 187 Courtesy of MART.

Chapter 9

198 Courtesy of MART; 204 Courtesy of RC&M; 209 Courtesy of Greenpeace; 217 Courtesy of R. K. Jha; 218 Courtesy of MART; 219 'Rural Marketing Snapshot' Courtesy of MART; 220 Courtesy of Ashish Gajera; 222 Courtesy of Impact Communications; 226 Courtesy of RC&M; 227 Courtesy of O&M; 228 Courtesy of RC&M; 229 Courtesy of RC&M; 229 Courtesy of MART.

Chapter 10

236 Courtesy of Byrraju Foundation; 238 'Rural Marketing Snapshot' Courtesy of MART; 240 Courtesy of Airtel; 241 Courtesy of Idea Cellular; 242 Courtesy of IndiaTechOnline.com; 244 Courtesy of ITC; 245 Courtesy of MART; 259 Courtesy of National Rural Health Mission, Government of Rajasthan.

Chapter 11

268 Courtesy of MART; 271 'Rural Marketing Snapshot' Courtesy of MART; 275 Courtesy of S. Das; 276 Courtesy of Tata Motors; 278 Courtesy of MART.

Chapter 12

284 Courtesy of MART Ericsson.

INDEX

Abadi, 18, 207
Accredited social health activist, 259–260
Advertisements for rural audiences, 197, 212
After-sales service, 126, 129
Agricultural inputs, 14, 166, 284
Agricultural marketing, 14, 38, 297–298
AICDA model of communication, 201
Anganwadi workers, 48, 65, 69, 210, 260
ASHA. see activated social health activist, 260

B

Banking services, 165, 248, 251, 266, 284
Behavioural segmentation, 96, 106
Brand ambassadors, 52, 194, 279
Brand building in rural markets, 130
Brand identity, 120, 129, 232
Brand image, 120, 129, 210
Brand loyalty, 120, 171, 174, 284
  versus brand stickiness, 120
Brand name, 53, 122, 232, 279
Brand stickiness, 97, 120
Buyer decision process, 54, 59

C

Captive-product pricing, 143
Cash discount, 144, 210
Caste system, 21–22
Causal research, 67
Channel partner, 159, 174, 231
Channel promotion, 168, 170
Channels of distribution, 156, 178, 191, 245
Chapati diagram, 65, 77, 83
Chit funds, 212, 254–255
Coinage pricing, 149–150
Common service centre, 244, 290
Communication mix, 200, 209, 211, 229
  decision, 47, 49
  strategy, 76, 97, 106
Communication process, 199, 229
Community health centres, 259, 261
Company depot, 156–157
Consumer behavior, 44
  Cultural factors, 44
  psychological factors, 52
  social factors, 47
Concentrated marketing, 102, 106
Credit instruments, 253
Credit patterns, 169
CSC, see common service centre, 169

D

Daily activity clock, 77, 83
Data analysis, 75
  bivariate, 75
  multivariate, 75
  univariate, 75
Demographic segmentation, 93, 95
Descriptive research, 67
Dhoni effect, 277
Differentiated marketing, 102
Diffusion of management, 57
Direct marketing, 210, 229
Discriminatory pricing, 146, 150
Disposable income, 10, 19, 272, 276, 280
Distribution channels, 129, 155, 176, 249
  channel dynamics, 156
  evolution of, 155
  rural channel members, 156
Distribution model, 156, 171, 175, 181
  for durables, 175
  for FMCGs, 49, 302
  modern, 163
  rural–centric, 180
Dry sampling, 225
Durables, distribution model for, 175
Dyads, 68, 70

E

Economic census, 29–30
Economic environment, 24, 39, 128
Economic liberalization, 24
Economic liberation, 104
Economy pricing, 145, 150
Events and experiences, 224, 226
Experiential marketing, 226
Exploratory research, 67, 87
Extension counters, 60, 185

F

Fair price shop, 157, 184
Fake brands, 121
Farm sector, 5, 16, 27, 29, 38
Feeder town, 57, 155, 189, 216
FGD, see focus group discussion, 57, 68, 204
Financial services in rural India banking services, 248–249
  insurance, 255
  microfinance and credit services, 252
  rural banking, cloud computing for, 251
First mover advantage, 119
Fixed costs, 136–137
FMCGs, distribution models for, 171–172
FMCG market, 112, 192
Focus group, 68, 70, 74, 204
Focus group discussion, 57, 68, 83, 204
Folk media, 218, 222, 230
Forward innovation, 303
Franchisee, 145, 166
Free gifts, 224
Frugal engineering, 127–128

INDEX

G

Geographic factors, 91
Geographic segmentation, 91, 105
Grameenon ke beech, 228
Green revolution, 14, 23, 38
Gyandoot, 243

H

Haat, 119, 178
Handicrafts, 14, 179, 181, 303
Health centres, 48, 258, 267
Health insurance, 192, 262
Hub and spoke model, 188, 244

I

ICDS, see integrated child development scheme, 69, 259
Inclusive marketing, 304
Income class, 18, 274
Income levels, 89, 274
individual marketing, 91
individual product decisions, 115
industrial sector, 15, 38
innovation, 57, 76, 303
innovative rural distribution, 303, 306
insurance, 15, 114, 184, 223, 244
integrated child development scheme, 69, 259
internet kiosks, 245

J

Joint families, 16, 49

K

Kisan credit card, 50, 253, 295
Kish grid, 71–72
Kshatriyas, 21–22

L

Latent demand, 33, 112, 264
Life insurance, 255–256
Literacy level, 10, 25, 198
Local brands, 91, 112, 186
Local marketing, 91
Low price points, 139
Low-involvement products, 121

M

Mahatma Gandhi national rural employment guarantee
act, 37, 40
Mandis, 55, 76
Market access map, 84
Marketing mix, 6, 10, 88, 110, 242
Mart market attractiveness score, 99
Mass marketing, 90
Mass media advertising, 54
Mass media, 7, 54, 57, 88, 213, 232
Mela, 50, 52, 208
MFI-bank linkage, 266
Microfinance, 252–253
Micro-savings, 248
middle class, 8–9
MNREGA, see mahatma Gandhi
National rural employment generation act, 37
Mobile traders, 186
Mobility map, 77, 83
Moneylenders, 248, 252
Multi-attribute segmentation, 98, 106

N

National rural health mission, 260–262
Need assessment map, 77, 83
Need recognition, 54–55
New product development, 127, 130
Niche marketing, 90
Non-farm sector, 28, 38
Non-life insurance, 256, 264
Non-personal communication channels, 208
NRHM, see national rural health mission, 260, 292

O

Opinion leaders, 56, 58, 206, 209
Outdoor media, 216, 230

P

Packaging, 123–124
aesthetics, 125
for rural markets, 196
material, 123, 136
pack size and convenience, 124
sachet revolution, the, 125
Participatory rural appraisal, 67, 76, 84, 150
Penetration pricing, 142–143
Personal communication channels, 207–208
Personalized media, 217, 230
Photo ethnography, 68, 83
Point of purchase displays, 197, 217
Positioning, 103–104
communication the concept, 105
developing the concept, 105
selecting the positioning concepts, 105
Potential product, 111, 129
PRA, see participatory rural appraisal, 57, 76, 84
Pradhan Mantri Rojgar Yojna, 37
Price sensitivity, 139
Pricing by channel, 168, 170
Pricing strategies, 132, 139, 142
by companies, 142
consumer psychology and, 135
external factors in, 138

INDEX

in rural India, 286
internal factors in, 136
price adjustment strategies, 144
product mix pricing strategies, 143
setting the price for rural products and services, 136
Primary research, 55, 69
Probability proportion to size method, 71, 83
Product, 56, 110, 115
adoption process, 56, 84
decisions and strategies, 114
lifecycle strategies, 118
Product line and mix decisions, 117
Product warranty and after-sales service, 126–127
Product mix, 117, 143
Product-bundle pricing, 143
Project shakti, 3, 15, 101, 181
Psychographic segmentation, 95, 106
Psychological pricing, 146, 150
Public-private partnerships, 283
Public distribution system, 184
Purchase decision, 49, 55, 191
Purchasing power, 9, 40, 136, 197

Q

Qualitative research, 67–68, 74
Quantitative research, 67–68

R

Research process, 66, 75, 83
attributes of a researcher, 81
collecting and analysis data, 66
defining objectives, 66
designing research instrument, 73
determining budget, 66
dos and don'ts in, 79
field procedures, 79
limitations of, 81
new age innovation in rural research, 76
organizing field and collecting data, 74
reporting findings, 75
research design, 66
sampling, 69
tools used in, 77
Rural-centric distribution models, 178, 181
Rural economic structure, 26–27, 39
farm sector, 27
non-farm sector and rural industries, 28
Rural environment, 7, 15
changing face of rural environment, 25
demographic environment, 15
physical environment, 18
political environment, 22
rural economic environment, 24
social and cultural environment, 19
technological environment, 23
Rural India, 5, 7, 9, 18, 25, 36, 44
data collection in, 80
facts about, 9
pricing in, 136
Rural marketing environment, 15, 17, 19, 21, 29, 35
Rural marketing research, 65, 67, 69, 71, 75, 79, 81 ,83
Rural marketing mix, challenging in, 6–7
Rural marketing, evolution of, 55
Rural marketing, defined, 4
Rural mobile traders, 186
Rural myths, 5, 10
Rural research business, 82
Rural settlements, 8
Rural infrastructure, 19, 25, 33, 190, 288
Rural housing, 19
Rural employment generation programmes, 36
Ration shops, 184–185
Reference group, 48, 60
traditional, 186
Regional brands, 112, 140, 197
Regional rural banks, 248, 253
Reverse innovation, 127, 303
Road connectivity, 34, 35, 156, 183, 288
Rural audience, 52, 205, 212
Rural banks, 4, 212, 216
Rural boom, 302, 306
Rural communication, 184, 202, 209, 211
budgeting the communication mix strategy, 209
challenges in, 198
changing means of, 218
designing message, 202
determining objectives, 201
development of effective communication, 22, 260
measuring the impact of, 211
selecting communication channels, 200
Rural development, 3, 25, 181, 288
Rural dividend, 304
Rural economy, 26, 35, 238
Rural enterprises, 29
Rural healthcare, 257
challenges in, 257
government initiatives in, 259
growth drivers of, 260
infrastructure, 258
market, 259
Rural healthcare services, 257
Rural housing pattern, 19
Rural India, 5, 8
financial services in, 166, 248
government initiatives in, 259
information and communications technology in, 243
telecom revolution in, 238
telecommunication in, 35, 44
Rural industries, 28
Rural infrastructure, 33, 288
Rural logistics, 188
Rural marketing research, 64, 76, 79, 83
business, 66, 78
designing, 66, 73
dos and don'ts of, 79

INDEX

limitations of, 81
Rural markets, 3, 15, 86, 119
building brands in, 119
definition of, 4
distribution models in, 171, 181
distribution of, 258
heterogeneity in, 88
new product development in, 127
product branding in, 119
Rural media, 213–214
conventional, 214
non-conventional, 218
Rural products, classification of, 110
Rural research, 66–67, 75, 81, 83
Rural retail shelf, 161
Rural retail, 158, 161
modern, 163
shelf, 161
spread, 159
traditional, 158
Rural retail environment, 158
changing face of, 25
emergence of modern retail in rural areas, 163
Rural services, 236, 249, 261
financial, 244, 248
healthcare, 142, 257
ICT, 112, 238
telecommunications, 35, 243, 260
Rural spending, 31, 39, 305
Rural-centric distribution models, 178
NGOs, 48, 187
shandies, 178
youth entrepreneurs, 178, 183

S

Sachet revolution, 124, 129
Sales promotion, 209, 224
Sarpanch, 22, 56, 120, 206
Satellite distribution, 188–189
Savings, 11, 51, 104, 141, 248, 256
SEC, see socio economic classification, 61
Secondary research, 69, 83
Secondary sector, 28
Segment marketing, 90
Segmentation, 38, 88
bases for segmenting rural consumer markets, 91
coverage of segments, 101
degrees of, 90
evaluation of segments, 101
prerequisites for, 89
selection of segments, 101
Semi-pucca, 19, 21, 38, 92
SGSY, see swarnjayanti gram swarojgar yojna, 37
Shandies, 97, 178
SHG-bank linkage, 266
Skimming pricing, 142
Slice of life observation, 68, 83
Small towns, 270, 272
as agricultural linkage, 284
as hub for availing services, 283
as place for leisure and, 284
changing face of, 25, 161, 273
defined, 274
entertainment, 284
potential of, 273
strategic importance for rural marketers, 282
Sociability, 48, 52
Social and cultural environment, 19, 51
Social class, 46, 95
Social factors, 47
Social infrastructure, 39, 178
Socio-economic classification, 46, 106
SOLO, see slice of life observation, 68, 83
Source of income, 50
Special-event pricing, 145
Spell-alikes, 121
Spurious products, 122, 130
Status symbols, 51–52, 130
Stock turnover, 163
Sourcing of stock and purchase cycles, 168
Swarnjayanti Gram Swarojgar Yojna, 37
Syndicated distribution, 190

T

Targeted marketing, 102
Targeting, 87, 89, 95, 99, 105, 166, 274
Tehsil, 23, 187, 242
Telecommunications , 35, 238
Telemedicine, 260–261
Transfer of capital, 168, 170

U

Undifferentiated marketing, 101
Unique selling, 105, 203

V

Value-for-money, 125, 134
Van operation, 176
Video vans, 202, 218
Village community, 20, 65, 246
Village internet kiosks, 245

W

Wall painting, 7, 164, 216
Wealth map, 77, 83
Wet sampling, 225
White revolution, 14, 35, 38
Word-of-mouth, 120, 166

Z

Zamindari, 22

BRAND INDEX

3 Roses Tea, 119
502 Pataka Chai, 119
555 Detergent Bar, 119
Adidas, 271
Aircel, 53, 57, 240
Airtel, 114, 126
Ala bleach, 118
Annapurna, 118
Asian paints, 101, 149
Ayush, 102, 260
Babool toothpaste, 104, 203
Bajaj, 15, 113, 175, 256, 281
Bayer, 115
BPCL, 104, 164
Breeze, 102, 118
Britannia tiger, 120, 222
Bru, 107, 225, 304
Byrraju foundation, 237, 264
Cadbury, 110, 148
Cavinkare, 112, 124, 138, 175
Chik shampoo, 124, 139
Chocobix, 110
Cibaca, 90
Clinic plus, 119, 138, 179, 302
Close-up, 118, 125
CMIE, 69
Coca-cola, 53, 96, 102, 124, 150, 127
Colgate, 57, 90, 98, 104, 155, 194
Colgate-Palmolive, 90, 98, 101, 112, 194
CSO, 69
Cycle Agarbatti, 119
Dabur Hajmola, 119
Dove, 118, 135
Drishtee, 243, 246
DSCL, 164–165
Dupont, 76, 127
e-choupal, 24, 38, 101, 137, 243
Ericsson, 76, 301, 307
Escorts, 14, 114, 120, 222
Eveready, 119, 175, 184
Eveready white, 119
Fair & Lovely, 121, 125, 133, 281
Fairever, 140
Fena washing soaps, 139
FMCG products, 98, 113, 124, 180, 275, 281
Future group, 167, 304
Ghari Detergent, 90, 101, 119
Gillette, 135, 171
Glaxo Smithkline, 124, 206
Godrej, 112, 117, 120, 124, 127, 185, 209
Godrej Aadhaar, 164, 167, 191
Godrej Chotu Kool, 117
Hajmola, 117, 148
Hamam, 90, 118
HDFC bank, 167, 295
Heinz, 185
Hero Honda, 104, 113, 149, 278
Himani, 103
Hindustan unilever
See also HUL, 3, 5, 15, 90, 103, 118, 182, 201
Honeywell, 15
Horlicks, 7, 24, 150
HPCL, 58, 60, 104, 149
HUL, 3, 49, 118, 125, 135, 148, 156, 172, 175
HUL Project Shakti, 304
ICICI, 114, 256, 278
Idea cellular, 133, 217
IFFCO, 14, 192, 241
IFFCO Kisaan Sanchar Limited, 241
IMRB, 82, 159, 310
Intel, 116
IOCL, 104
IRDA, 4, 256
ITC, 5, 24, 114
Kala Ghoda, 121
Kisaan Bazaar, 45, 166, 193
KVIC, 14
Lakme, 118
Lal sabun, 120
Lamsa, 121
LG electronics, 4, 110, 148
Liberty, 273
Life Insurance Corporation, 121, 186, 213, 258
Lifebuoy, 90, 18, 121, 208, 211
Lipton, 118
Liril, 103, 118
Lotto, 273
Lux, 103, 181, 283
Mahindra & Mahindra, 14, 113, 114, 127, 317
Marico, 15, 98, 112, 125, 218, 317
Marico industries, 98
Marketing mix, 6, 7, 10, 60, 88, 110, 134, 136, 140, 242, 268
MART, 17, 31, 99, 100, 200, 281, 309
Maruti, 15, 113, 227, 275
Max Vijay, 6
Micromax mobile, 111
Micromax, 111
Microsoft, 15, 254
MNREGA scheme, 36
Monsanto, 114
Murphy, 14, 317
National Rural Employment Guarantee Act (NREGA), 37, 40, 294
NCAER, 31, 51, 69, 100, 255, 257
Nielsen company, 82, 154
Nirma, 14, 33, 39, 141, 174, 296, 304
Nokia, 90
Nokia life tools, 239, 241, 242, 245
NSSO, 30, 69, 238
Panchayat Bhawan, 74, 216
Panchayati Raj, 8, 20, 22, 98, 296
Pantene, 133
Pears, 118
Pepsi, 76, 119, 125, 140, 148
Philips, 14, 110, 113, 123, 127, 142, 175, 193, 285
Planning Commission, 4, 26, 29, 185

BRAND INDEX

Pradhan Mantri Gram Sadak Yojna, 34
Project Shakti, 15, 101, 119, 136, 172, 181, 208, 304
Pudin Hara, 117
Puma, 271
Rallis India, 114
Rediffusion DY&R, 65, 197
Reliance Communication, 115, 240, 244
Reuters, 210, 241, 242
Rexona, 118
Sahara, 4
Samsung, 15, 113, 139, 179, 200
Shell Foundation, 15, 130
Shriram Consolidated Ltd, 14
SKS Finance, 304
TATA ACE, 104, 109, 218, 289
Tata Chemicals, 166, 185
Tata Group, 90, 137
Tata Kisan Sansar, 163, 164, 166, 191
TATA Motors, 104, 109, 128, 278, 289
Tata Nano, 127, 137, 280
Tata Shaktee, 120, 205, 230, 234, 236
Tata Swach, 128, 139
Tata Tea, 189, 220
Titan, 114
Ujala, 138
UNICEF, 65, 127, 292
Usha, 14, 114, 177, 281
UTV, 123, 153
Vaseline, 118, 281
Videocon, 114, 127, 144, 186, 239
Vodafone, 143, 239
Wall's, 118
Wheel, 11, 52, 55, 95, 104, 109, 129
Woodland, 271